THE *unofficial* GUIDE®
TO Walt Disney World® with Kids

2016

COME CHECK US OUT!

Supplement your valuable guidebook with tips, news, and deals by visiting our website:

theunofficialguides.com

Also, while there, sign up for The Unofficial Guide newsletter for even more travel tips and special offers.

Join the conversation on social media:

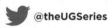 @theUGSeries

theUnofficialGuides

 theUGSeries

 theUGSeries

 theUGSeries

#theUGseries

Other *Unofficial Guides*

Beyond Disney: The Unofficial Guide to Universal Orlando, SeaWorld, & the Best of Central Florida

The Disneyland Story: The Unofficial Guide to the Evolution of Walt Disney's Dream

Mini Mickey: The Pocket-Sized Unofficial Guide to Walt Disney World

Universal vs. Disney: The Unofficial Guide to American Theme Parks' Greatest Rivalry

The Unofficial Guide Color Companion to Walt Disney World

The Unofficial Guide to Disney Cruise Line

The Unofficial Guide to Disneyland

The Unofficial Guide to Las Vegas

The Unofficial Guide to Universal Orlando

The Unofficial Guide to Walt Disney World

The Unofficial Guide to Washington, D.C.

THE *unofficial* GUIDE®

TO Walt Disney World® with Kids

2016

BOB SEHLINGER *and*
LILIANE J. OPSOMER
with LEN TESTA

(Walt Disney World® is officially known as Walt Disney World® Resort.)

keen
communications

Please note that prices fluctuate in the course of time and that travel information changes under the impact of many factors that influence the travel industry. We therefore suggest that you write or call ahead for confirmation when making your travel plans. Every effort has been made to ensure the accuracy of information throughout this book, and the contents of this publication are believed to be correct at the time of printing. Nevertheless, the publishers cannot accept responsibility for errors or omissions, for changes in details given in this guide, or for the consequences of any reliance on the information provided by the same. Assessments of attractions and so forth are based upon the authors' own experiences; therefore, descriptions given in this guide necessarily contain an element of subjective opinion, which may not reflect the publisher's opinion or dictate a reader's own experience on another occasion. Readers are invited to write the publisher with ideas, comments, and suggestions for future editions.

Published by:
Keen Communications, LLC
2204 First Avenue South, Suite 102
Birmingham. AL 35233

Unofficial Guide is a registered trademark of Google Inc. in the United States and other countries and may not be used without written permission. Used under license. All other trademarks are the property of their respective owners. Google Inc. is not associated with any product or vendor mentioned in this book.

Cover design by Scott McGrew

Text design by Vertigo Design with modifications by Annie Long

For information on our other products and services or to obtain technical support, please contact us from within the United States at 888-604-4537 or by fax at 205-326-1012.

Keen Communications, LLC, also publishes its books in a variety of electronic formats. Some content that appears in print may not be available in electronic formats.

ISBN: 978-1-62809-038-3; eISBN: 978-162809-039-0

Distributed by Publishers Group West

Manufactured in the United States of America

5 4 3 2

CONTENTS

List of Maps vii
Acknowledgments viii

INTRODUCTION 1
Why "Unofficial"? 1
About This Guide 5
A Quick Tour of a Big World 12

PART ONE Basic Considerations 19
Is Walt Disney World for You? 19
The Age Thing 21
About Inviting Your Children's Friends 26
A Few Words for Single Parents 27
"He Who Hesitates Is Launched!"
   Tips and Warnings for Grandparents 28
Order and Discipline on the Road 30

PART TWO Getting Your Act Together 36
Gathering Information 36
Allocating Time 44
Planning Your Walt Disney World Vacation Budget 59
Babysitting 71
Special Programs for Children 73

PART THREE Where to Stay 78
Things to Consider 79
Walt Disney World Lodging 87
Walt Disney World Hotels: Strengths and Weaknesses for Families 91
How to Get Discounts on Lodging at Walt Disney World 105
Lodging Outside Walt Disney World 113
How to Childproof a Hotel Room 133

PART FOUR Dining 134
Eating Outside Walt Disney World 134
Dining in Walt Disney World 140

PART FIVE **Know Before You Go 184**
The Brutal Truth About Family Vacations 184
Mental and Emotional Preparation 185
Physical Preparation 197
Developing a Good Plan 201
Logistic Preparation 203
Walt Disney World for Guests with Special Needs 216
Remembering Your Trip 217
Trial Run 219

PART SIX **Ready, Set, Tour! 221**
Touring Recommendations 221
Character Analysis 245
Strollers 255
When Kids Get Lost 258

PART SEVEN **The Magic Kingdom 262**
Main Street, U.S.A. 266
Adventureland 270
Frontierland 272
Liberty Square 275
Fantasyland 277
Tomorrowland 285
Live Entertainment and Parades in the Magic Kingdom 290
Magic Kingdom Touring Plans 294
Magic Kingdom Trivia Quiz 297

PART EIGHT **Epcot 298**
Kidcot Fun Stops 302
Future World 302
World Showcase 311
Live Entertainment at Epcot 318
Epcot Touring Plans 321
Epcot Trivia Quiz 323

PART NINE **Disney's Animal Kingdom 324**
The Oasis 328
Discovery Island 329
Africa 331
Asia 334
DinoLand U.S.A. 336
Live Entertainment at Animal Kingdom 338
Animal Kingdom Touring Plans 340
Disney's Animal Kingdom Trivia Quiz 341

PART TEN **Disney's Hollywood Studios 342**
Disney's Hollywood Studios Attractions 347
Live Entertainment at Disney's Hollywood Studios 355
Disney's Hollywood Studios Touring Plans 359
Disney's Hollywood Studios Trivia Quiz 360

PART ELEVEN **Universal Orlando and SeaWorld 361**
Universal Orlando 361
Universal's Islands of Adventure 371
Islands of Adventure Attractions 374
Islands of Adventure Touring Plan 392
Universal Studios Florida 393
Universal Studios Florida Attractions 396
Live Entertainment at Universal Studios 414
Universal Studios Florida Touring Plans 416
SeaWorld 417

PART TWELVE **The Best of the Rest 421**
The Water Theme Parks 421
Wet 'n Wild 426
Aquatica by SeaWorld 427
Disney Springs 429
Outdoor Recreation 435

INDEX **438**
CLIP-OUT TOURING PLANS **455**

LIST *of* MAPS

South Orlando & Walt Disney
    World Area 8–9
Walt Disney World 10–11
Hotel Concentrations Around
    Walt Disney World 114
The Magic Kingdom 264–265
Epcot 300–301
Where to View *IllumiNations* 321
Disney's Animal Kingdom 326–327

Disney's Hollywood Studios
    344–345
Universal Orlando 362–363
Universal's Islands of Adventure
    372–373
Universal Studios Florida
    394–395
Disney Springs 430–431

ACKNOWLEDGMENTS

THANKS TO OUR TEAM OF YOUNG PUNDITS, Isaac and Ethan Leifert, Julia Aronberg, Erin Haffreingue, Alex and Kieran Duncan, and Ricky Vosburgh-Tyson, for their unique wisdom and fun-loving attitude (gotta have attitude, right?). Also thanks to Hannah Testa, Katie Sutton, Eve Zibart, Idan Menin, Ian Geiger, and Shelton Siegel.

Kudos to entertainment reporter Jim Hill, who provided insightful and funny glimpses of the World behind the scenes. The cartoons were drawn by Tami Knight, possibly the nuttiest artist in Canada, and Chris Eliopoulos, a talented illustrator–Disney fanatic based in New Jersey. A big thank-you goes to Alexa and Kendall (also known as Anna and Elsa) and their family from Seattle, Washington, for allowing us to take and use their picture for the cover of this book.

For research and contributions concerning family dynamics and child behavior, thanks to psychologists Karen Turnbow, Susan Corbin, Gayle Janzen, and Joan Burns. Kudos also to Unofficial Guide Research Director Len Testa and his team for the data collection and programming behind the touring plans in this guide.

To the Ortiz-Valle gang: We love your reports from the parks and the insights from your annual takeover of the Disney fleet.

Thanks also to Amber Kaye Henderson and Ritchey Halphen for their editorial and production work on this book. Scott McGrew, Steve Jones, and Cassandra Poertner created the maps, and Ann Cassar prepared the index.

—*Bob Sehlinger, Liliane Opsomer, and Len Testa*

INTRODUCTION

 ## WHY "UNOFFICIAL"?

DECLARATION OF INDEPENDENCE

THE AUTHORS AND RESEARCHERS OF THIS GUIDE specifically and categorically declare that they are and always have been totally independent of the Walt Disney Company, Inc.; of Disneyland, Inc.; of Walt Disney World, Inc.; and of any and all other members of the Disney corporate family not listed.

The authors believe in the wondrous variety, joy, and excitement of the Walt Disney World attractions. At the same time, we recognize that Walt Disney World is a business. In this guide, we represent and serve you, the consumer. If a restaurant serves bad food, or a gift item is overpriced, or a certain ride isn't worth the wait, we can say so, and in the process we hope to make your visit more fun, efficient, and economical.

YOUR UNOFFICIAL TOOLBOX

WHEN IT COMES TO WALT DISNEY WORLD, a couple with kids needs different advice than does a party of seniors going to the Epcot International Flower & Garden Festival. Likewise, adults touring without children, honeymooners, and folks with only a day or two to visit all require their own special guidance.

To meet the varying needs of our readers, we've created *The Unofficial Guide to Walt Disney World,* or what we call the Big Book. At more than 850 pages, it contains all the information that anyone traveling to Walt Disney World needs to have a super vacation. More than 30 years in the making, it's our cornerstone.

As thorough as we try to make the main guide, there still isn't sufficient space for all the tips and resources that may be useful to certain readers. Therefore, we've developed additional guides that provide information tailored to specific visitors. Though some advice from the Big Book, such as arriving early at the theme parks, is echoed in these guides, most of the information is unique.

Here's what's in the toolbox:

The guide you're reading now presents detailed planning and touring tips for a family vacation, along with more than 20 special touring plans for families that you won't find anywhere else. *The Unofficial Guide to Walt Disney World with Kids* is the only Unofficial Guide created with the guidance of a panel of kids, all of varying ages and backgrounds.

The Unofficial Guide Color Companion to Walt Disney World, by Bob Sehlinger and Len Testa, is a visual feast that proves a picture is worth a thousand words. In the Big Book, for instance, you can learn about the best guest rooms to request at Disney's Wilderness Lodge, but in the *Color Companion* you can *see* the rooms, along with the pool and the magnificent lobby. Full-color photos illustrate how long the lines get at different times of day, how wet riders get on Splash Mountain, and how the parks are decked out for various holidays. The *Color Companion* whets your appetite for Disney fun, pictures all the attractions, serves as a keepsake, and, as always, helps make your vacation more enjoyable. Most of all, the *Color Companion* is for fun and allows us to use photography to express our zany Unofficial sense of humor. Think of it as Monty Python meets Walt Disney . . . in Technicolor.

Mini Mickey: The Pocket-Sized Unofficial Guide to Walt Disney World, by Bob Sehlinger and Ritchey Halphen with Len Testa, is a portable CliffsNotes-style version of the Big Book. It distills information to help short-stay or last-minute visitors decide quickly how to plan their limited hours at Disney World. It is a great book for convention goers.

Beyond Disney: The Unofficial Guide to Universal Orlando, SeaWorld, & the Best of Central Florida, by Bob Sehlinger and Seth Kubersky with Len Testa, is a guide to non-Disney theme parks, attractions, restaurants, outdoor recreation, and nightlife in Orlando and Central Florida.

The Unofficial Guide to Universal Orlando, by Seth Kubersky with Bob Sehlinger and Len Testa, is the first comprehensive guide ever published that is dedicated to Universal Orlando. It is filled with proven tips and touring advice, including how to best experience the amazing new Wizarding Worlds of Harry Potter.

THE MUSIC OF LIFE

THOUGH IT'S COMMON in our culture to see life as a journey from cradle to grave, Alan Watts, a noted late-20th-century philosopher, saw it differently. He viewed life not as a journey but as a dance. In a journey, he said, you are trying to get somewhere, and are consequently always looking ahead, anticipating the way stations, and thinking about the end. Though the journey metaphor is popular, particularly in the West, it is generally characterized by a driven, goal-oriented mentality: a way of living and being that often inhibits those who subscribe to the journey metaphor from savoring each moment of life.

When you dance, by contrast, you hear the music and move in harmony with the rhythm. Like life, a dance has a beginning and an end. But unlike a journey, your objective is not to get to the end but to enjoy the dance while the music plays. You are totally in the moment and care nothing about where on the floor you stop when the dance is done.

As you begin to contemplate your Walt Disney World vacation, you may not have much patience for a philosophical discussion about journeys and dancing. But you see, it is relevant. If you are like most travel guide readers, you are apt to plan and organize, to anticipate and control, and you like things to go smoothly. And truth be told, this leads us to suspect that you are a person who looks ahead and is outcome-oriented. You may even feel a bit of pressure concerning your vacation. Vacations, after all, are special events and expensive ones as well. So you work hard to make the most of your vacation.

We also believe that work, planning, and organization are important, and at Walt Disney World they are essential. But if they become your focus, you won't be able to hear the music and enjoy the dance. Though a lot of dancing these days resembles highly individualized seizures, there was a time when each dance involved specific steps, which you committed to memory. At first you were tentative and awkward, but eventually the steps became second nature and you didn't think about them anymore.

Metaphorically, this is what we want for you and your children or grandchildren as you embark on your Walt Disney World vacation. We want you to learn the steps ahead of time, so that when you're on your vacation and the music plays, you will be able to hear it, and you and your children will dance with grace and ease.

YOUR PERSONAL TRAINERS

WE'RE HERE TO WHIP YOU INTO SHAPE by helping you plan and enjoy your Walt Disney World vacation. Together we'll make sure that it really *is* a vacation, as opposed to, say, an ordeal or an expensive way to experience heatstroke. Our objective, simply put, is to ensure that you and your children have fun.

Because this book is specifically for adults traveling with children, we'll concentrate on your special needs and challenges. We'll share our most useful tips as well as the travel secrets of more than 59,000 families interviewed over the years we've covered Walt Disney World.

So who *are* we? There's a bunch of us, actually. Your primary personal trainers are Liliane and Bob. Helping out bigtime are Isaac, Ethan, and Julia, our Florida-based crew; Erin and Ricky, who live in New York; and Alex and Kieran, who reside in the United Kingdom.

Ethan   Kieran   Erin

Ricky   Alex   Isaac   Julia

Isaac, 15, is our easygoing King of Patience. He calms the troops and makes sure that nobody misses their favorite attractions. Isaac plays football and rows crew; he also enjoys music and has performed at Walt Disney World with his school's orchestra and choir.

Ethan is 12 years old and always on the go. On his agenda: action, adventure, and what's new. In addition, he's a dedicated tennis player who loves to travel.

Julia, 11, loves face painting, Disney pin trading, autographs, and parades. She's a great soccer player in addition to being a talented singer and dancer.

Erin is 16 years old; he loves to paint, and the creative side of Disney appeals to him. His French-born mom takes him to the parks regularly. Erin loves the thrill rides at Disney's Hollywood Studios, and he delights in seeing his mom's expressions when they ride The Twilight Zone Tower of Terror together. He also makes sure that his little brother, Max, always has a good time when they visit the parks.

New to our team are Ricky, Alex, and Kieran. Kieran is 10 years old and lives in England, where he enjoys playing the trumpet, cricket, and soccer. He is often in Florida, where his family has a holiday home, but he would rather live on the *Disney Dream*. His goal is to become the captain of the ship and a Disney Legend. We refer to him as Captain Kieran.

Kieran's sister, Alex, is 12 years old. She loves all things Disney, and like Harry Potter, she is a wizard. She dislikes One Direction but loves the Vamps. She excels at karate and, together with Captain Kieran, visits the parks regularly. This year marks her 41st visit.

Ricky is 10 years old and lives on a small horse farm in Westchester County, New York. He loves playing video games and watching YouTube videos. He has just begun making his own videos and shot several during a recent trip to Disney World. Ricky is a foodie and is always game for experiencing a new restaurant.

This year we are saying goodbye to Hannah Testa, who for years has kept the gang in check. May all your wishes come true, princess, and remember the rule: NEVER grow up! Thank you for your witty contributions. Together with Ian, Sheldon, and Idan, you will always be part of the Unofficial family.

Liliane, a native of Belgium, moved to Birmingham, Alabama, in 2014 after having spent 25 years in New York City. She's funny and very charming in the best European tradition, and she puts more energy into being a mom than you think possible without performance-enhancing drugs. Optimistic and happy, she loves the sweet and sentimental side of Walt Disney World. You might find her whooping it up at the *Hoop-Dee-Doo Musical Revue,* but you'll never see her riding a roller coaster with Bob.

Speak of the devil, Bob isn't a curmudgeon exactly, but he likes to unearth Disney's secrets and show readers how to beat the system. His idea of a warm fuzzy might be the Rock 'n' Roller Coaster, but he'll help you save lots of money, find the best hotels and restaurants, and

BOB

LILIANE

return home less than terminally exhausted. The caricatures above pretty much sum up the essence of Bob and Liliane.

If you're thinking that the cartoons paint a somewhat conflicted picture of your personal trainers, well, you're right. Admittedly, Bob and Liliane have been known to disagree on a thing or two. Together, however, they make a good team. You can count on them to give you both sides of every story. Let's put it this way: Liliane will encourage you to bask in the universal-brotherhood theme of It's a Small World. Bob will show up later to help you get the darned song out of your head.

Len is our research dude. His really complicated scientific wizardry will help you save a bundle of time—would you believe 4 hours in a single day?—by staying out of those pesky lines.

Oops, almost forgot: There's another team member you need to meet. Called a Wuffo, she's our very own character. She'll warn you when rides are too scary, too dark, too wet, or too rough, and she'll tell you which rides to avoid if you have motion sickness. You'll bump into her throughout the book doing, well, what characters do.

So why did we create our own character when Disney has dozens just sitting around? Simple—Disney characters toe the company line. We needed a tough (but lovable) independent character who would give you the skinny on what Disney rides do to your stomach and central nervous system.

ABOUT *This* GUIDE

WALT DISNEY WORLD HAS BEEN OUR BEAT for more than three decades, and we know it inside out. During those years, we've observed many thousands of parents and grandparents trying—some successfully, others less so—to have a good time at Walt Disney World. Some of these, owing to unfortunate dynamics within the family, were handicapped right from the start. Others were simply overwhelmed by the size and complexity of Walt Disney World; still others fell victim to a lack of foresight, planning, and organization.

Walt Disney World is a better destination for some families than for others. Likewise, some families are more compatible on vacation than others. The likelihood of experiencing a truly wonderful Walt Disney World vacation transcends the theme parks and attractions offered. In fact, the theme parks and attractions are the only constants in the equation. The variables that will define the experience and determine its success are intrinsic to your family: things like attitude, sense of humor, cohesiveness, stamina, flexibility, and conflict resolution.

The simple truth is that Walt Disney World can test you as a family. It will overwhelm you with choices and force you to make decisions about how to spend your time and money. It will challenge you physically as you cover miles on foot and wait in lines touring the theme parks. You will have to respond to surprises (both good and bad) and deal with hyperstimulation.

This guide will forewarn and forearm you. It will help you decide whether a Walt Disney World vacation is a good idea for you and your family at this particular time. It will help you sort out and address the attitudes and family dynamics that can affect your experience. Most important, it will provide the confidence that comes with good planning and realistic expectations.

THE SUM OF ALL FEARS

EVERY WRITER WHO EXPRESSES an opinion is accustomed to readers who strongly agree or disagree—it comes with the territory. Extremely troubling, however, is the possibility that our efforts to be objective have frightened some readers away from Walt Disney World or made others apprehensive. For the record, if you enjoy theme parks, Disney World is as good as it gets, absolute nirvana. It's upbeat, safe, fun, eye-popping, happy, and exciting. If you arrive without knowing a thing about the place and make every possible mistake, chances are about 90% that you'll have a wonderful vacation anyway. In the end, guidebooks don't make or break great destinations. Rather, they are simply tools to help you enhance your experience and get the most for your money.

BOB Be prepared to read experienced Disney World visitors' opinions of the parks in this book and to apply them to your own travel circumstances.

As wonderful as Walt Disney World is, however, it's a complex destination. Even so, it isn't nearly as challenging or difficult as New York, San Francisco, Paris, Acapulco, or any other large city or destination. And, happily, there are numerous ways to save money, minimize hassle, and make the most of your time. That's what this guide is about: giving you a heads-up regarding potential problems or opportunities. Unfortunately, some *Unofficial Guide* readers add up the warnings and critical advice and conclude that Walt Disney World is too intimidating, too expensive, or too much work. They lose track of the wonder of Disney World and focus instead on what might go wrong.

Our philosophy is that knowledge is power (and time and money too). You're free to follow our advice—or not—at your discretion. But you can't exercise that discretion if we fail to present the issues. With or without a guidebook, you'll have a great time at Walt Disney World. If you let us, we'll help you smooth the potential bumps. We're certain that we can help you turn a great vacation into an absolutely superb one. Either way, once there, you'll get the feel of the place and quickly reach a comfort level that will allay your apprehensions and allow you to have a great experience.

LETTERS AND COMMENTS FROM READERS

MANY WHO USE *The Unofficial Guide to Walt Disney World with Kids* write us to comment or share their own touring strategies. We appreciate all such input, both positive and critical, and encourage our readers to continue writing. Their comments and observations are frequently incorporated into revised editions of the guide and have contributed immeasurably to its improvement.

Privacy Policy

If you write us or complete our reader survey, rest assured that we won't release your name and address to any mailing-list companies, direct mail advertisers, or other third parties. Unless you instruct us otherwise, we'll assume that you don't object to being quoted in the guide.

How to Contact the Authors

Bob, Liliane, and Len
The Unofficial Guide to Walt Disney World with Kids
2204 First Ave. S, Ste. 102
Birmingham, AL 35233
unofficialguides@menasharidge.com

When e-mailing us, please tell us where you're from. If you snail mail us, put your address on both your letter and envelope; the two sometimes get separated. It's also a good idea to include your phone number. Because we're travel writers, we're often out of the office for long periods of time, so forgive us if our response is slow. *Unofficial Guide* e-mail isn't forwarded to us when we're traveling, but we'll respond as soon as possible after we return.

Online Reader Survey

Express your opinions about your Walt Disney World visit at **touring plans.com/walt-disney-world/survey.** This online questionnaire lets every member of your party, regardless of age, tell us what he or she thinks about attractions, hotels, restaurants, and more.

If you'd rather print out and mail us the survey, send it to the address above. In any case, let us know what you think!

Continued on page 12

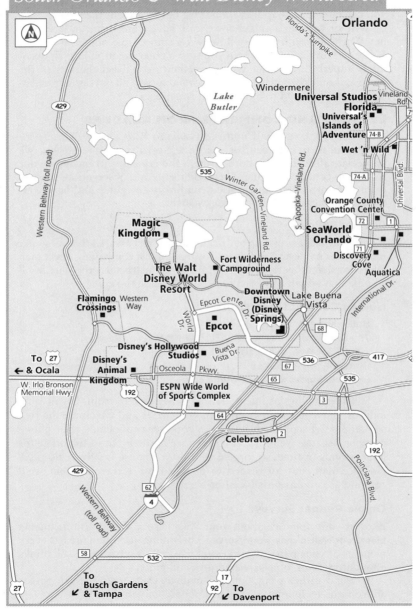

South Orlando & Walt Disney World Area

Orlando

Florida's Turnpike

Windermere

Lake
Butler

429

Universal Studios Vineland
Florida Rd.

Universal's
Islands of
Adventure 74-B

Wet 'n Wild

535

Winter Garden-Vineland Rd.

74-A

S. Apopka-Vineland Rd.

Western Beltway (toll road)

Orange County
Convention Center

72

SeaWorld
Orlando

Magic
Kingdom

71

Discovery
Cove
Aquatica

Fort Wilderness
Campground

The Walt
Disney World
Resort

Flamingo Western
Crossings Way

Epcot Center Dr.

Downtown
Disney
(Disney
Springs)

Lake Buena
Vista

World Dr.

Epcot

68

International Dr.

To 27
← & Ocala

Disney's Hollywood
Studios

Disney's
Animal
Kingdom

W. Irlo Bronson
Memorial Hwy.

192

Osceola Pkwy.

ESPN Wide World
of Sports Complex

Buena
Vista Dr.

536

417

67

65

535

64

3

Celebration 2

192

Poinciana Blvd.

429

62

Western Beltway
(toll road)

4

58

532

27

To
Busch Gardens
↙ & Tampa

17

92 To
↙ Davenport

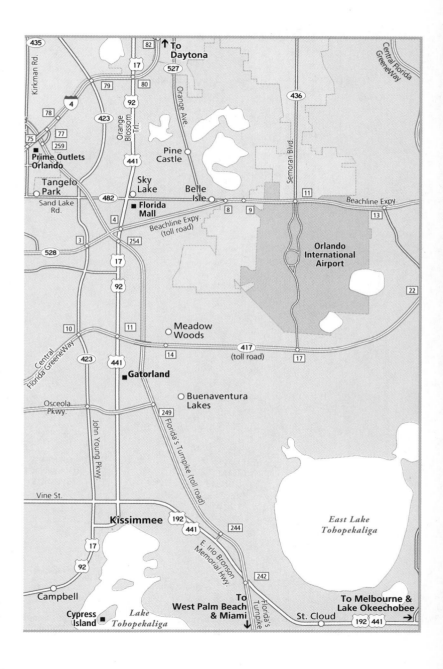

Walt Disney World

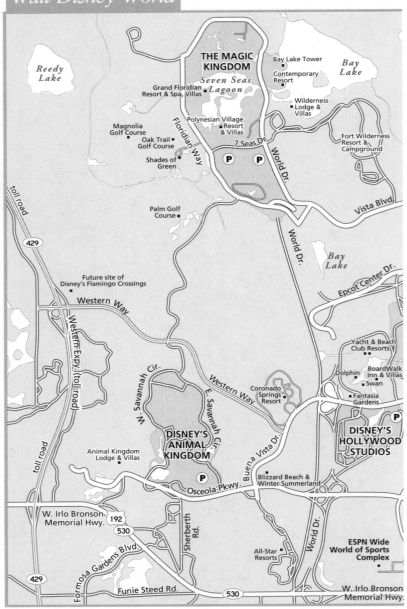

Reedy
Lake

**THE MAGIC
KINGDOM**

*Seven Seas
Lagoon*

Grand Floridian
Resort & Spa, Villas

Bay Lake Tower

Contemporary
Resort

*Bay
Lake*

Wilderness
Lodge &
Villas

Magnolia
Golf Course

Oak Trail
Golf Course

Polynesian Village
Resort
& Villas

7 Seas Dr.

Fort Wilderness
Resort &
Campground

Shades of
Green

Floridian Way

P   P

World Dr.

Palm Golf
Course

Vista Blvd.

World Dr.

*Bay
Lake*

429

Future site of
Disney's Flamingo Crossings

Western Way

Epcot Center Dr.

toll road

Western Expy. (toll road)

Yacht & Beach
Club Resorts

Dolphin

BoardWalk
Inn & Villas

Swan

Fantasia
Gardens

W. Savannah Cir.

E. Savannah Cir.

Western Way

Coronado
Springs
Resort

**DISNEY'S
HOLLYWOOD
STUDIOS**

P

**DISNEY'S
ANIMAL
KINGDOM**

Animal Kingdom
Lodge & Villas

P

Buena Vista Dr.

Blizzard Beach &
Winter Summerland

Osceola Pkwy.

toll road

W. Irlo Bronson
Memorial Hwy.

192

530

Sherberth Rd.

World Dr.

**ESPN Wide
World of Sports
Complex**

Formosa Gardens Blvd.

All-Star
Resorts

429

Funie Steed Rd.

530

W. Irlo Bronson
Memorial Hwy.

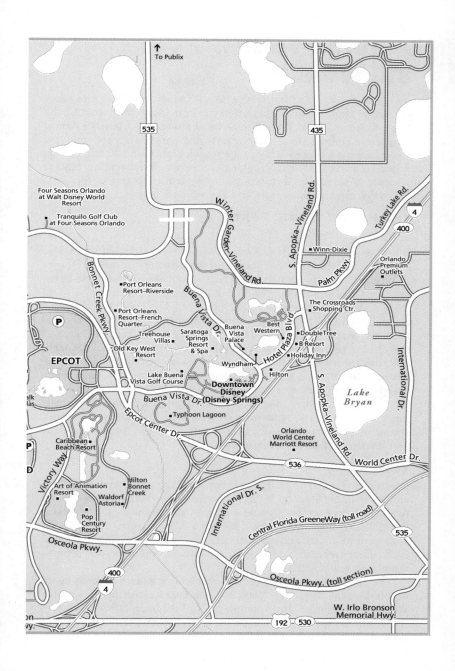

Continued from page 7

A **QUICK TOUR** *of a* **BIG WORLD**

WALT DISNEY WORLD COMPRISES 43 square miles, an area twice as large as Manhattan. Situated strategically in this vast expanse are the **Magic Kingdom, Epcot, Disney's Hollywood Studios,** and **Disney's Animal Kingdom** theme parks; 2 swimming theme parks; a sports complex; 5 golf courses; 43 hotels and a campground; more than 100 restaurants; 4 interconnected lakes; 2 shopping complexes; 8 convention venues; a nature preserve; and a transportation system consisting of four-lane highways, elevated monorails, and a network of canals.

THE MAJOR THEME PARKS

The Magic Kingdom

When people think of Walt Disney World, most think of the Magic Kingdom, opened in 1971. It consists of the adventures, rides, and shows featuring the Disney cartoon characters, as well as Cinderella Castle. It's only one element of Disney World, but it remains the heart.

The Magic Kingdom is divided into six "lands," with five arranged around a central hub. First you come to **Main Street, U.S.A.,** which connects the Magic Kingdom entrance with the hub. Clockwise around the hub are **Adventureland, Frontierland, Liberty Square, Fantasyland,** and **Tomorrowland.** Five hotels (**Bay Lake Tower;** the **Contemporary, Polynesian Village & Villas,** and **Grand Floridian Resorts;** and **The Villas at the Grand Floridian**) are connected to the Magic Kingdom by monorail and boat. Two other hotels, **Shades of Green** (operated by the US Department of Defense) and **Wilderness Lodge & Villas,** are nearby but aren't served by the monorail. Also nearby and served by boat and bus is **Fort Wilderness Resort & Campground.**

Epcot

Opened in October 1982, Epcot is twice as big as the Magic Kingdom and comparable in scope. It has two major areas: **Future World** consists of pavilions concerning human creativity and technological advancement; **World Showcase,** arranged around a 40-acre lagoon, presents the architectural, social, and cultural heritages of almost a dozen nations, each country represented by replicas of famous landmarks and settings familiar to world travelers.

The Epcot resort hotels—the **BoardWalk Inn & Villas, Caribbean Beach Resort, Dolphin, Swan,** and **Yacht & Beach Club Resorts and Beach Club Villas**—are within a 5- to 15-minute walk of the International Gateway, the World Showcase entrance to the theme park. The hotels are also linked to Epcot and Disney's Hollywood Studios by canal and walkway. Epcot is connected to the Magic Kingdom and its hotels by monorail.

Disney's Hollywood Studios

Opened in 1989 as Disney-MGM Studios and a little larger than the Magic Kingdom, Disney's Hollywood Studios consists of two areas. One, occupying about 75% of the Studios, is a theme park focused on movies, music, and television. Park highlights include a re-creation of Hollywood and Sunset Boulevards from Hollywood's Golden Age, four high-tech rides, several musical shows, and a movie stunt show. The second area encompasses soundstages, a back lot of streets and sets, and an outdoor theater for an automobile stunt show.

Disney's Hollywood Studios is connected to other Walt Disney World areas by highway and canal but not by monorail. Guests can park in the Studios' pay parking lot or commute by bus. Guests at Epcot resort hotels can reach the Studios by boat or on foot.

Disney's Animal Kingdom

About five times the size of the Magic Kingdom, Disney's Animal Kingdom combines zoological exhibits with rides, shows, and live entertainment. The park is arranged in a hub-and-spoke configuration somewhat like the Magic Kingdom. A lush tropical rain forest serves as Main Street, funneling visitors to **Discovery Island,** the park's hub. Dominated by the park's central icon, the 14-story-tall, hand-carved **Tree of Life,** Discovery Island offers services, shopping, and dining. From there, guests can access the themed areas: **Africa, Asia,** and **DinoLand U.S.A.** Discovery Island, Africa, and DinoLand U.S.A. opened in 1998, followed by Asia in 1999. Africa, the largest themed area at 100 acres, features free-roaming herds in a re-creation of the Serengeti Plain.

Camp Minnie-Mickey, the park's former character-greeting area, closed in 2014 to make way for a new "land" based on James Cameron's *Avatar* films, with construction ongoing until 2017.

Disney's Animal Kingdom has its own parking lot and is connected to other Walt Disney World destinations by the Disney bus system. Though no hotels lie within Animal Kingdom proper, the **All-Star Resorts, Animal Kingdom Lodge & Villas,** and **Coronado Springs Resort** are all nearby.

THE WATER PARKS

DISNEY WORLD HAS TWO MAJOR water parks: **Typhoon Lagoon** and **Blizzard Beach.** Opened in 1989, Typhoon Lagoon is distinguished by a wave pool capable of making 6-foot waves. Blizzard Beach is newer, having opened in 1995, and it features more slides. Both parks are beautifully landscaped, and great attention is paid to atmosphere and aesthetics. Typhoon Lagoon and Blizzard Beach have their own adjacent parking lots and can be reached by Disney bus.

OTHER WALT DISNEY WORLD VENUES

Disney Springs

Disney Springs is a large shopping, dining, and entertainment complex that encompasses the **Marketplace** on the east, the **West Side** on the west, and **Town Center** in the middle. The Marketplace contains the world's largest Disney-character-merchandise store, upscale resort wear and specialty shops, and several restaurants, including **Rainforest Cafe** and **T-REX.** The West Side combines nightlife, shopping, dining, and entertainment. **House of Blues** serves Cajun-Creole dishes in its restaurant and electric blues in its music hall. **Bongos Cuban Café,** a nightclub and café created by Gloria Estefan and her husband, Emilio, offers Latin rhythms and flavors. **Wolfgang Puck Grand Cafe,** sandwiched among pricey boutiques, is the West Side's prestige eatery. For entertainment, you'll find a 24-screen **AMC Theater; Splitsville,** an upscale bowling alley and restaurant; a permanent showplace for the extraordinary 70-person cast of **Cirque du Soleil La Nouba;** and **DisneyQuest,** an interactive virtual reality and electronic-games venue. Access Disney Springs via Disney buses from Disney resorts.

Since the nighttime-entertainment venues at the former Pleasure Island were shuttered in 2008, The Big Mouse has suffered great angst in trying to arrive at an overall vision for Downtown Disney. After several false starts, Disney embarked on an expansion with a Florida-waterfront-town theme. Called **Disney Springs,** it encompasses the current three areas and adds a fourth. Pleasure Island will become **Town Center** and be built out toward the parking lot. Adjacent to the waterfront is **The Landing,** with shops, restaurants, docks, and a promenade. A desperately needed multistory parking garage opened in 2015. Construction will be completed in 2016.

Disney's BoardWalk

Near Epcot, the BoardWalk is an idealized replication of an East Coast 1930s waterfront resort. Open all day, the BoardWalk features upscale restaurants, shops and galleries, a brewpub, and an ESPN sports bar. In the evening, a nightclub with dueling pianos and a DJ dance club join the lineup; both are for guests age 21 and up only. There's no admission fee for the BoardWalk, but the piano bar levies a cover charge at night. This area is anchored by the BoardWalk Inn & Villas, along with its adjacent convention center. The BoardWalk is within walking distance of the Epcot resorts, Epcot's International Gateway, and Disney's Hollywood Studios. Boat transportation is available to and from Epcot and Disney's Hollywood Studios; buses serve other Disney World locations.

ESPN Wide World of Sports Complex

The 220-acre Wide World of Sports is a state-of-the-art competition and training facility consisting of a 9,500-seat ballpark, two field houses, and venues for baseball, softball, tennis, track and field, volleyball, and dozens of other sports. The spring-training home of the Atlanta Braves, the complex also hosts a mind-boggling calendar of professional and amateur competitions. Walt Disney World guests not participating in events may pay admission to watch any of the scheduled competitions.

Disney Cruise Line: The Mouse at Sea

In 1998, the Walt Disney Company launched (literally) its own cruise

line with the 2,400-passenger *Disney Magic.* Its
sister ship, the *Disney Wonder,* first sailed in 1999.
Most cruises depart from Port Canaveral, Florida
(about a 90-minute drive from Walt Disney
World), or Miami on three-, four-, or seven-night
itineraries. Caribbean and Bahamian cruises
include a day at **Castaway Cay,** Disney's private
island. Cruises can be packaged with a stay at

LILIANE Check out our
*Unofficial Guide to
Disney Cruise Line*
for in-depth infor-
mation on DCL,
including our advice on
cruising with kids and teens.

Disney World. In 2011 and 2012, respectively, two new ships, the *Disney
Dream* and the *Disney Fantasy,* joined the fleet, enabling Disney Cruise
Line to expand sailings to California, Alaska, the Mediterranean, and
northern Europe.

Disney cruises are perfect for families and for kids of all ages.
Though the cruises are family-oriented, extensive children's programs
and elaborate child-care facilities allow grown-ups plenty of opportunities to relax and do adult stuff. The ships are modern ocean liners
with classic steamship lines. Cabins are among the most spacious in
the cruise industry, and the staff is very attentive and accommodating.
From the waitstaff at breakfast, lunch, and dinner to the cabin stew-
ards, yours truly has not experienced any better.

Cabin design reveals Disney's finely tuned sense of the needs of
families and children and offers a cruise-industry first: a split bathroom with a bathtub and shower combo and sink in one room, and
toilet, sink, and vanity in another. This configuration, found in all but
standard inside cabins, allows any family member to use the bathroom without monopolizing it. All bathrooms
have a tub and shower, except rooms for persons with disabilities (shower only). Decor
includes unusual features such as bureaus
designed to look like steamer trunks. Cabins
also have a telephone, TV, hair dryer, and a
cooling box. In some cabins, pull-down Mur-
phy beds or drop-down bunk beds allow for
additional daytime floor space. Storage is generous, with deep drawers and large closets.

LILIANE Board the ship as
early as possible. Check on
your dining rotation, and
reserve Palo or Remy, spa

treatments, and kids'
programs. Relax and
get ready for the
departure party.

A big party with appearances by Mickey and Minnie marks depar-
tures, when the ship's horn toots "When You Wish Upon a Star." Halfway through your voyage Disney throws a deck party, where Mickey
saves all passengers from Captain Hook and his evil plans.

Dining is a true pleasure. Each night, passengers move to a different
family restaurant—each with its own unique theme and menu—and
take their table companions and waitstaff with them. In addition to
the family restaurants, the ships have a range of
cafés offering pizza, burgers, sandwiches, and
ice cream bars. Room service is available 24/7.

For a night out without kids, Palo, which
offers tables with a view, is a must. Reservations are also a must, and a surcharge of $30 is
added for this service to your onboard bill. The

LILIANE Disney strictly
enforces a minimum age

limit (18) for dining
at Palo and Remy,
and a jacket (tie
optional) is a must.

food is excellent, the ambience sophisticated. Disney enforces a strict policy for diners at Palo to be 18 years of age or older.

In addition to Palo, the *Dream* and the *Fantasy* crank it up a notch with Remy. Chefs Scott Hunnel of Victoria & Albert's and Arnaud Lallement from L'Assiette Champenoise—a Michelin two-star restaurant outside Reims, France—created the French-inspired menu, served in an Art Nouveau–style dining room. This upscale dining experience on the high seas costs $75. If you think this is a little over the top, we completely agree. Whatever happened to the no-frills, great-food philosophy we learned from Remy in *Ratatouille*?

The Disney ships offer 15,000-plus square feet of playrooms and other kids' facilities. Programs include interactive activities, play areas supervised by trained counselors, and a children's drop-off service in the evening. Passengers can register their children for the nursery, and group babysitting is available for select hours every day. Cost is $9 per child for the first child and $8 an hour for each additional child in the same family. **Oceaneer Club,** featuring a Never Land theme on the *Wonder* and subdivided into differently themed spaces (*Toy Story, The Avengers,* and the like) on the other ships, is perfect for kids ages 3–7, though children up to age 12 can participate. **Oceaneer's Lab** offers high-tech play. Kids wear ID bracelets, and parents receive pagers. There are also special clubs for tweens (**Edge**) and teens (**Vibe**).

Big with kids of all ages are the pools and the nightly entertainment on board, which show Disney at its best. The **Walt Disney Theatre** stages several musical productions each cruise, and the **Buena Vista Theatre,** with its full-screen cinema, shows first-run and digital 3-D movies as well as classic Disney films. Movies are also played poolside on a state-of-the-art 24-by-14-foot LED screen affixed to the forward funnel in the ships' family-pool areas.

The *Dream* and the *Fantasy* feature the first-ever onboard water coaster. At 765 feet long and the height of four decks, **AquaDuck** is a major attraction for kids and grown-ups alike (the *Magic*'s counterpart, similar though not identical, is **AquaDunk**). Following an initial drop, guests glide through a translucent tube in a loop that extends 12 feet over the side of the vessel, allowing them to look down on the ocean 150 feet below. The ride lasts about 90 seconds and comes with climbs and drops, twists and turns. If you can keep your eyes open while riding, the AquaDuck will provide you with a spectacular view of the ship.

Senses Spa & Salon on the *Dream, Magic,* and *Fantasy* is a great place to relax not just for adults but also for teens, who get their own separate area called **Chill Spa.** (**Vista Spa & Salon** on the *Wonder* is strictly for Mom and Dad.) The treatments are pricey, and there's a surcharge ($16–$25 per day depending on the ship) for the use of the spa's Rainforest suite of saunas, steam rooms, and aromatic showers. The fitness center's showers and lockers are free of charge.

Keys, the piano bar on the *Magic,* and **Cadillac Lounge,** on the *Wonder,* are the most relaxing and beautiful lounges on the Seven Seas. Make a before- or after-dinner drink there part of your routine.

Shore excursions depend on the itinerary, but all Caribbean and Bahamian cruises make at least one call at **Castaway Cay,** Disney's 1,000-acre private island. The natural environment and miles of white-sand beaches have been nicely preserved. The best way to enjoy the island is to disembark first thing in the morning and secure a prime spot at the beach complete with hammock and shade. **Castaway Family Beach** is served by a tram running every 5 minutes. We walked the quarter-mile to the beach but realize that it could be tiresome to walk in the blistering summer heat. **Cookie's BBQ** and **Cookie's Too** serve an array of food that is included in the price of your cruise. Programs for kids on Castaway Cay give parents a chance to enjoy **Serenity Bay,** the adults-only beach.

Another great family experience is a wedding or vow renewal, offered both at sea and on Castaway Cay. In 2014 Liliane joined 26 family members with the mission of getting her cousin Sergio and his bride, Nancy, hitched on Castaway Cay. She still chuckles when she thinks about the frantic efforts of the wedding coordinator and the photographer trying to make sense of the unruly group. With the help of some pixie dust, though, the ceremony went off without a hitch.

Disney's Fairy Tale Wedding packages on Castaway Cay start at $4,000 for a party of eight guests plus the couple; the charge for additional guests is $20 per person age 3 years and older. Each package includes the ceremony, a wedding coordinator, concierge service, and the officiant. Also included are live music during and after the wedding, a bouquet for the bride and a boutonniere for the groom, and a reception aboard the ship. The couple is also treated to dinner at Palo and a $100 onboard stateroom credit. A photographer, a surprise visit by Disney characters, and much more can be booked for an additional cost. For more information, check out **disneyweddings.com/cruise.**

Disney Cruise Line fared better than most of its competitors during the recession and is thriving as of this writing. Sailings enjoy high occupancy these days, and a number of new itineraries have been added. Friends of Disney's *Frozen* can experience the country that inspired the icy kingdom of Arendelle on a Norwegian Fjord cruise of 7, 9, or 11 nights.

Cruises are a terrific value in travel. Deals abound. Check websites such as **cruisecritic.com, cruisemates.com, vacationstogo.com,** and **last minutetravel.com** for the latest discounts. Search engine **kayak.com** is another great resource for uncovering cruise bargains. If you prefer to buy directly from Disney, here's how to get in touch:

Disney Cruise Line
☎ 800-951-6499 or 800-951-3532
disneycruise.com

Disney Cruise Line offers a free planning DVD that tells you all you need to know about Disney cruises and then some. To obtain a copy, call ☎ 888-DCL-2500, or order online at **disneycruise.com.**

Finally, to get the most out of your cruise, we recommend *The Unofficial Guide to Disney Cruise Line,* by Len Testa with Laurel Stewart,

Erin Foster, and Ritchey Halphen, which presents advice for first-time cruisers; money-saving tips for booking your cruise; and detailed profiles for restaurants, shows, and nightclubs, along with deck plans and thorough coverage of the ports visited by DCL.

DISNEY-SPEAK POCKET TRANSLATOR

THOUGH IT MAY COME AS A SURPRISE to many, Walt Disney World has its own somewhat peculiar language. Here are some terms you're likely to bump into.

DISNEY-SPEAK	ENGLISH DEFINITION
ADVENTURE	Ride
ATTRACTION	Ride or theater show
ATTRACTION HOST	Ride operator
AUDIENCE	Crowd
BACKSTAGE	Behind the scenes, out of view of customers
CAST MEMBER	Employee
CHARACTER	Disney character impersonated by an employee
COSTUME	Work attire or uniform
DARK RIDE	Indoor ride
DAY GUEST	Any customer not staying at a Disney resort
FACE CHARACTER	A character who does not wear a head-covering costume (Snow White, Cinderella, Jasmine, and the like)
GENERAL PUBLIC	Same as day guest
GREETER	Employee positioned at an attraction entrance
GUEST	Customer
HIDDEN MICKEYS	Frontal silhouette of Mickey's head worked subtly into the design of buildings, railings, vehicles, golf greens, attractions, and just about anything else
ONSTAGE	In full view of customers
PRESHOW	Entertainment at an attraction prior to the feature presentation
RESORT GUEST	A customer staying at a Disney resort
SECURITY HOST	Security guard
SOFT OPENING	Opening a park or attraction before its stated opening date
TRANSITIONAL EXPERIENCE	An element of the queuing area and/or preshow that provides a story line or information essential to understanding the attraction

PART ONE

BASIC CONSIDERATIONS

 IS WALT DISNEY WORLD *for* YOU?

ALMOST ALL VISITORS ENJOY WALT DISNEY WORLD on some level and find things to see and do that they like. In fact, for many, the theme park attractions are just the tip of the iceberg. The more salient question, then—this is a family vacation, after all—is whether the members of your family basically like the same things. If you do, fine. If not, how will you handle the differing agendas?

A mother from Toronto described her husband's aversion to Disney's (in his terms) "phony, plastic, and idealized version of life." Touring the theme parks, he was a real cynic and managed to diminish the experience for the rest of the family. As it happened, however, Dad's pejorative point of view didn't extend to the Disney golf courses. So Mom packed him up and sent him golfing while the family enjoyed the parks.

If you have someone in your family who doesn't like theme parks or, for whatever reason, doesn't care for Disney's brand of entertainment, it helps to get that attitude out in the open. Our recommendation is to deal with the person up front. Glossing over or ignoring the contrary opinion and hoping that "Tom will like it once he gets there" is naive and unrealistic. Either leave Tom at home or help him discover and plan activities that he will enjoy, resigning yourself in the process to the fact that the family won't be together at all times.

DIFFERENT FOLKS, DIFFERENT STROKES

IT'S NO SECRET THAT WE AT THE UNOFFICIAL GUIDES believe that thorough planning is an essential key to a successful Walt Disney World vacation. It's also no secret that our emphasis on planning rubs some folks the wrong way. Bob's sister and her husband, for example, are spontaneous people and do not appreciate the concept of detailed planning or, more particularly, following one of our touring plans when they visit the theme parks. To them the most important thing is to relax, take things as they come, and enjoy the moment. Sometimes they arrive at Epcot at 10:30 in the morning (impossibly late for us Unofficial Guide types), walk around enjoying the landscaping and architecture, and then sit with a cup of espresso, watching other guests race around the park like maniacs. They would be the first to admit that they don't see many attractions, but experiencing attractions is not what lights their sparklers.

Not coincidentally, most of our readers are big on planning. When they go to the theme park, they want to experience the attractions, and the shorter the lines, the better. They are willing to sacrifice some spontaneity for touring efficiency.

We want you to have the best possible time, whatever that means to you, so plan (or not) according to your preference. The point here is that most families (unlike Bob's sister and her husband) are not entirely in agreement on this planning versus spontaneity issue. If you are a serious planner and your oldest daughter and husband are free spirits, you have the makings of a problem. In practice, the way this and similar scenarios shake out is that the planner (usually the more assertive or type-A person) just takes over. Sometimes daughter and husband go along and everything works out, but just as often they feel resentful. There are as many ways of developing a win–win compromise as there are well-intentioned people on different sides of this situation. How you settle it is up to you. We're simply suggesting that you examine the problem and work out the solution *before* you go on vacation.

THE NATURE OF THE BEAST

THOUGH MANY PARENTS DON'T REALIZE IT, there is no law that says you must take your kids to Walt Disney World. Likewise, there's no law that says you will enjoy Walt Disney World. And though we will help you make the most of any visit, we can't change the basic nature of the beast . . . er, mouse. A Walt Disney World vacation is an active and physically demanding undertaking. Regimentation, getting up early, lots of walking, waiting in lines, fighting crowds, and (often) enduring heat and humidity are as intrinsic to a Walt Disney World vacation as stripes are to a zebra. Especially if you're traveling with children, you'll need a sense of humor, more than a modicum of patience, and the ability to roll with the punches.

BOB Sehlinger's Law postulates that the number of adults required to take care 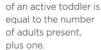 of an active toddler is equal to the number of adults present, plus one.

KNOW THYSELF AND NOTHING TO EXCESS

THIS GOOD ADVICE WAS MADE AVAILABLE to ancient Greeks courtesy of the oracle of Apollo at Delphi, who gave us permission to pass it along to you. First, concerning the "know thyself" part, we want you to do some serious thinking about what you want in a vacation. We also want you to entertain the notion that having fun on your vacation may be very different from doing and seeing as much as possible.

Because Walt Disney World is expensive, many families confuse "seeing everything" in order to "get our money's worth" with having a great time. Sometimes the two are compatible, but more often they are not. So if sleeping in, relaxing with the paper over coffee, sunbathing by the pool, or taking a nap ranks high on your vacation hit parade, you need to accord them due emphasis on your Disney visit (are you listening?), even if it means you see less of the theme parks.

Which brings us to the "nothing to excess" part. At Walt Disney World, especially if you are touring with children, less is definitely more. Trust us—you cannot go full tilt dawn to dark in the theme parks day after day. First you'll get tired, then you'll get cranky, and then you'll

LILIANE You can enjoy a perfectly wonderful time in the World if you're realistic, organized, and prepared.

adopt a production mentality ("We have three more rides, and then we can go back to the hotel"). Finally, you'll hit the wall because you just can't maintain the pace.

Plan on seeing Walt Disney World in bite-size chunks with plenty of sleeping, swimming, napping, and relaxing in-between. Ask yourself over and over in both the planning stage and while you are at Walt Disney World: What will contribute the greatest contentedness, satisfaction, and harmony? Trust your instincts. If

BOB Get a grip on your needs and preferences before you leave home, and develop an itinerary that incorporates all the things that make you happiest.

stopping for ice cream or returning to the hotel for a dip feels like more fun than seeing another attraction, do it—even if it means wasting the remaining hours of an expensive admissions pass.

The AGE THING

THERE IS A LOT OF SERIOUS REFLECTION among parents and grandparents in regard to how old a child should be before embarking on a trip to Walt Disney World. The answer, not always obvious, stems from the personalities and maturity of the children, as well as the personalities and parenting style of the adults.

Walt Disney World for Infants and Toddlers

We believe that traveling with infants and toddlers is a great idea. Developmentally, travel is a stimulating learning experience for even the youngest of children. Infants, of course, will not know Mickey Mouse from a draft horse but will respond to sun and shade, music, bright colors, and the extra attention they receive from you. From first steps to full mobility, toddlers respond to the excitement and spectacle of Disney World, though of course in a much different way than you do. Your toddler will prefer splashing in fountains and clambering over curbs and benches to experiencing most attractions, but no matter: He or she will still have a great time.

Somewhere between 4 and 6 years of age, your child will experience the first vacation that he or she will remember as an adult. Though more likely to remember the comfortable coziness of the hotel room than the theme parks, the child will be able to experience and comprehend many attractions and will be a much fuller participant in your vacation. Even so, his or her favorite activity is likely to be swimming in the hotel pool.

As concerns infants and toddlers, there are good reasons and bad reasons for vacationing at Walt Disney World. A good reason for taking your little one to Disney World is that you want to go and there's no one available to care for your child during your absence. Philosophically, we are very much against putting your life (including your vacation) on hold until your children are older.

LILIANE Traveling with infants and toddlers sharpens parenting skills and makes the entire family more mobile and flexible, resulting in a richer, fuller life for all.

Especially if you have children of varying ages (or plan to, for that matter), it's better to take the show on the road than to wait until the youngest reaches the perceived ideal age. If your family includes a toddler or infant, you will find everything from private facilities for breast-feeding to changing tables in both men's and women's restrooms to facilitate baby's care. Your whole family will be able to tour together with fewer hassles than on a picnic outing at home.

An illogical reason, however, for taking an infant or toddler to Disney World is that you think it's the perfect vacation destination for babies. It's not, so think again if you are contemplating Disney World primarily for your child's enjoyment. For starters, attractions are geared more toward older children and adults. Even designer play areas such as Tom Sawyer Island in the Magic Kingdom are developed with older children in mind.

That said, let us stress that for the well prepared, taking a toddler to Disney World can be a totally glorious experience. There's truly nothing like watching your child respond to the color, the sound, the festivity, and, most of all, the characters. You'll return home with scrapbooks of photos that you will treasure forever. Your little one won't remember much, but never mind. Your memories will be unforgettable.

LILIANE Baby supplies— including disposable diapers, formula, and baby food—are for sale, and there are rockers and special chairs for nursing mothers.

If you elect to take your infant or toddler to Disney World, rest assured that their needs have been anticipated. The major theme parks have centralized facilities for infant and toddler care. Everything necessary for changing diapers, preparing formula, and warming bottles and food is available. Dads in charge of little ones are welcome at the centers and can use most services offered. In addition, men's rooms in the major theme parks have changing tables.

Infants and toddlers are allowed to experience any attraction that doesn't have minimum height or age restrictions. A Minneapolis mom suggests using a baby sling:

> We used a baby sling on our trip and thought it was great when standing in the lines—much better than a stroller, which you have to park before getting in line (and navigate through crowds). My baby was still nursing when we went to Disney World. The only really

great place I found to nurse in the Magic Kingdom was a hidden bench in the shade in Adventureland between the snack stand (next to the Enchanted Tiki Room) *and the small shops. It is impractical to go to the baby station every time, so a nursing mom better be comfortable about nursing in very public situations.*

Two points in our reader's comment warrant elaboration. First, the rental strollers at all of the major theme parks are designed for toddlers and children up to 3 and 4 years old but are definitely not for infants. If you bring pillows and padding, the rental strollers can be made to work. You can bring your own stroller, but unless it's collapsible, you will not be able to take it on Disney trams, buses, or boats.

Even if you opt for a stroller (your own or a rental), we nevertheless recommend that you also bring a baby sling or baby/child backpack. Simply put, there will be many times in the theme parks when you will have to park the stroller and carry your child. As an aside, if you haven't checked out baby slings and packs lately, you'll be amazed by some of the technological advances made in these products.

The second point that needs addressing is our reader's perception that there are not many good places in the theme parks for breast-feeding unless you are accustomed to nursing in public. Many nursing moms recommend breast-feeding during a dark Disney theater presentation. This works, however, only if the presentation is long enough for the baby to finish nursing. *The Hall of Presidents* at the Magic Kingdom and *The American Adventure* at Epcot will afford you about 23 and 29 minutes, respectively.

Many Disney shows run back to back with only 1 or 2 minutes in between to change the audience. If you want to breast-feed and require more time than the length of the show, tell the cast member on entering that you want to breast-feed and ask if you can remain in the theater and watch a second showing while your baby finishes. Also keep in mind that many shows may have special effects or loud sound tracks that may make children even as old as 7 uncomfortable.

If you can adjust to nursing in more public places with your breast and the baby's head covered with a shawl or some such, nursing will not be a problem at all. Even on the most crowded days, you can always find a back corner of a restaurant or a comparatively secluded park bench or garden spot to nurse. Finally, the Baby Care Centers, with their private nursing rooms, are centrally located in all of the parks except the Studios.

LILIANE In addition to providing an alternative to carrying your child, a stroller serves as a handy cart for diaper bags, water bottles, and other items you deem necessary.

A mom from Georgia wrote to us, and we totally agree with her:

Many women have no problem nursing uncovered, and they have the right to do so in public without being criticized. Even women who want to cover up may have a baby who won't cooperate and flings off the cover; plus, it's not necessary to sit through all of The Hall of Presidents *to feed your child. I understand that peace and quiet help, but babies will eat almost anywhere, and mothers shouldn't feel pressured to sneak off when a baby is hungry. A lot of people read your books, and it would be nice to see you refer to breast-feeding as normal and not something that needs to be hidden or covered.*

Walt Disney World for 4-, 5-, and 6-Year-Olds

Children ages 4–6 vary immensely in their capacity to comprehend and enjoy Walt Disney World. With this age group, the go–no-go decision is a judgment call. If your child is sturdy, easygoing, fairly adventuresome, and demonstrates a high degree of independence, the trip will probably work. On the other hand, if your child tires easily, is temperamental, or is a bit timid or reticent in embracing new experiences, you're much better off waiting a few years. Whereas the travel and sensory-overload problems of infants and toddlers can be addressed and (usually) remedied on the go, discontented 4- to 6-year-olds have the ability to stop a family dead in its tracks, as this mother of three from Cape May, New Jersey, attests:

My 5-year-old was scared pretty badly on a dark ride our first day at Disney World. From then on, for the rest of the trip, we had to coax and reassure her before each and every ride before she would go. It was like pulling teeth.

If you have a tiring, clinging, and/or difficult 4- to 6-year-old who, for whatever circumstances, will be part of your group, you can side-step or diminish potential problems with a bit of pretrip preparation. Even if your preschooler is plucky and game, the same prep measures (described later in this section) will enhance his or her experience and make life easier for the rest of the family.

Parents who understand that a visit with 3- to 6-year-old children is going to be more about the cumulative experience than it is about seeing it all will have a blast, as well as wonderful memories of their children's amazement.

The Ideal Age

Though our readers report both successful trips and disasters with children of all ages, the consensus is that the ideal children's ages for family compatibility and togetherness at Walt Disney World are 8–12 years. This age group is old enough, tall enough, and sufficiently stalwart to experience, understand, and appreciate practically all Disney attractions. Moreover, they are developed to the extent that they can get around the parks on their own steam without being carried or collapsing. Best of all, they're still young enough to enjoy being with Mom and Dad. From our experience, ages 10–12 are better than 8 and 9, though what you gain in maturity is at the cost of that irrepressible, wide-eyed wonder so prevalent in the 8- and 9-year-olds.

Walt Disney World for Teens

Teens love Walt Disney World, and for parents of teens the World is a nearly perfect, albeit expensive, vacation choice. Though your teens might not be as wide-eyed and impressionable as their younger sibs, they are at an age where they can sample, understand, and enjoy practically everything Disney World has to offer.

For parents, Disney World is a vacation destination where you can permit your teens an extraordinary amount of freedom. The entertainment is wholesome, the venues are safe, and the entire complex of hotels, theme parks, restaurants, and shopping centers is accessible via the Disney World transportation system. The transportation system allows you, for example, to enjoy a romantic dinner and an early bedtime while your teens take in the late-night fireworks at the theme parks. After the fireworks, a Disney bus, boat, or monorail will deposit them safely back at the hotel.

Because most adolescents relish freedom, you may have difficulty keeping your teens with the rest of the family. Thus, if one of your objectives is to spend time with your teenage children during your Disney World vacation, you will need to establish some clear-cut guidelines regarding togetherness and separateness before you leave home. Make your teens part of the discussion and try to meet them halfway in crafting a decision everyone can live with. For your teens, touring on their own at Walt Disney World is tantamount to being independent in a large city. It's intoxicating, to say the least, and can be an excellent learning experience, if not a rite of passage. In any event, we're not suggesting that you just turn them loose. Rather, we are just attempting to sensitize you to the fact that for your teens, there are some transcendent issues involved.

Most teens crave the company of other teens. If you have a solitary teen in your family, do not be surprised if he or she wants to invite a friend on your vacation. If you are invested in sharing intimate, quality time with your solitary teen, the presence of a friend will make this difficult, if not impossible. However, if you turn down the request to bring a friend, be prepared to go the extra mile to be a companion to your teen at Disney World. Expressed differently, if you're a teen, it's not much fun to ride Space Mountain by yourself.

One specific issue that absolutely should be addressed before you leave home is what assistance (if any) you expect from your teen in regard to helping with younger children in the family. Once again, try to carve out a win-win compromise. Consider the case of the mother from Indiana who had a teenage daughter from an earlier marriage and two children under age 10 from a second marriage. After a couple of vacations where she thrust the unwilling teen into the position of being a surrogate parent to her stepsisters, the teen declined henceforth to participate in family vacations.

Many parents have written *The Unofficial Guide* asking if there are unsafe places at Walt Disney World or places where teens simply should not be allowed to go. Though the answer depends more on your family values and the relative maturity of your teens than on Disney World, the basic answer is no. Though it's true that teens (or adults, for that matter) who are looking for trouble can find it anywhere, there is absolutely nothing at Disney World that could be construed as a precipitant or a catalyst.

As a final aside, if you allow your teens some independence and they are getting around on the Walt Disney World transportation system, expect some schedule slippage. There are no posted transportation schedules other than when service begins in the morning and when service terminates at night. Thus, to catch a bus, for example, you just go to a bus station and wait for the next bus to your Disney World destination. If you happen to just miss the bus, you might have to wait 15–45 minutes (more often 15–20 minutes) for the next one. If punctuality is essential, advise your independent teens to arrive at a transportation station an hour before they are expected somewhere to allow sufficient time for the commute.

About **INVITING** *Your* **CHILDREN'S FRIENDS**

IF YOUR CHILDREN WANT TO INVITE FRIENDS on your Walt Disney World vacation, give your decision careful thought. There's more involved here than might be apparent. First, consider the logistics of numbers. Is there room in the car? Will you have to leave something at home that you had planned on taking to make room in the trunk for the friend's luggage? Will additional hotel rooms or a larger condo be required? Will the increased number of people in your group make it hard to get a table at a restaurant?

If you determine that you can logistically accommodate one or more friends, the next step is to consider how the inclusion of the friend will affect your group's dynamics. Generally speaking, the presence of a friend will make it harder to really connect with your own children. So if one of your vacation goals is an intimate bonding experience with your children, the addition of friends will probably frustrate your attempts to realize that objective.

If family relationship building is not necessarily a primary objective of your vacation, it's quite possible that the inclusion of a friend will make life easier for you. This is especially true in the case of only children, who may otherwise depend exclusively on you to keep them happy and occupied. Having a friend along can take the pressure off and give you some much-needed breathing room.

If you decide to allow a friend to accompany you, limit the selection to children you know really well and whose parents you also know. Your Disney World vacation is not the time to include "my friend Eddie from school" whom you've never met. Your children's friends who have spent time in your home will have a sense of your parenting style, and you will have a sense of their personality, behavior, and compatibility with your family. Assess the prospective child's potential to fit in well on a long trip. Is he or she polite, personable, fun to be with, and reasonably mature? Does he or she relate well to you and to the other members of your family?

Because a Disney World vacation is not, for most of us, a spur-of-the-moment thing, you should have adequate time to evaluate potential candidate friends. A trip to the mall including a meal in a sit-down restaurant will tell you volumes about the friend. Likewise, inviting the friend to share dinner with the family and then spend the night will provide a lot of relevant information. Ideally this type of evaluation should take place early on in the normal course of family events, before you discuss the possibility of a friend joining you on your vacation. This will allow you to size things up without your child (or the friend) realizing that an evaluation is taking place.

By seizing the initiative, you can guide the outcome. Ann, a Springfield, Ohio, mom, for example, anticipated that her 12-year-old son would ask to take a friend on their vacation. As she pondered the various friends her son might propose, she came up with four names. One, an otherwise sweet child, had a medical condition that Ann felt unqualified to monitor or treat. A second friend was overly aggressive with younger children and was often socially inappropriate for his age. Two other friends, Chuck and Marty, with whom she'd had a generally positive experience, were good candidates for the trip. After orchestrating some opportunities to spend time with each of the boys, she made her decision and asked her son, "Would you like to take Marty with us to Disney World?" Her son was delighted, and Ann had diplomatically preempted having to turn down friends her son might have proposed.

We recommend that you do the inviting instead of your child and that you extend the invitation to the parent (to avoid disappointment, you might want to sound out the friend's parent before broaching the issue with your child). Observing this recommendation will allow you to query the friend's parents concerning food preferences, any medical conditions, how discipline is administered in the friend's family, how the friend's parents feel about the way you administer discipline, and the parents' expectation regarding religious observations while their child is in your care.

Before you extend the invitation, give some serious thought to who pays for what. Make a specific proposal for financing the trip a part of your invitation. For example: "There's room for Marty in the hotel room, and transportation's no problem because we're driving. So we'll just need you to pick up Marty's meals, theme park admissions, and spending money."

A FEW WORDS *for* SINGLE PARENTS

BECAUSE SINGLE PARENTS GENERALLY are also working parents, planning a special getaway with your children can be the best way to spend some quality time together. But remember, the vacation is not just for your child—it's for you too. You might invite a grandparent or a favorite aunt or uncle along; the other adult provides nice company for you, and your child will benefit from the time with family members. You might likewise consider inviting an adult friend.

Though bringing along an adult friend or family member is the best option, the reality is that many single parents don't have friends, grandparents, or favorite aunts or uncles who can make the trip. And while spending time with your child is wonderful, it is very difficult to match the energy level of your child if you are the sole focus of his or her world.

One alternative: Try to meet other single parents at Walt Disney World. It may seem odd, but most of them are in the same boat as you; besides, all you have to do is ask. Another option, albeit expensive, is to take along a trustworthy babysitter (18 or up) to travel with you.

The easiest way to meet other single parents at the World is to hang out at the hotel pool. Make your way there on the day you arrive, after traveling by car or plane and without enough time to blow a full admission ticket at a theme park. In any event, a couple of hours spent poolside is a relaxing way to start your vacation.

If you visit Walt Disney World with another single parent, get adjoining rooms; take turns watching all the kids; and, on at least one night, get a sitter and enjoy an evening out.

Throughout this book we mention the importance of good planning and touring. For a single parent, this is an absolute must. In addition, make sure that you set aside some downtime back at the hotel every day.

Finally, don't try to spend every moment with your children on vacation. Instead, plan some activities for your children with other children. Disney educational programs for children, for example, are worth considering. Then take advantage of your free time to do what you want to do: Read a book, have a massage, take a long walk, or enjoy a catnap.

While pricey, one of the best ways for single parents to relax is to add a three- or four-night cruise to their Disney stay. Onboard activities will keep your child occupied and give you time to relax.

"HE WHO HESITATES IS LAUNCHED!" *Tips and Warnings for Grandparents*

SENIORS OFTEN GET INTO PREDICAMENTS caused by touring with grandchildren. Run ragged and pressured to endure a blistering pace, many seniors just concentrate on surviving Walt Disney World rather than enjoying it. The theme parks have as much to offer older visitors as they do children, and seniors must either set the pace or dispatch the young folks to tour on their own.

An older reader from Alabaster, Alabama, writes:

> *Being a senior is not for wusses. At Disney World particularly, it requires courage and pluck. Things that used to be easy take a lot of effort, and sometimes your brain has to wait for your body to catch up. Half the time, your grandchildren treat you like a crumbling ruin and then turn around and trick you into getting on a roller coaster in the dark. What you need to tell seniors is that they have to be alert and not trust anyone. Not their children or even the Disney people, and especially not their grandchildren. When your grandchildren want you to go on a ride, don't follow along blindly like a lamb to the slaughter. Make sure you know what the ride is all about. Stand your ground and do not waffle. He who hesitates is launched!*

If you don't get to see much of your grandchildren, you might think that Walt Disney World is the perfect place for a little bonding and togetherness. Wrong! Disney World can potentially send children into system overload and can precipitate behaviors that pose a challenge even to adoring parents, never mind grandparents. You don't take your grandchildren straight to Disney World for the same reason you don't buy your 16-year-old son a Ferrari: Handling it safely and well requires some experience.

Begin by spending time with your grandchildren in an environment that you can control. Have them over one at a time for dinner and to spend the night. Check out how they respond to your oversight and discipline. Determine that you can set limits and that they will accept those limits. When you reach this stage, you can contemplate some outings to the zoo, the movies, the mall, or the state fair. Gauge how demanding your grandchildren are when you are out of the house. Eat a meal or two in a full-service restaurant to get a sense of their social skills and their ability to behave appropriately. Don't expect perfection, and be prepared to modify your own behavior a little too. As a senior friend of mine told her husband (none too decorously), "You can't see Walt Disney World sitting on a stick."

If you have a good relationship with your grandchildren and have had a positive one-on-one experience taking care of them, you might consider a trip to Disney World. If you do, we have two recommendations. First, visit Disney World without them to get an idea of what you're getting into. A scouting trip will also provide you with an opportunity to enjoy some of the attractions that won't be on the itinerary when you return with the grandkids. Second, if you are considering a trip of a week's duration, you might think about buying a Disney package that combines four days at Disney World with a three-day cruise. In addition to being a memorable experience for your grandchildren, the cruise provides plenty of structure for children of almost every age, thus allowing you to be with them but also to have some time off. Call Disney Cruise Line at ☎ 800-951-3532 or visit **disneycruise.com.**

Tips for Grandparents

1. It's best to take one grandchild at a time, two at the most. Cousins can be better than siblings because they don't fight as much. To preclude sibling jealousy, try connecting the trip to a child's milestone, such as finishing the sixth grade.

2. Let your grandchildren help plan the vacation, and keep the first one short. Be flexible and don't overplan. Take a break in the afternoon.

3. Discuss mealtimes and bedtime. Fortunately, many grandparents are on an early dinner schedule, which works nicely with younger children. Also, if you want to plan a special evening out, be sure to make the reservation ahead of time.

4. Gear plans to your grandchildren's age levels, because if they're not happy, you won't be happy. Take a day off between visits to the parks.

5. Create an itinerary that offers some supervised activities for children in case you need a rest.

6. If you're traveling by car, this is the one time we highly recommend headphones. Kids' musical tastes are vastly different from most grandparents'. It's simply more enjoyable when everyone can listen to his or her own preferred style of music, at least for some portion of the trip.

7. Take along a night-light.

8. Carry a notarized statement from parents for permission for medical care in case of an emergency. Also be sure you have insurance information and copies of any prescriptions for medicines the kids may take. Ditto for eyeglass prescriptions.

9. Tell your grandchildren about any medical problems you may have, so they can be prepared if there's an emergency.

10. Many attractions and hotels offer discounts for seniors, so check ahead of time for bargains.

11. Plan your evening meal early to avoid long waits. And make advance reservations if you're dining in a popular spot, even if it's early. Take some crayons and paper to keep younger kids occupied.

ORDER *and* **DISCIPLINE** *on the* **ROAD**

OK, OK, WIPE THAT SMIRK OFF YOUR FACE. Order and discipline on the road may seem like an oxymoron to you, but you won't be hooting when your 5-year-old launches a screaming stem-winder in the middle of Fantasyland. Your willingness to give this subject serious consideration before you leave home may well be the most important element of your pretrip preparation.

Discipline and maintaining order are more difficult when traveling because everyone is, as a Boston mom put it, "in and out" (in strange surroundings and out of the normal routine). For children, it's hard to contain excitement and anticipation that pop to the surface in the form of fidgety hyperactivity, nervous energy, and, sometimes, acting out. Confinement in a car, plane, or hotel room only exacerbates the situation, and kids are often louder than normal, more aggressive with siblings, and much more inclined to push the envelope of parental patience and control. Once in the theme parks, it doesn't get much better. There's more elbow room, but there's also overstimulation, crowds, heat, and miles of walking. All this coupled with marginal or inadequate rest can lead to meltdown in the most harmonious of families.

The following discussion was developed by leading child psychologist Dr. Karen Turnbow, who has contributed to The Unofficial Guides for years and who has spent many days at Walt Disney World conducting research and observing families.

LILIANE Discuss your vacation needs with your children and explore their wants and expectations well before you depart on your trip.

Sound parenting and standards of discipline practiced at home, applied consistently, will suffice to handle most situations on vacation. Still, it's instructive to study the hand you are dealt when traveling. For starters, aside from being jazzed and ablaze with adrenaline, your kids may believe that rules followed at home are somehow suspended when traveling. Parents reinforce this misguided intuition by being inordinately lenient in the interest of maintaining peace in the family. While some of your home protocols (cleaning your plate, going to bed at a set time, and such) might be relaxed to good effect on vacation, differing from your normal approach to discipline can precipitate major misunderstanding.

Children, not unexpectedly, are likely to believe that a vacation (especially a vacation to Walt Disney World) is expressly for them. This reinforces their focus on their own needs and largely erases any consideration of yours. Such a mind-set dramatically increases their sense of hurt and disappointment when you correct them or deny them something they want. An incident that would hardly elicit a pouty lip at home could well escalate to tears or defiance when traveling.

The stakes are high for everyone on a vacation—for you because of the cost in time and dollars but also because your vacation represents a rare opportunity for rejuvenation and renewal. The stakes are high for your children too. Children tend to romanticize travel, building anticipation to an almost unbearable level. Discussing the trip in advance can ground expectations to a certain extent, but a child's imagination will, in the end, trump reality every time. The good news is that you can take advantage of your children's emotional state to preestablish rules and conditions for their conduct while on vacation. Because your children want what's being offered *sooooo* badly, they will be unusually accepting and conscientious regarding whatever rules are agreed upon.

According to Dr. Turnbow, successful response to (or avoidance of) behavioral problems on the road begins with a clear-cut disciplinary policy at home. Both at home and on vacation, the approach should be the same and should be based on the following key concepts:

1. LET EXPECTATIONS BE KNOWN. Discuss what you expect from your children, but don't try to cover every imaginable situation. Cover expectations in regard to compliance with parental directives, treatment of siblings, resolution of disputes, schedule (including wake-up and bed-times), courtesy and manners, staying together, and who pays for what.

2. EXPLAIN THE CONSEQUENCES OF NONCOMPLIANCE. Detail very clearly and firmly the consequences of unmet expectations. This should be very straightforward and unambiguous. If you do X (or don't do X), this is what will happen.

3. WARN YOUR KIDS. You're dealing with excited, expectant children, not machines, so it's important to issue a warning before meting out discipline. It's critical to understand that we're talking about one unequivocal warning rather than multiple warnings or nagging. These undermine your credibility and make your expectations appear relative or less than serious. Multiple warnings or nagging also effectively pass control of the situation from you to your child (who may continue to act out as an attention-getting strategy).

4. FOLLOW THROUGH. If you say that you're going to do something, do it. Period. Children must understand that you are absolutely serious and committed.

5. BE CONSISTENT. Inconsistency makes discipline a random event in the eyes of your children. Random discipline encourages random behavior, which translates to a nearly total loss of parental control. Long-term, both at home and on the road, your response to a given situation or transgression must be perfectly predictable. Structure and repetition, essential for a child to learn, cannot be achieved in the absence of consistency.

Though the previous five are the biggies, several other corollary concepts and techniques are worthy of consideration.

First, understand that whining, tantrums, defiance, sibling friction, and even holding the group up are ways in which children communicate with parents. Frequently the object or precipitant of a situation has little or no relation to the unacceptable behavior. On the surface, a fit may appear to be about the ice cream you refused to buy little Robby, but there's almost always something deeper, a subtext that is closer to the truth (this is the reason why ill behavior often persists after you give in to a child's demands). As often as not the real cause is a need for attention. This need is so powerful in some children that they will subject themselves to certain punishment and parental displeasure to garner the attention they crave.

To get at the root cause of the behavior in question requires both active listening and empowering your child with a "feeling vocabulary." Active listening is a concept that's been around for a long time. It involves being alert not only to what a child says but also to the context in which it is said, to the language used and possible subtext, to the child's emotional state and body language, and even to what's not said. Sounds complicated, but it's basically being attentive to the larger picture and, more to the point, being aware that there is a larger picture.

Helping your child to develop a feeling vocabulary consists of teaching your child to use words to describe what's going on. The idea is to teach the child to articulate what's really troubling him, to be able to identify and express emotions and mood states in language.

It all begins with convincing your child that you're willing to listen attentively and take what he's saying seriously. Listening to your child, you help him transcend the topical by reframing the conversation to address the underlying emotional state(s). That his brother hit him may have precipitated the mood, but the act is topical and of secondary importance. What you want is for your child to be able to communicate how that makes him feel and to get in touch with those emotions. When you reduce an incident (hitting) to the emotions triggered (anger, hurt, rejection, and so on), you have the foundation for helping him to develop constructive coping strategies. A child who can tell his mother why he is distressed is a child who has discovered a coping strategy far more effective (not to mention easier for all concerned) than a tantrum.

SIX MORE TIPS

UNTIL YOU GET THE ACTIVE LISTENING and feeling vocabulary going, be careful not to become part of the problem. There's a whole laundry list of adult responses to bad behavior that only make things worse. Hitting, swatting, yelling, name calling, insulting, belittling, using sarcasm, pleading, nagging, and inducing guilt ("We've spent thousands of dollars to bring you to Disney World and now you're spoiling the trip for everyone!") figure prominently on the list.

Responding to a child appropriately in a disciplinary situation requires thought and preparation. Following are key things to keep in mind and techniques to try when your world blows up while waiting in line for Dumbo.

1. BE THE ADULT. It's well understood that children can punch their parents' buttons faster and more lethally than just about anyone or anything else. They've got your number, know precisely how to elicit a response, and are not reluctant to go for the jugular. Fortunately (or unfortunately) you're the adult, and to deal with a situation effectively, you must act like one. If your kids get you ranting and caterwauling, you effectively abdicate your adult status. Worse, you suggest by way of example that being out of control is an acceptable expression of hurt or anger. No matter what happens, repeat the mantra, "I am the adult in this relationship."

2. FREEZE THE ACTION. Being the adult and maintaining control almost always translates to freezing the action, to borrow a sports term. Instead of a knee-jerk response (at a maturity level closer to your child's than yours), freeze the action by disengaging. Wherever you are or whatever the family is doing, stop in place and concentrate on one thing and one thing only: getting all involved to calm down. Practically speaking, this usually means initiating a time-out. It's essential that you take this action immediately. Grabbing your child by the arm or collar and dragging him toward the car or hotel room only escalates the turmoil by prolonging the confrontation and by adding a coercive physical dimension to an already volatile emotional event. If, for the sake of people around you (as when a toddler throws a tantrum in church), it's essential to retreat to a more private place, choose the first place available. Firmly sit the child down and refrain from talking to him until you've both cooled off. This might take a little time, but the investment is worthwhile.

3. ISOLATE THE CHILD. You'll be able to deal with the situation more effectively and expeditiously if the child is isolated with one parent. Dispatch the uninvolved members of your party for a Coke break or have them go on with the activity or itinerary without you (if possible) and arrange to rendezvous later at an agreed time and place. In addition to letting the others get on with their day, isolating the offending child with one parent relieves him of the pressure of being the group's focus of attention and object of anger. Equally important, isolation frees you from the scrutiny and expectations of the others in regard to how to handle the situation.

4. REVIEW THE SITUATION WITH THE CHILD. If, as discussed previously, you've made your expectations clear, stated the consequences of failing those expectations, and administered a warning, review the situation with the child and follow through with the discipline warranted. If, as often occurs, things are not so black and white, encourage the child to communicate his feelings. Try to uncover what occasioned the acting out. Lecturing and accusatory language don't work well here, nor do threats. Dr. Turnbow suggests that a better approach (after the child is calm) is to ask, "What can we do to make this a better day for you?"

5. FREQUENT TANTRUMS OR ACTING OUT. The preceding four points relate to dealing with an incident as opposed to a chronic condition. If a child frequently acts out or throws tantrums, you'll need to employ a somewhat different strategy.

Tantrums are cyclical events evolved from learned behavior. A child learns that he can get your undivided attention by acting out. When you respond, whether by scolding, admonishing, threatening, or negotiating, your response further draws you into the cycle and prolongs the behavior. When you accede to the child's demands, you reinforce the effectiveness of the tantrum and raise the cost of capitulation next time around. When a child thus succeeds in monopolizing your attention, he effectively becomes the person in charge.

To break this cycle, you must disengage from the child. The object is to demonstrate that the cause-and-effect relationship (that is, tantrum elicits parental attention) is no longer operative. This can be accomplished by refusing to interact with the child as long as the untoward behavior continues. Tell the child that you're unwilling to discuss his problem until he calms down. You can ignore the behavior, remove yourself from the child's presence (or vice versa), or isolate the child with a time-out. The important thing is to disengage quickly and decisively with no discussion or negotiation.

Most children don't pick the family vacation as the time to start throwing tantrums. The behavior will be evident before you leave home, and home is the best place to deal with it. Be forewarned, however, that bad habits die hard, and a child accustomed to getting attention by throwing tantrums will not simply give up after a single instance of disengagement. More likely, the child will at first escalate the intensity and length of his tantrums. By your consistent refusal over several weeks (or even months) to respond to his behavior, however, he will finally adjust to the new paradigm.

LILIANE Tantrums are about getting attention. Giving your child attention when things are on an even keel often preempts acting out.

Children are cunning as well as observant. Many understand that a tantrum in public is embarrassing to you and that you're more likely to cave in than you would at home. Once again, consistency is the key, along with a bit of anticipation. When traveling, it's not necessary to retreat to the privacy of a hotel room to isolate your child. You can carve out space for time-out almost anywhere: on a theme park bench, in a park, in your car, in a restroom, even on a sidewalk. You can often spot the warning signs of an impending tantrum and head it off by talking to the child before he reaches an explosive emotional pitch.

6. SALVAGE OPERATIONS. Children are full of surprises, and sometimes the surprises are not good. If your sweet child manages to make a mistake of mammoth proportions, what do you do? This happened to an Ohio couple, resulting in the offending kid pretty much being grounded for life. Fortunately there were no injuries or lives lost, but the parents had to determine what to do for the remainder of the vacation. For starters, they split the group. One parent escorted the offending child back to the hotel, where he was effectively confined to his guest room for the duration. That evening, the parents arranged for in-room sitters for the rest of the stay. Expensive? You bet, but better than watching your whole vacation go down the tubes.

A family at the Magic Kingdom had a similar experience, though the offense was of a more modest order of magnitude. Because it was their last day of vacation, they elected to place the child in time-out, in the theme park, for the rest of the day. One parent monitored the culprit while the other parent and the siblings enjoyed the attractions. At agreed times the parents would switch places. Once again, not ideal, but preferable to stopping the vacation.

PART TWO

GETTING *Your* ACT TOGETHER

Visiting Walt Disney World is a bit like childbirth—you never really believe what people tell you, but once you've been through it yourself, you know exactly what they were saying!

—Hilary Wolfe, a mother and *Unofficial Guide* reader from Swansea, Wales, United Kingdom

GATHERING INFORMATION

IN ADDITION TO USING THIS GUIDE, we recommend that you visit our website, **touringplans.com,** which has interactive trip-planning tools that aren't possible to replicate in a printed book. These tools will save you time and money during your trip. The companion blog, **blog .touringplans.com,** has breaking news for Walt Disney World, Universal Orlando, Disney Cruise Line, and Disneyland. Here's a quick rundown of the site's features:

DETAILED 365-DAY CROWD CALENDAR FOR EACH THEME PARK See which parks will be the least crowded every day of your trip, using a 1-to-10 scale. With the Crowd Calendar, you'll be able to plan which park to visit each day to avoid long lines.

CUSTOMIZABLE TOURING PLANS Create custom touring plans tailored to your family's favorite attractions, restaurants, and more, and save up to 4 hours in line. These plans can be updated even while you're in the parks. *Our best and most effective touring plans are those provided in this guide.* In a number of situations, however, you may be better served by a customized plan—for instance, if you want to integrate personal preferences such as meals and breaks into your touring plan.

HOTEL ROOM VIEWS AND ONLINE FAX SERVICE We have photos of the views from every hotel room in Walt Disney World—more than 30,000 images—and we'll give you the exact wording to use with Disney to request a specific room. We'll even automatically fax your room request to Disney right before you arrive.

TICKET DISCOUNTS A customizable search helps you find the cheapest tickets for your specific needs. The average family can save $20–$80 by purchasing admission from one of our recommended ticket wholesalers.

FASTPASS+ INFORMATION We show every FastPass+ reservation available at every attraction in the parks on a single page of our site.

ANSWERS TO YOUR TRIP-PLANNING QUESTIONS Our online community includes tens of thousands of Disney experts and fans willing to help with your vacation plans. Ask questions and offer your own helpful tips.

Much of our online content, including new research, menus, and updates and changes to this guide, is completely free. Access to parts of the site, including the Crowd Calendar, hotel-room views, and custom touring plans, requires a small subscription fee (current-book owners get a substantial discount). This nominal charge—less than a meal at most Disney counter-service restaurants—subsidizes our research and keeps the site up and running day and night.

Our online app, **Lines,** available free to **touringplans.com** subscribers, is designed to accompany you in the parks. It provides ride and park information that Disney doesn't, including:

- **Posted and actual wait times at attractions** Lines is the only Disney-parks app that displays both posted wait times and the actual times you'll wait in line. The wait time you see posted outside of a ride is often much higher than the real wait time because Disney wants you to go to another part of the park—it's a simple form of crowd control. With Lines, you can make better decisions about what to see.

- **"Ride now or wait" recommendations** Lines shows you whether ride wait times are likely to get longer or shorter. If you find a long line at a particular attraction, Lines tells you the best time to come back.

- **Real-time touring plan updates while you're in a park** Lines automatically updates your custom touring plan to reflect actual crowd conditions at a given moment. You can also restart your plan and add or change attractions, breaks, meals, and more.

- **In-park chat feature with our Lines community** Have a quick question while you're in the parks? Ask our community of thousands of Liners and get a response within seconds.

The Unofficial Guide and **touringplans.com,** along with the Lines app, were created to work together to provide the most comprehensive planning and touring support possible. This mom from St. Louis, Missouri, shares her experience using all the tools in our toolbox:

I loved having the book to read cover to cover and then easily refer back to. After reading the book, I had a good idea of what hotels I was interested in and had must-do and must-eat places somewhat picked out. I then took the knowledge from the book and switched to the website to personalize our touring plans and use as an easy reference when needed. The book and the website together made our trip INCREDIBLE. My husband even complimented me on our touring plans—they worked perfectly and were super-easy to use and manipulate.

The Unofficial Guides' website, **theunofficialguides.com,** features free content, and we invite you to follow us on Facebook (**facebook.com/TheUnofficialGuideToWaltDisneyWorldWithKids**) and Twitter (**@LilianeOpsomer**) for daily tips and updates.

Next, we recommend that you obtain the following:

BOB Request information as far in advance as possible and allow 6 weeks for delivery. Make a checklist of information you request, and follow up if you haven't received your materials within 6 weeks.

1. THE WALT DISNEY TRAVEL COMPANY FLORIDA VACATIONS BROCHURE AND DVD These cover Walt Disney World in its entirety, list rates for all Disney resort hotels and campgrounds, and describe Disney World package vacations. They're available from most travel agents, by calling the Walt Disney Travel Company at ☎ 407-828-8101 or 407-934-7639, or by visiting **disneyworld.com.** Be prepared to hold. When you get a representative, ask for the DVD vacation planner.

2. DISNEY CRUISE LINE BROCHURE AND DVD This brochure provides details on vacation packages that combine a cruise on Disney Cruise Line with a stay at Disney World. Disney Cruise Line also offers a free DVD that tells you all you need to know about Disney cruises and then some. To obtain a copy, call ☎ 800-951-3532 or order at **disneycruise.com,** where you can also view the entire DVD.

3. ORLANDO MAGICARD If you're considering lodging outside Disney World or if you think you might patronize out-of-the-World attractions and restaurants, obtain an Orlando Magicard, a Vacation Planner, and the *Orlando Official Vacation Guide* (all free) from the Orlando Official Visitor Center. The Magicard entitles you to discounts for hotels, restaurants, ground transportation, shopping malls, dinner theaters, and non-Disney theme parks and attractions. The Orlando Magicard can be conveniently downloaded for printing at **visitorlando.com/magicard.** To order the accommodations guide, call ☎ 800-643-9492. For more information and materials, call ☎ 407-363-5872 weekdays during business hours and 9 a.m.–3 p.m. Eastern time weekends, or go to **visitorlando.com.**

4. *HOTELCOUPONS.COM FLORIDA GUIDE* Another good source of discounts on lodging, restaurants, and attractions statewide is the *HotelCoupons.com Florida Guide.* You can sign up at **hotelcoupons.com** to have a free monthly guide sent to you by e-mail, or you can view the guide online. If you prefer a hard copy over a digital version, you can request one by calling ☎ 800-222-3948 Monday–Friday, 8 a.m.–5 p.m. Eastern time. The guide is free, but you pay $4 for handling ($6 if it's shipped to Canada).

5. KISSIMMEE VISITOR'S GUIDE This full-color guide is one of the most complete resources available and is of particular interest to those who intend to lodge outside of Disney World, featuring ads for hotels, rental houses, time-shares, and condominiums, as well as a directory of attractions, restaurants, special events, and other useful info. For a copy, call the Kissimmee Convention and Visitors Bureau at ☎ 800-327-9159 or 407-742-8200, or view it online at **experiencekissimmee.com.**

6. *GUIDEBOOK FOR GUESTS WITH DISABILITIES* Available at Guest Relations when entering the theme/water parks, at resort front desks, and wheelchair-rental areas (listed in each theme park chapter). More-limited information is available at **disneyworld.disney.go.com/plain-text.**

DISNEY ONLINE: OFFICIAL AND OTHERWISE

THE WALT DISNEY COMPANY HAS ROLLED OUT a set of high-tech enhancements to its theme parks and hotels. This collection of initiatives, officially known as **MyMagic+,** includes issuing rubber wristbands (**MagicBands**) with embedded computer chips that function as admission tickets and hotel keys; it also involved major changes to Disney's FastPass ride-reservation system, restaurants, and attractions.

The changes to FastPass—now known as **FastPass+**—require that you make reservations months in advance to ride Disney's headliner attractions, if you want any chance of avoiding long waits in line. Other features, such as MagicBands and restaurant reservations, require you to enter detailed information about your traveling party.

Disney's website (**disneyworld.com**) and mobile app are the "glue" binding all of this together. Because you have to plan so much before you leave home, we're covering the basics of Disney's website and app in this section. While we provide navigational instructions here, Disney's Web designers change direction faster than hypercaffeinated squirrels in traffic, so you may have to hunt around to find some features. Full coverage of MagicBands starts on page 69; details on the FastPass+ system start on page 232.

My Disney Experience at DisneyWorld.com

A lot of work has gone into the Disney website. You can make hotel, dining, and recreation reservations; buy admission; and get park hours, attraction information, and much more.

The most important of the site's features support My Disney Experience. To make use of some of these, you'll need to register by providing your e-mail address and choosing a password. You'll also need to have reserved a room at a Disney-owned hotel or have in your possession a valid theme park ticket.

GETTING STARTED In the upper-right corner of the home page, click "My Disney Experience" to access a welcome page with links to any existing hotel and dining reservations. Click the "My Family & Friends" link, and then enter the names and ages of everyone traveling with you. You'll need this information when you make your FastPass+ and dining reservations.

Back on the "My Disney Experience" page, click "My Itinerary" in the top right corner of the page. A calendar will then appear—if you have a Disney-hotel reservation, the calendar should display those dates of travel. If not, you'll need to manually enter your reservation number, and then select your travel dates using the calendar.

For each day of your trip, the website will display operating hours for the theme and water parks. Select the theme park you'll be visiting on a particular day; if you're visiting more than one, select the one at which you want to make reservations now.

MAKING FASTPASS+ RESERVATIONS Click the "FastPass+ Service" link from the menu on your screen. Next, select one of your displayed travel dates, and then indicate which members of your group will be with you and which park you'll be visiting on that date. At press time, you could use FastPass+ at just one park per day and make only three reservations in advance—this may change, however.

Now you'll see a list of your chosen park's participating FastPass+ attractions. Select the ones you'd like to reserve. Attractions that no longer have FastPass+ reservations available for the day of your choice will be marked with an exclamation sign in a red triangle and the following sentence, also in red: "FastPass+ Distribution Has Ended for Selected Day."

At this point, the website will give you a "Best Match" set of Fast-Pass+ reservations and return times for your attractions, plus three optional sets of return times. Select the set that most closely fits the rest of your plans for the day, or if you're using our touring plans, select the set that most closely matches the suggested FastPass+ return times on the plans. After confirming your selections, you can check for alternative return-time windows for each attraction.

You'll need to repeat these steps for every day for which you want to use FastPass+ in the theme parks. If you're unsure of the attractions or times of day for which you should use FastPass+, our touring plan software can make recommendations that will minimize your time in line. See page 226 for details.

You must use all three FastPass+ reservations before you can get a new FastPass+ at a FastPass+ kiosk or via the My Disney Experience app. If you got a FastPass+ for evening fireworks, you will not be able to get another FastPass+ until after the last pass is used.

Also, if you ride an attraction for which you have a FastPass+ without using the pass, you must cancel that pass before you can add another one. It is not enough to have the time elapse, as was the case with the old FastPass system. We strongly recommend that you install the My Disney Experience app on your phone to avoid going to a FastPass+ kiosk for changes or additional passes.

MAKING DINING RESERVATIONS From the "My Itinerary" page, go to "Add Plans," and click "Make a Dining Reservation." Pick the date for which you wish to make a reservation. A list of every Disney World eatery will be displayed. Use the filtering criteria at the top of the page to narrow the list.

Once you've settled on a restaurant, click the restaurant's name to check availability for your dining time and the number of people in your party. If space is available and you want to make a reservation, you'll need to indicate which members of your party will be joining you. If you want to make other dining reservations, you'll need to repeat this process for every reservation.

All reservations come with a cancellation fee of at least $10 per person. Make sure you read all the instructions and cancel in time to avoid any fees. Furthermore, some reservations, such as the *Hoop-Dee-Doo Musical Revue,* are instantly charged to your credit card for the full amount.

Once you've made your initial set of FastPass+ and dining reservations, you'll be able to view and edit them (along with your hotel reservation) in the "My Reservation" section of My Disney Experience.

My Disney Experience Mobile App

Along with the website, Disney offers a companion app for iOS and Android devices. It includes park hours, attraction operating hours and descriptions, restaurant hours and descriptions, the ability to make FastPass+ and dining reservations online, GPS-based directions, and more. My Disney Experience is optimized for the latest phones and tablets, so some features may not be available on all devices.

You still see only Disney's "official" information, including intentionally wrong attraction wait times so you'll go somewhere else in the park. Search for "My Disney Experience" on iTunes, Google Play, or the Amazon Appstore for Android.

Our Recommended Websites

Searching online for Disney information is like navigating an immense maze for a very small piece of cheese: There's a lot of information available, but you may find a lot of dead-ends before getting what you want. Our picks follow.

BEST Q&A SITE Who knew? Walt Disney World has a **Mom's Panel** all chosen from among 10,000-plus applicants. The panelists have a website, **disneyworldmoms.com,** where they offer tips and discuss how to plan a Disney World vacation. Several moms have specialized experience in areas such as Disney Cruise Line; some speak Spanish too.

BEST GENERAL UNOFFICIAL WALT DISNEY WORLD WEBSITE Besides **touringplans.com,** Deb Wills's **allears.net** is the first website we recommend to friends who want to make a trip to Disney World. Updated several times a week, the site includes breaking news, tons of photos, Disney restaurant menus, resort and ticket information, tips for guests with special needs, and more. We also check **wdwmagic.com** for news and happenings around Walt Disney World.

BEST MONEY-SAVING SITE MouseSavers (**mousesavers.com**) keeps an updated list of discounts and reservation codes for use at Disney resorts. Codes are separated into categories such as "For the general public" and "For residents of certain states." Anyone who calls or books online can use a current code and get the discounted rate. Savings can be considerable—up to 40% in many cases. MouseSavers also has discount codes for rental cars and non-Disney hotels in the area.

BEST WALT DISNEY WORLD PREVIEW SITE If you want to see what a particular attraction is like, **touringplans.com** offers free videos or photos of every attraction. Videos of indoor ("dark") rides are sometimes inferior to those of outdoor rides due to poor lighting, but even the videos and photos of indoor rides generally provide a good sense of what the attraction is about. **YouTube** is also an excellent place to find videos of Disney and other Central Florida attractions.

SOCIAL MEDIA   Facebook, Twitter, and **Instagram** are popular places for Disney fans to gather online and share comments, tips, and photos. Following fellow Disneyphiles as they share their in-park experiences can make you feel like you're there, even as you're stuck in a cubicle at work. You can also join more than 5,600 fans for daily news and insights on our very own Facebook page: **facebook.com/TheUnofficial GuideToWaltDisneyWorldWithKids.**

BEST INTERNET RADIO STATION   MouseWorld Radio (mouseworldradio .com) plays everything from attraction themes and hotel background music to sound clips from old TV ads for Disney resorts. What makes MouseWorld Radio special is that the tracks match what the Disney parks are playing at the time of day you're listening.

BEST THEME PARK–INSIDER SITE   It's been said that people who eat sausage should never watch it being made. If you have the stomach to learn how theme parks get built, take a look around **jimhillmedia.com.** Jim has insider accounts of the politics, frantic project management, and pipe dreams that somehow combine to create the attractions that Disney and Universal build.

BEST DISNEY DISCUSSION BOARDS   There are tons of these; among the most active are **disboards.com, forums.wdwmagic.com,** our own **forum .touringplans.com,** and, for Brits, **thedibb.co.uk** (*DIBB* stands for "Disney Information Bulletin Board").

BEST SITES FOR TRAFFIC, ROADWORK, CONSTRUCTION, AND SAFETY INFORMATION   Visit **expresswayauthority.com** for the latest information on roadwork in the Orlando and Orange County areas. The site also contains detailed maps, directions, and toll-rate information for the most popular tourist destinations. A seven-year construction project to improve I-4 was launched in 2015. Information on the northern section between Kirkman Road (near Universal) and downtown Orlando can be found at **i4ultimate.com.** Construction updates on the southern section from Kirkman Road to US 27 in Polk County are available at **i4express.com.** Check **flhsmv.gov/fhp/cps** to learn about state child-restraint requirements. Finally, we like **Google Maps** for driving directions.

Liliane's Favorite Podcasts

If you just can't make it through the year without the Mouse, don't despair. Sounds, images, and news from the World are available in abundance online. Here are some of my favorites.

WDW TODAY   Unofficial Guide Research Director Len Testa cohosts three podcasts a week (Monday, Wednesday, and Friday) on all things Disney. Subscriptions are available free through iTunes. These programs consistently rank among the top 10 iTunes travel podcasts, drawing almost 40,000 listeners per show. Visit **wdwtoday.com.**

BE OUR GUEST   This fun, high-energy, Disney-related podcast has three episodes a week. Visit **beourguestpodcast.blogspot.com** for more info.

INSIDE THE MAGIC Operated by Ricky Brigante, the show focuses primarily on Disney, but Ricky also covers Universal Orlando, SeaWorld, Busch Gardens, and many other theme parks and independent attractions in the area. Visit **insidethemagic.net.**

SOUNDS OF DISNEY Every other Sunday you can join Jeff Davis, also known as The Sorcerer, as he delights his audience with music, news, and Disney songs right from the parks. In addition to the podcast, Davis's website, **srsounds.com,** provides music, videos, pictures, and a message board.

DISNEY DREAM GIRLS Recorded in the UK, this all-female podcast promotes "Disney Girl Power." Visit **facebook.com/disneydreamgirls podcast** or **twitter.com/disdreamgirls.**

IMPORTANT WALT DISNEY WORLD TELEPHONE NUMBERS

WHEN YOU CALL THE MAIN INFORMATION NUMBER, you'll be offered a menu of options for recorded information on operating hours, recreation areas, shopping, entertainment, tickets, reservations, and driving directions. If you have a question not covered by recorded information, press 8 at any time to speak to a representative. See the table below for a list of phone numbers.

Important WDW Telephone Numbers

General Information ☎ 407-824-4321 or 407-824-2222

General Information for the Hearing-Impaired (TTY) ☎ 407-827-5141

General Information for Guests with Disabilities ☎ 407-939-7807

Accommodations/Reservations ☎ 407-W-DISNEY (934-7639)

Blizzard Beach Information ☎ 407-560-3400

Centra Care   Kissimmee ☎ 407-390-1888   Lake Buena Vista ☎ 407-934-2273
  Universal–Dr. Phillips ☎ 407-291-8975

Dining Advance Reservations ☎ 407-WDW-DINE (939-3463)

Disabled Guests Special Requests ☎ 407-939-7807

DisneyQuest ☎ 407-828-4600

ESPN Wide World of Sports Complex ☎ 407-939-GAME (4263)

Golf Reservations and Information ☎ 407-WDW-GOLF (939-4653)

Guided-Tour Information ☎ 407-WDW-TOUR (939-8687)

Lost and Found
  Yesterday or before (all Disney parks) ☎ 407-824-4245
  Yesterday or before (Disney Springs) ☎ 407-828-3150
  Today at Disney's Animal Kingdom ☎ 407-938-2784
  Today at Disney's Hollywood Studios ☎ 407-560-4668
  Today at Epcot ☎ 407-560-7500
  Today at the Magic Kingdom ☎ 407-824-4521
  Today at Universal Orlando ☎ 407-224-4233

Continued on next page

Important WDW Telephone Numbers

Outdoor Recreation Reservations and Information ☎ 407-WDW-PLAY (939-7529)

Resort Dining and Information ☎ 407-WDW-DINE (939-3463)

Security ☎ 407-560-7959 *(routine)* or 407-560-1990 *(urgent)*

Tennis Reservations/Lessons ☎ 321-228-1146

Ticket Inquiries ☎ 407-566-4985

Typhoon Lagoon Information ☎ 407-560-4120

Walt Disney Travel Company ☎ 407-939-6244

Weather Information ☎ 407-827-4545

Wrecker Service ☎ 407-824-0976 *(or call Security after hours; see above)*

ALLOCATING TIME

YOU SHOULD ALLOCATE 6 days for a whirlwind tour (7–10 days if you're old-fashioned and insist on some relaxation during your vacation). If you don't have 6-plus days, then you need to be prepared to make some hard choices.

BOB If you must visit during the busy summer season, cut your visit short by one or two days so that you will have the weekend or a couple of vacation days remaining to recuperate when you get home.

A seemingly obvious point lost on many families is that Walt Disney World is not going anywhere. There's no danger that it will be packed up and shipped to Iceland anytime soon. This means that you can come back if you don't see everything this year. Disney has planned it this way, of course, but that doesn't matter. It's infinitely more sane to resign yourself to the reality that seeing everything during one visit is impossible. We recommend, therefore, that you approach Disney World the same way you would an eight-course Italian dinner: leisurely, with plenty of time between courses.

WHEN TO GO TO WALT DISNEY WORLD

LET'S CUT TO THE ESSENCE: Walt Disney World between mid-June and mid-August is rough. You can count on large summer crowds as well as Florida's trademark heat and humidity. Avoid these dates if you can. Ditto for Memorial Day weekend at the beginning of the summer and Labor Day weekend at the end. Other holiday periods (Thanksgiving, Christmas, Easter, Halloween, spring break, and so on) are extremely crowded, but the heat is not as bad.

BOB Though crowds have grown in September and October as a result of promotions aimed at families without school-age children and the international market, these months continue to be good for touring.

The least-busy time is from Labor Day in September through the beginning of October. Next slowest are the weeks in mid-January after the Martin Luther King Jr. holiday weekend up to Presidents' Day in February (except when the Walt Disney World Marathon runs after MLK Day). The weeks after Thanksgiving and before Christmas are less crowded than average, as is mid-April–mid-May, after spring break and before Memorial Day.

Late February, March, and early April are dicey. Crowds ebb and flow according to spring break schedules and the timing of Presidents' Day weekend. Besides being asphalt-melting hot, July brings throngs of South American tourists on their winter holiday.

So, parents, what to do? If your children are of preschool age, definitely go during a cooler, less-crowded time. If you have school-age children, look first for an anomaly in your school-year schedule: in other words, a time when your kids will be out of school when most schools elsewhere are in session. Anomalies are most often found at the beginning or end of the school year (for example, school starts late or lets out early), at Christmas, or at spring break. In the event that no such anomalies exist, and providing that your kids are good students, our recommendation is to ask permission to take your children out of school either just before or after the Thanksgiving holiday. Teachers can assign lessons that can be made up at home over the Thanksgiving holiday, either before or after your Disney World vacation.

If none of these options are workable for your family, consider visiting Disney World the week immediately before school starts (excluding Labor Day weekend) or the week immediately after school lets out (excluding Memorial Day weekend). This strategy should remove you from the really big mob scenes by about a week or more.

The time that works best for kids is the week before school ends. Because grades must be finalized earlier, there is often little going on at school during that week. Check far in advance with your child's teacher to determine if any special exams or projects will occur in that last week. If no major assignments are on the child's schedule, then go for it.

Incidentally, taking your kids out of school for more than a few days is problematic. We have received well-considered letters from parents and teachers who don't think taking kids out of school is such a hot idea. A Fairfax, Virginia, dad put it thus:

> My wife and I do not encourage families to take their children out of school. My wife is an eighth-grade science teacher. She has parents pull their children, some honor roll students, out of school for vacations, only to discover when they return that the students are unable to comprehend the material. Several students have been so thoroughly lost in their assignments that they ask if they can be excused from the tests. Parental suspicions about the quality of their children's education should be raised when children go to school for 6 hours a day yet supposedly can complete this same instruction with less than an hour of homework each night.

A Martinez, California, teacher offers this compelling analogy:

> There are a precious 180 days for us as teachers to instruct our students, and there are 185 days during the year for Disney World. I have seen countless students struggle to catch up the rest of the year due to a week of vacation during critical instructional periods. The

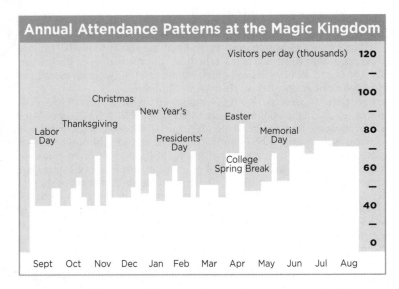

Annual Attendance Patterns at the Magic Kingdom

Visitors per day (thousands)

analogy I use with my students' parents is that it's like walking out of a movie after watching the first 5 minutes, and then returning for the last 5 minutes and trying to figure out what happened.

But a schoolteacher from Penn Yan, New York, expresses a different opinion:

I've read the comments by teachers saying that they all think it's horrible for a parent to take a child out for a vacation. As a teacher and a parent, I disagree. If a parent takes the time to let us know that a child is going to be out, we help them get ready for upcoming homework the best we can. If the child is a good student, why shouldn't they go have a wonderful experience with their family? I also don't understand when teachers say they can't get something together for the time the student will be out. We all have to plan ahead, and we know what we are teaching days, if not weeks, in advance. Take 20 minutes out of your day and set something up. Learn to be flexible!

Though we strongly recommend going to Disney World in the fall, winter, or spring, there are a few trade-offs. The parks often close early during the off-season, either because of low crowds or special events such as the Halloween and Christmas parties at the Magic Kingdom. This drastically reduces touring hours. Even when crowds are small, it's difficult to see big parks such as the Magic Kingdom between 9 a.m. and 7 p.m. Early closing also usually means no evening parades or fireworks. And because these are slow times, some rides and attractions may be closed. Finally, Central Florida temperatures fluctuate wildly during late fall, winter, and early spring; daytime highs in the 40s and 50s aren't uncommon.

Walt Disney World Climate

	JAN	FEB	MAR	APR	MAY	JUN	JUL	AUG	SEP	OCT	NOV	DEC
Average Daily Low (°F)												
	47	50	54	59	65	71	73	73	72	66	58	51
Average Daily High (°F)												
	71	73	78	83	89	91	92	92	90	84	78	72
Average Daily Temperature (°F)												
	60	61	67	71	77	81	82	83	81	75	68	62
Average Daily Humidity Percentage												
	62	73	71	70	71	70	74	76	76	75	74	73
Average Rainfall per Month (Inches)												
	2.9	2.7	4.0	2.3	3.1	8.3	7.0	7.7	5.1	2.5	2.1	2.9
Number of Days of Rain per Month												
	6	7	8	6	8	14	17	16	14	9	6	6

On the other hand, Disney generally has the best lodging offers during these times of the year, including free dining plans. If you plan to stay on-property, this could represent some serious savings.

BE UNCONVENTIONAL The Orange County Convention Center in Orlando hosts some of the largest conventions and trade shows in the world. Hotel rooms anywhere near Walt Disney World are hard to find when there's a big convention—rooms less than $75 or more than $200 a night (that is, budget and upscale) go quickly. Check the convention schedule for the next seven months at **occc.net/global/calendar.**

DON'T FORGET AUGUST Kids go back to school pretty early in Florida (and in a lot of other places too). This makes mid- to late August a good time to visit Disney World for families who can't vacation during the off-season. A New Jersey mother of two school-age children spells it out:

> The end of August is the PERFECT time to go. There were virtually no wait times, 20 minutes at the most.

JUNE AND THE EARLY BIRD It's not an easy turnaround, but heading for Walt Disney World in late May or early June as soon as school is out will net big rewards. Late May through about June 12 is still considered shoulder season, so the crowds will not have spiked to summer levels. Also the weather is usually cooler than in late August. An exception to the above is Memorial Day weekend, though the week following the holiday is one of the best of the whole summer crowd-wise.

HOLIDAYS AND SPECIAL EVENTS AT WALT DISNEY WORLD

YOU CAN'T BEAT THE HOLIDAYS for live entertainment, special events, parades, fireworks, and elaborate decorations at the theme parks and resort hotels. Unfortunately, you also can't beat holiday periods for crowds. A mom from Ogden, Utah, puts it this way:

We know the lines will be outrageous, but the special shows, parades, and decorations more than make up for it. For first-timers who want to see the rides, Christmas is not ideal, but for us it's the most colorful and exciting time to go.

Here's a look at the larger special events and major holidays at Walt Disney World.

JANUARY Usually held the second weekend after New Year's, the **Walt Disney World Marathon** pulls in more runners and their families every year. In 2015, more than 50,000 runners participated in the event—enough people to affect crowd conditions and pedestrian traffic throughout Disney World. Information on all Disney running events can be found at **rundisney.com.**

Each year the China Pavilion in Epcot has a **Chinese New Year** celebration (which is usually in late January or early February). There are typically Chinese acrobats and special activities for kids.

FEBRUARY **Black History Month** is celebrated throughout Walt Disney World with displays, artisans, storytellers, and entertainers. The Kinsey Collection at Epcot's United States Pavilion is a highlight.

Mardi Gras is February 9, 2016, and **Presidents' Day** is February 15, 2016. These holidays will bring increases in attendance starting the weekend before. Usually held at the end of Presidents' Day week is the **Princess Half-Marathon** event, February 18–21 in 2016. The schedule for that weekend includes a health expo, kids' races, a family 5K, a 10K, and the big race. The 2014 event—in which *Unofficial Guide* coauthor Liliane Opsomer ran her third half-marathon—drew more than 25,000 runners, enough to increase park attendance and affect vehicular and pedestrian traffic.

MARCH The **Epcot International Flower & Garden Festival** runs annually from mid-March to May. Expert horticulturists showcase exotic floral displays and share gardening tips. The 30 million blooms from some 1,200 species will make your eyes pop, and best of all, the event doesn't seem to affect crowd levels at Epcot. Food and beverage kiosks at the festival make it more like September's Food & Wine event (see page 49), only with flowers. Check out **tinyurl.com/epcotflowerpower** for a review with lots of pictures.

The **Atlanta Braves** hold spring training and play exhibition games at the ESPN Wide World of Sports Complex mid-February–March. You can get the exhibition schedule and purchase tickets by calling Ticketmaster at ☎ 800-745-3000 or visiting **ticketmaster.com.** You can watch the training sessions at no charge when you buy general admission to the complex ($16.50 for adults, $11.50 for ages 3–9).

In Disney Springs, the **Mighty St. Patrick's Day Festival,** a week-long celebration culminating on St. Patrick's Day (March 17), pays tribute to Irish music, dance, and food. Check out **tinyurl.com /disneystpattysday** for coauthor Liliane Opsomer's 2014 review.

Easter falls on March 27 in 2016, so expect most of March and early April to be peak spring break season. The **Easter Parade** at the

Magic Kingdom showcases outstanding floats carrying Mickey, Minnie, and the gang, all dressed in their Sunday best, in a special parade. Of course, the appearance of the Easter Bunny is guaranteed. Ask at the front desk about special activities (such as egg hunts) at your hotel and other Disney resorts.

MAY Disney's Hollywood Studios hosts *Star Wars* **Weekends** annually beginning this month, with appearances from that franchise's actors and technicians. These events draw mainly local sci-fi fans, but some come from all over the country.

JUNE Events this month include both *Star Wars* Weekends and **Gay Days,** May 31–June 6 in 2016. Since 1991, gay, lesbian, bisexual, and transgender (GLBT) people from around the world have been converging on and around the World in early June for a week of events centered on the theme parks. Today, Gay Days attracts more than 160,000 GLBT visitors and their families and friends. Universal Studios and Wet 'n Wild also participate. For additional information, visit **gaydays.com.**

All summer long, you can dance to classic rock-and-roll hits under the skies of the open-air America Gardens Theatre at Epcot. The **Sounds Like Summer Concert Series** features a lineup of cover bands performing timeless tunes. The concerts are included in your park admission; check the daily *Times Guide* for the performance schedule.

JULY Independence Day at Disney World basically means crowds and more crowds. All parks are in a festive and patriotic mood, and the fireworks are incredible. A very special place to visit is *The Hall of Presidents* at the Magic Kingdom. We recommend leaving the parks prior to the evening fireworks and watching them from the Polynesian Village Resort. Most parks will reach full capacity by 10 a.m., and no advance reservations will get you into a park once it has closed. So pick your park and be prepared to stay there all day. If partying is your thing, consider Disney Springs, which throws a DJ dance party and a fireworks show of its own.

SEPTEMBER Night of Joy, a Christian-music festival, is staged at the Magic Kingdom the first or second weekend of the month (September 11–12 in 2015). About 16 nationally known acts perform concerts on Friday and Saturday evenings after the park has closed. For information or to purchase tickets, call ☎ 407-W-DISNEY (934-7639) or visit **tinyurl.com/wdwnightofjoy.** One-day tickets are $69.23 per person for adults and children, including tax; two-day tickets are $122.48. Same-day tickets cost $85.20 per person for adults and children, including tax.

Those who say Christmas is the most wonderful time of year have never been to the **Epcot International Food & Wine Festival.** Held in World Showcase from mid-September through mid-November, the celebration represents 25 nations and cuisines, including demonstrations, wine seminars, tastings, and opportunities to see some of the world's top chefs. Though many activities are included in Epcot admission, some workshops and tastings are by reservation only and cost more than $100. Call ☎ 407-WDW-DINE (939-3463) starting around the beginning of August for more information. We think the culinary demos and the wine-and-beverage seminars (about $15–$20 each) are the best values at the festival. Because most of the food kiosks are set up around World Showcase, it can be difficult to walk through the crowds at some of the popular spots. Wait times at Epcot's attractions, however, are affected only slightly.

Held two dozen or so nights each year mid-September–October 31 (and occasionally into November), **Mickey's Not-So-Scary Halloween Party** runs 7 p.m.–midnight at the Magic Kingdom. The event includes trick-or-treating in costume, parades, live music, storytelling, and a fireworks show. See **tinyurl.com/mickeysnotsoscary** for more information. Several times that evening, Disney villains will put on a great show followed by a **Villains' Mix and Mingle** in front of Cinderella Castle. Aimed primarily at younger children, the party is happy and upbeat rather than spooky and frightening.

The park will be crowded, so arrive early (we recommend arriving an hour before the beginning of the party, as Disney starts letting guests with party tickets inside the park around 4 p.m. Upon entering the park, you will be issued a wristband identifying you as a party guest. Also, get the special map for the event with details and hours of all the happenings. Go straight to the rides that are on your must-do list, and after that just enjoy the party. If trick-or-treating is a priority, do that first thing after you arrive or toward the end of the night, when crowds thin out and there are no long lines in front of the trick-or-treating stations.

An absolute must-ride is The Haunted Mansion, which is spooky but only in the sweetest way. Look for the ghost in the garden of the mansion when you're queuing up; his hilarious tales and interaction with the guests will make you forget you are standing in line. Characters are out in force all over the park, and the **Boo to You Parade** is pretty amazing. Our two favorite parts of the parade are the Headless Horseman riding at full speed through the park and The Haunted Mansion's groundskeeper, with his dim lantern in one hand and his bloodhound, followed by a large group of ghosts and gravediggers. Don't be shy: Wear a costume—about 50% of all the adults will be wearing a getup of some kind. The party has become very popular, and you won't be able to see or do it all. Pick your favorite events, forget about the rides, and enjoy the night.

Advance tickets for the 2015 events cost (including tax) $68–$87 for adults, $63–$82 for kids; same-day tickets cost $74–$87 for adults, $69–$82 for kids. Discounts are available for members of the US military, Disney Annual Pass holders, and Disney Vacation Club members. The least-crowded events are typically in September and on Tuesdays; tickets for the late-October dates usually sell out one to four days in advance.

In addition to activities in the theme parks, Disney's **Fort Wilderness Resort & Campground** offers haunted carriage rides. The carriage rides include a performer who tells the story of Ichabod Crane and the Headless Horseman from Washington Irving's story "The Legend of

Sleepy Hollow." The rides leave from Pioneer Hall and cost $60 per carriage. A carriage can accommodate four adults, or two adults with three small children. This excursion can be booked up to 180 days in advance by calling ☎ 407-WDW-PLAY (939-7529).

Also check out the different Halloween activities organized at the Disney properties. Activities range from pet-costume parades, Halloween movies under the stars, and trick-or-treating to costume parades and contests. Check at the reception for a detailed schedule of events happening during your stay.

Teens and young adults looking for a non-Disney Halloween happening should check out the party at **Universal CityWalk**. And if you'd rather have a monster with a chain saw running after you, consider attending Universal theme parks' **Halloween Horror Nights.** (*Note:* No costumes are allowed at the parks on these special nights.) For more information, visit **halloweenhorrornights.com.**

NOVEMBER The **Wine and Dine Half-Marathon** early this month revolves around a 13.1-mile race that ends with a party amid Epcot's International Food & Wine Festival. The number of runners (13,000 in 2014) and their "cheer squads"—combined with the guests who descend on Epcot for the food festival alone—blows up the crowd levels like an agitated puffer fish. Vehicular and pedestrian traffic is disturbed by the running courses throughout Disney property.

There are no special Thanksgiving events or decorations in the parks, so if you're looking for the equivalent of the Macy's Thanksgiving Parade, you're out of luck, though many of the Christmas decorations are normally in place the day after Thanksgiving. But the kids are out of school, and this is the busiest travel weekend of the year. Your best bet for the least-crowded park will be Epcot.

Remember to make your dining arrangements long before your visit, especially if you want a traditional Thanksgiving meal. While there is plenty of food at the World, note that not all restaurants offer turkey with all the trimmings. Some that do include **Liberty Tree Tavern** at the Magic Kingdom; **50's Prime Time Cafe** at Disney's Holly-wood Studios; **Cítricos** at the Grand Floridian; **Artist Point** at Wilderness Lodge; and **'Ohana** (which means "family" in Hawaiian) at the Polynesian Village Resort, which is perfect for families with small children. For information and reservations, call ☎ 407-WDW-DINE (939-3463).

The annual **Disney Parks Christmas Day Parade,** televised on December 25, is usually taped at the Magic Kingdom on the weekend that falls nine days after Thanksgiving, roughly the last weekend in November or first week of December. The parade ties up pedestrian traffic on Main Street, U.S.A. all day.

DECEMBER If you're visiting during Christmas week, don't expect to see all the attractions in a single day of touring at any park. All parks, especially the Magic Kingdom, will be filled to capacity, and Disney will stop admitting visitors as early as 10 a.m. (Not to mention that women will have to wait up to 20 minutes to use the restrooms in the Magic

Kingdom during Christmas week.) As you might have guessed by now, your only way in is getting there early. Be at the gates with admission passes in hand at least 1 hour before scheduled opening time. Most of all, bring along a humongous dose of patience and humor. The daily tree-lighting ceremonies and the parades are wonderful. Again, most parks will reach full capacity by 10 a.m., and no advance reservations will get you into the park once it is closed. So *pick your park* and be prepared to stay there all day.

LILIANE Did I mention that it's going to be packed? This is not a good time for first-time visitors, but fun can be had by all at the parks even at peak times. (I actually stayed at Disney World on Christmas Eve and Christmas Day and loved it.)

Also, be sure to make dinner reservations long before your visit, especially if you are spending Christmas Eve and Christmas Day at the parks. Christmas festivities at Disney World usually run November 24–December 30. From the Monday following Thanksgiving weekend until December 20 or so, you can enjoy the decorations and holiday events without the crowds. This between-holidays period is one of our favorite times of year at Disney World.

The **Magic Kingdom** is home to a stunning display of holiday decorations, a **tree-lighting ceremony** on Main Street, and **Mickey's Once Upon a Christmastime Parade** on select days. Check the *Times Guide* for days and hours. The Magic Kingdom is also the scene of **Mickey's Very Merry Christmas Party,** staged 7 p.m.–midnight (after regular hours) on about 20 evenings in November and December. Advance tickets for the 2015 events cost (including tax) $74–$82 for adults, $69–$77 for kids; same-day tickets cost $79–$82 for adults, $74–$77 for kids. Tickets for busier dates usually sell out one to four days in advance. Included in the cost is the use of all attractions during party hours, holiday-themed stage shows featuring Disney characters, cookies and hot chocolate, performances of Mickey's Once Upon a Christmastime Parade, carolers, "a magical snowfall" on Main Street, white lights on Cinderella Castle, and fireworks. The least crowded dates are usually the weeks before Thanksgiving week and the week after. Tuesday (and the rare Wednesday) parties are the slowest,too. See **tinyurl.com/mickeysverymerryxmas** for more details. We don't recommend the party for first-time visitors.

With about twice the land of the Magic Kingdom, **Epcot** is a good option on Christmas Day, but this doesn't mean it's a ghost town, just somewhat less crowded than the Magic Kingdom. Again, if your heart is set on touring a park on Christmas Day, you'll have to get up early.

At Epcot don't miss the **Candlelight Processional,** featuring a celebrity narrator accompanied by a huge live choir and a full orchestra. The show takes place daily at the America Gardens Theatre and is included with regular Epcot admission. Special lunch and dinner packages are available for an additional charge and include preferred seating for the processional (call ☎ 407-WDW-DINE [939-3463] for reservations). If you don't want to spring for one of the packages, we recommend lining up at least 1 hour prior to the show of your choice. Guests with preferred seating are well advised not to come at the last minute, either—instead, arrive at the reserved-seating entrance 30 minutes before the beginning of the show. Seats within this section are available on a first-come, first-serve basis and are opened to general admission 15 minutes before the beginning of the show. Check the *Times Guide* for performance hours and information on the day's narrator.

The nightly fireworks, water, and laser show ***IllumiNations: Reflections of Earth*** is always worth watching and has an extra-special holiday finale.

Our favorite Epcot holiday event, however, is **Holidays from Around the World** (check out Liliane's review online at **theunofficialguides .com/2014/12/02/christmas-around-world-showcase**). While strolling from land to land, visitors can enjoy storytellers in each country. At the **United Kingdom Pavilion,** Father Christmas tells of his country's holiday customs. **France** is the home of Père Noël. In **Morocco,** guests can listen to stories about many festivals held throughout the country; the storytelling is exquisite, interactive, and educational. In **Japan,** the Daruma Seller talks about how Japanese celebrate the New Year. (*Daruma* dolls are symbols of the New Year and are said to bring good luck.)

At the **American Adventure Rotunda,** Santa himself is on hand to tell Christmas stories. Special programs are held for Kwanzaa and Hanukkah as well. (To learn more about Kwanzaa, an African American celebration of family, community, and culture, visit **kwanzaaguide.com.** The History Channel offers a nice description of Hanukkah, the Jewish Festival of Lights, at **history.com/topics/hanukkah.**)

In **Italy,** meet La Befana, the good witch who brings gifts to children on Epiphany. (For more information on La Befana, check out **en .wikipedia.org/wiki/befana.**) **Germany** honors St. Nicholas on December 6, and he welcomes visitors throughout the afternoon. Visitors can also hear the story of the nutcracker's origin.

Visit **China** and enjoy the Chinese Lion Dancers, a typical part of any Chinese New Year celebration. The show replaced the tales of the Monkey King in 2015 and is a huge improvement; make sure to watch it. In **Norway,** meet the Christmas elf Julenisse, who represents simplicity and peace (to learn more, visit **tinyurl.com/norwaysanta**). In **Mexico,** the Three Kings have been replaced by Fiesta de Navidad, and while the performance of the dancers and the Mariachi Cobre band is great, we miss the wonderful story of Los Tres Reyes Magos. Read about them at **mexonline.com/history-lostresreyes.htm.**

At **Disney's Hollywood Studios,** the park is also dressed for the season, but the big attraction is the **Osborne Family Spectacle of Dancing Lights.** Millions—yes, millions—of lights decorate the buildings on the Streets of America, and snow machines provide the perfect atmosphere. There is no additional fee to see the display, but be prepared for huge crowds. A little background: Jennings Osborne of Little Rock, Arkansas, began putting up Christmas lights on his house in 1986 and expanded his display by buying the two houses next to his. As his collection grew, so did the displeasure of his neighbors. Eventually the matter was brought to court, and in 1994 the Arkansas Supreme Court ruled that his houses, with their 3 million lights, were a public nuisance. The Walt Disney Company brought Osborne's Christmas lights to Disney's Hollywood Studios in 1995 and has a special agreement with him to keep the display. For a review by Liliane featuring lots of pictures, check out **tinyurl.com/osbornelights.**

Disney's Animal Kingdom has festive holiday decorations and a gigantic Christmas tree with carolers performing throughout the day. Kids can meet Santa Goofy and other favorite Disney characters all dressed in their holiday finest. If you don't mind the lines, this is the perfect place for taking holiday photographs.

You thought we were done? No way—there's much more to see outside of the parks.

The **holiday decorations** at the Walt Disney World resorts are attractions in their own right. Generally speaking, each resort incorporates its theme into its holiday finery. At **Port Orleans Resort,** for example, expect Mardi Gras colors in the trees, while the **Yacht Club** has trees adorned with miniature sailboats. Also make sure to visit the **Grand Floridian,** where the mother of all Christmas trees—five stories tall!—dominates the lobby, flanked by a gingerbread dollhouse and a miniature railroad. Don't miss the free daily classes in decorating gingerbread houses, led by a Grand Floridian pastry chef; guests get a free recipe brochure and a taste of freshly made gingerbread. At the **Beach Club,** poinsettias, artificial snow, and a gingerbread carousel are the big draw. For a more natural approach, visit the **Wilderness Lodge** and **Animal Kingdom Lodge.**

LILIANE A word of advice for families with small children: Reassure the kids that Santa knows where the family is on Christmas Day. You don't want your little ones to suddenly worry that Santa won't find them on Christmas because they're not at home. Consider shipping a small tree and holiday decorations to your hotel. Kids can decorate the window of your hotel room with their drawings.

Check out Liliane's 2014 write-up about Christmas decorations at the resorts—again, with lots of pictures—at **theunofficialguides .com/2014/12/16/disney-resort-holiday-decorations.**

If you're staying at a Disney resort over Christmas, check with the concierge to see what holiday events might be going on. Happenings can range from carolers, brass bands, and country singers to Christmas-cookie decorating, visits with Santa, and readings of *The Night Before Christmas.*

During December, Disney offers 25-minute **"sleigh" rides** through the woods from the Fort Wilderness Campground. (The horse-drawn vehicle is wheeled but made to look like a red sleigh, complete with sleigh bells!) Rides are offered every half hour 5:30–9:30 p.m., departing from Crockett's Tavern at Fort Wilderness. The cost is $60 per sleigh. (Each sleigh can accommodate up to four adults or two adults plus up to three children age 9 and under.) You can book up to 180 days in advance by calling ☎ 407-WDW-PLAY (939-7529).

Disney Springs features holiday decor and offers photo ops with Santa but is mainly about shopping. The atmosphere is festive, and shops and restaurants have special window dressings. If you're looking for the perfect Christmas card, this is the place to get it. Santa appears in his chalet at Marketplace, and you can take pictures with your own camera or use Disney's Memory Maker service. For a less classical picture, Santa Goofy appears in the chalet December 25–January 3. Ask at Guest Relations for the daily schedule.

Ring in the New Year with Mickey and friends. If you're in the mood for a night of partying and live entertainment, there's no better place than **Disney Springs** or **Universal CityWalk**. Both offer a choice of parties and midnight fireworks. The Magic Kingdom shows fireworks on both December 30 and 31 for those who either wish to see fireworks in multiple parks or who don't wish to be caught in the largest crowds of the year on New Year's Eve.

Though all parks, with the exception of Animal Kingdom, have spectacular fireworks at midnight, here are a few different options for the last night of the year:

- **Cirque du Soleil** offers a special New Year's production of *La Nouba.* For more information, visit **cirquedusoleil.com.**

- Forget the rides—the lines will be looong. Relax at your hotel pool and go out for a great dinner that night. If you have little children, get a babysitter. The trick is to arrive a day before New Year's, settle in, go to a water park, and start the touring after January 2, when crowds thin out.

- At Epcot, welcome the New Year several times. Have a drink before 6 p.m. at the Biergarten in Germany. (When the clock strikes 6, it will be midnight in Germany.) Then go over to the Rose & Crown Pub in the United Kingdom and repeat the celebration at 7 p.m., as guests and staff alike will be welcoming the New Year in the United Kingdom. Best of all, you get to start all over again a few hours later when the clock finally strikes midnight at Epcot.

HIGH-LOW, HIGH-LOW, IT'S OFF TO DISNEY WE GO

THOUGH WE RECOMMEND OFF-SEASON TOURING, we realize that's not possible for many families. We want to make it clear, therefore, that you can have a wonderful experience regardless of when you go. Our advice, irrespective of season, is to arrive early at the parks and avoid the crowds by using one of our touring plans. If attendance is light, kick back and forget the touring plans.

Selecting the Day of the Week for Your Visit

We receive thousands of e-mails and letters from readers each year asking which park is the best bet on a particular day. To make things easier for you (and us!), we provide at **touringplans.com** a calendar covering the next year (click "Crowd Calendar" on the home page). For each date, we offer a crowd-level index based on a scale of 1–10, with 1 being least crowded and 10 being most crowded. The calendar also lists the best and worst park(s) to visit in terms of crowd conditions on any given day.

Extra Magic Hours (EMHs)

This program is a perk for families staying at a Walt Disney World resort, including the Swan, Dolphin, and Shades of Green, and the Hilton in the Downtown Disney Resort Area. On selected days of the week, Disney resort guests will be able to enter a Disney theme park 1 hour earlier or stay in a selected theme park about 2 hours later than the official park-operating hours. Theme park visitors not staying at a Disney resort may stay in the park for Extra Magic Hour evenings, but they can't experience any rides, attractions, or shows. In other words, they can shop and eat. The swimming theme parks, Typhoon Lagoon and Blizzard Beach, rarely offer EMHs. If they do, it's usually during the summer.

BOB You'll need to have a Park Hopper option on your theme park admission to take advantage of Extra Magic Hours at more than one park on the same day.

BOB Extra Magic Hours draw more Disney resort guests to the host park, which results in longer lines than you would otherwise experience.

WHAT'S REQUIRED? A valid admission ticket or MagicBand wristband is required to enter the park, and you must show your Disney resort ID or have your MagicBand scanned when entering. For evening EMHs, you may be asked to show your Disney resort ID or MagicBand to experience rides or attractions.

WHEN ARE EMHs OFFERED? You can check the Crowd Calendar at **touringplans.com** for the dates of your visit, check the parks calendar at **disneyworld.com,** or call Walt Disney World Information at ☎ 407-824-4321 or 407-939-6244 (press *0* for a live representative).

In addition to these, it's common for Epcot to have evening EMHs on Wednesdays in September and October and for Animal Kingdom to have morning EMHs on Mondays later in the year.

SAMPLE EXTRA MAGIC HOURS SCHEDULE *(frequently varies)*						
MORNING						
MON	**TUES**	**WED**	**THUR**	**FRI**	**SAT**	**SUN**
—	Epcot	Animal Kingdom	Magic Kingdom	—	DHS	Animal Kingdom
EVENING						
MON	**TUES**	**WED**	**THUR**	**FRI**	**SAT**	**SUN**
DHS	—	—	—	Epcot	Magic Kingdom	—

WHAT DO EXTRA MAGIC HOURS MEAN TO YOU? Disney seems to use EMHs in two ways: to provide Disney resort guests some extra park time on days when those parks are traditionally crowded, and as an incentive to visit one park on days when another park is typically more crowded.

Crowds typically range from slightly below average to average at Animal Kingdom and the Magic Kingdom on days when those parks host Extra Magic Hours. Crowds are higher than average at Disney's Hollywood Studios, and slightly higher at Epcot, on days when they have EMHs.

Not many families have the stamina to take advantage of morning and evening EMHs on consecutive days. If you have to choose between morning or evening Extra Magic Hour sessions, consider first whether your family functions better getting up early or staying up late. Also, consider the time at which the parks close to day guests. Evening EMHs are most useful when the crowds are low and the parks close relatively early to the general public, so your family doesn't have to stay up past midnight to take advantage of the perk.

MORNING EXTRA MAGIC HOURS (A.K.A. EARLY ENTRY) These are offered at all four theme parks throughout the year, and rarely (during summer) at Blizzard Beach and Typhoon Lagoon water parks. Several days of the week, Disney resort guests are invited to enter a designated theme park 1 hour before the general public. During this hour, guests can enjoy selected attractions opened early just for them.

Morning Extra Magic Hours strongly affect attendance at Disney's Hollywood Studios and Epcot, especially during busier times of year. Crowds at those parks are usually larger than average, as a Winston-Salem, North Carolina, mom discovered:

> *Disney's Hollywood Studios was a MADHOUSE. Do NOT go on Extra Magic Hours days. After spending about 3 hours to ride three rides, I just wanted to trample the people stampeding to the exit.*

Magic Kingdom crowds are about average when it has morning EMHs (usually Thursday). Because Disney's Animal Kingdom typically has two morning EMHs but no evening EMHs, crowds are spread out, resulting in lower-than-average waits on both days.

If you're staying at a Disney resort, remember these three things about Extra Magic Hours:

1. The Magic Kingdom has more attractions open for morning EMHs than any other park. We think the Magic Kingdom's morning session, coupled with a good touring plan, is the most worthwhile of any EMHs at any park.

2. Morning EMHs are least useful at Disney's Animal Kingdom because it has fewer rides overall. There's simply not as much benefit for the lost sleep.

3. If you think don't think you'll be at the park with morning Extra Magic Hours 30 minutes before it opens, visit another park instead.

During holiday periods and summer, when Disney hotels are full, getting in early makes a tremendous difference in crowds at the designated park. The program funnels so many people into the EMH park that it fills by about 10 a.m. and is practically gridlocked by noon. A mother of three from Lee's Summit, Missouri, writes:

> *Our first full day at WDW, we went to the Magic Kingdom on an early-entry day for resort guests. We were there at 7:30 a.m. and were able to walk onto all the rides in Fantasyland with no wait. At 8:45 a.m. we positioned ourselves at the Adventureland rope and ran toward Splash Mountain when the rope dropped. We were able to ride Splash Mountain with no wait and then Big Thunder with about*

a 15-minute wait. We then went straight to the Jungle Cruise and the wait was already 30 minutes, so we skipped it. The park became incredibly crowded as the day progressed, and we were all exhausted from getting up so early. We left the park around noon. After that day, I resolved to avoid early-entry days and instead be at a non–early-entry park about a half hour before official opening time.

Note that during holidays, the Magic Kingdom opens to regular guests at 8 a.m. Morning Extra Magic Hours begin at 7 a.m., so you'll need to be at the Magic Kingdom entrance at around 6:30 a.m. You won't be alone, but relatively few people are willing to get up that early for a theme park, and your first hour in the parks will be (please pardon us) magical.

This note from a North Bend, Washington, dad emphasizes the importance of arriving at the beginning of the early-entry period.

We only used early entry once—to Disney's Hollywood Studios. We got there 20 minutes after early entry opened, and the wait for Tower of Terror was 1½ hours long without FastPass+. We skipped it.

An alternative strategy for Disney resort guests is to take advantage of morning Extra Magic Hours, but only until the designated park gets crowded. At that time, move to another park.

A Dillsburg, Pennsylvania, mom has another tip:

If you have FastPass+ opportunities [see page 232], schedule them for the park you're visiting second.

This works particularly well at the Magic Kingdom for families with young children who love the attractions in Fantasyland. However, it will take you about an hour to commute to the second park of the day. If, for example, you depart the Magic Kingdom for Disney's Hollywood Studios at 11 a.m., you'll find the Studios pretty crowded when you arrive at about noon, as this Texas mom found:

We made the mistake of doing a morning at the Magic Kingdom and an afternoon at the Studios. Worst idea ever. By the time we got to the Studios, all the [FastPass+ reservations] were gone for Toy Story Midway Mania!, the Tower of Terror, and Rock 'n' Roller Coaster. And all three rides had at least 90-minute waits.

Keeping these and other considerations in mind, here are some guidelines:

1. Use the morning-EMH–park-hopping strategy during the less busy times of year when the parks close early. You'll get a jump on the general public and add an hour to what, in the off-season, is an already short touring day.

2. Use the morning-EMH–park-hopping strategy to complete touring a second park that you've already visited on a previous day, or specifically to see live entertainment in the second park.

Don't hop to Disney's Animal Kingdom if it closes before 7 p.m. Crowds generally start leaving between 3 and 4 p.m. If the park closes at 5 or 6, you'll have only 1–3 hours of touring with lower crowds.

On any day except its EMH days, hopping to Epcot is usually good. Epcot is equipped to handle large crowds better than any other Disney park, minimizing the effects of a midday arrival. Also, World Showcase has a large selection of interesting dining options, making it a good choice for evening touring.

Don't hop to the park with morning EMHs. The idea is to avoid crowds, not join them. Finally, limit your hopping to two parks per day. Hopping to a third park in one day would result in more time spent commuting than saved by avoiding crowds.

EVENING EXTRA MAGIC HOURS These let Disney resort guests enjoy a different theme park on specified nights for about 2 hours after it closes to the general public. Guests pay no additional charge to participate but must scan their MagicBands (see page 69) at each ride or attraction they wish to experience. You can also show up at the turnstiles at any point after evening Extra Magic Hours have started. Note that if you've been in another park that day, you'll need the Park Hopper feature on your admission ticket to enter. Evening Extra Magic Hours are offered at the Magic Kingdom, Epcot, and Disney's Hollywood Studios, but not at Disney's Animal Kingdom.

Evening sessions are usually more crowded at the Magic Kingdom and the Studios than at Epcot. Those evening EMH crowds can be just as large as those throughout the day. During summer, when the Magic Kingdom's evening EMH session runs until 1 a.m., lines at headliner attractions can still be long at midnight. A mom from Fairhaven, Massachusetts, doesn't mince words:

> I say steer clear of a park that is open late. There are only a few attractions open and tons of people trying to get on them.

More attractions operate during evening EMHs than during morning EMHs. Certain fast-food and full-service restaurants remain open as well.

PLANNING *Your* WALT DISNEY WORLD VACATION BUDGET

HOW MUCH YOU SPEND DEPENDS on how long you stay at Walt Disney World. But even if you stop by only for an afternoon, be prepared to drop a bundle. Later we'll show you how to save money on lodging. This section will give you some sense of what you can expect to pay for admissions and food. And we'll help you decide which admission option will best meet your needs.

WALT DISNEY WORLD ADMISSION OPTIONS

DISNEY OFFERS A NUMBER of different admission options to accommodate various vacation needs. These range from the humble

1-Day Base Ticket, good for a single day's entry into one Disney theme park, to the blinged-out **Premium Annual Pass,** good for 365 days of admission into every Disney theme or water park, plus DisneyQuest.

The number of ticket options available makes it difficult to sort out which option represents the least expensive way to see and do everything you want. The average family staying for a week at an off-World hotel and planning a couple of activities outside the theme parks has about a dozen different ticket options to consider.

Adding to the complexity, Disney's reservation agents are trained to avoid answering subjective questions about which ticket option is "best." Many families, we suspect, become overwhelmed trying to sort out the different options and simply purchase an expensive ticket with more features than they'll use.

As an example, a family of two adults and two children who want to visit the theme parks for five days and a water park for one day could buy everyone a 5-Day Base Ticket plus the Water Park Fun and More option, for $1,572 total. Or they could buy separate admissions to the theme and water parks from a third-party vendor for $1,376, a savings of $196. The problem is that comparing options requires detailed knowledge of the myriad perks included with specific admissions.

THIS IS A JOB FOR . . . A COMPUTER!

IT'S COMPLICATED ENOUGH that we wrote a computer program to solve it. Visit **touringplans.com** and try our **Park Ticket Calculator,** on the home page. It aggregates ticket prices from Disney and a number of online ticket vendors. Just answer a few simple questions relating to the size of your party and the theme parks you intend to visit, and the calculator will identify your four least expensive ticket options. It'll also show you how much you'll save.

The program will also make recommendations for considerations other than price. For example, Annual Passes might cost more, but they make sense in certain circumstances because Disney often offers substantial resort discounts and other deals to Annual Pass holders. Those resort discounts, especially during the off-season, can more than offset a small incremental charge for the Annual Pass.

The Park Ticket Calculator has saved readers millions of dollars over the past few years, as this husband discovered:

You just saved me from making a $408 mistake and needless expense!

MAGIC YOUR WAY

WALT DISNEY WORLD OFFERS AN ARRAY of theme park ticket options, grouped into a program called Magic Your Way. The simplest option, visiting one theme park for one day, is called a **1-Day Base Ticket.** Other features, such as the ability to visit more than one park per day ("park-hopping") or the inclusion of admission to Disney's minor venues (Typhoon Lagoon, Blizzard Beach, DisneyQuest, mini-golf, and the like), are available as individual add-ons to the Base Ticket.

In 2013 Disney introduced separate pricing for a single day's admission to the Magic Kingdom versus the World's other theme parks. An adult 1-Day Base Ticket for the Magic Kingdom costs $111.83, while one day's admission to any other theme park is $103.31 (including tax).

Multiday pricing is still uniform across the parks. The more days of admission you buy, the lower the cost per day. For example, if you buy an adult 5-Day Base Ticket for $335.48 (tax included), each day costs $67.10, compared with $103.31 a day for a one-day pass to Epcot, the Studios, or Animal Kingdom and $111.83 for the Magic Kingdom. Tickets can be purchased from 1 up to 10 days and admit you to exactly one theme park per day; you can reenter your chosen park as many times as you like on that day.

Disney says its tickets expire within 14 days of the first day of use. In practice, they really mean 13 days after the first day of use. If, say, you purchase a 4-Day Base Ticket on June 1 and use it that day for admission to the Magic Kingdom, you'll be able to visit a single Disney theme park on any of your three remaining days from June 2 through June 14. After that, the ticket expires and any unused days will be lost.

BASE-TICKET ADD-ONS

NAVIGATING THE MAGIC YOUR WAY PROGRAM is like ordering dinner à la carte at an upscale restaurant: many choices, mostly expensive, virtually all of which require some thought.

Two add-on options are offered with the Magic Your Way Ticket, each at an additional cost:

PARK HOPPER This add-on you lets you visit more than one theme park per day. The cost is a flat rate of $53.25 (tax included) on top of the price of a 1-Day Base Ticket to the Magic Kingdom or $61.77 (tax included) to Epcot, Disney's Hollywood Studios, or Animal Kingdom. For 2- or 3-Day Base Tickets, the add-on is $53.25 (tax included)—exorbitant for one or two days but more affordable the longer you stay. For tickets of four or more days, the cost is a flat $68.16 (tax included). As an add-on to a 7-Day Base ticket, the flat fee works out to $9.74 per day for park-hopping privileges. If you want to visit the Magic Kingdom in the morning and eat at Epcot in the evening, this is the feature to request.

WATER PARK FUN AND MORE (WPFAM) This option gives you a single admission to one of Disney's water parks (Blizzard Beach and Typhoon Lagoon), DisneyQuest, Oak Trail Golf Course, Fantasia Gardens or Winter Summerland mini-golf, or the ESPN Wide World of Sports Complex. The cost is a flat $63.90, including tax. Except for the single-day WPFAM ticket, which gives you two admissions, the number of admissions equals the number of days on your ticket. If you buy an 8-Day Base Ticket, for example, and add the WPFAM option, you get eight WPFAM admissions. What you *can't* do is, say, buy a 10-Day Base Ticket with only three WPFAM admissions or a 3-Day Base Ticket with four WPFAM admissions. You can, however, skip WPFAM entirely and buy an

WDW Theme Park Ticket Options

	1-DAY	2-DAY	3-DAY	4-DAY	5-DAY
BASE TICKET AGES 3–9					
MK: $105.44 EP/AK/DHS: $96.92	$190.64	$272.64	$303.53	$314.18
—	($95.32/day)	($90.88/day)	($75.88/day)	($62.84/day)
BASE TICKET AGE 10 AND UP					
MK: $111.83 EP/AK/DHS: $103.31	$204.48	$292.88	$324.83	$335.48
—	($102.24/day)	($97.63/day)	($81.21/day)	($67.10/day)
Base Ticket admits guest to one theme park each day of use.					
PARK HOPPER ADD-ON *(1-day prices include admission)*					
Ages 3–9: $158.69 Age 10+: $165.08	$68.16 (+ admission)	$68.16 (+ admission)	$68.16 (+ admission)	$68.16 (+ admission)
—	($34.08/day)	($22.72/day)	($17.04/day)	($13.63/day)
Park Hopper option entitles guest to visit more than one theme park on each day of use.					
WPFAM ADD-ON *(1-day prices include admission)*					
Ages 3–9: $173.60 Age 10+: $179.99	$63.90 (+ admission)	$63.90 (+ admission)	$63.90 (+ admission)	$63.90 (+ admission)
2 visits	2 visits	3 visits	4 visits	5 visits
Water Park Fun and More option entitles guest to a specified number of visits (between 2 and 10) to a choice of entertainment and recreation venues.					
PARK HOPPER + WPFAM *(1-day prices include admission)*					
Ages 3–9: $201.29 Age 10+: $207.68	$95.85 (+ admission)	$95.85 (+ admission)	$95.85 (+ admission)	$95.85 (+ admission)
—	($47.93/day)	($31.95/day)	($23.96/day)	($19.17/day)

individual admission to any of these minor parks—that's frequently the best deal if you want to visit only one of the previous venues.

Disney also offers a **Park Hopper–WPFAM combo** for $95.85, including tax. If you plan to spend a lot of time at the water parks and other WPFAM venues, the combo will save you $36 over buying the two options separately.

The foregoing add-ons are available for purchase in any combination. If you buy a ticket and then decide later on that you want one or more of the options, you can upgrade the ticket to add the feature(s) you desire. Disney doesn't prorate the cost, so you'll pay the same price regardless of when you buy the option: If you add the Park

Note: All ticket and add-on prices include 6.5% sales tax.				
6-DAY	**7-DAY**	**8-DAY**	**9-DAY**	**10-DAY**
BASE TICKET AGES 3–9				
$324.83	$335.48	$346.13	$356.78	$367.43
($54.14/day)	($47.93/day)	($43.27/day)	($39.64/day)	($36.74/day)
BASE TICKET AGE 10 AND UP				
$346.13	$356.78	$367.43	$378.08	$388.73
($57.69/day)	($50.97/day)	($45.93/day)	($42.01/day)	($38.87/day)
Park choices are Magic Kingdom, Epcot, Disney's Hollywood Studios, or Disney's Animal Kingdom.				
PARK HOPPER ADD-ON *(1-day prices include admission)*				
$68.16 (+ admission)	$68.16 (+ admission)	$68.16 (+ admission)	$68.16 (+ admission)	$68.16 (+ admission)
($11.36/day)	($9.74/day)	($8.52/day)	($7.57/day)	($6.82/day)
Park choices are any combination of Magic Kingdom, Epcot, Disney's Hollywood Studios, or Disney's Animal Kingdom on each day of use.				
WPFAM ADD-ON *(1-day prices include admission)*				
$63.90 (+ admission)	$63.90 (+ admission)	$63.90 (+ admission)	$63.90 (+ admission)	$63.90 (+ admission)
6 visits	7 visits	8 visits	9 visits	10 visits
Choices are Disney's Blizzard Beach water park, Disney's Typhoon Lagoon water park, DisneyQuest, Oak Trail Golf Course, ESPN Wide World of Sports Complex, or Winter Summerland or Fantasia Gardens mini-golf.				
PARK HOPPER + WPFAM *(1-day prices include admission)*				
$95.85 (+ admission)	$95.85 (+ admission)	$95.85 (+ admission)	$95.85 (+ admission)	$95.85 (+ admission)
($15.98/day)	($13.69/day)	($11.98/day)	($10.65/day)	($9.59/day)
Note: Check **touringplans.com** for the latest ticket prices, which are subject to change. All tickets expire 13 days after first use.				

Hopper option on the last day of your trip, you'll pay the same $61.70 as if you'd bought it before you left home.

Annual Passes

An **Annual Pass** provides unlimited use of the major theme parks for one year; a **Premium Annual Pass** also provides unlimited use of the minor parks. Annual Pass holders also get perks, including free parking and seasonal offers such as room-rate discounts at Disney resorts. The Annual Pass is not valid for special

LILIANE I keep my Annual Passes in the same place as my passport, insurance papers, and other travel documents. And I always keep a copy of my credit card receipt documenting the purchase. I even make a digital copy because receipts fade as time goes by.

events, such as admission to Mickey's Very Merry Christmas Party. Tax included, Annual Passes run $696.51 for both adults and kids age 3 and up. A Premium Annual Pass, at $829.64 for adults and kids age 3 and up, provides unlimited admission to Blizzard Beach, Typhoon Lagoon, DisneyQuest, and Oak Trail Golf Course, in addition to the four major theme parks, plus mini-golf discounts.

Florida Resident Passes

Disney offers several special admission options to Florida residents. The **Florida Resident Annual Pass** ($563.39 for adults and kids age 3 and up) and the **Florida Resident Premium Annual Pass** ($691.19 for adults and kids age 3 and up) both offer unlimited admission and park-hopping privileges to the four major theme parks. The Florida Resident Premium Annual Pass also provides unlimited admission to Blizzard Beach, Typhoon Lagoon, DisneyQuest, and Oak Trail Golf Course, in addition to the four major theme parks, plus mini-golf discounts. And the **Florida Resident Seasonal Pass** ($350.39 for adults and kids age 3 and up) provides unlimited admission to the four major theme parks except on blackout dates. In addition to Annual Passes, Florida residents are eligible for discounts on one-day Park Hopper Tickets (about $4) as well as on various add-on options. The **Florida Resident Weekday Select Pass** is $239.63 for all ages and provides admission to the four major theme parks Monday–Friday except on blackout days. For $211.94 Florida residents can purchase the **Epcot After 4 Annual Pass,** which provides admission to Epcot on any day after 4 p.m. Florida residents can also purchase a full year's admission to Disney's water parks—any day after 2 p.m.—for $69.23 for adults and $62.84 for kids age 10 and up.

ANOTHER ONE BITES THE DUST

DISNEY CLOSES MONEY-SAVING LOOPHOLES each time it updates admission prices and options. The most recent casualty was the No Expiration option, which allowed you to roll over any unused admission days on your ticket to a subsequent trip. Assuming you could keep that ticket in a safe place, you'd pay for two trips' worth of admission now and avoid years of Disney ticket price increases on your next visit.

Well, they couldn't let *that* continue, could they? If you previously purchased theme park tickets with the No Expiration option, your tickets will still be honored.

HOW TO GET THE MOST FROM MAGIC YOUR WAY

FIRST, BE REALISTIC about what you want out of your vacation. A seven-day theme park ticket with seven WPFAM admissions might seem like a wonderful idea when you're snowbound in February and planning your trip. But actually trying to visit all those parks in a week in July might end up feeling more like Navy SEAL training. If you're going to visit only one water park, DisneyQuest, or the ESPN Wide World of Sports Complex, you're almost always better off purchasing that admission separately rather than in the WPFAM option. If you plan to visit two or more WPFAM venues, you're better off buying the add-on.

ANTICIPATING PRICE INCREASES

DISNEY USUALLY RAISES PRICES ONCE A YEAR: The latest hike came in February 2015 and the one before that in February 2014, the three before came in June, and the five before that in August. We wouldn't be surprised to see a second round of price increases in late 2015. Price increases have generally run about 5% a year, but specific ticket categories are frequently bumped much more. In 2015, the average increase for Base Tickets was 3%, and 4% for add-on options. If you're putting a budget together, assume at least a 5% increase, but know that it could be higher.

A Georgia dad puts Disney's price hikes in perspective:

In the spring of 1983 as a working student, I purchased a [pre–Magic Your Way] 3-Day Park Hopper for $35 (including tax). Minimum wage was $3.35/hour, meaning it took less than 11 hours of work to pay for that ticket. With the latest increase, a 3-Day Base Ticket plus Park Hopper costs $361, or about 50 hours of work at today's minimum wage of $7.25/hour.

A Wayne, Pennsylvania, reader, takes a different tack:

Disney has gotten more expensive, and it's a shame that this makes it difficult for some people to visit. However, the dollar comparison is not accurate, as Disney was much smaller years ago.

TICKETS, BIOMETRICS, WRISTBANDS, AND RFID

TO THIS POINT IN THE BOOK, we've used the word *ticket* to describe that thing you carry around as proof of your admission to the park. In fact, Disney admission media come in two forms—neither of which is a ticket. While we use *ticket* as shorthand for "admission medium," you'll be better prepared by knowing what you'll actually be handed when you plunk down your money.

If you're staying at a Disney resort, your admission medium is a rubber wristband about the size and shape of a small wristwatch. Called a **MagicBand**, it contains a tiny radio frequency identifier (RFID) chip, on which is stored a link to the record of your admission purchase in Disney's computers. Your MagicBand also functions as your hotel-room key, and it can (optionally) work as a credit card for most food and merchandise purchases throughout the park.

If you don't want a MagicBand, you get a **Key to the World Card,** which looks like a credit card. If you're staying off-property or you bought your admission from a third-party vendor, your ticket is a flexible, credit card–size piece of plastic-coated paper. For $13 you can upgrade these cards to a MagicBand. The inner workings of RFID are discussed in detail starting on page 69.

In addition to using RFID chips, Disney's computer systems store the dimensions of one finger from your right hand, a reference to which is also stored on your MagicBand or laminated card. Recording this biometric information requires a quick and painless measurement, taken the first time you use the ticket. When you use it again, you'll be asked to scan the same finger to validate your identity. If the scans don't match—say, you use a different finger—you may be asked to present photo identification.

If you're buying admission for your entire family and you're worried that you won't be able to keep everyone's tickets straight, Disney's computer system should have every family member's data linked to every ticket, allowing anyone in your group to enter with anyone else's ticket. We've confirmed this by having a platoon of Unofficial Guide researchers (including men, women, and children) swap MagicBands with each other; all were admitted.

WHERE TO PURCHASE MAGIC YOUR WAY TICKETS

YOU CAN BUY YOUR ADMISSION PASSES on arrival at Walt Disney World or buy them in advance. Passes are available at Disney World resorts and theme parks, at some non-Disney hotels and shopping centers, and through independent ticket brokers. Because Disney admissions are only marginally discounted in the Walt Disney World–Orlando area, the chief reason for you to buy from an independent broker is convenience. Offers of free or heavily discounted tickets abound, but they generally require you to attend a time-share sales presentation.

Magic Your Way tickets are available at Disney Stores and at **disney world.com** for the same prices listed in the chart on pages 62–63.

If you're trying to keep costs to an absolute minimum, consider using an online ticket wholesaler, such as the **Official Ticket Center, Undercover Tourist, Kissimmee Guest Services,** or **Maple Leaf Tickets,** especially for trips with five or more days in the parks. The savings can range from $4 to more than $60, depending on the ticket and options chosen. If any options don't make sense for your specific vacation plans, the representatives will tell you so.

All four companies offer discount tickets for almost all Central Florida attractions, including Disney, Universal, SeaWorld, and Cirque du Soleil. Discounts for the major theme parks range from about 6% to 12%; tickets for other attractions are more deeply discounted. The **Official Ticket Center** (3148 Vineland Rd., Kissimmee; daily, 8 a.m.–8:30 p.m. Eastern time; ☎ 407-396-9020 or 877-406-4836; **official ticketcenter.com**) offers delivery by USPS Certified Mail for free; you may also pick up tickets at its office for free. For $10, it will deliver via Priority Mail or to area hotels. **Undercover Tourist** (US: ☎ 800-846-1302; Monday–Friday, 9 a.m.–4 p.m. Eastern time; UK: ☎ 0800 081 1702; Monday–Friday, 2 p.m.–9 p.m. Greenwich mean time; ☎ +1 386-239-8624 worldwide; **undercovertourist.com**) offers free delivery and has a sweetheart relationship with **MouseSavers** (**mouse savers.com**). If you subscribe to the MouseSavers e-newsletter, you can access Undercover Tourist through a special "secret" link that provides additional savings on top of the normal discount. **Kissimmee Guest Services** (950 Celebration Blvd., Ste. H, Celebration; ☎ 888-206-6040 or 321-939-2057; Monday–Saturday, 8 a.m.–5 p.m., Sunday, 8 a.m.–noon, Eastern time; UK: ☎ 0208 432 4024; **kgstickets.com**) offers free ticket delivery to area hotels for tickets ordered by phone, but tickets ordered online are cheaper. **Maple Leaf Tickets** (4647 W. Irlo Bronson Memorial Hwy., Kissimmee; daily, 8 a.m.–6 p.m. Eastern time; ☎ 407-396-0300 or 800-841-2837; **mapleleaftickets.com**) offers free pickup at its store. For $6.95 per order, it will deliver via USPS Priority Mail or to area hotels.

Where *Not* to Buy Passes

In addition to the many authorized sellers of Disney admissions, a number of bricks-and-mortar sellers exist. They buy unused days on legitimately purchased passes, and then resell them as if they were newly issued. These resellers are easy to identify: They insist that you specify exactly which dates you plan to use the ticket. They know, of course, how many days are left on the pass and when it expires. If you tell them you plan to use it tomorrow and the next two days, they'll sell you a ticket that has three days remaining and expires in three days. Naturally, because they don't tell you this, you assume the usual 14-day expiration period from the date of first use. In the case of your tickets, however, the original purchaser triggered the 14-day expiration period. If you decide to skip a day instead of using the pass on the next three consecutive days, you'll discover to your chagrin that it has expired.

LILIANE Also steer clear of passes offered on eBay, Craigslist, and the like.

FOR ADDITIONAL INFORMATION ON PASSES

IF YOU HAVE A QUESTION OR CONCERN regarding admissions that can be addressed only through a person-to-person conversation, contact **Disney Ticket Inquiries** at ☎ 407-566-4985 or **ticket.inquiries @disneyworld.com**. If you call, be aware that you may spend a considerable time on hold; if you e-mail, be aware that it can take up to three days to get a response. In contrast, the ticket section of the Disney World website—**disneyworld.disney.go.com/tickets**—is surprisingly straightforward in showing how ticket prices breaks down.

HOW MUCH DOES IT COST PER DAY?

A TYPICAL DAY WOULD COST $738.52, excluding lodging and transportation, for a family of four—Mom, Dad, 12-year-old Abner, and 8-year-old Agnes—driving their own car and staying outside the World. They plan to stay a week, so they buy 5-Day Base Tickets with the Park Hopper option.

A Birmingham, Alabama, mom of two begs to differ with our budget recommendation above for souvenirs:

> Sorry, but Uncle Bob is totally out of touch when he says "you won't have to buy souvenirs every day." In my experience, you'll head home with several sets of character ears; enough dress-up costumes to outfit the neighborhood; and countless pins, toys, and knickknacks.

BACK TO THE SALT MINES! Our math could be off, but it appears that the cost of a Disney vacation has increased roughly three times faster

HOW MUCH DOES A DAY COST?	
Breakfast for four at Denny's with tax and tip	$43.15
Epcot parking fee (free for pass holders and resort guests)	$17.00
Four day admission on a 5-Day Ticket with Park Hopper	$318.66
Dad: *Adult 5-Day with tax is $403.64 divided by five days = $80.73*	
Mom: *Adult 5-Day with tax is $403.64 divided by five days = $80.73*	
Abner: *Adult 5-Day with tax is $403.64 divided by five days = $80.73*	
Agnes: *Child 5-Day with tax is $382.34 divided by five days = $76.47*	
Morning break (soda or coffee)	$11.25
Fast-food lunch (sandwich or burger, fries, soda), no tip	$58.28
Afternoon break (soda and popcorn)	$26.63
Dinner at Italy (3 appetizers, 4 entrées, 3 desserts), with tax and tip	$210.41
Souvenirs (Mickey T-shirts for Abner and Agnes) with tax*	$53.14
One-day total (without lodging or transportation)	**$738.52**

Cheer up—you won't have to buy souvenirs every day.

than US workers' median wages (6.0% vs. 1.8%) since 2005. To put that in perspective, it took the average worker about 3.8 hours to earn enough money for a 1-Day Base Ticket in 2005. Today it's 4.2 hours.

A Cincinnati, Ohio, man didn't hold back:

> *We were distressed by the obvious trend toward "pay more but get less" that we observed in almost every area of our Disney vacation. We travel to Walt Disney World with frequency. We were all disgusted at various points throughout our stay when we could clearly see that we were paying much more to get much less than we have on previous trips. Don't even get me started on our costly but crummy dining experiences. Unfortunately, the trend appears to be completely on the side of Disney profits rather than overall guest satisfaction.*

From a Shreveport, Louisiana, family:

> *We went to Disney World four years ago; we were shocked at how much the prices in restaurants have gone up. We spent $75 for four people for breakfast!*

The *Unofficial* No-Frills Guide to Walt Disney World

With even a bare-bones visit to the World now out of reach of many families, being frugal is becoming ever more necessary. These tips can help:

1. Buy your admission online from one of the sellers on page 66. Get tickets only for the number of days you plan to visit, and skip all add-on options.

2. Book a hotel outside of Walt Disney World. Hotels on US 192 (Irlo Bronson Memorial Highway) are usually the least expensive. Also, consider renting a vacation home (see discussion starting on page 130) if you have four or more people in your group.

3. Eat breakfast in your hotel room from a cooler; take lunch, snacks, and drinks from your cooler to the park; and eat dinner outside the World using discount coupons from local visitor guides or from the Internet.

4. Avoid parking fees by using your hotel's shuttle service or by taking Disney transportation from Disney Springs or the water parks, where parking is free. Note that the second suggestion eats up a lot of time, so do it only if you're budgeting to the penny.

5. Buy discounted Disney merchandise from one of Orlando's two **Disney Character Warehouse** outlets (4951 International Dr., ☎ 407-354-3255; 8200 Vineland Ave., ☎ 407-477-0222; **premiumoutlets.com/orlando**).

RFID: IT'S ALL IN THE WRIST

WITH ITS MYMAGIC+ CAMPAIGN (see page 39), Disney introduced **MagicBands**—reusable rubber wristbands—as a sort of wearable theme park ticket. Small and reusable across trips, a MagicBand is imprinted with your first name, an ID number, and some legalese, along with a Mickey logo. A tiny radio-frequency-identification (RFID) chip embedded in the wristband holds your ticket and travel information.

BOB Old non-RFID tickets must be converted to the new medium before you can enter the theme parks or use FastPass+. You can get this done only at Guest Relations, just outside each park.

Each RFID chip—not much larger than the end of a pencil—sends a unique serial number over short distances via radio waves. When you purchase theme park admission, Disney's computers will store that serial number, along with your ticket information. To enter a theme park, you'll touch your MagicBand to an RFID reader instead of going through a turnstile. The RFID reader will collect your MagicBand's serial number, compare your biometric information, and verify with Disney's computer systems that you have the correct admission to enter the park.

Disney hotel guests get a MagicBand by default but may request a plastic **Key to the World (KTTW) Card** instead. If you're staying off-site or you bought your admission through a third party, you can upgrade to a MagicBand for $13; otherwise you get a credit card–size laminated ticket. Like the MagicBand, the two card options use RFID.

Each member of your family gets his or her own MagicBand, each with a unique serial number. Along with the wristband, each family member will be asked to select a four-digit personal-identification number (PIN) for purchases—more on that on the following page. The wristbands are resizable and waterproof, and they have ventilation holes for cooling. Eight colors are available: red, black, blue, green, pink, orange, yellow, and gray (the default). You can choose your colors and personalize your bands when you book your resort stay at the Disney World website.

BOB At **magicyourband .com** you can create stickers of almost any color or design for your MagicBand.

You'll feel a little clumsy using the MagicBand at first. The RFID chip in the band is located under a Mickey-head symbol about the size of a dime. To open your guest room door, use FastPass+, or enter a park, you have to line up the Mickey head almost exactly with the RFID reader in question. It gets better with practice, but many guests go through wrist contortions, or actually take the

MagicBand off, to align the chip with a reader. Quite a few, particularly men, simply carry the MagicBand in their pocket instead of wearing it.

RFID for Payment, Hotel-Room Access, and Photos

Disney's hotel-room doors have RFID readers, allowing you to enter your room simply by tapping your wristband or KTTW Card against the reader. The same technology has been in use for years at upscale hotels around the world.

RFID readers are also installed at virtually every Disney cash register on property, allowing you to pay for food, drinks, and souvenirs by tapping your MagicBand/KTTW Card against the reader. You'll be asked to verify your identity by entering your PIN on a small keypad to complete your purchase. This technology, known as contactless payment, has been in use worldwide for many years too.

If you're using Disney's **Memory Maker** service (**disneyworld.disney .go.com/memory-maker**), your MagicBand/KTTW Card serves as the link between your photos and your family. Each photographer carries a small RFID reader, against which you tap your MagicBand before having your photo taken. The Memory Maker system will link your photos to you, and you'll be able to view them on the Disney World website.

Disney's onboard ride-photo computers incorporate RFID technology too. As you begin down the big drop near the finale of Splash Mountain, for example, RFID sensors read the serial number on your MagicBand and pass it to Splash Mountain's cameras. When those cameras snap your family plunging into the briar patch, they attach your MagicBand's serial number to the photo, allowing you to see your ride photos together after you've returned home. Because ride sensors may not pick up the signal from an RFID card sitting in a wallet or purse, we're fairly sure that onboard ride photos require MagicBands.

The Future of RFID

Other innovative uses of RFID technology are rumored to be in the works. In one scenario we've heard, you'll provide Disney with some information about your child before your visit, such as his or her favorite color and pet's name. Later, when your child visits Cinderella, an RFID reader next to Cinderella will recognize your child's wristband and display the previously gathered information on a hidden prompter for Cinderella to work into conversation. And because Disney's computer systems will know from your MagicBand which rides you've been on and where you've eaten, Cinderella may mention those details too.

But as impressive as all this sounds, many people are understandably concerned about multinational corporations tracking their movements. As noted earlier, guests who prefer not to wear MagicBands can instead obtain KTTW Cards, which are somewhat more difficult to track (inexpensive RFID-blocking wallets are available online). Disney claims that guests who opt out of MagicBands don't get the full range of ride experiences, though, so there's a trade-off to be made.

RFID and MagicBands are hot topics with our readers. Here are a few typical comments. First from a Buckley, Michigan, mom:

> *MagicBands and MyMagic+: AMAZING! We had everything we needed right in our wristbands! If we didn't want to take anything with us when we left the room, we didn't have to. The MagicBands acted as our room key, charge card, park passes, FastPasses, and dining plan vouchers.*

This from a newlywed couple:

> *I cannot say enough about how awesome the MagicBands are! Not having to root around for a room key after a long day of touring was bliss. The fact that they could be worn in the water made going to the pool or water park a snap. Also, they were linked to my wife's credit card, so we didn't have to bring cash everywhere. Plus, they survived Summit Plummet!*

Finally, a mom from Plano, Texas, chipped in with this:

> *Loved the MagicBands! They make it so convenient to spend lots of money. And you can use them at the Disney store in the airport too. When we ate lunch at Sunshine Seasons, a coupon printed out at the bottom of my receipt for 20% off a purchase at select stores in the Disney resort that was good only until 1 p.m. each day. I had never heard of coupons being given out at Disney, but I used it later in the week.*

BABYSITTING

CHILD-CARE CENTERS Child care isn't available inside the theme parks, but two Magic Kingdom resorts connected by monorail or boat (Polynesian Village Resort and Wilderness Lodge & Villas), four Epcot resorts (the Yacht & Beach Club Resorts, the Swan, and the Dolphin), and Animal Kingdom Lodge, along with the Hilton at Walt Disney World, have child-care centers for potty-trained children age 3 and older (see table on following page). Services vary, but children generally can be left between 5 p.m. and midnight. (At the Dolphin and Swan, hours are 5:30 p.m.–midnight, and the price is $10 per child, per hour.) Milk and cookies and blankets and pillows are provided at all centers, and dinner is provided at most. Play is supervised but not organized, and toys, videos, and games are plentiful. Guests at any Disney resort or campground may use the services.

The most elaborate of the child-care centers (variously called "clubs" or "camps") is **Lilo's Playhouse** at the Polynesian Village Resort. The rate for ages 3–12 is $15 per hour, per child (2-hour minimum).

All the clubs accept reservations (some six months in advance!) with a credit card guarantee. Call the club directly, or reserve through Disney at ☎ 407-WDW-DINE (939-3463). Most clubs require a

CHILD-CARE CLUBS*		
HOTEL NAME OF PROGRAM	AGES	PHONE
ANIMAL KINGDOM LODGE		
Simba's Cubhouse	3–12	☎ 407-938-4785
DOLPHIN AND SWAN		
Camp Dolphin	4–12	☎ 407-934-4241
POLYNESIAN VILLAGE RESORT		
Lilo's Playhouse	3–12	☎ 407-824-1639
YACHT & BEACH CLUB RESORTS		
Sandcastle Club	3–12	☎ 407-934-3750
WILDERNESS LODGE & VILLAS		
Cub's Den	3–12	☎ 407-824-1083

* Child-care clubs operate afternoons and evenings. Before 4 p.m., call the hotels rather than the numbers listed above. All programs require reservations; call ☎ 407-WDW-DINE (939-3463).

24-hour cancellation notice and levy a hefty penalty of 2 hours' time or $30 per child for no-shows. A limited number of walk-ins are usually accepted on a first-come, first-serve basis.

If you're staying in a Disney resort that doesn't offer a child-care club and you *don't* have a car, then you're better off using in-room babysitting. Trying to take your child to a club in another hotel by Disney bus requires a 50- to 90-minute trip each way. By the time you've deposited your little one, it will almost be time to pick him or her up again.

IN-ROOM BABYSITTING Two companies provide in-room sitting in Walt Disney World and surrounding areas: **Kid's Nite Out** and **Fairy Godmothers** (no kidding). Kid's Nite Out also serves hotels in the greater Orlando area, including downtown. Both provide sitters older than age 18 who are insured, bonded, screened, reference-checked,

Babysitting Services

KID'S NITE OUT	FAIRY GODMOTHERS
☎ 407-828-0920 or 800-696-8105 kidsniteout.com	☎ 407-277-3724
HOTELS SERVED All WDW and Orlando-area hotels	**HOTELS SERVED** All WDW hotels and those in the general WDW area
SITTERS Men and women	**SITTERS** Mothers and grandmothers, female college students
MINIMUM CHARGES 4 hours	**MINIMUM CHARGES** 4 hours
BASE HOURLY RATES • 1 child, $18 • 2 children, $21 3 children, $24 • 4 children, $26	**BASE HOURLY RATES** 1 child, $16 • 2 children, $16 3 children, $16 • 4 children and up, $18
EXTRA CHARGES Transportation fee, $10; starting before 8 a.m. or after 9 p.m., +$2 per hour; additional fee for holidays	**EXTRA CHARGES** Transportation fee, $16; starting after 10 p.m., +$2 per hour
CANCELLATION DEADLINE 24 hours before service	**CANCELLATION DEADLINE** 3 hours before service
FORM OF PAYMENT AE, D, MC, V; tips in cash	**FORM OF PAYMENT** Cash or traveler's checks for actual payment; tips in cash
THINGS SITTERS WON'T DO Transport children in private vehicle, take children swimming, give baths	**THINGS SITTERS WON'T DO** Transport children, give baths. Swimming is at sitter's discretion.

police-checked, and trained in CPR. In addition to caring for your kids in your room, the sitters will, if you direct (and pay), take your children to the theme parks or other venues. Both services offer bilingual sitters. (See table on previous page for details.)

SPECIAL PROGRAMS
for CHILDREN

SEVERAL CHILDREN'S PROGRAMS ARE AVAILABLE at Walt Disney World parks and resorts.

BEHIND THE SEEDS AT EPCOT This 1-hour walking tour of the Land greenhouses and labs at Epcot has plenty of interaction for the kids, including guessing games and feeding fish at the fish farm. The greenhouses are home to more than 60 crops from around the world. Did you know that the food grown in The Land is used at restaurants throughout Epcot? The price is $20 per adult and $16 per child (ages 3–9). Call ☎ 407-WDW-TOUR (939-8687) for additional information and reservations.

DINE WITH AN ANIMAL SPECIALIST We highly recommend this experience at Sanaa, one of the restaurants at Animal Kingdom Lodge. Not only will you and your family be treated to a fabulous African-inspired lunch, but you'll also get to spend time with a caretaker who shares fun facts about his or her work with the animals. After lunch, guests are taken outside and behind the gates to meet an endangered animal.

Limited to 12 participants, the lunch is offered Wednesdays and Saturdays at noon. The price—$49 for adults and $29 for kids ages 3–9 (it's best suited for ages 8 and up)—includes tax, tip, and a $5 donation to the Disney Conservation Fund. It's educational, fun, and a great value. Check out Liliane's review at **tinyurl.com /lunchwithanimalspecialist.**

LILIANE Be aware that Disney is tinkering with prices and availability of packages now more than ever. Check ahead of time before promising your kids any activity.

DISNEY'S FAMILY MAGIC TOUR This is a 1½- to 2-hour guided tour of the Magic Kingdom for the entire family. Even children in strollers (no younger than age 3) are welcome. The tour combines information about the Magic Kingdom with the gathering of clues that ultimately solve "diabolical" problems. There's usually a marginal plot such as saving Wendy from Captain Hook, in which case the character at the end of the tour is Wendy. The tour departs daily at 10 a.m. The cost is about $34 per person with tax, plus a valid Magic Kingdom admission. Maximum group size is 20 persons. Reservations can be made up to a year in advance by calling ☎ 407-WDW-TOUR (939-8687).

DISNEY'S THE MAGIC BEHIND OUR STEAM TRAINS Kids must be age 10 or older for this 3-hour tour, presented Monday–Saturday. At the 7:30 a.m. start time, join the crew of the Walt Disney World Railroad as they prepare their steam locomotives for the day. Cost is about $54 per person with tax, plus a valid Magic Kingdom admission. Call ☎ 407-WDW-TOUR (939-8687) for information and reservations.

DISNEY'S PIRATE ADVENTURE CRUISES Children ages 4–12 get to don bandannas, hoist the Jolly Roger, and set out on a boat trip to search for buried treasure by following a map. At the final port of call, the kids find the hidden treasure (doubloons, beads, and rubber bugs!) and wolf down light snacks. The treasure is split among the kids. The adventure costs about $37 per child with tax and is offered at Port Orleans Riverside (Bayou Pirate Adventure), the Grand Floridian (Pirate Adventure), the Yacht Club (Albatross Cruise), and the Caribbean Beach Resort (Islands of the Caribbean Pirate Cruise). Each kids-only excursion takes place daily (weather permitting), 9:30–11:30 a.m. Call ☎ 407-WDW-PLAY (939-7529) for days offered and other information. Boys and girls alike really love this outing—many report it as the highlight of their vacation. *Note:* No parents allowed.

If you want to go whole hog, check out **The Pirates League** in Adventureland at the Magic Kingdom, where scoundrels, rogues, and mermaids of all ages can acquire special costumes and accessories. Different packages are available:

First Mate Package: Includes bandanna; your child's choice of facial effects (scars, tattoos, fake teeth, earring, and eye patch); sword and sheath; pirate-coin necklace; and personalized pirate oath for $34.95, plus tax.

Empress Package: Comes with bandanna; shimmering makeup (face gem, tattoos, nail polish, earring, and eye patch); sword and sheath; pirate-coin necklace; and personalized pirate oath for $34.95 plus tax.

LILIANE If you want to treat your child to a costume or makeover, do it on a day when you're not at the parks. The **Bibbidi Bobbidi Boutique** in Disney Springs offers all of the packages mentioned here, and you won't lose precious touring time.

Mermaid Package: Comes with a mermaid makeup application along with a take-home makeup kit, a hairstyle and color-changing hair clip, a mermaid necklace, nail polish, and a mermaid sash to top it all off for $39.95 plus tax. Add a mermaid costume T-shirt and tutu, and be ready to pay a whopping $74.95 plus tax.

Jake and the Never Land Pirates Package: Inspired by the popular kids' TV series on the Disney Junior channel. For $29.95 plus tax, kids receive a bandanna, a sword and sheath, a Pirates League bag, a necklace, and pirate coins. The deluxe version of this package includes a Jake and the Never Land Pirates costume T-shirt, for $44.95 plus tax.

These packages are available for boys, girls, and adults. Call ☎ 407-WDW-CREW (939-2739) to make an appointment.

WONDERLAND TEA PARTY This event is held at 1900 Park Fare restaurant at the Grand Floridian Monday–Friday, 2–3 p.m. The price tag is $49 plus tax per child (ages 4–12). The program consists of decorating and eating cupcakes and having tea with characters from *Alice in Wonderland*. Small children might get scared meeting the White Rabbit.

Reservations can be made by calling ☎ 407-WDW-DINE (939-3463) 180 days in advance.

MY DISNEY GIRL'S PERFECTLY PRINCESS TEA PARTY It certainly takes a princely sum to cover the tab on this Grand Floridian shindig, hosted by Rose Petal, an enchanted storytelling rose. Your little princess gets to sip tea with Princess Aurora. Girls receive an 18-inch My Disney Girl doll dressed in a matching Princess Aurora gown plus accessories. Other loot includes a ribbon tiara, silver link bracelet, fresh rose, scrapbook set, and "Best Friend" certificate. A luncheon is served as well. The cost is about $250 with tax and gratuity for one adult and one child ages 3–11; add an additional adult for $85 or an additional child for $165 (adults-only bookings not available). Princes who attend the tea party will receive a plush Duffy (the Disney bear) and a crown. **Note: This event is not covered by the Disney Dining Plan.** Your credit card will be charged beforehand, and you can book up to 180 days in advance. The tea party is held on select days, 10:30 a.m.–noon. Call ☎ 407-939-6983 for reservations and information. Check in 15 minutes prior to reservation time.

An Illinois mom ponied up for two of the programs:

We splurged and went to the Perfectly Princess Tea Party. It was nice but a bit too long with all the singing and stories. Not easy for a 4-year-old to sit that long. I'm not sure it was worth the cost, and I would not do it again. We also booked the Wonderland Tea Party. That was a much better cost, and I thought my daughter would love decorating a cupcake. She was so freaked out by the Mad Hatter that the nice workers there called me and asked me to come get her. They said many kids are scared of him, so I'm not sure why they don't have Alice and another character. I was pleased that they gave me a full refund (she was in there maybe 10 minutes).

ULTIMATE DAY FOR YOUNG FAMILIES–VIP TOUR EXPERIENCE, ULTIMATE DAY OF THRILLS–VIP EXPERIENCE These two tours (7 hours and $299 each) include rides on 12 attractions at the Magic Kingdom, Animal Kingdom, and Disney's Hollywood Studios, plus lunch at the Wilderness Lodge's Whispering Canyon Cafe. The Young Families tour features rides such as Dumbo, Peter Pan's Flight, and Toy Story Midway Mania!, while the Thrills tour includes headliner thrill rides such as Space Mountain and Tower of Terror. Transportation among parks is included, but park admission is not. You'll need the Park Hopper feature on your Magic Your Way ticket. Annual Pass holders, Disney Vacation Club members, and Disney Visa Card holders get a 15% discount.

FORT WILDERNESS ARCHERY EXPERIENCE Loyal fans of Princess Merida, this is your activity! Guests 7 years of age and up can learn how to hold and fire a compound bow in this 90-minute archery program. With class sizes limited to 10 guests, this is a wonderful experience held at the campsites at Disney's Fort Wilderness Resort. The fee for the program is $39. For reservations call ☎ 407-WDW-PLAY (939-7529).

ESCAPE TO WALT'S WILDERNESS This tour, available twice a week, 8 a.m.–1 p.m., begins at the Contemporary Resort Marina, where guides take participants on pontoon boats for an eco-history tour of Bay Lake. Next, at Fort Wilderness, guests head to the beach beside a bonfire to enjoy a camp-style breakfast. A horse-drawn wagon next takes guests to the Settlement and Pioneer Hall for archery practice. During a walk along the railroad tracks, guides reveal more about Walt's fascination with trains. The tour ends at the Tri-Circle-D Ranch horse barn to meet the celebrity horses who live and work at Walt Disney World. The cost is $109, plus tax, and participants must be at least 7 years old. For reservations call ☎ 407-WDW-TOUR (939-8687).

WILD AFRICA TREK This backstage tour of Disney's Animal Kingdom is not made for the faint of heart, but you and especially your kids will get a real sense of adventure. On this 3-hour walking and driving tour, you will visit Harambe Wildlife Reserve and the savanna for up close encounters with giraffes, rhinos, tigers, and lions. At some point in the tour, secured to an overhead track with a safety harness, you will walk a wobbly bridge and get incredible views of hippos and crocodiles. The tour includes a meal at Boma, an African restaurant at the Animal Kingdom Lodge, as well as digital photos the guide took while on tour. You can bring your own camera or iPhone too, but only if you have a strap that can be attached to the provided vest or if you can hang the camera securely around your neck. Wear comfortable clothes and sneakers, and bring a strap for your glasses or sunglasses. A keepsake water bottle that clips to your vest will be provided to you. For anything you cannot attach to your vest, Disney will provide lockers. The guides are incredibly knowledgeable, and a wireless headset allows you to hear the guide at all times. The price is $201.29 per person and jumps up to $265 during peak seasons such as December and Easter. Participants must be 8 years of age or older, at least 48 inches tall, and 45–300 pounds with the harness gear on. Call ☎ 407-WDW-TOUR (939-8687) for reservations.

LILIANE Love, love, love this tour. I wish I could go on it every time I visit and capture tigers and lions and more with my camera.

KIERAN If you can go on only one tour, this is the one. It's amazing! You feel like a real VIP. Pick your time slot wisely though, so that lunch is served when you're hungry; otherwise, it's a bit of a waste.

SPECIAL CHRISTMASTIME TOURS If you're visiting at the end of the year, we recommend **Disney's Holiday D-Lights,** a 5-hour tour for $209 plus tax, and **Disney's Yuletide Fantasy** tour, which runs $89 plus tax.

BIRTHDAYS AND SPECIAL OCCASIONS

GUESTS WHO ARE CELEBRATING A BIRTHDAY or visiting Walt Disney World for the first time can pick up a button corresponding to the celebration at Guest Relations when entering any of the parks. Often upon check-in, clerks at the Disney resorts will ask if any member of your party is celebrating a special event. It's especially fun for birthday kids, as cast members will congratulate your child throughout the day in the hotel, on the bus, in the park, and at restaurants throughout the World. A Lombard, Illinois, mom put the word out and was glad she did:

> My daughter was turning 5 while we were there, and I asked about special things that could be done. Our hotel asked me who her favorite character was and did the rest. We came back to our room on her birthday and there were helium balloons, a card, and a Cinderella 5-by-7-inch photo autographed in ink! When we entered the Magic Kingdom, we received an It's My Birthday Today pin (FREE!), and at the restaurant she got a huge cupcake with whipped cream, sprinkles, and a candle. IT PAYS TO ASK!!

Another great and reasonably priced treat is to have your child's hair cut at the **Harmony Barber Shop** on Main Street, U.S.A. at the Magic Kingdom. Rest assured that your kid will walk away with a good haircut, and you may even be treated to a song by the Dapper Dans, Disney's famous barber-shop quartet. The best time to go is during a parade. You get a good view, and the staff sings along with the parade music. It's a great photo op. An Ohio mom celebrated her child's first haircut at the barber shop:

> The barber shop makes a big deal with baby's first haircut—pixie dust, photos, a certificate, and "free" mouse ears hat! ($14 total).

Lest you think the Harmony Barber Shop is strictly a boys' domain, a fashion- and dollar-conscious Kalamazoo, Michigan, mom writes that it's a great alternative to the Bibbidi Bobbidi Boutique (see page 432) for little girls who want to get gussied up Disney princess–style:

> I think I spent about $12, including tip. You don't need reservations, and in my opinion they do a better job than Bibbidi Bobbidi Boutique. They put my daughter's hair into a teased bun and used brightly colored paints and colorful confetti to match whatever princess dress she had on.

PART THREE

WHERE *to* STAY

WHEN TRAVELING WITH CHILDREN, your hotel is your home away from home, your safe harbor, and your sanctuary. Staying in a hotel is in itself a great adventure for children. They take in every detail and delight in such things as having a pool at their disposal and obtaining ice from a noisy machine. Of course, it's critical that your children feel safe and secure, but it adds immeasurably to the success of the vacation if they really like the hotel.

In truth, because of their youth and limited experience, children are far less particular about hotels than adults, but kids' memories are like little steel traps, so once you establish a lodging standard, that's pretty much what they'll expect every time. A couple from Gary, Indiana, stayed at the pricey Yacht Club Resort at Walt Disney World because they heard that it offered a knockout swimming area (which it does). When they returned two years later and stayed at Disney's All-Star Resorts for about a third of the price, their 10-year-old carped all week. If you're on a budget, it's better to begin with modest accommodations and move up to better digs on subsequent trips as finances permit.

BOB In our opinion, if you're traveling with a child age 12 or younger, one of your top priorities should be to book a hotel within easy striking distance of the parks.

"YOU CAN'T ROLLER-SKATE IN A BUFFALO HERD"

THIS WAS A SONG TITLE FROM THE 1960s. If we wrote that song today, we'd call it "You Can't Have Fun at Disney World if You're Drop-Dead Tired." Believe us, Walt Disney World is an easy place to be penny-wise and pound-foolish. Many families who cut lodging expenses by booking a budget hotel end up so far away from Disney World that it's a major hassle to return to the hotel in the middle of the day for swimming and a nap. By trying to spend the whole day at the theme parks, however, they wear themselves out quickly, and the dream vacation suddenly disintegrates into short tempers and exhaustion. And don't confuse this advice with a sales pitch for Disney hotels. There are, you will find, dozens of hotels outside Disney World that are as close or closer to certain Disney parks than some of the resorts inside the World. Our main point—our only point, really—is that you should be able to return to your hotel easily when the need arises.

THINGS *to* CONSIDER

COST

AT WALT DISNEY WORLD, STANDARD HOTEL-ROOM RATES range from about $100 to more than $1,600 per night during the holidays. Outside, rooms are as low as $35 a night. Clearly, if you are willing to sacrifice some luxury and don't mind a 10- to 25-minute commute, you can really cut your lodging costs by staying outside Walt Disney World. Hotels in the World tend to be the most expensive, but they also offer some of the highest quality, as well as a number of perks not enjoyed by guests who stay outside of the World.

Animal Kingdom Villas, Bay Lake Tower, Beach Club Villas, Board-Walk Villas, The Villas at Grand Floridian Resort & Spa, Old Key West Resort, Polynesian Villas, Saratoga Springs Resort & Spa, and **Wilderness Lodge Villas** offer condo-type accommodations with one-, two-, and (at Animal Kingdom Villas, Bay Lake Tower, BoardWalk Villas, Grand Floridian Villas, Old Key West, and Saratoga Springs) three-bedroom units with kitchens, living rooms, DVD players, and washers and dryers. Studios have a kitchenette (with microwave, mini-fridge, and sink) but no washer or dryer. Prices range from $358 per night for a studio suite at Animal Kingdom Villas to more than $3,400 per night for a two-bedroom bungalow at the Polynesian. Fully equipped cabins (minus a washer and dryer) at **Fort Wilderness Resort & Campground** cost $336–$562 per night. Family Suites at the All-Star Music and Art of Animation Resorts have kitchenettes, separate bedrooms, and two bathrooms. A few suites without kitchens are available at the more expensive Disney resorts.

For any extra adults in a room (more than two), the nightly surcharge for each extra adult is $10 at Value resorts, $15 at Moderate resorts, and $25 at Deluxe resorts, plus tax. DDV resorts do not levy a surcharge.

Also at Disney World are the seven hotels of the **Downtown Disney Resort Area (DDRA).** Accommodations range from fairly luxurious to motel-like. While the DDRA is technically part of Disney World, staying there is like visiting a colony rather than the motherland. Free parking at theme parks isn't offered—nor is early entry, with one exception, the Hilton—and hotels operate their own buses rather than use Disney transportation. For more information on DDRA properties, see the discussion starting on page 104.

LOCATION AND TRANSPORTATION OPTIONS

ONCE YOU'VE DETERMINED YOUR BUDGET, think about what you want to do at Walt Disney World. Will you go to all four theme

COSTS PER NIGHT OF DISNEY HOTEL ROOMS, LATE 2015 *(rack rate)*	
Rates are for standard rooms except where noted.	
All-Star Resorts	$104–$199
All-Star Music Resort Family Suites	$244–$443
Animal Kingdom Lodge	$320–$556
Animal Kingdom Villas *(studio, Jambo/Kidani)*	$358–$674
Art of Animation Resort	$129–$224
Art of Animation Family Suites	$304–$514
Bay Lake Tower at Contemporary Resort *(studio)*	$500–$740
Beach Club Resort	$400–$672
Beach Club Villas *(studio)*	$415–$687
BoardWalk Inn	$429–$683
BoardWalk Villas *(studio)*	$415–$687
Caribbean Beach Resort	$191–$285
Contemporary Resort *(Garden Building)*	$400–$630
Coronado Springs Resort	$197–$290
Dolphin *(Sheraton)*	$189–$430
Fort Wilderness Resort & Campground *(cabins)*	$336–$562
Grand Floridian Resort & Spa	$582–$856
Grand Floridian Villas *(studio)*	$570–$890
Old Key West Resort *(studio)*	$368–$531
Polynesian Village Resort	$483–$760
Polynesian Villas & Bungalows *(studio)*	$494–$772
Pop Century Resort	$115–$209
Port Orleans Resort *(French Quarter & Riverside)*	$191–$285
Saratoga Springs Resort & Spa *(studio)*	$368–$531
Swan *(Westin)*	$189–$430
Treehouse Villas	$818–$1,377
Wilderness Lodge	$325–$561
Wilderness Lodge Villas *(studio)*	$421–$621
Yacht Club Resort	$400–$672

parks or will you concentrate on one or two? If you'll be driving a car, the location of your Disney hotel isn't especially important unless you plan to spend most of your time at the Magic Kingdom. (Disney transportation is always more efficient than your car in this case because it deposits you right at the theme park entrance.)

Most convenient to the Magic Kingdom are the three resorts linked by monorail: the **Grand Floridian** and its **Villas,** the **Contemporary** and **Bay Lake Tower,** and the **Polynesian Village.**

Wilderness Lodge & Villas, along with **Fort Wilderness Resort & Campground,** are linked to the Magic Kingdom by boat and to everywhere else in the World by bus. **Shades of Green** only has bus service.

WHAT IT COSTS TO STAY IN THE DOWNTOWN DISNEY RESORT AREA	
Best Western Lake Buena Vista Resort Hotel	$80–$170
B Resort	$119–$237
Buena Vista Palace Hotel & Spa	$139–$169
DoubleTree Guest Suites	$119–$229
Hilton Orlando Lake Buena Vista	$139–$289
Holiday Inn in the WDW Resort	$104–$190
Wyndham Lake Buena Vista Resort	$104–$300

The most centrally located resorts in Walt Disney World are the Epcot hotels—**BoardWalk Inn & Villas, Yacht & Beach Club Resorts, Beach Club Villas, Swan,** and **Dolphin**—and **Coronado Springs,** near the Animal Kingdom. The Epcot hotels are within easy walking distance of Disney's Hollywood Studios and Epcot's International Gateway. Except at Coronado Springs, boat service is also available at these resorts, with vessels connecting to DHS.

Caribbean Beach Resort, Pop Century Resort, and **Art of Animation Resort** are just south and east of Epcot and DHS. Along Bonnet Creek, **Disney's Old Key West** and **Port Orleans Resorts** also offer quick access to those parks. **Saratoga Springs** is connected to Disney Springs via a pedestrian bridge; boat and bus service are available.

BOB If you plan to use Disney transportation to visit all four major parks and one or both of the water parks, book a centrally located resort that has good transportation connections. The Epcot resorts and the Polynesian Village, Caribbean Beach, Art of Animation, Pop Century, Coronado Springs, and Port Orleans Resorts fill the bill.

Though not centrally located, the **All-Star Resorts** and **Animal Kingdom Lodge & Villas** have good bus service to all Disney World destinations and are closest to Animal Kingdom.

Wilderness Lodge & Villas and Fort Wilderness have the most inconvenient transportation service of the Disney hotels. Also, buses run less frequently to and from Old Key West than they do at other Disney resorts. Spotty bus service is also a drawback shared by Saratoga Springs and Treehouse Villas.

LILIANE Just for the record, the Epcot resorts within walking distance of the International Gateway are a long, long walk from Future World, the section of Epcot where families tend to spend most of their time.

COMMUTING TO AND FROM THE THEME PARKS

FOR VISITORS LODGING INSIDE WALT DISNEY WORLD With three important exceptions, the fastest way to commute from your hotel to the theme parks and back is in your own car. And though many Walt Disney World guests use the Disney transportation system and appreciate not having to drive, based on timed comparisons, it's almost always less time-consuming to drive. The exceptions are these: (1) commuting to the Magic Kingdom from the hotels on the monorail (Grand Floridian, Polynesian Village, and Contemporary Resorts and Bay Lake Tower); (2) commuting to the Magic Kingdom from any Disney hotel

DRIVING TIME TO THE THEME PARKS

MINUTES TO:	MAGIC KINGDOM PARKING LOT	EPCOT PARKING LOT	DISNEY'S HOLLYWOOD STUDIOS PARKING LOT	DISNEY'S ANIMAL KINGDOM PARKING LOT
FROM				
Downtown Orlando	35	31	33	37
North International Drive and Universal Studios	24	21	22	26
Central International Drive and Lake Road	26	23	24	27
South International Drive and SeaWorld	18	15	16	20
FL 535	12	9	10	13
US 192, north of I-4	10-15	7-12	5-10	5-10
US 192, south of I-4	10-18	7-15	5-13	5-12

by bus or boat; and (3) commuting to Epcot on the monorail from the Polynesian Village Resort via the Transportation and Ticket Center.

If you stay at the Polynesian, you can catch a direct monorail to the Magic Kingdom, and by walking 100 yards or so to the Transportation and Ticket Center, you can catch a direct monorail to Epcot. At the nexus of the monorail system, the Polynesian is certainly the most convenient resort. From either the Magic Kingdom or Epcot, you can return to your hotel quickly and easily whenever you want. The downside: A standard room costs $483–$760 a night depending on the season.

Second to the Polynesian in terms of convenience are the Grand Floridian and Contemporary, also on the Magic Kingdom monorail, but they cost as much as or more than the Polynesian. Less expensive Disney hotels transport you to the Magic Kingdom by bus or boat. For reasons described below, this is more efficient than driving a car.

DRIVING TIME TO THE THEME PARKS FOR VISITORS LODGING OUTSIDE WALT DISNEY WORLD For vacationers staying outside Walt Disney World, we've calculated the approximate commuting time to the major theme parks' parking lots from several off-World lodging areas. Add a few minutes to our times to pay your parking fee and to park. Once parked at the Transportation and Ticket Center (Magic Kingdom parking lot), it takes an average of 20–30 more minutes to reach the Magic Kingdom. At Epcot and Disney's Animal Kingdom, the lot-to-gate transit time is 10–15 minutes; at Disney's Hollywood Studios, it's 8–12 minutes. If you haven't purchased your theme park admission in advance, tack on another 10–20 minutes.

Our WDW Resorts Chart on pages 108–110 shows the commuting time, with no consideration of getting to and from the parking lot to the turnstiles, to the Disney theme parks from each hotel listed. Those commuting times represent an average of several test runs. Your actual time may be shorter or longer depending on many variables.

SHUTTLE SERVICE FROM HOTELS OUTSIDE WALT DISNEY WORLD
Many hotels in the Walt Disney World area provide shuttle service to the theme parks. They represent a fairly carefree alternative for getting to and from the parks, letting you off near the entrance (except for the Magic Kingdom) and saving you the cost of parking. The rub is that they might not get you there as early as you desire (a critical point if you take our touring advice) or be available at the time you wish to return to your lodging. Also, be forewarned that most shuttle services do not add vehicles at park opening or closing times. In the morning, your biggest problem is that you might not get a seat. At closing time, however, and sometimes following a hard rain, you can expect a lot of competition for standing space on the bus. If there's not room for everyone, you might have to wait 30 minutes to an hour for the next shuttle.

CONVENIENCE, CONVENIENTLY DEFINED Conceptually, it's easy to grasp that a hotel that is closer is more convenient than one that is far away. But nothing is that simple at Walt Disney World, so we'd better tell you exactly what you're in for. If you stay at a Walt Disney World resort and use the Disney transportation system, you'll have a 5- to 10-minute walk to the bus stop, monorail station, or dock (whichever applies). Once there, buses, trains, or boats generally run about every 15–25 minutes, so you might have to wait a short time for your transportation to arrive. Once you're on board, most conveyances make additional stops en route to your destination, and many take a less-than-direct route. Upon arrival, however, they deposit you fairly close to the entrance of the theme park. Returning to your hotel is the same process in reverse and takes about the same amount of time.

Regardless of whether or not you stay in Walt Disney World, if you use your own car, here's how your commute shakes out. After a 1- to 5-minute walk from your room to your car, you drive to the theme park, stopping to pay a parking fee or showing your MagicBand for free parking (if you're a Disney resort guest). Disney cast members then direct you to a parking space. If you arrive early, your space may be close enough to the park entrance (Magic Kingdom excepted) to walk. If you park farther afield, a Disney tram will come along every 5 minutes to collect you and transport you to the entrance.

At the Magic Kingdom, the entrance to the park is separated from the parking lot by the Transportation and Ticket Center (TTC) and the Seven Seas Lagoon. After parking at the Magic Kingdom lot, you take a tram to the TTC and then board a ferry or monorail (your choice) for the trip across the lagoon to the park. All this is fairly time-consuming and is to be avoided if possible. The only way to avoid it, however, is to lodge in a Disney hotel and commute directly to the Magic Kingdom entrance via Disney bus, boat, or monorail. Happily, all of the other theme parks are situated adjacent to their parking lots.

Because families with children tend to spend more time on average at the Magic Kingdom than at the other parks, and because it's so important to return to your hotel for rest, the business of getting around the lagoon can be a major consideration when choosing a place to stay; the extra hassle of crossing the lagoon (to get back to your car) makes coming and going much more difficult. The half hour it takes to commute to your hotel via car from the Animal Kingdom, Disney's Hollywood Studios, or Epcot takes an hour or longer from the Magic Kingdom. If you stay in a Disney hotel and use the Disney transportation system, you may have to wait 5–25 minutes for your bus, boat, or monorail, but it will take you directly from the Magic Kingdom entrance to your hotel, bypassing the lagoon and the TTC.

DINING

DINING FIGURES INTO THE DISCUSSION of where to stay only if you don't plan to have a car at your disposal. If you plan on using the Disney transportation system (for Disney hotel guests) or the courtesy shuttle of your non-Disney hotel, you will either have to dine at the theme parks or at or near your hotel. If your hotel offers a lot of choices or if other restaurants are within walking distance, then there's no problem. If your hotel is somewhat isolated and offers limited selections, you'll feel like Bob did on a canoe trip once when he ate northern pike at every meal for a week because that's all he could catch.

At Walt Disney World, though it's relatively quick and efficient to commute from your Disney hotel or campground to the theme parks, it's a long, arduous process requiring transfers to travel from hotel to hotel. Disney hotels that are somewhat isolated and that offer limited dining choices include Old Key West, Caribbean Beach, All-Star, Pop Century, Art of Animation, Animal Kingdom Lodge, Coronado Springs, and Wilderness Lodge Resorts, as well as the Fort Wilderness Campground and most of the Saratoga Springs Resort.

If you want a condo-type accommodation so that you have more flexibility for meal preparation than eating out of a cooler, the best deals in Disney World are the prefab log cabins at Fort Wilderness Resort & Campground. Other Disney lodgings with kitchens are available at the Animal Kingdom Villas, Bay Lake Tower, Beach Club Villas, BoardWalk Villas, Old Key West, Polynesian Villas, Saratoga Springs, and Wilderness Lodge Villas, but all are much more expensive than the cabins at the campground. Outside Disney World, an ever-increasing number of condos are available, and some are very good deals. See our discussion of lodging outside Disney World later in this chapter.

LILIANE If you share a room with your children, you all need to hit the sack at the same time. Establish a single compromise bedtime, probably a little early for you and a bit later than the children's usual weekend bedtime. Observe any nightly rituals you practice at home, such as reading a book before lights-out.

THE SIZE OF YOUR GROUP

LARGER FAMILIES AND GROUPS may be interested in how many people can stay in a Disney resort room, but only Lilliputians would be comfortable in a room filled to capacity. Groups requiring two or more rooms should consider condo, suite, or villa accommodations,

HOTEL | MAXIMUM OCCUPANCY PER ROOM

All-Star Resorts | Standard room: 4 people plus child under age 3 in crib; Family Suite: 6 people plus child in crib

Animal Kingdom Lodge | 2–5 people plus child under age 3 in crib

Animal Kingdom Villas: Jambo House | Studio: 4 people; 1-bedroom: 4 or 5 people; 2-bedroom: 8 or 9 people; Grand Villa: 12 people; all plus child in crib

Animal Kingdom Villas: Kidani Village | Studio: 4 people; 1-bedroom: 5 people; 2-bedroom: 9 people; Grand Villa: 12 people; all plus child in crib

Art of Animation | Little Mermaid buildings: 4 people; Cars, Finding Nemo, and Lion King buildings: 6 people; all plus child in crib

Bay Lake Tower at the Contemporary Resort | Studio: 4 people; 1-bedroom: 5 people; 2-bedroom: 9 people; Grand Villa: 12 people; all plus child in crib

Beach Club Resort | 5 people plus child in crib

Beach Club Villas | Studio and 1-bedroom: 4 people; 2-bedroom: 8 people; Grand Villa: 12 people; all plus child in crib

BoardWalk Inn | 4 people plus child in crib

BoardWalk Villas | Studio and 1-bedroom: 4 people; 2-bedroom: 8 people; Grand Villa: 12 people; all plus child in crib

Caribbean Beach Resort | 4 people plus child in crib; 5 people in rooms with Murphy bed

Contemporary Resort | 5 people plus child in crib

Coronado Springs Resort | 4 people plus child in crib

Dolphin (Sheraton) | 4 people

Fort Wilderness Cabins | 6 people plus child in crib

Grand Floridian Resort | 5 people plus child in crib

Grand Floridian Villas | Studio and 1-bedroom: 5 people; 2-bedroom: 9 or 10 people; Grand Villa: 12 people; all plus child in crib

Old Key West Resort | Studio: 4 people; 1-bedroom: 5 people; 2-bedroom: 9 people; Grand Villa: 12 people; all plus child in crib

Polynesian Village Resort | 5 people plus child in crib

Polynesian Villas & Bungalows | Studio: 5 people plus child in crib; 2-bedroom bungalow: 8 people plus child in crib

Pop Century Resort | 4 people plus child in crib

Port Orleans French Quarter | 4 people plus child in crib

Port Orleans Riverside | 4 people plus child in crib or trundle bed; 5 people in rooms with Murphy bed

Saratoga Springs | Studio and 1-bedroom: 4 people; 2-bedroom: 8 people; Grand Villa: 12 people; all plus child in crib

Swan (Westin) | 4 people

Treehouse Villas | 9 people plus child in crib

Wilderness Lodge | 4 people plus child in crib; junior suites with bunk beds accommodate 6 people

Wilderness Lodge Villas | Studio and 1-bedroom: 4 people; 2-bedroom: 8 people

Yacht Club Resort | 5 people plus child in crib

either in or out of Disney World. If there are more than six in your party, you will need either two hotel rooms, a suite (see Wilderness Lodge), a villa, or a condo.

STAYING IN OR OUT OF THE WORLD: WEIGHING THE PROS AND CONS

1. COST If cost is your primary consideration, you'll lodge much less expensively outside Walt Disney World.

2. EASE OF ACCESS Even if you stay in Disney World, you're dependent on some mode of transportation. It may be less stressful to use the Disney transportation system, but with the exception of commuting to the Magic Kingdom, the fastest, most efficient, and most flexible way to get around is usually a car. If you're at Epcot, for example, and want to take the kids back to Disney's Contemporary Resort for a nap, forget the monorail. You'll get back much faster by car.

A reader from Raynham, Massachusetts, who stayed at the Caribbean Beach Resort, writes:

> *Even though the resort is on the Disney bus line, I recommend renting a car if it fits one's budget. The buses don't go directly to many destinations, and often you have to switch buses. Getting a bus back to the hotel after a hard day can mean a long wait in line.*

A Havertown, Pennsylvania, dad concurs regarding bus service:

> *WDW bus transportation is quite inefficient. When traveling from the BoardWalk to anywhere else, we had to pick up other passengers at the Swan, Dolphin, and Yacht and Beach Clubs before heading off to the parks. Same story on return.*

Though it's only for the use and benefit of Disney guests, the Disney transportation system is nonetheless public, and users must expect inconveniences: conveyances that arrive and depart on their schedule, not yours; the occasional need to transfer; multiple stops; time lost loading and unloading passengers; and, generally, the challenge of understanding and using a large, complex transportation network.

3. YOUNG CHILDREN Though the hassle of commuting to most non-Disney hotels is only slightly (if at all) greater than that of commuting to Disney hotels, a definite peace of mind results from staying in the World. Regardless of where you stay, make sure you get your young children back to the hotel for a nap each day.

4. SPLITTING UP If your party will likely split up to tour (as frequently happens in families with children of widely varying ages), staying in Walt Disney World offers more transportation options, and thus more independence.

5. SLOPPIN' THE HOGS If you have a large crew that chows down like pigs at the trough, you may do better staying outside the World, where food is far less expensive.

6. VISITING OTHER ORLANDO-AREA ATTRACTIONS If you plan to visit SeaWorld, Kennedy Space Center, the Universal theme parks, or other area attractions, it may be more convenient to stay outside Disney World. Remember the number-one rule, though: Stay close enough to the World to return to your hotel for rest in the middle of the day.

WALT DISNEY WORLD LODGING

BENEFITS OF STAYING IN WALT DISNEY WORLD

IN ADDITION TO PROXIMITY—especially easy access to the Magic Kingdom—Walt Disney World resort hotel and campground guests are accorded other privileges and amenities unavailable to those staying outside the World. Though some of these perks are only advertising gimmicks, others are potentially quite valuable. Here are the benefits and what they mean:

1. EARLY ACCESS TO RIDE AND RESTAURANT RESERVATIONS Disney hotel and campground guests, along with guests staying at the Swan and Dolphin resorts, can make FastPass+ ride reservations 60 days before they arrive—30 days earlier than the general public. Disney resort guests can also make dining reservations up to 190 days before their visit, 10 more than the general public.

2. EXTRA MAGIC HOURS AT THE THEME PARKS Disney World lodging guests (including guests at the Hilton Orlando Lake Buena Vista) are invited to enter a designated park 1 hour earlier than the general public each day or to enjoy a designated theme park for up to 2 hours after it closes to the general public in the evening. Extra Magic Hours can be quite valuable if you know how to use them; they can also land you in gridlock.

3. THEME All of the Disney hotels are themed, in pointed contrast to non-Disney hotels, which are, well, mostly just hotels. Each Disney hotel is designed to make you feel that you're in a special place or period of history. See the table on page 88 that lists the various hotels and summarizes their respective themes.

Themed rooms are a huge attraction for children, firing their imaginations and really making the hotel an adventure and a memorable place. Some resorts carry off their themes better than others, and some themes are more exciting. **Wilderness Lodge & Villas,** for example, is extraordinary. The lobby opens eight stories to a timbered ceiling supported by giant columns of bundled logs. One look eases you into the Northwest wilderness theme. The isolated lodge is heaven for kids.

Animal Kingdom Lodge & Villas replicates the grand safari lodges of Kenya and Tanzania and overlook its own African-inspired game preserve. By far the most exotic of the Disney resorts, it's made to order for families with children.

Another kids' favorite is **Treehouse Villas at Saratoga Springs Resort.** Designed in the adventurous image of their 1970s predecessors, the treehouses are nestled in the woods alongside the Lake Buena Vista Golf Course.

The **Polynesian Village Resort & Villas** convey the feeling of the Pacific islands. It's great for families. Kids don't know Polynesia from amnesia, but they like those cool "lodge" buildings and all the torches at night. The new Bora Bora Bungalows offer perfect views of Cinderella Castle and the Magic Kingdom fireworks across the Seven Seas Lagoon.

WALT DISNEY WORLD RESORT HOTEL THEMES

HOTEL THEME	
ALL-STAR RESORTS	Sports, movies, and music
ANIMAL KINGDOM LODGE & VILLAS	East African game-preserve lodge
ART OF ANIMATION RESORT	Disney's animated films
BAY LAKE TOWER AT THE CONTEMPORARY	Ultramodern high-rise
BEACH CLUB RESORT & VILLAS	New England beach club of the 1870s
BOARDWALK INN	East Coast boardwalk hotel of the early 1900s
BOARDWALK VILLAS	East Coast beach cottages of the early 1900s
CARIBBEAN BEACH RESORT	Caribbean islands
CONTEMPORARY RESORT	The future as envisioned by past and present generations
CORONADO SPRINGS RESORT	Northern Mexico and the American Southwest
DOLPHIN (SHERATON)	Modern Florida resort
GRAND FLORIDIAN RESORT & VILLAS	Turn-of-the-20th-century luxury hotel
OLD KEY WEST RESORT	Florida Keys
POLYNESIAN VILLAGE RESORT & VILLAS	Hawaii and South Seas islands
POP CENTURY	Popular-culture icons from various decades of the 20th century
PORT ORLEANS FRENCH QUARTER	Turn-of-the-19th-century New Orleans
PORT ORLEANS RIVERSIDE	Antebellum Louisiana plantation and bayou
SARATOGA SPRINGS RESORT	1880s Victorian lakeside resort
SWAN (WESTIN)	Modern Florida resort
TREEHOUSE VILLAS	Rustic vacation homes with modern amenities
WILDERNESS LODGE & VILLAS	Grand national park lodge of the early 1900s
YACHT CLUB RESORT	New England seashore hotel of the 1880s

Grandeur, nostalgia, and privilege are central to the **Grand Floridian Resort & Villas,** the **Yacht & Beach Club Resorts,** the **Beach Club Villas, Saratoga Springs Resort,** and **BoardWalk Inn & Villas.** Kids appreciate the creative swimming facilities of these resorts but are relatively neutral toward their shared Eastern-seaboard theme.

LILIANE Coronado Springs and the Port Orleans Resorts are among my favorite resorts.

Port Orleans Resort lacks the mystery and sultriness of New Orleans's French Quarter, but it's hard to replicate the Big Easy in a sanitized Disney version. The Riverside section of Port Orleans, however, hits the mark with its antebellum Mississippi River theme, as does **Old Key West Resort** with its Florida Keys theme. Children like each of these resorts, even though the themes are a bit removed from their frame of reference. The **Caribbean Beach Resort**'s theme is much more effective at night, thanks to creative lighting. By day, the resort looks like a Miami condo development. Its pirate-themed suites are a big hit with little buccaneers, and the playground and swimming pool fit in nicely with the pirate theme.

Coronado Springs Resort offers several styles of Mexican and southwestern American architecture. Though the lake setting is lovely and the resort is attractive, the theme (with the exception of the main swimming area) isn't especially stimulating for kids, but like the Caribbean, it's beautiful at night.

The **All-Star Resorts** comprise almost 35 three-story, T-shaped hotels with almost 6,000 guest rooms. There are 15 themed areas: 5 celebrate sports (surfing, basketball, tennis, football, and baseball), 5 recall Hollywood movies, and 5 have musical motifs. The resort's design, with entrances shaped like giant Dalmatians, Coke cups, footballs, and the like, is pretty adolescent, sacrificing grace and beauty for energy and novelty. Guest rooms are small, with decor reminiscent of a teenage boy's bedroom. **Pop Century Resort** is pretty much a clone of All-Star Resorts, only here the giant icons symbolize decades of the 20th century (Big Wheels, 45-rpm records, silhouettes of people doing period dances, and such), and period memorabilia decorates the rooms. Across the lake from Pop Century is **Art of Animation Resort,** with icons and decor based on *Cars, Finding Nemo, The Lion King,* and *The Little Mermaid.*

Pretense aside, the **Contemporary, Bay Lake Tower, Swan,** and **Dolphin** are essentially themeless but architecturally interesting. The Contemporary is a 15-story, A-frame building with monorails running through the middle. Views from guest rooms in the Contemporary are among the best at Walt Disney World. Bay Lake Tower at the Contemporary Resort is a sleek, curvilinear high-rise offering bird's-eye views of Bay Lake. The Swan and Dolphin resorts are massive yet whimsical. Designed by Michael Graves, they're excellent examples of "entertainment architecture." Children are blown away by the giant sea creature and swans atop the Dolphin and Swan and love the idea of the monorail running through the middle of the Contemporary.

4. GREAT SWIMMING AREAS Walt Disney World resorts offer some of the most imaginative swimming facilities that you are likely to encounter anywhere. Exotically themed, beautifully landscaped, and equipped with slides, fountains, and smaller pools for toddlers, Disney resort swimming complexes are a quantum leap removed from the typical rectangular hotel pool. Some resorts, such as the Grand Floridian and the Polynesian, even offer a sand beach on Seven Seas Lagoon in addition to swimming pools. Others, such as the Caribbean Beach and Port Orleans Resorts, have elaborately themed playgrounds near their swimming areas.

LILIANE Just in case your luggage is delayed or your room isn't ready, always pack a change of clothes and bathing suits for all family members in your carry-on luggage. Also keep your MagicBand in your carry-on; you'll be asked for it before boarding Disney's Magical Express.

5. DISNEY'S MAGICAL EXPRESS If you arrive in Orlando by air, Disney will collect your checked baggage and send it by bus directly to your Walt Disney World resort, allowing you to bypass baggage claim. Baggage service is available daily, 5 a.m.–10 p.m.; free bus service to your hotel is available 24 hours a day. If your flight arrives in Orlando close to or

DISNEY WORLD RESORT SWIMMING POOLS: RATED AND RANKED	
RANK/HOTEL	POOL RATING
1. YACHT & BEACH CLUB RESORTS & BEACH CLUB VILLAS (shared complex)	★★★★★
2. ANIMAL KINGDOM VILLAS (Kidani Village)	★★★★½
3. GRAND FLORIDIAN RESORT & VILLAS	★★★★½
4. WILDERNESS LODGE & VILLAS	★★★★½
5. SARATOGA SPRINGS RESORT AND TREEHOUSE VILLAS	★★★★½
6. CORONADO SPRINGS RESORT	★★★★
7. PORT ORLEANS RESORT	★★★★
8. CARIBBEAN BEACH RESORT	★★★★
9. POLYNESIAN VILLAGE, VILLAS, & BUNGALOWS	★★★★
10. ANIMAL KINGDOM LODGE & VILLAS (Jambo House)	★★★★
11. DOLPHIN	★★★★
12. SWAN	★★★★
13. BAY LAKE TOWER	★★★★
14. BOARDWALK INN & VILLAS	★★★½
15. CONTEMPORARY RESORT	★★★½
16. ART OF ANIMATION RESORT	★★★
17. OLD KEY WEST RESORT	★★★
18. FORT WILDERNESS RESORT & CAMPGROUND	★★★
19. ALL-STAR RESORTS	★★★
20. POP CENTURY RESORT	★★★
21. SHADES OF GREEN	★★★

after 10 p.m., you must collect your own bags and bring them with you on the bus.

When it's time to go home, you can check your baggage and receive your boarding pass at the front desk of your Disney resort. This service is available to all guests at Disney-owned resorts—but not the Swan, Dolphin, Shades of Green, or Downtown Disney resorts—even those who don't use the Magical Express service (folks who have rental cars, for example). Resort check-in counters are open 5 a.m.–1 p.m., and you must check in no later than 3 hours before your flight (within the United States and Puerto Rico) or 4 hours before international flights. Participating airlines are **AirTran, Alaska, American, Delta, JetBlue, Southwest, United,** and **US Airways.** All of the preceding airlines have restrictions on the number of bags, checking procedures, and related items; consult your carrier before leaving home for specifics.

If your flight departs from Orlando before 8 a.m., Magical Express will pick you up before the Magical Express desk at your resort is open. In this case, because the desk isn't manned until 5 a.m., you cannot use the resort check-in for your bags or get your boarding pass. You'll need to handle your own luggage and get your boarding pass at the airport.

Travel agents report few complaints about Magical Express, though it's not without its faults. Luggage is transported by truck to Walt Disney World instead of accompanying you on the bus. Readers have complained of luggage delivered to their hotel rooms hours late, sometimes in the middle of the night. If you want, you can collect your own luggage at the baggage claim and bring it along with you on the bus; if your room isn't ready when you arrive, the hotel will store your luggage and provide a number you can call to check the status of your room. Some buses go directly to your resort while others make multiple stops at other resorts. Regarding the return trip to the airport, some readers report barely getting to the airport in time for their flight, while others have been made to depart from their hotel very early.

6. BABYSITTING AND CHILD-CARE OPTIONS Disney hotel and campground guests have several options for babysitting, child care, and children's programs. The **Polynesian Village Resort** and **Animal Kingdom Lodge,** along with several other Disney hotels, offer "clubs"—themed child-care centers for potty-trained children ages 3–12.

Though somewhat expensive, the clubs do a great job and are highly regarded by children and parents. On the negative side, they're open only in the evening, and not all Disney hotels have them. If you're staying at a Disney hotel that doesn't have a child-care club, you're better off using a private in-room babysitting service (see page 72). In-room babysitting is also available at hotels outside Disney World.

7. PRIORITY THEME PARK ADMISSIONS On days of unusually heavy attendance, Disney may restrict admission into the theme parks, in which case priority is given to guests staying at Disney resorts.

8. CHILDREN SHARING A ROOM WITH THEIR PARENTS There's no extra charge per night for children younger than age 18 sharing a room with their parents. Many hotels outside Disney World also offer this perk.

9. FREE PARKING Disney resort guests with cars pay nothing to park in theme park lots or at hotels. This saves $17 per day at the parks and up to $20 per day at the hotels.

WALT DISNEY WORLD HOTELS: *Strengths and Weaknesses for Families*

FOR THE SAKE OF ORIENTATION, we've grouped the Disney resorts by location. Closest to the Magic Kingdom are the **Contemporary Resort** and **Bay Lake Tower, Grand Floridian Resort,** and **Polynesian Village Resort, Villas, & Bungalows,** all on the monorail; **Fort Wilderness Resort & Campground** and the **Wilderness Lodge & Villas,** which are connected to the Magic Kingdom by boat; and the US military resort, **Shades of Green,** served exclusively by bus.

Close to Epcot are the **BoardWalk Inn & Villas, Caribbean Beach,** the non-Disney-owned **Swan** and **Dolphin,** the **Yacht & Beach Club Resorts,** and the **Beach Club Villas.** These are also the closest hotels to Disney's Hollywood Studios.

Closer to Disney Springs and Bonnet Creek are **Old Key West, Port Orleans,** and **Saratoga Springs Resorts.** Also nearby are the seven independent hotels of the **Downtown Disney Resort Area.**

The **All-Star, Art of Animation, Coronado Springs,** and **Pop Century Resorts** are near both Disney's Hollywood Studios and Disney's Animal Kingdom. Closest to the Animal Kingdom is **Animal Kingdom Lodge & Villas.**

MAGIC KINGDOM RESORTS

Disney's Contemporary Resort & Bay Lake Tower

STRENGTHS	
• On the Magic Kingdom monorail	• Recreational options, including super games arcade
• Easy walk to the Magic Kingdom	• Excellent dining options on-site and via monorail
• Iconic architecture; the only hotel that the monorail goes *through*	
	WEAKNESSES
• Large, very attractive guest rooms with nice views of Bay Lake	• Monorail aside, the theme leaves children cold
• Character meals	• No on-site child care
• Excellent children's pool	• Bus transportation to DHS, Animal Kingdom, water parks, and Disney Springs is shared with other resorts
• Convenient parking	
• Marina	

THE CONTEMPORARY RESORT has a sleek, ultramodern look, with an A-frame design that allows the monorail to pass through. And it has lots to offer the active family: six lighted tennis courts, three swimming pools, a health club, volleyball courts, a beach, and a marina that rents sailboats of various sizes—you must be at least 18 years old, which helps limit the traffic a little—and offers parasailing and waterskiing. Guest rooms are quite stunning and, in our opinion, the nicest to be found at Walt Disney World. There's no compelling theme, but then show us a child who isn't wowed by monorails tearing though the inside of a hotel. Bay Lake Tower is a high-rise Disney Vacation Club property situated on Bay Lake between the Contemporary Resort and the Magic Kingdom. Like other DVC developments, it offers studios and one-, two-, and three-bedroom suites. Features include a fireworks-viewing deck, a rooftop lounge, a lakeside pool, and a sky bridge linking the tower to the Contemporary Resort's monorail station.

Disney's Fort Wilderness Resort & Campground

IF CAMPING IS ONE OF YOUR HOBBIES, you can rough it in beautiful territory at Fort Wilderness for as little as $56 per campsite. Either set up a tent and use the restrooms, showers, and laundry down the lane, or borrow your parents' RV. With the accessibility of two markets

STRENGTHS	WEAKNESSES
• Informality	• Isolated location
• Children's play areas	• Complicated bus service
• Best recreational options at WDW	• Confusing campground layout
• Special day and evening programs	• Lack of privacy
• Campsite amenities	• Very limited on-site dining options
• Plentiful showers and toilets	• No on-site child care
• *Hoop-Dee-Doo Musical Revue* dinner show	• Extreme distance to store and restaurant facilities from many campsites
• Convenient self-parking	• Crowding at beaches and pools
• Off-site dining options via boat at the Magic Kingdom	• Small baths in cabins

on-site, most visitors here choose to do their own cooking; if you do so, this becomes the absolute rock-bottom-priced Disney World vacation.

799 CAMPSITES $56–$120 per night; boat and bus service

409 WILDERNESS HOMES AND CABINS $299–$500 per night (sleep 4–6); boat and bus service

BOB All loops have a comfort station with showers, toilets, phones, an ice machine, and a coin laundry.

Fort Wilderness is ideal for nature lovers. For the less active, electric carts are for rent. Also available are pools, a marina, a beach, and outdoor games such as basketball, volleyball, shuffleboard, fishing, canoeing, biking, and even tennis and horseback riding. If you really get into the mood, you can sit around the evening campfire and watch a movie with the other happy campers. The campsites are the only accommodations that allow you to have pets (not running loose, of course).

Here's what you *can't* do: drive anywhere *within* the campground (of course, you can drive to enter or exit the campground), not even from your campsite back to the trading post. You must take the bus, rent a bike or golf cart, or walk (it's not far). And bus or boat transportation to the theme parks can be laborious.

Obviously, Fort Wilderness draws a lot of families (did we mention the petting farm and the hay rides?), and in hot weather, a lot of bugs and thunderstorms. If you want things a little more comfortable, ask for a full-service hookup and get water, electricity, an outdoor grill, sanitary disposal, and even a cable-TV connection. If you want super privacy and even more amenities, rent one of the prefab log cabins, which get you a full kitchen, housekeeping services, air-conditioning, a daily newspaper, voice mail, and, yes, cable TV.

Disney's Grand Floridian Resort & Spa, Grand Floridian Villas

THE GRAND FLORIDIAN HAS A LOT TO OFFER: a white-sand beach, a spa and fitness center, tennis courts, elaborate theatrical dining from high tea to personal butler service, and so on. But the tone strikes some people as rather hoity-toity, the music in the lobby can be disconcertingly loud, the rooms are not as expansive or as good-looking as the

STRENGTHS	WEAKNESSES
• Boat and monorail transportation to the Magic Kingdom	• Most expensive WDW resort
• Large rooms with day beds	• Children don't get the theme
• Children's programs, character meals	• Only one on-site restaurant suitable for younger children
• Fantastic kids' *Alice in Wonderland*-themed splash area	• Self-parking is across the street
• Diverse recreational options	• Close to construction at the Polynesian Village through at least winter 2015
• Good restaurant selection via monorail	• Bus transportation to DHS, Animal Kingdom, water parks, and Disney Springs is shared with other resorts
	• No on-site child care

public spaces, and the complex is frequently crowded with sightseers. Also, because a wedding chapel is on the grounds, there are frequently receptions, photo sessions, and bridezilla fits—which, depending on your outlook, add charm or are inconveniences. The Villas at the Grand Floridian, a Disney Vacation Club property, opened in fall 2013. This T-shaped building, situated between the main building and the Polynesian Village Resort, along Seven Seas Lagoon, has 200 rooms in studio, one-, two-, and three-bedroom configurations, along with a 0.25-acre kids' pool.

Disney's Polynesian Village Resort, Villas, & Bungalows

STRENGTHS	
• Most family-friendly dining on the monorail loop	• Beach and marina
• Fun South Seas theme that kids love	• Excellent swimming complex and recreational options
• WDW's best child-care facility on-site	• Easily accessible self-parking
• Boat and monorail transportation to the Magic Kingdom; walking distance to Epcot monorail	**WEAKNESSES**
• Rooms among the nicest at WDW	• Ongoing DVC/DDV construction through at least winter 2015
• Children's programs, character meals	• Bus transportation to DHS, Animal Kingdom, water parks, and Disney Springs is shared with other resorts

THE POLYNESIAN IS ARRAYED along the Seven Seas Lagoon facing the Magic Kingdom. It's a huge complex, but the hotel buildings, laid out like a South Seas–island village around a ceremonial house, are of a decidedly human scale compared with the hulking Grand Floridian and Contemporary Resorts. From the tiki torches at night to the bleached-sand beach, kids love the Polynesian. The new villas and bungalows are part of Disney Vacation Club. The bungalows, built on stilts on the Seven Seas Lagoon, offer spectacular views of Cinderella Castle and the Magic Kingdom fireworks but obstruct the view for some buildings that previously had it. The resort's location at WDW's transportation nexus makes it the most convenient resort for those without a car. However, we advise not booking a stay here until the current construction project is complete.

Shades of Green

STRENGTHS	• Video arcade and game room with pool tables
• Large guest rooms	
• Discount tickets for military personnel	**WEAKNESSES**
	• No interesting theme
• Views of golf course from guest rooms	• Limited on-site dining
• Convenient self-parking	• Limited bus service
• Swimming complex, fitness center	• No on-site child care
• On-site car rental (Alamo)	• Daily parking fee ($5); no free parking at the theme parks

THIS DELUXE RESORT IS OWNED and operated by the US Armed Forces and is open only to US military personnel (including members of the National Guard and reserves, retired military, and employees of the US Public Health Service and the Department of Defense; others may be eligible; call for additional information). Shades of Green consists of one three-story building nestled among three golf courses that are open to all Disney guests. Tastefully nondescript, Shades of Green is at the same time pure peace and quiet. There's no beach or lake, but there are two pools, one shaped like Mickey's head. If you qualify to stay here, don't even think about staying anywhere else.

Disney's Wilderness Lodge & Villas

STRENGTHS	• Convenient self-parking
• Along with Animal Kingdom Lodge, it's the least expensive Deluxe resort	**WEAKNESSES**
	• Transportation to Magic Kingdom is by bus or boat only
• Magnificently rendered theme that children can't get enough of	
• Good on-site dining	• Bus transportation to the Magic Kingdom sometimes shared with Fort Wilderness
• Great views from guest rooms	
• Close to recreational options at Fort Wilderness	• No character meals
	• Rooms sleep only four people (plus child in crib)
• Elaborate swimming complex	
• On-site child care	• Ongoing construction through 2016

THIS DELUXE RESORT IS INSPIRED by national park lodges of the early 20th century. Wilderness Lodge & Villas ranks with Animal Kingdom Lodge & Villas as one of the most impressively themed and meticulously detailed Disney resorts. It's also by far the hands-down favorite hotel of children. You won't have any trouble convincing the kids to abandon the theme parks for rest and a swim if you stay at Wilderness Lodge.

On the shore of Bay Lake, the lodge consists of an eight-story central building flanked by two seven-story guest wings and a wing of studio and one- and two-bedroom condominiums. The hotel features exposed timber columns, log cabin–style facades, and dormer windows. The grounds are landscaped with evergreen pines and pampas grass. The lobby boasts an 82-foot-tall stone fireplace and two 55-foot Pacific Northwest totem poles. Timber pillars, giant tepee chandeliers, and stone- and wood-inlaid floors accentuate the lobby's rustic luxury. Though the resort isn't on vast acreage, it does have a beach and a delightful pool modeled on a mountain stream complete with waterfall and geyser; a children's water-play area was added to it in 2014. Adjoining the Wilderness Lodge are the Wilderness Lodge Villas, a Disney Vacation Club property. Parts of the Wilderness Lodge & Villas property will be a construction zone through 2016, as Disney adds 26 new lakeside villas.

EPCOT RESORTS

Disney's BoardWalk Inn & Villas

STRENGTHS	
• Lively seaside and amusement-pier theme	• Views from waterside guest rooms
• Walking distance to Epcot's International Gateway and Disney's Hollywood Studios	**WEAKNESSES**
	• Limited quick-service dining options suitable for kids; no character meals
• Boat service to DHS and Epcot	• Limited children's activities
• Modest but well-themed swimming complex	• No on-site child care
	• No transportation to Epcot main entrance
• 3-minute walk to BoardWalk midway and dining options	• Bus service to the Magic Kingdom, Animal Kingdom, water parks, and Disney Springs is shared with other Epcot resorts
• Health and fitness center	

ALSO ON CRESCENT LAKE, the BoardWalk Inn is another of the Walt Disney World Deluxe resorts. The complex is a detailed replica of an early-20th-century Atlantic coast boardwalk. Facades of hotels, diners, and shops create an inviting and exciting waterfront skyline. In reality, behind the facades, the BoardWalk Inn & Villas are a single integrated structure. Restaurants and shops occupy the boardwalk level, while accommodations rise up to six stories above. Painted bright red and yellow along with weathered pastel greens and blues, the BoardWalk resorts are the only Disney hotels that use neon signs as architectural detail. The inn and villas share one pool with an old-fashioned amusement-park theme and also have two quiet pools. The BoardWalk Villas will finish a resort-wide interior and exterior refurbishment project in late 2015.

Disney's Caribbean Beach Resort

STRENGTHS	WEAKNESSES
• Colorful Caribbean theme	• Lackluster on-site dining; no character meals
• Children's play areas	
• Rooms with *Pirates of the Caribbean* and *Finding Nemo* themes	• No on-site child care
• Lakefront setting	• Check-in is far from rest of resort
	• Multiple bus stops
• Large food court	• Some "villages" are a good distance from restaurants and shops
• One of two Moderate resorts that can sleep five (in a Murphy bed)	

THE CARIBBEAN BEACH RESORT OCCUPIES 200 acres surrounding a 45-acre lake called Barefoot Bay. This midpriced resort, modeled after resorts in the Caribbean, consists of the registration area (Custom House) and six two-story "villages" named after Caribbean islands. Each village has its own pool, laundry room, and beach. The Caribbean motif is maintained with blue-metal roofs, widow's walks, and wooden-railed porches. The atmosphere is cheerful, with buildings painted blue, lime green, and sherbet orange. Rooms in the Trinidad South village are themed to *Finding Nemo* and *Pirates of the Caribbean*. In addition to the six village pools, the resort's main swimming pool is themed as an old Spanish fort, complete with slides and water cannons.

The Walt Disney World Swan & Walt Disney World Dolphin

STRENGTHS	
• Best-priced location on Crescent Lake	• Participates in Extra Magic Hours program
• Extremely nice guest rooms	**WEAKNESSES**
• Good on-site and nearby dining	• Primarily adult convention and business clientele
• Very nice swimming complex	• Somewhat dated architecture
• On-site child care	• Distant guest self-parking; daily resort and parking fees
• Children's programs, character meals	• No Disney's Magical Express or Disney Dining Plan
• Only hotels within walking distance to mini-golf (Fantasia Gardens)	• Bus service to the Magic Kingdom, Animal Kingdom, water parks, and Disney Springs is shared with other Epcot resorts
• On-site car rental (National and Alamo)	
• Walking distance to both Epcot International Gateway and DHS	

THE SWAN AND DOLPHIN RESORTS were not designed by Disney Imagineers, though you might certainly think they were. They were the playgrounds of postmodern architect Michael Graves; in fact, they are not Disney-owned properties at all, though guests have most of the perks. The Swan and Dolphin are patronized by business types and adult travelers rather than families, and their theme runs more to the surrealistic rather than to the whimsical. That being said, a quick glance at the Swan and Dolphin's strengths will verify that they have as much or more to offer families than the Disney resorts. Rooms at the Swan and Dolphin are undergoing a complete renovation through late 2016; public spaces will not be affected.

Disney's Yacht & Beach Club Resorts & Beach Club Villas

SITUATED ON CRESCENT LAKE across from Disney's BoardWalk, the Yacht & Beach Club Resorts are connected and share a boardwalk, marina, and swimming complex. The Yacht Club Resort has a breezy Nantucket and Cape Cod atmosphere with its own lighthouse, lots of polished wood, and burnished brass. Its sibling resort, the Beach Club, shares most of the facilities but is a little sportier and more casual in atmosphere. The Disney Vacation Club Villas at the Beach Club are

STRENGTHS	
• Fun and nautical New England theme	• Best pool complex of any WDW resort
• Attractive guest rooms	• Convenient self-parking
• Relatively affordable full-service restaurant (Captain's Grille)	• View from waterside guest rooms
	• On-site child care
• Children's programs, character meals	**WEAKNESSES**
• Boat service to DHS	• Bus service to the Magic Kingdom, Animal Kingdom, water parks, and Disney Springs is shared with other Epcot resorts
• Walking distance to Epcot's International Gateway	
• Close to many BoardWalk and Epcot dining options	• No convenient counter-service food
	• Views and balcony size are hit-or-miss

available for rent, have their own small pool, and may offer more privacy. The resorts offer a shared mini–water park, Stormalong Bay, with a white-sand beach and marina, and an unusual number of sports facilities, such as tennis and volleyball, plus fitness rooms, and so on. Many of the rooms have balconies, though a relatively small percentage look across the lake toward the BoardWalk. The Beach Club Resort will be undergoing an extensive refurbishment through late 2016, including new room decor and furniture and renovations to public spaces.

BONNET CREEK/DISNEY SPRINGS AREA RESORTS

Disney's Old Key West Resort

STRENGTHS	WEAKNESSES
• Largest villas of the DVC/DDV resorts, with full kitchens	• Old Key West theme meaningless to children
• Quiet, lushly landscaped setting	• Large, confusing layout
• Convenient self-parking	• Multiple bus stops
• Small, more private swimming pools in each accommodations cluster	• Mediocre on-site dining, no character meals
• Nice family pool with waterslide and free sauna for parents inside lighthouse	• No easily accessible off-site dining
• Recreation options	• Extreme distance of many guest rooms from dining and services
• Boat service to Disney Springs	• No on-site child care

THIS WAS THE FIRST DISNEY VACATION CLUB PROPERTY. Though the resort is a time-share property, units not being used by owners are rented on a nightly basis. Old Key West is a large aggregation of two- to three-story buildings modeled after Caribbean-style residences and guesthouses of the Florida Keys. Arranged subdivision-style around a golf course and along Bonnet Creek, the buildings are in small neighborhood-like clusters. They feature pastel facades, white trim, and shuttered windows. The registration area—along with a full-service restaurant, modest fitness center, marina, and sundries shop—is in Conch Flats Community Hall. Each cluster of accommodations has a quiet pool; a larger pool is at the community hall. A waterslide in the shape of a giant sand castle is the primary kid pleaser at the main pool.

Disney's Port Orleans Resort: French Quarter and Riverside

STRENGTHS	WEAKNESSES
• Creative swimming areas	• Boat service to Disney Springs
• Riverside is one of two Moderate resorts that can sleep five (in a Murphy bed at Alligator Bayou)	**WEAKNESSES**
	• No full-service dining at French Quarter; mediocre full-service restaurant at Riverside doesn't offer character meals
• Disney princess–themed rooms at Riverside	• No on-site child care
• Food courts	• Extreme distance of many guest rooms from dining and services
• Convenient self-parking	• French Quarter and Riverside share bus service during slower times of year
• Children's play areas	
• Varied recreational offerings	

PORT ORLEANS RIVERSIDE AND FRENCH QUARTER RESORTS are good-looking, lower-cost hotel alternatives that combine steamboat-era Southern decor and fairly easy access to Disney Springs, and they're pretty popular among families too.

The 1,008-room French Quarter section is a sanitized Disney version of the New Orleans French Quarter. Consisting of seven three-story buildings next to the Sassagoula River, the resort suggests what New Orleans would look like if its buildings were painted every year and its garbage collectors never went on strike. Prim pink-and-blue guest buildings are festooned with wrought iron filigree, shuttered windows, and old-fashioned iron lampposts. In keeping with the Crescent City theme, the French Quarter is landscaped with magnolia trees and overgrown vines. The centrally located Mint contains the registration area and food court and is a reproduction of a turn-of-the-19th-century building where Mississippi Delta farmers sold their harvests. The registration desk features a vibrant Mardi Gras mural and old-fashioned bank-teller windows. The section's Doubloon Lagoon swimming complex surrounds a colorful fiberglass creation depicting Neptune riding a sea serpent. We think that French Quarter has the most attractive and tasteful rooms of any of the Disney Moderate resorts.

Port Orleans's Riverside Resort draws on the lifestyle and architecture of Mississippi River communities in antebellum Louisiana. Spread along Sassagoula River, which encircles Ol' Man Island (the section's main swimming area), Riverside is subdivided into two more themed areas: the "mansion" area, featuring plantation-style architecture, and the "bayou" area, with tin-roofed imitation-rustic wooden buildings. Mansions are three stories tall, while bayou guesthouses are a story shorter. Riverside's food court houses a working cotton press powered by a 35-foot waterwheel. A set of 512 rooms is themed to Disney's *The Princess and the Frog.*

Disney's Saratoga Springs Resort & Spa & Treehouse Villas

THE MAIN POOL IS THIS RESORT'S FOCAL POINT. Called High Rock Spring, it tumbles over boulders into a clear, free-form heated pool. The area offers a waterslide that winds among the rocks, two

STRENGTHS	• Limited dining options
• Extremely nice studio rooms and villas	• No character meals
• Lushly landscaped setting	• No on-site child care
• Very nice spa and fitness center	• Most distant of all Disney resorts from the theme parks
• Convenient self-parking	
• Closest resort to Disney Springs and Typhoon Lagoon	• Theme and atmosphere not very kid-friendly
• Nice themed swimming complex	• Limited number of units makes the Treehouses among the most difficult accommodations to book at WDW
• Hiking, jogging, and water recreation	
WEAKNESSES	• Bus service can take some time to get out of the (huge) resort
• Villas are beginning to show some wear	

whirlpool spas, and an interactive wet-play area for children. The Saratoga Springs complex will eventually be the largest Vacation Club resort, with well over 800 units. It's expanding toward the Disney Springs shopping area (across the lake) via a path and a pedestrian bridge. There is boat as well as bus service at the facility, though the boats are prohibited from running if lightning threatens. The resort's decor plays on the history and retro-Victorian style of the upstate New York racing resort, with traditional horse-country prints and drawings, stable boy uniforms for the bellhops, and so on. The spa, probably Disney's best, has a fitness center attached. The Disney Springs fireworks are visible from some areas.

Favorites of kids are the Treehouse Villas, nestled in a pinewoods bordering the golf course. With the entire living and sleeping area about 12 feet off the ground, you really do feel like you're living in a tree house. There are only 60 three-bedroom units, so if you want to reserve one of those, book well in advance.

ANIMAL KINGDOM RESORTS

Disney's Animal Kingdom Lodge & Villas

STRENGTHS	• On-site child care
• Exotic theme	• Proximity to non-Disney restaurants on US 192
• Uniquely appointed guest rooms	
• Most rooms have private balconies	**WEAKNESSES**
• View of savanna and animals from guest rooms	• Remote location
	• Savanna views can be hit-or-miss
• Creatively themed swimming areas	
• Excellent on-site dining, including a buffet	• No counter-service dining other than pool bar
• On-site nature programs and storytelling	• Jambo House villas are smaller than those at Kidani Village

ANIMAL KINGDOM LODGE is a snazzy take on safari chic, with balcony views of wildlife that alone may be worth the tab, but its distance from the other parks may be a drawback for those planning to explore all of Disney World. On the other hand, if you have a car, it's the closest resort to all of the affordable family restaurants lining US 192 (Irlo Bronson Memorial Highway). By far the most exotic Disney resort, it's tailor-made for families.

Designed by Peter Dominick of Wilderness Lodge fame, Animal Kingdom Lodge fuses African tribal architecture with the rugged style of grand East African national park lodges. Five-story thatched-roof wings fan out from a vast central rotunda housing the lobby and featuring a huge mud fireplace. Public areas and many rooms offer panoramic views of a private 43-acre wildlife preserve punctuated with streams and elevated kopje (rock outcrops) and populated with some 200 free-roaming animals and 130 birds. Most guest rooms boast hand-carved furnishings and richly colored upholstery. Almost all rooms have full balconies.

Studio and one-, two-, and three-bedroom villa accommodations are available in Jambo House (the main building) and at adjacent Kidani Village, a Disney Vacation Club property. Having stayed at Kidani Village, we think it's a quieter, more relaxed resort. The lobby and rooms have a smaller, more personal feel than Jambo House's. The building's exterior isn't anything special—essentially a set of green rectangles with oversize African-themed decorations attached. Kidani's distance from Jambo House makes it feel remote. The bus stops are a fair distance from the main building too, and it's easy to head in the wrong direction when you're coming back from the parks at night.

Disney's All-Star Resorts: Movies, Music, & Sports

STRENGTHS	WEAKNESSES
• Least expensive of the Disney resorts	• Small standard rooms
• Super-kid-friendly theme	• No full-service dining; food courts often overwhelmed at mealtimes
• Lots of pools	• No character meals
• Food courts and in-room pizza delivery	• No on-site child care
• Family suites at All-Star Music are less expensive than those at Art of Animation	• All three resorts share buses during slower times of year; bus stops often crowded
• Convenient parking	• Limited recreation options

DISNEY'S VERSION OF A BUDGET RESORT features three distinct themes executed in the same hyperbolic style. Spread over a vast expanse, the resorts comprise almost 35 three-story motel-style guest-room buildings. Each resort has its own lobby, food court, and registration area. All-Star Sports Resort features huge sports equipment: bright football helmets, tennis rackets, and baseball bats—all taller than the buildings they adorn. Similarly, All-Star Music Resort features 40-foot guitars, maracas, and saxophones, while All-Star Movies Resort showcases giant popcorn boxes and icons from Disney films. Lobbies of all are loud (in both decibels and brightness) and cartoonish, with checkerboard walls and photographs of famous athletes, musicians, or film stars.

At 260 square feet, guest rooms are very small—so small, in fact, that a family of four attempting to stay in one room might redefine *family values* by week's end. The All-Stars are the noisiest Disney resorts, though guest rooms are well soundproofed and quiet.

All-Star Music has 192 Family Suites in the Jazz and Calypso Buildings. Suites measure roughly 520 square feet, slightly larger than the cabins at Fort Wilderness but slightly smaller than Art of Animation's Family Suites. Each suite, formed from the combination of two formerly separate rooms, includes a kitchenette with mini-refrigerator, microwave, and coffeemaker. Sleeping accommodations include a queen bed in the bedroom, plus a pullout sleeper sofa, a chair bed, and an ottoman bed. A hefty door separates the two rooms.

We receive a lot of letters commenting on the All-Star Resorts. From a Massachusetts family of four:

> *I would never recommend the All-Star for a family. It was like dormitory living. Our room was about 1 mile from the bus stop, and the room was tiny—you needed to step into the bathroom, shut the door, and then step around the toilet that blocked half the tub.*

But a Baltimore family had a very positive experience:

> *We were pleasantly surprised by All-Star Movies. Yes, the rooms are small, but the overall magic there is amazing. The lobby played Disney movies, which is perfect if you get up early and the buses aren't running yet. There are great photo ops everywhere (Donald and Daisy were awesome). Customer service was impeccable.*

Disney's Art of Animation Resort

STRENGTHS	WEAKNESSES
• Exceptional theming	• Most expensive Value resort
• Family Suites are well designed	• No on-site child care
• Best pool of the Value resorts	• No full-service dining or character meals
• Food court and in-room pizza delivery	• Terrible in-room mobile reception
• One bus stop	• Limited recreation options

ART OF ANIMATION RESORT DRAWS its inspiration from four Disney animated films: *The Lion King, The Little Mermaid,* and Disney-Pixar's *Finding Nemo* and *Cars.*

The Value resort, located across Hour Glass Lake from Pop Century, has 864 rooms and 1,120 family suites. The latter have two separate bathrooms, a master bedroom, three separate sleeping areas within the living space, and a kitchenette. The resort consists of four-story buildings and a series of themed swimming pools, including a large feature pool at the *Finding Nemo* courtyard. A water-play area, as well as a 68,800-square-foot commercial building with shopping and dining space, completes the picture. As at Pop Century, large, colorful icons stand in the middle of each group of buildings; here, though, they represent film characters rather than pop-culture touchstones. An interesting departure from the other Value resorts is the outside paint schemes: Rather than using pastels, Disney has decorated the exteriors with giant murals stretching the length of each structure. The *Cars* buildings, for example, each display a four-story panoramic vista of the American desert, with the movie's iconic characters in the middle, while the *Lion King* buildings capture a single verdant jungle scene.

Three of the four sets of themed buildings have pools; the *Lion King* complex has a playground instead. Like the other Value resorts, Art of Animation has a central building—here called Animation Hall—for check-in and bus transportation; it also holds the resort's food court, Landscape of Flavors; a gift shop; and a video game arcade.

Reader reports on Art of Animation have mostly been positive. A mom from Blountville, Tennessee, says:

> *The Art of Animation Resort was the highlight of our trip! Out daughter loves* The Little Mermaid, *and the rooms, while small and basic, were adorable. The courtyards, the pools, the main lobby areas, etc.— Disney is fantastic at attention to detail. Our daughter loved pointing out* Lion King, Finding Nemo, *and* Little Mermaid *characters every day.*

Disney's Coronado Springs Resort

STRENGTHS	WEAKNESSES
• Nice guest rooms	• Conventioneers may be off-putting to vacationing families
• Food court	
• Mayan-themed swimming area with waterslides	• Insufficient on-site dining; no character meals
• Setting is beautiful at night	• No on-site child care
	• Multiple bus stops
	• *Extreme* distance of many guest rooms from dining and services

TO SAVE A LITTLE MONEY without giving up services, consider the Coronado Springs Resort, a rich, Old Mexico–style complex with courtyards, fountains, stucco and terra-cotta buildings, a few Mayan ruins here and there, several swimming pools, a mini–water park, a white-sand beach, a fitness center, a walking path circling a 22-acre lake, and a nightclub. Because it's also a convention hotel, expect a high percentage of guests to be business travelers. Coronado Springs has particularly good access to Animal Kingdom and Blizzard Beach.

Disney's Pop Century Resort

STRENGTHS	WEAKNESSES
• Large swimming pools	• Theming holds more appeal for adults than for kids and teens
• Food court and in-room pizza delivery	
• Convenient self-parking	• Small rooms are the same size as All-Stars' but slightly more expensive
• Fast check-in	• No full-service dining or character meals
• One bus stop	• No on-site child care
	• Limited recreation options

ON VICTORY WAY near the ESPN Wide World of Sports Complex is Pop Century Resort. Originally designed to be completed in phases, the first section opened in 2004. The long-planned second phase of Pop

Century was canceled in favor of a new Value resort, Art of Animation (see profile on page 102).

Pop Century is an economy resort and a near-clone of the All-Star Resorts (that is, four-story, motel-style buildings around a central pool, food court, and registration area). Decorative touches make the difference. Where the All-Star Resorts display larger-than-life icons from sports, music, and movies, Pop Century draws its icons from decades of the 20th century. Look for such oddities as building-size Big Wheels, hula hoops, and the like, punctuated by silhouettes of people dancing the decade's fad dance.

The public areas at Pop Century are marginally more sophisticated than the ones at the All-Star Resorts, with 20th-century period furniture and decor rolled up in a saccharine, those-were-the-days theme. A food court, bar, playground, pools, and so on emulate the All-Star Resorts model in size and location. A Pop Century departure from the All-Star precedent has merchandise retailers thrown in with the fast-food concessions in a combination dining-and-shopping area. This apparently is what happens when a giant corporation tries to combine selling pizza with hawking Goofy hats. (You just know the word *synergy* was used like cheap cologne in those design meetings.) The resort is connected to the rest of Walt Disney World by bus, but because of the limited dining options, we recommend having a car.

If you're considering one of the Disney Value resorts, this reader from Dublin, Georgia, thinks Pop Century beats the All-Star Resorts hands-down.

(1) It's far superior to the All-Star Resorts. (2) There's a lake and a view of fireworks. (3) The courtyards have Twister games and neat pools for little children. (4) The memorabilia is interesting to us of a certain age. (5) I love the gift shop, food court, and bar combo. The [dinner entrées are among] the best bargains and the best food anywhere. (6) Bus transportation is better than anywhere else, including Grand Floridian! (7) The layout is more convenient to the food court. (8) The noise from neighbors is not worse than anywhere else. (9) Where else do the cast members do the shag to oldies?

INDEPENDENT HOTELS OF THE DOWNTOWN DISNEY RESORT AREA

THE SEVEN HOTELS of the Downtown Disney Resort Area (DDRA) were created in the days when Disney had far fewer of its own resorts. The hotels—**Best Western Lake Buena Vista Resort Hotel, B Resort, Buena Vista Palace Hotel & Spa, DoubleTree Guest Suites, Hilton Orlando Lake Buena Vista, Holiday Inn in the Walt Disney World Resort,** and **Wyndham Lake Buena Vista Resort**—are chain properties with minimal or nonexistent theming, though the Buena Vista Palace, especially, is pretty upscale. All were hit hard by the recession, and several of the larger properties shifted their focus to convention and business travelers.

The main advantage to staying in the DDRA is being in Disney World and proximal to Disney Springs. Guests at the Hilton,

AMENITIES AT DOWNTOWN DISNEY RESORT AREA HOTELS

HOTEL	CHILDREN'S PROGRAMS	DINING	KID-FRIENDLY	POOL(S)	RECREATION
Best Western LBV Resort	—	★★½	★★★	★★½	★★
B Resort	—	★★★½	★★½	★★½	★★★
Buena Vista Palace	★★★★	★★	★★★½	★★★½	★★★★
DoubleTree Guest Suites	—	★★	★★★	★★½	★★½
Hilton Orlando LBV	—	★★½	★★½	★★★	★★½
Holiday Inn WDW Resort	—	★★	★★	★★★	★★
Wyndham LBV Resort	★★½	★★½	★★★	★★★	★★★

Wyndham, Buena Vista Palace, and Holiday Inn are an easy 5- to 15-minute walk from the Marketplace on the east side of Disney Springs. Guests at Best Western, B Resort, and DoubleTree are about 10 minutes farther by foot. Disney transportation can be accessed at Disney Springs, though the Disney buses take a notoriously long time to leave due to the number of stops throughout the shopping and entertainment complex. Though all DDRA hotels offer shuttle buses to the theme parks, the service is provided by private contractors and is somewhat inferior to Disney transportation in frequency of service, number of buses, and hours of operation. All these hotels are easily accessible by car and are only marginally farther from the Disney parks than several of the Disney resorts (and DDRA hotels are quite close to Typhoon Lagoon water park).

All DDRA hotels try to appeal to families, even the business and meeting hotels. Some have pool complexes that rival those at any Disney resort, whereas others offer a food court or all-suite rooms. A few sponsor Disney-character meals and organized children's activities; all have counters for buying Disney tickets, and most have Disney gift shops.

Hilton Orlando Lake Buena Vista is the only DDRA hotel that offers Extra Magic Hours. However, a reservation here cannot be connected to your **mydisneyexperience.com** account, so you won't be able to make FastPass+ reservations 30 days in advance.

Take a peek at the combined website for the DDRA hotels at **down towndisneyhotels.com**. Finally, check the cost table on page 81 and the comparative table above.

HOW *to* GET DISCOUNTS *on* LODGING *at* WALT DISNEY WORLD

THERE ARE SO MANY GUEST ROOMS in and around Disney World that competition is brisk, and everyone, including Disney, wheels and deals to fill them. Here are some tips for getting price breaks at Disney properties:

1. SEASONAL SAVINGS You can save 15–35% or more per night on a Walt Disney World hotel room by scheduling your visit during the slower times of the year.

2. ASK ABOUT SPECIALS When you talk to Disney reservationists, ask specifically about specials. For example, "What special rates or discounts are available at Disney hotels during the time of our visit?"

3. KNOW THE SECRET CODE The folks at **MouseSavers** (**mousesavers .com**) maintain an updated list of discounts and reservation codes for Disney resorts. The codes are separated into categories such as "for anyone," "for residents of certain states," and "for Annual Pass holders." Anyone calling ☎ 407-W-DISNEY can use a current code and get the discounted rate. You can also sign up for the MouseSavers newsletter, with discount announcements, Disney news, and exclusive offers not available to the general public.

Be aware that Disney targets people with PIN codes in e-mails and direct mailings. PIN-code discounts are offered to specific individuals and are correlated with a given person's name and address. When you try to make a reservation using the PIN, Disney will verify that the street or e-mail address to which the code was sent is yours.

To get your name in the Disney system, call the Disney Reservation Center at ☎ 407-W-DISNEY and request that written info or the free trip-planning DVD be sent to you. If you've been to Walt Disney World before, your name and address will of course already be on record, but you won't be as likely to receive a PIN-code offer as you would by calling and requesting to be sent information. On the web, go to **disneyworld.com** and sign up (via the trip-planning DVD) to automatically be sent offers and news at your e-mail address. You might also consider getting a **Disney Rewards Visa Card,** which entitles you to around two days' advance notice when a discount is released (visit **disney.go.com/visa** for details).

4. INTERNET SELLERS Online travel sellers **Expedia** (**expedia.com**), **One Travel** (**onetravel.com**), **Priceline** (**priceline.com**), and **Travelocity** (**travel ocity.com**) offer discounted rooms at Disney hotels, but usually at a price approximating the going rate obtainable from the Walt Disney Travel Company or Walt Disney World Central Reservations. Most breaks are in the 7–25% range, but they can go as deep as 40%. Always check these websites' prices against Disney's—while updating this guide, we noticed that for the same dates during summer 2015, Priceline was charging $30 more per night than Disney for the same standard-view room at the Beach Club.

5. WALT DISNEY WORLD WEBSITE Disney still offers deals when it sees lower-than-usual future demand. Go to **disneyworld.com** and look for "Explore Our Special Offers" on the home page. In the same place, also look for seasonal discounts, usually listed as "Summertime Savings" or

"Fall Savings" or something similar. You can also go to "Places to Stay" at the top right of the home page, where you'll find a link to Special Offers. You must click on the particular special to get the discounts: If you fill out the information on "Price Your Vacation," you'll be charged the full rack rate.

6. RENTING DISNEY VACATION CLUB POINTS The Disney Vacation Club (DVC) is Disney's time-share condominium program. DVC resorts (also known as Disney Deluxe Villa resorts) at Walt Disney World are **Animal Kingdom Villas, Bay Lake Tower** at the Contemporary Resort, **Beach Club Villas, BoardWalk Villas, Grand Floridian Villas, Old Key West Resort, Polynesian Villas & Bungalows, Saratoga Springs Resort & Spa, Treehouse Villas at Saratoga Springs,** and **Wilderness Lodge Villas.** Each resort offers studios and one- and two-bedroom villas (some resorts also offer three-bedroom villas; the Polynesian only has studios and two-bedroom bungalows). Studios are equipped with kitchenettes, wet bars, and fridges; the villas come with full kitchens. Most accommodations have patios or balconies.

DVC members receive a number of points annually that they use to pay for their Disney accommodations. Sometimes members elect to "rent" (sell) their points instead of using them in a given year. Though Disney is not involved in the transaction, it allows DVC members to make these points available to the general public. The going rental rate is usually in the range of $13–$14 per point. Renting a studio for a summer week at Animal Kingdom Lodge & Villas would run you $3,930 with tax during Regular season if you booked through the Disney Reservation Center. The same studio costs the DVC member 76 points for a week. If you rented those points at $14 per point, the same studio would cost you $1,120 with tax—more than $2,800 less.

You have two options when renting points: Go through a company that specializes in DVC points rental, or locate and deal directly with the selling DVC member. For a fixed rate of around $14 per point, the folks at **David's Disney Vacation Club Rentals** (**dvcrequest.com**) will act on your behalf as a points broker, matching your request for a specific resort and dates to their available supply. They'll also take requests months in advance and notify you as soon as something becomes available. We've used these folks for huge New Year's Eve events and last-minute trips, and they're tops. Plus they accept major credit cards.

When you deal directly with the selling DVC member, you pay him or her directly, such as by certified check (few members take credit cards). The DVC member makes a reservation in your name and pays Disney the requisite number of points. Arrangements vary, but the going rate seems to be around $12 per point. Usually your reservation is documented by a confirmation sent from Disney to the owner and then passed along to you. Though the deal you cut is strictly up to you and the owner, you should always insist on receiving the aforementioned confirmation before making more than a one-night deposit.

Continued on page 110

WDW RESORTS CHART

All-Star Movies Resort ★★★
1901 W. Buena Vista Dr.
Lake Buena Vista, FL 32830
☎ 407-939-7000
tinyurl.com/allstarmovies

ROOM RATING	73
COST ($ = $50)	$$$-

Commuting times to parks (*in minutes*):

MAGIC KINGDOM	6:15
EPCOT	5:45
ANIMAL KINGDOM	4:15
DHS	5:15

All-Star Music Resort ★★★
1801 W. Buena Vista Dr.
Lake Buena Vista, FL 32830
☎ 407-939-6000
tinyurl.com/allstarmusicresort

ROOM RATING	73
COST ($ = $50)	$$$-

Commuting times to parks (*in minutes*):

MAGIC KINGDOM	6:15
EPCOT	5:45
ANIMAL KINGDOM	4:15
DHS	5:15

All-Star Sports Resort ★★★
1701 W. Buena Vista Dr.
Lake Buena Vista, FL 32830
☎ 407-939-5000
tinyurl.com/allstarsports

ROOM RATING	73
COST ($ = $50)	$$$-

Commuting times to parks (*in minutes*):

MAGIC KINGDOM	6:15
EPCOT	5:45
ANIMAL KINGDOM	4:15
DHS	5:15

Art of Animation Resort ★★★½
1850 Animation Way
Lake Buena Vista, FL 32830
☎ 407-938-7000
tinyurl.com/artofanimationresort

ROOM RATING	80
COST ($ = $50)	$$$$-

Commuting times to parks (*in minutes*):

MAGIC KINGDOM	12:00
EPCOT	10:00
ANIMAL KINGDOM	12:00
DHS	3:00

Bay Lake Tower at Contemporary Resort ★★★★½
4600 N. World Dr.
Lake Buena Vista, FL 32830
☎ 407-824-1000
tinyurl.com/baylaketower

ROOM RATING	95
COST ($ = $50)	$- x 12

Commuting times to parks (*in minutes*):

MAGIC KINGDOM	on monorail
EPCOT	11:00
ANIMAL KINGDOM	17:15
DHS	14:15

Beach Club Resort ★★★★½
1800 Epcot Resorts Blvd.
Lake Buena Vista, FL 32830
☎ 407-934-8000
tinyurl.com/beachclubresort

ROOM RATING	90
COST ($ = $50)	$+ x 9

Commuting times to parks (*in minutes*):

MAGIC KINGDOM	7:15
EPCOT	5:15
ANIMAL KINGDOM	6:45
DHS	4:00

Caribbean Beach Resort ★★★½
900 Cayman Way
Lake Buena Vista, FL 32830
☎ 407-934-3400
tinyurl.com/caribbeanbeachresort

ROOM RATING	80
COST ($ = $50)	$$$$+

Commuting times to parks (*in minutes*):

MAGIC KINGDOM	8:00
EPCOT	6:00
ANIMAL KINGDOM	7:15
DHS	4:15

Contemporary Resort ★★★★½
4600 N. World Dr.
Lake Buena Vista, FL 32830
☎ 407-824-1000
tinyurl.com/contemporarywdw

ROOM RATING	93
COST ($ = $50)	$+ x 9

Commuting times to parks (*in minutes*):

MAGIC KINGDOM	on monorail
EPCOT	11:00
ANIMAL KINGDOM	17:15
DHS	14:15

Coronado Springs Resort ★★★★
1000 W. Buena Vista Dr.
Orlando, FL 32830
☎ 407-939-1000
tinyurl.com/coronadosprings

ROOM RATING	83
COST ($ = $50)	$- x 5

Commuting times to parks (*in minutes*):

MAGIC KINGDOM	5:30
EPCOT	4:00
ANIMAL KINGDOM	4:45
DHS	4:45

Grand Floridian Villas ★★★★½
4401 Floridian Way
Lake Buena Vista, FL 32830
☎ 407-824-3000
tinyurl.com/grandfloridianvillas

ROOM RATING	93
COST ($ = $50)	$- x 13

Commuting times to parks (*in minutes*):

MAGIC KINGDOM	on monorail
EPCOT	4:45
ANIMAL KINGDOM	11:45
DHS	6:45

Old Key West Resort ★★★★½
1510 North Cove Rd.
Lake Buena Vista, FL 32830
☎ 407-827-7700
tinyurl.com/oldkeywest

ROOM RATING	90
COST ($ = $50)	$+ x 8

Commuting times to parks (*in minutes*):

MAGIC KINGDOM	10:45
EPCOT	6:00
ANIMAL KINGDOM	14:30
DHS	10:30

Polynesian Village Resort ★★★★½
1600 Seven Seas Dr.
Lake Buena Vista, FL 32830
☎ 407-824-2000
tinyurl.com/polynesianresort

ROOM RATING	92
COST ($ = $50)	$- x 12

Commuting times to parks (*in minutes*):

MAGIC KINGDOM	12:00
EPCOT	8:00
ANIMAL KINGDOM	16:15
DHS	12:30

Animal Kingdom Lodge
★★★★
2901 Osceola Pkwy.
Lake Buena Vista, FL 32830
☎ 407-938-3000
tinyurl.com/aklodge

ROOM RATING	89
COST ($ = $50)	$ x 8

Commuting times to parks (*in minutes*):

MAGIC KINGDOM	8:15
EPCOT	6:15
ANIMAL KINGDOM	2:15
DHS	6:00

Animal Kingdom Villas (Jambo House) ★★★★½
2901 Osceola Pkwy.
Lake Buena Vista, FL 32830
☎ 407-938-3000
tinyurl.com/akjambo

ROOM RATING	91
COST ($ = $50)	$ x 8

Commuting times to parks (*in minutes*):

MAGIC KINGDOM	8:15
EPCOT	6:15
ANIMAL KINGDOM	2:15
DHS	6:00

Animal Kingdom Villas (Kidani Village) ★★★★½
3701 Osceola Pkwy.
Lake Buena Vista, FL 32830
☎ 407-938-7400
tinyurl.com/akkidani

ROOM RATING	95
COST ($ = $50)	$- x 10

Commuting times to parks (*in minutes*):

MAGIC KINGDOM	8:15
EPCOT	6:15
ANIMAL KINGDOM	2:15
DHS	6:00

Beach Club Villas ★★★★½
1800 Epcot Resorts Blvd.
Lake Buena Vista, FL 32830
☎ 407-934-8000
tinyurl.com/beachclubvillas

ROOM RATING	90
COST ($ = $50)	$- x 10

Commuting times to parks (*in minutes*):

MAGIC KINGDOM	7:15
EPCOT	5:15
ANIMAL KINGDOM	6:45
DHS	4:00

BoardWalk Inn ★★★★
2101 N. Epcot Resorts Blvd.
Lake Buena Vista, FL 32830
☎ 407-939-6200
tinyurl.com/boardwalkinn

ROOM RATING	89
COST ($ = $50)	$+ x 10

Commuting times to parks (*in minutes*):

MAGIC KINGDOM	7:15
EPCOT	5:30
ANIMAL KINGDOM	7:00
DHS	3:00

BoardWalk Villas ★★★★½
2101 N. Epcot Resorts Blvd.
Lake Buena Vista, FL 32830
☎ 407-939-6200
tinyurl.com/boardwalkvillas

ROOM RATING	90
COST ($ = $50)	$- x 10

Commuting times to parks (*in minutes*):

MAGIC KINGDOM	7:15
EPCOT	5:30
ANIMAL KINGDOM	7:00
DHS	3:00

Dolphin ★★★★½
1500 Epcot Resorts Blvd.
Lake Buena Vista, FL 32830
☎ 407-934-4000
swandolphin.com

ROOM RATING	90
COST ($ = $50)	$$$$+

Commuting times to parks (*in minutes*):

MAGIC KINGDOM	6:45
EPCOT	5:00
ANIMAL KINGDOM	6:15
DHS	4:00

Fort Wilderness Resort (cabins) ★★★★
4510 N. Fort Wilderness Trail
Lake Buena Vista, FL 32830
☎ 407-824-2837
tinyurl.com/ftwilderness

ROOM RATING	86
COST ($ = $50)	$- x 8

Commuting times to parks (*in minutes*):

MAGIC KINGDOM	13:15
EPCOT	8:30
ANIMAL KINGDOM	20:00
DHS	14:00

Grand Floridian Resort & Spa ★★★★½
4401 Floridian Way
Lake Buena Vista, FL 32830
☎ 407-824-3000
tinyurl.com/grandflresort

ROOM RATING	93
COST ($ = $50)	$- x 14

Commuting times to parks (*in minutes*):

MAGIC KINGDOM	on monorail
EPCOT	4:45
ANIMAL KINGDOM	11:45
DHS	6:45

Polynesian Village, Villas, & Bungalows (studios) ★★★★½
1600 Seven Seas Dr.
Lake Buena Vista, FL 32830
☎ 407-824-2000
tinyurl.com/polynesianresort

ROOM RATING	92
COST ($ = $50)	$+ x 11

Commuting times to parks (*in minutes*):

MAGIC KINGDOM	12:00
EPCOT	8:00
ANIMAL KINGDOM	16:15
DHS	12:30

Pop Century Resort ★★★
1050 Century Dr.
Lake Buena Vista, FL 32830
☎ 407-938-4000
tinyurl.com/popcenturywdw

ROOM RATING	71
COST ($ = $50)	$$$+

Commuting times to parks (*in minutes*):

MAGIC KINGDOM	8:30
EPCOT	6:30
ANIMAL KINGDOM	6:15
DHS	5:00

Port Orleans Resort– French Quarter ★★★★
2201 Orleans Dr.
Lake Buena Vista, FL 32830
☎ 407-934-5000
tinyurl.com/portorleansfq

ROOM RATING	84
COST ($ = $50)	$- x 5

Commuting times to parks (*in minutes*):

MAGIC KINGDOM	12:00
EPCOT	8:00
ANIMAL KINGDOM	16:15
DHS	12:30

WDW RESORTS CHART (continued)

Port Orleans Resort–Riverside ★★★★
1251 Riverside Dr.
Lake Buena Vista, FL 32830
☎ 407-934-6000
tinyurl.com/portorleansriverside

| ROOM RATING | 83 |
| COST ($ = $50) | $- x 5 |

Commuting times to parks (*in minutes*):
MAGIC KINGDOM	12:00
EPCOT	8:00
ANIMAL KINGDOM	16:15
DHS	12:30

Saratoga Springs Resort & Spa ★★★★½
1960 Broadway
Lake Buena Vista, FL 32830
☎ 407-827-1100
tinyurl.com/saratogawdw

| ROOM RATING | 90 |
| COST ($ = $50) | $+ x 8 |

Commuting times to parks (*in minutes*):
MAGIC KINGDOM	14:45
EPCOT	8:45
ANIMAL KINGDOM	18:15
DHS	14:30

Shades of Green ★★★★½
1950 W. Magnolia Palm Dr.
Lake Buena Vista, FL 32830
☎ 407-824-3400
shadesofgreen.org

| ROOM RATING | 91 |
| COST ($ = $50) | $$- |

Commuting times to parks (*in minutes*):
MAGIC KINGDOM	3:30
EPCOT	4:45
ANIMAL KINGDOM	9:30
DHS	6:15

Swan ★★★★½
1200 Epcot Resorts Blvd.
Lake Buena Vista, FL 32830
☎ 407-934-3000
swandolphin.com

| ROOM RATING | 90 |
| COST ($ = $50) | $$$$+ |

Commuting times to parks (*in minutes*):
MAGIC KINGDOM	6:30
EPCOT	4:45
ANIMAL KINGDOM	6:15
DHS	4:00

Treehouse Villas at Saratoga Springs Resort & Spa ★★★★½
1960 Broadway
Lake Buena Vista, FL 32830
☎ 407-827-1100
tinyurl.com/saratogawdw

| ROOM RATING | 90 |
| COST ($ = $50) | $- x 20 |

Commuting times to parks (*in minutes*):
MAGIC KINGDOM	12:45
EPCOT	7:15
ANIMAL KINGDOM	16:45
DHS	12:30

Wilderness Lodge ★★★★
901 Timberline Dr.
Lake Buena Vista, FL 32830
☎ 407-824-3200
tinyurl.com/wildernesslodge

| ROOM RATING | 86 |
| COST ($ = $50) | $- x 9 |

Commuting times to parks (*in minutes*):
MAGIC KINGDOM	*
EPCOT	10:00
ANIMAL KINGDOM	15:15
DHS	13:30

Wilderness Lodge Villas ★★★★½
901 Timberline Dr.
Lake Buena Vista, FL 32830
☎ 407-824-3200
tinyurl.com/wlvillas

| ROOM RATING | 90 |
| COST ($ = $50) | $- x 10 |

Commuting times to parks (*in minutes*):
MAGIC KINGDOM	*
EPCOT	10:00
ANIMAL KINGDOM	15:15
DHS	13:30

Yacht Club Resort ★★★★
1700 Epcot Resorts Blvd.
Lake Buena Vista, FL 32830
☎ 407-934-7000
tinyurl.com/yachtclubwdw

| ROOM RATING | 89 |
| COST ($ = $50) | $- x 10 |

Commuting times to parks (*in minutes*):
MAGIC KINGDOM	7:15
EPCOT	5:15
ANIMAL KINGDOM	6:45
DHS	4:00

*Primary transportation is by ferry rather than by car.

Continued from page 107

We suggest checking online at one of the various Disney discussion boards if you're not picky about where you stay and when you go and you're willing to put in the effort to ask around. If you're trying to book a particular resort, especially during a busy time of year, there's something to be said for the low-hassle approach of a points broker.

7. TRAVEL AGENTS We believe a good travel agent is the best friend a traveler can have. And though we at *The Unofficial Guide* know a thing or two about the travel industry, we always give our agent a chance to beat any deal we find. If she can't beat it, we let her book it anyway if she can get commission from it. We nurture a relationship that gives her plenty of incentive to roll up her sleeves and work on our behalf.

As you might expect, some travel agents and agencies specialize, sometimes exclusively, in selling Walt Disney World. These Disney specialists are so good that we use them ourselves. The needs of our research team are many, and our schedules are complicated. When we work with an Authorized Disney Vacation Planner, we know we're dealing with someone who knows Disney inside and out, including where to find the deals and how to use all the tricks of the trade that keep our research budget under control. Simply stated, they save us time and money—sometimes lots of both.

Each year we ask our readers to rate the travel agent who helped plan their Disney trip. We received more than 4,000 responses this year. The best of the best include **Sue Pisaturo** of **Small World Vacations,** whom we've used many times and who contributes to this guide (**sue@smallworldvacations.com**); **Coleen Bolton** (**coleen@mei-travel .com**), who also made our list in the 2013 and 2014 editions of this guide; **Minnie Babb** (**minnie@smallworldvacations.com**) and **Darren Wittko** (**darren@magicalvacationstravel.com**), both of whom made the list a second year in a row; and newcomers **Caroline Baggerly** (**caroline @mei-travel.com**), **Holly Biss** (**holly@magicalvacationstravel.com**), and **Belle Meyers** (**belle@smallworldvacations.com**).

WALT DISNEY TRAVEL COMPANY MAGIC YOUR WAY PACKAGES

DISNEY'S MAGIC YOUR WAY travel-package program mirrors the admission-ticket program of the same name. Here's how it works: You begin with a base package room and tickets. Tickets can be customized to match the number of days you intend to tour the theme parks, and range in length from 1 to 10 days. As with theme park admissions, the package program offers strong financial incentives to book a longer stay. An adult 1-Day Base Ticket for the Magic Kingdom (with tax) costs $111.83, whereas if you buy a 7-Day Base Ticket, the average cost per day drops to $50.97. You can purchase add-ons to your Base Tickets, such as hopping between theme parks; playing mini-golf; and visiting water parks, DisneyQuest, or the ESPN Wide World of Sports Complex.

With Magic Your Way packages, you can avoid paying for features you don't intend to use. On a one-week vacation, for example, you might want to spend only five days in the Disney parks, saving a day each for Universal Studios and SeaWorld. With Magic Your Way, you can buy only five days of admission on a seven-day package. Likewise, if you don't normally park-hop, you can purchase multiday admissions that don't include the Park Hopper feature. Best of all, you can buy the various add-ons at any time during your vacation.

The basic components of a Magic Your Way package are as follows:

- One or more nights of accommodations at your choice of any Disney resort

- Base Ticket for the number of days you tour the theme parks
- Unlimited use of the Disney transportation system
- Free theme park parking
- Official Walt Disney Travel Company luggage tag (one per person)

The various **Magic Your Way Dining Plans,** an optional but very popular component, are covered in detail beginning on page 171.

Number-Crunching

Comparing a Magic Your Way package with purchasing the package components separately is a breeze.

1. Pick a Disney resort and decide how many nights you want to stay.
2. Next, work out a rough plan of what you want to do and see so you can determine the admission passes you'll require.
3. When you're ready, call the Disney Reservation Center (DRC) at ☎ 407-W-DISNEY and price a Magic Your Way package with tax for your selected resort and dates. The package will include both admissions and lodging. It's also a good idea to get a quote from a Disney-savvy travel agent (see page 110).
4. Now, to calculate the costs of buying your accommodations and admission passes separately, call the DRC a second time. This time, price a room-only rate for the same resort and dates. Be sure to ask about the availability of any special deals. While you're still on the line, obtain the prices, with tax, for the admissions you require. If you're not sure which of the various admission options will best serve you, consult our free Ticket Calculator at **touringplans.com.**
5. Add the room-only rates and the admission prices. Compare this sum to the DRC quote for the Magic Your Way package.
6. Check for deals and discounts on packages, room-only rates, and theme park admission.

Throw Me a Line!

If you buy a package from Disney, don't expect reservationists to offer suggestions or help you sort out your options. Generally, they respond only to your specific questions, ducking queries that require an opinion. A reader from North Riverside, Illinois, complains:

> *The representatives from WDW were very courteous, but they only answered the questions posed and were not eager to give advice on what might be most cost-effective. I feel a person could spend 8 hours on the phone with WDW reps and not have any more input than you get from reading the literature.*

If you can't get the information you need from a Disney reservationist, get in touch with a good travel agent (see page 110 for our recommendations).

LODGING *Outside*
WALT DISNEY WORLD

AT THIS POINT YOU'RE PROBABLY WONDERING how a hotel outside Walt Disney World could be as convenient as one inside Walt Disney World. Well, Mabel, Disney World is a *muy largo* place, but like any city or state, it has borders. By way of analogy, let's say you want to stay in a hotel in Cincinnati but can't find one you can afford. Would you rather book a hotel in Toledo or Cleveland, which are both still in Ohio but pretty darn far away, or would you be willing to leave Ohio and stay just across the river from Cincy in Covington, Kentucky?

Just south of Walt Disney World on US 192 are a bunch of hotels and condos, some great bargains, that are closer to Animal Kingdom and Disney's Hollywood Studios than are many hotels in Disney World. Similarly, there are hotels along Disney's east border, FL 535, that are exceptionally convenient if you plan to use your own car.

Lodging costs outside Walt Disney World vary incredibly. If you shop around, you can find a clean motel with a pool within a few minutes of Walt Disney World for as low as $40 a night. You also can find luxurious, expensive hotels. Because of hot competition, discounts abound.

GOOD NEIGHBOR HOTELS

SOME HOTELS PAY DISNEY a marketing fee to display a "Good Neighbor" designation. Usually a ticket shop in the lobby sells full-price Disney tickets. Other than that, the designation means nothing for the consumer. It doesn't guarantee quality—some Good Neighbor hotels are very nice, others not so much. Some are close to Disney World, while others are quite far away. Disney requires Good Neighbor hotels to provide free shuttle service to Walt Disney World but prohibits them from offering shuttle service to Universal or SeaWorld.

SELECTING AND BOOKING A HOTEL
OUTSIDE WALT DISNEY WORLD

THERE ARE FOUR PRIMARY out-of-the-World areas to consider:

1. INTERNATIONAL DRIVE AREA This area, about 15–25 minutes northeast of Walt Disney World, parallels I-4 on its eastern side and offers a wide selection of both hotels and restaurants. Accommodations range from about $56 to $400 per night. The chief drawbacks of the International Drive area are its terribly congested roads, countless traffic signals, and inadequate access to westbound I-4. While the biggest bottleneck is the intersection with Sand Lake Road, the mile of International Drive between Kirkman Road and Sand Lake Road stays in near-continuous gridlock. It's common to lose 25–35 minutes trying to navigate this 1-mile stretch.

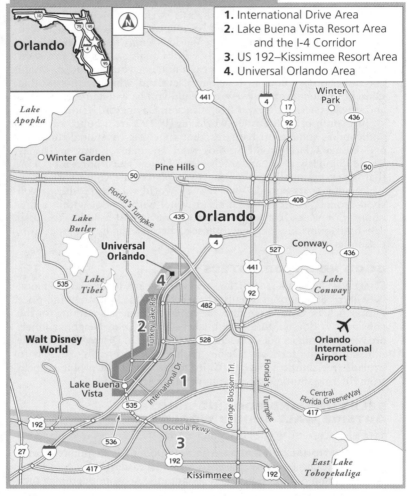

Hotel Concentrations Around Walt Disney World

Orlando

1. International Drive Area
2. Lake Buena Vista Resort Area and the I-4 Corridor
3. US 192–Kissimmee Resort Area
4. Universal Orlando Area

Lake Apopka

Winter Park

Winter Garden

Pine Hills

Lake Butler

Orlando

Florida's Turnpike

Universal Orlando

Conway

Lake Tibet

Lake Conway

Walt Disney World

Turkey Lake Rd.

International Dr.

Orlando International Airport

Lake Buena Vista

Orange Blossom Trl.

Florida's Turnpike

Osceola Pkwy.

Central Florida GreeneWay

Kissimmee

East Lake Tohopekaliga

Hotels in the International Drive area are listed in the *Official Vacation Guide* published by the Orlando–Orange County Convention and Visitors Bureau. For a copy, call ☎ 800-972-3304 or 407-363-5872, or go to **visitorlando.com**.

2. LAKE BUENA VISTA AND THE I-4 CORRIDOR A number of hotels are situated along FL 535 and west of I-4 between Walt Disney World and

I-4's intersection with the Florida Turnpike. These properties are easily reached from the interstate and are near a large number of restaurants, including those on International Drive. Most hotels in this area are listed in the *Official Vacation Guide*. This area includes Disney's new Flamingo Crossings Value-priced resort area (see page 115).

3. US 192 (IRLO BRONSON MEMORIAL HIGHWAY) This is the highway to Kissimmee, south of Walt Disney World. In addition to a number of large, full-service hotels, many small, privately owned motels often offer a good value. Several dozen properties on US 192 are closer to the Disney theme parks than are the more expensive hotels in the Downtown Disney Resort Area. The number and variety of restaurants on US 192 has increased markedly in the past several years, easing the area's primary shortcoming. Hotels on US 192 and in Kissimmee can be found in the *Kissimmee Visitor's Guide;* call ☎ 800-327-9159 or check **experiencekissimmee.com.**

4. UNIVERSAL ORLANDO AREA In the triangular area bordered by I-4 on the southeast, Vineland Road on the north, and Turkey Lake Road on the west are Universal Orlando and the hotels most convenient to it. Running north–south through the middle of the triangle is Kirkman Road, which connects to I-4. On the east side of Kirkman are a number of independent hotels and restaurants. Universal hotels, theme parks, and CityWalk are west of Kirkman. Traffic in this area is not nearly as congested as on nearby International Drive, and there are good interstate connections in both directions.

THE BEST HOTELS FOR FAMILIES OUTSIDE WALT DISNEY WORLD

WHAT MAKES A SUPER FAMILY HOTEL? Roomy accommodations, in-room fridge, great pool, complimentary breakfast, child-care options, and programs for kids are a few of the things *The Unofficial Guide* hotel team researched in selecting the top hotels for families from among hundreds of properties in the Disney World area. Some of our picks are expensive, others are more reasonable, and some are a bargain. Regardless of price, be assured that these hotels understand a family's needs.

Though all the hotels in the next section offer some type of shuttle to the theme parks, some offer very limited service. Call the hotel before you book and ask what the shuttle schedule will be when you visit. Because families, like individuals, have different wants and needs, we haven't ranked the following properties here. They're listed geographically and then alphabetically.

Disney's Flamingo Crossings

In 2007, right before the global financial meltdown, Disney announced ambitious plans for a new 450-acre, Value-oriented hotel and restaurant complex, just beyond the western edge of the main Disney World property, at the intersection of Western Way and FL 429. Plans were quietly dropped when the Great Recession came. Fast-forward to 2015, and construction has begun on the first two hotels, scheduled to open in early 2016. Both are Marriott brands: **TownePlace Suites,** an extended-stay hotel, and **SpringHill Suites** will have about 250 rooms each; we expect them to be near the $150- to $250-per-night price point. As budget suites, these rooms are targeting the sports groups that participate in events at the ESPN Wide World of Sports Complex. These two hotels will be adjacent and share parking, a pool, and a gym. Other planned amenities include batting cages, a basketball court, and a practice field capable of being configured for different sports. Assuming there's a market for these, the developer plans to build up to five more hotels in the same area.

INTERNATIONAL DRIVE & UNIVERSAL AREAS

CoCo Key Hotel and Water Resort–Orlando ★★★½

7400 International Dr.
Orlando
☎ 407-351-2626 or
877-875-4681
cocokeyorlando.com

Rate per night $75–$108. **Pools** ★★★★. **Fridge in room** Yes. **Shuttle to parks** Yes (Aquatica, SeaWorld, Universal, Wet 'n Wild). **Maximum number of occupants per room** 4. **Special comments** Daily $24 resort fee for use of the water park; day guests may use the water park for $24.95/person Monday–Friday ($26.95 on weekends and $21.95 for Florida residents).

NOT FAR FROM THE UNIVERSAL ORLANDO theme parks, CoCo Key combines a tropical-themed hotel with a canopied water park featuring 3 pools and 14 waterslides, as well as poolside food and arcade entertainment. A full-service restaurant serves breakfast and dinner; a food court offers family favorites such as burgers, chicken fingers, and pizza.

A unique feature of the resort is its cashless payment system, much like that on a cruise ship. At check-in, families receive bar-coded wristbands that allow purchased items to be easily charged to their room.

The unusually spacious guest rooms include 37-inch flat-panel TVs, free Wi-Fi, granite showers and countertops, and plenty of accessible outlets for electronics.

DoubleTree by Hilton Orlando at SeaWorld ★★★★½

10100 International Dr.
Orlando
☎ 407-352-1100 or
800-327-0363
doubletreeorlando
idrive.com

Rate per night $129–$179. **Pools** ★★★½. **Fridge in room** Standard in some rooms; available in others for $10/day. **Shuttle to parks** Yes (fee varies depending on destination). **Maximum number of occupants per room** 4. **Special comments** Good option if you're visiting SeaWorld or Aquatica. Pets welcome (1 per room, 25-pound limit, $75).

ON 28 LUSH, TROPICAL ACRES, the DoubleTree is adjacent to SeaWorld and Aquatica water park. The 1,094 rooms and suites—classified as resort or tower—are suitable for business travelers or families. We recommend the tower rooms for views and the resort rooms for convenience. Laguna serves steak and seafood, along with breakfast; you can also get a quick bite at Bangli Lounge, the deli, or the pool bar. Relax and cool off at one of the three pools (there are two more just for kids), or indulge in a spa treatment. A fitness center, mini-golf course, children's day camp, and game area afford even more diversions. The resort is about a 15-minute drive to Walt Disney World, a 12-minute drive to Universal, or a short walk to SeaWorld.

Hard Rock Hotel Orlando ★★★★½

Rate per night $259–$464. **Pool** ★★★★. **Fridge in room** Yes. **Shuttle to parks** Yes (Universal, SeaWorld, Discovery Cove, Aquatica, Wet 'n Wild). **Maximum number of occupants per room** 5 (double-queen) or 3 (king). **Special comments** Microwaves available for $15/day. Character dinner on Saturday. Pets welcome ($50/night).

5800 Universal Blvd.
Orlando
☎ 407-503-2000 or
888-464-3617
hardrockhotelorlando
.com

THE HARD ROCK HOTEL IS THE CLOSEST resort to Universal's theme parks. The exterior has white stucco walls, arched entryways, and rust-colored roof tiles. Inside, the lobby is a tribute to rock-and-roll style, all marble, chrome, and stage lighting.

The eight floors hold 650 rooms and 29 suites, with the rooms categorized into standard, deluxe, and club-level tiers. Standard rooms measure 375 square feet and are furnished with two queen beds, a flat-panel LCD television, refrigerator, coffeemaker, and an alarm clock with a 30-pin iPhone docking port.

A six-drawer dresser and separate closet with sliding doors ensure plenty of storage space. In addition, most rooms have a reading chair and a small desk with two chairs. An optional rollaway bed, available at an extra charge, allows standard rooms to sleep up to five people.

Each room's dressing area features a sink and hair dryer. The bathroom is probably large enough for most adults to get ready in the morning while another person gets ready in the dressing area.

Guests staying in standard rooms can choose from one of three views: standard, which can include anything from walkways and parking lots to lawns and trees; garden view, which includes the lawn, trees, and (in some rooms) the waterway around the resort; and pool view, which includes the Hard Rock's expansive pool.

That pool is an attraction unto itself. Situated in the middle of the resort's C-shaped main building, the 12,000-square-foot pool includes a 250-foot waterslide, a sand beach, and underwater speakers so you can hear the music while you swim. Adjacent to the pool are a fountain play area for small children, a sand-volleyball court, hot tubs, and a poolside bar. The Hard Rock also has a small, functional fitness center. Like all Universal Orlando Resort hotels, the Hard Rock has a business center and video arcade.

On-site dining includes The Kitchen, a casual full-service restaurant open for breakfast, lunch, and dinner, featuring American food such as burgers, steaks, and salads. The Palm Restaurant is an upscale steak house available for dinner only. And, of course, the Hard Rock Café is just a short distance away at Universal CityWalk.

After its much-needed refurbishment in early 2015, we rate the rooms at Hard Rock slightly ahead of the more-expensive Portofino Bay.

Loews Portofino Bay Hotel ★★★★½

Rate per night $294–$479. **Pools** ★★★★. **Fridge in room** Minibar; fridge available for $15/day. **Shuttle to parks** Yes (Universal, SeaWorld, Discovery Cove,

Aquatica, Wet 'n Wild). **Maximum number of occupants per room** 5 (double-queen) or 3 (king). **Special comments** Character dinner on Friday. Pets welcome ($50/night).

5601 Universal Blvd.
Orlando
☎ 407-503-1000 or
888-464-3617
tinyurl.com/portofinobay

UNIVERSAL'S TOP-OF-THE-LINE HOTEL evokes the Italian seaside city of Portofino, complete with a man-made bay past the lobby. To Universal's credit, the layout, color, and theming of the guest-room buildings are a good approximation of the architecture around the harbor in the real Portofino (Universal's version has fewer yachts, though).

Inside, the lobby is decorated with pink marble floors, white-wood columns, and arches. The space is both airy and comfortable, with side rooms featuring seats and couches done in bold reds and deep blues.

Most guest rooms are 450 square feet and have either one king bed or two queen beds. King rooms sleep up to three people with an optional rollaway bed; the same option allows queen rooms to sleep up to five. Two room-view options are available: Garden rooms look out over the landscaping and trees; bay-view rooms face either west or south and overlook Portofino Bay, with a view of the piazza behind the lobby too.

Rooms come furnished with a 32-inch LCD flat-panel TV, a refrigerator, a coffeemaker, and an alarm clock with a 30-pin iPhone docking port. Other amenities include a small desk with two chairs, a comfortable reading chair with lamp, a chest of drawers, and a standing closet.

Guest bathrooms at Portofino Bay are the best on Universal property. The shower has enough water pressure to strip paint from old furniture, not to mention an adjustable spray nozzle that varies the water pulses to simulate everything from a tropical monsoon to the thumps of wildebeest hooves during migrating season.

Portofino Bay has three pools, the largest of which is the Beach Pool, on the west side of the resort. Two smaller quiet pools sit at the far end of the east wing and to the west of the main lobby. The Beach Pool has a zero-entry design and a waterslide themed after a Roman aqueduct, plus a children's play area, hot tubs, and a poolside bar and grill. The Villa Pool has private cabana rentals for that Italian Riviera feeling. Rounding out the luxuries are the full-service Mandara Spa; a complete fitness center with weight machines, treadmills, and more; a business center; and a video arcade. On-site dining includes three sit-down restaurants serving Italian cuisine; a deli; a pizzeria; and a café serving coffee and gelato.

Loews Royal Pacific Resort ★★★★½

6300 Hollywood Way
Orlando
☎ 407-503-1000 or
888-464-3617
tinyurl.com/royalpacific

Rate per night $234–$404. **Pools** ★★★★. **Fridge in room** Yes. **Shuttle to parks** Yes (Universal, SeaWorld, Discovery Cove, Aquatica, Wet 'n Wild). **Maximum number of occupants per room** 5 (double-queen) or 3 (king). **Special comments** Microwaves available for $15/day. Character breakfast on Sunday; character dinners on Monday, Wednesday, and Thursday. Pets welcome ($50/night).

YOU MAY BE TEMPTED, as we were initially, to write off the Royal Pacific as a knockoff of Disney's Polynesian Village Resort. There are indeed similarities, but the Royal Pacific is attractive enough, and has enough strengths of its own, for us to recommend that you try a stay there to compare for yourself.

The South Seas–inspired theming is both relaxing and structured. Guests enter the lobby from a walkway two stories above an artificial stream that surrounds the resort. Once you're inside, the lobby's dark teakwood accents contrast nicely with the enormous amount of light coming in from the windows and three-story A-frame roof. Palms line the walkway through the lobby, and through these you see that the whole lobby surrounds an enormous outdoor fountain.

The 1,000 guest rooms are spread among three Y-shaped wings attached to the main building. Standard rooms are 335 square feet and feature one king or two queen beds, fitted with 300-thread-count sheets. The rooms and hallways of Royal Pacific's first tower were refurbished in 2015, and the remainder will be done by early 2016, with modern monochrome wall treatments and carpets, accented with boldly colored floral graphics. Rooms include a 32-inch flat-panel LCD TV, a refrigerator, a coffeemaker, and an alarm clock with a 30-pin iPhone docking port. Other amenities include a small desk with two chairs, a comfortable reading chair, a chest of drawers, and a large closet. A dressing area with sink is separated from the rest of the room by a wall. Next to the dressing area is the bathroom, with a tub, shower, and toilet.

As at the Hard Rock, the Royal Pacific's zero-entry pool includes a sand beach, volleyball court, play area for kids, hot tub, and cabanas for rent, plus a poolside bar and grill.

Amenities include a 5,000-square-foot fitness facility ($10 per day, free with club-level rooms), a business center, a video arcade, two full-service restaurants, three bars, and a luau. Of the table-service restaurants, only the Islands Dining Room is open for breakfast. Emeril Lagasse's Tchoup Chop, the other table-service option, is open for lunch and dinner (reservations recommended).

Loews Sapphire Falls Resort *(opening 2016)*

Rate per night $229–$264. **Pools** ★★★★. **Fridge in room** Yes. **Shuttle to parks** Yes (Universal, SeaWorld, Discovery Cove, Aquatica, Wet 'n Wild). **Maximum number of occupants per room** 5 (double-queen) or 3 (king). **Special comment** Opens July 2016.

6601 Adventure Way
Orlando
☎ 407-503-5000 or
888-464-3617
loewshotels.com
/sapphire-falls-hotel

UNIVERSAL'S FIFTH ON-SITE LOEWS HOTEL, Sapphire Falls Resort, seeks to bring a sunny Caribbean island vibe to the moderate-price market when its 1,000 rooms open in July 2016. Sandwiched between Royal Pacific and Cabana Bay—both physically and price wise—Sapphire Falls will sport all of the amenities of Universal's three Deluxe hotels, including water taxi transportation to the parks, with the crucial exception of complimentary Express Passes.

Water figures heavily at Sapphire Falls, whose namesake waterfalls form the scenic centerpiece of the resort. The zero-entry main pool features a white-sand beach, waterslide, children's play areas, fire pit, and cabanas for rent. A fitness room holds a sauna and hot tub. For dinner, Amatista Cookhouse offers table-service Caribbean dining, with an open kitchen and waterfront views. Club Katine serves tapas-style small plates near the pool bar's fire pit. New Dutch Trading Co. is an island-inspired grab-and-go marketplace, and Strong Water Tavern in the lobby has rum tastings and tableside ceviche.

Sapphire Falls also contains 131,000 square feet of meeting space and a business center. Covered walkways connect to a parking structure, which in turn connects to the meeting facilities at Royal Pacific, making the new sister proper-ties ideal for conventions.

The rooms range from 364 square feet in a standard queen or king to 529 square feet in the 36 Kids' Suites, up to 1,358 square feet in the 15 Hospitality Suites. All rooms have a 49-inch flat-panel HDTV, mini-fridge, and coffeemaker. Universal has already begun accepting reservations for 2016.

Nickelodeon Suites Resort ★★★½

14500 Continental Gateway, Orlando
☎ 407-387-5437 or 877-NICK-111
nickhotel.com

Rate per night $149–$209. **Pools** ★★★★. **Fridge in room** Yes. **Shuttle to parks** Yes (Disney, Universal, SeaWorld, Aquatica, Wet 'n Wild). **Maximum number of occupants per room** 8. **Special comments** Daily character breakfast; resort fee of $35/night.

SPONGEBOB SQUAREPANTS, eat your heart out. This resort is as kid-friendly as they come. Decked out in all themes Nickelodeon, the hotel is sure to please any fan of TV shows the likes of *SpongeBob SquarePants, Dora the Explorer,* or *Avatar: The Last Airbender,* to name a few. Nickelodeon characters from the channel's many shows hang out in the resort's lobby and mall area, greeting kids while parents check in.

Guests can choose from among 777 suites—one-bedroom Family Suites and two- and three-bedroom KidSuites—executed in a number of different themes, all very brightly and creatively decorated. All suites include kitchenettes or full kitch-ens; also standard are a microwave, fridge, coffeemaker, TV, iron and board, hair dryer, and safe. KidSuites feature a semiprivate kids' bedroom with bunk or twin beds, pullout sleeper bed, 32-inch TV, CD player, and activity table.

Additional amenities include a video arcade, Studio Nick (which hosts several game shows a night for a live audience), a buffet (kids age 3 and younger eat free with a paying adult), a food court offering Subway and other choices, the full-service Nicktoons Cafe (offers character breakfasts), a convenience store, a lounge, a gift shop, a fitness center, a washer and dryer in each courtyard, and a guest-activities desk (buy Disney tickets and get recommendations on babysitting). Not to be missed—don't worry, your kids won't let you—are the resort's two pools, Oasis and Lagoon. Oasis features a water park complete with water cannons, rope lad-ders, geysers, and dump buckets, as well as a hot tub for adults (with a view of the rest of the pool so you can keep an eye on little ones) and a smaller play area for younger kids. Kids will love the huge, zero-entry Lagoon Pool with its 400-gallon dump bucket, plus a nearby basketball court and nine-hole mini-golf course. Pool activities for kids are scheduled several times a day, seasonally; some games fea-ture the infamous green slime. Whatever you do, avoid letting your kids catch you saying the phrase "I don't know" while you're here—trust us.

Universal's Cabana Bay Beach Resort ★★★★

6550 Adventure Way Orlando
☎ 407-503-4000 or 888-464-3617
tinyurl.com/cabanabay

Rate per night $119–$210 standard rooms, $174–$294 suites. **Pools** ★★★★. **Fridge in room** Suites only. **Shuttle to parks** Yes (Universal, SeaWorld, Discovery Cove, Aquatica, Wet 'n Wild). **Maximum number of occupants per room** 4 (standard rooms) or 6 (suites).

OPENED IN SPRING 2014, Cabana Bay was Universal's first on-site hotel aimed at the value and moderate markets. The theme is midcentury modern, with lots of windows, bright colors, and period-appropriate lighting and furniture.

Kids will love the two large and well-themed pools (one with a lazy river), the amount of space they have to run around in, the video arcade, and the vintage cars parked outside the hotel lobby. Adults will appreciate the sophisticated kitsch of the decor, the multiple lounges, the business center, and the on-site Starbucks. We think Cabana Bay is an excellent choice for price- and/or space-conscious families visiting Universal.

Each family suite has a small bedroom with two queen beds, divided from the living area and kitchenette by a sliding screen; a pullout sofa in the living area offers additional sleeping space. (Standard rooms also have two queen beds.) The bath is divided into three sections: toilet, sink area, and shower room with additional sink. The kitchenette has a microwave, coffeemaker, and mini-fridge. A bar area allows extra seating for quick meals, and a large closet has enough space to store everyone's luggage. Built-in USB charging outlets for your devices are a thoughtful touch.

Recreational options include the 10-lane Galaxy Bowl (about $15 per person with shoe rental), poolside table tennis and billiards, and a large Jack LaLanne fitness center. Outdoor movies are shown nightly near the pool. We're also told that Cabana Bay guests can use the pools at the other three Universal hotels.

In addition to the Starbucks, a food court with seating area shows 1950s TV clips. Swizzle Lounge in the lobby, two pool bars, in-room pizza delivery, and the Galaxy Bowl round out the on-site dining options. You'll find more restaurants and clubs nearby at the Royal Pacific Resort and Universal CityWalk.

Unlike the other Universal resorts, Cabana Bay offers no watercraft service to the parks—it's either take the bus or walk. In November 2014, a new pedestrian bridge opened, connecting Cabana Bay to CityWalk and the rest of Universal Orlando, but we still recommend the bus service for most people. Bus service from Cabana Bay to the parks is superior to any bus transportation from Disney hotels to Disney parks. Cabana Bay guests are eligible for early entry at Universal but do not get a complimentary Universal Express Pass.

LAKE BUENA VISTA & I-4 CORRIDOR

B Resort ★★★½

Rate per night $135–$172. Pools ★★★½. Fridge in room Yes. Shuttle to parks Yes (Disney only). Maximum number of occupants per room 4 plus child in crib. Special comments $22.50/ night resort fee.

1905 Hotel Plaza Blvd.
☎ 407-828-2828 or 800-66-BHOTELS
bresortlbv.com

B RESORTS, a Florida hotel chain, relaunched the former Royal Plaza in summer 2014 after an extensive multiyear renovation. Located within walking distance of shops and restaurants and situated 5 miles or less from the Disney parks, the 394-room hotel targets couples, families, groups, and business travelers.

Decorated in cool blues, whites, and grays, guest rooms and suites afford views of downtown Orlando, area lakes, and theme parks. Along with B Resorts–exclusive Blissful Beds, each room is outfitted with sleek modern furnishings and a large interactive flat-planel TV. Additional touches include a mini-fridge, in-room snacks, and gaming consoles (available on request). Some rooms are also equipped with bunk beds, kitchenettes, or wet bars.

The bathroom is spacious, with plenty of storage. The glass shower is well-designed and has good water pressure. There's absolutely nothing wrong with this hotel at this price point, except for the terrible traffic you have to endure every night because of Disney Springs.

Amenities include free Wi-Fi, a spa, beauty salon, and fitness center. The main restaurant, American Q, serves a modern upscale take on classic barbecue in regional styles ranging from Carolina to Kansas City. Hungry guests can also choose from a poolside bar and grill; The Pickup, a grab-and-go shop just off the lobby that serves quick breakfasts, snacks, picnic lunches, and ice cream; and 24/7 in-room dining.

Other perks: a zero-entry pool with interactive water features; a kids' area; loaner iPads; Monscierge, a digital touch screen concierge and destination guide in the lobby; and more than 25,000 square feet of meeting and multiuse space. Though not served by Disney transportation, B Resort provides bus service to the parks and other Disney World venues.

Buena Vista Palace Hotel & Spa   ★★★½

1900 E. Buena Vista Dr.
Lake Buena Vista
☎ 407-827-2727 or
866-397-6516
buenavistapalace.com

Rate per night $121–$226. **Pools** ★★★½. **Fridge in room** Yes. **Shuttle to parks** Yes (Disney only). **Maximum number of occupants per room** 4. **Special comments** Sunday character brunch available; $22/night resort fee.

THE BUENA VISTA PALACE IS UPSCALE and convenient. Surrounded by an artificial lake and plenty of palms, the spacious pool area comprises three heated pools, the largest of which is partially covered; a whirlpool and sauna; a basketball court; and a sand volleyball court. A pool concierge will fetch your favorite magazine or fruity drink. On Sunday, the Watercress Café hosts a character brunch ($25 for adults, $12 for children). The 897 guest rooms are posh and spacious; each comes with a desk, coffeemaker, hair dryer, satellite TV with pay-per-view movies, iron and board, and mini-fridge. There are also 117 suites. In-room babysitting is available. One lighted tennis court, a European-style spa offering 60 services, a fitness center, an arcade, a playground, and a beauty salon round out the amenities. Two restaurants and a mini-market are on-site. And if you aren't wiped out after time in the parks, consider dropping by the Lobby Lounge or the full-menu sports bar for a nightcap.

Four Seasons Resort Orlando at Walt Disney World Resort   ★★★★★

10100 Dream Tree Blvd.
Golden Oak
☎ 407-313-7777
or 800-267-3046
fourseasons.com
/orlando

Rate per night $545–$845. **Pools** ★★★★★. **Fridge in room** Yes. **Shuttle to parks** Yes (Disney only). **Maximum number of occupants per room** 4 (3 adults or 2 adults and 2 children). **Special comments** The best pool complex in Walt Disney World.

OPENED IN SUMMER 2014, the plush Four Seasons is the best deluxe resort in the area, with comfort, amenities, and personal service that far surpass anything Disney's Deluxes offer. The Spanish Revival–inspired architecture calls to mind Florida's grand resorts of the early 20th century.

Most of the 444 guest rooms have an 80-square-foot balcony with table and chairs. Standard-view rooms look out onto the resort's lawns, gardens, and nearby homes in Golden Oak. Lake-view rooms overlook the lake, the Tom Fazio–designed Tranquilo Golf Club (formerly Disney's Osprey Ridge Golf Course), or the pool. Park-view rooms offer views of the Magic Kingdom's nightly fireworks. (Suites are available with views of Epcot too.)

Standard guest rooms average around 500 square feet and feature either one king bed with a sleeper sofa or two double beds (a crib is available in double rooms). Amenities include two flat-panel TVs, a coffeemaker, a small refrigerator, a work desk with two chairs, a personal DVR to record TV shows, and Bluetooth speakers for your personal audio. Each nightstand has four electrical outlets and two USB ports. Bathrooms have glass-walled showers, a separate tub, marble vanities with two sinks, mosaic-tile floors, hair dryers, lighted mirrors, and a TV in the mirror above the sink.

If you're looking for family activities, the Four Seasons has them. Explorer Island comprises an adult pool, family pool, 242-foot waterslide, children's splash zone, playground, and lazy river. The free Kids for All Seasons program runs daily, 9 a.m.–5 p.m. Other amenities include a full-service spa and fitness center.

Capa, a Spanish-themed rooftop restaurant, serves seafood and steaks. Ravello serves upscale Italian dishes for dinner as well as a Disney-character breakfast on Thursdays, Saturdays, and select Tuesdays. PB&G (Pool Bar and Grill) serves barbecued meats and salads by the main pool.

Hilton Orlando Bonnet Creek ★★★★

Rate per night $119–$249. **Pool** ★★★★½. **Fridge in room** Yes. **Shuttle to parks** Yes (Disney only). **Maximum number of occupants per room** 4. **Special comments** $22/night resort fee.

14100 Bonnet Creek Resort Lane
Orlando
☎ 407-597-3600
hiltonbonnetcreek.com

THE HILTON BONNET CREEK is one of our favorite non-Disney hotels in Lake Buena Vista, and the value for the money beats anything in Disney's Deluxe category. Behind Disney's Caribbean Beach and Pop Century Resorts, this Hilton is much nicer than the one in the Downtown Disney Resort Area.

Standard rooms measure around 414 square feet and have either one king bed or two queen beds. The beds' mattresses and linens are very comfortable. Other features include a 37-inch flat-panel TV, a spacious work desk, an armoire, a small reading chair with floor lamp, a nightstand, and a digital clock. A coffeemaker, small refrigerator, and iron and board are all standard, along with free wired and wireless Internet. Bathrooms include tile floors with glass showers and a hair dryer. Unfortunately, the layout isn't as up-to-date as other hotels'—where many upscale hotel bathrooms have two sinks (so two people can primp at once), the Hilton's has only one.

Families will enjoy the huge zero-entry pool, complete with waterslide, as well as the 3-acre lazy river. Even better, the Hilton staff run arts-and-crafts activities poolside during the day, allowing parents to grab a quick swim and a cocktail. Pool-facing cabanas are available for rent at around $300 per day or $150 per half-day. If you're trying to stay in swimsuit shape, a nice fitness center sits on the ground floor.

The Hilton participates in the Waldorf Astoria's Kids Club next door, for children ages 5–12. A daytime program is available 10:30 a.m.–2:30 p.m., and an evening program is available 6–10 p.m. on Friday and Saturday. Price is $75 for the first child, $25 for each additional child.

More than a dozen restaurants and lounges are between the Hilton and the Waldorf Astoria, with cuisine including steak, Italian, sushi, and tapas; a coffee bar, an American bistro, and breakfast buffet round out the choices. Reservations are recommended for the fancy places.

This hotel is also an excellent choice for avid runDisney fans; it offers many special programs and treats for runners on race days.

Hilton Orlando Lake Buena Vista ★★★★

1751 Hotel Plaza Blvd.
☎ 407-827-4000
hilton-wdwv.com

Rate per night $161–$241. **Pools** ★★★½. **Fridge in room** Minibar; mini-fridge available free on request. **Shuttle to parks** Yes (Disney theme and water parks only). **Maximum number of occupants per room** 4. **Special comments** Sunday character breakfast and Disney Extra Magic Hours program; $22/night resort fee.

THE HILTON IS THE ONLY HOTEL in the Downtown Disney Resort Area (DDRA) that offers Disney's Extra Magic Hours program to its guests (though we hear the perk may be discontinued at the end of 2015). Though the resort fees are outrageous and the decor is dated, the rooms are comfortable and nicer than some others in the DDRA. On-site dining includes Covington Mill Restaurant, offering sandwiches and pasta; Andiamo, an Italian bistro; and Benihana, a Japanese steak house and sushi bar. Covington Mill hosts a Disney-character breakfast on Sundays. The two pools are matched with a children's spray pool and a 24-hour fitness center. An exercise room and a game room are on-site, as is a 24-hour market. Babysitting is available, but there are no organized children's programs.

Holiday Inn Resort Lake Buena Vista ★★★½

Rate per night $80–$164 **Pool** ★★★. **Fridge in room** Yes. **Shuttle to parks** Yes (Disney only). **Maximum number of occupants per room** 4–6. **Special comments** Resort fee of $15/night entitles guests to numerous perks,

13351 FL 535, Orlando
☎ 407-239-4500
or 866-808-8833
hiresortlbv.com

including use of fitness center and daily fountain drinks for kids. Pets welcome ($50–$75/night depending on weight).

THE BIG LURE HERE IS KIDSUITES—405-square-foot rooms, each with a separate children's area. The kids' area sleeps two to four children in one or two sets of bunk beds. The separate adult area has its own TV, safe, hair dryer, and mini-kitchenette with fridge, microwave, sink, and coffeemaker. Standard guest rooms offer these adult amenities. Other kid-friendly amenities include the tiny Castle Movie Theater, which shows movies all day, every day; a playground; an arcade with video games and air hockey, among its many games; and a basketball court. Other amenities include a fitness center for the grown-ups and a large free-form pool complete with kiddie pool and two whirlpools. Applebee's serves breakfast and dinner and offers an à la carte menu for dinner. There's also a minimart. More perks: Kids age 12 and younger eat free from a special menu when dining with one paying adult (maximum four kids per adult), and "Dive-Inn" poolside movies are shown on Saturday nights.

Hyatt Regency Grand Cypress ★★★★½

Rate per night $169–$334. **Pool** ★★★★★. **Fridge in room** Yes, plus minibar. **Shuttle to parks** Yes (Disney, Universal, SeaWorld). **Maximum number of occupants per room** 4. **Special comments** $29/night resort fee.

THERE ARE MYRIAD REASONS to stay at the 1,500-acre Grand Cypress, but the pool ranks as reason number one. The 800,000-gallon tropical paradise has two 45-foot waterslides, waterfalls, and a suspension bridge, along with a waterslide tower, a splash zone, a pool bar, and kids' rock-climbing facilities.

1 Grand Cypress Blvd.
Orlando
☎ 407-239-1234
grandcypress.hyatt.com

The 769 standard guest rooms are 360 square feet and have a Florida ambience, with green and reddish hues, touches of rattan, and private balconies. Amenities include a minibar, iron and board, safe, hair dryer, ceiling fan, and cable/satellite TV with pay-per-view movies and video games. Suite and villa accommodations offer even more amenities. Camp Hyatt provides supervised programs for kids ages 3–12; in-room babysitting is available. Six restaurants offer dining options, and four lounges provide nighttime entertainment.

Marriott Village at Lake Buena Vista ★★★

8623 Vineland Ave.
Orlando
☎ 407-938-9001
or 800-761-7829
marriottvillage.com

Rate per night $74–$189. **Pools** ★★★. **Fridge in room** Yes. **Shuttle to parks** Yes (Disney only, $7). **Maximum number of occupants per room** 4 (Courtyard and Fairfield) or 5 (Spring-Hill). **Special comments** Free Continental breakfast at Fairfield and SpringHill.

THIS GATED HOTEL COMMUNITY INCLUDES a 388-room Fairfield Inn (★★★½), a 400-suite SpringHill Suites (★★★), and a 312-room Courtyard (★★★½). Amenities at all three properties include fridge, cable TV, iron and board, hair dryer, and microwave. Cribs and roll-away beds are available at no extra charge at all locations. Swimming pools at all three hotels are attractive and medium-sized, featuring children's interactive splash zones and whirlpools; in addition, each property has its own fitness center. The incredibly convenient Village Marketplace food court includes Pizza Hut, Village Grill, Village Coffee House, and a 24-hour convenience store. Bahama Breeze and Golden Corral full-service restaurants are within walking distance. Other services and amenities include a Disney planning station and ticket sales, an arcade, and a Hertz car-rental desk.

Sheraton Lake Buena Vista Resort ★★★★

12205 S. Apopka–
Vineland Rd.
Orlando
☎ 407-239-0444
or 800-325-3535
sheratonlakebuena
vistaresort.com

Rate per night $163–$200. **Pool** ★★★★. **Fridge in room** Yes. **Shuttle to parks** Yes (Disney only). **Maximum number of occupants per room** 4–6. **Special comments** Dogs 80 pounds and under allowed; $19.95/night resort fee.

COMPRISING 400 GUEST ROOMS and 90 family junior suites, this resort has a sleek, modern feel. Amenities in each room include Sheraton Sweet Sleeper beds, free Wi-Fi, 42-inch HDTV, refrigerator, coffeemaker, hair dryer, safe, clock-radio, and iron and board. The family junior suites also provide bunk beds for children. Microwaves are available at an extra charge. The relaxing pool area features cabanas with food service (for a fee), and youngsters can enjoy the cascading waterfall and waterslide.

The Top of the Palms Spa offers massages, facials, manicures, and pedicures. Also on-site are two restaurants, a business center, a fitness center, an arcade, and a gift shop.

Sheraton Vistana Resort Villas   ★★★★

8800 Vistana Centre Dr.
Orlando
☎ 407-239-3100 or
866-208-0003
tinyurl.com/vistanaresort

Rate per night $127–$254. **Pools** ★★★½. **Fridge in room** Yes. **Shuttle to parks** Yes (Disney free; other parks for a fee). **Maximum number of occupants per room** 4–8. **Special comments** Though time-shares, the villas are rented nightly as well.

THE SHERATON VISTANA is deceptively large, stretching across both sides of Vistana Centre Drive. If you want a serene retreat from your days in the theme parks, this is an excellent base. The spacious villas come in one-bedroom, two-bedroom, and two-bedroom-with-lock-off models (which can be reconfigured as one studio room and a one-bedroom suite). Each villa has a full kitchen (including fridge/freezer, microwave, oven/range, dishwasher, toaster, and coffeemaker, with an option to prestock with groceries and laundry products), clothes washer and dryer, TVs in the living room and each bedroom (one with DVD player), stereo with CD player in some villas, separate dining area, and private patio or balcony in most. Grounds offer seven swimming pools (three with bars), four playgrounds, two restaurants, game rooms, fitness centers, a mini-golf course, sports equipment rental (including bikes), and courts for basketball, volleyball, tennis, and shuffleboard. A mind-boggling array of activities for kids (and adults) ranges from crafts to games and sports tournaments. Of special note: Vistana is highly secure, with locked gates bordering all guest areas, so children can have the run of the place without parents worrying about them wandering off. The one downside: noise, both above (from being on the flight path of a helicopter tour company) and below (from International Drive).

Waldorf Astoria Orlando   ★★★★½

14200 Bonnet Creek
Resort Lane, Orlando
☎ 407-597-5500
waldorfastoria
orlando.com

Rate per night $234–$424. **Pool** ★★★★. **Fridge in room** Yes. **Shuttle to parks** Yes (Disney only) **Maximum number of occupants per room** 4 plus child in crib. **Special comments** Good alternative to Disney Deluxe resorts; $30/night resort fee.

THE WALDORF ASTORIA is between I-4 and Disney's Pop Century Resort, near the Hilton Orlando at the back of the Bonnet Creek Resort property. Beautifully decorated and well manicured, the Waldorf is more elegant than any Disney resort. Service is excellent, and the staff-to-guest ratio is far lower than at Disney properties.

At just under 450 square feet, standard rooms feature either two queen beds or one king. A full-size desk allows you to get work done if it's absolutely necessary, and rooms also have flat-panel televisions, high-speed Internet, and Wi-Fi. The bathrooms are spacious and gorgeous, with cool marble floors, glass-walled showers, separate tubs, and enough counter space for a Broadway makeup artist. This space is so nice that we've debated whether we'd rather stay at Pop Century with three others or sleep in a Waldorf bathroom by ourselves.

Amenities include a fitness center, a spa, a golf course, six restaurants, and two pools (including one zero-entry pool for kids). Poolside cabanas are available for rent. Runners will enjoy the relative solitude—it's about a 1-mile round-trip to the nearest busy road. Waldorf Astoria guests have full access to the specials that Hilton Orlando Bonnet Creek (a sister property) offers on runDisney race days.

Wyndham Bonnet Creek Resort ★★★★½

Rate per night $229–$359. **Pool** ★★★★. **Fridge in room** Yes.
Shuttle to parks Yes (Disney only). **Maximum number of occupants per room** 4–12 depending on room/suite. **Special comments** A non-Disney suite hotel within Walt Disney World.

9560 Via Encinas
Lake Buena Vista
☎ 407-238-3500
or 888-743-2687
wyndhambonnet
creek.com

THIS CONDO HOTEL lies on the south side of Buena Vista Drive, about a quarter-mile east of Disney's Caribbean Beach Resort. It's part of a luxury-hotel complex on the same site that includes a 500-room Waldorf Astoria (see previous profile), a 400-room Wyndham Grand, and a 1,000-room Hilton (see page 123). The development is surrounded on three sides by Disney property and on one side by I-4.

One- and two-bedroom condos have fully equipped kitchens, washers and dryers, jetted tubs, and balconies. Activities and amenities include two outdoor swimming pools, a lazy river float stream, a children's activities program, a game room, a playground, and miniature golf. One-bedroom units are furnished with a king bed in the bedroom and a sleeper sofa in the living area; two-bedroom condos have two double beds in the second bedroom, a sleeper sofa in the living area, and an additional bath.

US 192 AREA

Clarion Suites Maingate ★★★½

Rate per night $99–$169. **Pool** ★★★. **Fridge in room** Yes.
Shuttle to parks Yes (Disney, Universal, SeaWorld). **Maximum number of occupants per room** 6 for most suites. **Special comments** Free Continental breakfast served daily for up to two guests; additional breakfast $5.99 advance, $6.99 day of.

7888 W. Irlo Bronson
Memorial Hwy.
Kissimmee
☎ 407-390-9888 or
888-390-9888
clarionsuites
kissimmee.com

THIS PROPERTY HAS 150 SPACIOUS one-room suites, each with a double sofa bed, microwave, fridge, coffeemaker, TV, hair dryer, and safe. The suites aren't lavish, but they're clean and contemporary, with muted deep-purple and beige tones. Extra bathroom counter space is especially convenient for larger families. The heated pool is large and has plenty of lounge chairs and moderate landscaping. A kiddie pool, whirlpool, and poolside bar complete the courtyard. Other amenities include an arcade and a gift shop. But Maingate's big plus is its location next door to a shopping center with about everything a family could need. There, you'll find 10 dining options, including Outback Steakhouse, Red Lobster, Subway, T.G.I. Friday's, and Chinese, Italian, and Japanese eateries; a Winn-Dixie Marketplace; a liquor store; and a tourist-information center with park passes for sale, among other services. All this is a short walk from your room.

Gaylord Palms Resort & Convention Center
★★★★½

Rate per night $257–$283. **Pool** ★★★★. **Fridge in room** Yes.
Shuttle to parks Yes (Disney only). **Maximum number of occupants per room** 4. **Special comments** Probably the closest you'll get to Disney-level extravagance out of the World. Resort fee of $20/day.

6000 W. Osceola Pkwy.
Kissimmee
☎ 407-586-2000
gaylordpalms.com

THIS UPSCALE RESORT has a colossal convention facility and caters to business clientele, but it's still a nice (if pricey) family resort. Hotel wings are defined by the three themed glass-roofed atriums they overlook: Key West's design is reminiscent of island life in the Florida Keys; Everglades is an overgrown spectacle of shabby swamp chic, complete with piped-in cricket noise and a robotic alligator; and the immense, central St. Augustine harks back to Spanish Colonial Florida. Lagoons, streams, and waterfalls cut through and connect all three, and walkways and bridges abound. A fourth wing, Emerald Bay Tower, overlooks the Emerald Plaza shopping and dining area of the St. Augustine atrium. These rooms are the nicest and the most expensive, and they're mostly used by convention-goers. Though rooms have fridges and alarm clocks with CD players (as well as other perks such as high-speed Internet access), the rooms themselves really work better as retreats for adults than for kids. However, children will enjoy wandering the themed areas and playing in the family pool (with water-squirting octopus). In-room child care is provided by Kid's Nite Out (see page 72).

Orange Lake Resort ★★★★½

8505 W. Irlo Bronson Memorial Hwy. Kissimmee
☎ 407-239-0000 or 800-877-6522
orangelake.com

Rate per night $107–$159. **Pools ★★★★. Fridge in room** Yes. **Shuttle to parks** Yes (fee varies depending on destination). **Maximum number of occupants per room** 4 (one-bedroom) up to 16 (four-bedroom). **Special comments** This is a time-share property, but if you rent directly through the resort as opposed to the sales office, you can avoid time-share sales pitches; $8/night resort fee.

YOU COULD SPEND YOUR ENTIRE VACATION never leaving this property, about 6–10 minutes from the Disney theme parks. From its 10 pools and two mini-water parks to its golfing opportunities (36 holes of championship greens plus two 9-hole executive courses), Orange Lake offers an extensive menu of amenities and recreational opportunities. If you tire of lazing by the pool, try waterskiing, wakeboarding, tubing, fishing, or other activities on the 80-acre lake. There's also a live alligator show, exercise programs, organized competitive sports and games, arts-and-crafts sessions, and miniature golf. Activities don't end when the sun goes down. Karaoke, live music, a Hawaiian luau, and movies at the resort cinema are some of the evening options.

The 2,412 units, ranging from suites and studios to three-bedroom villas, are tastefully decorated and comfortably furnished, all with fully equipped kitchens. If you'd rather not cook on vacation, seven restaurants are scattered across the resort: two cafés, three grills, one pizzeria, and a fast-food eatery. If you need help with (or a break from) the kids, babysitters are available to come to your villa, accompany your family on excursions, or take your children to attractions for you.

Radisson Resort Orlando-Celebration ★★★★

2900 Parkway Blvd. Kissimmee
☎ 407-396-7000 or 800-634-4774
radissonorlando resort.com

Rate per night $99–$155. **Pool ★★★★½. Fridge in room** Yes. **Shuttle to parks** Yes (Disney only). **Maximum number of occupants per room** 5. **Special comments** $20/day resort fee; kids age 10 and younger eat free with a paying adult at Mandolin's restaurant.

THE POOL ALONE IS WORTH A STAY HERE, but the Radisson Resort gets high marks in all areas. The free-form pool is huge, with a waterfall and waterslide surrounded by palms and flowering plants, plus a smaller heated pool, two whirlpools, and a kiddie pool. Other outdoor amenities include two lighted tennis courts, sand volleyball, a playground, and jogging areas. Kids can also blow off steam at the arcade, while adults might visit the fitness center. Rooms are elegant, featuring Italian furnishings and marble baths. They're of ample size and include a minibar (some rooms), coffeemaker, TV, iron and board, hair dryer, and safe. Dining options include Mandolin's for breakfast (buffet) and dinner and a 1950s-style diner serving burgers, sandwiches, shakes, and Pizza Hut pizza, among other fare. A sports lounge with a 6-by-11-foot TV offers nighttime entertainment. Guest services can help with tours, park passes, car rental, and babysitting. While the hotel doesn't offer children's programs per se, there are plenty of activities, such as face painting by a clown, juggling classes, bingo, and arts and crafts at the pool.

GETTING A GOOD DEAL ON A ROOM OUTSIDE WALT DISNEY WORLD

UNABLE TO COMPETE WITH Disney resorts for convenience or perks, out-of-World hotels lure patrons with bargain rates. The extent of the bargain depends on the season, day of the week, and local events. Here are tips and strategies for getting a good deal on a room outside Walt Disney World.

1. ORLANDO MAGICARD This discount program is sponsored by Visit Orlando. Cardholders are eligible for discounts of 12–50% at about 50 hotels. The Magicard is also good for discounts at some area attractions, three dinner theaters, museums, performing-arts venues, restaurants, shops, and more. Valid for up to six persons, the card isn't available for larger groups or conventions.

To obtain a free Magicard and a list of participating hotels and attractions, call ☎ 800-643-9492 or 407-363-5872. On the Web, go to **visitorlando.com/magicard;** the Magicard and accompanying brochure can be printed from your computer. If you miss getting one before you leave home, obtain one at the Convention and Visitors Bureau Information Center at 8723 International Dr. When you call for your Magicard, also request the *Official Vacation Guide.*

2. *HOTELCOUPONS.COM FLORIDA GUIDE* This book of coupons for lodging statewide is free in many restaurants and motels on main highways leading to Florida. Because most travelers make reservations before leaving home, picking up the book en route doesn't help much. To view it online or sign up for a free monthly e-guide, visit **hotelcoupons.com.** For a hard copy ($3 for handling, $5 if shipped to Canada), call ☎ 800-222-3948 Monday–Friday, 8 a.m.–5 p.m. Eastern time.

3. HOTEL SHOPPING ONLINE The secret to shopping on the Internet is . . . shopping. When we're really looking for a deal, we scour sites such as the ones on the next page for unusually juicy hotel deals that meet our criteria (location, quality, price, amenities).

OUR FAVORITE ONLINE HOTEL RESOURCES
mousesavers.com Best site for hotels in Disney World
hotelcoupons.com Self-explanatory
experiencekissimmee.com Primarily US 192–Kissimmee area hotels
visitorlando.com Good info; not user-friendly for booking
orlandovacation.com Great rates for condos and home rentals

If we find a hotel that fills the bill, we check it out at other websites and comparative travel search engines such as **Kayak** (**kayak.com**) and **Mobissimo** (**mobissimo.com**) to see who has the best rate. (As an aside, Kayak used to be purely a search engine but now sells travel products, raising the issue of whether products not sold by Kayak are equally likely to come up in a search. Mobissimo, on the other hand, only links potential buyers to provider websites.) Your initial shopping effort should take about 15–20 minutes, faster if you can zero in quickly on a particular hotel.

Next, armed with your insider knowledge of hotel economics, call the hotel or have your travel agent call. Start by asking about specials. If there are none, or if the hotel can't beat the best price you've found on the Internet, share your findings and ask if the hotel can do better. Sometimes you'll be asked for proof of the rate you've discovered online—to be prepared for this, go to the site and enter the dates of your stay, and make sure the rate you've found is available. If it is, print the page with this information and have it handy for your travel agent or for when you call the hotel.

4. IF YOU MAKE YOUR OWN RESERVATION Call and ask about specials before you inquire about corporate rates. Don't hesitate to bargain, but do it before you check in. If you're buying a weekend package, for example, and want to extend your stay, you can often obtain at least the corporate rate for the extra days.

BOB Always call the hotel in question, not the hotel chain's national 800 number.

CONDOMINIUMS AND VACATION HOMES

IN A CONDO, if something goes wrong, someone will be on hand to fix the problem. Vacation homes rented from a property-management company likewise will have someone to come to the rescue, though responsiveness tends to vary vastly from company to company. If you rent directly from an owner, correcting problems is often more difficult, particularly if the owner doesn't live in the same area as the rental home.

Because condos tend to be part of large developments (frequently time-shares), amenities such as pools, playgrounds, game arcades, and fitness centers often rival those found in the best hotels. In a vacation home, all the amenities are contained in the home (though in planned developments, there may be community amenities as well). Depending on the specific home, you might find a small pool, hot tub, two-car garage, family room, game room, and even a home theater. Features found in both condos and vacation homes include full kitchens, laundry rooms, TVs, and DVD players. Time-shares are clones when it comes to furniture and decor, but single-owner condos and vacation homes are furnished and decorated in a style that reflects the taste of the owner. Vacation homes very rarely afford interesting views (though some overlook lakes or natural areas), while condos, especially the high-rise variety, sometimes offer exceptional ones.

The Price Is Nice

The best deals in lodging in the Walt Disney World area are vacation homes and single-owner condos. Prices range from about $65 a night for two-bedroom condos and town homes to $200–$500 a night for three- to seven-bedroom vacation homes. Forgetting about taxes to keep the comparison simple, let's compare renting a vacation home to staying at one of Disney's Value resorts. A family of two parents, two teens, and two grandparents would need three hotel rooms at Disney's All-Star Resorts. At the lowest rate obtainable, that would run you $98 per night, per room, or $294 total. Rooms are 260 square feet each, so you'd have a total of 780 square feet. Each room has a private bath and TV.

Renting at the same time of year from **All Star Vacation Homes** (no relation to Disney's All-Star Resorts), you can stay at a 2,053-square-foot, four-bedroom, three-bath vacation home with a private pool 3 miles from Disney World for $304—not quite as economical as Disney's Value resorts, but plenty of value all the same: With four bedrooms, each of the teens can have his or her own room. Further, for the dates we checked, All Star Vacation Homes was running a special in which they threw in a free rental car with a one-week home rental.

Location, Location, Location

The best vacation home is one that is within easy commuting distance of the theme parks. If you plan to spend some time at SeaWorld and the Universal parks, you'll want something just to the northeast of Walt Disney World (between the World and Orlando). If you plan to spend most of your time in the World, the best selection of vacation homes is along US 192 to the south of the park.

To get the most from a vacation home, you need to be close enough to commute in 20 minutes or less to your Walt Disney World destination. This proximity will allow for naps, quiet time, swimming, and dollar-saving meals you prepare yourself. Though traffic and road conditions are as important as the distance from a vacation home to your Disney destination, we recommend a home no farther than 5 miles away in areas northeast of Disney World and no farther than 4.5 miles away in areas south of the park.

Recommended Websites

The only practical way to shop for a rental home is on the Web. The problem is that there are so many owners, rental companies, and individual homes from which to choose that you could research yourself into a stupor. The best websites provide the following:

- Ease of navigation
- The ability to browse without having to log in or divulge personal information
- Photos and in-depth descriptions of individual homes
- Overview maps or text descriptions that reflect how distant specific homes or developments are from Walt Disney World
- The ability to book the specific rental home of your choice on the site
- A prominently displayed phone number for non-Internet bookings and questions

After checking out dozens upon dozens of sites, we narrowed our recommendations to the following:

All Star Vacation Homes (allstarvacationhomes.com) is easily the best of the sites run by vacation-home management companies, with plenty of photographs and details about featured homes. Properties are within either 4 miles of Walt Disney World or 3 miles of Universal. **#1 Dream Homes (floridadreamhomes.com)** also has a good reputation for customer service.

Orlando's Finest Vacation Homes (orlandosfinest.com) represents both homeowners and management companies. It's not quite as comprehensive as sites such as All Star Vacation Homes, but friendly sales agents can help you fill in the blanks.

Vacation Rental by Owner (vrbo.com) is a nationwide vacation-homes listings service that puts prospective renters in direct contact with owners of rental homes. The site is straightforward and lists a large number of rental properties in Celebration, Disney's planned community situated about 8–10 minutes from the theme parks. Two similar listings services with good websites are **Vacation Rentals 411 (vacationrentals411.com)** and **Last Minute Villas (lastminutevillas.net)**.

Visit Orlando (visitorlando.com) is the way to go when it comes to shopping for time-shares (click "Places to Stay" on the home page), because you can bypass these developments' notoriously high-pressure sales pitches. The site also lists hotels and vacation homes.

We frequently receive letters from readers extolling the virtues of renting a condo or vacation home. This endorsement from a New Jersey family of five is typical:

I cannot stress enough how important it is that large families (more than two kids) rent a house for their stay! We stayed at Windsor Hills Resort, booked through **globalresorthomes.com**. *It took about 10 minutes to drive to the parks in the morning, and we had no traffic issues at all. We had a brand-new four-bedroom, four-bath house with our own pool—all for $215 a night! This was in October, but rates never climb above $300, even in the high season. We loved getting away from the hubbub of Disney and relaxing back at the house in "our" pool.*

HOW *to* CHILDPROOF
a HOTEL ROOM

SMALL CHILDREN UP TO 3 YEARS OLD (and sometimes older) can wreak mayhem—if not outright disaster—in a hotel room. Chances are that you're pretty experienced when it comes to spotting potential dangers, but just in case you need a refresher course, here's what to look for.

Begin by checking for hazards that you can't fix yourself: balconies, chipping paint, cracked walls, sharp surfaces, shag carpeting, and windows that can't be secured shut. If you encounter anything that you don't like or is too much of a hassle to fix, ask for another room.

If you use a crib supplied by the hotel, make sure that the mattress is firm and covers the entire bottom of the crib. The mattress cover, if there is one, should fit tightly. Slats should be 2½ inches (about the width of a soda can) or less apart. Make sure the drop sides work properly. Check for sharp edges and potentially toxic substances. Wipe down surfaces with disinfectant. Finally, position the crib away from drapery cords, heaters, wall sockets, and air conditioners.

A Monteno, Illinois, mom offers this suggestion:

> *You can request bed rails at the Disney resorts. Our 2½-year-old was too big for the pack-and-play; the bed rails worked perfectly for us.*

If your infant can turn over, we recommend changing him or her on a pad on the floor. Likewise, if you have a child seat of any sort, place it where it cannot be knocked over, and always strap your child in.

If your child can roll, crawl, or walk, you should bring about eight electrical outlet covers and some cord to tie cabinets shut and to bind drape cords and the like out of reach. Check for appliances, lamps, ice buckets, and anything else that your child might pull down on him- or herself. Have the hotel remove coffee tables with sharp edges, and both real and artificial plants that are within your child's reach. Round up items from tables and countertops such as courtesy toiletries and drinking glasses, and store them out of reach.

If the bathroom door can be accidentally locked, cover the locking mechanism with duct tape or a doorknob cover. Use the security chain or upper latch on the room's entrance door to ensure that your child doesn't open it without your knowledge.

Inspect the floor and remove pins, coins, and other foreign objects that your child might find. Don't forget to check under beds and furniture. *Tip:* Crawl around the room on your hands and knees to see possible hazards from your child's perspective.

If you rent a suite or a condo, you'll have more territory to childproof and will have to deal with things such as cleaning supplies, a stove, a refrigerator, cooking utensils, and low cabinet doors, among other things. Sometimes the best option is to seal off the kitchen with a safety gate.

PART FOUR

DINING

DINING OPTIONS ABOUND BOTH IN AND OUT of Walt Disney World, and if you're so inclined, there are a lot of ways to save big bucks while keeping your crew nourished and happy.

EATING *Outside*
WALT DISNEY WORLD

1. **A CAR HELPS** Access to restaurants outside of Walt Disney World can really cut the cost of your overall vacation, but you need to have wheels. If you eat only your evening meal outside the World, the savings will more than pay for a rental car.

2. **PLENTY OF CHOICES** Eating outside of Walt Disney World doesn't relegate you to dining in lackluster restaurants. The range of choices is quite broad and includes elegant dining options, as well as familiar chain restaurants and local family eateries.

3. **DISCOUNTS ARE EVERYWHERE** Visitor magazines and booklets containing discount coupons to dozens of out-of-the-World restaurants are available everywhere except in Disney World. The coupons are good at a broad selection of eateries, ranging from burger joints to some of the best restaurants in the area. Though coupon booklets and freebie visitor mags are pretty much everywhere, the mother lode can be found at the **Visit Orlando Official Visitor Center** at 8723 International Dr., Ste. 101, at the corner of Austrian Row, open 8:30 a.m.–6:30 p.m.; ☎ 407-363-5872. Here you'll find copies of every magazine and booklet available. The center also sells slightly discounted tickets to the theme parks. Also see **visitorlando.com.** The **Kids Eat Free Card** may be a good investment if you have young children and plan to eat off Disney property frequently. It provides free kids' meals at more than 50 restaurants in the Orlando area. To see a full listing, visit **kidseatfreecard.com.** Each $20 card is valid for one child age 11 or younger and requires that the child be accompanied by one adult paying for a full-price entrée.

You can save money at some Disney World–area restaurants by purchasing discounted gift certificates from **restaurant.com.** Most certificates are for a specific amount (usually $25) at a discounted price (usually $10). cates do not expire and can be printed at home. You can only use one cer per restaurant per month (but that means you could use one certificate at eac. restaurant during your vacation). Occasionally there are other restrictions, so be sure to read the information provided on the site carefully. Some restaurants require you to buy a certain number of entrées, for instance. Note that restaurants occasionally drop out of the program, so call the restaurant before you go to reconfirm that it is still participating. If a restaurant is no longer a participant, you can change the certificate for another restaurant by contacting the site's customer service.

BUFFETS AND MEAL DEALS OUTSIDE WALT DISNEY WORLD

BUFFETS, RESTAURANT SPECIALS, and discount dining abound in the area surrounding Walt Disney World, especially on US 192 (known locally as Irlo Bronson Memorial Highway) and along International Drive. The local visitor magazines, distributed free at non-Disney hotels, among other places, are packed with advertisements and discount coupons for seafood feasts, Chinese buffets, Indian buffets, and breakfast buffets, as well as specials for everything from lobster to barbecue. For a family trying to economize, some of the come-ons are mighty sweet. But are these places any good? Is the food fresh, tasty, and appealing? Are the restaurants clean and inviting? Armed with little more than a roll of Tums, the *Unofficial* research team tried all the eateries that advertise heavily in the free tourist magazines. Here's what we discovered.

CHINESE SUPER BUFFETS *Whoa!* Talk about an oxymoron. If you've ever tried preparing Chinese food, especially a stir-fry, you know that split-second timing is required to avoid overcooking. So it should come as no big surprise that Chinese dishes languishing on a buffet lose their freshness, texture, and flavor in a hurry.

For the past few editions of this guide, we were able to find several Chinese buffets that we felt comfortable recommending; unfortunately, we would return the next year only to discover that their quality had slipped precipitously. We then searched for new buffets to replace the ones we removed from the book, and we can tell you that wasn't fun work. At the end of the day, **Dragon Court Chinese Buffet & Sushi Bar** (12384 S. Apopka–Vineland Road, just after FL 535 turns 90 degrees to the west; ☎ 407-238-9996; **dragoncourtchinese.com**) and **Ace Plus Chinese Buffet** (8701 W. Irlo Bronson Memorial Hwy.; ☎ 407-390-7588; **acepluschinesebuffet.com**) are the only Asian buffets we've elected to list. Dragon Court is friendly and low-key, with a good selection of mainly Chinese dishes. Ace Plus is a good choice if you're staying near where US 192 intersects the FL 429 toll road. We rate both buffets at two and a half stars: Dragon Court has fewer selections than Ace Plus, but the overall quality is less hit-and-miss; Ace Plus, while not as good as Dragon Court, has so much to choose from that, if you pick your way through the minefield, you'll find enough for an enjoyable

...AWAY 12551 FL 535, Orlando; ☎ 407-827-1111; **johnnies** ...oderate–expensive. Seafood and steaks, with an emphasis on Florida

...OUS PIG* 1234 N. Orange Ave., Winter Park; ☎ 407-628-2333; **the** ra...**.com;** moderate–expensive. New American cuisine with an award-winning menu ...hanges frequently, with seasonal ingredients.

BARBECUE

BUBBALOU'S BODACIOUS BAR-B-QUE 5818 Conroy Rd., Orlando (near Universal Orlando); ☎ 407-295-1212; **bubbalous.com;** inexpensive. Tender, smoky barbecue; tomato-based Killer Sauce.

4 RIVERS SMOKEHOUSE 11764 University Blvd., Orlando; ☎ 844-474-8377; **4rsmokehouse.com;** inexpensive. Award-winning beef brisket, fried pickles, cheese grits, fried okra, and collard greens.

CHINESE

MING COURT 9188 International Dr., Orlando; ☎ 407-351-9988; **ming-court.com;** inexpensive. Dim sum, crispy roast pork, and roast duck. Beautiful setting.

CUBAN/SPANISH

COLUMBIA 649 Front St., Celebration; ☎ 407-566-1505; **columbiarestaurant .com;** moderate. Cuban/Spanish creations such as paella and the 1905 Salad.

FRENCH

LE COQ AU VIN* 4800 S. Orange Ave., Orlando; ☎ 407-851-6980; **lecoqauvin restaurant.com;** moderate–expensive. Country French cuisine in a relaxed atmosphere. Reservations suggested.

INDIAN

AMERICAN GYMKHANA 7559 W. Sand Lake Rd., Orlando; ☎ 407-985-2900; **americangymkhana.com;** moderate. Blend of Indian, Pakistani, and Middle Eastern cuisines prepared with locally sourced ingredients.

MEMORIES OF INDIA 8204 Crystal Clear Ln., Orlando; ☎ 407-370-3277; **memoriesofindiacuisine.com;** inexpensive–moderate. Classic tandoori dishes, samosas, *tikka masala,* and Sunday Champagne brunch with buffet.

ITALIAN

ANTHONY'S COAL-FIRED PIZZA 8031 Turkey Lake Rd., Orlando; ☎ 407-363-9466; **acfp.com;** inexpensive. Pizza, eggplant, pasta, beer and wine.

BICE ORLANDO RISTORANTE Loews Portofino Bay Hotel, 5601 Universal Blvd., Orlando; ☎ 407-503-1415; **orlando.bicegroup.com;** expensive. Authentic Italian; great wines.

JAPANESE/SUSHI

AMURA 7786 W. Sand Lake Rd., Orlando; ☎ 407-370-0007; **amura.com;** moderate. A favorite sushi bar for locals. The tempura is popular too.

NAGOYA SUSHI 7600 Dr. Phillips Blvd., Ste. 66, in the very rear of The Marketplace at Dr. Phillips; ☎ 407-248-8558; **nagoyasushi.com;** moderate. A small, intimate restaurant with great sushi and an extensive menu.

MEXICAN

CHEVYS FRESH MEX 12547 FL 535, Lake Buena Vista; ☎ 407-827-1052; **chevys.com;** inexpensive–moderate. Across from the FL 535 entrance to WDW.

EL PATRON 12167 S. Apopka-Vineland Rd., Orlando; ☎ 407-238-5300; **elpatron orlando.com;** inexpensive. Family-owned restaurant serving freshly prepared Mexican dishes. Full bar.

*20 minutes or more from Walt Disney World

MEXICAN *(continued)*

TAQUITOS JALISCO* 1041 S. Dillard St., Winter Garden; ☎ 407-654-0363; inexpensive. Low-key. Flautas, chicken mole, fajitas, hearty burritos, good vegetarian.

SEAFOOD

BONEFISH GRILL 7830 W. Sand Lake Rd., Orlando; ☎ 407-355-7707; **bonefish grill.com;** moderate. Casual setting along busy Restaurant Row on Sand Lake Road. Choose your fish; then choose a sauce to accompany. Also has steaks and chicken.

CELEBRATION TOWN TAVERN 721 Front St., Celebration; ☎ 407-566-2526; **thecelebrationtowntavern.com;** moderate. Popular hangout for locals, with New England–style seafood. Clam chowder is a big hit.

STEAK/PRIME RIB

BULL & BEAR Waldorf Astoria Orlando, 14200 Bonnet Creek Resort Ln., Orlando; ☎ 407-597-5500; **waldorfastoriaorlando.com/dining/bullandbear;** expensive. Classic steak house with a clubby ambience. Steaks, seafood, lamb chops, and more.

TEXAS DE BRAZIL 5259 International Dr., Orlando; ☎ 407-355-0355; **texasde brazil.com;** expensive. All-you-can-eat Brazilian-style *churrascaria.* Ribs, filet mignon, chicken, lamb, and salad bar. Kids ages 3–5 eat for $5, ages 6–12 for half price.

VITO'S CHOP HOUSE 8633 International Dr., Orlando; ☎ 407-354-2467; **vitoschophouse.com;** moderate. Upscale meat house with a taste of Tuscany.

THAI

THAI SILK 6803 S. Kirkman Rd. at International Dr., Orlando; ☎ 407-226-8997; **thaisilkorlando.com;** moderate. Acclaimed by Orlando dining critics for its authentic Thai dishes. Delicious vegetarian options; impressive wine list.

THAI THANI 11025 International Dr., Orlando; ☎ 407-239-9733; 600 Market St., Celebration, ☎ 407-239-9733; **thaithani.net;** moderate. Thai duck preparations; some Chinese stir-fry.

*20 minutes or more from Walt Disney World

meal. Finally, sushi at Chinese buffets is, almost without exception, pretty dismal—if it's sushi that lures you, go to a Japanese restaurant.

INDIAN BUFFETS Indian food works better on a buffet than Chinese food; in fact, it actually improves as the flavors marry. In the Disney World area, most Indian restaurants offer a buffet at lunch only—not too convenient if you're spending your day at the theme parks. If you're out shopping or taking a day off, these Indian buffets are worth trying:

AASHIRWAD INDIAN CUISINE 5748 International Dr., at the corner of International Drive and Kirkman Road; ☎ 407-370-9830; **aashirwadrestaurant.com**

PUNJAB INDIAN RESTAURANT 7451 International Dr.; ☎ 407-352-7887; **punjabindianrestaurant.com**

CHURRASCARIAS A number of these South American–style meat emporiums have sprung up along International Drive. Our picks are **Café Mineiro** (6432 International Dr.; ☎ 407-248-2932; **cafemineirosteak house.com**), north of Sand Lake Road, and **Bio Brazil Churrascaria** (5668 International Dr.; ☎ 407-354-0260; **biobrazil.com**). Both offer good value. More expensive are the Argentinean churrasco specialties at **The Knife** (12501 FL 535; ☎ 321-395-4892; **thekniferestaurant.com**); be sure to try the sweetbreads, an Argentine specialty rarely found in the United

States. If you prefer chain restaurants, the pricey **Texas de Brazil** and **Fogo de Chão** also have locations in Orlando.

SEAFOOD AND LOBSTER BUFFETS These affairs don't exactly fall under the category of inexpensive dining. The main draw (no pun intended) is all the lobster you can eat. The problem is that lobsters, like Chinese food, don't wear well on a steam table. After a few minutes on the buffet line, they make better tennis balls than dinner, so try to grab your lobster immediately after a fresh batch has been brought out. Two lobster buffets are on International Drive, and another is on US 192. Though all three do a reasonable job, we prefer **Boston Lobster Feast** (6071 W. Irlo Bronson Memorial Hwy.; ☎ 407-396-2606; and 8731 International Dr., five blocks north of the Convention Center; ☎ 407-248-8606; **bostonlobsterfeast.com**). Both locations are distinguished by a vast variety of seafood in addition to the lobster. The International Drive location is cavernous and noisy, which is why we prefer the Irlo Bronson location, where you can actually have a conversation over dinner. The International Drive location has ample parking, while the Irlo Bronson restaurant does not. At about $40 for early birds (4–6 p.m.) and $44 after 6 p.m., dining is expensive at both locations.

SALAD BUFFETS The most popular of these in the Walt Disney World area is **Sweet Tomatoes** (6877 S. Kirkman Rd., ☎ 407-363-1616; 12561 S. Apopka–Vineland Rd., ☎ 407-938-9461; 3236 Rolling Oaks Blvd., off US 192 near the FL 429 western entrance to Disney World, ☎ 407-966-4664; **souplantation.com**). During lunch and dinner, you can expect a line out the door, but fortunately one that moves fast. The buffet features prepared salads and an extensive array of ingredients for building your own. In addition, Sweet Tomatoes offers a variety of soups, a modest pasta bar, a baked-potato bar, an assortment of fresh fruit, and ice cream sundaes. Dinner runs $11.79 for adults, $6 for children ages 6–12, and $4 for children ages 3–5. Lunch is $9.79 for adults and the same prices as dinner for children.

BREAKFAST AND ENTRÉE BUFFETS Most chain steak houses in the area, including **Ponderosa, Sizzler,** and **Golden Corral,** offer entrée buffets. Among them, they have 15 locations in the Walt Disney World area. All serve breakfast, lunch, and dinner. At lunch and dinner, you get the buffet when you buy an entrée, usually a steak; breakfast service is a straightforward buffet (that is, you don't have to buy an entrée). As for the food, it's chain-restaurant quality but decent all the same. Prices are a bargain, and you can get in and out at lightning speed—important at breakfast when you're trying to get to the parks early. Some locations offer lunch and dinner buffets at a set price without your having to buy an entrée.

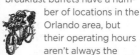

BOB Most chain-restaurant breakfast buffets have a number of locations in the Orlando area, but their operating hours aren't always the same. If you want to eat early or late, your best bet is to contact the restaurant to confirm that it will be open at your preferred time.

Though you can argue about which chain serves the best steak, **Golden Corral** wins the buffet contest hands-down, with at least twice as many offerings as its three competitors. While buffets at Golden Corral and Ponderosa are pretty consistent from location to location, the buffets at the different Sizzlers vary a good deal. Our pick of the Sizzlers is the one at 7602 W. Irlo Bronson Memorial Hwy. (☎ 407-397-0997). In addition to the steak houses, WDW-area **Shoney's** also offer breakfast, lunch, and dinner buffets. Local freebie visitor magazines are full of discount coupons for all of the previous restaurants.

A New Hampshire reader notes that some off-site breakfast buffets don't open early enough:

You mention quite a few buffets for off-site dining, but it would have been nice to know their normal morning business hours. Some buffets (like Ponderosa) didn't open until 8 a.m. for breakfast. This is way too late if you're trying to get to the park at opening time.

DISNEY BUFFETS VS. OFF-SITE BUFFETS Most off-site buffets are long on selection but don't compare favorably to Disney buffets in terms of quality; likewise, the setting and ambience of Disney buffets is generally superior. If you're trying to save money, however, non-Disney buffets offer excellent value. At a Disney buffet, you can expect well-prepared dishes across all food categories. At an off-site buffet, though some dishes may be below par, you should find enough that's palatable to put together a more-than-acceptable meal. At any buffet, we recommend starting with small samples to sort out the winners and losers, and then going back for larger portions of your favorites.

MEAL DEALS Discount coupons are available for a wide range of restaurants, including some wonderful upscale-ethnic places such as **Ming Court** (Chinese; 9188 International Dr., Orlando; ☎ 407-351-9988; **ming-court.com**).

A meat eater's delight is the Feast for Four at **Sonny's Real Pit Bar-B-Q.** For $44 per family of four, you get sliced pork and beef plus chicken, ribs, your choice of three sides (choose from beans, slaw, fries, among others), garlic bread or corn bread, and soft drinks or tea, all served family-style. The closest Sonny's location to Walt Disney World and Universal is at 7423 S. Orange Blossom Trail in Orlando (☎ 407-859-7197; **sonnysbbq.com**.) No coupons are available (or needed) for Sonny's, but they're available for the other "meateries."

COUPONS Find discounts and two-for-one coupons for many of the restaurants mentioned in freebie visitor guides available at most hotels outside Walt Disney World. The **Visit Orlando Official Visitors Center** (8723 International Dr.; ☎ 407-363-5872; open daily, 8:30 a.m.–6:30 p.m., except December 25) offers a treasure trove of coupons and free visitor magazines. In Kissimmee, visit the **Osceola County Welcome Center and History Museum** (4155 W. Vine St.; ☎ 407-396-8644; **osceolahistory.org**). In addition to visitor information and restaurant coupons, the center also houses an excellent free museum tracing the colorful history of Central Florida. On the Internet, check out **coupons alacarte.com** and **orlandocoupons.com** for printable coupons.

THE GREAT ORLANDO PIZZA SCAM　Plenty of reputable local pizza joints deliver to hotels in and around the theme parks; many Disney and Universal resorts offer pizza delivery as well. But for a few years now, con artists have been distributing fliers advertising delivery to hotel guests—they ask for your credit card number over the phone, but the pizza never arrives. Disregard any such fliers you find.

DINING *in* WALT DISNEY WORLD

OVER THE YEARS, Disney's food-and-beverage department has not only vastly expanded but has succeeded in upgrading the full-service restaurants around the World. Now there are 9 or 10 first-class restaurants and perhaps an equal number of B+ establishments. The wine lists have been seriously improved and expanded.

Of course, if the average parents roaming Walt Disney World were primarily concerned with pleasing their palates, the hottest dinner ticket in the parks wouldn't be the *Hoop-Dee-Doo Musical Revue*. In fact, if you want to know what Disney World visitors really like, look at the numbers: Every year, they consume 1.2 million pounds of turkey legs, 7 million hamburgers, 5 million hot dogs, 50 million sodas, and 5.3 million bags of popcorn.

LILIANE　One thing parents should be aware of is that both full- and counter-service restaurants at Walt Disney World serve very substantial portions. You can easily put aside parts of dinners for lunches the next day (if you have a fridge in your room), split an entrée, or load up at lunch and go light on dinner.

So for many families, food is a secondary consideration, but if you do care about dining out on your vacation or you'd like to experiment with different cuisines, *The Unofficial Guide to Walt Disney World*, also known as the Big Book, includes detailed reviews of the sit-down establishments in the World.

"WAITER, THESE PRICES ARE GIVING ME HEARTBURN!"

INCREASES IN DISNEY'S TICKET COSTS are always sure to grab headlines, but most people don't notice that Disney's restaurant prices rise about as fast. For example, while the cost of a one-day theme park ticket has increased about 33% since 2010, the average entrée price at Le Cellier has gone from around $30 to just under $42—an increase of 39%. In prior years, Disney has levied a dining surcharge during the summer and other busy times of year. Factoring in the surcharge, an adult breakfast at The Crystal Palace has increased almost 45% during the same time.

You might need a stiff drink after seeing those menu prices, but alcohol is no bargain either. While the average bottle of wine in WDW costs three times as much as retail, some wines have much higher markups. For example, a $9 bottle of Placido Pinot Grigio costs $39 in Epcot and various Disney resort lounges—more than four times as much as

ADVANCE RESERVATIONS: The Official Line

YOU CAN RESERVE THE FOLLOWING up to 180 days in advance:

AFTERNOON TEA AND CHILDREN'S PROGRAMS at the Grand Floridian Resort & Spa

ALL DISNEY TABLE-SERVICE RESTAURANTS and character-dining venues

FANTASMIC! DINING PACKAGE at Disney's Hollywood Studios

HOOP-DEE-DOO MUSICAL REVUE at Fort Wilderness Resort & Campground

MICKEY'S BACKYARD BBQ at Fort Wilderness Resort & Campground

SPIRIT OF ALOHA DINNER SHOW at the Polynesian Village Resort

Guests staying at Walt Disney World resorts—these do not include the Swan, the Dolphin, Shades of Green, or the hotels of the Downtown Disney Resort Area—can book their dining 180 days before their arrival date and can book dining reservations for their entire length of stay (up to 10 days).

the retail price. If you rent a car and eat dinner each day at non-Disney restaurants, you'll save enough to more than pay for the rental cost.

This comment from a New Orleans mom spells it out:

> *Disney keeps pushing prices up and up. For us, the sky is NOT the limit. We won't be back.*

ADVANCE RESERVATIONS: WHAT'S IN A NAME?

THOUGH THEY'RE CALLED ADVANCE RESERVATIONS, most reservations at Disney World don't guarantee you a table at a specific time, as they would at your typical hometown restaurant. The Disney rep usually explains that you'll be seated ahead of walk-ins—that is, those who do not have Advance Reservations.

BOB Disney charges a $10-to-$25-per-person penalty for missing an Advance Reservation, or if you cancel on the day of the meal.

GETTING ADVANCE RESERVATIONS AT POPULAR RESTAURANTS

BREAKFAST AND DINNER at the Magic Kingdom's **Be Our Guest** restaurant and the 8 a.m. breakfast slots at **Cinderella's Royal Table** are the hardest-to-get reservations in Walt Disney World. Why? Be Our Guest has the best food in the park, awesome atmosphere, and good word of mouth; Cinderella's Royal Table is Disney's tiniest character restaurant, accommodating only about 130 diners at a time. You'll have to put in some effort to secure an Advance Reservation at these places.

The easiest and fastest way to get a reservation is go to **disney world.disney.go.com/dining** starting at 6 a.m. Eastern time, a full hour before phone reservations open. To familiarize yourself with how the site works, try it out a couple of days before you actually need to make reservations. You'll also save time by setting up an account online before your 180-day booking window, making sure to enter any credit card information needed to guarantee your reservations. If

ADVANCE RESERVATIONS: The *Unofficial* Scoop

BECAUSE DISNEY CHARGES a $10-to-$25-per-person no-show penalty at its restaurants, no-show rates are close to zero. The penalty ensures that serious diners have some chance to get into Disney's better restaurants.

These days you'll need to reserve only a few breakfast venues in advance most times of the year. The most popular of these are **Be Our Guest** and **Cinderella's Royal Table** at the Magic Kingdom. If you don't care what time you eat, you'll need to call about 10 weeks out to get in for breakfast. If you're visiting during a holiday or peak season, or you want a specific time such as 8 a.m., you'll need to call a full 180 days in advance. If these are unavailable, we recommend **'Ohana** at the Polynesian Village Resort, which can be booked as little as a week before your trip.

Likewise, only a handful of restaurants require lunch reservations. The most popular are **Be Our Guest,** which fills up six months in advance, Epcot's **Le Cellier Steakhouse,** in the Canada Pavilion, which fills up about three months in advance; Cinderella's Royal Table, which fills up during about the same time frame; and **Akershus Royal Banquet Hall** in the Norway Pavilion, which fills up about 7–10 weeks out.

Except for **Be Our Guest Restaurant**, for which reservations are snapped up as soon as they're available, dinner reservations are generally easy to get within 60 days at most locations, as long as you're not particular about the time you eat. (If that's critical to your family's happiness, click or call 180 days in advance.)

you live in California and have to get up at 3 a.m. Pacific time to make a reservation, Disney couldn't care less.

Disney's website is usually within a few seconds of the official time as determined by the US Naval Observatory or the National Institute of Standards and Technology, accessible online at **time.gov.** Using this site, synchronize your computer to the second the night before your 180-day window opens.

Early on the morning you want to make reservations, take a few moments to type the date of your visit into a word processor in MM/DD/YYYY format (for example, 11/16/2016 for November 16, 2016). Select the date and copy it to your computer's clipboard by pressing the **Ctrl** and **C** keys simultaneously (**Command-C** on Mac) or right-clicking your mouse and selecting "Copy." This will save you from having to type in the date when the site comes online.

Next, start trying Disney's website about 3 minutes before 6 a.m. You'll see a text box where you can specify the date of your visit. Click the text box and press **Ctrl-A,** then **Ctrl-V** (substitute **Command** for **Ctrl** on Mac) to paste the date; then press the tab key on your keyboard. (You can also click on the blue calendar icon to flip through a month-by-month calendar, or you can select the entire date in the text box, right-click your mouse, and select "Paste," but these are slower.) You'll also see a place to specify the time of your meal and your party size; you can fill these in ahead of time too.

Above the "Party Size" widget is a text box with the words "Search within Dining." Start typing your restaurant name in that text box. As soon as you start typing, the website will start guessing which restaurant you want and offer a list of suggestions. It's faster if you just type a few letters—*bog* or *cin* are enough for the site to know you mean Be Our Guest and Cinderella's Royal Table, respectively. Click on the desired restaurant in the list of suggestions. Finally, click "Find a Table" or hit the Enter key on your keyboard—both submit your request.

If your date isn't yet available, a message will appear saying "There is a problem searching for reservations at this time" or something similar. If this happens, refresh the browser page and start over. If you don't see an error message, however, the results returned will tell you whether your restaurant has a table available.

Note that while you're typing, other guests are trying to make Advance Reservations too, so you want the transaction to go down as quickly as possible. Flexibility on your part counts—it's much harder to get a seating for a large group, so give some thought to breaking your group into numbers that can be accommodated at tables for four. Also make sure that you have your credit card out where you can read it.

BOB For Advance Reservations, be sure you bring your confirmation number to the restaurant.

All Advance Reservations for Cinderella's Royal Table character meals, the *Fantasmic!* Dining Package, the *Hoop-Dee-Doo Musical Revue*, the *Spirit of Aloha Dinner Show*, and *Mickey's Backyard BBQ* require complete prepayment with a credit card at the time of the booking. The name on the booking can't be changed after the Advance Reservation is made. Reservations may be canceled, with the deposit refunded in full, by calling ☎ 407-WDW-DINE at least 24 hours (Cindy's) or 48 hours (*Fantasmic!* and the dinner shows) before seating time.

While many readers have been successful using our strategies, some have not:

> *I got up extra-early 180 days before our trip to get Thanksgiving reservations at Le Cellier for my husband's birthday. Even though I logged on to Disney's website right at 6 a.m., by the time I got done typing and clicking, the only table that was available was for 8:40 p.m.—too late for our children, and we would have missed IllumiNations.*

On most days, a couple hundred users slam Disney's computer system within milliseconds of one another. With this volume, a 20th of a second or less can make the difference between getting a table and not getting one. As it happens, there are variables beyond your control. One is the number of computers through which your request passes before it reaches Disney's reservation system. The explanation—covered in excruciating detail in the Big Book—is rather technical, but the same principle applies whether you're trying to get dining reservations online with Disney or concert seats through Ticketmaster.

If you don't have access to a computer at 6 a.m. on the morning you need to make reservations, Disney's phone agents begin taking calls at 7 a.m. Eastern time. Call ☎ 407-WDW-DINE and follow the prompts to speak to a live person. You may still get placed on hold, and you'll be an hour behind the early birds with computers. Still, you'll be well ahead of those who couldn't make it up before sunrise.

Also, if you're on the Disney Dining Plan and you want to book the *Fantasmic!* package, Cinderella's Royal Table, or one of the dinner shows, you may be better off reserving by phone. The online system may not recognize your table-service credits, but you can book and pay with a credit card and then call ☎ 407-WDW-DINE after 7 a.m. and have them credit the charge for the meal back to your card (a potential hassle if you get an uncooperative cast member). When you get to Walt Disney World, you'll use credits from your dining plan to "pay" for the meal. (Sometimes the online system has glitches and shows no availability; in this case, call after 7 a.m. to confirm if the online system is correct.)

Last-Ditch Efforts

Because a fee is charged for failing to cancel an Advance Reservation in time (see below), you can often score a last-minute reservation. As long as the reservation-holder calls to cancel before midnight the day before, he or she won't be charged, so your best shot at picking up a canceled reservation is to repeatedly call ☎ 407-WDW-DINE or ping **disneyworld .disney.go.com/dining** as often as possible between 10 and 11 p.m.

If you *still* can't get an Advance Reservation, go to the restaurant on the day you wish to dine and try for a table as a walk-in (most full-service restaurants take walk-ins between 2:30 and 4:30 p.m.). This is a long shot, though it's possible during the least busy times of year. There's also a fair shot at success on cold or rainy days during busier seasons, when there's a good chance of no-shows. If you try to walk in then, your chances are best during the last hour of serving.

Landing an Advance Reservation for Cinderella's Royal Table at dinner is somewhat easier than for breakfast or lunch, but the price is a whopping $73 for adults and $43 for children ages 3–9. If you're unable to lock up a table for breakfast or lunch, a dinner reservation will at least get your children inside the castle.

Canceling an Advance Reservation

Disney charges a per-person penalty if you fail to show up for an Advance Reservation the day of the meal. A $10 no-show fee is enforced at all Disney sit-down restaurants; at **Victoria & Albert's,** it's $25 for the main dining room, $50 for Queen Victoria's Room and Chef's Table (the latter two also require 48 hours' notice to cancel an Advance Reservation).

DRESS

DRESS IS INFORMAL at most theme park restaurants, but Disney has a business casual dress code for some of its resort restaurants: khakis, dress slacks, jeans, or dress shorts with a collared shirt for men and capris, skirts, dresses, jeans, and dress shorts for women. Restaurants with this dress code are **Jiko—The Cooking Place** at Animal Kingdom Lodge & Villas, the **Flying Fish Cafe** at the BoardWalk, the **California Grill** at the Contemporary Resort, **Monsieur Paul** at Epcot's France Pavilion, **Cítricos** and **Narcoossee's** at the Grand Floridian Resort & Spa, **Artist Point** at Wilderness Lodge & Villas, **Yachtsman Steakhouse** at the Yacht Club Resort, **Todd English's bluezoo** and **Shula's Steak House** at the Dolphin, and **Il Mulino New York Trattoria** at the Swan. **Victoria & Albert's** at the Grand Floridian is the only Disney restaurant that requires men to wear a jacket to dinner.

Also, be aware that smoking is banned at all restaurants and lounges on Walt Disney World property. Diners who puff must feed their nicotine fix outdoors—and in the theme parks, that might also mean going to a designated smoking area.

FOOD ALLERGIES AND SPECIAL REQUESTS

IF YOU HAVE FOOD ALLERGIES or observe some specific type of diet (such as eating kosher), make your needs known when you make your Advance Reservations. For more information, e-mail **specialdiets @disneyworld.com** or visit **tinyurl.com/wdwspecialdiets.**

A Phillipsburg, New Jersey, mom reports her family's experience:

My 6-year-old has many food allergies. When making my Advance Reservations, I indicated these to the clerk. When we arrived at the restaurants, the staff was already aware of my child's allergies and assigned our table a chef who double-checked the list of allergies with us. The chefs were very nice and made my son feel very special.

A Charlotte, North Carolina, mom offers this handy tip:

*A website called **AllergyEats** (**allergyeats.com/disney**) is a lifesaver. Put in your allergies and your park, and it shows you what you can eat.*

To request kosher meals at table-service restaurants, call ☎ 407-WDW-DINE (939-3463) 24 hours in advance. All Disney menus have vegetarian options; vegans may have to talk to the chef.

A FEW CAVEATS

BEFORE YOU BEGIN EATING your way through the World, you need to know:

1. Theme park restaurants rush their customers to make room for the next group of diners. Dining at high speed may appeal to a family with young, restless children, but for people wanting to relax, it's more like eating in a pressure chamber than fine dining.

2. Disney restaurants have comparatively few tables for parties of two, and servers are generally disinclined to seat two guests at larger tables. If you're a duo, you might have to wait longer—sometimes much longer—to be seated.

3. At full-service Disney restaurants, an automatic gratuity of 18% is added to your tab—even at buffets where you get your own food.

4. If you're dining in a theme park and cost is an issue, make lunch your main meal. Entrées are similar to those on the dinner menu, but prices are significantly lower.

WALT DISNEY WORLD RESTAURANT CATEGORIES

IN GENERAL, FOOD AND BEVERAGE offerings at Walt Disney World are defined by service, price, and convenience.

FULL-SERVICE RESTAURANTS Full-service restaurants are in all Disney resorts (except the All-Star Resorts, Art of Animation, Port Orleans French Quarter, and Pop Century), all major theme parks, and Disney Springs. Disney operates most of the restaurants in the theme parks and its hotels, while contractors or franchisees operate the restaurants in hotels of the Downtown Disney Resort Area (DDRA); the Swan and Dolphin resorts; and some in Disney's Animal Kingdom, Epcot, the BoardWalk, and Disney Springs. Advance Reservations (see page 141) are recommended for most full-service restaurants except those in the DDRA. The restaurants accept American Express, Diners Club, Discover Card, Disney gift cards, Disney Dream Reward Dollars, Disney Visa Instant Credit, Japan Credit Bureau, MasterCard, and Visa.

BUFFETS AND FAMILY-STYLE RESTAURANTS Many of these have Disney characters in attendance, and most have a separate children's menu featuring dishes such as hot dogs, burgers, chicken nuggets, pizza, macaroni and cheese, and spaghetti and meatballs. In addition to the buffets, several restaurants serve a family-style, all-you-can-eat, fixed-price meal.

Advance Reservations are required for character buffets and recommended for all other buffets and family-style restaurants. Most major credit cards are accepted.

If you want to eat a lot but don't feel like standing in yet another line, then consider one of the all-you-can-eat family-style restaurants. These feature platters of food brought to your table in courses by a server. You can eat as much as you like—even go back to a favorite appetizer after you finish the main course. The food tends to be a little better than what you'll find on a buffet line.

The table on page 147 lists buffets and family-style restaurants (where you can belly up for bulk loading) at Walt Disney World.

FOOD COURTS Featuring a collection of counter-service eateries under one roof, food courts can be found at the Moderate resorts (Coronado Springs, Caribbean Beach, Port Orleans) and Value resorts (All-Star, Art of Animation, and Pop Century). (The closest thing to a food court at the theme parks is **Sunshine Seasons** at Epcot; see page 163.) Advance Reservations are neither required nor available at these restaurants.

COUNTER SERVICE Counter-service fast food is available in all theme parks, at Disney Springs, and at the BoardWalk. The food compares in quality with Captain D's, McDonald's, or Taco Bell but is more expensive, though often served in larger portions.

FAST CASUAL Somewhere between burgers and formal dining are the establishments in Disney's "fast casual" category, including four in the theme parks: **Be Our Guest** (lunch service) and **Tomorrowland Terrace** in the Magic Kingdom, **Sunshine Seasons** in Epcot, and **Studio Catering Co.** in Disney's Hollywood Studios. Fast-casual restaurants feature menu choices a cut above what you'd normally see at a typical counter-service location. At Sunshine Seasons, for example, chefs will prepare grilled salmon on an open cooking surface while you watch, or you can choose from rotisserie chicken or pork, tasty noodle bowls, or large

WALT DISNEY WORLD BUFFETS and FAMILY-STYLE RESTAURANTS

RESTAURANT	LOCATION	CUISINE	MEALS SERVED	CHARACTERS
Akershus Royal Banquet Hall	Epcot	American (B), Norwegian (L, D)	B, L, D	Yes
Biergarten	Epcot	German	L, D	No
Boma—Flavors of Africa	Animal Kingdom Lodge	African (D), American (B)	B, D	No
Cape May Cafe	Beach Club Resort	American	B, D	Yes (B)
Captain's Grille	Yacht Club Resort	American	B*, L, D	No
Chef Mickey's	Contemporary Resort	American	B, Br, D	Yes
Cinderella's Royal Table	The Magic Kingdom	American	B*, L, D	Yes
The Crystal Palace	The Magic Kingdom	American	B, L, D	Yes
The Garden Grill	Epcot	American	D	Yes
Garden Grove	Swan	American	B*, L*, D	Yes (B**)
Hollywood & Vine	Disney's Hollywood Studios	American	B, L, D	Yes (B, L)
Hoop-Dee-Doo Musical Revue	Fort Wilderness	American	D	No
Liberty Tree Tavern	The Magic Kingdom	American	L, D*	No
Mickey's Backyard BBQ	Fort Wilderness	American	D	Yes
1900 Park Fare	Grand Floridian	American	B, D	Yes
'Ohana	Polynesian Village Resort	Polynesian	B, D	Yes (B)
Spirit of Aloha Dinner Show	Polynesian Village Resort	American	D	No
Trail's End Restaurant	Fort Wilderness	American	B***, L, D***	No
Tusker House Restaurant	Disney's Animal Kingdom	African (L, D), American (B)	B, L, D	Yes
Whispering Canyon Cafe	Wilderness Lodge	American	B, L, D	No

* Serves family-style meals only at the meal(s) indicated.
** Character-breakfast buffet served only on weekends.
*** Serves buffet-style meals only at the meal(s) indicated.

sandwiches made with artisanal breads. Entrées cost about $2 more on average than traditional counter service, but the variety and food quality more than make up for the difference.

VENDOR FOOD Vendors abound at the theme parks, Disney Springs, and the BoardWalk. The offerings include popcorn, ice cream bars, churros (Mexican pastries), soft drinks, bottled water, and (in theme parks) fresh fruit. Prices include tax; many vendors are set up to accept credit cards, charges to your room at a Disney resort, and the Disney Dining Plan. Others take only cash (look for a sign near the cash register).

HARD CHOICES

DINING DECISIONS WILL DEFINITELY affect your Walt Disney World experience. If you're short on time and you want to see the theme parks, avoid full service. Ditto if you're short on funds. If you do want full service, arrange Advance Reservations—again, they won't actually reserve you a table, but they can minimize your wait.

Integrating Meals into *The Unofficial Guide* Touring Plans

Arrive before the park of your choice opens. Tour expeditiously, using your chosen plan (taking as few breaks as possible), until about 11 or 11:30 a.m. Once the park becomes crowded around midday, meals and other breaks won't affect the plan's efficiency. If you intend to stay in the park for evening parades, fireworks, or other events, eat dinner early enough to be finished in time for the festivities.

Character Dining

A number of restaurants, primarily those that serve all-you-can-eat buffets and family-style meals, offer character dining. At character meals, you pay a fixed price and dine in the presence of one to five Disney characters who circulate throughout the restaurant, hugging children (and sometimes adults), posing for photos, and signing autographs. Character breakfasts, lunches, and dinners are served at restaurants in and out of the theme parks. See page 249 for more information about character meals.

FAST FOOD IN THE THEME PARKS

BECAUSE MOST MEALS DURING a Disney World vacation are consumed on the run while touring, we'll tackle counter-service and vendor foods first. Plentiful in all theme parks are hot dogs, hamburgers, chicken sandwiches, salads, and pizza. They're augmented by special items that relate to the park's theme or the part of the park you're touring. In Epcot's Germany, for example, counter-service bratwurst and beer are sold. In Frontierland in the Magic Kingdom, vendors sell smoked turkey legs. Counter-service prices are fairly consistent from park to park.

LILIANE Look for the **Mickey Check** icon on healthy menu items such as fresh fruit and low-fat milk.

Getting your act together in regard to counter-service restaurants in the parks is more a matter of courtesy than necessity. Rude guests rank fifth among reader complaints. A mother from Fort Wayne, Indiana, points out that indecision can be as maddening as outright discourtesy, especially when you're hungry:

> *Every fast-food restaurant has menu signs the size of billboards, but do you think anybody reads them? People still don't have a clue what they want when they finally get to the counter. If by some miracle they've managed to choose between the hot dog and the hamburger, they then fiddle around another 10 minutes deciding what size Coke to order. Folks, PULEEEZ get your orders together ahead of time!*

A North Carolina reader on counter-service food lines:

Many counter-service registers serve two queues each, one to the left and one to the right of each register. People are not used to this and will instinctively line up in one queue per register, typically on the right side, leaving the left vacant. We had register operators wave us up to the front several times to start a left queue instead of waiting behind others on the right.

Healthful Food at Walt Disney World

One of the most commendable developments in food service at Disney World has been the introduction of healthier foods and snacks. Health-conscious choices are available at most fast-food counters and even vendors. All the major theme parks have fruit stands, for example.

Cutting Your Dining Time at the Theme Parks

Even if you confine your meals to vendor and counter-service fast food, you lose a lot of time getting food in the theme parks. Here are some ways to minimize the time you spend hunting and gathering:

1. Eat breakfast before you arrive. Restaurants outside the World offer some outstanding breakfast specials. Plus, some hotels furnish small refrigerators in their guest rooms, or you can rent a fridge or bring a cooler. If you can get by on cold cereal, rolls, fruit, and juice, this will save a ton of time.

2. After a good breakfast, buy snacks from vendors in the parks as you tour, or stuff some snacks in a fanny pack.

3. All theme park restaurants are busiest between 11:30 a.m. and 2:15 p.m. for lunch and 6 and 9 p.m. for dinner. For shorter lines and faster service, don't eat during these hours, especially 12:30–1:30 p.m.

THE COST OF COUNTER-SERVICE FOOD

BAGEL OR MUFFIN	$2.79-$2.99
BROWNIE	$2.99-$3.99
BURRITO	$7.09-$7.59
CAKE OR PIE	$3.59-$5.19
CEREAL WITH MILK	$3.19-$3.69
CHEESEBURGER WITH FRIES	$8.79-$11.49
CHICKEN BREAST SANDWICH	$9.19-$9.99
CHICKEN NUGGETS WITH FRIES	$7.59-$9.29
CHILDREN'S MEAL (various)	$5.49-$5.99
CHIPS	$2.79-$3.25
COOKIE	$2.50-$3.99
FRIED-FISH BASKET WITH FRIES	$7.99-$9.49
FRIES	$2.99
FRUIT (whole)	$1.69-$3.59
FRUIT CUP / FRUIT SALAD	$3.79-$3.99
HOT DOG	$5.75-$10.29
ICE CREAM / FROZEN NOVELTIES	$3.99-$4.99
NACHOS WITH CHEESE	$3.99-$7.69
PB&J SANDWICH	$5.49 (kids' meal)
PIZZA (personal)	$9.19-$10.69
POPCORN	$3.50-$5.50
PRETZEL	$2.95-$4.79
SALAD (entrée)	$7.99-$11.69
SALAD (side)	$3.29
SMOKED TURKEY LEG	$10.50-$13.29
SOUP / CHILI	$3.29-$7.99
SUB / DELI SANDWICH	$7.50-$10.49
TACO SALAD	$8.19
VEGGIE BURGER	$8.59-$9.99

4. Many counter-service restaurants sell cold sandwiches. Buy a cold lunch minus drinks before 11:30 a.m., and carry it in small plastic bags until you're ready to eat (within an hour or so of purchase). Ditto for dinner. Buy drinks at the appropriate time from any convenient vendor.

5. Most fast-food eateries have more than one service window. Regardless of the time of day, check the lines at all windows before queuing. Sometimes a window that's staffed but out of the way will have a much shorter line or none at all. Note, however, that some windows may offer only certain items.

6. If you're short on time and the park closes early, stay until closing and eat dinner outside Disney World before returning to your hotel. If the park stays open late, eat dinner about 4 or 4:30 p.m. at the restaurant of your choice. You should sneak in just ahead of the dinner crowd.

THE COST OF COUNTER-SERVICE DRINKS

DRINKS	SMALL	LARGE
BEER	$5.75-$7.00	$7.50-$12.50
BOTTLED WATER	$2.50-$4.00	$2.50-$4.00
LATTE *(one size)*	$3.99	$3.99-$5.19
COFFEE *(one size)*	$2.29	$2.29
FLOAT, MILK SHAKE, OR SUNDAE *(one size)*	$4.49-$5.39	$4.49-$5.39
FRUIT JUICE	$2.59-$2.99	$3.29-$3.79
HOT TEA AND COCOA *(one size)*	$2.09-$2.29	$2.09-$2.29
MILK	$1.79	$2.39-$2.59
SOFT DRINKS, ICED TEA, AND LEMONADE	$2.59-$2.99	$3.29

Refillable souvenir mugs cost $17.56 including tax (free refills) at Disney resorts and $11 at water parks. Each person on a Disney Dining Plan gets a free mug, refillable only at his/her Disney resort. There is also a short wait between refills. A screen on the soda fountain shows the exact amount of time until guests can fill up their mug again.

Tips for Saving Money on Food

Every time you buy a soda at the theme parks, it's going to set you back about $3, and everything else from hot dogs to salad is comparably high. You can say, "Oh, well, we're on vacation," and pay the exorbitant prices, or you can plan ahead and save big bucks.

For comparison purposes, let's say that a family of two adults and two teens arrives at Disney World on Sunday afternoon and departs for home the following Saturday after breakfast. During that period the family eats six breakfasts, five lunches, and six dinners. What those meals cost depends on where and what they eat. They could rent a condo and prepare all of their own meals, but they didn't travel all the way to Disney World to cook. So let's be realistic and assume that they'll eat their evening meals out—which is what most families do, because, among other reasons, they're too tired to think about cooking.

That leaves breakfast and lunch to contend with. Here are just a few sensible options for our hypothetical family. Needless to say, there are dozens of other combinations.

1. Eat breakfast in their room out of their cooler or fridge and prepare sandwiches and snacks to take to the theme parks in their hip packs. Carry water bottles or rely on drinking fountains for water. Cost: $130 for family of four for six days (does not include dinners or food purchased on travel days).

2. Eat breakfast in their room out of their cooler or fridge, carry snacks in their hip packs, and buy lunch at Disney counter-service restaurants. Cost: $350 for family of four for six days (does not include dinners or food purchased on travel days).

3. Eat breakfast at their hotel restaurant, buy snacks from vendors, and eat lunch at Disney counter-service restaurants. Cost: $700 for family of four for six days (does not include dinners or food purchased on travel days).

In case you're wondering, these are the foods on which we've based our grocery costs for those options where breakfast, lunch, and/ or snacks are prepared from the cooler:

BREAKFAST Cold cereal (choice of two), breakfast pastries, bananas, orange juice, milk, and coffee.

LUNCH Cold cuts or peanut butter and jelly sandwiches, condiments (mayo, mustard, and such), boxed juice, and apples.

SNACKS Packaged cheese or peanut butter crackers, boxed juice, and trail mix (combination of chocolate candies, nuts, raisins, and so on).

Projected costs for snacks purchased at the theme parks are based on drinks (coffee or sodas) twice a day and popcorn once each day. Counter-service-meal costs assume basic fare (hot dogs, burgers, fries, and a drink). Hotel breakfast expenses assume eggs, bacon, and toast or pancakes with bacon and juice, milk, or coffee.

If you opt to buy groceries, you can stock up on food for your cooler at the Publix at the intersection of Silver Lake Park Drive and FL 535. There's also a Winn-Dixie on Apopka–Vineland Road, about a mile north of Crossroads Shopping Center. The Winn-Dixie at US 192 on the west side of I-4 is the closest and largest grocery for visitors staying near the Sherberth Road or World Drive entrances to Disney World. The Super Target on Rolling Oaks Boulevard is the closest to the Western Way entrance.

DISNEY DINING SUGGESTIONS

FOLLOWING ARE SUGGESTIONS for dining at each of the major theme parks. If you want to try a theme-park full-service restaurant, be aware that the restaurants continue to serve after the park's official closing time. We once showed up at the Hollywood Brown Derby just as Disney's Hollywood Studios closed at 8 p.m. We were seated almost immediately and enjoyed a leisurely dinner while the crowds cleared out. Don't worry if you are depending on Disney transportation: Buses, boats, and monorails run 1–2 hours after the parks close.

The Magic Kingdom

Of the park's six full-service restaurants, **Be Our Guest** (dinner) in Fantasyland is the best, followed by **Liberty Tree Tavern** in Liberty Square and **The Plaza Restaurant** on Main Street. **Cinderella's Royal Table** in the castle and **The Crystal Palace** on Main Street serve decent-but-expensive character buffets. Avoid **Tony's Town Square Restaurant** on Main Street.

KIERAN I am way too young to drink, but if your mum likes a glass of wine with her food, then dinner at Be Our Guest is perfect. It's the only restaurant in the Magic Kingdom that serves alcohol.

AUTHORS' FAVORITE COUNTER-SERVICE RESTAURANTS

- Be Our Guest (breakfast and lunch)   *Fantasyland*
- Columbia Harbour House   *Liberty Square*

These two restaurants offer the most variety within the Magic Kingdom. Be Our Guest serves a tasty tuna niçoise salad (with seared tuna), a grilled-ham-and-cheese sandwich that's better than you'd expect, and a juicy braised-pork entrée. Columbia Harbour House's offerings include lobster rolls, grilled salmon, and a delicious hummus sandwich on multigrain bread. Otherwise, the Magic Kingdom's fast-food eateries are undistinguished. They're also about twice as expensive as McDonald's, for about the same quality. On the positive side, portions are large, sometimes large enough for children to share.

Epcot

Since the beginning, dining has been an integral component of Epcot's entertainment product. World Showcase has many more restaurants than attractions, and Epcot has added bars, tapas-style eateries, and full-service restaurants faster than any park in memory.

For the most part, Epcot's restaurants have always served decent food, though the World Showcase restaurants have occasionally been timid about delivering honest representations of their host nations' cuisine. That seems to be changing faster in some areas (Mexico) than others (Morocco), but we're hopeful that we see a trend. It's still true that the less adventuresome diner can find steak and potatoes on virtually every menu, but the same kitchens will serve up the real thing for anyone willing to ask.

Many Epcot restaurants are overpriced, most conspicuously **Monsieur Paul** (France) and **Coral Reef Restaurant** (The Seas). Representing decent value with their combination of attractive ambience and well-prepared food are **Via Napoli** (Italy), **Biergarten** (Germany), and **La Hacienda de San Angel** (Mexico). Biergarten (along with **Restaurant Marrakesh** in Morocco) also features live entertainment.

AUTHORS' FAVORITE COUNTER-SERVICE RESTAURANTS

- Les Halles Boulangerie–Patisserie *France*
- Sommerfest *Germany*
- Sunshine Seasons *The Land*
- Tangierine Café *Morocco*

Les Halles Boulangerie–Patisserie sells pastries, sandwiches, and quiches. The pastries are made on-site, and the sandwiches are as close to actual French street food—in taste, size, and price—as you'll get anywhere in Epcot. (We had one of those *Ratatouille* flashback scenes while eating one, only ours was in the Marais.) Another favorite is the chicken-and-lamb shawarma platter at Morocco's **Tangierine Café**. Besides juicy lamb, it comes with some of the best tabbouleh we've tasted in Florida.

In addition to these, we recommend the following ethnic counter-service specialties:

GERMANY • **Sommerfest** for bratwurst and Altenmünster Oktoberfest beer
JAPAN • **Katsura Grill** for noodle dishes, teriyaki, and tempura
NORWAY • **Kringla Bakeri Og Kafe** for pastries, open-face sandwiches, and Carlsberg beer
UNITED KINGDOM • **Rose & Crown Pub** for fish-and-chips and Guinness, Harp, and Bass beers

LILIANE'S TOP 10 DISNEY WORLD SNACKS

FOLLOWING IS A TOP-10 LIST of particularly decadent or unusual snacks available at WDW. We've omitted the usual funnel cakes, popcorn, and ice cream available anywhere. Also absent are the truly bizarre snacks, such as the squid treats sold at the Mitsukoshi Department Store in the Japan Pavilion at Epcot's World Showcase. These are the goodies worth scouring the parks and resorts for, in ascending order:

10. KAKIGŌRI at the Japan Pavilion, Epcot World Showcase A little on the sweet side but lighter than ice cream, the shaved ice at this small stand comes in such unique flavors as honeydew melon, strawberry, and tangerine. And at $3.75, it's a bargain.

9. TURKEY LEGS Available at every theme park, these must come from 85-pound turkeys because they're huge, not to mention extra-juicy and flavorful. Grab some napkins and go primal on one of these bad boys, and don't worry about the stares you might attract—they're all just jealous.

8. TIE-DYED CHEESECAKE at Disney's Pop Century Resort A colorful and delicious treat. Part red velvet cake and part cheesecake, the dessert is so popular that many discussion boards offer recipes such as this one: **tinyurl.com /tie-dyedcheesecake.**

7. LES HALLES BOULANGERIE–PATISSERIE at the France Pavilion, Epcot World Showcase There are simply no words to adequately describe the pastries at this bakery. Try the frangipane or the Napoleon. Oh, did we mention the flan tart, the crème brûlée, and the chocolate mousse?

6. CADBURY CHOCOLATE BARS at the United Kingdom Pavilion, Epcot World Showcase If you've never had a genuine English Cadbury bar, you just don't know what you're missing.

5. MILK SHAKES from Beaches & Cream at the Beach Club Resort Hand-dipped, thick, and creamy. When was the last time you sported a milk shake mustache? For large crowds, or large appetites, try the Kitchen Sink: a huge sundae consisting of mountains of ice cream and toppings that is actually served in a kitchen sink.

4. SELMA'S COOKIES at the BoardWalk Oddly enough, these are available at the candy store, Seashore Sweets, rather than at the BoardWalk Bakery (go figure), but they're worth tracking down for their rich, buttery, homemade taste.

3. GHIRARDELLI SODA FOUNTAIN AND CHOCOLATE SHOP at Disney Springs Marketplace Everything is good, and the atmosphere has a sophisticated ice-cream-shop-plus-coffee-bar vibe. *Very* San Fran.

2. ZEBRA DOMES at Animal Kingdom Lodge Offered as a dessert on the Boma buffet, they're also available at the Mara food court, on the lower level of the resort near the pool. They consist of a layer of sponge cake topped with chocolate mousse, and then covered in white- and dark-chocolate ganache stripes. Fun and yum rolled into one!

And the number-one snack at Walt Disney World is . . .

1. Two words: DOLE WHIP! Available in Adventureland at the Magic Kingdom, a Dole Whip is a soft-serve pineapple–ice cream dream.

(PS: Bob has a favorite snack, too. Keep reading to find it!)

Disney's Animal Kingdom

Because touring the Animal Kingdom takes less than a day, crowds are heaviest 9:30 a.m.–3:30 p.m. Expect a mob at lunch and thinner crowds at dinner. We recommend that you tour early after a good

BOB Don't expect a broad choice of exotic dishes at Animal Kingdom.

breakfast, and then eat a very late lunch or graze on vendor food. If you tour later in the day, eat lunch before you arrive, and then enjoy dinner in or out of the theme park.

Animal Kingdom offers a lot of counter-service fast food, along with **Tusker House,** a buffet-style restaurant, and **Yak & Yeti,** a table-service restaurant, in Asia. You'll find plenty of traditional Disney-theme-park food—hot dogs, hamburgers, and the like—but even the fast food is superior to typical Disney fare. The third full-service restaurant in the Animal Kingdom, **Rainforest Cafe,** has entrances both inside and outside the theme park, meaning you don't have to buy park admission to eat there.

AUTHORS' FAVORITE COUNTER-SERVICE RESTAURANTS

- Flame Tree Barbecue *Discovery Island*   • Yak & Yeti Local Food Cafes *Asia*

We like Flame Tree Barbecue for its waterfront dining pavilions and Yak & Yeti Local Food Cafes (just outside the full-service Yak & Yeti) for casual Asian dishes from egg rolls to crispy honey chicken. The sit-down Yak & Yeti also serves above-average dishes from China, Thailand, Vietnam, and Japan.

Disney's Hollywood Studios

Dining at Disney's Hollywood Studios is more interesting than in the Magic Kingdom and less ethnic than at Epcot. The Studios has five restaurants where Advance Reservations are recommended: **The Hollywood Brown Derby, 50's Prime Time Cafe, Sci-Fi Dine-In Theater Restaurant, Mama Melrose's Ristorante Italiano,** and the **Hollywood & Vine** buffet. The upscale Brown Derby is by far the best restaurant at the Studios. For simple Italian food, including pizza, Mama Melrose's is fine; just don't expect anything fancy. At the Sci-Fi Dine-In, you eat in little cars at a simulated drive-in movie of the 1950s. Though you won't find a more entertaining restaurant in Walt Disney World, the food is quite disappointing. Somewhat better is the 50's Prime Time Cafe, where you sit in Mom's time-warp kitchen and scarf down meat loaf while watching clips of vintage TV sitcoms. It's a hoot, and the food is a step up. The best way to experience either restaurant is to stop in for dessert or a drink 2:30–4:30 p.m. Hollywood & Vine features singing and dancing characters from the Disney Channel during breakfast and lunch.

AUTHORS' FAVORITE COUNTER-SERVICE RESTAURANTS

- ABC Commissary *Echo Lake*   • Backlot Express *Echo Lake*
- Min and Bill's Dockside Diner *Echo Lake*
- Toluca Legs Turkey Company *Sunset Boulevard*

READERS' COMMENTS ABOUT WALT DISNEY WORLD DINING

EATING IS A POPULAR TOPIC AMONG *Unofficial Guide* readers. In addition to participating in our annual restaurant survey, many readers like to share their thoughts with us. The following comments are representative of those we receive.

A reader from Glendale, Illinois, had a positive experience with Disney food, writing:

> *In general, we were pleasantly surprised. I expected it to be over-priced, generally bad, and certainly unhealthy. There were a lot of options, and almost all restaurants (including counter service) had generally good food and some healthy options. It's not the place to expect fine cuisine—and it's certainly overpriced—but if you understand the parameters, you can eat quite well.*

We've received consistent raves for Boma—Flavors of Africa:

> *Please stop telling everyone how wonderful Boma is. I love it so much there, and I don't want everyone to know the secret—it's already difficult to get a table! Prime rib and Zebra Domes—yum!*

A Lombard, Illinois, mom underscores the need to make Advance Reservations:

> *Please stress that if you want a "normal" dining hour at a specific restaurant, call them 90 or 60 days in advance—IT IS WORTH IT! I wanted to change one reservation about two weeks before our arrival date, and I had a choice of dinner times of either 7:45 or 9 p.m. (not feasible with little ones).*

A Greenwood, Indiana, family had this to say:

> *The food was certainly expensive, but contrary to many of the views expressed in* The Unofficial Guide, *we all thought the quality was excellent. Everything we had, from chicken strips and hot dogs in the parks to dinner at the Coral Reef, tasted great and seemed very fresh.*

A family from Youngsville, Louisiana, got a leg up on other guests:

> *The best thing we ate were the smoked turkey legs.*

A mom from Aberdeen, South Dakota, writes:

> *When we want great food, we'll be on a different vacation. Who wants to waste fun time with the kids at a sit-down restaurant when you know the food will be mediocre anyway?*

On the topic of saving money, a Seattle woman offered this:

> *For those wanting to save a few bucks (or in some cases several bucks), we definitely suggest eating outside WDW for as many meals as possible. To keep down our costs, we ate a large breakfast before leaving the hotel, had a fast-food lunch in the park, a snack later to hold us over, and then ate a good dinner outside the park. Several good restaurants*

in the area have excellent food at reasonable prices, notably Café Tu Tu Tango and Ming Court, both on International Drive.

COUNTER-SERVICE RESTAURANT MINI-PROFILES

TO HELP YOU FIND PALATABLE FAST FOOD that suits your taste, we provide thumbnail profiles of the theme park counter-service restaurants, listed alphabetically by park. They're rated for quality, portion size, and value. The value rating ranges A–F as follows:

A = Exceptional value, a real bargain **B** = Good value
C = Fair value, you get exactly what you pay for
D = Somewhat overpriced **F** = Significantly overpriced

THE MAGIC KINGDOM

Aloha Isle

QUALITY Excellent	VALUE B+	PORTION Medium	LOCATION Adventureland
READER-SURVEY RESPONSES 97% 👍	3% 👎	DISNEY DINING PLAN? No	

Selections Soft-serve ice cream; ice cream floats; fresh pineapple spears; chips; juice, bottled water, coffee, tea.

Comments The pineapple Dole Whip soft-serve is a must-try.

Be Our Guest Restaurant

QUALITY Excellent	VALUE B+	PORTION Medium	LOCATION Fantasyland
READER-SURVEY RESPONSES 91% 👍	9% 👎	DISNEY DINING PLAN? Yes	

Selections Breakfast: cured meats and cheese with fresh marmalade, open-faced bacon and poached egg sandwich with Brie, eggs Florentine in puff pastry, steel-cut oatmeal, scrambled egg whites with roasted tomatoes, signature fried doughnuts. Lunch: tuna niçoise salad, croque monsieur, carved turkey and roast-beef sandwiches, braised pork with bacon mashed potatoes, veggie quiche, quinoa salad. Kids' meals include seared mahimahi, carved turkey sandwich, slow-cooked pork, a tasty meat loaf, grilled cheese and tomato soup, or whole-grain macaroni with marinara sauce.

Comments The best counter-service restaurant in the Magic Kingdom, and one of the best in all of Disney World. Our favorite breakfast selections are the open-faced bacon-and-egg sandwich with Brie and the signature fried doughnuts topped with banana-caramel sauce and chocolate ganache. For lunch we like the slow-cooked pork coq au vin–style, with mushrooms, carrots, onions, and bacon; it's served with mashed potatoes for soaking up the rich sauce, plus a side of green beans. The croque monsieur is a grown-up version of grilled ham and cheese, with carved ham, Gruyère cheese, and béchamel sauce and *pommes frites* on the side. For a healthier option, the generous seared-tuna niçoise salad hits the spot.

Note: Breakfast is served only 8–10 a.m. and is still in a testing phase, though we doubt this popular dining experience will end. Lines for lunch start forming as early as 9:30 a.m. Expect at least a 30-minute wait if you go 11 a.m.–1 p.m. Advance Reservations for lunch are available online at **disneyworld.disney.go.com/dining.** Disney has also rolled out advance ordering for lunch via its My Disney Experience mobile app.

Casey's Corner

QUALITY Good	VALUE B	PORTION Medium	LOCATION Main Street, U.S.A.
READER-SURVEY RESPONSES 84% 👍 16% 👎		DISNEY DINING PLAN? Yes	

Selections Hot dogs, corn-dog nuggets, fries, and brownies.

Comments Best to stop at Casey's when it's extra-busy—that's the best guarantee of a fresh bun and hot fries. Len recommends the barbecue slaw dog; our dining insider favors the Polish sausage with grilled onions and stone-ground mustard, or the addictive corn-dog nuggets.

Columbia Harbour House

QUALITY Good	VALUE B	PORTION Medium	LOCATION Liberty Square
READER-SURVEY RESPONSES 94% 👍 6% 👎		DISNEY DINING PLAN? Yes	

Selections Choose wisely with the grilled salmon with couscous and broccoli, tuna on multigrain bread, broccoli peppercorn salad, or the Lighthouse Sandwich with hummus and broccoli slaw. Or indulge with fried shrimp or battered fish. The lobster roll falls somewhere in between. Other choices: fried chicken or fish nuggets, New England clam chowder, vegetarian chili, coleslaw, or garden salad; chocolate cake, seasonal cobbler, or strawberry yogurt for dessert. For kids: macaroni and cheese, PB&J sandwich, chicken nuggets, or tuna sandwich with grapes.

Comments No trans fats in the fried items, and the soups and sandwiches are a cut above most fast-food fare.

Cosmic Ray's Starlight Cafe

QUALITY Good	VALUE B	PORTION Large	LOCATION Tomorrowland
READER-SURVEY RESPONSES 80% 👍 20% 👎		DISNEY DINING PLAN? Yes	

Selections Rotisserie chicken; burgers (and vegetarian burgers); hot dogs; Greek salad; chicken, turkey, and vegetable sandwiches; chicken nuggets; chili-cheese dog; barbecue-pork sandwich; chicken-noodle soup; chili-cheese fries; gelato or cake for dessert. Kosher choices available on request.

Comments Plenty of options, but the setup can be a little confusing. Each of the three "bays" has different offerings, so make sure you look at each menu before deciding—and note that some items show up on more than one menu. Generous toppings bar.

Friar's Nook

QUALITY Good	VALUE B	PORTION Medium–large	LOCATION Fantasyland
READER-SURVEY RESPONSES 92% 👍 8% 👎		DISNEY DINING PLAN? Yes	

Selections Hot dogs, specialty macaroni and cheese (bacon cheeseburger, beef pot roast), veggies and chips with hummus, lemonade slush.

Comments We prefer the plain version of the mac and cheese, with crunchy panko topping. A little pricey, but filling.

Gaston's Tavern

QUALITY Good	VALUE C	PORTION Medium	LOCATION Fantasyland
READER-SURVEY RESPONSES 91% 👍 9% 👎		DISNEY DINING PLAN? Yes	

Selections Roast pork shank (the porcine equivalent of the giant turkey leg), hummus with chips, cinnamon rolls, chocolate croissants, LeFou's Brew (frozen apple juice flavored with toasted marshmallow).

Comments Clever setting, limited menu. The supersweet Le Fou's Brew is basically expensive apple juice.

Golden Oak Outpost

QUALITY Good	VALUE B+	PORTION Medium-large	LOCATION Frontierland
READER-SURVEY RESPONSES	76% 👍	24% 👎	DISNEY DINING PLAN? Yes

Selections Waffle fries topped with barbecue pork and slaw or brown gravy and white Cheddar; BLT waffle fries with bacon, lettuce, tomato, and ranch dressing; Tex-Mex waffle fries with black bean relish, jalapeños, Cheddar, and sour cream.

Comments Served with apple slices or carrots. Sweet potato nuggets with powdered sugar for dessert.

The Lunching Pad

QUALITY Good	VALUE B-	PORTION Medium	LOCATION Tomorrowland
READER-SURVEY RESPONSES	71% 👍	29% 👎	DISNEY DINING PLAN? Yes

Selections Sweet cream-cheese pretzel; frozen sodas; classic Coney Island dog with chili, onion, and mustard.

Comments The frozen carbonated drinks—cola, cherry, or blue raspberry—are a treat in summer's heat.

Main Street Bakery

QUALITY Fair	VALUE C	PORTION Small	LOCATION Main Street, U.S.A.
READER-SURVEY RESPONSES	93% 👍	7% 👎	DISNEY DINING PLAN? Yes

Selections Coffee drinks and teas; breakfast sandwiches and pastries.

Comments Disney-themed Starbucks, with the same food and drinks you'd find in any other. Very crowded at park opening and mealtimes.

Pecos Bill Tall Tale Inn & Cafe

QUALITY Good	VALUE B	PORTION Medium-large	LOCATION Frontierland
READER-SURVEY RESPONSES	84% 👍	16% 👎	DISNEY DINING PLAN? Yes

Selections One-third-pound Angus cheeseburgers; grilled-chicken sandwich with bacon and pepper Jack cheese; barbecue-pork sandwiches; veggie burgers; Southwest chicken salad; chili; child's plate with burger, grilled cheese, turkey sandwich, or barbecue-pork sandwich and child's beverage; fries and chili-cheese fries; chocolate cake, yogurt, and carrot cake.

Comments Garnish your burger at the fixin's station.

The Pinocchio Village Haus

QUALITY Fair	VALUE C	PORTION Medium	LOCATION Fantasyland
READER-SURVEY RESPONSES	78% 👍	22% 👎	DISNEY DINING PLAN? Yes

Selections Flatbreads; Italian flatbread sub; chicken nuggets; fries; Caesar salad with chicken; meatball sub sandwiches; Mediterranean salad; kids' meals of pizza, chicken nuggets, mac and cheese, or PB&J.

Comments An easy stop for families in Fantasyland, but it's usually crowded. Consider Columbia Harbour House only a few minutes' walk away (it's tastier too).

Tomorrowland Terrace Restaurant *(open seasonally)*

QUALITY Fair	VALUE C	PORTION Medium-large	LOCATION Tomorrowland
READER-SURVEY RESPONSES	83% 👍	17% 👎	DISNEY DINING PLAN? Yes

Selections One-third-pound Angus bacon cheeseburger; chicken nuggets; pasta primavera with chicken; lobster roll; beef-and-blue-cheese salad; citrus shrimp salad; chocolate cake, carrot cake, or yogurt for dessert.

Comments The lobster roll, served with homemade potato chips, is our favorite item on the menu.

Tortuga Tavern *(open seasonally)*

QUALITY Fair	VALUE B	PORTION Medium–large	LOCATION Adventureland
READER-SURVEY RESPONSES 86% 👍	14% 👎	DISNEY DINING PLAN? Yes	

Selections Southwest chicken salad; beef or chicken rice bowl; chicken, beef, or vegetarian burritos; chicken Caesar salad; macaroni and cheese tortillas for kids.

Comments Large, shaded eating area. Generous toppings bar with tomatoes, lettuce, cheese, and salsa.

EPCOT

L'Artisan des Glaces

QUALITY Excellent	VALUE C	PORTION Large	LOCATION France
READER-SURVEY RESPONSES 97% 👍	3% 👎	DISNEY DINING PLAN? Yes	

Selections Flavors change but can include vanilla, chocolate, mint chocolate, pistachio, hazelnut, profiterole, caramel with salt, cherry, white chocolate with coconut, and coffee ice creams. Sorbet flavors can include strawberry, mango, melon, lemon, pomegranate, and mixed berry. Over-21s can enjoy two scoops in a martini glass, topped with a shot of Grand Marnier, rum, or whipped cream–flavored vodka.

Comments Hands-down, the best ice cream at Disney World, freshly made on the spot. Our profiterole sample had chunks of chocolate-covered cookie pieces, and our white chocolate–coconut had fresh shaved coconut in it. The chocolate macaroon ice cream sandwich is worth every calorie.

La Cantina de San Angel

QUALITY Good	VALUE B	PORTION Medium–large	LOCATION Mexico
READER-SURVEY RESPONSES 84% 👍	16% 👎	DISNEY DINING PLAN? Yes	

Selections Tacos with seasoned beef; nachos with ground beef; fried cheese empanada; Mexican salad with cabbage, lettuce, black beans and corn; guacamole and chips; churros and frozen fruit pops; margaritas. For kids, empanadas or chicken tenders.

Comments The Cantina is a popular spot for a quick meal, with 150 covered outdoor seats. When it's extra-busy, the back of La Hacienda's dining room is opened for air-conditioned seating.

Crêpes des Chefs de France

QUALITY Excellent	VALUE B+	PORTION Medium	LOCATION France
READER-SURVEY RESPONSES 84% 👍	16% 👎	DISNEY DINING PLAN? No	

Selections Crepes filled with chocolate, strawberry preserves, ice cream, or sugar; ice cream; specialty beer (Kronenbourg 1664); espresso.

Comments These crepes rate high—even with French guests.

Electric Umbrella

QUALITY Fair	VALUE B–	PORTION Medium	LOCATION Innoventions East
READER-SURVEY RESPONSES 67% 👍	33% 👎	DISNEY DINING PLAN? Yes	

Selections Angus bacon cheeseburger; French Dip burger; sausage-and-pepper sub; veggie flatbread; veggie naan-wich with tofu; Caesar salad with chicken; chicken nuggets; child's plate with cheeseburger, mac and cheese, veggie flatbread, or chicken wrap; cheesecake; no-sugar-added brownie; chocolate cupcake.

Comments In a word, uninspired. Much better choices elsewhere.

Fife & Drum Tavern

QUALITY Fair	VALUE C	PORTION Large	LOCATION United States
READER-SURVEY RESPONSES 86% 👍 14% 👎		DISNEY DINING PLAN? Yes	

Selections Turkey legs, popcorn, pretzels, ice cream, frozen slushes, beer.

Comments Great place to grab a bite for a show in American Gardens Theatre. Seating is also available in and around the Liberty Inn, behind the Fife & Drum.

Fountain View

QUALITY Fair	VALUE C	PORTION Small	LOCATION Future World Plaza
READER-SURVEY RESPONSES 94% 👍 6% 👎		DISNEY DINING PLAN? Yes	

Selections Coffee drinks and teas; breakfast sandwiches and pastries.

Comments Disney-themed Starbucks, with the same food and drinks you'd find in any other.

Les Halles Boulangerie–Patisserie

QUALITY Good	VALUE A	PORTION Small-medium	LOCATION France
READER-SURVEY RESPONSES 96% 👍 4% 👎		DISNEY DINING PLAN? Yes	

Selections Tuna niçoise salad, sandwiches (ham and cheese; turkey BLT; chicken breast; grilled eggplant; Brie, cranberry, and apple); imported-cheese plates; quiches; soups; pastries.

Comments Les Halles opens at 9 a.m.—2 hours before World Showcase—so it's a wonderful spot for a quiet breakfast. Usually crowded starting at lunch and stays that way throughout the day.

Kabuki Café

QUALITY Fair	VALUE C	PORTION Small	LOCATION Japan
READER-SURVEY RESPONSES 93% 👍 7% 👎		DISNEY DINING PLAN? Yes	

Selections Sushi, including California roll with cucumber, crab, and avocado, and *temari* roll with tuna, salmon, and shrimp; edamame; shaved ice flavored with fruit or milk; green tea, caramel ginger, or strawberry ice cream; Japanese beer, including a frozen Kirin, slushy-style; wine and sake; sodas.

Comments The sushi are frequently premade and come as four bite-size pieces, small enough to be a snack without ruining your appetite for something else later in World Showcase. Share a frozen Kirin.

Katsura Grill

QUALITY Good	VALUE B	PORTION Small-medium	LOCATION Japan
READER-SURVEY RESPONSES 89% 👍 11% 👎		DISNEY DINING PLAN? Yes	

Selections Sushi; udon noodle bowls (beef, curry, or tempura shrimp); chicken, beef, or salmon teriyaki; chicken-cutlet curry; Japanese curry rice with beef; edamame; miso soup; green tea cheesecake; green tea or adzuki bean ice cream; teriyaki chicken kid's plate; Kirin beer, sake, and plum wine.

Comments Great spot to grab some sushi and sit outside.

Kringla Bakeri og Kafe

QUALITY Good–excellent	VALUE B	PORTION Small–medium	LOCATION Norway
READER-SURVEY RESPONSES 95% 👍 5% 👎		DISNEY DINING PLAN? Yes	

Selections Pastries and cakes; rice cream; unusual sandwiches (smoked salmon and egg or Norwegian club with lingonberry mayo); vegetable torte; espresso, cappuccino, and imported beers (Carlsberg for $8.25).

Comments Try the ham-and-apple sandwich with Jarlsberg and Muenster cheeses or the rice cream (not a typo). Shaded outdoor seating.

Liberty Inn

QUALITY Fair	VALUE C	PORTION Medium	LOCATION United States
READER-SURVEY RESPONSES 80% 👍 20% 👎		DISNEY DINING PLAN? Yes	

Selections Angus bacon cheeseburger; surf-and-turf burger with beef and crab; Louisiana-style shrimp with rice; grilled-chicken BLT; Maryland crab cakes; New York strip with red-wine butter, fries, and steamed broccoli; chili; Southwest salad with chicken and black bean salsa; Red, White, & Blue Salad with dried cranberries, pecans, apples, and blue cheese; hot dogs; veggie "chicken" sandwich; chicken nuggets; child's plate of grilled chicken or pasta with marinara.

Comments They've freshened up the menu here, but quality could be better. Still, the New York strip is a relative bargain at $11.49. Kosher items also available.

Lotus Blossom Café

QUALITY Fair	VALUE C	PORTION Medium	LOCATION China
READER-SURVEY RESPONSES 70% 👍 30% 👎		DISNEY DINING PLAN? Yes	

Selections Pork and vegetable egg rolls, pot stickers, Hong Kong–style vegetable curry (chicken optional), sesame chicken salad, shrimp fried rice, orange chicken, beef-noodle soup bowl, caramel-ginger or lychee ice cream, plum wine, Tsingtao beer.

Comments The menu never changes, and the food remains mediocre.

Promenade Refreshments

QUALITY Fair	VALUE C	PORTION Large	LOCATION World Showcase Promenade
READER-SURVEY RESPONSES 79% 👍 21% 👎		DISNEY DINING PLAN? Yes	

Selections Chili dogs, hot dogs, frozen yogurt, beer.

Comments Seating is limited to nonexistent. Be prepared to walk and chew.

Refreshment Cool Post

QUALITY Good	VALUE B-	PORTION Small	LOCATION Between Germany and China
READER-SURVEY RESPONSES 85% 👍 15% 👎		DISNEY DINING PLAN? Yes	

Selections Hot dogs, soft-serve in a waffle cone, slushes, coffee or tea, draft Safari Amber beer ($7).

Comments Home of the Doofenslurper—frozen lemonade topped with passion fruit sorbet foam.

Refreshment Port

QUALITY Good	VALUE B-	PORTION Medium	LOCATION Near Canada
READER-SURVEY RESPONSES 93% 👍 7% 👎		DISNEY DINING PLAN? Yes	

Selections Fried favorites—croissant doughnut, chicken nuggets, and fries—plus flavored coffees, hot chocolate, and soft-serve ice cream.

Comments Almost everyone in line is here for the calorie-laden croissant doughnut.

Rose & Crown Pub

QUALITY Good	VALUE C+	PORTION Medium	LOCATION United Kingdom
READER-SURVEY RESPONSES 91% 👍 9% 👎		DISNEY DINING PLAN? No	

Selections Fish-and-chips; Scotch egg (hard-boiled, wrapped in sausage, and deep-fried); corned beef; shepherd's pie; bangers and mash; British cheese plate; Guinness, Harp, and Bass beers, as well as other spirits.

Comments Most of the crowd Is here to drink in an authentic British pub. Outside the pub is Yorkshire County Fish Shop (see below), which serves food to go.

Sommerfest

QUALITY Good	VALUE B–	PORTION Medium	LOCATION Germany
READER-SURVEY RESPONSES 86% 👍 14% 👎		DISNEY DINING PLAN? Yes	

Selections Bratwurst, curry wurst, and frankfurter sandwiches with kraut; *nudelgratin* (baked macaroni with Cheddar and Swiss); cold potato salad; house-made paprika chips; apple strudel; Black Forest cake; German wine and beer.

Comments Grab a spot in the courtyard to indulge in one of the hearty sausages and a cold Pilsner. Skip the *nudelgratin*.

Sunshine Seasons

QUALITY Excellent	VALUE A	PORTION Medium	LOCATION The Land
READER-SURVEY RESPONSES 95% 👍 5% 👎		DISNEY DINING PLAN? Yes	

Selections Comprise the following four areas: (1) wood-fired grills and rotisseries, with rotisserie half-chicken or slow-roasted pork chop and wood-grilled fish with seasonal vegetables; (2) a sandwich shop with made-to-order sandwiches such as oak-grilled veggie flatbread, spicy fish tacos, and turkey-and-cheese on ciabatta; (3) Asian shop, with noodle bowls and various stir-fry combos; (4) soup-and-salad shop, with soups made daily and unusual creations such as the Power Salad (quinoa, almonds, and chicken) and roasted-beet-and-goat-cheese salad. Breakfast includes the usual suspects: pastries, bacon, eggs, and the like.

Comments One of the best quick-service spots in Epcot. The breakfast panini (eggs, bacon, roast pork, and cheese) is an *Unofficial* favorite.

Tangierine Café

QUALITY Good	VALUE B	PORTION Medium	LOCATION Morocco
READER-SURVEY RESPONSES 93% 👍 7% 👎		DISNEY DINING PLAN? Yes	

Selections Chicken and lamb shawarma; hummus; tabbouleh; lentil salad; couscous salad; chicken, lamb, or falafel wraps; marinated olives; child's burger or chicken tenders with carrot sticks and applesauce; Moroccan wine and beer; baklava.

Comments It's rarely busy, and the food is decent if not totally authentic. Grab a seat outdoors.

Yorkshire County Fish Shop

QUALITY Good	VALUE B+	PORTION Medium	LOCATION United Kingdom
READER-SURVEY RESPONSES 94% 👍 6% 👎		DISNEY DINING PLAN? Yes	

Selections Fish-and-chips, shortbread, Bass Ale draft, and Harp Lager.

Comments There's usually a line for the crisp, hot fish-and-chips at this convenient fast-food window attached to the Rose & Crown Pub. Outdoor seating overlooks the lagoon.

DISNEY'S ANIMAL KINGDOM
Creature Comforts

QUALITY Fair	VALUE C	PORTION Small	LOCATION Discovery Island near Africa
READER-SURVEY RESPONSES	Too new to rate	DISNEY DINING PLAN?	Yes

Selections Coffee drinks and teas; breakfast sandwiches and pastries.
Comments Disney-themed Starbucks. The fare is largely the same you'd find at any other, plus the occasional Animal Kingdom–themed treat.

Flame Tree Barbecue

QUALITY Excellent	VALUE B–	PORTION Large	LOCATION Discovery Island
READER-SURVEY RESPONSES	92% 👍 8% 👎	DISNEY DINING PLAN?	Yes

Selections Half-slab St. Louis–style ribs; smoked half-chicken; smoked-pork sandwiches; smoked-chicken salad; jumbo turkey leg; fruit plate with honey yogurt; child's plate of baked chicken drumstick, chicken sandwich, hot dog, or PB&J sandwich; fries, coleslaw, and onion rings; Key lime or chocolate mousse pie; Safari Amber beer, Bud Light, and wine.
Comments It recently expanded its outdoor seating, so there's more shaded space overlooking the water. One of our favorites for lunch.

Harambe Market

QUALITY Good	VALUE B	PORTION Large	LOCATION Africa
READER-SURVEY RESPONSES	Too new to rate	DISNEY DINING PLAN?	Yes

Selections Spice-rubbed ribs with green papaya–carrot slaw and chickpea, cucumber, and tomato salad; curry corn dog, grilled-chicken kebabs, or ground beef–kebab flatbread sandwich, each served with a roasted broccoli–tomato salad. Beer and South African wines available. Kids' menu includes child-size versions of the adult selections or a snack pack with yogurt, apple slices, carrots, and crackers.
Comments Plenty of shaded seating. Modeled after a typical real-life market in an African nation during the 1960s colonial era. The curry corn dog and the chicken skewers are our favorites.

Kusafiri Coffee Shop and Bakery

QUALITY Good	VALUE B	PORTION Medium	LOCATION Africa
READER-SURVEY RESPONSES	92% 👍 8% 👎	DISNEY DINING PLAN?	Yes

Selections Cupcakes, turnovers, Danish, muffins, croissants, cookies, brownies, cake, fruit cups, yogurt, coffee, cocoa, and juice. Breakfast wrap (egg, sausage, spinach, and goat cheese) served until 10:30 a.m.
Comments The only savory offering is the breakfast wrap. The colossal cinnamon roll is a favorite anytime.

Pizzafari

QUALITY Fair	VALUE B	PORTION Medium	LOCATION Discovery Island
READER-SURVEY RESPONSES	80% 👍 20% 👎	DISNEY DINING PLAN?	Yes

Selections Cheese, pepperoni, or veggie personal pizzas; meatball salad; wedge salad with chicken; pasta Bolognese. Kids' choices: mac and cheese, pasta with turkey marinara, cheese pizza, or PB&J. Chocolate mousse or tiramisu for dessert. Beer and wine available.

Comments Hectic at peak mealtimes, but there's lots of seating. The pizza is unimpressive. Kosher menu is available.

Restaurantosaurus

QUALITY Good	VALUE B+	PORTION Medium–large	LOCATION DinoLand U.S.A.
READER-SURVEY RESPONSES 77% 👍	23% 👎	DISNEY DINING PLAN? Yes	

Selections Angus bacon cheeseburger; chicken nuggets; black bean burger; mac-and-cheese hot dog; chicken BLT salad; grilled-chicken sandwich; kids' turkey wrap, corn-dog nuggets, cheeseburger, or PB&J.

Comments Plenty of seating and a good burger-toppings bar.

Royal Anandapur Tea Company

QUALITY Good	VALUE B	PORTION Medium	LOCATION Asia
READER-SURVEY RESPONSES 91% 👍	9% 👎	DISNEY DINING PLAN? No	

Selections Wide variety of hot and iced teas and coffees (fantastic frozen chai); lattes, espresso, and cappuccino; pastries.

Comments Halfway between Expedition Everest and Kali River Rapids, this is the kind of small, eclectic, Animal Kingdom–specific food stand that you wish other parks had. Nine loose-leaf teas from Asia and Africa can be ordered hot or iced.

Yak & Yeti Local Food Cafes

QUALITY Fair	VALUE B	PORTION Large	LOCATION Asia
READER-SURVEY RESPONSES 90% 👍	10% 👎	DISNEY DINING PLAN? Yes	

Selections Crispy honey chicken with steamed rice, Korean stir-fry barbecue chicken, ginger chicken salad, Asian chicken sandwich, roasted-vegetable couscous wrap, teriyaki beef bowl, egg rolls, chicken fried rice. Kids' menu: chicken tenders, PB&J, or cheeseburger with applesauce and carrots.

Comments For filling up when you're in a hurry. Everything is a little too sweet, except the couscous wrap.

DISNEY'S HOLLYWOOD STUDIOS

ABC Commissary

QUALITY Fair	VALUE B–	PORTION Medium–large	LOCATION Echo Lake
READER-SURVEY RESPONSES 69% 👍	31% 👎	DISNEY DINING PLAN? Yes	

Selections New York strip steak; roasted salmon; Asian salad (chicken or salmon); chicken club sandwich; Angus cheeseburger with sriracha aioli and fried shrimp; shrimp platter; seafood platter; couscous, quinoa, and arugula salad; child's chicken nuggets, cheeseburger, or turkey sandwich; chocolate mousse, cupcakes, or no-sugar-added strawberry parfait for dessert; wine and beer.

Comments You're bound to find something you like on this diverse menu. Indoors, centrally located, but hard to find. Offers kosher meals.

Backlot Express

QUALITY Fair	VALUE C	PORTION Medium–large	LOCATION Echo Lake
READER-SURVEY RESPONSES 83% 👍	17% 👎	DISNEY DINING PLAN? Yes	

Selections Angus cheeseburger; Buffalo chicken nuggets; chili dog; Southwest salad with chicken, black bean relish, and avocado; pressed turkey club; grilled-vegetable sandwich; cantaloupe-and-cucumber salad. For kids, chicken nuggets, PB&J, or grilled-veggie sandwich. Beer.

Comments Fun props—some actually used in movies—decorate this spacious dining area.

Catalina Eddie's

QUALITY Fair	VALUE B	PORTION Medium–large	LOCATION Sunset Boulevard
READER-SURVEY RESPONSES 60% 👍 40% 👎		DISNEY DINING PLAN? Yes	

Selections Cheese and pepperoni pizzas, hot Italian deli sandwich, Caesar salad, banana parfait, cupcakes, and vanilla cake with chocolate custard.
Comments Seldom crowded.

Fairfax Fare

QUALITY Fair	VALUE B	PORTION Medium–large	LOCATION Sunset Boulevard
READER-SURVEY RESPONSES 81% 👍 19% 👎		DISNEY DINING PLAN? Yes	

Selections Barbecue chicken and ribs; pulled-pork sandwiches; "designer" hot dogs (barbecue pork and coleslaw, macaroni and cheese with truffle oil); chili dogs; turkey legs; Fairfax Salad with barbecue pork, bacon, and corn-tomato salsa; banana parfait or vanilla cake for dessert.
Comments The mac-and-cheese–truffle-oil hot dog is a standout. Ask to have your bun warmed before your dog is served.

Min and Bill's Dockside Diner

QUALITY Fair	VALUE C	PORTION Small–medium	LOCATION Echo Lake
READER-SURVEY RESPONSES 81% 👍 19% 👎		DISNEY DINING PLAN? Yes	

Selections Turkey legs, frankfurter in a pretzel roll, barbecue-pork mac and cheese, shakes and soft drinks, chips and cookies, beer.
Comments The hot dog in a pretzel roll is genius. Limited seating at nearby picnic tables.

Pizza Planet

QUALITY Good	VALUE B+	PORTION Medium	LOCATION Streets of America
READER-SURVEY RESPONSES 76% 👍 24% 👎		DISNEY DINING PLAN? Yes	

Selections Cheese, pepperoni, and vegetarian pizzas; meatball sub; salads; child's chicken sub or cheese pizza; cookies and cupcakes.
Comments It's all about the arcade games. Retire to the outdoor seating with umbrella-shaded tables if you want to avoid the din inside.

Rosie's All-American Café

QUALITY Fair	VALUE C	PORTION Medium	LOCATION Sunset Boulevard
READER-SURVEY RESPONSES 97% 👍 3% 👎		DISNEY DINING PLAN? Yes	

Selections Cheeseburgers; black bean burgers; chicken nuggets; soups; child's turkey sandwich or chicken nuggets with carrot sticks and applesauce; banana parfait, cupcakes, or vanilla cake with chocolate custard.
Comments A quick stop on the way to Tower of Terror or Rock 'n' Roller Coaster. Plenty of shaded seating and a good fixin's bar.

Starring Rolls Cafe

QUALITY Good	VALUE B	PORTION Small–medium	LOCATION Sunset Boulevard
READER-SURVEY RESPONSES 93% 👍 7% 👎		DISNEY DINING PLAN? Yes	

Selections Deli sandwiches, sushi, pastries and desserts, coffee.
Comments Slowest counter service in the Studios.

Studio Catering Co.

QUALITY Good	VALUE B	PORTION Small–medium	LOCATION Streets of America
READER-SURVEY RESPONSES 85% 👍 15% 👎		DISNEY DINING PLAN? Yes	

Selections Pulled beef brisket sandwich, spicy chipotle ranch chicken, vegetable wrap, deli sandwich, turkey-and-cheese panini, and Greek salad. Kids' menu includes chicken nuggets and a mini vegetable wrap. The adjacent High Octane Refreshments serves margaritas and other cocktails.

Comments You might miss this spot unless your kids are burning off energy at Honey, I Shrunk the Kids Movie Set Adventure. Grab a frozen drink to sip while the youngsters play. Plenty of shaded seating.

Toluca Legs Turkey Company

QUALITY Good	VALUE B	PORTION Medium–large	LOCATION Sunset Boulevard
READER-SURVEY RESPONSES 83% 👍 17% 👎		DISNEY DINING PLAN? Yes	

Selections Smoked turkey legs and pork shanks; bottled soda and beer.

Comments For fans of giant meat.

Trolley Car Cafe

QUALITY Fair	VALUE C	PORTION Small	LOCATION Sunset Boulevard
READER-SURVEY RESPONSES 90% 👍 10% 👎		DISNEY DINING PLAN? Yes	

Selections Coffee drinks and teas; breakfast sandwiches and pastries.

Comments Disney-themed Starbucks. The pink-stucco Spanish Colonial exterior calls to mind old Hollywood, while the industrial-style interior is themed to evoke a trolley-car switching station. The fare is largely the same you'd find at any other Starbucks, plus such signature Studios treats as the mountainous chocolate-Butterfinger cupcake.

DISNEY'S FULL-SERVICE RESTAURANTS: A QUICK ROMP AROUND THE WORLD

LILIANE Young children are the rule, not the exception, at Disney World restaurants.

DISNEY RESTAURANTS OFFER an excellent (though expensive) opportunity to introduce young children to the variety and excitement of ethnic food. No matter how formal a restaurant appears, the staff is accustomed to wiggling, impatient, and often boisterous children. **Les Chefs de France** at Epcot, for example, may be the nation's only French restaurant where most patrons wear shorts and T-shirts and at least two dozen young diners are attired in basic black . . . mouse ears.

Almost all Disney restaurants offer children's menus, and all have booster seats and high chairs. They understand how tough it may be for kids to sit for an extended period of time, and waiters will supply little ones with crackers and rolls and serve your dinner much faster than in comparable restaurants elsewhere. Letters from readers suggest that being served too quickly is much more common than having a long wait.

In **Epcot**, preschoolers most enjoy **Biergarten** in Germany, **San Angel Inn** in Mexico, and **Coral Reef** at The Seas with Nemo & Friends Pavilion in Future World. The Biergarten combines a rollicking and noisy atmosphere with good basic food, including pork roast and German sausages; a

RICKY At Coral Reef you can eat fish, but I would rather just look at them and eat chicken.

German oompah band entertains. Children often have the opportunity to participate in Bavarian dancing. San Angel Inn Restaurante is in the Mexican village marketplace. From the table, children can watch boats on Gran Fiesta Tour drift beneath a smoking volcano. With a choice of chips, tacos, and other familiar items, picky children usually have no difficulty finding something to eat. Be aware that the service is sometimes glacially slow. Coral Reef, with tables beside windows looking into The Seas' aquarium, offers a colorful mealtime diversion for all ages. If your kids don't eat fish, Coral Reef also serves beef and chicken. The downside is that the food is extremely expensive. For a more affordable splurge, forget lunch or dinner and drop in during off-hours for one of the Coral Reef's decadent desserts. The San Angel Inn is likewise overpriced but not in the same league as Coral Reef. The Biergarten offers reasonable value, plus good food.

Epcot's newest restaurant, while certainly not cheap, provides the added value of a great location. **Spice Road Table**, situated along the edge of World Showcase Lagoon in the Morocco Pavilion, serves up Mediterranean-inspired small plates similar to Spanish tapas, and its outdoor terrace provides perfect views for *IllumiNations* at night. Kids will like sitting outside, and the small plates can be shared. The entire family will enjoy the fireworks while Mom and Dad have a nice glass of wine.

LILIANE Spice Road Table is my new favorite spot for watching *Illumi-Nations*. Read my review here: **tinyurl .com/spiceroadtable.**

Be Our Guest Restaurant and **Cinderella's Royal Table,** both in Fantasyland, are the hot tickets in the Magic Kingdom, but reservations are often well-nigh impossible to get. For the best combination of food and entertainment, book a character meal at **The Crystal Palace.** From a strictly foodie standpoint, we think the best kids' fare is at the **Liberty Tree Tavern,** and it's easy to book too.

A new restaurant is scheduled to open in Adventureland in late 2015 or early 2016, in the area across from Swiss Family Treehouse. The working name is **Skipper's Cantina,** the theme is reportedly tied to the Jungle Cruise, and it will reportedly operate along the lines of Fantasyland's Be Our Guest, with counter-service lunches and sit-down dinners.

At **Disney's Hollywood Studios,** all ages enjoy the atmosphere and entertainment at the **Sci-Fi Dine-In Theater Restaurant** and the **50's Prime Time Cafe.** Unfortunately, the Sci-Fi's food is close to dismal except for dessert, and the Prime Time's is uneven. Theme aside, children enjoy the character meals at **Hollywood & Vine,** and the pizza at **Mama Melrose's** never fails to please.

RICKY At the Sci-Fi Dine-In Theater try the fried pickles. I love fried pickles!

The three full-service restaurants at Disney's Animal Kingdom are **Tusker House Restaurant** (actually a buffet); **Rainforest Cafe,** a great favorite of children; and **Yak & Yeti Restaurant.**

As you've undoubtedly noticed by now, Disney World is a trend-savvy place, and every market share has its niche. But Disney World is also about stars, fantasies, and meeting characters. So if you've become habituated to oak-fired filet of beef, the **California Grill** atop the Contemporary Resort will oblige. Great sushi can be had at **Teppan Edo** at Japan in Epcot and at **Kimonos** in the Swan. The best and biggest steaks are at **Shula's Steak House** in the Dolphin, **Le Cellier Steakhouse** in the Canada Pavilion, or **Yachtsman Steakhouse** at the Yacht Club, albeit way overpriced. In Italy **Via Napoli,** an authentic Neapolitan pizzeria, features wood-burning ovens and imports water from a source that most resembles the water in Naples, Italy, home of some of the world's best pizza dough. The 300-seat pizzeria is inspired by the Naples 45 pizzeria on East 45th Street in New York City and has both indoor and outdoor dining. In Mexico, the counter-service **La Cantina de San Angel** and the full-service **La Hacienda de San Angel** (dinner only) offer a combined 400 seats with alfresco seating for lunch and a perfect place for viewing *IllumiNations,* the nightly Epcot fireworks spectacular.

Planet Hollywood at Disney Springs (teens love it) famously belongs to and has memorabilia from the likes of Demi Moore, Bruce Willis, and Sylvester Stallone. At The Landing, **The Boathouse** is a new upscale seafood restaurant on the waterfront; kids will enjoy watching the amphibious cars drive by. The West Side has two celebrity-connected restaurant-nightclubs: **House of Blues,** part of the chain of New Orleans–style music halls–restaurants once partly owned by surviving Blues Brother Dan Aykroyd; and **Bongos,** a Cuban-flavored café created by Gloria Estefan and her husband, Emilio.

Not only film and sports stars but also the Food Network and food-magazine stars have been enlisted in the Disney World parade. Paul Bocuse was one of the eponymous **Chefs de France** who designed the menu for that restaurant and for **Monsieur Paul** in Epcot. Boston star chef Todd English created **bluezoo** for the Dolphin. California's Wolfgang Puck is so celebrity-kitchen-conscious that the TV monitors at **Wolfgang Puck Grand Cafe** on the West Side show not sports or movies but the cooks at work, a fad English has also adopted.

Celebrity status notwithstanding, neither Puck's café nor the Estefans' Bongos has drawn much praise from diners, though bluezoo is very good (but also quite adult). House of Blues, surprisingly enough, has done much better with its Louisiana-inspired fare and gospel brunch.

If your kids haven't had their fill of robotic crocodiles, Abraham Lincolns, singing parrots, and the like, **T-REX** and **Rainforest Cafe** will serve up all they can handle. T-REX features animatronic dinosaurs and an occasional woolly mammoth, while Rainforest Cafe is stuffed with jungle critters. Both, of course, have gift shops. There are not one but two Rainforest Cafe branches, one at Disney Springs Marketplace and a supertheatrical version at the entrance to Disney's Animal Kingdom, where the decor and animatronic elephants make it fit right into the scenery there. Not surprisingly in a place where the sky "rains" and the stars flicker overhead, more thought went into naming the dishes than perfecting the recipes. Also, note that the Animal Kingdom Rainforest Cafe serves breakfast.

If your kids prefer dinosaurs to pachyderms, try T-REX, which is located within spitting distance of the Rainforest Cafe and operated by the same folks. The food is better than Rainforest, and children go nuts about being surrounded by a life-size animatronic brontosaurus, triceratops, and such.

In fact, though the official guides to Walt Disney World describe various restaurants as *delicious, delectable,* and *delightful,* the truth is that only perhaps a dozen of the nearly 100 full-service establishments are first-rate. And some of the most disappointing restaurants, in general, are the often attractive but commissary-bland ethnic kitchens.

Though a blessing in disguise to many children and picky eaters of all ages, most of the "ethnic" food at Walt Disney World is Americanized, or rather homogenized, especially at Epcot, where visitors from so many countries, as well as the United States, tend to have preconceived notions of egg rolls and enchiladas. **Teppan Edo** in the Japan Pavilion happens to be one of the better restaurants in the World, with pretty good teppanyaki (and good tempura next door)—but it specializes in a particularly Westernized form of Japanese cuisine, first produced in New York only about 30 years ago. **Nine Dragons Restaurant** in the China Pavilion serves satisfying dim sum along with handmade noodles (taffy pulled in the dining room), a respectable five-spiced fish, and crisp vegetables. The **San Angel Inn** in the Mexico Pavilion is associated with the famous Debler family of Mexico City. **Les Chefs de France** and **Monsieur Paul,** the brainchildren of master chefs Paul Bocuse, the late Gaston Lenôtre, and Roger Vergé, are serious dining destinations. When making your reservation, check Bocuse's schedule with a cast member.

BOB OK, because you've been good, I'll tell you the one junk food to blow your calorie budget on: In Epcot's France Pavilion, there's a cart that sells bags of cinnamon-glazed pecans and almonds. Don't say we never spoil you.

Liliane loves meeting the princesses at Norway's **Akershus Royal Banquet Hall,** but Bob finds the buffet stodgy, smoky, and cheese- and mayonnaise-heavy. (If smoked meats are your thing, he thinks the smoked turkey legs from the outdoor vendors are far better.)

Among the places the culinary staff actually recommends (off the record) are the classic-Continental prix-fixe **Victoria & Albert's** at the Grand Floridian, where you pay $150 a head to have every waitress introduce herself as Vicky and all the waiters as Al; the **Flying Fish Cafe; Artist Point; Jiko; Sanaa;** and the ultra-chic **California Grill.**

Another thing: A lot of the food at Disney World, particularly the fast food, isn't exactly healthy. (Funnel cakes? Happy Meals?) But this is an area that the parks have started to address. **Artist's Palette** at Saratoga Springs Resort and **Sunshine Seasons** in the Land Pavilion at Epcot are fast-casual spots where the food is freshly prepared, often when you order it, but can be carried out or taken to nearby tables. At Sunshine Seasons, there are four different fully staffed kitchens, one preparing entrée salads with seared tuna or roasted beets with goat cheese, as well as soups du jour; another stir-frying veggies and preparing Asian noodle soup; a third wood-grilling chicken and beef to be wrapped in grilled flatbread or salmon with pesto; and a fourth preparing deluxe focaccia sandwiches. Artist's Palette offers everything from French toast to individual flatbreads to gourmet-prepared entrées for carryout. Try the **Turf Club Bar & Grill** next door for roasted and grilled specialties.

Beyond that, there are fruit stands and juice bars scattered around, veggie sandwiches, wraps, rotisserie chicken, soft pretzels as well as the deceptively simple popcorn, baked potatoes (not, frankly, prepared with the apparent care of the turkey legs but about a tenth of the calories and salt), as well as the frozen fruit bars in the ice cream freezers and frozen yogurt or smoothies at the ice cream shops. Yes, it's hard, especially with all those fudge and cookie stands practically pelting you with sugary goodness as you saunter past, but stick to your guns. Look for the fruit markets in Liberty Square in the Magic Kingdom, on Sunset Boulevard in Disney's Hollywood Studios, and at the Harambe Village marketplace in Disney's Animal Kingdom.

MAGIC YOUR WAY DINING PLANS

DISNEY OFFERS DINING PLANS to accompany its Magic Your Way lodging packages (see page 60). They're available to all Disney resort guests except those staying at the Swan, the Dolphin, the hotels of the Downtown Disney Resort Area, and Shades of Green. Guests must also purchase a Magic Your Way package from Disney (not through an online reseller), have Annual Passes, or be members of the Disney Vacation Club (DVC) to participate in the dining plan. Except for DVC members, a three-night minimum stay is typically also required. The overall cost is determined by the number of nights you stay at a Disney resort hotel. All plans include tax but not gratuity.

You must purchase a Disney package vacation to be eligible for a dining plan, as a family of five from Waldron, Michigan, learned:

> We read through The Unofficial Guide and noticed that it said not to book a package during slow season. We were overwhelmed with the decisions that we had to make, so we booked the resort first, then the tickets, and then we wanted the dining plan. Well, they wouldn't add the dining plan because we had already booked everything.

In addition to food, all the plans include "sweeteners" such as a free round of miniature golf, discounts on spa treatments and salon services, and deals on recreational activities such as fishing and water sports.

Disney ceaselessly tinkers with the dining plans' rules, meal definitions, and participating restaurants. Here are some recent examples:

- At sit-down restaurants, you can substitute dessert for a side salad, cup of soup, or fruit plate.
- For guests on the Deluxe, Premium, and Platinum Dining Plans, Disney makes no distinction between adult and child dining credits. Ditto for counter-service restaurants using any plan. If you have two child and two adult dining credits available and you'd like to pay for four adult meals using those credits, you can.

- You may exchange one sit-down or counter-service meal credit for three snacks, as long as you do so within the same transaction. It is not a good deal to exchange a sit-down credit for three snacks.

- Finally, you can use your meal credits to pay for the meals of people who are not on any dining plan.

MAGIC YOUR WAY PLUS DINING PLAN This plan provides, for each member of your group, for each night of your stay, one counter-service meal, one full-service meal, and one snack at participating Disney dining locations and restaurants, including room service at some Disney resorts (type "Disney Dining Plan Locations" into your favorite search engine to find sites with the entire list). The plan also includes one refillable drink mug per person, per package, but it can be filled only at Disney resort counter-service restaurants. For guests age 10 and up, the price is $61.82, tax included; for guests ages 3–9, the price is $20.98 per night, tax included. Children younger than age 3 eat free from an adult's plate.

For instance, if you're staying for three nights, you'll be credited with three counter-service meals, three full-service meals, three snacks, and one refillable mug for each member of your party. All those meals will be put into a group meal account. Meals in your account can be used by anyone in your group, on any combination of days—for example, you can skip a full-service meal one day and have two on another day.

The counter-service meal includes a main course (sandwich, dinner salad, pizza, or the like) or a complete combo meal (a main course and a side dish—think burger and fries), plus dessert and a nonalcoholic drink. The full-service sit-down meals include a main course, dessert, and nonalcoholic drink. If you're dining at a buffet, the full-service meal includes the buffet and a nonalcoholic drink. The snack includes items normally sold from carts or stands throughout the parks and resorts: ice cream, soft drinks, soup, fruit, side items, and the like. When in doubt, ask a cast member what else might count.

Disney's top-of-the-line restaurants (dubbed **Disney Signature** restaurants in the plan), along with Cinderella's Royal Table, all the dinner shows, regular room service, and in-room pizza delivery, count as two full-service meals on the standard (Plus) dining plan. If you dine at one of these locations, two full-service meals will be deducted from your account for each person dining.

In addition to the preceding, the dining plan comes with several other important rules:

- Everyone staying in the same resort room must participate in the dining plan.

- Alcoholic and some nonalcoholic drinks are not included in the plan.

- A full-service meal can be breakfast, lunch, or dinner. The greatest savings occur when you use your full-service-meal credits for dinner.

- The meal plan expires at midnight **on the day you check out** of the Disney resort. **Unused meals are nonrefundable.**

- Neither the Disney Dining Plan nor Disney's Free Dining can be added to a discounted room-only reservation.

QUICK-SERVICE DINING PLAN This plan includes meals, snacks, and nonalcoholic drinks at most counter-service eateries in Walt Disney World. The cost (including tax) is $42.77 per day for guests age 10 and up, $17.54 per day for kids ages 3–9. The plan includes two counter-service meals and one snack per day, in addition to one refillable drink mug per person, per package (eligible for refills only at counter-service locations in your Disney resort).

MAGIC YOUR WAY DELUXE DINING PLAN This plan offers a choice of full-service or counter-service meals for three meals a day at any participating restaurant. In addition to the three meals a day, the plan also includes two snacks per day and a refillable drink mug. The Deluxe Plan costs $111.73 per night for guests age 10 and older, and $32.56 per night for kids ages 3–9, tax included.

MAGIC YOUR WAY PREMIUM PACKAGE Along with park tickets and lodging, you get breakfast, lunch, and dinner (including two snacks per day plus gratuities and one refillable resort drink mug per person), character meals, and dinner shows; unlimited golf, tennis, fishing excursions, and water sports; select theme park tours; Cirque du Soleil show tickets; unlimited use of child-care facilities—everything you can think of except for alcoholic beverages. The Premium Package costs $204 for adults and $149 for kids ages 3–9 (tax included) in addition to the cost of the standard Magic Your Way package. *Note:* A minimum three-night stay at Walt Disney World is required to book the Premium Package.

MAGIC YOUR WAY PLATINUM PACKAGE The favorite of high rollers who want to prepay for everything they might desire while at Walt Disney World, the Platinum Package gets you lodging; Base Tickets; breakfast, lunch, and dinner in full-service restaurants; unlimited golf, tennis, boating, and recreation; unlimited dinner shows and character breakfasts; primo Cirque du Soleil seats; private in-room child care; unlimited use of child-care facilities; personalized itinerary planning; a ride on the Characters in Flight balloon at Disney Springs; a spa treatment; a fireworks cruise; admission to select tours; reserved seating for *Fantasmic!;* and (here's the kicker) nightly turndown service! Everything you can think of, in other words, except alcoholic beverages. Per diem prices (including tax) for the Platinum Package are $264 for adults and $194 for kids in addition to the cost of a standard Magic Your Way package— but anyone who buys this package doesn't give a Goofy fart what the prices are anyway. As with the Premium Package, a minimum three-night stay is required.

Things to Consider When Evaluating the Plus Dining Plan

If you prefer to always eat at counter-service restaurants, you'll be better off with the Quick-Service plan. Other poor candidates for the Plus plan include finicky eaters, light eaters, families who can't agree on restaurants, and those who can't get reservations at their first- or second-choice sit-down restaurants. It's usually not cost-effective during the holidays or summer either. In addition, if you have children age 10 and older, be sure that they can eat an adult-size dinner at a sit-down restaurant every night; if not, you'd probably come out ahead just paying for everyone's meals without the plan.

If you opt for the plan, skipping one full-service meal during a visit of five or fewer days can mean the difference between saving and losing money. In our experience, having a scheduled sit-down meal for every day of a weeklong vacation can be mentally exhausting, especially for kids. One option might be to schedule a meal at a Disney Signature restaurant, which requires two full-service credits, and have no scheduled sit-down meal on another night in the middle of your trip, allowing everyone to decide on the spot if they're up for something formal.

As already noted, many of the most popular restaurants are fully booked as soon as their reservation windows open. If you're still interested in the dining plan, book your restaurants as soon as possible, typically 180 days before you visit. Then decide whether the plan makes economic sense for you and your family. (For more on Advance Reservations, see page 141.)

If you're making reservations to eat at Disney hotels other than your own, a car allows you to easily access them. When you use the Disney transportation system, dining at the various resorts can be a logistical nightmare. Those without a car may want to weigh the immediate services of a taxi—typically $10–$15 each way across Disney property, versus a 50- to 75-minute trip on Disney transportation each way.

When Disney offers Free Dining discounts (typically in September), it generally charges rack rate for the hotel. You should work out the math, but Free Dining is typically a good deal for families who have two children under age 10, are staying at a Value resort, and book lots of character meals. Light eaters and childless couples, especially those staying at Deluxe resorts, may find it cheaper to take a room discount and pay for food separately.

For an in-depth discussion of the various plans, including number crunching (with algebra, even!), visit **touringplans.com** (scroll down and click "Dining" on the home page, then "Disney Dining Plan").

Readers who try the Disney dining plans have varying experiences. A St. Louis family of three comments:

We got the dining plan and would never do it again. Far too expensive, far too much food, and then you have to tip on top of the expense. Much easier to buy what you want, where and when you want.

A Belmont, Massachusetts, dad likes the Quick-Service Dining Plan:

If you intend to eat Disney food, the counter-service meal plan is a good option. We didn't want the full plan because the restaurants seemed overpriced, and the necessity of reservations months in advance seemed crazy and a bar to flexibility. You get two counter-service meals (entrée/combo, dessert, drink) and two snacks (food item or drink) per person as part of the plan, and even though kids' meals are cheaper, there is no distinction when you order—kids can order (more-expensive) adult meals.

But a reader from The Woodlands, Texas, laments that the plan has altered the focus of her vacation:

> For me, the dining plan has taken a lot of the fun out of going to Disney World. Now, dining for each day must be planned months in advance unless one is to eat just hot dogs, pizza, and other walk-up items. I want to have fun. I don't want to be locked into a tight schedule, always worrying about where we need to be when it's time to eat, and I don't want to eat when I'm not hungry just because I have a reservation somewhere.

A mom from Orland Park, Illinois, comments on the difficulty of getting Advance Reservations:

> It's impossible to get table reservations anywhere good—the restaurants that are available are available for a reason. We found ourselves taking whatever was open and were unhappy with every sit-down meal we had, except for lunch at Liberty Tree Tavern. I don't enjoy planning my day exclusively around eating at a certain restaurant at a certain time, but that is what you must do six months in advance if you want to eat at a good sit-down restaurant in Disney. That is ridiculous.

In a similar vein, a San Jose, California, reader says that guests who are not on the dining plan need to know how it affects Advance Reservations:

> When planning 90 days out for the off-season, I was told by the Disney rep to make all my Advance Reservations then because the restaurants are booked by people on the dining plan. In fact, I was told that most of the sit-down restaurants don't even take walk-ins anymore. Sure enough, even though I was well over 90 days away from my vacation, a lot of my restaurant choices were unavailable. I had to rearrange my entire schedule to fit the open slots at the restaurants I didn't want to miss.

On a positive note, many readers report that Disney cast members are much more knowledgeable about the dining plan these days than in the past. A Washington, D.C.–area couple writes:

> The kinks are worked out, and everyone at the parks we talked to seemed to get it, but we still spent $40 or more at most sit-down dinners on drinks and tips.

A mum from Sutton Coldfield, England, warns that toddlers fall through the cracks:

> We were traveling with two 6-year-olds and a 2-year-old. My youngest did not qualify for the dining plan, which worked well in the buffet-style restaurants where he could eat free. However, if you eat in a full-service restaurant and your 2-year-old is eating off the menu, there's no infant option—you have to pay for a child's meal.

A Land O' Lakes, Florida, dad bumped into this problem:

We had some trouble with our Deluxe Dining Plan being "invalidated" after checkout, though it was supposed to be valid until midnight of our checkout date. That was annoying because calls to the resort were needed to verify the meals left on our passes for The Crystal Palace and for some snacks later.

The dining plan left a family of five from Nashville, Tennessee, similarly dazed and confused:

What was annoying was the inconsistency. You can get a 16-ounce chocolate milk on the kids' plan, but only 8 ounces of white milk at many places. At Earl of Sandwich, you can get 16 ounces of either kind. A pint of milk would count as a snack (price $1.79), but they wouldn't count a quart of milk (price $2.39) because it wasn't a single serving. However, in Animal Kingdom, my husband bought a water-bottle holder (price $3.75) and used a snack credit.

Reader Tips for Getting the Most Out of the Plan

A mom from Radford, Virginia, shares the following:

Warn people to eat lunch early if they have dinner reservations before 7 p.m. Disney doesn't skimp on food—if you eat a late lunch, you WILL NOT be hungry for dinner.

A mom from Brick Township, New Jersey, found that the dining plan streamlined her touring:

We truly enjoyed our Disney trip, and this time we purchased the dining plan. This was great for the kids because we did a character-dining experience every day. This helped us in the parks because we didn't have to wait in line to see the characters. Instead, we got all of our autographs during our meals.

A Saskatoon, Saskatchewan, father of three says it's important to be vigilant when it comes to the outdoor food vendors:

We had a problem with a vendor who charged us meal service for each of the ice cream bars we purchased. This became evident at our final sit-down meal, when we didn't have any meal vouchers left. Check the receipts after every purchase!

CHARACTER DINING

ALL THE RAGE AT WALT DISNEY WORLD, character dining combines a meal with meeting the characters. The characters circulate throughout the meal, stopping at each table to sign autographs, pose for photos, and lavish attention on mostly adoring (but sometimes stupefied) children. For a detailed description of this Disney ritual, see the discussion starting on page 249.

WALT DISNEY WORLD DINNER THEATERS

SEVERAL DINNER-THEATER SHOWS play each night at Walt Disney World, and unlike other Disney dining venues, they make hard reservations instead of Advance Reservations, meaning you must guarantee your reservation ahead of time with a credit card. You'll receive a confirmation number and be told to pick up your tickets at a Disney-hotel Guest Relations desk. Unless you cancel your tickets at least 48 hours before your reservation time, your credit card will still be charged the full amount. Dinner-show reservations can be made 180 days in advance; call ☎ 407-939-3463.

Hoop-Dee-Doo Musical Revue
Pioneer Hall, Fort Wilderness Resort & Campground

Showtimes 4, 6:15, and 8:30 p.m. nightly. **Cost** *Category 1:* $66–$70 adults, $34–$36 children ages 3–9. *Category 2:* $59–$63 adults, $29–$31 children. *Category 3:* $55–$59 adults, $28–$30 children. Prices include tax and gratuity. **Discounts** Seasonal. **Type of seating** Tables of various sizes to fit the number in each party, set in an Old West–style dance hall. **Menu** All-you-can-eat barbecue ribs, fried chicken, corn, and strawberry shortcake. **Vegetarian alternative** On request (at least 24 hours in advance). **Beverages** Unlimited beer, wine, sangria, and soft drinks.

SIX WILD WEST PERFORMERS arrive by stagecoach (sound effects only) to entertain the crowd inside Pioneer Hall. There isn't much of a plot, just corny jokes interspersed with song or dance. The humor is of the *Hee Haw* ilk, but it's presented enthusiastically.

Audience participation includes sing-alongs, hand clapping, and a finale that uses volunteers to play parts on stage. Performers are accompanied by a banjo player and pianist who also play quietly while the food is being served. The fried chicken and corn on the cob are good, and the ribs are very tasty.

Traveling to Fort Wilderness and absorbing the rustic atmosphere of Pioneer Hall augments the adventure. For repeat Disney World visitors, an annual visit to the revue is a tradition of sorts. Plus, warts and all, the revue is all Disney, and for some folks that's enough. The fact that performances sell out far in advance gives the experience a special aura. To make reservations for the *Hoop-Dee-Doo Musical Revue,* call as soon as you're certain of the dates of your visit. The earlier you call, the better your seats will be.

If you go to *Hoop-Dee-Doo,* allow plenty of driving time (about an hour) to get there. Or do as this California dad suggests:

> Take the boat from the Magic Kingdom rather than any bus. This is contrary to the "official" directions. The boat dock is a short walk from Pioneer Hall in Fort Wilderness, while the bus goes to the main Fort Wilderness parking lot, where one has to transfer to another bus to Pioneer Hall.

Boat service may be suspended during thunderstorms, so if it's raining or it looks like it's about to rain, Disney will provide bus service from the parks.

Mickey's Backyard BBQ Fort Wilderness Resort & Campground

Showtimes Thursday and Saturday at 5, 6:30, and 7 p.m. **Cost** $60 adults, $36 children ages 3–9. Prices include tax and gratuity. **Type of seating** Picnic tables. **Menu** Baked chicken, barbecue-pork ribs, burgers, hot dogs, corn, beans, mac and cheese, salads and slaw, bread, and watermelon and ice cream bars for dessert. **Vegetarian alternatives** On request. **Beverages** Unlimited beer, wine, lemonade, and iced tea.

SITUATED ALONG BAY LAKE and held in a covered pavilion, *Mickey's Backyard BBQ* features Mickey, Minnie, Chip 'n' Dale, and Goofy, along with a country band and line dancing. Though the pavilion gets some breeze off Bay Lake, we recommend going during the spring or fall, if possible. The food is pretty good, as is, fortunately, the insect control.

The easiest way to get to the barbecue is to take a boat from the Magic Kingdom or, from one of the Disney resorts, take the Magic Kingdom monorail. Give yourself at least 45 minutes if you plan to arrive by boat. Ferry service may be suspended during thunderstorms, so if it's raining or it looks like it's about to rain, Disney will provide bus service from the parks. From a Rhode Island dad:

> *Mickey's Backyard BBQ was a surprise hit. It was easy to get there from the Magic Kingdom. The food at the BBQ was nice, and watching little kids line dance with the characters was about the most adorable thing I've ever seen.*

Spirit of Aloha Dinner Show Polynesian Village Resort

Showtimes Tuesday–Saturday, 5:15 and 8 p.m. **Cost** *Category 1:* $70–$74 adults, $36–$40 children ages 3–9. *Category 2:* $63–$67 adults, $31–$33 children. *Category 3:* $59–$63 adults, $30–$32 children. Prices include tax and gratuity. **Discounts** Seasonal. **Type of seating** Long rows of tables, with some separation between individual parties. The show is performed on an outdoor stage, but all seating is covered. Ceiling fans provide some air movement, but it can get warm, especially at the early show. **Menu** Tropical fruit, roasted chicken, island pork ribs, mixed vegetables, rice, and pineapple bread; chicken tenders, PB&J sandwiches, mac and cheese, and hot dogs are also available for children. **Vegetarian alternative** On request. **Beverages** Beer, wine, and soft drinks.

THIS SHOW FEATURES South Seas–island native dancing followed by an all-you-can-eat "Polynesian-style" meal. The dancing is interesting and largely authentic, and the dancers are attractive though definitely PG-rated in the Disney tradition. We think the show has its moments and the meal is adequate, but neither is particularly special.

The show follows (tenuously) the common "girl leaves home for the big city, forgets her roots, and must rediscover them" theme. The story, however, never really makes sense as anything other than a slender thread between musical numbers. Our show lasted for more than 2 hours and 15 minutes.

The food does little more than illustrate how difficult it must be to prepare the same meal for hundreds of people simultaneously. The roasted chicken is better than the ribs, but neither is anything special. We conditionally recommend *Spirit of Aloha* for special occasions, when the people celebrating get to go on stage. But go to the early show and get dessert somewhere else in the World.

WALT DISNEY WORLD RESTAURANTS: RATED AND RANKED

OVERALL RATING This represents the entire dining experience: style, service, ambience, and food quality. Five stars is the highest rating attainable. Four-star restaurants are above average, and three-star restaurants offer good, though not necessarily memorable, meals. Two-star restaurants serve mediocre fare, and one-star restaurants are below average. Our star ratings don't correspond to ratings awarded by AAA, Mobil, Zagat, or other restaurant reviewers.

COST RANGE The next rating tells you how much you'll spend on a full-service entrée. Appetizers, sides, soups/salads, desserts, drinks, and tips aren't included. Costs are categorized as inexpensive (less than $13), moderate ($13–$23), or expensive ($24 and up).

QUALITY RATING The food quality is rated on a scale of one to five stars, five being the best. The criteria are taste, freshness of ingredients, preparation, presentation, and creativity of food served. Price is not a consideration.

VALUE RATING If you are looking for both quality and value, then you should check the value rating, expressed as stars.

★★★★★	Exceptional value, a real bargain
★★★★	Good value
★★★	Fair value, you get exactly what you pay for
★★	Somewhat overpriced
★	Significantly overpriced

WALT DISNEY WORLD RESTAURANTS BY CUISINE

CUISINE	LOCATION	OVERALL RATING	COST	QUALITY RATING	VALUE RATING
AFRICAN					
JIKO—THE COOKING PLACE	Animal Kingdom Lodge	★★★★½	Exp	★★★★½	★★★½
BOMA—FLAVORS OF AFRICA	Animal Kingdom Lodge	★★★★	Exp	★★★★	★★★★½
SANAA	Animal Kingdom Villas–Kidani Village	★★★★	Exp	★★★★	★★★★
TUSKER HOUSE RESTAURANT	Animal Kingdom	★★★	Mod	★★★	★★★
AMERICAN					
CALIFORNIA GRILL	Contemporary	★★★★★	Exp	★★★★★	★★★
BE OUR GUEST RESTAURANT	Magic Kingdom	★★★★	Exp	★★★★	★★★★
THE HOLLYWOOD BROWN DERBY	DHS	★★★★	Exp	★★★★	★★★
ARTIST POINT	Wilderness Lodge	★★★½	Exp	★★★★	★★★
CAPE MAY CAFE	Beach Club	★★★½	Mod	★★★½	★★★★
WHISPERING CANYON CAFE	Wilderness Lodge	★★★	Mod	★★★½	★★★★
CAPTAIN'S GRILLE	Yacht Club	★★★	Mod	★★★½	★★★
THE CRYSTAL PALACE	Magic Kingdom	★★★	Mod	★★★½	★★★
HOUSE OF BLUES	Disney Springs	★★★	Mod	★★★½	★★★
50'S PRIME TIME CAFE	DHS	★★★	Mod	★★★	★★★

WALT DISNEY WORLD RESTAURANTS BY CUISINE (continued)

CUISINE	LOCATION	OVERALL RATING	COST	QUALITY RATING	VALUE RATING
AMERICAN (continued)					
LIBERTY TREE TAVERN*	Magic Kingdom	★★★	Mod	★★★	★★★
TUSKER HOUSE RESTAURANT	Animal Kingdom	★★★	Mod	★★★	★★★
CINDERELLA'S ROYAL TABLE	Magic Kingdom	★★★	Exp	★★★	★★
OLIVIA'S CAFE	Old Key West	★★★	Mod	★★★	★★
T-REX	Disney Springs	★★★	Mod	★★	★★
THE WAVE . . . OF AMERICAN FLAVORS	Contemporary	★★★	Mod	★★	★★
CHEF MICKEY'S	Contemporary	★★½	Exp	★★★	★★★
ESPN CLUB	BoardWalk	★★½	Mod	★★★	★★★
ESPN WIDE WORLD OF SPORTS GRILL	ESPN Wide World of Sports Complex	★★½	Mod	★★★	★★★
HOLLYWOOD & VINE	DHS	★★½	Mod	★★★	★★★
1900 PARK FARE	Grand Floridian	★★½	Mod	★★★	★★★
BOATWRIGHT'S DINING HALL	Port Orleans	★★½	Mod	★★★	★★
GRAND FLORIDIAN CAFE	Grand Floridian	★★½	Mod	★★★	★★
BEACHES & CREAM SODA SHOP	Beach Club	★★½	Inexp	★★½	★★½
FRESH MEDITERRANEAN MARKET	Dolphin	★★½	Mod	★★½	★★
SPLITSVILLE	Disney Springs	★★½	Mod	★★½	★★
PLANET HOLLYWOOD	Disney Springs	★★½	Mod	★★	★★
RAINFOREST CAFE	Animal Kingdom and Disney Springs	★★½	Mod	★★	★★
GARDEN GROVE	Swan	★★	Mod	★★★	★★
TURF CLUB BAR & GRILL	Saratoga Springs	★★	Mod	★★★	★★
LAS VENTANAS	Coronado Springs	★★	Mod	★★½	★★
SCI-FI DINE-IN THEATER RESTAURANT	DHS	★★	Mod	★★½	★★
GARDEN GRILL RESTAURANT	Epcot	★★	Exp	★★	★★★
BIG RIVER GRILLE & BREWING WORKS	BoardWalk	★★	Mod	★★	★★
THE FOUNTAIN	Dolphin	★★	Mod	★★	★★
THE PLAZA RESTAURANT	Magic Kingdom	★★	Mod	★★	★★
TRAIL'S END RESTAURANT	Fort Wilderness Resort	★★	Mod	★★	★★
WOLFGANG PUCK GRAND CAFE	Disney Springs	★★	Exp	★½	★½
MAYA GRILL	Coronado Springs	★	Exp	★	★

WALT DISNEY WORLD RESTAURANTS BY CUISINE (continued)

CUISINE	LOCATION	OVERALL RATING	COST	QUALITY RATING	VALUE RATING
BUFFET					
BOMA—FLAVORS OF AFRICA	Animal Kingdom Lodge	★★★★	Exp	★★★★	★★★★½
CAPE MAY CAFE	Beach Club	★★★½	Mod	★★★½	★★★★
THE CRYSTAL PALACE	Magic Kingdom	★★★	Mod	★★★½	★★★
TUSKER HOUSE RESTAURANT	Animal Kingdom	★★★	Mod	★★★	★★★
CHEF MICKEY'S	Contemporary	★★½	Exp	★★★	★★★
HOLLYWOOD & VINE	DHS	★★½	Mod	★★★	★★★
1900 PARK FARE	Grand Floridian	★★½	Mod	★★★	★★★
GARDEN GROVE	Swan	★★	Mod	★★★	★★
AKERSHUS ROYAL BANQUET HALL	Epcot	★★	Exp	★★	★★★★
BIERGARTEN	Epcot	★★	Exp	★★	★★★★
TRAIL'S END RESTAURANT	Fort Wilderness Resort	★★	Mod	★★	★★
CAJUN					
BOATWRIGHT'S DINING HALL	Port Orleans	★★½	Mod	★★★	★★
CHINESE					
NINE DRAGONS RESTAURANT	Epcot	★★★	Mod	★★★	★★
CUBAN					
BONGOS CUBAN CAFE	Disney Springs	★★	Mod	★★	★★
ENGLISH					
ROSE & CROWN DINING ROOM	Epcot	★★★	Mod	★★★½	★★
FRENCH					
MONSIEUR PAUL	Epcot	★★★★	Exp	★★★★½	★★★
BE OUR GUEST RESTAURANT	Magic Kingdom	★★★★	Exp	★★★★	★★★★
LES CHEFS DE FRANCE	Epcot	★★★	Exp	★★★	★★★
GERMAN					
BIERGARTEN	Epcot	★★	Exp	★★	★★★★
GLOBAL					
PARADISO 37	Disney Springs	★★½	Inexp	★★★	★★★
GOURMET					
VICTORIA & ALBERT'S	Grand Floridian	★★★★★	Exp	★★★★★	★★★★
INDIAN					
SANAA	Animal Kingdom Villas-Kidani Village	★★★★	Exp	★★★★	★★★★

WALT DISNEY WORLD RESTAURANTS BY CUISINE *(continued)*

CUISINE	LOCATION	OVERALL RATING	COST	QUALITY RATING	VALUE RATING
IRISH					
RAGLAN ROAD IRISH PUB & RESTAURANT	Disney Springs	★★★★	Mod	★★★½	★★★
ITALIAN					
TUTTO ITALIA RISTORANTE	Epcot	★★★★	Exp	★★★★	★★★
VIA NAPOLI	Epcot	★★★★	Mod	★★★½	★★★
TRATTORIA AL FORNO	BoardWalk	★★★½	Mod	★★★½	★★
IL MULINO NEW YORK TRATTORIA	Swan	★★★	Exp	★★★	★★
MAMA MELROSE'S RISTORANTE ITALIANO	DHS	★★½	Mod	★★★	★★
PORTOBELLO	Disney Springs	★★½	Exp	★★★	★★
TONY'S TOWN SQUARE RESTAURANT	Magic Kingdom	★★½	Mod	★★★	★★
JAPANESE/SUSHI					
KIMONOS	Swan	★★★★	Mod	★★★★½	★★★
TEPPAN EDO	Epcot	★★★½	Exp	★★★★	★★★
TOKYO DINING	Epcot	★★★	Mod	★★★★	★★★
MEDITERRANEAN					
CÍTRICOS	Grand Floridian	★★★½	Exp	★★★★½	★★★
FRESH MEDITERRANEAN MARKET	Dolphin	★★½	Mod	★★½	★★
MEXICAN					
LA HACIENDA DE SAN ANGEL	Epcot	★★★	Exp	★★★½	★★½
SAN ANGEL INN RESTAURANTE	Epcot	★★★	Exp	★★★	★★
MAYA GRILL	Coronado Springs	★	Exp	★	★
MOROCCAN					
SPICE ROAD TABLE	Epcot	★★★½	Mod	★★★★	★★★
RESTAURANT MARRAKESH	Epcot	★★	Mod	★★½	★★
NORWEGIAN					
AKERSHUS ROYAL BANQUET HALL	Epcot	★★	Exp	★★	★★★★
POLYNESIAN/PAN-ASIAN					
'OHANA	Polynesian Village	★★★	Mod	★★★½	★★★
KONA CAFE	Polynesian Village	★★★	Mod	★★★	★★★★
TRADER SAM'S GROG GROTTO	Polynesian Village	★★★	Mod	★★★	★★★
YAK & YETI RESTAURANT	Animal Kingdom	★★	Exp	★★½	★★

WALT DISNEY WORLD RESTAURANTS BY CUISINE (continued)

CUISINE	LOCATION	OVERALL RATING	COST	QUALITY RATING	VALUE RATING
SEAFOOD					
NARCOOSSEE'S	Grand Floridian	★★★★½	Exp	★★★½	★★
FLYING FISH CAFE	BoardWalk	★★★★	Exp	★★★★	★★★
ARTIST POINT	Wilderness Lodge	★★★½	Exp	★★★★	★★★
TODD ENGLISH'S BLUEZOO	Dolphin	★★★	Exp	★★★★	★★
THE BOATHOUSE	Disney Springs	★★★	Exp	★★★	★★½
FULTON'S CRAB HOUSE	Disney Springs	★★½	Exp	★★½	★★
CORAL REEF RESTAURANT	Epcot	★★½	Exp	★★	★★
SHUTTERS AT OLD PORT ROYALE	Caribbean Beach	★★	Mod	★★½	★★
STEAK					
SHULA'S STEAK HOUSE	Dolphin	★★★★	Exp	★★★★	★★
LE CELLIER STEAKHOUSE	Epcot	★★★½	Exp	★★★½	★★★
YACHTSMAN STEAKHOUSE	Yacht Club	★★★	Exp	★★★½	★★
SHUTTERS AT OLD PORT ROYALE	Caribbean Beach	★★	Mod	★★½	★★

PART FIVE

KNOW BEFORE YOU GO

The **BRUTAL TRUTH** *About* **FAMILY VACATIONS**

IT HAS BEEN SUGGESTED THAT THE PHRASE *family vacation* is a bit of an oxymoron. This is because you can never take a vacation from the responsibilities of parenting if your children are traveling with you. Though you leave your work and normal routine far behind, your children require as much attention, if not more, when traveling as they do at home.

Parenting on the road is an art. It requires imagination and organization. Think about it: You have to do all the usual stuff (feed, dress, bathe, supervise, teach, comfort, discipline, put to bed, and so on) in an atmosphere where your children are hyperstimulated, without the familiarity of place and the resources you take for granted at home. Though it's not impossible—and can even be fun—parenting on the road is not something you want to learn on the fly, particularly at Walt Disney World.

The point we want to drive home is that preparation, or the lack thereof, can make or break your Walt Disney World vacation. Believe us, you do *not* want to leave the success of your expensive Disney vacation to chance. But don't confuse chance with good luck. Chance is what happens when you fail to prepare. Good luck is when preparation meets opportunity.

Your preparation can be organized into several categories, all of which we will help you undertake. Broadly speaking, you need to prepare yourself and your children mentally, emotionally, physically, organizationally, and logistically. You also need a basic understanding of Walt Disney World and a well-considered plan for how to go about seeing it.

MENTAL *and* EMOTIONAL PREPARATION

THIS IS A SUBJECT THAT WE WILL TOUCH on here and return to many times in this book. Mental preparation begins with realistic expectations about your Disney vacation and consideration of what each adult and child in your party most wants and needs from their Walt Disney World experience. Getting in touch with this aspect of planning requires a lot of introspection and good, open family communication.

DIVISION OF LABOR

TALK ABOUT WHAT YOU AND YOUR PARTNER NEED and what you expect to happen on the vacation. This discussion alone can pre-empt some unpleasant surprises mid-trip. If you are a two-parent family, do you have a clear understanding of how the parenting workload is to be distributed? We've seen some distinctly disruptive misunderstandings in two-parent households where one parent is (pardon the legalese) the primary caregiver. Often, the other parent expects the primary caregiver to function on vacation as she (or he) does at home. The primary caregiver, on the other hand, is ready for a break. She expects her partner to either shoulder the load equally or perhaps even assume the lion's share so she can have a *real* vacation. However you divide the responsibility, of course, is up to you. Just make sure you negotiate a clear understanding *before* you leave home.

TOGETHERNESS

ANOTHER DIMENSION TO CONSIDER is how much togetherness seems appropriate to you. For some parents, a vacation represents a rare opportunity to really connect with their children, to talk, exchange ideas, and get reacquainted. For others, a vacation affords the time to get a little distance, to enjoy a round of golf while the kids are participating in a program organized by the resort.

At Walt Disney World you can orchestrate your vacation to spend as much or as little time with your children as you desire, but more about that later. The point here is to think about your and your children's preferences and needs concerning your time together. A typical day at a Disney theme park provides the structure of experiencing attractions together, punctuated by periods of waiting in line, eating, and so on, which facilitate conversation and sharing. Most attractions can be enjoyed together by the whole family, regardless of age ranges. This allows for more consensus and less dissent when it comes to deciding what to see and do. For many parents and children, however, the rhythms of a Walt Disney World day seem to consist of passive entertainment experiences alternated with endless discussions of where to go and what to do next. As a mother from Winston-Salem, North Carolina, reported:

Our family mostly talked about what to do next with very little sharing or discussion about what we had seen. The conversation was pretty task-oriented.

Two observations: First, fighting the crowds and keeping the family moving along can easily escalate into a pressure-driven outing. Having an advance plan or itinerary eliminates moment-to-moment guesswork and decision making, thus creating more time for savoring and connecting. Second, external variables such as crowd size, noise, and heat, among others, can be so distracting as to preclude any meaningful togetherness. These negative impacts can be moderated, as previously discussed, by your being selective concerning the time of year, day of the week, and time of day you visit the theme parks. The bottom line is that you can achieve the degree of connection and togetherness you desire with a little advance planning and a realistic awareness of the distractions you will encounter.

LIGHTEN UP

PREPARE YOURSELF MENTALLY to be a little less compulsive on vacation about correcting small behavioral deviations and pounding home the lessons of life. Certainly, little Mildred will have to learn eventually that it's very un-Disney-like to take off her top at the pool. But there's plenty of time for that later. So what if Matt eats hamburgers for breakfast, lunch, and dinner every day? You can make him eat peas and broccoli when you get home and are in charge of meal preparation again. Roll with the little stuff, and remember when your children act out that they are wired to the max. At least some of that adrenaline is bound to spill out in undesirable ways. Coming down hard will send an already frayed little nervous system into orbit.

SOMETHING FOR EVERYONE

IF YOU TRAVEL WITH AN INFANT, TODDLER, or any child who requires a lot of special attention, make sure that you have some energy and time remaining for your other children. In the course of your planning, invite each child to name something special to do or see at Walt Disney World with Mom or Dad alone. Work these special activities into your trip itinerary. Whatever else, if you commit, write it down so you don't forget. Remember, though, that a casually expressed willingness to do this or that may be perceived as a promise by your children.

LILIANE Try to schedule some time alone with each of your children, if not each day, then at least a couple of times during the trip.

Liliane

WHOSE IDEA WAS THIS, ANYWAY?

THE DISCORD THAT MANY VACATIONING FAMILIES experience arises from the kids being on a completely different wavelength from Mom and Dad. Parents and grandparents are often worse than children when it comes to conjuring up fantasy scenarios of what a Walt Disney

World vacation will be like. A Disney vacation can be many thi
believe us when we tell you that there's a lot more to it than just r
Dumbo and seeing Mickey.

In our experience, most parents and nearly all grandparents expect children to enter a state of rapture at Walt Disney World, bouncing from attraction to attraction in wide-eyed wonder, appreciative beyond words of their adult bene-factors. What they get, more often than not, is not even in the same ballpark. Preschoolers will, without a doubt, be wide-eyed, often with delight but also with a general sense of being

LILIANE Short for
the parks inter-
spersed with naps,
swimming, and
quiet activities
such as reading to your
children will go a long
way toward keeping
things on an even keel.

overwhelmed by noise, crowds, and Disney characters as big as tool-sheds. We have substantiated through thousands of interviews and surveys that the best part of a Disney vacation for a preschooler is the hotel swimming pool. With some grade-schoolers and pre-driving-age teens, you get near-manic hyperactivity coupled with periods of stud-ied nonchalance. This last, which relates to the importance of being cool at all costs, translates into a maddening display of boredom and a "been there, done that" attitude. Older teens are frequently the exponential version of the younger teens and grade-schoolers, except without the manic behavior.

As a function of probability, you may escape many—but most likely not all—of the aforementioned behaviors. Even in the event that they are all visited on you, however, take heart—there are antidotes.

LILIANE The more information your children have
before arriving at
Walt Disney World,
the less likely they
will be to act out.

For preschoolers keep things light and happy by limiting the time you spend in the theme parks. The most critical point is that the overstimulation of the parks must be balanced by adequate rest and more mellow activities. For grade-schoolers and early teens, moderate the hyperactivity and false apathy by enlisting their help in planning the vacation, especially by allowing them to take a leading role in determining the itinerary for days at the theme parks. Being in charge of specific responsibilities that focus on the happiness of other family members also works well. One reader, for example, turned a 12-year-old liability into an asset by asking him to help guard against attractions that might frighten his 5-year-old sister.

Knowledge enhances anticipation and at the same time affords a level of comfort and control that helps kids understand the big picture. The more they feel in control, the less they will act out of control.

DISNEY, KIDS, AND SCARY STUFF

DISNEY ATTRACTIONS, BOTH RIDES AND SHOWS, are adven-tures. They focus on themes common to adventures: good and evil, life and death, beauty and the grotesque, fellowship and enmity. As you

Continued on page 191

LD FRIGHT-POTENTIAL TABLE

to identify attractions to be wary of, and why. The table rep-
, and all kids are different. It relates specifically to kids ages
n at the younger end of the range are more likely to be
n in their 6th or 7th year.

THE MAGIC KINGDOM

SORCERERS OF THE MAGIC KINGDOM Loud but not frightening.

MAIN STREET, U.S.A.

TOWN SQUARE THEATER MEET AND GREETS Not frightening in any respect.

WALT DISNEY WORLD RAILROAD Not frightening in any respect.

ADVENTURELAND

JUNGLE CRUISE Moderately intense, some macabre sights. A good test attraction for little ones.

THE MAGIC CARPETS OF ALADDIN Much like Dumbo. A favorite ride of most younger children.

PIRATES OF THE CARIBBEAN Slightly intimidating queuing area; intense boat ride with gruesome (though humorously presented) sights and a short, unexpected slide down a flume.

SWISS FAMILY TREEHOUSE Kids who are afraid of heights may want to skip it.

WALT DISNEY'S ENCHANTED TIKI ROOM A thunderstorm, loud volume level, and simulated explosions frighten some preschoolers.

FRONTIERLAND

BIG THUNDER MOUNTAIN RAILROAD Visually intimidating from outside, with moderately intense visual effects. The roller coaster is wild enough to frighten many adults, particularly seniors. Switching-off option provided (see page 243).

COUNTRY BEAR JAMBOREE Not frightening in any respect.

SPLASH MOUNTAIN Visually intimidating from outside, with moderately intense visual effects. The ride culminates in a 52-foot plunge down a steep chute. Switching-off option provided (see page 243).

TOM SAWYER ISLAND AND FORT LANGHORN Some very young children are intimidated by dark walk-through tunnels that can be easily avoided.

LIBERTY SQUARE

THE HALL OF PRESIDENTS Not frightening, but boring for young ones.

THE HAUNTED MANSION Name raises anxiety, as do sounds and sights of waiting area. Intense attraction with humorously presented macabre sights. The ride itself is gentle.

LIBERTY BELLE RIVERBOAT Not frightening in any respect.

FANTASYLAND

ARIEL'S GROTTO Not frightening in any respect.

THE BARNSTORMER May frighten some preschoolers.

DUMBO THE FLYING ELEPHANT A tame midway ride; a great favorite of most young children.

ENCHANTED TALES WITH BELLE Not frightening in any respect.

IT'S A SMALL WORLD Not frightening in any respect.

MAD TEA PARTY Midway-type ride can induce motion sickness in all ages.

MICKEY'S PHILHARMAGIC Some preschoolers may be a little scared at first, but taking the 3-D glasses off tones down the effect.

SMALL-CHILD FRIGHT-POTENTIAL TABLE

FANTASYLAND (continued)

THE MANY ADVENTURES OF WINNIE THE POOH Frightens a few preschoolers.

PETER PAN'S FLIGHT Not frightening in any respect.

PETE'S SILLY SIDESHOW Not frightening in any respect.

PRINCE CHARMING REGAL CARROUSEL Not frightening in any respect.

PRINCESS FAIRYTALE HALL Long lines may have parents running for the hills.

SEVEN DWARFS MINE TRAIN Marginally wild ride, dark scenes, and special effects may frighten children age 7 and under.

UNDER THE SEA: JOURNEY OF THE LITTLE MERMAID Animatronic octopus character frightens some preschoolers.

TOMORROWLAND

ASTRO ORBITER Visually intimidating waiting area, but a relatively tame ride.

BUZZ LIGHTYEAR'S SPACE RANGER SPIN May frighten some preschoolers.

MONSTERS, INC. LAUGH FLOOR May frighten some preschoolers.

SPACE MOUNTAIN Very intense roller coaster in the dark; the Magic Kingdom's wildest ride and a scary roller coaster by any standard. Switching-off option provided (see page 243).

STITCH'S GREAT ESCAPE! Very intense (and smelly). May frighten children age 9 and younger. Switching-off option provided (see page 243).

TOMORROWLAND SPEEDWAY The noise of the waiting area slightly intimidates preschoolers; otherwise, not frightening.

TOMORROWLAND TRANSIT AUTHORITY PEOPLEMOVER Not frightening in any respect.

WALT DISNEY'S CAROUSEL OF PROGRESS Not frightening in any respect.

EPCOT

FUTURE WORLD

CAPTAIN EO Extremely intense visual effects and loudness frighten many young children.

THE CIRCLE OF LIFE Not frightening in any respect.

JOURNEY INTO IMAGINATION WITH FIGMENT Loud noises and unexpected flashing lights startle younger children.

LIVING WITH THE LAND Not frightening in any respect, but loud.

MISSION: SPACE Extremely intense space-simulation ride that has been known to frighten guests of all ages. Switching-off option provided (see page 243).

THE SEAS MAIN TANK AND EXHIBITS Not frightening in any respect.

THE SEAS WITH NEMO & FRIENDS Very sweet but may frighten some toddlers.

SOARIN' May frighten kids age 7 and younger, or anyone with a fear of heights. Otherwise a very mellow ride.

SPACESHIP EARTH Dark, imposing presentation intimidates a few preschoolers.

SUM OF ALL THRILLS Intense roller-coaster simulator may frighten some kids.

TEST TRACK Intense thrill ride may frighten guests of any age. Switching-off option provided (see page 243).

TURTLE TALK WITH CRUSH Not frightening in any respect.

UNIVERSE OF ENERGY: ELLEN'S ENERGY ADVENTURE Dinosaur segment frightens some preschoolers; visually intense, with some intimidating effects.

SMALL-CHILD FRIGHT-POTENTIAL TABLE
EPCOT *(continued)*

WORLD SHOWCASE

AGENT P'S WORLD SHOWCASE ADVENTURE Not frightening in any respect.

THE AMERICAN ADVENTURE Not frightening in any respect.

FROZEN EVER AFTER Dark. The previous ride ended with a plunge down a 20-foot flume, which, if it was kept, may frighten a few preschoolers.

GRAN FIESTA TOUR STARRING THE THREE CABALLEROS Not frightening in any respect.

ILLUMINATIONS Not frightening in any respect.

IMPRESSIONS DE FRANCE Not frightening in any respect.

O CANADA! Not frightening, but audience must stand.

REFLECTIONS OF CHINA Not frightening in any respect.

ROYAL SOMMERHUS MEET AND GREET Not frightening in any respect.

WORLD SHOWCASE PAVILIONS Not frightening in any respect.

DISNEY'S ANIMAL KINGDOM

THE OASIS Not frightening in any respect.

DISCOVERY ISLAND

MEET FAVORITE DISNEY PALS AT ADVENTURERS OUTPOST Not frightening in any respect.

THE TREE OF LIFE/*IT'S TOUGH TO BE A BUG!*** Very intense and loud, with special effects that startle viewers of all ages and potentially terrify little kids.

AFRICA

CONSERVATION STATION AND AFFECTION SECTION Not frightening in any respect.

FESTIVAL OF THE LION KING A bit loud, but otherwise not frightening.

KILIMANJARO SAFARIS A "collapsing" bridge and the proximity of real animals make a few young children anxious.

PANGANI FOREST EXPLORATION TRAIL Not frightening in any respect.

WILDLIFE EXPRESS TRAIN Not frightening in any respect.

ASIA

EXPEDITION EVEREST Can frighten guests of all ages. Switching-off option provided (see page 243).

FLIGHTS OF WONDER Swooping birds startle some younger children.

KALI RIVER RAPIDS Potentially frightening and certainly wet for guests of all ages. Switching-off option provided (see page 243).

MAHARAJAH JUNGLE TREK Some children may balk at the bat exhibit.

DINOLAND U.S.A.

DINOSAUR High-tech thrill ride rattles riders of all ages. Switching-off option provided (see page 243).

PRIMEVAL WHIRL A beginner roller coaster. Most children age 7 and older will take it in stride. Switching-off option provided (see page 243).

THEATER IN THE WILD/*FINDING NEMO—THE MUSICAL*** Not frightening in any respect, but loud.

TRICERATOP SPIN A midway-type ride that will frighten only a small percentage of younger children.

SMALL-CHILD FRIGHT-POTENTIAL TABLE
DISNEY'S HOLLYWOOD STUDIOS

HOLLYWOOD BOULEVARD

THE GREAT MOVIE RIDE Intense in parts, with very realistic special effects and some visually intimidating sights. Frightens many preschoolers.

SUNSET BOULEVARD

***BEAUTY AND THE BEAST—LIVE ON STAGE*/THEATER OF THE STARS** Not frightening in any respect.

FANTASMIC! Loud and intense with fireworks and some scary villains, but most young children like it.

ROCK 'N' ROLLER COASTER The wildest coaster at Walt Disney World. May frighten guests of any age. Switching-off option provided (see page 243).

THE TWILIGHT ZONE TOWER OF TERROR Visually intimidating to young children; contains intense and realistic special effects. The plummeting elevator at the ride's end frightens many adults as well as kids. Switching-off option provided (see page 243).

ECHO LAKE

FOR THE FIRST TIME IN FOREVER—A FROZEN SING-ALONG CELEBRATION Not frightening in any respect.

INDIANA JONES EPIC STUNT SPECTACULAR! An intense show with powerful special effects, including explosions, but young kids generally handle it well.

JEDI TRAINING ACADEMY Not frightening in any respect.

STAR TOURS—THE ADVENTURES CONTINUE Extremely intense visually for all ages; too intense for kids under age 8. Switching-off option provided (see page 243).

STREETS OF AMERICA

JIM HENSON'S MUPPET-VISION 3-D Intense and loud, but not frightening.

LIGHTS, MOTORS, ACTION! EXTREME STUNT SHOW Super stunt spectacular; intense with loud noises and explosions, but not threatening in any way.

PIXAR PLACE

TOY STORY MIDWAY MANIA! Dark ride may frighten some preschoolers.

MICKEY AVENUE

WALT DISNEY: ONE MAN'S DREAM Not frightening in any respect.

ANIMATION COURTYARD

DISNEY JUNIOR—LIVE ON STAGE! Not frightening in any respect.

VOYAGE OF THE LITTLE MERMAID Some children are creeped out by Ursula.

Continued from page 187

sample the attractions at Walt Disney World, you transcend the spinning and bouncing of midway rides to thought-provoking and emotionally powerful entertainment. All of the endings are happy, but the adventures' impact, given Disney's gift for special effects, often intimidates and occasionally frightens young children.

There are rides with burning towns and ghouls popping out of their graves, all done with a sense of humor, provided you're old enough to understand the joke. And bones. There are bones everywhere: human bones, cattle bones, dinosaur

BOB Before lining up for any attraction, check out our description of it and see our Small-Child Fright-Potential Table above and on the preceding pages.

bones, even whole skeletons. There's a stack of skulls at the headhunter's camp on the Jungle Cruise, a platoon of skeletons sailing ghost ships in Pirates of the Caribbean, and a haunting assemblage of skulls and skeletons in The Haunted Mansion. Skulls, skeletons, and bones punctuate Peter Pan's Flight and Big Thunder Mountain Railroad. And in Disney's Animal Kingdom, there's an entire children's playground made up exclusively of giant bones and skeletons.

On the other hand, the monsters and special effects at Disney's Hollywood Studios seem more real and sinister than those in the other theme parks. If your child has difficulty coping with the ghouls of The Haunted Mansion, think twice about exposing him or her to machine-gun battles, earthquakes, explosions, and the creature from *Alien* at the Studios.

One reader tells of taking his preschool children on Star Tours:

We took a 4-year-old and a 5-year-old, and they had the *^%#! scared out of them at Star Tours. We did this first thing in the morning, and it took hours of Tom Sawyer Island and Small World to get back to normal.

Our kids were the youngest by far in Star Tours. I assume that other adults had more sense or were not such avid readers of your book. Preschoolers should start with Dumbo and work up to the Jungle Cruise in late morning, after being revved up and before getting hungry, thirsty, or tired. Pirates of the Caribbean is out for preschoolers. You get the idea.

LILIANE You know I scream a lot on roller coasters, but did you know that I don't leave my feet on the floor during the *It's Tough to Be a Bug!* 3-D show at the Animal Kingdom? Well, now you know I do not like bugs, and they sting too; they do, they do.

At Walt Disney World, anticipate the almost inevitable emotional overload of your young children. Be sensitive, alert, and prepared for practically anything, even behavior that is out of character for your child at home. Most young children take Disney's macabre trappings in stride, and others are easily comforted by an arm around the shoulder or a squeeze of the hand. Parents who know that their children tend to become upset should take it slow and easy, sampling more benign adventures, gauging reactions, and discussing with the children how they felt about what they saw.

Some Tips

1. START SLOW AND WARM UP Though each major theme park offers several fairly nonintimidating attractions that you can sample to determine your child's relative sensitivity, the Magic Kingdom is probably the best testing ground. At the Magic Kingdom, try Buzz Lightyear's Space Ranger Spin in Tomorrowland, Peter Pan's Flight in Fantasyland, and the Jungle Cruise in Adventureland to measure your child's reaction to unfamiliar sights and sounds. If your child takes these in stride, try Pirates of the Caribbean. Try the Astro Orbiter in Tomorrowland, the Mad Tea Party in Fantasyland, or The Barnstormer also in

Fantasyland to observe how your child tolerates certain ride speeds and motions.

Do not assume that because an attraction is a theater presentation, it will not frighten your child. Trust us on this one. An attraction does not have to be moving to trigger unmitigated, panic-induced hysteria. Rides such as Big Thunder Mountain Railroad and Splash Mountain may look scary, but they do not have even one-fiftieth the potential for terrorizing children as do theater attractions such as *Stitch's Great Escape!*

2. BE ATTUNED TO PEER AND PARENT PRESSURE Sometimes young children will rise above their anxiety in an effort to please parents or siblings. This doesn't necessarily indicate a mastery of fear, much less enjoyment. If children leave a ride in apparently good shape, ask if they would like to go on it again (not necessarily now, but sometime). The response usually will indicate how much they actually enjoyed the experience. There's a big difference between having a good time and just mustering the courage to get through.

3. ENCOURAGE AND EMPATHIZE Evaluating a child's capacity to handle the visual and tactile effects of Disney World requires patience, understanding, and experimentation. Each of us, after all, has our own demons. If a child balks at or is frightened by a ride, respond constructively. Let your children know that lots of people, adults and children, are scared by what they see and feel. Help them understand that it's OK if they get frightened and that their fear doesn't lessen your love or respect. Take pains not to compound the discomfort by making a child feel inadequate; try not to undermine self-esteem, impugn courage, or ridicule. Most of all, don't induce guilt by suggesting the child's trepidation might be ruining the family's fun. It is also sometimes necessary to restrain older siblings' taunting or teasing.

A visit to Disney World is more than just an outing or an adventure for a young child. It's a testing experience, a sort of controlled rite of passage. If you help your little one work through the challenges, the time can be immeasurably rewarding and a bonding experience for you both.

The Fright Factor

Of course, each youngster is different, but there are eight attraction elements that alone or combined can push a child's buttons:

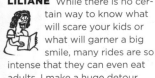

LILIANE While there is no certain way to know what will scare your kids or what will garner a big smile, many rides are so intense that they can even eat adults. I make a huge detour around The Twilight Zone Tower of Terror or Space Mountain, but I can't get enough of Star Tours, Mission: SPACE, and Kali River Rapids—and I have survived the Mad Tea Party and Expedition Everest. Parents know their children best. I do remember braving The Twilight Zone Tower of Terror once because I felt that I could not deprive my then-10-year-old just because I was a chicken. I didn't let on that this was not my cup of tea. My prayers to exit the attraction were answered when he asked me shyly if we could ask a cast member to get out. The request was granted instantly by both me and the cast member.

1. NAME OF THE ATTRACTION Young children will naturally be apprehensive about something called The Haunted Mansion or The Twilight Zone Tower of Terror.

2. VISUAL IMPACT OF THE ATTRACTION FROM OUTSIDE Big Thunder Mountain Railroad and Splash Mountain look scary enough to give even adults second thoughts, and they visually terrify many young children.

3. VISUAL IMPACT OF THE INDOOR QUEUING AREA Pirates of the Caribbean's caves and dungeons and The Haunted Mansion's "stretch rooms" can frighten kids even before they board the ride.

4. INTENSITY OF THE ATTRACTION Some attractions are overwhelming, inundating the senses with sights, sounds, movement, and even smell. *It's Tough to Be a Bug!* at Animal Kingdom, for example, combines loud sounds, lights, smoke, animatronic insects, and 3-D cinematography to create a total sensory experience. For some preschoolers, this is two or three senses too many.

5. VISUAL IMPACT OF THE ATTRACTION ITSELF Sights in various attractions range from falling boulders to lurking buzzards, from grazing dinosaurs to attacking white blood cells. What one child calmly absorbs may scare the bejabbers out of another.

6. DARK Many Disney World attractions operate indoors in the dark. For some children, darkness alone triggers fear. A child who is frightened on one dark ride (The Haunted Mansion, for example) may be unwilling to try other indoor rides.

7. THE RIDE ITSELF; THE TACTILE EXPERIENCE Some rides are wild enough to cause motion sickness, to wrench backs, and to discombobulate patrons of any age.

8. LOUD The sound levels in some attractions and live shows are so loud that younger children flip out even though the general content of the presentation is quite benign. For toddlers and preschoolers especially, it's good to have a pair of earplugs handy.

Disney Orientation Course

We receive many tips from parents telling how they prepared their young children for the Disney experience. A common strategy is to acquaint children with the characters and stories behind the attractions by reading Disney books and watching Disney videos at home. A more direct approach is to watch videos that show the attractions. A Lexington, Kentucky, mom reports:

> *My timid 7-year-old daughter and I watched rides and shows on YouTube, and we cut out all the ones that looked too scary.*

You can also order a free **Walt Disney World Vacation Planning DVD** by clicking on "Free Vacation Planning DVD" at the **disneyworld .com** home page or by calling ☎ 407-w-DISNEY (934-7639). As a YouTube supplement, it gives your kids an adequate sense of what they'll see. Allow at least one month for delivery. For more immediate gratification, you can also watch the **Travel Channel**'s Disney World specials on Hulu or Netflix streaming.

LILIANE My first roller coaster experience ever was with my son. We rode The Barnstormer. I screamed his ears off. Next I took a ride with you-know-who: Bob. He tricked me into riding The Incredible Hulk Coaster at Universal's Islands of Adventure. One cannot print what I said to him. (*Editor's note:* Bob is still deaf in one ear.)

A MAGICAL TIME FOR MOM AND DAD

OK, LILIANE WRITING HERE. Because Bob's idea of a romantic evening is watching *Monday Night Football* on the sofa with his honey instead of sitting in his La-Z-Boy, I'm going to tackle this subject solo.

Let's face it: We all know that moms and dads deserve some special time. But the reality on the ground is that the kids come first. And when the day is over, Mom and Dad are way too tired to think about having a special evening alone. It's difficult enough to catch a movie or go out for a romantic dinner in our hometowns, so how realistic is a romantic parents' night out while on vacation at Walt Disney World?

The answer is: No planning, no romance! With a little magic and some advance preparation, you can make it happen. Here we offer a few suggestions.

Staying at a hotel that offers great kids' programs is a big plus. Consider signing up small children for a half-day program with lunch or dinner while you enjoy your resort. Go to the pool and read a book, and then have a meal in calm and peace. Rent a bike, a boat, or just take off outside the World. This is also a great opportunity to enjoy the thrill rides you passed up when you were busy worshipping at the altar of Dumbo.

PREPARING YOUR CHILDREN TO MEET THE CHARACTERS

ALMOST ALL DISNEY CHARACTERS are quite large; several, like Baloo, are huge! Young children don't expect this and can be intimidated if not terrified. Discuss the characters with your children before you go. If there is a high school or college with a costumed mascot nearby, arrange to let your kids check it out. If not, then Santa Claus or the Easter Bunny will do.

ISAAC Tell kids in advance that the headpiece characters don't talk.

On the first encounter at Walt Disney World, don't thrust your child at the character. Allow the little one to deal with this big thing from whatever distance feels safe to him or her. If two adults are present, one should stay near the youngster while the other approaches the character and demonstrates that it's safe and friendly. Some kids warm to the characters immediately; some never do. Most take a little time and several encounters.

There are two kinds of characters: "furs," or those whose costumes include face-covering headpieces (including animal characters and such humanlike characters as Captain Hook), and "face characters," those for whom no mask or headpiece is necessary. These include Tiana, Anna, Elsa, Mary Poppins, Ariel, Jasmine, Aladdin, Cinderella, Belle, Snow White, Merida, and Prince Charming, among others.

LILIANE If a character appears to be ignoring your child, ask the character's handler to get its attention.

Only face characters speak. Headpiece characters don't make noises of any kind. Because cast members couldn't possibly imitate the distinctive cinema voice of the character, Disney has determined that it's more effective to keep them silent. Lack of speech notwithstanding, headpiece characters are very warm and responsive and communicate very effectively with gestures. Disney is currently testing new technology that will allow headpiece characters

to speak. It is assumed that the technology is a portable version of that used in *Turtle Talk with Crush* at Epcot, where an animated turtle converses in real time with audience members. A less advanced option is a menu-driven selection of recorded phrases such as, "Hi, I'm Mickey," or "What's your name?"

BOB If your child wants to collect character autographs, it's a good idea to carry a pen the width of a Magic Marker. Costumes make it exceedingly difficult for characters to wield a pen, so the bigger the writing instrument, the better. Unfortunately, a few characters, such as Buzz Lightyear, can't sign autographs at all but will gladly pose for photos.

Some character costumes are cumbersome and limit cast members' ability to see and maneuver. (Eye holes frequently are in the mouth of the costume or even on the neck or chest.) Children who approach the character from the back or side may not be noticed, even if the child touches the character. It's possible in this situation for the character to accidentally step on the child or knock him or her down. It's best for a child to approach a character from the front, but occasionally not even this works. Duck characters (such as Donald, Daisy, and Uncle Scrooge), for example, have to peer around their bills.

It's OK for your child to touch, pat, or hug the character. Understanding the unpredictability of children, the character will keep his feet very still, particularly refraining from moving backward or sideways. Most characters will sign autographs or pose for pictures.

ALEX If you ask a face character about the movie he or she is in, the person will go right into character. My dad will always kiss female "non-human" hands, and watch the reaction!

Another great way to show young children how the characters appear in the parks is to rent or buy a *Disney SingAlong Songs* DVD. These programs show Disney characters interacting with real kids. At a minimum, the videos will give your kids a sense of how big the characters are. The best two are *Flik's Musical Adventure SingAlong Songs at Disney's Animal Kingdom* and *Campout SingAlong Songs at Walt Disney World*. *It's a Small World SingAlong Songs—Disneyland Fun* is a third offering . . . but then there's THAT SONG. No sense turning your brain to mush before even leaving home.

KIERAN If you want a character to sign a clothing item, make sure you are not wearing it. If you want a hat signed, you will have to take it off.

See "Character Analysis," page 245, for an in-depth discussion of the Disney characters.

PHYSICAL PREPARATION

YOU'LL FIND THAT SOME physical conditioning, coupled with a realistic sense of the toll that Walt Disney World takes on your body, will preclude falling apart in the middle of your vacation. As one of our readers put it, "If you pay attention to eat, heat, feet, and sleep, you'll be OK."

As you contemplate the stamina of your family, it's important to understand that somebody is going to run out of steam first, and when they do, the whole family will be affected. Sometimes a cold drink or a snack will revive the flagging member. Sometimes, however, no amount of cajoling or treats will work. In this situation it's crucial that you recognize that the child, grandparent, or spouse is at the end of his or her rope. The correct decision is to get them back to the hotel. Pushing the exhausted beyond their capacity will spoil the day for them—and you. Accept that stamina and energy levels vary and be prepared to administer to members of your family who poop out. One more thing: no guilt trips. "We've driven a thousand miles to take you to Disney World and now you're going to ruin everything!" is not an appropriate response.

THE AGONY OF THE FEET

HERE'S A LITTLE FACTOID TO CHEW ON: If you spend a day at Epcot and visit both sections of the park, you will walk 5–9 miles! The walking, however, will be nothing like a 5-mile hike in the woods. At Epcot (and the other Disney parks as well) you will be in direct sunlight most of the time, will have to navigate through huge jostling crowds, will be walking on hot pavement, and will have to endure waits in line between bursts of walking. The bottom line, if you haven't figured it out, is that Disney theme parks (especially in the summer) are not for wimps!

BOB If your children (or you, for that matter) do not consider it cool to wear socks, get over it! Bare feet, whether encased in Nikes, Weejuns, Docksides, or Birkenstocks, will turn into lumps of throbbing red meat if you tackle a Disney park without socks.

Though most children are active, their normal play usually doesn't condition them for the exertion of touring a Disney theme park. We recommend starting a program of family walks six weeks or more before your trip. A Pennsylvania mom who did just that offers the following:

We had our 6-year-old begin walking with us a bit every day one month before leaving—when we arrived [at Walt Disney World], her little legs could carry her and she had a lot of stamina.

The first thing you need to do, immediately after making your hotel reservation, is to get thee to a "footery." Take the whole family to a shoe store and buy each member the best pair of walking, hiking, or running shoes you can afford. Wear exactly the kind of socks to try on the shoes that you will wear when using them. Do not under any circumstances attempt to tour Walt Disney World shod in sandals, flip-flops, loafers, or any kind of high heel or platform shoe.

LILIANE Be sure to give your kids adequate recovery time between training walks (48 hours will usually be enough), however, or you'll make the problem worse.

Good socks are as important as good shoes. When you walk, your feet sweat like a mule in a peat bog, and moisture increases friction. To minimize friction, wear a pair of SmartWool or Coolmax hiking socks, available at most outdoor retail (camping equipment) stores. To further combat moisture, dust your feet with some antifungal powder.

All right, now you have some good shoes and socks. The next thing to do is to break the shoes in. You can accomplish this painlessly by wearing the shoes in the course of normal activities for about three weeks.

Once the shoes are broken in, it's time to start walking. The whole family will need to toughen up their feet and build endurance. As you begin, remember that little people have little strides, and though your 6-year-old may create the appearance of running circles around you, consider that (1) he won't have the stamina to go at that pace very long, and (2) more to the point, he probably has to take two strides or so to every one of yours to keep up when you walk together.

BOB If your child is age 8 or younger, we recom- mend regular foot inspections whether he or she understands the hot-spot idea or not. Even the brightest and most well-intentioned child will fail to sound off when distracted.

Start by taking short walks around the neighborhood, walking on pavement, and increasing the distance about a quarter of a mile on each outing. Older children will shape up quickly. Younger children should build endurance more slowly and incrementally. Increase distance until you can manage a 6- or 7-mile hike without requiring CPR. And remember, you're not training to be able to walk 6 or 7 miles just once; at Walt Disney World you will be hiking 5–9 miles or more almost *every day*. So unless you plan to crash after the first day, prepare your feet to walk long distances for three to five consecutive days.

Let's be honest and admit up front that not all feet are created equal. Some folks are blessed with really tough feet, whereas the feet of others sprout blisters if you look at them sideways. Assuming that there's nothing wrong with either shoes or socks, a few brisk walks will clue you in to what kind of feet your family have. If you have a tenderfoot in your family, walks of incrementally increased distances will usually toughen up his or her feet to some extent. For those whose feet refuse to toughen, your only alternative is preventive care. After several walks, you will know where your tenderfoot tends to develop blisters. If you can anticipate where blisters will develop, you can cover sensitive spots in advance with moleskin (a friction-resistant adhesive dressing) or a blister bandage.

When you initiate your walking program, teach your children to tell you if they feel a hot spot on their feet. This is the warning that a blister is developing. If your kids are too young, too oblivious, or too preoccupied, or they don't understand the concept, your best bet is to make regular foot checks. Have your children remove their shoes and socks and present their feet for inspection. Look for red spots and blisters, and ask if they have any places on their feet that hurt.

LILIANE If you have a child who will physically fit in a stroller, rent one, no matter how well conditioned your family is.

During your conditioning, and also at Walt Disney World, carry a foot emergency kit in your day pack or hip pack. The kit should contain gauze, antibiotic ointment, an assortment of Band-Aid Advanced Healing Blister Bandages, a sewing needle or some such to drain blisters, as well as matches or a lighter to sterilize the needle. An extra pair of dry socks and foot powder are optional.

If you discover a hot spot, dry the foot and cover the spot immediately with a blister bandage. If you find that a blister has fully or partially developed, first air out and dry the foot. Next, using your sterile needle, drain the fluid, but do not remove the top skin. Clean the area with antiseptic cleaner and place a blister bandage over the blister. If you do not have blister bandages, do not try to cover the hot spot or blister with regular Band-Aid bandages. Regular ones slip and wad up. Head to First Aid instead.

A stroller will provide the child the option of walking or riding, and, if he collapses, you won't have to carry him. Even if your child hardly uses the stroller at all, it serves as a convenient rolling depository for water bottles and other stuff you may not feel like carrying. Strollers at Walt Disney World are covered in detail starting on page 255.

SLEEP, REST, AND RELAXATION

OK, WE KNOW THAT THIS SECTION is about physical preparation *before you go,* but this concept is so absolutely critical that we need to tattoo it on your brain right now.

Physical conditioning is important but is *not* a substitute for adequate rest. Even marathon runners need recovery time. If you push too hard and try to do too much, you'll either crash or, at a minimum, turn what should be fun into an ordeal. Rest means plenty of sleep at night, naps during the afternoon on most days, and planned breaks in your vacation itinerary. And don't forget that the brain needs rest and relaxation as well as the body. The stimulation inherent in touring a Disney theme park is enough to put many children and some adults into system overload. It is imperative that you remove your family from this unremitting assault on the senses, preferably for part of each day, and do something relaxing and quiet like swimming or reading.

The theme parks are huge; don't try to see everything in one day. Tour in the early morning and return to your hotel around 11:30 a.m. for lunch, a swim, and a nap. Even during off-season, when the crowds are smaller and the temperature more pleasant, the size of the major theme parks will exhaust most children under age 8 by lunchtime. Return to the park in late afternoon or early evening and continue touring. A family from Texas underlines the importance of naps and rest:

> *Despite not following any of your "tours," we did follow the theme of visiting a specific park in the morning, leaving midafternoon for either a nap back at the room or a trip to the pool, and then returning to one of the parks in the evening. On the few occasions when we skipped your advice, I was muttering to myself by dinner. I can't tell you what I was muttering . . .*

When it comes to naps, this mom does not mince words:

*One last thing for parents of small kids—take the book's advice and
get out of the park and take the nap, take the nap, TAKE THE NAP!
Never in my life have I seen so many parents screaming at, ridiculing,
or slapping their kids. (What a vacation!) Walt Disney World is overwhelming for kids and adults. Even though the rental strollers recline
for sleeping, we noticed that most of the toddlers and preschoolers
didn't give up and sleep until 5 p.m., several hours after the fun had
worn off, and right about the time their parents wanted them to be
awake and polite in a restaurant.*

A mom from Rochester, New York, was equally adamant:

*You absolutely must rest during the day. Kids went 8 a.m.–9 p.m. in
the Magic Kingdom. Kids did great that day, but we were all completely worthless the next day. Definitely must pace yourself. Don't
ever try to do two full days of park sightseeing in a row. Rest during
the day. Go to a water park or sleep in every other day.*

If you plan to return to your hotel in midday and would like your
room made up, let housekeeping know before you leave in the morning.

DEVELOPING *a* GOOD PLAN

ALLOW YOUR CHILDREN to participate in the planning of your time
at Disney World. Guide them diplomatically through the options, estab-
lishing advance decisions about what to do each day and how the day
will be structured. Begin with your trip *to* Walt Disney World, deciding
what time to depart, who sits by the window, whether to stop for meals
or eat in the car, and so on. For the Disney World part of your vacation,
build consensus for wake-up call, bedtime, and building naps into the
itinerary, and establish ground rules for eating, buying refreshments,
and shopping. Determine the order for visiting the different theme parks
and make a list of must-see attractions. To help you with filling in the
blanks of your days, and especially to prevent
you from spending most of your time standing
in line, we offer a number of field-tested touring plans. The plans are designed to minimize
your waiting time at each park by providing
step-by-step itineraries that route you counter
to the flow of traffic. The plans are explained
in detail starting on page 226.

Generally it's better to just sketch in the
broad strokes on the master plan. The detail
of what to do when you actually arrive at
the park can be decided the night before you
go or with the help of one of our touring
plans once you get there. Above all, be flexible. One important caveat, however: Make
sure you keep any promises or agreements

BOB To keep your thinking
fresh and to ade-
quately cover all
bases, develop your
plan in a series of
family meetings no longer
than 30 minutes each. You'll
discover that all members of
the family will devote a lot of
thought to the plan both
during and between meet-
ings. Don't try to anticipate
every conceivable contin-
gency, or you'll end up with
something as detailed and
unworkable as the tax code.

that you make when planning. They may not seem important to you, but they will to your children, who will remember for a long, long time that you let them down.

The more that you can agree to and nail down in advance, the less potential you'll have for disagreement and confrontation once you arrive. Because children are more comfortable with the tangible than the conceptual, and also because they sometimes have short memories, we recommend typing up all of your decisions and agreements and providing a copy to each child. Create a fun document, not a legalistic one. You'll find that your children will review it in anticipation of all the things they will see and do, will consult it often, and will even read it to their younger siblings.

By now you're probably wondering what one of these documents looks like, so we've provided a sample below. Incidentally, this itinerary reflects the preferences of its creators, the Langston family, and is not meant to be offered as an example of an ideal itinerary. It does, however, incorporate many of our most basic and strongly held recommendations, such as setting limits and guidelines in advance, getting enough rest, getting to the theme parks early, touring the theme parks in shorter visits with naps and swimming in between, and saving time and money by having a cooler full of food for breakfast. As you will see, the Langstons go pretty much full-tilt without much unstructured time and will probably be exhausted by the time they get home, but that's their choice. One more thing—the Langstons visited Walt Disney World in late June, when all of the theme parks stay open late.

THE GREAT WALT DISNEY WORLD EXPEDITION

COCAPTAINS Mary and Jack Langston

TEAM MEMBERS Lynn and Jimmy Langston

EXPEDITION FUNDING The main Expedition Fund will cover everything except personal purchases. Each team member will receive $40 for souvenirs and personal purchases. Anything above $40 will be paid for by team members with their own money.

EXPEDITION GEAR Each team member will wear an official expedition T-shirt and carry a hip pack.

PREDEPARTURE Jack makes Advance Reservations at Disney World restaurants. Mary, Lynn, and Jimmy make up trail mix and other snacks for the hip packs.

Notice that the Langstons' itinerary on pages 204–205 provides minimal structure and maximum flexibility. It specifies which park the family will tour each day without attempting to nail down exactly what the family will do there. No matter how detailed your itinerary is, be prepared for surprises at Walt Disney World, both good and bad. If an unforeseen event renders part of the plan useless or impractical, just roll with it. And always remember that it's your itinerary; you created it, and you can change it. Just try to make any changes the result of family discussion, and be especially careful not to scrap an element of the plan that your children perceive as something you promised them.

Routines That Travel

If when at home you observe certain routines—for example, reading a book before bed or having a bath first thing in the morning—try to incorporate these familiar activities into your vacation schedule. They will provide your children with a sense of security and normalcy.

Maintaining a normal routine is especially important with toddlers, as a mother of two from Lawrenceville, Georgia, relates:

> *The first day, we tried an early start, so we woke the children (ages 2 and 4) and hurried them to get going. BAD IDEA with toddlers. This put them off schedule for naps and meals the rest of the day. It is best to let young ones stay on their regular schedule and see Disney at their own pace, and you'll have much more fun.*

We offer a sleepyhead touring plan for each park, perfect for families like this reader's.

LOGISTIC PREPARATION

WHEN WE RECENTLY LAUNCHED into our spiel about good logistic preparation for a Walt Disney World vacation, a friend from Indianapolis said, "Wait, what's the big deal? You pack clothes, a few games for the car, then go!" So OK, we confess, that will work, but life can be sweeter and the vacation smoother (as well as less expensive) with the right gear.

CLOTHING

LET'S START WITH CLOTHES. We recommend springing for vacation uniforms. Buy for each child several sets of jeans (or shorts) and T-shirts, all matching, and all the same. For a one-week trip, as an example, get each child three or so pairs of khaki shorts, three or so light yellow T-shirts, three pairs of SmartWool or Coolmax hiking socks. What's the point? First, you don't have to play fashion designer, coordinating a week's worth of stylish combos. Each morning the kids put on their uniform. It's simple, it's time-saving, and there are no decisions to make or arguments about what to wear. Second, uniforms make your children easier to spot and keep together in the theme parks. Third, the uniforms give your family, as well as the vacation itself, some added identity. You might even go so far as to create a logo for the trip to be printed on the shirts.

When it comes to buying your uniforms, we have a few suggestions. Purchase well-made, durable shorts or jeans that will serve your

LILIANE Give your teens the job of coming up with the logo for your shirts. They will love being the family designers.

Continued on page 206

LANGSTON FAMILY ITINERARY

DAY 1: FRIDAY

6:30 p.m.	Dinner
After dinner	Pack car
10 p.m.	Lights out

DAY 2: SATURDAY

7 a.m.	Wake up!
7:15 a.m.	Breakfast
8 a.m.	Depart Chicago for Hampton Inn, Chattanooga; Confirmation #DE56432; Lynn rides shotgun
About noon	Stop for lunch; Jimmy picks restaurant
7 p.m.	Dinner
9:30 p.m.	Lights out

DAY 3: SUNDAY

7 a.m.	Wake up!
7:30 a.m.	Depart Chattanooga for Walt Disney World, Port Orleans Resort–Riverside; confirmation #L124532; Jimmy rides shotgun
About noon	Stop for lunch; Lynn picks restaurant
5 p.m.	Check in, buy park admissions (if you haven't already), and unpack
6–7 p.m.	Mary and Jimmy shop for breakfast food for cooler
7:15 p.m.	Dinner at Boatwright's at Port Orleans Riverside
After dinner	Walk along Bonnet Creek
10 p.m.	Lights out

DAY 4: MONDAY

7 a.m.	Wake up! Cold breakfast from cooler in room
8 a.m.	Depart room to catch bus for Epcot
Noon	Lunch at Epcot
1 p.m.	Return to hotel for swimming and a nap
5 p.m.	Return to Epcot for touring, dinner, and *IllumiNations*
9:30 p.m.	Return to hotel
10:30 p.m.	Lights out

DAY 5: TUESDAY

7 a.m.	Wake up! Cold breakfast from cooler in room
7:45 a.m.	Depart room to catch bus for Disney's Hollywood Studios
Noon	Lunch at Studios
2:30 p.m.	Return to hotel for swimming and a nap
6 p.m.	Drive to dinner at cafe at Wilderness Lodge
7:30 p.m.	Return to Studios via car for touring and *Fantasmic!*
10 p.m.	Return to hotel
11 p.m.	Lights out

DAY 6: WEDNESDAY

ZZZZZZ!	Lazy morning—sleep in!
10:30 a.m.	Late-morning swim
Noon	Lunch at Riverside Mill Food Court at Port Orleans
1 p.m.	Depart room to catch bus for Animal Kingdom; tour until park closes
8 p.m.	Dinner at Rainforest Cafe at Animal Kingdom
9:15 p.m.	Return to hotel via bus
10:30 p.m.	Lights out

DAY 7: THURSDAY

6 a.m.	Wake up! Cold breakfast from cooler in room
6:45 a.m.	Depart via bus for early entry at Magic Kingdom
11:30 a.m.	Return to hotel for lunch, swimming, and a nap
4:45 p.m.	Drive to Contemporary for dinner at Chef Mickey's
6:15 p.m.	Walk from the Contemporary to the Magic Kingdom for more touring, fireworks, and parade
11 p.m.	Return to Contemporary via walkway or monorail; get car and return to hotel
11:45 p.m.	Lights out

DAY 8: FRIDAY

8 a.m.	Wake up! Cold breakfast from cooler in room
8:40 a.m.	Drive to Blizzard Beach water park
Noon	Lunch at Blizzard Beach
1:30 p.m.	Return to hotel for nap and packing
4 p.m.	Revisit favorite park or do whatever we want
Dinner	When and where we decide
10 p.m.	Return to hotel
10:30 p.m.	Lights out

DAY 9: SATURDAY

7:30 a.m.	Wake up!
8:30 a.m.	After fast-food breakfast, depart for Executive Inn, Nashville; confirmation #SD234; Lynn rides shotgun
About noon	Stop for lunch; Jimmy picks restaurant
7 p.m.	Dinner
10 p.m.	Lights out

DAY 10: SUNDAY

7 a.m.	Wake up!
7:45 a.m.	Depart for home after fast-food breakfast; Jimmy rides shotgun
About noon	Stop for lunch; Lynn picks restaurant
4:30 p.m.	Home, sweet home!

Continued from page 203

children well beyond the vacation. Buy short-sleeve T-shirts in light colors for warm weather or long-sleeve, darker-colored T-shirts for cooler weather. We suggest that you purchase your colored shirts from a local screen printing company. You can select from a wide choice of colors not generally available in retail clothing stores and will not have to worry about finding the sizes you need. Plus, the shirts will cost a fraction of what a clothing retailer would charge. All-cotton shirts are a little cooler and more comfortable in hot, humid weather; polyester-cotton blends dry a bit faster if they get wet.

LABELS A great idea, especially for younger children, is to attach labels with your family name, hometown, the name of your hotel, the dates of your stay, and your mobile number inside the shirt. For example:

**Carlton Family of Frankfort, KY; Port Orleans Riverside
May 5–12; 502-555-2108**

Instruct your smaller children to show the label to an adult if they get separated from you. Elimination of the child's first name (which most children of talking age can articulate in any event) allows you to order labels that are all the same, that can be used by anyone in the family, and that can also be affixed to such easily lost items as caps, hats, jackets, hip packs, ponchos, and umbrellas. If fooling with labels sounds like too much of a hassle, check out "When Kids Get Lost" (pages 258–261) for some alternatives.

TEMPORARY TATTOOS An easier and trendier option is a temporary tattoo with your child's name and your phone number. Unlike labels, ID bracelets, or wristbands, the tattoos cannot fall off or be lost. Temporary tattoos last about two weeks, won't wash or sweat off, and are not irritating to the skin. They can be purchased online from **SafetyTat** at **safetytat.com,** or from **Tattoos With A Purpose** at **tattooswithapurpose .com.** Special tattoos are available for children with food allergies or cognitive impairment such as autism.

DRESSING FOR COOLER WEATHER Central Florida experiences temperatures all over the scale November–March, so it could be a bit chilly if you visit during those months. Our suggestion is to layer: For example, a breathable, waterproof or water-resistant Windbreaker over a light, long-sleeved polypropylene shirt over a long-sleeved T-shirt. As with the baffles of a sleeping bag or down coat, it is the air trapped between the layers that keeps you warm. If all the layers are thin, you won't be left with something bulky to cart around if you want to pull one or more off. Later in this section, we'll advocate wearing a hip pack. Each layer should be sufficiently compactible to fit easily in that hip pack, along with whatever else is in it.

ACCESSORIES

I (BOB) WANTED TO CALL THIS PART "Belts and Stuff," but Liliane (who obviously spends a lot of time at Macy's) thought "Accessories" put a finer point on it. In any event, we recommend pants for your children with reinforced elastic waistbands that eliminate the need to wear a belt (one less thing to find when you're trying to leave). If your children like belts or want to carry an item suspended from their belts, buy them military-style 1-inch-wide web belts at any Army/Navy surplus or camping-equipment store. The belts weigh less than half as much as leather, are cooler, and are washable.

SUNGLASSES The Florida sun is so bright and the glare so blinding that we recommend sunglasses for each family member. For children and adults of all ages, a good accessory item is a polypropylene eyeglass strap for spectacles or sunglasses. The best models have a little device for adjusting the amount of slack in the strap. This allows your child to comfortably hang sunglasses from his or her neck when indoors or, alternately, to secure them fast to his or her head while experiencing a fast ride outdoors.

HIP PACKS AND WALLETS Unless you are touring with an infant or toddler, the largest thing anyone in your family should carry is a hip pack, or fanny pack. Each adult and child should have one. They should be large enough to carry at least a half-day's worth of snacks, as well as other items deemed necessary (lip balm, bandanna, antibacterial hand gel, and so on), and still have enough room left to stash a hat, poncho, or light Windbreaker. We recommend buying full-size hip packs as opposed to small, child-size hip packs at outdoor retailers. The packs are light; can be made to fit any child large enough to tote a hip pack; have slip-resistant, comfortable, wide belting; and will last for years.

BOB Unless you advise the front desk to the contrary, all MagicBands (or Disney resort room keys) can be used for park admission and as credit cards. They are definitely something you don't want to lose. Our advice is to void the charge privileges on your preteen children's bands or cards, and then collect them and put them together someplace safe when not in use.

Do not carry billfolds or wallets, car keys, park tickets, or room keys in your hip packs. We usually give this advice because hip packs are vulnerable to thieves (who snip them off and run), but pickpocketing and theft are not all that common at Walt Disney World. In this instance, the advice stems from a tendency of children to inadvertently drop their wallet in the process of rummaging around in their hip packs for snacks and other items.

You should weed through your billfold and remove to a safe place anything that you will not need on your vacation (family photos, local library card, department store credit cards, business cards, and so on). In addition to having a lighter wallet to lug around, you will decrease your exposure in the event that your wallet is lost or stolen. When we're working at Walt Disney World, we carry a small profile billfold with a driver's license, a credit card, our hotel room key, and a small amount of cash. Think about it: You don't need anything else.

LILIANE Equip each child with a big bandanna. Though bandannas come in handy for wiping noses, scouring ice cream from chins and mouths, and dabbing sweat from the forehead, they can also be tied around the neck to protect from sunburn.

DAY PACKS We see a lot of folks at Disney World carrying day packs (that is, small, frameless backpacks) and/or water bottle belts that strap around the waist. Day packs might be a good choice if you plan to carry a lot of camera equipment or if you need to carry baby supplies on your person. Otherwise, try to travel as light as possible. Packs are hot, cumbersome, not very secure, and must be removed every time you get on a ride or sit down for a show. Hip packs, by way of contrast, can simply be rotated around the waist from your back to your abdomen if you need to sit down. Additionally, our observation has been that the contents of one day pack can usually be redistributed to two or so hip packs.

CAPS Caps protect young eyes from damaging ultraviolet rays, but the lifespan of a child's hat is usually pretty short. Simply put, kids pull caps on and off as they enter and exit attractions, restrooms, and restaurants, and . . . big surprise, they lose them. In fact, they lose them by the thousands. You could provide a ball cap for every Little Leaguer in America from the caps that are lost at Walt Disney World each summer.

LILIANE If your kids are little and don't mind a hairdo change, consider getting them a short haircut before you leave home. Not only will they be cooler and more comfortable, but—especially with your girls—you'll save them (and yourselves) the hassle of tangles and about 20 minutes of foo-fooing a day. Don't try this with your confident teen or preteen, though. Braids will do the trick for girls, and your Mick Jagger in the party will be grateful for the bandanna or sports headband, unless of course the hair is meant to keep the monsters and dinosaurs out of sight!

If your children are partial to caps, there is a device sold at ski and camping supply stores that might increase the likelihood of the cap returning home with the child. Essentially, it's a short, light cord with little alligator clips on both ends. Hook one clip to the shirt collar and the other to the hat. It's a great little invention. Bob uses one when he skis in case his ball cap blows off.

RAINGEAR Rain in central Florida is a fact of life, though persistent rain day after day is unusual (it is the Sunshine State, after all!). Our suggestion is to check out The Weather Channel or weather forecasts on the Internet for three or so days before you leave home to see if there are any major storm systems heading for central Florida. If it appears that you might see some rough weather during your visit, you're better off bringing raingear from home. If, however, nothing big is on the horizon weatherwise, you can take your chances.

We at *The Unofficial Guide* usually do not bring raingear. Scattered thundershowers are more the norm than are prolonged periods of rain. At Disney World, ponchos are available in seemingly every retail shop for about $10. If you insist on bringing raingear, however, any dollar store has them for exactly that: $1!

If you do find yourself in a big storm, you'll want to have both a poncho and an umbrella. As one *Unofficial* reader put it:

> Umbrellas make the rain much more bearable. When rain isn't beating down on your ponchoed head, it's easier to ignore.

Another advantage of buying ponchos before you leave home is that you can choose the color. At Walt Disney World all the ponchos are clear, and it's quite a sight when 30,000 differently clad individuals suddenly transform themselves into what looks like an army of really big larvae. If your family is wearing blue ponchos, they'll be easier to spot.

And consider this tip from a Memphis, Tennessee, mom:

Scotchgard your shoes. The difference is unbelievable.

MISCELLANEOUS ITEMS

MEDICATION Some parents of hyperactive children on medication discontinue or decrease the child's normal dosage at the end of the school year. If you have such a child, be aware that Disney World might overly stimulate him or her. Consult your physician before altering your child's medication regimen. Also, if your child has attention

LILIANE Often little ones fall asleep in their strollers (hallelujah!). Bring a large lightweight cloth to drape over the stroller to cover your child from the sun. A few clothespins will keep it in place.

deficit disorder, remember that especially loud sounds can drive him or her right up the wall. Unfortunately, some Disney theater attractions are almost unbearably loud.

SUNSCREEN Overheating and sunburn are among the most common problems of younger children at Disney World. Carry and use full-spectrum sunscreen of SPF 30 or higher. Be sure to put some on children in strollers, even if the stroller has a canopy. Some of the worst cases of sunburn we've seen were on the exposed foreheads and feet of toddlers and infants in strollers. To avoid overheating, rest regularly in the shade or in an air-conditioned restaurant or show.

WATER BOTTLES Don't count on keeping young children hydrated with soft drinks and stops at water fountains. Long lines may hamper buying refreshments, and fountains may not be handy. Furthermore, excited children may not realize or tell you that they're thirsty or hot. We recommend renting a stroller for children age 6 and younger and carrying plastic bottles of water. Plastic squeeze bottles with caps run about $3 in all major parks. You can save oodles of money by buying your own water outside the parks (Disney allows you to bring water to the parks). If you are staying in a rental home, freeze the water and use it to keep sandwiches cool. By the time you are thirsty, the water should be just right to quench your thirst. You can also refill the water bottles at any Disney counter-service restaurant by asking for free tap water.

LILIANE About two weeks before I arrive at WDW, I always ship a box to my hotel containing food, plastic cutlery, and toiletries, plus pretty much any other consumables that might come in handy during my stay. If you fly, this helps

COOLERS AND MINI-FRIDGES If you drive to Walt Disney World, bring two coolers: a small one for drinks in the car and a large one for the hotel room. If you fly and rent a car, stop and

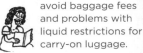

avoid baggage fees and problems with liquid restrictions for carry-on luggage.

purchase a large Styrofoam cooler, which can be discarded at the end of the trip. Refrigerators in all Disney resort rooms are free of charge. If you arrive at your room and there is no refrigerator, call housekeeping and request one. Along with free fridges, coffeemakers have also been added in the rooms.

Coolers and mini-fridges allow you to have breakfast in your hotel room, store snacks and lunch supplies to take to the theme parks, and supplant expensive vending machines for snacks and beverages at the hotel. To keep the contents of your cooler cold, we suggest freezing a 2-gallon milk jug full of water before you head out. In a good cooler, it will take the jug five or more days to thaw. If you buy a Styrofoam cooler in Florida, you can use bagged ice and ice from the ice machine at your hotel. Even if you have to rent a mini-fridge, you will save a bundle of cash, as well as significant time, by reducing dependence on restaurant meals and expensive snacks and drinks purchased from vendors.

FOOD-PREP KIT If you plan to make sandwiches, bring along your favorite condiments and seasonings from home. A good travel kit will include mayonnaise, ketchup, mustard, salt and pepper, and packets of sugar or artificial sweetener. Also bring some plastic knives and spoons, paper napkins, plastic cups, and a box of zip-top plastic bags. For breakfast you will need some plastic bowls for cereal. Of course, you can buy this stuff in Florida, but you probably won't consume it all, so why waste the money? If you drink bottled beer or wine, bring a bottle opener and corkscrew.

ENERGY BOOSTERS Kids get cranky when they're hungry, and when that happens, your entire group has a problem. Like many parents you might, for nutritional reasons, keep a tight rein on snacks available to your children at home. At Walt Disney World, however, maintaining energy and equanimity trumps between-meal snack discipline. For maximum zip and contentedness, give your kids snacks containing complex carbohydrates (fruits, crackers, nonfat energy bars, and the like) *before* they get hungry or show signs of exhaustion. You should avoid snacks that are high in fats and proteins because these foods take a long time to digest and will tend to unsettle your stomach if it's a hot day.

Bob enthusiastically recommends **Clif Shot Bloks,** chewable cubes that replace electrolytes in the body. They're light, come in several different flavors (all tasty), and don't melt even on the hottest days. Bob uses them when needed on mountain bike rides. They really work wonders.

ELECTRONICS Regardless of your children's ages, always bring a nightlight. Flashlights are also handy for finding stuff in a dark hotel room after the kids are asleep. If you are big coffee drinkers and if you drive, bring along a coffeemaker if it's not included in your room.

Smartphones, tablets, digital music players with headphones, and electronic games are often controversial gear for a family outing. We recommend compromise. Headphones allow kids to create their own space even when they're with others, and that can be a safety valve. That said, try to agree before the trip on some headphone parameters, so you

RESPECT FOR THE SUN

Health and science writer **Avery Hurt** sheds some light on the often confusing products and methods for avoiding sunburn. Here's the basic advice from the medical experts.

• **Choose a sunscreen that is convenient for you to use.** Some prefer sprays, others lotions. The form of sunscreen doesn't matter as much as the technique of applying it.

• **Apply sunscreen a half hour before going out,** and be sure to get enough on you. One ounce per application is recommended—that means a full shot glass worth each time you apply. The 1-ounce amount was calculated for average adults in swimsuits; an average 7-year-old will probably take two-thirds of an ounce (20 cc). It's a good idea to measure that ounce in your hands at home, so you'll be familiar with what an ounce looks like in your palms. It's far more sunscreen than you tend to think.

• **Get a generous covering on all exposed skin.** Then reapply (another full shot glass) every 2 hours or after swimming or sweating. No matter what it says on the label, water resistance of sunscreen is limited. And none of them last all day.

• **There is very little difference in protection** between 30 or so SPF and 45 or 50 or greater. There is no need to spend more for higher SPF numbers. In fact, it is much safer to choose a lower (and typically less expensive) SPF (as long as it is at least 30) and apply it more often. However, do be sure to choose a product that has broad-spectrum coverage, meaning that it filters out both UVA and UVB rays. As long as the SPF is at least 30 and offers broad-spectrum protection, one brand can serve the whole family. There's no need to pay extra for special formulas made for children.

• **It is best to keep babies under 6 months old covered** and out of the sun. However, the American Academy of Pediatrics condones a small amount of sunscreen on vulnerable areas, such as the nose and chin, when you have your baby out. Be very careful to monitor your baby even if he is wearing a hat and sitting under an umbrella.

• **Use a lip balm** with an SPF of 15 and reapply often to your own lips and those of your kids. Again, the brand is less important than choosing something that you will use—and remembering to use it.

• **Sunglasses are also a must.** Too much sun exposure can contribute to age-related macular degeneration (among other things). Not all sunglasses filter out damaging rays. Be sure to choose shades (for adults and kids) that have 99% UV protection. Large lenses and wraparound styles might not look as cool, but they offer much better protection. You may have to spend a little more to be sure you are getting adequate protection, but you don't want to skimp on this.

• **If you do get a burn,** cool baths, aloe gels, and ibuprofen (or for adults, aspirin) usually help ease the suffering. Occasionally sunburns can be as dangerous in the short term as they are in the long term. If you or your child experience nausea, vomiting, high fever, severe pain, confusion, or fainting, seek medical care immediately.

don't begin to feel as if they're being used to keep other family members and the trip itself at a distance.

POWERING UP Speaking of smart devices, their use has become standard in the parks. In addition to taking photos, guests also use apps to check on waiting lines and score seats at restaurants. All that technology comes at a price: dead batteries. You spend all day using your phone to e-mail photos to Great-Aunt Fern, but at the end of the day, you can't find the missing members of your party because you don't have enough power to place a call or even send a text. Having experienced the problem firsthand, Liliane has a few suggestions:

First, bring an extra charged battery, and always, *always* bring the charging cable.

You can drop off your phone to be charged at any Guest Relations desk in any park. While they usually have cords and plugs for most phones, it helps to bring yours along. You'll be issued a claim check to pick up your phone, which will be done charging in an hour or two.

Six charging stations are also available at the **D-Zone,** near the *Tangled*-themed bathrooms in Fantasyland in the Magic Kingdom. They're built into the faux-wood posts near the seating area.

You can also recharge at the Baby Care Centers in the parks and at restrooms. Charging policies at restaurants vary—our experience has been that the upscale places will fuss about a request, while the counter-service places don't mind.

Here are a few good choices during lunch- or dinnertime: In the Magic Kingdom, several tables at the **Columbia Harbour House** (especially upstairs) are near electrical outlets. At **Pecos Bill Tall Tale Inn and Cafe,** a table opposite the condiments station is next to a power outlet. At Disney's Hollywood Studios, don't count on the sit-down restaurants; rather, head for **Backlot Express,** which has lots of tables nestled next to power outlets. At Epcot, you'll find outlets at **Sunshine Seasons** and **Electric Umbrella,** as well as in the single-rider line at **Soarin',** which is good for a quick 5- or 10-minute charge. At Animal Kingdom, try outlets at **Pizzafari** or **Tusker House.**

For a rundown of additional charging locations in the parks, charging etiquette, and tips for extending your device's battery life, go to **blog.touringplans.com** and type "phone charging" in the search box.

DON'T FORGET THE TENT *Bob here:* This is not a joke, and it has nothing to do with camping. When my daughter was preschool-age, I about went crazy trying to get her to sleep in a shared hotel room. She was accustomed to having her own room at home and was hyperstimulated whenever she traveled. I tried makeshift curtains and room dividers and even rearranged the furniture in a few hotel rooms to create the illusion of a more private, separate space for her. It was all for naught. It wasn't until she was around 4 years old and I took her camping that I seized on an idea that had some promise. She liked the cozy, secure, womblike feel of a backpacking tent and quieted down much more readily than she ever had in hotel rooms. So the next time the family stayed in a hotel,

I pitched my backpacking tent in the corner of the room. In she went, nested for a bit, and fell asleep.

Since the time of my daughter's childhood, there has been an astounding evolution in tent design. Responding to the needs of climbers and paddlers who often have to pitch tents on rocks (where it's impossible to drive stakes), tent manufacturers developed a broad range of tents with self-supporting frames that can be erected virtually anywhere without ropes or stakes. Affordable and sturdy, many are as simple to put up as opening an umbrella. So, if your child is too young for a room of his or her own, or you can't afford a second hotel room, try pitching a small tent. Modern tents are self-contained, with floors and an entrance that can be zipped up (or not) for privacy but cannot be locked. Kids appreciate having their own space and enjoy the adventure of being in a tent, even one set up in the corner of a hotel room. Sizes range from children's play tents with a 2- to 3-foot base to models large enough to sleep two or three husky teens. Light and compact when stored, a two-adult-size tent in its own storage bag (called a stuff sack) will take up about one-tenth or less of a standard overhead bin on a commercial airliner. Another option for infants and toddlers is to drape a sheet over a portable crib or playpen to make a tent.

"THE BOX" *Bob again:* On one memorable Walt Disney World excursion when my children were young, we started each morning with an immensely annoying, involuntary scavenger hunt. Invariably, seconds before our scheduled departure to the theme park, we discovered that some combination of shoes, billfolds, sunglasses, hip packs, or other necessities were unaccountably missing. For the next 15 minutes we would root through the room like pigs hunting truffles in an attempt to locate the absent items. Now I don't know about your kids, but when my kids lost a shoe or something, they always searched where it was easiest to look, as opposed to where the lost article was most likely to be. I would be jammed under a bed feeling around, while my children stood in the middle of the room intently inspecting the ceiling. As my friends will tell you, I'm as open to a novel theory as the next guy, but we never did find any shoes on the ceiling. Not once. Anyway, here's what I finally did: I swung by a liquor store and mooched a big empty box. From then on, every time we returned to the room, I had the kids deposit shoes, hip packs, and other potentially wayward items in the box. After that the box was off-limits until the next morning, when I doled out the contents.

PLASTIC GARBAGE BAGS On two attractions, the **Kali River Rapids** raft ride in Animal Kingdom and **Splash Mountain** in the Magic Kingdom, you are certain to get wet and possibly soaked. If it's really hot and you don't care, then fine. But if it's cool or you're just not up for a soaking, bring a large plastic trash bag to the park. By cutting holes in the top and on the sides, you can fashion a sack poncho that will keep your clothes from getting wet. On the raft ride, you will also get your feet wet. If you're not up for walking around in squishy, soaked shoes, bring a second, smaller plastic bag to wear over your feet while riding.

SUPPLIES FOR INFANTS AND TODDLERS

BASED ON RECOMMENDATIONS from hundreds of *Unofficial Guide* readers, here's what we suggest you carry with you when touring with infants and toddlers:

- A disposable diaper for every hour you plan to be away from your hotel room
- A plastic (or vinyl) diaper wrap with Velcro closures
- A cloth diaper or kitchen towel to put over your shoulder for burping
- Two receiving blankets: one to wrap the baby and one to lay the baby on or to drape over you when you nurse; bring a few clothespins, and you can use a blanket as a makeshift canopy to shelter baby from the sun by attaching it to the roof of the stroller.
- Ointment for diaper rash
- Moistened towelettes such as Wet Ones
- Prepared formula in bottles if you are not breast-feeding
- A washable bib, baby spoon, and baby food if your infant is eating solid foods
- For toddlers, a small toy for comfort and to keep them occupied during attractions

Baby Care Centers at the theme parks will sell you just about anything that you forget or run out of. As with all things Disney, prices will be higher than elsewhere, but at least you won't need to detour to a drugstore in the middle of your touring day.

TIPS FOR PREGNANT MOTHERS

LET'S FACE IT: A visit to Walt Disney World is not the ideal vacation for an expecting mom, but we also know that quite a lot of pregnant moms visit the World every year. The most important advice for pregnant moms is to take it easy. If you travel by car or plane, make sure you prepare your schedule in such a manner that you have plenty of rest. Don't stay on your feet all day; stick to a healthy, balanced diet, but most of all don't skip meals; and drink plenty of fluids. Keep the dining options flexible; morning sickness or sudden aversions or preferences to food can be dealt with easily if you don't make reservations and go for whatever you feel like eating. Always carry some snacks and bottled water with you. A plastic bag folded in your pocket in case you feel unwell takes no space but gives peace of mind. You also should discuss your upcoming Walt Disney World visit with your physician. He or she will certainly have valuable tips.

Comfortable clothes are a must, and so are well-worn-in supporting shoes. You may consider getting a maternity support belt to keep your back from hurting. If you're using a special pillow at night to support your belly, don't forget to bring it with you. If you do not have enough space for it in your suitcase, consider shipping one ahead in a care box. Of course the hotel will provide you with extra pillows if needed.

Maternity bathing suit: If you don't own one, purchase a maternity bathing suit; you will be glad you did. A relaxing afternoon at the pool or a float down the lazy river in the water parks is wonderful.

At the parks take frequent breaks; put your legs up! The Baby Care Centers also welcome expectant moms, and you can sit and relax in a pleasant atmosphere. Go back to the hotel for a nap during the day, and plan a day away from the parks. Go splurge and have a massage; your back and feet will be grateful. Sleep is precious, so don't overdo it; a good night of sleep is better than all the fireworks in the sky.

Heed the warnings! Here is a short list of rides that are absolutely not suitable for expecting moms: **The Barnstormer, Big Thunder Mountain Railroad, DINOSAUR, Expedition Everest, Kali River Rapids, Kilimanjaro Safaris, Mission: SPACE, Rock 'n' Roller Coaster, Seven Dwarfs Mine Train, Space Mountain, Splash Mountain, Star Tours, Test Track, Tomorrowland Speedway,** and **The Twilight Zone Tower of Terror.** Remember, this is just a short list; use your own best judgment.

A word about the water parks: Obviously, experiencing the offerings of **Crush 'n' Gusher** at Typhoon Lagoon or barreling down **Summit Plummet** at Blizzard Beach is ill-advised if you're in the family way, but the water parks offer great lazy rivers and pools, as well as shady beaches where you can relax and let the rest of your group enjoy the wild things.

Tips for Nursing Mothers

Baby Care Centers are available at all Walt Disney World parks, and nursing mothers will not have difficulty finding a comfortable, clean, and pleasant place to take care of their infants. In addition to breastfeeding rooms equipped with rocking chairs and love seats, the childcare facilities have sinks for washing and a room with toys and videos for your older children. Should you need diapers, baby clothes, children's medicines, and other small necessities, Disney has those items available right there for a fee.

Here are some tips to remember when visiting:

- Getting there by plane: Remember to nurse your child at takeoff and landing. It helps to open the baby's ears and also eliminates discomfort due to pressure changes.

- Nurse your infant at the first sign of hunger. You and the baby will be calmer, and you will attract much less attention if you feed the baby before he or she gets fussy and screams at the top of his or her lungs.

- Wear comfortable clothes. While you can access the Baby Care Centers at any time, there is nothing wrong with nursing your infant in a calm, shady spot anywhere at Walt Disney World or at the pool of your hotel. A dress with buttons in the front and a small baby blanket to put over your shoulder will do the trick. A large T-shirt that allows the baby to nurse "from under" is another option. In case you feel self-conscious, remember that Florida was the first state to protect breast-feeding in public by law in 1993.

- Pick a quiet place to nurse your baby.

- Adequate rest is another must. Schedule several breaks into your day and go back to the hotel for a nap.

- Make sure you plan regular healthy meals. A nursing mom, much like an expecting mother, has increased nutritional needs. In addition to eating a well-balanced diet and drinking plenty of fluids, it is always a good idea to take along some snacks.

- It is hot in Florida, and while it is important for all visitors to drink lots of water, it is crucial for nursing moms, so stay hydrated!

- Schedule a down day into your trip. If you have older children, let Dad take them to the park while you stay behind with the baby. A day of rest works wonders.

- If you plan on a parent's evening out, consider pumping milk for later use or supplementing breast milk with a bottle of formula.

- Nursing is exhausting, and so is touring Walt Disney World. Fatigue can reduce milk flow. Get enough rest and don't stay up past your bedtime. The night of a nursing mom is already short. Leave the park whenever you feel tired and get enough sleep.

- A bath and a massage calm most fussy babies and are good for mom as well. Bring along some Epsom salts for a relaxing bath, or stop at Basins at Disney Springs and splurge on bath bombs. At $12 for three, they're a bargain.

We also suggest reading *Baby Massage: A Practical Guide to Massage and Movement for Babies and Infants,* by Peter Walker.

WALT DISNEY WORLD *for* GUESTS *with* SPECIAL NEEDS

FIRST, CHECK OUT SERVICES and facilities at **disneyworld.disney.go .com/guest-services/guests-with-disabilities,** as well as the frequently asked questions page. For specific requests, such as those for special accommodations at hotels or on the Disney transportation system, call ☎ 407-939-7807 or 407-939-7670 (TTY). When booking your room, let the reservation agent know of any special needs you have.

Much of the Disney transportation system is disabled-accessible. Most attractions, restrooms, and restaurants accommodate the nonambulatory disabled. All Disney lots have close-in parking for disabled visitors. All monorails and most rides, shows, restrooms, and restaurants accommodate wheelchairs. Even if the attraction doesn't accommodate wheelchairs or electric convenience vehicles, nonambulatory guests may ride if they can transfer from their wheelchair to the ride's vehicle. Disney staff, however, aren't trained or permitted to assist with transfers; guests must be able to board the ride unassisted or have a member of their party assist them. Either way, members of the nonambulatory guest's party will be permitted to ride with him or her. Make sure to ask for boarding instructions as soon as you arrive at an attraction.

Guest Relations at the parks provide free assistive-technology devices to visually- and hearing-impaired guests. Braille guidebooks are available at Guest Relations at the parks, and Braille menus are available at some theme park restaurants. Disney provides sign-language interpretations of live shows at the theme parks on certain days of the week. Get confirmation of the interpreted-performance schedule a minimum of one week in advance by calling Disney World information at ☎ 407-824-4321 (voice) or 407-827-5141 (TTY). You'll be contacted before your visit with a show schedule that lists the names, dates, and times of the interpreted performances.

Service animals are welcome in all Disney resorts and in the parks. The relief areas for the service animals are marked on hotel and theme park maps. Service animals are even allowed on some rides. Read more at **disneyworld.disney.go.com/guest-services/service-animals.**

Disney's "Guide for Guests with Cognitive Disabilities" is available for download at **tinyurl.com/cognitivedisabilitiesguide.** If you have a family member with a developmental disability, we recommend visiting **autismattheparks.com,** which was awarded the 2015 Sunshine Blog Award for Best Cause Blog.

Disney's Disability Access Service (DAS) is designed to accommodate guests who can't wait in regular standby lines. You must obtain a DAS card at the Guest Relations window of the first theme park you visit. The same card works in every subsequent park you visit. Check Disney's website to find out what is needed for DAS prior to leaving home.

▮❚ REMEMBERING *Your* TRIP

1. Purchase a notebook for each child and spend some time each evening recording the events of the day. If your children have trouble getting motivated or don't know what to write about, start a discussion; otherwise, let them write or draw whatever they want to remember from the day's events.

2. Collect mementos along the way and create a treasure box in a small tin or cigar box. Months or years later, it's fun to look at postcards, pins, or ticket stubs to jump-start a memory.

3. Add inexpensive postcards to your photographs to create an album; then write a few words on each page to accompany the images.

4. Give each child a disposable camera to record his or her version of the trip. One 5-year-old snapped an entire series of photos that never showed anyone above the waist—his view of the world—and the photos were priceless.

5. Nowadays, many families travel with a camcorder or make videos with their smartphones/tablets, though we recommend using one sparingly—parents end up viewing the trip through the lens rather than being in the moment. If you must, take your device of choice along, but record only a few moments

of major sights (too much is boring anyway). And let the kids record and narrate. On the topic of narration, speak loudly so as to be heard over the not-insignificant background noise of the parks. Make use of lockers at all of the parks when the recorder becomes a burden or when you're going to experience an attraction that might damage it or get it wet. Unless you have a waterproof camcorder or smart device, leave it behind on Splash Mountain, Kali River Rapids, and any other ride where water is involved.

6. Another inexpensive way to record memories is a palm-size voice recorder. Let all family members describe their experiences. Hearing a small child's voice years later is so endearing, and those recorded descriptions will trigger an album's worth of memories, far more focused than what many novices capture on video.

7. At the Magic Kingdom collect any button that applies to your visit (such as First Visit, Birthday, Just Married, Engaged, and so on); each is available for free at City Hall/Guest Relations.

ALEX We always collect park maps on our last day. They're a nice reminder of our trip and are very useful for our scrapbooks.

8. At the Main Street Fire Station, you can get a pack of the Sorcerers of the Magic Kingdom cards for each member of the family. Get them even if you don't play the game—they're great keepsakes. Each guest gets a new package every day!

Finally, when it comes to taking photos and collecting mementos, don't let the tail wag the dog. You're not going to Disney World to build the biggest scrapbook in history. Or as this Houston mom put it:

Tell your readers to get a grip on the photography thing. We were so busy shooting pictures that we kind of lost the thread.

HOW TO HAVE FUN BEFORE AND AFTER YOUR VISIT —OR, THINGS THAT BOB WOULD NEVER DO

PREPARING FOR YOUR Walt Disney World vacation is important, but it is equally important to have a good time. Doing so before you leave is yet another way to get the whole family involved.

The weekend before your departure, plan a party for all who are going to Walt Disney World. Pick a Disney movie the entire family will enjoy and plan a meal in front of the TV. A chocolate cake or cookies shaped like the famous mouse head will be a guaranteed success and add to the fun. This is the perfect time to go over the must-see list and reiterate the do's and dont's.

A similar event can be planned upon your return, when it is time to share the pictures and maybe even the movie you made during your visit to Walt Disney World.

BOB Liliane will throw a party at the least provocation— Groundhog Day, National Tulip Day, Bless the Reptiles Day, you name it. But scheduling a wingding the weekend before you go to Disney World is to me like holding an Easter-egg hunt in a cattle stampede—just a little too much going on to add one more thing.

Great Websites

Arts and crafts and party tips: **family.go.com/crafts, family.go.com/parties**

Some serious cooking: **magicalkingdoms.com/wdw /recipes**

LILIANE
Don't forget to send Bob an invitation.

◨ TRIAL RUN

IF YOU GIVE THOUGHTFUL CONSIDERATION to all areas of mental, physical, organizational, and logistical preparation discussed in this chapter, what remains is to familiarize yourself with Walt Disney World itself, and of course, to conduct your field test. Yep, that's right, we want you to take the whole platoon on the road for a day to see if you are combat ready. No joke, this is important. You'll learn who poops out first, who is prone to developing blisters, who has to pee every 11 seconds, and, given the proper forum, how compatible your family is in terms of what you like to see and do.

For the most informative trial run, choose a local venue that requires lots of walking, dealing with crowds, and making decisions on how to spend your time. Regional theme parks and state fairs are your best bets, followed by large zoos and museums. Devote the whole day. Kick off the morning with an early start, just like you will at Walt Disney World, paying attention to who's organized and ready to go and who's dragging his or her butt and holding up the group. If you have to drive an hour or two to get to your test venue, no big deal. You'll have to do some commuting at Disney World too. Spend the whole day, eat a couple meals, and stay late.

Don't bias the sample (that is, mess with the outcome) by telling everyone you are practicing for Walt Disney World. Everyone behaves differently when they know they are being tested or evaluated. Your objective is not to run a perfect drill but to find out as much as you can about how the individuals in your family, as well as the family as a group, respond to and deal with everything they experience during the day. Pay attention to who moves quickly and who is slow; to who is adventuresome and who is reticent; to who keeps going and who needs frequent rest breaks; to who sets the agenda and who is content to follow; to who is easily agitated and who stays cool; to who tends to dawdle or wander off; to who is curious and who is bored; to who is demanding and who is accepting. You get the idea.

Discuss the findings of the test run with your spouse the next day. Don't be discouraged if your test day wasn't perfect; few (if any) are. Distinguish between problems that are remediable and problems that are intrinsic to your family's emotional or physical makeup (no amount of hiking, for example, will toughen up some people's feet).

Establish a plan for addressing remediable problems (further conditioning, setting limits before you go, trying harder to achieve family consensus, and so on) and develop strategies for minimizing or working around problems that are a fact of life (waking sleepyheads 15 minutes early, placing moleskin on likely blister sites before setting out, packing familiar food for the toddler who balks at restaurant fare). If you are an attentive observer, a fair diagnostician, and a creative problem solver, you'll be able to work out a significant percentage of the problems you're likely to encounter at Walt Disney World before you ever leave home.

PART SIX

READY, SET, TOUR!

TOURING RECOMMENDATIONS

HOW MUCH TIME IS REQUIRED TO SEE EACH PARK?

THE MAGIC KINGDOM AND EPCOT offer such a large number of attractions and special live-entertainment options that it is impossible to see everything in a single day, with or without a midday break. For a reasonably thorough tour of each, allocate a minimum of one and a half days and preferably two days. The Animal Kingdom and Disney's Hollywood Studios can each be seen in a day, though planning on a day and a half allows for a more relaxed visit.

WHICH PARK TO SEE FIRST?

THIS QUESTION IS LESS ACADEMIC than it appears, especially if your party includes children or teenagers. Children who see the Magic Kingdom first expect the same type of entertainment at the other parks. At Epcot, they're often disappointed by the educational orientation and serious tone (many adults react the same way). Disney's Hollywood Studios (DHS) offers some wild action along with family-friendly stage shows and attractions. Children may not find Animal Kingdom as exciting as the Magic Kingdom or DHS because animals can't be programmed to entertain on cue.

First-time visitors should see Epcot first; you'll be able to enjoy it without having been preconditioned to think of Disney entertainment as solely fantasy or adventure.

See Disney's Animal Kingdom second. Like Epcot, it's educational, but its live animals provide a change of pace.

Next, see Disney's Hollywood Studios, which helps all ages transition from the educational Epcot and Animal Kingdom to the fanciful Magic Kingdom. Also, because DHS is smaller, you won't walk as much or stay as long. Save the Magic Kingdom for last.

If you can't postpone the Magic Kingdom without a major revolt, at least see Epcot first. Adult orientation notwithstanding, there's lots that children 7 and up will love, younger children not so much. Be sure to participate in the Agent P and Kidcot programs, described in Part Eight. They'll be the highlight of your child's day. If seeing Mickey is your kid's top priority, be advised that you can see him in each of the major theme parks. Any cast member can tell you where to find him.

OPERATING HOURS

THE DISNEY WORLD WEBSITE publishes preliminary park hours 180 days in advance, but schedule adjustments can happen at any time, including the day of your visit. Check **disneyworld.com** or call ☎ 407-824-4321 for the exact hours before you arrive. Off-season, parks may be open as few as 8 hours (9 a.m.–5 p.m.). At busy times (particularly holidays), they may operate 8 a.m.–2 a.m.

OFFICIAL OPENING VERSUS REAL OPENING

WHEN YOU CALL, you're given "official" hours. Sometimes parks open earlier. If the official hours are 9 a.m.–9 p.m., for example, Main Street in the Magic Kingdom might open at 8:30 a.m., and the remainder of the park at 9 a.m.

Disney surveys local hotel reservations, estimates how many visitors to expect on a given day, and opens the theme parks early to avoid bottlenecks at parking facilities and ticket windows, as well as to absorb crowds as they arrive.

Rides and attractions shut down at approximately the official closing time. Main Street in the Magic Kingdom remains open 30 minutes to an hour after the rest of the park has closed.

THE RULES

SUCCESSFUL TOURING OF THE MAGIC KINGDOM, Animal Kingdom, Epcot, or Disney's Hollywood Studios hinges on five rules:

1. Determine in Advance What You Really Want to See

What rides and attractions appeal most to you? Which additional rides and attractions would you like to experience if you have some time left? What are you willing to forgo?

To help you set your touring priorities, we describe each theme park and its attractions later in this book. In each description, we include the authors' evaluation of the attraction and the opinions of Walt Disney World guests expressed as star ratings. Five stars is the best possible rating.

Finally, because attractions range from midway-type rides and horse-drawn trolleys to colossal, high-tech extravaganzas, we have developed a hierarchy of categories to pinpoint an attraction's magnitude:

SUPER-HEADLINERS The best attractions the theme park has to offer. Mind-boggling in size, scope, and imagination, they represent the cutting edge of modern attraction technology and design.

HEADLINERS Full-blown, multimillion-dollar, full-scale themed adventures and theater presentations. Modern in technology and design and employing a complete range of special effects.

MAJOR ATTRACTIONS Themed adventures on a more modest scale but incorporating state-of-the-art technologies. Or, larger-scale attractions of older design.

MINOR ATTRACTIONS Midway-type rides, small dark rides (cars on a track, zigzagging through the dark), small theater presentations, transportation rides, and elaborate walk-through attractions.

DIVERSIONS Exhibits, both passive and interactive. Include playgrounds, video arcades, and street theater.

Though not every Walt Disney World attraction fits neatly into these descriptions, the categories provide a comparison of attractions' size and scope. Remember that bigger and more elaborate doesn't always mean better. Peter Pan's Flight, a minor attraction in the Magic Kingdom, continues to be one of the park's most beloved rides. Likewise, for many young children, no attraction, regardless of size, surpasses Dumbo.

2. Arrive Early! Arrive Early! Arrive Early!

This is the single most important key to efficient touring and avoiding long lines. First thing in the morning, there are no lines and fewer people. The same four rides you experience in 1 hour in early morning can take as long as 3 hours after 10:30 a.m. Eat breakfast before you arrive; don't waste prime touring time sitting in a restaurant.

The earlier a park opens, the greater your advantage. This is because most vacationers won't rise early and get to a park before it opens. Fewer people are willing to make an 8 a.m. opening than a 9 a.m. opening. If you visit during midsummer, arrive at the turnstile 30–40 minutes before opening. During holiday periods, arrive 45–60 minutes early.

If getting the kids up earlier than usual makes for rough sailing, don't despair: You'll have a great time no matter when you get to the park. Many families with young children have found that it's better to accept the relative inefficiencies of arriving at the park a bit late than to jar the children out of their routine. We include a number of touring plans for sleepyheads in this guide.

LILIANE Still, you'll be able to see and do much more if you arrive early.

3. Avoid Bottlenecks

Crowd concentrations and/or faulty crowd management cause bottlenecks. Avoiding bottlenecks involves being able to predict where, when, and why they occur. Concentrations of hungry people create bottlenecks at restaurants during lunch and dinner. Concentrations of people moving toward the exit at closing time create bottlenecks in gift shops en route to the gate. Concentrations of visitors at new and popular rides and at rides slow to load and unload create bottlenecks and long lines. To help you get a grip on which attractions cause bottlenecks, we've developed a Bottleneck Scale with a range of 1–10. If an attraction ranks high on the Bottleneck Scale, try to experience it during the first 2 hours the park is open. The scale is included in each attraction profile in Parts Seven through Eleven.

The best way to avoid bottlenecks, however, is to use one of our field-tested touring plans available in clip-out form, complete with a map, on pages 455–480. The plans will save you as much as 4½ hours of standing in line in a single day.

4. Go Back to Your Hotel for a Rest in the Middle of the Day

You may think we're beating the dead horse with this midday nap thing, but if you plug away all day at the theme parks, you'll understand how the dead horse feels. No joke; resign yourself to going back to the hotel in the middle of the day for swimming, reading, and a snooze.

5. Let Off Steam

Time at a Disney theme park is extremely regimented for younger children. Often held close for fear of losing them, they are ushered from line to line and attraction to attraction throughout the day. After a couple of hours of being on such a short leash, it's not surprising that they're in need of some physical freedom and an opportunity to discharge that pent-up energy. As it happens, all of the major theme parks except Epcot offer some sort of elaborate, creative playground perfect for such a release. Be advised that each playground (or plaza) is fairly large, and it's pretty easy to misplace a child while they're exploring. All children's playgrounds, however, have only one exit, so though your kids might get lost within the playground, they cannot wander off into the rest of the park without passing through the single exit (usually staffed by a Disney cast member).

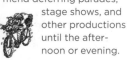

LILIANE If you can't calm them—dunk them. Whenever my son was too wound up to nap or go to bed at night, I took him to the pool—water works wonders.

YOUR DAILY ITINERARY

BOB We strongly recommend deferring parades, stage shows, and other productions until the afternoon or evening.

PLAN EACH DAY in three blocks:

1. Early morning theme park touring
2. Midday break
3. Late-afternoon and evening theme park touring

Choose the attractions that interest you most and check their bottleneck ratings along with what time of day we recommend you visit. If your children are 8 years old or younger, review the attraction's fright-potential rating. Use one of our touring plans or work out a step-by-step plan of your own and write it down. Experience attractions with a high bottleneck rating as early as possible, transitioning to attractions with ratings of 6–8 around midmorning. Plan on departing the park for your midday break by 11:30 a.m. or so.

For your late-afternoon and evening touring block, you do not necessarily have to return to the same theme park. If you have purchased one of the Disney admission options that allow you to "park-hop"—that is, visit more than one theme park on a given day—you may opt to spend the afternoon/evening block somewhere different. In any event, as you start your afternoon/evening block, see attractions with low bottleneck ratings until about 5 p.m. After 5 p.m., any attraction with a rating of 1–7 is fair game. If you stay into the evening, try attractions with ratings of 8–10 during the hour just before closing.

In addition to attractions, each theme park offers a broad range of special live-entertainment events. In the morning, concentrate on the attractions. For the record, we regard live shows that offer five or more daily performances a day (except for street entertainment) as attractions. Thus, *Indiana Jones* at Disney's Hollywood Studios is an attraction, as is *Festival of the Lion King* at the Animal Kingdom. *IllumiNations* at Epcot or the parades at the Magic Kingdom, on the other hand, are live-entertainment events. A schedule of live performances is listed in the *Times Guide* available at the entrance of each park. When planning your day, also be aware that major live events draw large numbers of guests from the attraction lines. Thus, a good time to see an especially popular attraction is during a parade or other similar event.

TOURING PLANS

OUR TOURING PLANS ARE STEP-BY-STEP GUIDES for seeing as much as possible with a minimum of standing in line. They're designed to help you avoid crowds and bottlenecks on days of moderate-to-heavy attendance. On days of lighter attendance (see "When to Go to Walt Disney World," pages 44–47), the plans will still save time, but they won't be as critical to successful touring. *Unofficial Guide* touring plans, it seems, have side effects. As two readers attest, the plans can fan the embers of love and help you impress your friends. First from a 30-something mother of two from Oconomowoc, Wisconsin:

LILIANE Don't get obsessed with the touring plans. It's your vacation, after all. You can amend or even scrap the plans if you want.

> My husband was a bit doubtful about using a touring plan, but on our first day at Magic Kingdom, when we had done all of the Fantasyland attractions and ridden Splash Mountain twice before lunch, he looked at me with amazement and said, "I've never been so attracted to you."

And from a young Gardner, Massachusetts, reader:

> I went with my school for the Magic Music Days. I've been to Disney World before several times, and my parents have always used the guide. I looked crazy to my friends, with my huge book marked and well-worn and a stack of clip-out touring plans in my hand. The group that traveled around with me were amazed, commenting that it seemed like we were in front of a huge crowd. As soon as we left

a ride we had walked on with no wait minutes before, there'd be a line of 15–20 minutes! Thank you for helping me impress my friends!

What You Can Realistically Expect from the Touring Plans

The best way to see as much as possible with the least amount of waiting is to arrive early. Several of our touring plans require that you be on hand when the park opens. Because this is often difficult and sometimes impossible for families with young children or nocturnal teens, we've developed additional touring plans for families who get a late start. You won't see as much as with the early-morning plans, but you'll see significantly more than visitors without a plan.

Variables That Will Affect the Success of the Touring Plans

The plans' success will be affected by how quickly you move from ride to ride; when and how many refreshment and restroom breaks you take; when, where, and how you eat meals; and your ability (or lack thereof) to find your way around. Smaller groups almost always move faster than larger groups, and parties of adults generally cover more ground than families with young children. Switching off (see page 243), also known as "The Baby Swap" or child swapping, among other things, inhibits families with little ones from moving expeditiously among attractions.

Along with dining breaks, the appearance of a Disney character usually stops a touring plan in its tracks. While some characters stroll the parks, it's equally common that they assemble in a specific venue where families queue up for photos and autographs. Meeting characters, posing for photos, and getting autographs can burn hours of touring time.

If your kids collect character autographs, you need to anticipate these interruptions by including character greetings when creating your online touring plans, or else negotiate some understanding with your children about when you'll collect autographs. Note that queues for autographs, especially in the Magic Kingdom and Disney's Animal Kingdom, are sometimes as long as the queues for major attractions. The only time-efficient ways to collect autographs are to use FastPass+ where available or to line up at the character-greeting areas first thing in the morning. Early morning is also the best time to experience popular attractions, so you may have some tough choices to make.

LILIANE Character meals are another way to collect autographs and might be something you could promise your avid collector in exchange for a full day of touring when the signature hunt is off.

While we realize that following the touring plans isn't always easy, we nevertheless recommend continuous, expeditious touring until around noon. After noon, interruptions won't affect the plans significantly.

A multigenerational family from Aurora, Ohio, wonders how to know if you are on track or not, writing:

It seems like the touring plans were very time-dependent, yet there were no specific times attached to the plan outside of the early morning. On more than one day, I often had to guess as to whether we were on track. Having small children and a grandparent in our group, we couldn't move at a fast pace.

There is no objective measurement for being on track—each family's or touring group's experience will differ to some degree. Nevertheless, the sequence of attractions in the touring plans will allow you to enjoy the greatest number of attractions in the least possible amount of time. Two quickly moving adults will probably take in more attractions in a specific time period than will a large group made up of children, parents, and grandparents. However, each will maximize their touring time and experience as many attractions as possible.

What To Do if You Lose the Thread

If unforeseen events interrupt a plan:

1. If you're following a touring plan in our **Lines** app (**touringplans.com/lines**), just press the "Optimize" button when you're ready to start touring again. Lines will figure out the best possible plan for the remainder of your day.

2. If you're following a printed touring plan, skip a step on the plan for every 20 minutes' delay. For example, if you lose your wallet and spend an hour hunting for it, skip three steps and pick up from there.

3. Forget the plan and organize the remainder of the day using the standby wait times listed in Lines.

What to Expect When You Arrive at the Parks

Because most touring plans are based on being present when the theme park opens, you need to know about opening procedures. Disney transportation to the parks begins 1½–2 hours before official opening. The parking lots open at around the same time.

Each park has an entrance plaza outside the turnstiles. Usually, you're held there until 30 minutes before the official opening time, when you're admitted. What happens next depends on the season and the day's crowds.

1. **STANDARD OPENING PROCEDURES** At Epcot, Disney's Hollywood Studios, and Animal Kingdom, all guests are permitted through the turnstiles, and you'll find that one or several specific attractions are open early. At Epcot, Spaceship Earth and sometimes Test Track or Soarin' will be operating. At Animal Kingdom, you may find it's Kilimanjaro Safaris, Expedition Everest, and TriceraTop Spin. At Hollywood Studios, look for Tower of Terror, Toy Story Midway Mania!, and/or Rock 'n' Roller Coaster.

   At the Magic Kingdom, you may be admitted past the turnstiles 15 minutes before park opening, but you'll usually be confined to a small section of the park, such as Main Street, U.S.A., until official opening time. A human wall of Disney cast members keeps you there until opening, when the wall speedwalks you back to the headliner attractions (to prevent anyone from running or getting trampled).

2. **HIGH-ATTENDANCE DAYS** When large crowds are expected, you'll usually be admitted through the turnstiles up to 30 minutes before official opening, and most of the park will be operating.

In the first scenario above, you gain a big advantage if you're already past the turnstiles when the park opens. While everyone else is stuck in line waiting for the people ahead to find their tickets and figure out how the biometric scans work, the lucky few already in the park will be in line for their first attraction. You'll probably be done and on your way to your second before many of them are even in the park, and the time savings accrue throughout the rest of the day.

HOW TO FIND THE TOURING PLAN THAT'S BEST FOR YOU

THE DIFFERENT TOURING PLANS FOR EACH PARK are described in the chapter pertaining to that park. The descriptions will tell you for whom (for example, teens, parents with preschoolers, grandparents, and so on) or for what situation (such as sleeping late or enjoying the park at night) the plans are designed. The actual touring plans are located on pages 455–480 at the back of the book. Each plan includes a numbered map of the park in question to help you find your way around. Clip out the plan of your choice and take it with you to the park.

Our best touring plans are those provided in this guide. However, customized plans are available at **touringplans.com;** there you can create specific plans based on your family setup, your favorite attractions, restaurants, and more.

Will the Plans Continue to Work Once the Secret Is Out?

Yes! First, most of the plans require that a patron be there when a park opens. Many Disney World patrons simply won't get up early while on vacation. Second, less than 2% of any day's attendance has been exposed to the plans—too few to affect results. Last, most groups tailor the plans, skipping rides or shows according to taste.

How Frequently Are the Touring Plans Revised?

We revise them every year, and updates are always available at **touring plans.com.** Most complaints we receive come from readers using out-of-date editions of *The Unofficial Guide.* Even if you're up-to-date, though, be prepared for surprises. Opening procedures and showtimes may change, for example, and you can't predict when an attraction might break down.

"Bouncing Around"

Some readers object to crisscrossing a theme park as our touring plans sometimes require. A woman from Decatur, Georgia, told us she "got dizzy from all the bouncing around." Believe us, we empathize.

We've worked hard over the years to eliminate the need to crisscross a theme park in our touring plans. (In fact, our customized software can minimize walking instead of waiting in line, if that's important to you.) Occasionally, however, it's possible to save a lot of time in line with a few extra minutes of walking.

The reasons for this are varied. Sometimes a park is designed intentionally to require walking. In the Magic Kingdom, for example, the most popular attractions are positioned as far apart as possible—in the north, east, and west corners of the park—so that guests are more evenly distributed throughout the day. Other times, you may be visiting just after a new attraction has opened that everyone wants to try. In that case, a special trip to visit the new attraction may be required earlier in the day than normal, in order to avoid longer waits later. And live shows, especially at the Studios, sometimes have performance schedules so at odds with each other (and the rest of the park's schedule) that orderly touring is impossible.

If you want to experience headliner attractions in one day without long waits, you can see those first (requires crisscrossing the park), use FastPass+ (if available), or hope to squeeze in visits during parades and the last hour the park is open (may not work).

Touring Plans and the Obsessive-Compulsive Reader

We suggest sticking to the plans religiously, especially in the mornings, if you're visiting during busy times. The consequence of touring spontaneity in peak season is hours of standing in line. When using the plans, however, relax and always be prepared for surprises and setbacks.

If you find your type-A brain doing cartwheels, reflect on the advice of a woman from Trappe, Pennsylvania:

> I had planned for this trip for two years and researched it by use of guidebooks, websites, DVDs, and information received from WDW. On night three of our trip, I ended up taking an unscheduled trip to the emergency room. When the doctor asked what seemed to be the problem, I responded, "I don't know, but I can't stop shaking, and I can't stay here very long because I have to get up in a couple hours to go to Disney's Hollywood Studios." Diagnosis: an anxiety attack caused by my excessive itinerary.

However, a vet from Annandale, Virginia, warns:

> I'm retired Navy, and planning a Disney visit today is almost like planning an amphibious landing for the invasion! I pity any free spirit who blithely shows up at a Disney park for the first time without any advance planning and expects to flit from ride to ride without a care in the world. Disney World will eat you alive if you're not careful!

Touring Plan Rejection

Some folks don't respond well to the regimentation of a touring plan. If you encounter this problem with someone in your party, roll with the punches, as this Maryland couple did:

> The rest of the group was not receptive to the use of the touring plans. I think they all thought I was being a little too regimented about planning this vacation. Rather than argue, I left the touring

plans behind as we ventured off for the parks. You can guess the outcome. We took our camcorder with us and watched the movies when we returned home. About every 5 minutes or so, there's a shot of us all gathered around a park map trying to decide what to do next.

A reader from Royal Oak, Michigan, ran into trouble by not getting her family on board ahead of time:

If one member of the family is doing most of the research and planning (like I did), communicate what the book/touring plans suggest. I failed to do this and it led to some, shall we say, tense moments between my husband and me on our first day. However, once he realized how much time we were saving, he understood why I was so bent on following the plans.

Finally, note that our mobile app, **Lines,** can be used to find attractions with low wait times, even if you're not using a structured touring plan.

Touring Plans for Low-Attendance Days

We receive a number of letters each year similar to the following one from Lebanon, New Jersey:

The guide always assumed there would be large crowds. We had no lines. An alternate tour for low-traffic days would be helpful.

There are, thankfully, still days on which crowds are low enough that a full-day touring plan isn't needed. However, some attractions in each park bottleneck even if attendance is low:

- **MAGIC KINGDOM** Space Mountain, Splash Mountain, The Many Adventures of Winnie the Pooh, *Enchanted Tales with Belle,* Peter Pan's Flight, and Seven Dwarfs Mine Train

- **EPCOT** Test Track and Soarin'

- **DISNEY'S ANIMAL KINGDOM** Kilimanjaro Safaris, Expedition Everest, and Dinosaur

- **DISNEY'S HOLLYWOOD STUDIOS** Rock 'n' Roller Coaster, The Twilight Zone Tower of Terror, and Toy Story Midway Mania!

For this reason, we recommend that you follow a touring plan at least through the first five or six steps. If you're pretty much walking onto every attraction, scrap the remainder of the plan. Alternatively, you can see the attractions above immediately after the park is open, or use FastPass+.

Extra Magic Hours and the Touring Plans

If you're a Disney resort guest and use your morning Extra Magic Hours privileges, complete your early-entry touring before the general public is admitted and position yourself to follow the touring plan. When the public is admitted, the park will suddenly swarm. A Wilmington, Delaware, mother advises:

The early-entry times went like clockwork. We were finishing up the Great Movie Ride when Disney's Hollywood Studios opened to the public, and we had to wait in line quite a while for Voyage of the Little Mermaid, which sort of screwed up everything thereafter. Early-opening attractions should be finished up well before regular opening time so you can be at the plan's first stop as early as possible.

In the Magic Kingdom, early-entry attractions currently operate in Fantasyland and Tomorrowland. At Epcot, they're in the Future World section. At Disney's Animal Kingdom, they're in DinoLand U.S.A., Asia, Discovery Island, and Africa. At Disney's Hollywood Studios, they're dispersed. Practically speaking, see any attractions on the plan that are open for early entry, crossing them off as you do. If you finish all early-entry attractions and have time left before the general public is admitted, sample early-entry attractions not included in the plan. Stop touring about 10 minutes before the public is admitted, and position yourself for the first attraction on the plan that wasn't open for early entry. During early entry in the Magic Kingdom, for example, you can almost always experience Seven Dwarfs Mine Train and Under the Sea: Journey of the Little Mermaid in Fantasyland, plus Space Mountain in Tomorrowland. As official opening nears, go to the boundary between Fantasyland and Liberty Square and be ready to blitz Splash and Big Thunder Mountains according to the touring plan when the rest of the park opens.

Evening Extra Magic Hours, when a designated park remains open for Disney resort guests 2 hours beyond normal closing time, have less effect on the touring plans than early entry in the morning. Parks are almost never scheduled for both early entry and evening Extra Magic Hours on the same day. Thus a park offering evening Extra Magic Hours will enjoy a fairly normal morning and early afternoon. It's not until late afternoon, when park hoppers coming from the other theme parks descend, that the late-closing park will become especially crowded. By that time, you'll be well toward the end of your touring plan.

FASTPASS+

DISNEY INTRODUCED THE FASTPASS ride-reservation system in 1999 as a way to moderate the high wait times at some of its headliner attractions. A new version of the system, called FastPass+, completely replaced the old one in January 2014. Whereas the old system printed your reservation times on small slips of paper dispensed from ATM-like kiosks next to each attraction, the current FastPass+ system is (with one exception described later) entirely electronic: You must use a computer, mobile device, or in-park terminal to make and modify FastPass+ reservations, and you must use your RFID-enabled MagicBand, Key to the World Card, or day-guest card to redeem the reservation. As before, FastPass+ is free of charge to all Walt Disney World guests.

LILIANE Specific Fast-Pass+ information for each Disney theme park is provided in its respective chapter.

Because FastPass+ has a learning curve, understanding how to use it is important for success when using our touring plans, especially if you want to experience lots of attractions or you're unable to arrive at park opening. Somewhat like making a dinner reservation at a restaurant, FastPass+ allows you to reserve a ride on an attraction at a Disney theme park. You can request a specific time, such as 7:30 p.m., or you can let the system give you its first-available reservation.

Though we take issue with the current system's complicated rules and procedures, we do concede that it can help you see more with less waiting, provided you know how to use it. Like the old FastPass, it reduces waits for designated attractions by distributing guests at those attractions throughout the day. FastPass+ provides an incentive—a shorter wait—for guests willing to postpone experiencing a given attraction until later in the day. The system also, in effect, imposes a penalty—standby status—on guests who don't use it. However, spreading out guest arrivals sometimes decreases waits for standby guests as well.

FastPass+ does *not* eliminate the need to arrive early at a theme park. Because each park offers a limited number of FastPass+ attractions, you still have to make an early start if you want to avoid long lines at non-FastPass+ attractions. Plus, a limited supply of FastPasses is available for each attraction on any day. If you don't reserve in advance and you arrive at your park of choice after noon, you might find no more spots available for your favorites.

Making a FastPass+ Reservation

Anyone with an upcoming stay at a Walt Disney World hotel can make FastPass+ reservations up to 60 days in advance at **mydisneyexperience.com** and through the My Disney Experience (MDE) app; Annual Pass holders staying off-property may reserve up to 30 days in advance, as may day guests with a valid ticket. At press time, you could use FastPass+ at just one park per day.

If you buy your admission the day you arrive at the park or you want to change your previous FastPass+ selections once you're inside, you can do so using the mobile app or in-park computer terminals.

You should set aside *at least* 30 minutes to complete the advance-booking process. Before you begin, make sure that you have the following items on hand:

- A valid admission ticket or purchase-confirmation number for everyone in your group
- Your hotel reservation number, if you're staying on-site
- A computer, smartphone, or tablet connected to the Internet
- An e-mail account that you can access easily while traveling
- A My Disney Experience account
- A schedule of the parks you'll be visiting each day, including arrival and departure times, plus the times of any midday breaks
- The dates, times, and confirmation numbers of any dining or recreation reservations you've already made

We think it's easier to use **mydisneyexperience.com** than the MDE app, so here's how to make reservations using the website:

1. E-MAIL ACCESS Because the MDE site uses your e-mail address to identify you and send you new login credentials should you forget your old ones (see next step), you need to make sure you'll have easy access to your account while you're in the parks. If you don't have a mobile app for your e-mail account, download and configure it before you leave home. And if you don't have an account with a Web-based service such as Gmail, go ahead and set one up—it's much easier to configure for mobile devices than e-mail you get through your ISP.

2. MY DISNEY EXPERIENCE ACCESS Now go to the MDE site and click "Sign In or Create Account" in the upper right corner; then click "Create Account" on the screen that follows. You'll be asked for your e-mail address, along with your name, home address, and birthdate. (Disney uses your home address to send your MagicBands and, if applicable, hotel reservation information.) You'll also be asked to choose two security questions and answers—write these down and store them in a safe place, or save them as a text file. If you forget your MDE login information, Disney will ask you these questions to verify your identity.

3. DISNEY HOTEL INFORMATION Next, MDE asks whether you'll be staying at a Disney hotel. If you are, enter your reservation number. This associates your MDE account with your hotel stay in Disney's computer systems. If you've booked a travel package that includes theme park admission, Disney computers will automatically link the admission to your MDE account, allowing you to skip Step 5 below.

4. REGISTER FRIENDS AND FAMILY You'll now be asked for the names, ages, and e-mail addresses of everyone traveling with you. This is so you can make dining and FastPass+ reservations for your entire group at the same time later in the process. You can add family and friends at any time, but you might as well do it now.

5. REGISTER TICKETS If you've bought your admission from a third-party ticket reseller or you have tickets or MagicBands left over from a previous trip, you'll be asked to register those next. On each ticket is printed a unique ID code, usually a string of 12–20 numbers, located in one corner on the back; on MagicBands, look for a 12-digit number printed inside the band. Enter the ID code for each ticket you have.

You can make FastPass+ reservations for as many days as there are on your ticket. If you decide later to extend your stay, you'll be able to make reservations for additional days. If you have a voucher that needs to be converted to a ticket at the parks, you can still register it by calling Disney tech support at ☎ 407-939-7765.

6. SELECT A DATE Click on the My Disney Experience logo in the upper right corner of your screen. A menu should appear, with "FastPass+" as one of the choices. Click on "FastPass+."

The next screen should display a rolling seven-day calendar, beginning around the start of your trip's dates. Select one of these dates and click "Next."

7. SELECT TRAVEL PARTY On the screen that follows, you'll choose which of your friends and family will use the FastPass+ reservations you're making. Note that everyone you select during this step will get the same set of FastPass+ attractions and times: If your FastPass+ choices include, say, Space Mountain and your father-in-law doesn't do roller coasters, you'll need to tweak his selections in Step 10. For now, choose all the members of your group and click "Next."

8. SELECT ATTRACTIONS On this screen you choose your FastPass+ experiences from a list of eligible attractions. Because Disney has rules governing the combinations of FastPasses you can get at Epcot and Disney's Hollywood Studios (see page 237), the attractions will be grouped into the correct tiers for those parks, and you'll see how many opportunities you have in each tier. If all FastPasses for an attraction have been distributed, the message "Standby Available" will appear next to its name.

If you don't choose an attraction for every opportunity MDE gives you—for instance, if you choose only two attractions when MDE says you can choose three—you'll automatically be assigned random attractions for all remaining opportunities.

9. CHOOSE INITIAL RETURN TIMES Next, MDE will give you four different sets of FastPass+ return times, grouped as Options A, B, and C, plus

Best Match. Each option contains one return time for each attraction that you selected in Step 8. Choose the set of return times that's closest to what you want, and you'll be able to modify them in the next step.

10. MODIFY RETURN TIMES OR ATTRACTIONS If the initial set of FastPass+ return times conflicts with your plans, you can check whether alternate times are available that better fit your schedule. The good news is that you can change each attraction's return times separately. Plus, if none of the return times for a particular attraction work for you, you can pick another attraction at this stage without having to start over.

OK, you've booked one set of FastPasses for one park visit—now you'll need to repeat Steps 6–10 for every park you plan to visit, on every day of your trip. Simple, no?

Buying Tickets and Making FastPass+ Reservations On Arrival

If (1) you buy your admission the day you arrive at the parks or (2) you have to delay making your FastPass+ selections until you're inside, Disney has placed new computer terminals throughout the parks where you can make reservations; we've listed the specific locations in each theme park's chapter. Each set of terminals—look for the FP+ KIOSK signs—is staffed by a group of cast members who can walk you through the reservation process.

BOB You'll be notified of any issues with FastPass+ reservations through the My Disney Experience mobile app.

If you're tech-challenged, not to worry: You can use a paper FastPass+ form, sort of like a cafeteria menu, that lets you tick off check boxes next to the rides you want to experience. A cast member will take your form and enter your selections into the kiosk for you. You'll still need to provide your MDE username and password, however. Be aware that the number of kiosks is limited, and most locations can process reservations for no more than 150 people per hour.

RETURNING TO RIDE Each FastPass+ reservation lasts for an hour, and Disney officially enforces the ride return time. Thus, if you make a FastPass+ reservation to ride Space Mountain at 7:30 p.m., you have until 8:30 p.m. to either use it or change it to something else. Your FastPass+ may be canceled if you don't show up on time; in practice, however, we've found that you can usually be up to 5 minutes early or 15 minutes late to use your reservation.

When you return to Space Mountain at the designated time, you'll be directed to a FASTPASS+ RETURN line. Before you enter the line, you'll need to validate your reservation by touching your MagicBand or RFID ticket to a reader at the FastPass+ Return entrance. Then you'll proceed with minimal waiting to the attraction's preshow or boarding area.

If technical problems cause an attraction to be closed during your return time, Disney will automatically adjust your FastPass+ reservation in one of three ways:

1. If it's early in the day, Disney will offer you the chance to return to the attraction at any point in the day after it reopens.

2. Alternatively, Disney may let you choose another FastPass+ attraction in the same park, on the same day.

3. If it's late in the day, Disney will automatically give you another selection good for any FastPass+ attraction at any park the following day.

At the FastPass+ attractions listed below, the time gap between getting your pass and returning to ride can range from 3 to 7 hours. To ensure that you have enough time to ride on the day of your visit, either book FastPass+ in advance for these attractions or reserve them in the parks as early in the day as possible.

GET FASTPASS+ *BEFORE 11 A.M.* FOR THE FOLLOWING:						
MAGIC KINGDOM						
Buzz Lightyear's Space Ranger Spin	Evening parade	*Frozen* Meet and Greet	Peter Pan's Flight	Seven Dwarfs Mine Train	Space Mountain	Splash Mountain
EPCOT	*IllumiNations*		Mission: Space Orange		Soarin'	Test Track
ANIMAL KINGDOM	Expedition Everest		Kilimanjaro Safaris		Meet Mickey and Minnie at Adventurers Outpost	
DHS	Rock 'n' Roller Coaster		Toy Story Midway Mania!		The Twilight Zone Tower of Terror	

FastPass+ Rules

Disney has put rules in place to prevent guests from obtaining certain combinations of FastPass+ reservations before they get to the parks:

RULE #1: You can obtain only one advance FastPass+ reservation per attraction, per day, but you can get more once you're in the park and you've used your first set of three. You can't make multiple advance FastPass+ reservations for, say, Toy Story Midway Mania!—you must select three different attractions. But once you've entered Hollywood Studios for the day and your first three reservations have been used or have expired, you can obtain more for Toy Story Midway Mania! if they're available.

It's generally a bad idea to make advance FastPass+ reservations for any of the evening parades or fireworks, because you won't be able to get any more reservations while you're in the park. We suggest checking around 4 p.m. to see if any reservations are available for the fireworks and parades. If they are and you're done with the headliner attractions, go ahead and grab a FastPass+.

RULE #2: FastPass+ reservation times can't overlap—Disney's computer system doesn't allow it. If you have a FastPass+ reservation for 2–3 p.m., you can't make another reservation later than 2 p.m. or earlier than 3 p.m. in the same park.

FASTPASS+ TIERS Disney also prohibits guests from using FastPass+ on all of a park's headliner attractions. The practice, known informally as FastPass+ tiers, was in effect only at Epcot and Disney's Hollywood Studios at press time. At Epcot, by way of example, the FastPass+ attractions are divided into the following two tiers:

TIER A: Choose 1	TIER B: Choose 2
• *IllumiNations*	• *Captain EO*
• Living with the Land	• Epcot Character Spot
• Soarin'	• Journey into Imagination with Figment
• Test Track	• Mission: Space (Green or Orange)
	• Spaceship Earth
	• The Seas with Nemo & Friends
	• *Turtle Talk with Crush*

FastPass+ lets you choose only one attraction from Tier A and two attractions from Tier B. Note that Tier A comprises the attractions with the longest lines: This ensures that most guests get to choose either Soarin' or Test Track. Also, note that few of the attractions in Tier B actually require FastPass+ for most of the year.

Again, though, the tiers don't apply beyond your first three advance FastPass+ reservations—any reservations you make beyond the first three when you're in the parks are totally up to you.

Clearly, the FastPass+ rules are designed to do three things: encourage you to stay at a Disney resort, book your trip well in advance, and tell Disney exactly where you plan to be every day. These three things increase Disney's revenue. They also decrease Disney's operating expenses because Disney can adjust its staffing levels at each park based on how many people have made FastPass+ reservations. More important, by promising lower wait times in advance, Disney encourages you to spend more time at its parks and discourage you from last-minute trips to Universal or other parks.

BOB For now, assume it's going to take 1-5 minutes to get your FastPass+ scanned when you return to ride, plus a few minutes in the actual FastPass+ line before you ride.

How FastPass+ Affects Your Waits in Line

FastPass+ has a noticeable effect on standby lines. Standby wait times are down significantly at the following attractions:

- Rock 'n' Roller Coaster (–14 minutes)
- Toy Story Midway Mania! (–13 minutes)
- Expedition Everest (–11 minutes)
- Test Track (–11 minutes)

LILIANE Lines at Pirates of the Caribbean and Spaceship Earth? Give me a break!

Wait times are *up* at these attractions:

- Pirates of the Caribbean (+10)
- Dinosaur (+7 minutes)
- The Haunted Mansion (+7)
- Spaceship Earth (+7)
- The Magic Carpets of Aladdin (+6)
- Journey Into Imagination with Figment (+5)
- Primeval Whirl (+4)

How FastPass+ Affects Your Touring Plans

We think most *Unofficial Guide* readers will probably spend fewer minutes per day walking around the parks because they no longer need to walk to an attraction's FastPass machines. The time saved from walking is slightly more than the overall increases in standby waits at secondary attractions, so FastPass+—when it works—is roughly a break-even proposition for folks using our touring plans.

We say "when it works" because on a recent trip to the Magic Kingdom, we (Bob and Len) spent the better part of a day observing just how wrong things can go at a FastPass+ return point. The most common snafu we saw was a family arriving too early or too late for their reservation. That's understandable, because MagicBands don't display reservation times, and the times are cumbersome to find on My Disney Experience.

The next most frequent issue we saw was from families, particularly those who don't speak English as their first language, who simply didn't get how FastPass+ works. For example, many families seemed to think that simply wearing the MagicBand allowed them access to the FastPass+ line, without their having to make a reservation.

When a MagicBand doesn't work at a FastPass+ return point, a cast member can usually resolve the problem fairly quickly. When the problem is more complex, the line stops while the issue is sorted.

On the upside, Disney has made great progress in streamlining these "recovery" processes, and we expect them to continue to pour resources into further speed-ups.

Customized Touring Plans and FastPass+

The touring plans in this guide, which all incorporate FastPass+, are our most efficient, provided you're willing to arrive at the park 35–60 minutes before opening. Likewise, both our custom plans and our Lines app support FastPass+.

You can update your FastPass+ reservations while you're in the park too. If you decide to change a reservation from Splash Mountain to Big Thunder Mountain Railroad, you can tell Lines to re-optimize your plan based on your new FastPass+ times. This allows you to handle any situation while still minimizing your waits for the rest of the day.

That said, most of the Studios' and Animal Kingdom's shows never require FastPass+. The touring plans already do a good job of getting you to the show at least 15 minutes in advance (or earlier for *Fantasmic!*), in which case you'll almost always be able to get in to see that performance. In the worst-case scenario, you'll have to wait only until the next show. Also, because you can get a FastPass+ reservation for either *Fantasmic!* or Toy Story Midway Mania! at the Studios, you'll almost always end up with a shorter wait in line if you use the Toy Story FastPass+.

The same logic applies at Disney World's parades and fireworks. We don't usually recommend using FastPass+ for the Main Street Electrical Parade or *Wishes* fireworks at the Magic Kingdom, *IllumiNations* at Epcot, or many theater shows (unless you have extra FastPasses at the end of your second day). Using FastPass+ for these usually guarantees you only somewhere to sit or stand. Because you still have to arrive early to claim a prime viewing location, you end up not saving much time—as this Charleston, South Carolina, reader figured out:

> *FastPass+ for* IllumiNations *and shows like* Beauty and the Beast *is a waste. They give away many more reservations for* IllumiNations *than actually provide a good view, so unless you arrive early and stake out a place (which you can do without FastPass+), there really is no point.*

Readers React to FastPass+

FastPass+ generates more comments than anything we've seen in years. A mother from Kansas likes the ability to schedule rides in advance:

> *It was great to schedule our FastPasses ahead of time and know when and where we were going to be. If a ride was closed during our scheduled time, we got an e-mail, and we were able to go back at any time the rest of the day or switch the attraction or time.*

A Columbia, Maryland, woman, however, laments that ride reservations are yet another chore on her vacation to-do list:

> *Between the need for scheduling meals 180 days in advance and rides 60 days out, Disney World has become a vacation for those who enjoy planning every hour of their day.*

From a Ross-on-Rye, United Kingdom, grandfather:

> *This was our first trip with our grandchildren and FastPass+, and I found the amount of planning required to get appropriate Fast-Passes for our multigenerational group intimidating.*

A Pennsylvania mom of two found out that FastPass+ is inflexible when it comes to park hopping:

> *When we were about to leave the Magic Kingdom for Hollywood Studios, it was frustrating to know that I couldn't make a reservation at the kiosk for any park other than the one I was currently at.*

A Fort Collins, Colorado, woman discovered that the FastPass+ times recommended by the My Disney Experience mobile app usually aren't the most convenient:

> *Disney doesn't make it very clear that you don't have to take the times it gives you; you can try times other than its recommended ones.*

A common complaint is that FastPass+ is targeted to tech-savvy younger guests, as this 60-something from Bemidji, Minnesota, notes:

> *Many seniors, and a surprising number of others, aren't into technology. I know a lot of people can't go anywhere without their gadgets, but there are a LOT of us, young and old, who don't have them or don't want to use them on vacation. It seems that those without iPhones, etc., are at a disadvantage.*

As discussed earlier, you can make changes to your FastPass+ reservations, or set up new reservations, at FastPass+ kiosks in the park. An "up East" family of four reported their experience:

There were almost always lines at the in-park kiosks, especially after 11 a.m. By the time I'd used our first three selections (usually early afternoon), there were rarely any FastPass+ times left for the rides we wanted to go on. (Disney sometimes had a sandwich board near the kiosks, noting which attractions still had FastPass+ times available and their level of availability [for example, very limited or available].) Though Disney says you can get an additional FastPass+ after you've used your selections, I wouldn't count on it—the most popular attractions are usually out of FastPass+ times early in the day.

HEIGHT REQUIREMENTS

A NUMBER OF ATTRACTIONS require children to meet minimum height and age requirements; see the table on the next page. If you have children too short or too young to ride, you have several options, including switching off (described on page 243). Though the alternatives may resolve some practical and logistical issues, be forewarned that your smaller children might be resentful of their older (or taller) siblings who qualify to ride. A mom from Virginia bumped into just such a situation, writing:

You mention height requirements for rides but not the intense sibling jealousy this can generate. Frontierland was a real problem in that respect. Our very petite 5-year-old, to her outrage, was stuck hanging around while our 8-year-old went on Splash Mountain and Big Thunder Mountain with Grandma and Granddad, and the nearby alternatives weren't helpful (too long a line for rafts to Tom Sawyer Island, etc.). If we had thought ahead, we would have left the younger kid with one of the grown-ups for another roller coaster or two and then met up later at a designated point.

The reader makes a valid point, though in practical terms splitting the group and meeting up later can be more complicated than she might imagine. If you choose to split up, ask the Disney greeter at the entrance to the attraction(s) with height requirements how long the wait is. Tack 5 minutes for riding onto the anticipated wait, and then add 5 or so minutes to exit and reach the meeting point for an approximate sense of how long the younger kids (and their supervising adult) will have to do other stuff. Our guess is that even with a long line for the rafts, the reader would have had more than sufficient time to take her daughter to Tom Sawyer Island while the sib rode Splash Mountain and Big Thunder Mountain Railroad with the grandparents. For sure she had time to tour the Swiss Family Treehouse in adjacent Adventureland.

WAITING-LINE STRATEGIES FOR ADULTS WITH YOUNG CHILDREN

CHILDREN HOLD UP BETTER through the day if you minimize the time they spend in lines. Arriving early and using our touring plans immensely reduces waiting, along with these tips:

1. LINE GAMES Wise parents anticipate restlessness in line and plan activities to reduce the stress and boredom. In the morning, have waiting

ATTRACTION AND RIDE RESTRICTIONS

THE MAGIC KINGDOM

- **The Barnstormer** 35" minimum height
- **Big Thunder Mountain Railroad** 40" minimum height
- **Seven Dwarfs Mine Train** 38" minimum height
- **Space Mountain** 44" minimum height   • **Splash Mountain** 40" minimum height
- *Stitch's Great Escape!* 40" minimum height
- **Tomorrowland Speedway** 32" to ride, 54" to drive unassisted

EPCOT

- **Mission: Space** 44" minimum height   • **Soarin'** 40" minimum height
- **Sum of All Thrills** 48" minimum height, 54" for inversions
- **Test Track** 40" minimum height

DISNEY'S ANIMAL KINGDOM

- **Dinosaur** 40" minimum height   • **Expedition Everest** 44" minimum height
- **Kali River Rapids** 38" minimum height   • **Primeval Whirl** 48" minimum height

DISNEY'S HOLLYWOOD STUDIOS

- **Honey, I Shrunk the Kids Movie Set Adventure**
  10 years maximum recommended age
- **Rock 'n' Roller Coaster** 48" minimum height
- **Star Tours—The Adventures Continue** 40" minimum height
- **The Twilight Zone Tower of Terror** 40" minimum height

BLIZZARD BEACH WATER PARK

- **Chair Lift** 32" minimum height
- **Downhill Double Dipper slide** 48" minimum height
- **Slush Gusher slide** 48" minimum height
- **Summit Plummet slide** 48" minimum height
- **T-Bar (in Ski Patrol Training Camp)** 60" maximum height
- **Tike's Peak children's area** 48" maximum height

TYPHOON LAGOON WATER PARK

- **Bay Slides** 60" minimum height   • **Crush 'n' Gusher slide** 48" minimum height
- **Humunga Kowabunga slide** 48" minimum height
- **Ketchakiddee Creek children's area** 48" maximum height
- **Shark Reef saltwater reef swim** *Unless accompanied by adult:*
  10 years minimum age
- **Wave Pool** *Adult supervision required*

DISNEYQUEST

- **Buzz Lightyear's AstroBlasters** 51" minimum height
- **CyberSpace Mountain** 51" minimum height
- **Mighty Ducks Pinball Slam** 48" minimum height
- **Pirates of the Caribbean—Battle for Buccaneer Gold** 35" minimum height

children discuss what they want to see and do during the day. Later, watch for and count Disney characters or play simple guessing games such as 20 Questions. Lines move continuously, so games requiring pen and paper are impractical. The holding area of a theater attraction, however, is a different story. Here, tic-tac-toe, hangman, drawing, and coloring make the time fly by. As an alternative, we've provided a trivia game for each park at the end of each park chapter.

2. SWITCHING OFF Several attractions have minimum height and/or age requirements. Some couples with children too small or too young forgo these attractions, while others take turns riding. Missing some of Disney's best rides is an unnecessary sacrifice, and waiting in line twice for the same ride is a tremendous waste of time.

ATTRACTIONS WHERE SWITCHING OFF IS COMMON	
THE MAGIC KINGDOM	**DISNEY'S ANIMAL KINGDOM**
The Barnstormer	Dinosaur
Big Thunder Mountain Railroad	Expedition Everest
Seven Dwarfs Mine Train	Kali River Rapids
Space Mountain	Primeval Whirl
Splash Mountain	
Stitch's Great Escape!	
Tomorrowland Speedway	
EPCOT	**DISNEY'S HOLLYWOOD STUDIOS**
Mission: Space	Rock 'n' Roller Coaster
Soarin'	Star Tours—The Adventures Continue
Test Track	The Twilight Zone Tower of Terror

Instead, take advantage of "switching off," also known as "The Baby Swap" or "The Rider Swap" (or "The Baby/Rider Switch"). To switch off, there must be at least two adults. Adults and children wait in line together. When you reach a cast member, say you want to switch off. The cast member will allow everyone, including young children, to enter the attraction. When you reach the loading area, one adult rides while the other exits with the kids. Then the riding adult disembarks and takes charge of the children while the other adult rides. A third member of the party, either an adult or an older child, can ride twice, once with each switching-off adult, so that the switching-off adults don't have to ride alone.

3. COMBINING THE FASTPASS+ SYSTEM WITH SWITCHING OFF On most FastPass+ attractions, Disney handles switching off somewhat differently. When you tell the cast member that you want to switch off, he or she will issue you a special "rider exchange" FastPass good for three people. One parent and the nonriding child (or children) will at that point be asked to leave the line. When those riding reunite with the waiting adult, the waiting adult and two other persons from the party can ride using the special FastPass. This system eliminates confusion and congestion at the boarding area while sparing the nonriding adult

and child the tedium and physical exertion of waiting in line.

4. LAST-MINUTE COLD FEET If your young child gets cold feet just before boarding a ride where there's no age or height requirement, you usually can arrange a switch-off with the loading attendant. (This happens frequently in Pirates of the Caribbean's dungeon waiting area.)

No law says you have to ride. If you reach the boarding area and someone is unhappy, tell an attendant you've changed your mind and you'll be shown the way out.

5. CATCH-22 AT TOMORROWLAND SPEEDWAY Though Tomorrowland Speedway is a great treat for young children, they're required to be 54 inches tall to drive unassisted. Few children age 6 and younger measure up, so the ride is essentially withheld from the very age group that would most enjoy it. To resolve this Catch-22, go on the ride with your small child. The attendants will assume that you will drive. After getting into the car, shift your child over behind the steering wheel. From your position, you will still be able to control the foot pedals. Children will feel like they're really driving, and because the car travels on a self-guiding track, there's no way they can make a mistake while steering.

CHARACTER ANALYSIS

THE LARGE, FRIENDLY COSTUMED VERSIONS of Mickey, Minnie, Donald, Goofy, and others—known as Disney characters—provide a link between Disney animated films and the theme parks. To people emotionally invested, the characters in Disney films are as real as next-door neighbors, never mind that they're just cartoons. In recent years, theme park personifications of the characters also have become real to us. It's not just a person in a mouse costume we see; it is Mickey himself. Similarly, meeting Goofy or Snow White in Fantasyland is an encounter with a celebrity, a memory to be treasured.

BOB Check your *Times Guide* to find out any character's whereabouts in the parks.

While Disney animated-film characters number in the hundreds, only about 250 have been brought to life in costume. Of these, fewer than a fifth mix with guests; the others perform in shows or parades. Characters are found in all major theme parks and at Disney Deluxe resorts that host character meals.

See page 196 for tips on preparing your young children to meet the Disney characters for the first time.

CHARACTER WATCHING

CHARACTER WATCHING HAS BECOME a pastime. Families once were content to meet a character occasionally. They now pursue them

LILIANE The only way to meet The Beast is after dinner at Be Our Guest.

relentlessly, armed with autograph books and cameras. Some characters are only rarely seen, so character watching has become character collecting. (To cash in on character collecting, Disney sells autograph books

WDW CHARACTER-GREETING VENUES*

THE MAGIC KINGDOM

MICKEY AND HIS POSSE

- **Chip 'n' Dale** Frontierland
- **Daisy, Donald, Goofy, Minnie** Pete's Silly Sideshow (FastPass+)
- **Mickey** Town Square Theater (FastPass+)
- **Pluto** Town Square

DISNEY ROYALTY (*Princesses, Princes, Suitors, and Such*)

- **Aladdin, Jasmine** Adventureland   • **Anna, Elsa** Princess Fairytale Hall (FastPass+)
- **Ariel** Ariel's Grotto (FastPass+)   • **Belle** *Enchanted Tales with Belle* (FastPass+)
- **Cinderella, Rapunzel** Princess Fairytale Hall (FastPass+)
- **The Fairy Godmother, the Tremaines** Near Bibbidi Bobbidi Boutique at Cinderella Castle   • **Gaston** Fountain outside Gaston's Tavern
- **Merida** Fairytale Garden   • **Naveen, Tiana** Liberty Square
- **Snow White** Outside the Town Square Theater exit

FAIRIES

- **Tinker Bell and Friends** Town Square Theater (FastPass+)

MISCELLANEOUS

ALICE IN WONDERLAND **Alice, the White Rabbit** Mad Tea Party

THE ARISTOCATS **Marie** Town Square

LILO AND STITCH **Stitch** Tomorrowland

PETER PAN **Peter, Wendy** Adventureland

TOY STORY **Buzz Lightyear** Tomorrowland
   Woody Frontierland near Splash Mountain

EPCOT

MICKEY AND HIS POSSE

- **Chip 'n' Dale** Outside on the Land side of the Epcot Character Spot
- **Donald** Mexico, at the Mexico Promenade
- **Goofy, Minnie, Mickey** Epcot Character Spot (FastPass+)
- **Pluto** On the right as you enter Epcot through the main turnstiles

DISNEY ROYALTY

- **Aladdin, Jasmine** Morocco   • **Anna, Elsa,** *Frozen* **characters** Norway (in 2016)
- **Aurora, Belle** France   • **Mulan** China   • **Snow White** Germany

MISCELLANEOUS

- **Alice, Mary Poppins and Bert, Winnie the Pooh, Tigger, Eeyore** United Kingdom
- **Duffy the Disney Bear** World Showcase Plaza

*Characters are subject to change; check the *Times Guide* or **kennythepirate.com** for the latest information.

throughout the World.) Mickey, Minnie, and Goofy seem to be everywhere. But some characters, such as the Queen of Hearts and Friar Tuck, seldom come out, and quite a few appear only in parades or stage shows. Other characters appear only in a location consistent with their starring role. The Fairy Godmother is often near Cinderella Castle in Fantasyland, while Buzz Lightyear appears close to his eponymous attraction in Tomorrowland. (See the table on pages 246–247 for details.)

WDW CHARACTER-GREETING VENUES

DISNEY'S ANIMAL KINGDOM

MICKEY AND HIS POSSE

- **Chip 'n' Dale** Rafiki's Planet Watch at Conservation Station and The Oasis, just past the entrance turnstiles and to the right
- **Daisy** Discovery Island near the bridge to Africa
- **Donald** DinoLand U.S.A., to the left of the DINOSAUR exit on Cretaceous Trail
- **Goofy, Pluto** DinoLand U.S.A., near Primeval Whirl
- **Mickey, Minnie** Adventurers Outpost on Discovery Island (FastPass+)

DISNEY ROYALTY

- **Pocahontas** Discovery Island trails that run behind The Tree of Life

MISCELLANEOUS

THE JUNGLE BOOK **King Louie and Baloo** At Upcountry Landing on the walkway between Asia and Africa

THE LION KING **Rafiki** Rafiki's Planet Watch, at Conservation Station

UP **Dug, Russell** By *It's Tough to Be a Bug!*

DISNEY'S HOLLYWOOD STUDIOS

MICKEY AND HIS POSSE

- **Chip 'n' Dale, Daisy, Donald, Goofy, Pluto** In front of The Great Movie Ride
- **Minnie** In front of The Great Movie Ride and Center Stage Courtyard
- **Sorcerer Mickey** Streets of America near Studio Catering Co.

DISNEY CHANNEL STARS

- **Phineas and Ferb** At the exit of *Jim Henson's Muppet-Vision 3-D*
- **Sofia the First, Jake (*Jake and the Never Land Pirates*)** Animation Courtyard near *Disney Junior—Live on Stage!*

MISCELLANEOUS

MONSTERS, INC. **Mike, Sulley** Streets of America (Backlot)

TOY STORY **Buzz, Woody** Pixar Place

A Brooklyn dad complains that character collecting has gotten out of hand:

> This year, when we took our youngest child (who is now 8 years old), he had already seen his siblings' collection and was determined to outdo them. However, rather than random meetings, the characters are now available practically all day long at different locations, according to a printed schedule, which our son was old enough to read. We spent more time standing in line for autographs than we did for the most popular rides!

BOB Our advice for parents with preschoolers is to stay with the kids when they meet characters, stepping back only to take a quick picture.

A family from Birmingham, Alabama, found some benefit in their children's pursuit of characters:

> We had no idea we'd be caught up in this madness, but after my daughters grabbed your guidebook to get Pocahontas to sign it (we had no blank paper), we quickly bought a Disney autograph book and gave in.

It was actually the highlight of their trip, and my son even got into the act by helping get places in line for his sisters. They LOVED looking for characters. It was an amazing, totally unexpected part of our visit.

"THEN SOME CONFUSION HAPPENED" Children sometimes become lost at character encounters. Usually, there's a lot of activity around a character, with both adults and children touching it or posing for pictures. Most commonly, Mom and Dad stay in the crowd while Junior approaches the character. In the excitement and with the character moving around, Junior heads in the wrong direction to look for Mom and Dad. In the words of a Salt Lake City mom: "Milo was shaking hands with Dopey one minute, then some confusion happened and Milo was gone."

FROZEN FEVER

THERE IS NO DOUBT that the *Frozen* gals are here to stay. A sequel is in the works, and Princess Aurora moved out of Princess Fairytale Hall. Cindy learned to reckon with the power of a Northeaster, vacated the castle during the holiday season, and learned to "let it go."

We love the movie, and Liliane acquired a Queen Elsa costume for select events (though Merida will forever be her heroine). Here are our recommendations, for the first time in forever, on how to have the most *Frozen* fun while visiting Walt Disney World.

Magic Kingdom

As soon as possible, make FastPass+ reservations for a Princess Fairytale Hall meet and greet with Anna and Elsa. If you cannot get a FastPass+ reservation, try to get an early breakfast reservation at Be Our Guest. Enter the Magic Kingdom as soon as the gates open for breakfast guests, and once you're done eating, queue in the standby line to meet Anna and Elsa. If the park opens at 9 a.m. and you can score an 8 a.m. breakfast reservation, you should be in good shape. Alternatively, you can try breakfast at The Crystal Palace, but it would be a shame to hurry through a character breakfast just to see Anna and Elsa without a long wait.

The new Festival of Fantasy Parade is a must, and you can see Anna and Elsa on their float without standing in line.

Epcot

Maelstrom closed to make way for Frozen Ever After, set to open sometime in 2016. The new boat ride will take guests to Arendelle, the Norwegian-inspired home of Anna and Elsa. Royal Sommerhus, a meet and greet with Anna and Elsa, will also debut in 2016. Until the new attractions open, there is little hope of meeting the royals in Epcot. In the meantime, visit the stave church at the Norway Pavilion, and learn how the culture and beauty of Norway inspired the filmmakers of *Frozen*.

Disney's Hollywood Studios

For the First Time in Forever: A Frozen Sing-Along Celebration is a fun and interactive show where Anna, Elsa, Kristoff, and the royal historians of Arendelle tell the story of their kingdom. The show is staged at the Hyperion Theater, the former home of *The American Idol Experience.*

During the summer months only, Disney's Hollywood Studios hosts the Coolest Summer Ever. Twice daily, Anna, Elsa, and Kristoff take part in a festive mini-parade, accompanied by the Royal Arendelle Flag Corps and a flurry of skaters and skiers—along with the one and only Olaf. Several times each day, Olaf comes to the event stage, in front of The Great Movie Ride, to have a little fun with guests. There is a *Frozen* dance party, and as the sun goes down, Anna, Elsa, Kristoff, and Olaf come together at the event stage one more time for a grand finale to the day's festivities, kicking off a fireworks display set to the music of *Frozen* and, of course, "snow." Currently the Coolest Summer Ever activities are set to continue through September 7, 2015.

When All Els(a)e Fails

You will *not* find anything *Frozen* related at Disney's Animal Kingdom, as Colonel Hathi's Jungle Patrol joined forces with the future inhabitants of Pandora to put an end to the invasion. But there is always Disney Springs, where you can give your princess a total Anna or Elsa makeover at the Bibbidi Bobbidi Boutique. If this too fails, there is only one thing left to do: Let it go!

CHARACTER DINING: WHAT TO EXPECT

BECAUSE OF THE INCREDIBLE POPULARITY of character dining, reservations can be hard to come by if you wait until a couple of months

"Casting? There's been a mistake. We were supposed to get the Assorted Character Package with one Mickey, one Goofy, one Donald . . ."

before your vacation to book your choices. What's more, you must provide Disney with a credit card number. Your card will be charged $10 per person if you don't show or you cancel your reservation less than 24 hours in advance; you may, however, reschedule with no penalty. See "Getting Advance Reservations at Popular Restaurants" (page 141) for the full story.

At very popular character meals like the breakfast at Cinderella's Royal Table, you're required to make a for-real reservation and guarantee it with a for-real deposit.

LILIANE Even with Advance Reservations, expect to wait 10–20 minutes to be seated.

Character meals are bustling affairs held in hotels' or theme parks' largest full-service restaurants. Character breakfasts offer a fixed menu served individually, family-style, or on a buffet. The typical breakfast includes scrambled eggs; bacon, sausage, and ham; hash browns; waffles or French toast; biscuits, rolls, or pastries; and fruit. With family-style service, the meal is served in large skillets or platters at your table. The character breakfast at Akershus Royal Banquet Hall, for example, is served family-style and consists of typical breakfast fare such as eggs, bacon and sausage, and Danish pastries. Seconds (or thirds) are free. Buffets offer much the same fare, but you fetch it yourself.

Character dinners range from a set menu to buffets to ordering off the menu. Character-dinner buffets, such as those at 1900 Park Fare at the Grand Floridian and Chef Mickey's at the Contemporary Resort, separate the kids' fare from the grown-ups', though everyone is free to eat from both lines. Typically, the children's buffet includes hamburgers, hot dogs, pizza, fish sticks, chicken nuggets, macaroni and cheese, and peanut-butter-and-jelly sandwiches. Selections at the adult buffet usually include prime rib or other carved meat, baked or broiled Florida seafood, pasta, chicken, an ethnic dish or two, vegetables, potatoes, and salad.

At all meals, characters circulate around the room while you eat. During your meal, each of the three to five characters present will visit your table, arriving one at a time to cuddle the kids (and sometimes the adults), pose for photos, and sign autographs. Keep autograph books (with pens) handy and cameras or mobile phones at the ready. For the best photos, adults should sit across the table from their children. Seat the children where characters can easily reach them. If a table is against a wall, for example, adults should sit with their backs to the wall and children on the aisle.

Servers generally don't rush you to leave after you've eaten—you can stay as long as you wish to enjoy the characters. Remember, however, that lots of eager kids and adults are waiting not so patiently to be admitted.

When to Go

Attending a character breakfast usually prevents you from arriving at the theme parks in time for opening. Because early morning is best for touring and you don't want to burn daylight lingering over breakfast, we suggest the following:

1. Schedule your in-park character breakfast for the first seating if the park opens at 9 a.m. or later. You'll be admitted to the park before other guests (admission is still required) through a special line at the turnstiles. Arrive early to be among the first parties seated.

2. Go to a character dinner or lunch instead of breakfast. It'll be a nice break.

3. Schedule the last seating for breakfast. Have a light snack such as cereal or bagels before you head to the parks for opening, hit the most popular attractions until 10:15 or so, and then head to brunch. The buffet should keep you fueled until dinner, especially if you eat another light snack in the afternoon.

4. Go on your arrival or departure day. The day you arrive and check in is usually good for a character dinner. Settle at your hotel, swim, and then dine with the characters. This strategy has the added benefit of exposing your children to the characters before chance encounters at the parks. Some children, moreover, won't settle down to enjoy the parks until they have seen Mickey. Departure day also is good for a character meal. Schedule a character breakfast on your check-out day before you head for the airport or begin your drive home.

5. Go on a rest day. If you plan to stay five or more days, you'll probably take a day or half-day from touring to rest or do something else.

How to Choose a Character Meal

Many readers ask for advice about character meals. This question from a Waterloo, Iowa, mom is typical:

LILIANE If you've secured Advance Reservations for a character meal, I say roll out the costume chest. Dress up your little one—from princess to pirate, anything goes.

Are all character breakfasts pretty much the same, or are some better than others? How should I go about choosing one?

In fact, some are better, sometimes much better. When we evaluate character meals, we look for these things:

1. **THE CHARACTERS** The meals offer a diverse assortment of characters. Select a meal that features your kids' favorites. Check out our Character-Meal Hit Parade table (see pages 252–253) to see which characters are assigned to each meal. Most restaurants stick with the same characters. Even so, check the lineup when you call to make Advance Reservations.

2. **ATTENTION FROM THE CHARACTERS** At all character meals, characters circulate among guests, hugging children, posing for pictures, and signing autographs. How much time a character spends with you and your children depends primarily on the ratio of characters to guests. The more characters and fewer guests, the better. Because many character meals never fill to capacity, the character-to-guest ratios found in our Character-Meal Hit Parade table have been adjusted to reflect an average attendance. Even so, there's quite a range. The best ratio is at Cinderella's Royal Table, where there's approximately 1 character to every 26 guests.

   The worst ratio is theoretically at the Swan Resort's Garden Grove, where there could be as few as 1 character for every 198 guests. We say *theoretically*, however, because in practice there are far fewer guests at the Garden Grove than at character meals in Disney-owned resorts, and often more characters. During one recent meal, friends of ours were literally the only guests in the restaurant for breakfast and had to ask the characters to leave them alone to eat.

CHARACTER-MEAL HIT PARADE

1. CINDERELLA'S ROYAL TABLE   MAGIC KINGDOM

MEALS SERVED Breakfast, lunch, and dinner   SETTING ★★★★

CHARACTERS Cinderella, Ariel, Aurora, Jasmine, Snow White, Fairy Godmother (rare)

TYPE OF SERVICE Fixed menu   FOOD VARIETY & QUALITY ★★★

NOISE LEVEL Quiet   CHARACTER–GUEST RATIO 1:26

2. AKERSHUS ROYAL BANQUET HALL   EPCOT

MEALS SERVED Breakfast, lunch, and dinner   SETTING ★★★★

CHARACTERS 4–6 characters chosen from Ariel, Belle, Snow White, Aurora, Mary Poppins, and Cinderella

TYPE OF SERVICE Family-style and menu (all you care to eat)

FOOD VARIETY & QUALITY ★★★½

NOISE LEVEL Quiet   CHARACTER–GUEST RATIO 1:54

3. CHEF MICKEY'S   CONTEMPORARY

MEALS SERVED Breakfast, brunch, and dinner   SETTING ★★★

CHARACTERS Mickey, Minnie, Donald, Goofy, Pluto (sometimes Chip 'n' Dale)

TYPE OF SERVICE Buffet

FOOD VARIETY & QUALITY Breakfast and brunch ★★★   Dinner ★★★½

NOISE LEVEL Loud   CHARACTER–GUEST RATIO 1:56

4. THE CRYSTAL PALACE   MAGIC KINGDOM

MEALS SERVED Breakfast, lunch, and dinner   SETTING ★★★

CHARACTERS Pooh, Eeyore, Piglet, Tigger   TYPE OF SERVICE Buffet

FOOD VARIETY & QUALITY Breakfast ★★½   Lunch and dinner ★★★

NOISE LEVEL Very loud

CHARACTER–GUEST RATIO Breakfast 1:67 Lunch and dinner 1:89

5. 1900 PARK FARE   GRAND FLORIDIAN

MEALS SERVED Breakfast, dinner   SETTING ★★★

CHARACTERS *Breakfast:* Mary Poppins, Alice, Mad Hatter, Pooh, Tigger
Dinner: Cinderella, Prince Charming, Lady Tremaine, the two stepsisters

TYPE OF SERVICE Buffet   FOOD VARIETY & QUALITY Breakfast ★★★   Dinner ★★★½

NOISE LEVEL Moderate   CHARACTER–GUEST RATIO Breakfast 1:54 Dinner 1:44

6. GARDEN GRILL RESTAURANT   EPCOT

MEAL SERVED Dinner   SETTING ★★★★½

CHARACTERS Mickey, Pluto, Chip 'n' Dale

TYPE OF SERVICE Family-style   FOOD VARIETY & QUALITY ★★★½

NOISE LEVEL Very quiet   CHARACTER–GUEST RATIO 1:46

7. TUSKER HOUSE RESTAURANT   DISNEY'S ANIMAL KINGDOM

MEALS SERVED Breakfast, lunch, dinner   SETTING ★★★

CHARACTERS Donald, Daisy, Mickey, Goofy

TYPE OF SERVICE Buffet   FOOD VARIETY & QUALITY ★★★

NOISE LEVEL Very loud   CHARACTER–GUEST RATIO 1:112

8. CAPE MAY CAFE   BEACH CLUB

MEAL SERVED Breakfast SETTING ★★★ CHARACTERS Goofy, Donald, Minnie	
TYPE OF SERVICE Buffet FOOD VARIETY & QUALITY ★★½	
NOISE LEVEL Moderate CHARACTER–GUEST RATIO 1:67	

9. 'OHANA   POLYNESIAN VILLAGE

MEAL SERVED Breakfast   SETTING ★★
CHARACTERS Lilo and Stitch, Mickey, Pluto
TYPE OF SERVICE Family-style   FOOD VARIETY & QUALITY ★★½
NOISE LEVEL Moderate   CHARACTER–GUEST RATIO 1:57

10. HOLLYWOOD & VINE   DISNEY'S HOLLYWOOD STUDIOS

MEALS SERVED Breakfast, lunch   SETTING ★★½
CHARACTERS Handy Manny, Sofia the First, Doc McStuffins, Jake (*Jake and the Never Land Pirates*)
TYPE OF SERVICE Buffet   FOOD VARIETY & QUALITY ★★★
NOISE LEVEL Moderate   CHARACTER–GUEST RATIO 1:71

11. GARDEN GROVE   SWAN

MEALS SERVED Breakfast (Sat. and Sun.), dinner (Fri. and Sat.)   SETTING ★★★
CHARACTERS Chip 'n' Dale, Goofy, Pluto
TYPE OF SERVICE Buffet   FOOD VARIETY & QUALITY ★★★½
NOISE LEVEL Moderate   CHARACTER–GUEST RATIO 1:198, frequently much better

3. **THE SETTING** Some character meals are in exotic settings. For others, moving the event to an elementary-school cafeteria would be an improvement. Our table rates each meal's setting with the familiar scale of zero (worst) to five (best) stars. Two restaurants, Cinderella's Royal Table in the Magic Kingdom and The Garden Grill Restaurant in the Land Pavilion at Epcot, deserve special mention. Cinderella's Royal Table is on the first and second floors of Cinderella Castle in Fantasyland, offering guests a look inside the castle. The Garden Grill is a revolving restaurant overlooking several scenes from the Living with The Land boat ride. Also at Epcot, the popular Princesses Character Breakfast is held in the castlelike Akershus Royal Banquet Hall. Though Chef Mickey's at the Contemporary Resort is rather sterile in appearance, it affords a great view of the monorail running through the hotel. Themes and settings of the remaining character-meal venues, while apparent to adults, will be lost on most children.

4. **THE FOOD** Though some food served at character meals is quite good, most is average (palatable but nothing to get excited about). In variety, consistency, and quality, restaurants generally do a better job with breakfast than with lunch or dinner (if served). Some restaurants offer a buffet, while others opt for one-skillet family-style service, in which all hot items are served from the same pot or skillet. To help you sort it out, we rate the food at each character meal in our table using the five-star scale.

5. **THE PROGRAM** Some larger restaurants stage modest performances where the characters dance, head a parade around the room, or lead songs and cheers. For some guests, these activities give the meal a celebratory air; for others, they turn what was already mayhem into absolute chaos. Either way, the antics consume time the characters could spend with families at their table.

6. **NOISE** If you want to eat in peace, character meals are a bad choice. That said, some are much noisier than others. Our table gives you an idea of what to expect.

7. **WHICH MEAL** Though breakfasts seem to be most popular, character lunches and dinners are usually more practical because they don't interfere with early-morning touring. During hot weather, a character lunch can be heavenly.

8. **COST** Dinners cost more than lunches, and lunches cost more than breakfasts. Prices for meals vary considerably from the least expensive to the most expensive restaurant. Breakfasts run $25–$58 for adults and $15–$36 for kids ages 3–9. For character lunches, expect to pay $36–$60 for adults and $18–$36 for kids. Dinners are $36–$73 for adults and $17–$43 for children. Little ones age 2 years and younger eat free. The meals at the high end of the price range are at Cinderella's Royal Table in the Magic Kingdom and Akershus Royal Banquet Hall at Epcot.

9. **ADVANCE RESERVATIONS** Disney makes Advance Reservations for character meals 180 days before you wish to dine (Disney resort guests can reserve 190 days out, or 10 additional days in advance); moreover, Disney resort guests can make Advance Reservations for all meals during their stay. Advance Reservations for most character meals are easy to obtain even if you call only a couple of weeks before you leave home. Meals at Cinderella's Royal Table and Be Our Guest are another story. For these two, you'll need our strategy (see Part Four), as well as help from Congress and the Pope.

10. **"FRIENDS"** For some venues, Disney has stopped specifying characters scheduled for a particular meal. Instead, they say it's a given character "and friends"—for example, "Pooh and friends," meaning Eeyore, Piglet, and Tigger, or some combination thereof, or "Mickey and friends" with some assortment chosen among Minnie, Goofy, Pluto, Donald, Daisy, Chip, and Dale.

11. **THE BUM'S RUSH** Most character meals are leisurely affairs, and you can usually stay as long as you want. An exception is Cinderella's Royal Table in the Magic Kingdom. Because Cindy's is in such high demand, the restaurant does everything short of pre-chewing your food to move you through, as this European mother of a 5-year-old can attest:

We dined a lot, did three character meals and a few signature restaurants, and every meal was awesome except for lunch with Cinderella in the castle. While I'd often read it wouldn't be a rushed affair, it was exactly that. We had barely sat down when the appetizers were thrown on our table, the princesses each spent just a few seconds with our daughter—almost no interaction—and the side dishes were cold. We were out of there within 40 minutes and felt very stressed. Considering the price for the meal, I cannot recommend it.

12. **BOYS** To answer a common reader question, most character meals featuring Disney princesses include some element to appeal to the young roughnecks. A Texas mom shares her experience:

We ate at Cinderella's Royal Table for lunch, and my sons were made to feel very welcome. They loved the swords they received and have enjoyed "fighting off the dragons" with them.

(Presumably, "fighting off the dragons" didn't occur during the meal. Princesses *are* sticklers for decorum, after all.)

Getting an Advance Reservation at Cinderella's Royal Table

Once upon a time, breakfast was the only character meal at Cinderella Castle in the Magic Kingdom. Reservations for every table were gone within minutes of becoming available each morning. Disney responded to this popularity by adding character lunches and dinners—and jacking up the price to almost $60 per adult. As a result, it's now much easier to get into Cinderella's Royal Table for some meals during your stay. Also, the opening of the wildly popular Be Our Guest restaurant in Fantasyland has taken a lot of pressure off Cindy's. If you're visiting during peak periods or you have to have a reservation at a specific, popular time, see our Advance Reservation tips starting on page 141.

DISNEY'S ROYAL ALTERNATIVES If you're unwilling to fund Cinderella's shoe habit or you simply weren't able to get an Advance Reservation before young Ariel graduates from college, rest assured there are other venues that will feed you in the company of princesses.

Akershus Royal Banquet Hall, in the Norway Pavilion of Epcot's World Showcase, serves family-style breakfast, lunch, and dinner. Ariel, Cinderella, Snow White, and Belle are regulars. Entrées are a combination of traditional buffet fare and the occasional Scandinavian dish.

LILIANE The character meals at Akershus are my all-time favorite. There are plenty of princesses, and I love the food

Dinner at the Grand Floridian's **1900 Park Fare** features the whole crew from Cinderella, including Lady Tremaine and the stepsisters (breakfast is a supercalifragilisticexpialidocious affair with Mary Poppins and friends, which currently includes Alice in Wonderland, the Mad Hatter, Winnie the Pooh, and Tigger). At $45 per adult and $22 for children age 9 and under, this is a far more economical option for diners wishing to get their princess on, and the stepsisters are an absolute hoot. This meal is also a little more boy-friendly if you're entertaining a mixed crowd. Finally, remember that your princess may be feeding off your own excitement over eating in the Castle—she might be just as happy with a plastic crown purchased in the gift shop and a burger from Cosmic Ray's. We recommend visiting 1900 Park Fare on a day when you're not visiting the parks.

OTHER CHARACTER EVENTS

A CAMPFIRE AND SING-ALONG are held nightly (times vary with the season) near the Meadow Trading Post and Bike Barn at **Fort Wilderness Resort & Campground.** Chip 'n' Dale lead the songs, and a Disney film is shown. The program is free and open to Disney resort guests (☎ 407-824-2900). Another character encounter at Fort Wilderness is *Mickey's Backyard BBQ,* held seasonally on Thursday and Saturday. See page 177 for details.

▐ STROLLERS

STROLLERS ARE AVAILABLE for rent at all four theme parks and Disney Springs (single stroller, $15 per day with no deposit, $13 per day for the entire stay; double stroller, $31 per day with no deposit, $27 per

day for the entire stay; stroller rentals at Disney Springs require a $100 credit card deposit; double strollers not available at Disney Springs). Strollers are welcome at Blizzard Beach and Typhoon Lagoon, but no rentals are available. With multiday rentals, you can skip the rental line entirely after your first visit—just head over to the stroller-handout area, show your receipt, and you'll be wheeling out of there in no time. If you rent a stroller at the Magic Kingdom and you decide to go to Epcot, Disney's Animal Kingdom, or Disney's Hollywood Studios, turn in your Magic Kingdom stroller and present your receipt at the next park. You'll be issued another stroller at no additional charge.

With Disney pricing its own stroller rentals so high, several Orlando companies have sprung up, able to undercut Disney's prices, provide more comfortable strollers, and deliver them to your hotel. Most of the larger companies offer the same stroller models (the Baby Jogger City Mini Single, for example), so the primary differences between the companies are price and service.

LILIANE Rental strollers are too large for all infants and many toddlers. If you plan to rent a stroller for your infant or toddler, bring pillows, cushions, or rolled towels to buttress him in.

Regarding service, Disney currently allows just a handful of stroller companies to drop off and pick up at a Disney hotel without your having to be physically present to meet the delivery person, thus freeing you to run around the parks instead of waiting around at your hotel. The two companies reviewed below are part of the **Disney Preferred Stroller Provider** program, a fact they mention prominently on their websites. Before renting from another company, check to see if it's on the featured list too.

We had mom and **touringplans.com** blogger Angela Dahlgren rent strollers from different companies, use them in the parks, and then return them. Her evaluations cover the overall experience, from the ease with which the stroller was rented to the delivery of the stroller, its condition on arrival, usability in the parks, and the return process.

Kingdom Strollers (☎ 407-271-5301; **kingdomstrollers.com**) topped Angela's list, getting top marks for website ease of use, stroller selection, condition, and overall service. The stroller was also much easier to use than Disney's standard stroller, had more storage, and had an easier-to-use braking system. A rental of one to three nights costs $40, and four to seven nights is $60. That makes the break-even point for choosing Kingdom Strollers over Disney somewhere around five days.

Angela also recommends **Orlando Stroller Rentals, LLC** (☎ 800-281-0884; **orlandostrollerrentals.com**), which has the same prices, plus an excellent website that allows you to easily compare the features of different strollers.

Another important matter is protection against the sun. Liliane always used a stroller with an adjustable canopy and also had lightweight pieces of cloth handy to protect her child from the sun. You can use anything for that purpose; a receiving blanket works well. Liliane used clothespins and safety pins to attach the pieces to the canopy. Don't overdo it, though. While it's important to protect your child from the sun, make sure there is enough air circulating—temperatures climb quickly in enclosed spaces.

Strollers are a must for infants and toddlers, but we've observed many sharp parents renting strollers for somewhat older children (up to age 5 or so). The stroller keeps parents from having to carry kids when they sag and provides a convenient place to carry water and snacks.

A family from Tulsa, Oklahoma, recommends springing for a double stroller:

> We rent a double for baggage room or in case the older child gets tired of walking.

If you go to your hotel for a break and intend to return to the park, leave your rental stroller by an attraction near the park entrance, marking it with something personal, such as a bandanna. When you return, your stroller will be waiting.

A Charleston, West Virginia, mom recommends a backup plan:

> Strollers are not allowed in lines for rides, so if you have a small child (ours was 4) who needs to be held, you might end up holding him a long time. If I had it to do over, I'd bring along some kind of child carrier for when he was out of the stroller.

Bringing your own stroller is permitted. However, only collapsible strollers are allowed on monorails, parking lot trams, and buses. Your stroller is unlikely to be stolen, but mark it with your name.

Having her own stroller was indispensable to a Mechanicsville, Virginia, mother of two toddlers:

BOB Don't try to lock your stroller to a fence, post, or anything else at WDW. You'll get in big trouble.

> How I was going to manage to get the kids from the parking lot to the park was a big worry for me before I made the trip. I didn't read anywhere that it was possible to walk to the entrance of the parks instead of taking the tram, so I wasn't sure I could do it.
>
> I found that for me personally, since I have two kids aged 1 and 2, it was easier to walk to the entrance of the park from the parking lot with the kids in my own stroller than to take the kids out of the stroller, fold the stroller (while trying to control the two kids and associated gear), load the stroller and the kids onto the tram, etc. No matter where I was parked, I could always just walk to the entrance. It sometimes took awhile, but it was easier for me.

An Oklahoma mom, however, reports a bad experience with bringing her own stroller:

> *The first time we took our kids, we had a large stroller (big mistake). It is so much easier to rent one in the park. The large (personally owned) strollers are nearly impossible to get on the buses and are a hassle at the airport. I remember feeling dread when a bus pulled up that was even semifull of people. People look at you like you have a cage full of live chickens when you drag a heavy stroller onto the bus.*

STROLLER WARS Sometimes strollers disappear while you're enjoying a ride or show. Disney staff will often rearrange strollers parked outside an attraction. This may be done to tidy up or to clear a walkway. Don't assume that your stroller is stolen because it isn't where you left it. It may be neatly arranged a few feet away—or perhaps more than a few feet away.

Sometimes, however, strollers are taken by mistake or ripped off by people not wanting to spend time replacing one that's missing. Don't be alarmed if yours disappears. You won't have to buy it, and you'll be issued a new one.

You'd be surprised at how many people are injured by strollers pushed by parents who are aggressive or in a hurry. Given the number of strollers, pedestrians, and tight spaces, mishaps are inevitable on both sides. A simple apology and a smile are usually the best remediation.

A mom from New Hampshire reports:

> *If you're at park opening going toward a headliner attraction with a stroller, think of the stroller as a tractor-trailer during rush hour traffic—everyone cuts in front of you, and they get mad if you run into them. ABANDON the stroller and proceed on foot!*

WHEN KIDS GET LOST

IF ONE OF YOUR CHILDREN gets separated from you, don't panic. All things considered, Walt Disney World is about the safest place to get lost we can think of. Disney cast members are trained to watch for seemingly lost kids, and because children become detached from parents so frequently in the theme parks, cast members know exactly what to do.

If you lose a child in the Magic Kingdom, report it to a Disney employee, and then check at the Baby Care Center and at City Hall, where lost-children logs are kept. At Epcot, report the loss, then check at the Baby Care Center in the Odyssey Center. At Disney's Hollywood Studios, report the loss at the Guest Services Building, at the entrance end of Hollywood Boulevard. At Disney's Animal Kingdom, go to the Baby Care Center in Discovery Island. Paging isn't used, but in an emergency, an all-points bulletin can be issued throughout the park(s) via internal communications. If a Disney employee encounters a lost child, he or she will take the child immediately to the park's Baby Care Center.

As comforting as this knowledge is, however, it's nevertheless scary when a child turns up missing. Fortunately, circumstances surrounding a child becoming lost are fairly predictable and, for the most part, are also preventable.

Sew a label into each child's shirt that states his or her name, your name, the name of your hotel, and, if you have one, your cell phone number. Accomplish the same thing by writing the information on a strip of masking tape or by attaching a MagicBand to the child's clothing (resist the urge to put it on like a dog collar).

BOB We suggest that children younger than age 8 be color-coded by dressing them in vacation uniforms with distinctively colored T-shirts or equally eye-catching apparel.

Other than just blending in, children tend to become separated from their parents under remarkably similar circumstances:

1. PREOCCUPIED SOLO PARENT In this situation, the party's only adult is preoccupied with something like buying refreshments, loading the camera, or using the restroom. Junior is there one second and gone the next.

2. THE HIDDEN EXIT Sometimes parents wait on the sidelines while two or more young children experience a ride together. Parents expect the kids to exit in one place and, lo and behold, the youngsters pop out somewhere else. Exits from some attractions are distant from the entrances. Make sure you know exactly where your children will emerge before letting them ride by themselves. If in doubt, ask a cast member.

3. AFTER THE SHOW At the end of many shows and rides, a Disney staffer will announce, "Check for personal belongings and take small children by the hand." When dozens, if not hundreds, of people leave an attraction simultaneously, it's surprisingly easy for parents to lose contact with their children unless they have them directly in tow.

4. RESTROOM PROBLEMS Mom tells 6-year-old Tommy, "I'll be sitting on this bench when you come out of the restroom." Three possibilities: One, Tommy exits through a different door and becomes disoriented (Mom may not know there's another door). Two, Mom decides she also will use the restroom, and Tommy emerges to find her gone. Three, Mom pokes around in a shop while keeping an eye on the bench but misses Tommy when he comes out.

If you can't find a companion- or family-accessible restroom, make sure there's only one exit. The restroom on a passageway between Frontierland and Adventureland in the Magic Kingdom is the all-time worst for disorienting visitors. Children and adults alike have walked in from the Adventureland side and walked out on the Frontierland side (and vice versa). Adults realize quickly that something is wrong. Children, however, sometimes fail to recognize the problem. Designate a distinctive meeting spot and give clear instructions: "I'll meet you by this flagpole. If you get out first, stay right here." Have your child repeat the directions back to you.

5. PARADES There are many parades and shows at which the audience stands. Children tend to jockey for a better view. By moving a little this way and that, the child quickly puts distance between you before either of you notices.

6. MASS MOVEMENTS Be on guard when huge crowds disperse after fireworks or a parade, or at park closing. With 20,000–40,000 people at once in an area, it's very easy to get separated from a child or others in your party. Use extra caution after the evening parade and fireworks in the Magic Kingdom, *Fantasmic!* at Disney's Hollywood Studios, or *IllumiNations* at Epcot. Families should have specific plans for where to meet if they get separated.

7. CHARACTER GREETINGS Activity and confusion are common when the Disney characters appear, and children can slip out of sight. See "Then Some Confusion Happened" on page 248.

8. GETTING LOST AT DISNEY'S ANIMAL KINGDOM It's especially easy to lose a child in Animal Kingdom, particularly at the Oasis entryway, on the Maharajah Jungle Trek, and on the Pangani Forest Exploration Trail. Mom and Dad will stop to observe an animal. Junior stays close for a minute or so and then, losing patience, wanders to the exhibit's other side or to a different exhibit.

9. LOST . . . IN THE ZONE More often than you'd think, kids don't realize they're lost. They are so distracted that they sometimes wander around for quite a while before they notice that their whole family has mysteriously disappeared. Fortunately, Disney cast members are trained to look out for kids who have zoned out and will either help them find their family or deposit them at the Baby Care Center.

LILIANE'S TIPS FOR KEEPING TRACK OF YOUR BROOD

ON A GOOD DAY, it's possible for Liliane to lose a cantaloupe in her purse. Thus challenged, she works overtime developing ways to hang on to her possessions, including her child. Here's what she has to say:

I've seen parents write their cell phone numbers on a child's leg with a felt-tip marker . . . effective but crude. Before you resort to that, or perhaps a cattle brand, consider some of the tips I've busted my brain dreaming up. My friends—some much ditzier than I—have used them with great success.

- On your very first day in the parks, teach your kids how to recognize a Disney cast member by pointing out the Disney name tags that they all wear. Instruct your children to find someone with such a name tag if they get separated from you.

- Same-colored T-shirts for the whole family will help you gather your troops in an easy and fun way. You can opt for just a uniform color or go the extra mile and have the T-shirts printed with a logo such as "The Brown Family's Assault on the Mouse." You might also include the date or the year of your visit. Your imagination is the limit. Light-colored T-shirts can even be autographed by the Disney characters.

- Clothing labels are great, of course. If you don't sew, buy labels that you can iron on the garment. If you own a cell phone, be sure to include the number on the label. If you do not own a cell phone, put in the phone number of the hotel where you'll be staying. Another option is a custom-made temporary tattoo with all the pertinent info. They're cheap, last two weeks, don't wash off, and solve the problem of having to sew or iron a label on every garment. (They can be purchased online at **safetytat.com** or **tattooswithapurpose.com.**)

- In pet stores you can have name tags printed for a very reasonable price. These are great to add to necklaces and bracelets or attach to your child's shoelace or belt loop.

- When you check into the hotel, take a business card of the hotel for each member in your party, especially those old enough to carry wallets and purses.

- Always agree on a meeting point before you see a parade, fireworks, or nighttime spectacles such as *IllumiNations* and *Fantasmic!* Make sure the meeting place is in the park (as opposed to the car or someplace outside the front gate).

- If you have a digital camera or phone camera, take a picture of your kids every morning. If they get lost, the picture will show what they look like and what they're wearing.

- If all the members of your party have cell phones, it's easy to locate each other. Be aware, however, that the ambient noise in the parks is so loud that you probably won't hear your phone ring. Your best bet is to carry your phone in a front pants pocket and to program the phone to vibrate. If any of your younger kids carry cell phones, secure the phones with a strap. Even better, send text messages.

- Save key tags and luggage tags for use on items you bring to the parks, including your stroller, diaper bag, and backpack or hip pack.

- Don't underestimate the power of the permanent marker, such as a Sharpie. They are great for labeling pretty much anything. Mini-Sharpies are sold as clip-ons and are great for collecting character autographs. The Sharpie will also serve well for writing down the location of your car in the parking lot.

- Finally, a word about keeping track of your MagicBand admission wristbands: They're difficult, but not impossible, to lose. Most adults will be fine, but slender children without much articulation between the forearm and wrist need to wear the band more tightly. If you're worried about the band slipping off, ask for an RFID card instead (see page 69). Alternatively, have your child wear the MagicBand on a chain, much like a necklace. For very young children, I strongly recommend that an adult holds on to the MagicBand—no need to put yourself through all that stress.

PART SEVEN

The MAGIC KINGDOM

OPENED IN 1971, the Magic Kingdom was the first of Walt Disney World's four theme parks to be built. Many of the attractions found here are originals from that park opening, and a few—including **Cinderella Castle, Pirates of the Caribbean,** and **Splash Mountain**—have helped define the basic elements of theme park attractions the world over. Indeed, the Magic Kingdom is undoubtedly what most people think of when they think of Walt Disney World.

Stroller, wheelchair, and **ECV/ESV rentals** are to the right of the train station, and lockers are on the station's ground floor. On your left as you enter Main Street is **City Hall,** the center for information, lost and found, guided tours, and entertainment schedules. **ATMs** are underneath the Main Street railroad station, near the Transportation and Ticket Center (TTC), near City Hall, near the Frontierland shooting gallery, near Pinocchio Village Haus in Fantasyland, and inside the Tomorrowland Arcade. Down Main Street and left around the Central Plaza (toward Adventureland) are the **Baby Care Center** and **First Aid.** Across from Disney's Port Orleans Resort, **Best Friends Pet Resort** provides a comfortable home away from home for Fido, Fluffy, and all their pet pals.

If you don't already have a **handout park map,** get one at City Hall. The handout lists all attractions, shops, and eateries; provides helpful information about first aid, baby care, and assistance for the disabled; and gives tips for good photos. It also lists times for the day's special events, live entertainment, Disney character parades, concerts, and other activities. Additionally, it tells when and where to find Disney characters.

The guide map is supplemented by a daily entertainment schedule known as the *Times Guide,* which provides info on special Disney character appearances, shows and performances, parades, and street entertainment. It also identifies attractions that operate on a schedule different from normal park hours—for example, if you're staying at a Walt Disney World resort and the park is observing evening Extra

Magic Hours, the *Times Guide* will tell you which attractions are open late. All members of your party need to scan their MagicBands to participate in Extra Magic Hours.

Main Street, U.S.A., ends at the **Central Plaza,** from which branch the entrances to the other five sections of the Magic Kingdom: **Adventureland, Frontierland, Liberty Square, Fantasyland,** and **Tomorrowland.**

In this and the following three chapters, we rate the individual attractions at each of the four major Disney theme parks. **Appeal by Age ratings** are expressed on a scale of zero to five stars—the more stars, the better the attraction. The **authors' rating,** which uses the same scale, is from the perspective of an adult. The authors, for example, might rate a ride such as Dumbo much lower than the age group for which the ride is intended, in this case, children. The **bottleneck rating** ranges 1–10; the higher the rating, the more congested the attraction. In general, try to experience attractions with a high bottleneck rating early in the morning (that is, 8–10:30 a.m.) before the park gets crowded, or late in the day when the crowd has diminished.

With the opening of **Seven Dwarfs Mine Train** in 2014, the Magic Kingdom completed the expansion of Fantasyland begun in 2010. The first phase of New Fantasyland opened in 2012, with attractions and restaurants that quickly joined the Magic Kingdom's must-do list. Parents with small children now race each morning to **Princess Fairytale Hall**—a character greeting experience—for the chance to meet *Frozen's* Anna and Elsa the way teens head for Space Mountain. And Seven Dwarfs Mine Train is drawing Disney roller coaster fans to Fantasyland—be prepared for long lines, or make it your priority as soon as the park opens.

FASTPASS+ AT THE MAGIC KINGDOM

WHILE THE MAGIC KINGDOM offers FastPass+ for more than two dozen attractions (see table on page 266), our touring plan software identifies only five as frequently needing FastPass+: **Peter Pan's Flight,** *Enchanted Tales with Belle,* **Big Thunder Mountain Railroad, Splash Mountain,** and **Space Mountain.** Note that we haven't included the popular **Anna and Elsa Meet and Greet** at Princess Fairytale Hall among our FastPass+ musts. Lines do get incredibly long—approaching 4 hours in some cases!—but hourly capacity is only around 45–50 families, or roughly 500–600 people per day. You definitely need FastPass+, but your chances of scoring reservations are very low.

On the other hand, six Magic Kingdom attractions *never* seem to need FastPass+, either because our touring plans get you to them before long lines develop or because the attractions rarely see long waits: **The Barnstormer, It's a Small World, Mad Tea Party, The Magic Carpets of Aladdin,** *Mickey's PhilharMagic,* and *Monsters, Inc. Laugh Floor.*

FastPass+ kiosk locations in the Magic Kingdom are as follows:

- In the walkway between Adventureland and Liberty Square, near the Diamond Horseshoe Saloon and Swiss Family Treehouse

Continued on page 266

The Magic Kingdom

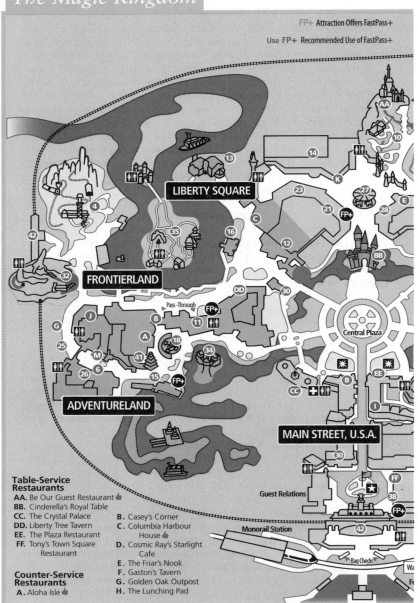

FP+ Attraction Offers FastPass+

Use FP+ Recommended Use of FastPass+

LIBERTY SQUARE

FRONTIERLAND

Pass-Through

Central Plaza

ADVENTURELAND

MAIN STREET, U.S.A.

Guest Relations

Monorail Station

Bag Checks

Table-Service Restaurants
AA. Be Our Guest Restaurant 🖐
BB. Cinderella's Royal Table
CC. The Crystal Palace
DD. Liberty Tree Tavern
EE. The Plaza Restaurant
FF. Tony's Town Square Restaurant

Counter-Service Restaurants
A. Aloha Isle 🖐

B. Casey's Corner
C. Columbia Harbour House 🖐
D. Cosmic Ray's Starlight Cafe
E. The Friar's Nook
F. Gaston's Tavern
G. Golden Oak Outpost
H. The Lunching Pad

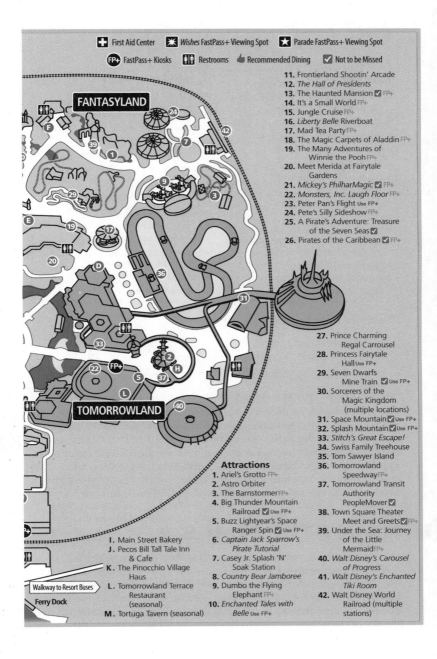

First Aid Center ✚   ✳ *Wishes* FastPass+ Viewing Spot   ★ Parade FastPass+ Viewing Spot

FP+ FastPass+ Kiosks   🚻 Restrooms   🍴 Recommended Dining   ✅ Not to be Missed

FANTASYLAND

TOMORROWLAND

Walkway to Resort Buses

Ferry Dock

11. Frontierland Shootin' Arcade
12. *The Hall of Presidents*
13. The Haunted Mansion ✅ FP+
14. It's a Small World FP+
15. Jungle Cruise FP+
16. *Liberty Belle* Riverboat
17. Mad Tea Party FP+
18. The Magic Carpets of Aladdin FP+
19. The Many Adventures of Winnie the Pooh FP+
20. Meet Merida at Fairytale Gardens
21. *Mickey's PhilharMagic* ✅ FP+
22. *Monsters, Inc. Laugh Floor* FP+
23. Peter Pan's Flight Use FP+
24. Pete's Silly Sideshow FP+
25. A Pirate's Adventure: Treasure of the Seven Seas ✅
26. Pirates of the Caribbean ✅ FP+

27. Prince Charming Regal Carrousel
28. Princess Fairytale Hall Use FP+
29. Seven Dwarfs Mine Train ✅ Use FP+
30. Sorcerers of the Magic Kingdom (multiple locations)
31. Space Mountain ✅ Use FP+
32. Splash Mountain ✅ Use FP+
33. *Stitch's Great Escape!*
34. Swiss Family Treehouse
35. Tom Sawyer Island
36. Tomorrowland Speedway FP+
37. Tomorrowland Transit Authority PeopleMover ✅
38. Town Square Theater Meet and Greets ✅ FP+
39. Under the Sea: Journey of the Little Mermaid FP+
40. *Walt Disney's Carousel of Progress*
41. *Walt Disney's Enchanted Tiki Room*
42. Walt Disney World Railroad (multiple stations)

Attractions

1. Ariel's Grotto FP+
2. Astro Orbiter
3. The Barnstormer FP+
4. Big Thunder Mountain Railroad ✅ Use FP+
5. Buzz Lightyear's Space Ranger Spin ✅ Use FP+
6. *Captain Jack Sparrow's Pirate Tutorial*
7. *Casey Jr. Splash 'N' Soak Station*
8. *Country Bear Jamboree*
9. Dumbo the Flying Elephant FP+
10. *Enchanted Tales with Belle* Use FP+

I. Main Street Bakery
J. Pecos Bill Tall Tale Inn & Cafe
K. The Pinocchio Village Haus
L. Tomorrowland Terrace Restaurant (seasonal)
M. Tortuga Tavern (seasonal)

MAGIC KINGDOM FASTPASS+ ATTRACTIONS

ADVENTURELAND
- Jungle Cruise
- The Magic Carpets of Aladdin
- Pirates of the Caribbean

FANTASYLAND
- Ariel's Grotto
- The Barnstormer
- Dumbo the Flying Elephant
- *Enchanted Tales with Belle*
- It's a Small World
- Mad Tea Party
- The Many Adventures of Winnie the Pooh
- *Mickey's PhilharMagic*
- Peter Pan's Flight
- Princess Fairytale Hall (Separate FastPass needed to meet Anna and Elsa or Cinderella and Rapunzel)
- Seven Dwarfs Mine Train
- Under the Sea: Journey of the Little Mermaid

FRONTIERLAND
- Big Thunder Mountain Railroad
- Splash Mountain

LIBERTY SQUARE
- The Haunted Mansion

MAIN STREET, U.S.A.
- Town Square Theater Meet and Greets (Separate FastPass needed to meet Mickey or Tinker Bell)

TOMORROWLAND
- Buzz Lightyear's Space Ranger Spin
- *Monsters, Inc. Laugh Floor*
- Space Mountain
- Tomorrowland Speedway

ENTERTAINMENT & PARADES
- *Celebrate the Magic*
- Festival of Fantasy Parade
- *Holiday Wishes: Celebrate the Spirit of the Season* (seasonal)
- Main Street Electrical Parade
- *Wishes* Fireworks

Continued from page 263

- At the entrance to Jungle Cruise in Adventureland
- Outside *Mickey's PhilharMagic* in Fantasyland
- Near *Stitch's Great Escape!* in Tomorrowland

Same-Day FastPass+ Availability

The preceding advice tells you which attractions to focus on when making your *advance* FastPass+ reservations before you get to the park. Once you're in the park, you can make more FastPass+ reservations once your advance reservations have been used or have expired (you must cancel your expired FastPass+ before you can book another). The table at right shows which attractions are likely to have day-of FastPasses available, and the approximate times at which they'll run out.

MAIN STREET, U.S.A.

BEGIN AND END YOUR VISIT ON MAIN STREET, which may open 30 minutes before and closes 30 minutes–1 hour after the rest of the park. It's easy to get sidetracked when entering Main Street, U.S.A.: This Disneyfied turn-of-the-19th-century small-town street is lovely, with exceptional attention to detail. But remember, time is of the essence, and the rest of the park is waiting to be discovered. The same goes for the one and only **Cinderella Castle.** Stick with your touring plan and return to the castle and Main Street after you've experienced the must-dos on your list.

MAGIC KINGDOM
When Same-Day FP+ Runs Out, by Crowd Level

ATTRACTION	LOW CROWDS*	MODERATE CROWDS*	HIGH CROWDS*
Ariel's Grotto	5 p.m.	6–9 p.m.	9–10 p.m.
The Barnstormer	6–7 p.m.	8–9 p.m.	10–11 p.m.
Big Thunder Mountain	4–6 p.m.	5 p.m.	2–3 p.m.
Buzz Lightyear's Space Ranger Spin	5–6 p.m.	7–8 p.m.	6–8 p.m.
Dumbo the Flying Elephant	6–7 p.m.	8–9 p.m.	10–11 p.m.
Enchanted Tales with Belle	5–6 p.m.	6–7 p.m.	7–9 p.m.
Festival of Fantasy Parade	3 p.m.	Unlikely day-of availability	Unlikely day-of availability
The Haunted Mansion	6 p.m.	7–8 p.m.	5–8 p.m.
It's a Small World	6–7 p.m.	8–9 p.m.	9–10 p.m.
Jungle Cruise	5–6 p.m.	7–9 p.m.	8–10 p.m.
Mad Tea Party	6–7 p.m.	8–9 p.m.	10–11 p.m.
The Magic Carpets of Aladdin	6–7 p.m.	8–9 p.m.	11 p.m.
Main Street Electrical Parade	noon–3 p.m.	Until first performance	Unlikely day-of availability
The Many Adventures of Winnie the Pooh	6–7 p.m.	8–9 p.m.	10–11 p.m.
Mickey's PhilharMagic	6–7 p.m.	7 p.m.	8–9 p.m.
Monsters, Inc. Laugh Floor	5–6 p.m.	8–9 p.m.	9–10 p.m.
Peter Pan's Flight	2–3 p.m.	3–4 p.m.	1–3 p.m.
Pirates of the Caribbean	5–6 p.m.	7–8 p.m.	3–5 p.m.
Princess Fairytale Hall: Anna and Elsa	5 p.m.	Unlikely day-of availability	Unlikely day-of availability
Princess Fairytale Hall: Cinderella and Rapunzel	5 p.m.	Unlikely day-of availability	Unlikely day-of availability
Seven Dwarfs Mine Train	1 p.m.	Unlikely day-of availability	Unlikely day-of availability
Splash Mountain	2–4 p.m.	3–6 p.m.	2–4 p.m.
Tomorrowland Speedway	5–6 p.m.	6–9 p.m.	7–9 p.m.
Town Square Mickey Mouse Meet and Greet	5–6 p.m.	5–9 p.m.	9–11 p.m.
Town Square Tinker Bell Meet and Greet	6 p.m.	8–10 p.m.	9–11 p.m.
Under the Sea: Journey of the Little Mermaid	5–6 p.m.	7–9 p.m.	8–9 p.m.
Wishes	3 p.m.	Until first performance	Unlikely day-of availability

* **LOW CROWDS** (Levels 1–3 on touringplans.com Crowd Calendar)

* **MODERATE CROWDS** (Levels 4–7 on touringplans.com Crowd Calendar)

* **HIGH CROWDS** (Levels 8–10 on touringplans.com Crowd Calendar)

When I walk into the Magic Kingdom
I immediately feel happy.

Ricky

DISNEY DISH WITH JIM HILL

WALKING THE BACK STREETS IN STYLE To keep guests who use the new overflow walkways behind Main Street, U.S.A., from having to see unthemed infrastructure, even for a minute, Disney recently added turn-of-the-20th-century theming to the back sides of all the buildings along the paths.

Sorcerers of the Magic Kingdom ★★★

**APPEAL BY AGE PRESCHOOL ★★★★   GRADE SCHOOL ★★★★½ TEENS ★★★★½
YOUNG ADULTS ★★★★   OVER 30 ★★★★   SENIORS ★★★½**

What it is Interactive game in which players must defeat villains spread around different lands. **Scope and scale** Minor attraction. **Fright potential** Loud but not frightening. **Bottleneck rating** 7. **When to go** Before 11 a.m. or after 8 p.m. **Special comments** Long lines to play. **Authors' rating** Great idea; ★★★. **Duration of experience** About 2 minutes per step, 4 or 5 steps per game. **Probable waiting time per step** 10–15 minutes.

Sorcerers of the Magic Kingdom combines aspects of role-playing games such as Dungeons and Dragons with Disney characters and theme park attractions. The wizard Merlin sends you on adventures in different parts of the Magic Kingdom to fight evildoers intent on taking over the park. Each land hosts a different adventure, with different villains in each.

This free game is played with a set of trading cards, with a different Disney character on each card. Each character possesses special properties that help it fight certain villains. Pick up the cards, plus a map showing where in the park you can play the game, at either the Fire Station on Main Street, U.S.A., or across from Sleepy Hollow Refreshments in Liberty Square.

You'll need your MagicBand to pick up your first set of cards and start the game. One card, known as your key, is special because it links you to your game. You'll need to present your key card when you pick up a set of cards to start your next adventure.

When you pick up your first set of cards, you'll view an instructional video; then you'll be sent to another location in another land to start your first adventure. Each location in the park is associated with a unique symbol such as an eye or a feather. Look for these symbols on the map to find the best route to your starting point.

Each adventure consists of four or five stops in a particular land. At each stop, another story will play on a computer screen, outlining what your villain is trying to do. Merlin will ask you to cast a spell, using your character cards, to stop the villain. Hold one or more of your cards up to the video display to cast your spell. Cameras in the display read your card, deploy the spell, and show you the results.

The game has three levels: easy, medium, and hard. In the easy version, appropriate for small children, holding up any one of your character cards is enough to defeat any villain. In more-advanced levels of the game, you need to display two or more character cards in specific combinations to defeat a particular villain; here, different card combinations produce different spells, and only some spells work on certain characters.

The audio at each step holds clues to which cards you should use against advanced villains. For example, if a villain says something like, "Don't toy with me!" then you should look for cards with characters that are toys, such as the *Toy Story* characters.

The game launched with an initial series of around 70 unique cards; you can obtain 5 new ones per day. Don't worry if you play more than once and end up with duplicate cards—a small trading market exists within the park.

Sorcerers is fun but is really more for return visitors as it takes up a good chunk of your touring time. You'll probably encounter a line of 5–10 people ahead of you at each portal, especially if you play during the afternoon. One complete adventure should take about 30–60 minutes to play, depending on how crowded the park is.

Town Square Theater Meet and Greets: Mickey Mouse, Tinker Bell and Friends (FastPass+) ★★★★

APPEAL BY AGE	PRESCHOOL ★★★★★	GRADE SCHOOL ★★★★★	TEENS ★★★★½
YOUNG ADULTS ★★★★	OVER 30 ★★★★½		SENIORS ★★★★½

What it is Character greeting venue. **Scope and scale** Minor attraction. **Fright potential** Not frightening in any respect. **Bottleneck rating** 7. **When to go** Before 10 a.m. or after 4 p.m., or use FastPass+. **Special comments** Mickey and the fairies have 2 separate queues, requiring 2 separate waits in line. **Authors' rating** It all started with this mouse; ★★★★. **Duration of experience** 2 minutes per character. **Probable waiting time** 15–25 minutes. **Queue speed** Slow.

Meet Mickey, along with Tinker Bell and her Pixie Hollow friends, throughout the day at the Town Square Theater on Main Street, to your right as you enter the park. Lines usually drop off after the afternoon parade.

Walt Disney World Railroad ★★★

APPEAL BY AGE	PRESCHOOL ★★★★	GRADE SCHOOL ★★★★	TEENS ★★★★
YOUNG ADULTS ★★★½	OVER 30 ★★★★		SENIORS ★★★★

What it is Scenic railroad ride around perimeter of the Magic Kingdom; provides transportation to Frontierland and Fantasyland. **Scope and scale** Minor attraction. **Fright potential** Not frightening in any respect. **Bottleneck rating** 6. **When to go** Anytime; closed during

Thumbs Up for the Whole Family

parades. **Special comment** Main Street is usually the least congested station. **Authors' rating** Plenty to see; ★★★. **Duration of ride** About 20 minutes for a complete circuit. **Average wait in line per 100 people ahead of you** 8 minutes; assumes 2 or more trains operating. **Loading speed** Moderate.

Later in the day, when you need a break, this full-circuit ride will give you and your feet 20 minutes of rest. Only folded strollers are permitted on the train, so you can't board with your rented Disney stroller. You can, however, obtain a replacement at your destination. Be advised that the railroad shuts down immediately preceding and during parades.

ADVENTURELAND

ADVENTURELAND IS THE FIRST LAND to the left of Main Street. It combines an African-safari theme with a tropical-island atmosphere.

Captain Jack Sparrow's Pirate Tutorial ★★★½

APPEAL BY AGE PRESCHOOL ★★★★½ GRADE SCHOOL ★★★★½ TEENS ★★★½
YOUNG ADULTS ★★★½ OVER 30 ★★★½ SENIORS ★★★½

What it is Outdoor stage show with guest participation. **Scope and scale** Diversion. **Fright potential** Not frightening in any respect. **Bottleneck rating** 8. **When to go** See *Times Guide* for show schedule. **Special comment** Audience stands. **Authors' rating** Sign us up; ★★★½. **Duration of presentation** About 20 minutes.

Outside Pirates of the Caribbean, Cap'n Jack and a crew member teach would-be knaves the skills needed for a career in piracy; some kids go on stage to train in the finer points of dueling. At the end, everyone takes the pirate's oath and sings a rousing round of "A Pirate's Life for Me." The shows attract decent crowds, but the first and last seem to be the least popular.

Jungle Cruise *(FastPass+)* ★★★½

APPEAL BY AGE PRESCHOOL ★★★★ GRADE SCHOOL ★★★★ TEENS ★★★½
YOUNG ADULTS ★★★★ OVER 30 ★★★★ SENIORS ★★★★

What it is Outdoor safari-themed boat ride adventure. **Scope and scale** Major attraction. **Fright potential** Moderately intense, some macabre sights; a good test attraction for little ones. **Bottleneck rating** 10. **When to go** Before 10:30 a.m., the

Thumbs Up for the Whole Family

last 2 hours the park is open, or use FastPass+. **Authors' rating** An enduring Disney masterpiece; ★★★½. **Duration of ride** 8–9 minutes. **Average wait in line per 100 people ahead of you** 3½ minutes. **Assumes** 10 boats operating. **Loading speed** Moderate.

You have to put things into perspective to truly enjoy this ride and realize that it once was a super-headliner attraction at the Magic Kingdom—it's fun and relaxing, but far from high-tech. Before you make a same-day Fast-Pass+ reservation, check the estimated wait time for the standby queue.

DISNEY DISH WITH JIM HILL

WE JUST USED WHAT WAS LION AROUND When Skipper's Cantina opens in late 2015 or early 2016, in the area across from Swiss Family Treehouse, you may notice a lot of familiar decor. According to the backstory the Imagineers cooked up for this new Magic Kingdom restaurant, the skippers "borrowed" a number of items from the Jungle Cruise to set up their restaurant. As you wander through the dining room, keep an eye out for items that used to be found in the attraction's queue or dangling from Trader Sam's belt.

The Magic Carpets of Aladdin *(FastPass+)* ★★½

APPEAL BY AGE PRESCHOOL ★★★★½ GRADE SCHOOL ★★★★ TEENS ★★★
YOUNG ADULTS ★★★ OVER 30 ★★★ SENIORS ★★★½

What it is Elaborate midway ride. **Scope and scale** Minor attraction. **Fright potential** Much like Dumbo; a favorite of most younger children. **Bottleneck rating** 10.

When to go Before 11 a.m. or after 7 p.m.; FastPass+ rarely necessary. **Authors' rating** An eye-appealing children's ride; ★★½. **Duration of ride** 1½ minutes. **Average wait in line per 100 people ahead of you** 16 minutes. **Loading speed** Slow.

Like Dumbo, Aladdin is a must for parents with preschoolers. Try to get your kids on in the first 30 minutes the park is open or just before park closing. Beware of the spitting camel positioned to spray jets of water on riders. The front-seat control moves your "carpet" up and down, while the backseat control pitches it forward or backward. Sweet, but oh-so-slow loading. Jasmine and Aladdin are often on hand for meeting and greeting.

This ride is inspired by the 1992 Disney movie Aladdin. *Did you know that Robin Williams was the voice of the Genie?*

A Pirate's Adventure: Treasure of the Seven Seas   ★★★½

**APPEAL BY AGE · PRESCHOOL ★★★½   GRADE SCHOOL ★★★★½   TEENS ★★★★
YOUNG ADULTS ★★★½   OVER 30 ★★★½   SENIORS ★★★★**

What it is Interactive game. **Scope and scale** Diversion. **Fright potential** Some exhibits may frighten small children when playing at night. **Bottleneck rating** 4. **When to go** Anytime. **Authors' rating** Simple, fast, and fun; ★★★½. **Duration of experience** About 25 minutes to play entire game. **Probable waiting time per step** 5 minutes or less.

Similar to Agent P's World Showcase Adventure at Epcot, A Pirate's Adventure features interactive areas with physical props and narrations that lead guests through a quest to find lost treasure, all within Adventureland.

Guests begin their journey at an old Cartography Shop near Golden Oak Outpost—this is the central hub for adventurers helping to locate missing treasure. Groups of up to six people are given a talisman (an RFID card) that will help them on their journey. The talisman activates a video screen that assigns your group to one of five different missions. Your group is then given a map and sent off to find your first location.

Once at the location, one member of the party touches the talisman to the symbol at the station, and the animation begins. Each adventure has four or five stops throughout Adventureland, and each stop contains 30–45 seconds of activity. No strategy or action is required: Watch what unfolds on the screen, get your next destination, and head off.

A Pirate's Adventure serves as a good introduction to other interactive games, such as Sorcerers of the Magic Kingdom (see page 268). The effects are better at night. While we think everyone should try A Pirate's Adventure, it isn't a must if time is tight.

Pirates of the Caribbean *(FastPass+)*   ★★★★

**APPEAL BY AGE PRESCHOOL ★★★½   GRADE SCHOOL ★★★★   TEENS ★★★★½
YOUNG ADULTS ★★★★   OVER 30 ★★★★½   SENIORS ★★★★½**

What it is Indoor pirate-themed adventure boat ride. **Scope and scale** Headliner. **Fright potential** Slightly intimidating queuing area; intense boat ride with gruesome (though humorously presented) sights and a short, unexpected slide down a flume. **Bottleneck rating** 7. **When to go** Before 11 a.m., after 7 p.m., or use Fast-Pass+. **Authors' rating** Disney Audio-Animatronics at their best; not to be missed; ★★★★. **Duration of ride** About 7½ minutes. **Average wait in line per 100 people ahead of you** 3 minutes; assumes one waiting line for FastPass+ and one for standby. **Loading speed** Fast.

Dark   Loud   Scary

This indoor ride cruises through a series of sets depicting a pirate raid on a Caribbean port. It's been a favorite for decades, but with the release of *Pirates of the Caribbean: The Curse of the Black Pearl* (2003), *Pirates of the Caribbean: Dead Man's Chest* (2006), *Pirates of the Caribbean: At World's End* (2007), *Pirates of the Caribbean: On Stranger Tides* (2011), and the upcoming *Pirates of the Caribbean: Dead Men Tell No Tales* (2017), its popularity has soared to new heights.

Rent the movies before you go to Walt Disney World. They're a blast.

Swiss Family Treehouse ★★★

APPEAL BY AGE	PRESCHOOL ★★★½	GRADE SCHOOL ★★★½	TEENS ★★★
YOUNG ADULTS ★★★	OVER 30 ★★★½		SENIORS ★★★

What it is Outdoor walk-through tree house. **Scope and scale** Minor attraction. **Fright potential** Kids who are afraid of heights might want to skip it; otherwise, not frightening. **Bottleneck rating** 6. **When to go** Anytime. **Special comment** Requires climbing a lot of stairs. **Authors' rating** A visual delight; ★★★. **Duration of tour** 10–15 minutes. **Average wait in line per 100 people ahead of you** 7 minutes.

Thumbs Up for the Whole Family

This king of all tree houses is perfect for the 10-and-under crowd. Though a minor attraction, it's a great place to expend pent-up energy. Parents might be inclined to sit across the walkway and watch their aspiring Tarzans, but in truth the tree house is fun for adults too.

Swiss Family Robinson is a 1960 film adaptation of the Johann David Wyss novel and was the inspiration for the Swiss Family Treehouse.

Walt Disney's Enchanted Tiki Room ★★★

APPEAL BY AGE	PRESCHOOL ★★★½	GRADE SCHOOL ★★★½	TEENS ★★★
YOUNG ADULTS ★★★	OVER 30 ★★★½		SENIORS ★★★★

What it is Audio-Animatronic Pacific Island musical-theater show. **Scope and scale** Minor attraction. **Fright potential** Young children might be frightened by the thunder-and-lightning storm, plus the theater is at times plunged into utter darkness. **Bottleneck rating** 4. **When to go** Before 11 a.m. or after 3:30 p.m. **Authors' rating** Very, very . . . unusual; ★★★. **Duration of show** 15½ minutes. **Preshow** Talking birds. **Probable waiting time** 15 minutes.

Dark   Loud

The Tiki Birds are a great favorite of the 8-and-under age set. The outright absurdity of the whole concept saves the show for older patrons—if you can look beyond the cheese, it's actually hilarious. The air-conditioned theater is a great place to cool off and rest your feet.

FRONTIERLAND

THIS "LAND" ADJOINS ADVENTURELAND as you move clockwise around the Magic Kingdom. Frontierland's focus is on the Old West, with stockade-type structures and pioneer trappings.

Big Thunder Mountain Railroad *(FastPass+)* ★★★★

| APPEAL BY AGE | PRESCHOOL ★★★½ | GRADE SCHOOL ★★★★½ | TEENS ★★★★½ |
| YOUNG ADULTS ★★★★½ | | OVER 30 ★★★★½ | SENIORS ★★★★ |

What it is Tame Western mining–themed roller coaster. **Scope and scale** Headliner. **Fright potential** Visually intimidating from outside, with moderately intense visual effects; wild roller coaster. **Bottleneck rating** 9. **When to go** Before 10 a.m., in the hour before closing, or use FastPass+. **Special comments** Must be 40" tall to ride; children younger than age 7 must ride with an adult. Switching-off option provided (see page 243). **Authors' rating** Great effects; not to be missed; ★★★★. **Duration of ride** Almost 3½ minutes. **Average wait in line per 100 people ahead of you** 2½ minutes; assumes 5 trains operating. **Loading speed** Moderate–fast.

Lose Things   Rough   Scary

Zooming on a runaway train around a mountain and through a deserted mining town is Disney at its best (if only one could concentrate on the scenery). The ride is rough, and if you don't like roller coasters, this one is going to remind you why. The air-conditioned queue features first-rate examples of Disney creativity: a realistic mining town, geysers, swinging possums, petulant buzzards, and the like. Ride after dark if you can. Regardless of when you ride, seats in the back offer a better experience.

It's fast and knocks you around a lot—it really rocks! There are lots of things to look at while you wait in line.

This is a fun ride at night. It's shaky and bumpy and at times really fast, with some very quick turns.

Isaac

Ethan

Country Bear Jamboree ★★★½

| APPEAL BY AGE | PRESCHOOL ★★★½ | GRADE SCHOOL ★★★½ | TEENS ★★★ |
| YOUNG ADULTS ★★★ | | OVER 30 ★★★½ | SENIORS ★★★★ |

What it is Audio-Animatronic country hoedown. **Scope and scale** Major attraction. **Fright potential** Not frightening in any respect. **Bottleneck rating** 6. **When to go** Anytime. **Authors' rating** Old and worn but pure Disney; ★★★½. **Duration of show** 11 minutes. **Probable waiting time** It's not terribly popular but has a comparatively small capacity. Waiting time between noon and 5:30 p.m. on a busy day will average 11–22 minutes.

A charming cast of Audio-Animatronic bears sings and stomps in a Western-style hoedown. Editing has cut a few minutes from the show, quickening its pace somewhat. Most songs remain the same, though, and *Country Bear Jamboree* has run for so long that the geriatric bears are a step away from assisted living. Reader comments tend to echo the need for something new. From a Sandy Hook, Connecticut, mom:

> *I know they consider it a classic, and kids always seem to love it, but could they PLEASE update it after half a century?*

Movie Tip

Kids will love watching The Country Bears, *a live-action film produced by Walt Disney Pictures based loosely on the* Country Bear Jamboree *show. It was Disney's first movie based on a ride or attraction, released in 2002, almost year before* Pirates of the Caribbean: The Curse of the Black Pearl.

Country Bear Jamboree is creepier than Five Nights at Freddy's because the animatronics are old.

Ricky

Frontierland Shootin' Arcade ★½

APPEAL BY AGE   PRESCHOOL ★★★½   GRADE SCHOOL ★★★½   TEENS ★★★★½
YOUNG ADULTS ★★★★   OVER 30 ★★★½   SENIORS ★★★★

What it is Electronic shooting gallery. **Scope and scale** Diversion. **Fright potential** Frightening to children scared of guns. **Bottleneck rating** 1. **When to go** Anytime. **Special comment** Costs $1 per play. **Authors' rating** Fun for kids but not a must; ★½.

Would-be gunslingers get around 30 shots per $1 play. Each shot is followed by a short delay before the next shot can be taken—this prevents small children from accidentally using all 30 shots in 5 seconds. It's barely noticeable for adults. Bring lots of quarters.

> Frontierland Shootin' Arcade can be addictive. If you want to shoot the whole train, aim for the first car, then don't move—just shoot each car as it goes by.

Ricky

Splash Mountain *(FastPass+)* ★★★★★

APPEAL BY AGE   PRESCHOOL ★★★★†   GRADE SCHOOL ★★★★½   TEENS ★★★★½
YOUNG ADULTS ★★★★½   OVER 30 ★★★★½   SENIORS ★★★★½

†Many preschoolers are too short to ride, and others freak out when they see it from the waiting line. Among preschoolers who actually ride, most love it.

What it is Indoor/outdoor water-flume adventure ride. **Scope and scale** Superheadliner. **Fright potential** Visually intimidating from outside, with moderately intense visual effects. The ride, culminating in a 52-foot plunge down a steep chute, is somewhat hair-raising for all ages. **Bottleneck rating** 10. **When to go** As soon as the park opens, during afternoon or evening parades, just before closing, or use FastPass+. **Special comments** Must be 40" tall to ride; children younger than age 7 must ride with an adult. Switching-off option provided (see page 243). **Authors' rating** A wet winner; not to be missed; ★★★★★. **Duration of ride** About 10 minutes. **Average wait in line per 100 people ahead of you** 3½ minutes; assumes ride is operating at full capacity. **Loading speed** Moderate.

Lose Things   Wet   Scary

Zip-a-dee-doo-dah, having fun yet? My-oh-my, will you get wet! This 0.5-mile ride through swamps, caves, and backwoods bayous is wonderful. Based on the 1946 Disney film *Song of the South,* the log flume ride takes you through Uncle Remus's tales of Br'er Rabbit. Three small drops lead up to the big one—a five-story plunge at 40 mph.

> Riding in log flumes is cool, and this ride has a couple of big drops. Water kind of splashes around you throughout the ride, and there's a possibility that you'll get soaked. Definitely fun!

Isaac

> A great ride, but be careful where you sit— your seat might already be wet before you even get in.

Ethan

> *Unavailable in the United States, Song of the South will become public domain in 2039, and Disney might rerelease the movie before they lose the rights to it. If you're interested in the history of this controversial movie, check out* **songofthesouth.net.**

Movie Tip

Tom Sawyer Island and Fort Langhorn ★★★

APPEAL BY AGE   PRESCHOOL ★★★★   GRADE SCHOOL ★★★★½   TEENS ★★★★
YOUNG ADULTS ★★★½   OVER 30 ★★★½   SENIORS ★★★

What it is Outdoor walk-through exhibit and rustic playground. **Scope and scale** Minor attraction. **Fright potential** Not frightening in any respect, other than dark tunnels that can be avoided. **Bottleneck rating** 4. **When to go** Midmorning–late afternoon. **Special comment** Closes at dusk. **Authors' rating** The place for rambunctious kids; ★★★.

Thumbs Up for the Whole Family

This is a great place for kids age 5 and up to unwind. The wildest and most uncooperative youngster will relax after exploring caves and climbing around in an old fort. It's also a great place for a picnic, but there is no food, so bring your own. Access is by raft with a (usually short) wait both coming and going. Plan to give your kids at least 20 minutes on the island—left to their own devices, they would likely stay all day.

I love Tom Sawyer Island. It's the perfect place to take a break or have a picnic; plus, it's a great place for nursing moms to find a quiet spot. Be aware, though, that raft transportation to the island stops at sunset.

Liliane

Tip for parents: If you're finding the going tough, head over to Tom Sawyer Island, and if your kids are sensible and old enough (like Alex and me), let them run around on their own and you can have a snooze (like my mum and dad) in the rocking chairs.

Kieran

LIBERTY SQUARE

LIBERTY SQUARE re-creates America at the time of the American Revolution. The architecture is Federal or Colonial. The **Liberty Tree,** a live oak more than 130 years old, lends dignity and grace to the setting.

The Hall of Presidents ★★★

APPEAL BY AGE	PRESCHOOL ★★½	GRADE SCHOOL ★★★	TEENS ★★★½
YOUNG ADULTS ★★★½	OVER 30 ★★★★		SENIORS ★★★★½

What it is Audio-Animatronic historical theater presentation. **Scope and scale** Major attraction. **Fright potential** Not frightening in any respect. **Bottleneck rating** 4. **When to go** Anytime. **Authors' rating** Impressive and moving; ★★★. **Duration of show** Almost 23 minutes.

Thumbs Up for the Whole Family

Probable waiting time The lines for this attraction look intimidating once you're inside the lobby, but they're swallowed up as the theater exchanges audiences. It would be exceptionally unusual not to be admitted to the next show.

Disney immortalizes the presidents of the United States with their own Audio-Animatronic counterparts. The last update was in 2009, when Barack Obama was added and the entire presentation revamped, including a new narration by Morgan Freeman and a new speech by George Washington. The Father of Our Country joins Presidents Lincoln and Obama as the only chief executives with speaking parts. Though the show is refreshed roughly every decade, the presentation remains inspirational and patriotic and highlights milestones in American history. *The Hall of Presidents* is definitely a must-see for adults, but kids are likely to fidget or fall asleep.

Did you know that famous Western actor Royal Dano is the voice of President Lincoln? Dano was also the voice of Lincoln for Disney's *Great Moments with Mr. Lincoln* program, first presented at the 1964–65 World's Fair in New York City.

Liliane

The Haunted Mansion *(FastPass+)* ★★★★½

APPEAL BY AGE	PRESCHOOL ★★★½	GRADE SCHOOL ★★★★	TEENS ★★★★½
YOUNG ADULTS ★★★★½	OVER 30 ★★★★½		SENIORS ★★★★½

What it is Haunted-house dark ride. **Scope and scale** Major attraction. **Fright potential** The name raises anxiety, as do the sounds and sights of the waiting area. An intense attraction with humorously presented macabre sights, the ride itself is gentle. **Bottleneck rating** 8. **When to go** Before 11 a.m. or the last 2 hours the park is open; use FastPass+ when touring for 2 days or more, or get it as your first in-park FastPass. **Authors' rating** Some of Disney World's best special effects; not to be missed; ★★★★½. **Duration of ride** 7-minute ride plus a 1½-minute preshow. **Average wait in line per 100 people ahead of you** 2½ minutes; assumes both "stretch rooms" operating. **Loading speed** Fast.

Dark   Scary

Don't let the apparent spookiness of the old-fashioned Haunted Mansion put you off. This is one of the best attractions in the Magic Kingdom (and, in fact, one that seems to get a few new twists each year). It's not scary, except in the sweetest of ways, but it will remind you of the days before ghost stories gave way to slasher flicks. The Haunted Mansion takes less than 10 minutes to ride, preshow included, but you may have to do it more than once—it's jam-packed with visual puns, special effects, Hidden Mickeys, and really lovely Victorian-spooky sets.

This ride is kind of creepy. Everything looks so real, even the ghosts. The end is cool, so make sure you keep your eyes open.

Ethan

DISNEY DISH WITH JIM HILL

OLD HAT IN A GOOD WAY As part of Disneyland's 60th-anniversary celebration, the long-gone-but-not-forgotten Hatbox Ghost returned to that theme park's Haunted Mansion. Walt Disney World's 50th anniversary is coming up in 2021, and according to what Imagineering insiders have recently told me, Disney World may get a hatbox-shaped birthday present at that time. But probably not sooner.

Liberty Belle Riverboat ★★½

APPEAL BY AGE	PRESCHOOL ★★★½	GRADE SCHOOL ★★★½	TEENS ★★★
YOUNG ADULTS ★★★½	OVER 30 ★★★½		SENIORS ★★★★

What it is Outdoor scenic boat ride. **Scope and scale** Major attraction. **Fright**

Thumbs Up for the Whole Family

potential Not frightening in any respect. **Bottleneck rating** 4. **When to go** Anytime. **Authors' rating** Slow, relaxing, and scenic; ★★½. **Duration of ride** About 16 minutes. **Average wait to board** 10–14 minutes.

This fully narrated 16-minute trip is relaxing and offers great photo ops. It's also a good choice at night, when the boat and the attractions along the waterfront are lighted. Did you know that the *Liberty Belle* runs on a track hidden just below the water?

FANTASYLAND

FANTASYLAND IS THE HEART OF THE MAGIC KINGDOM— a truly enchanting place spread gracefully like a miniature alpine village beneath the steepled towers of Cinderella Castle.

Fantasyland is divided into three distinct sections. Directly behind Cinderella Castle and set on a snowcapped mountain is **Beast's Castle,** part of a *Beauty and the Beast*–themed area. Most of this section holds dining and shopping. Outside Beast's Castle is **Belle's Village.** Nestled inside lush and beautifully decorated grounds, with gardens, meadows, and waterfalls, is **Maurice's Cottage,** home of *Enchanted Tales with Belle.*

The far-right corner of Fantasyland—including **Dumbo, The Barnstormer** kiddie coaster, and the Fantasyland train station—is called **Storybook Circus** as an homage to Disney's *Dumbo* film. These are low-capacity amusement park rides appropriate for younger children. Also located here is **Pete's Silly Sideshow,** a character greeting venue.

The middle of Fantasyland holds the headliners, including **Under the Sea: Journey of the Little Mermaid** and **Seven Dwarfs Mine Train.** The original part of Fantasyland contains classic attractions such as **Peter Pan's Flight** and **The Many Adventures of Winnie the Pooh.** It also hosts the incredibly popular **Princess Fairytale Hall** meet and greet, with waits of 4 hours or more to meet *Frozen*'s Anna and Elsa. (Lines for the other princesses are shorter.)

LILIANE The only way to visit Beast's Castle is by eating at Be Our Guest. Reservations are fully booked months in advance.

Finally, when nature (or technology) calls, don't miss the *Tangled-themed restrooms and outdoor seating* (with phone-charging stations), near Peter Pan's Flight and It's a Small World.

DISNEY DISH WITH JIM HILL

BEAUTIFUL FIXTURE, BEASTLY PROBLEM
The enormous chandelier that dangles over the Grand Ballroom in Be Our Guest Restaurant—12 feet tall and 11 feet wide, with 84 candles and 100 jewels—had to be partly disassembled at the last minute to fit through the restaurant's doors for installation.

Ariel's Grotto *(FastPass+)* ★★★

APPEAL BY AGE	PRESCHOOL ★★★★½	GRADE SCHOOL ★★★★½	TEENS ★★★★
YOUNG ADULTS ★★★★		OVER 30 ★★★½	SENIORS ★★★★

What it is Character greeting venue. **Scope and scale** Minor attraction. **Fright potential** Not frightening in any respect. **Bottleneck rating** 8. **When to go** Before 10:30 a.m. or the last 2 hours the park is open, or use FastPass+. **Authors' rating** Not quite as themed as other character greetings; ★★★. **Duration of experience** Maybe 30–90 seconds. **Average wait in line per 100 people ahead of you** 45 minutes. **Queue speed** Slow.

This is Ariel's home base, next to Under the Sea: Journey of the Little Mermaid. In the base of the seaside cliffs under Prince Eric's Castle, Ariel (in mermaid form) greets guests from a seashell throne. The queue isn't as detailed as other character greeting venues in the park.

The Grotto may close an hour before the rest of the park. The greeting area is set up almost as if to encourage guests to linger with Ariel, which keeps the line long. The queue isn't air-conditioned, which is surprising for a venue that's supposed to store fish.

The Barnstormer *(FastPass+)* ★★

APPEAL BY AGE PRESCHOOL ★★★★ GRADE SCHOOL ★★★★ TEENS ★★★½
YOUNG ADULTS ★★★   OVER 30 ★★★   SENIORS ★★★½

What it is Small roller coaster. **Scope and scale** Minor attraction. **Fright potential** A children's coaster; frightens some preschoolers. **Bottleneck rating** 9. **When to go** Before 11 a.m., during parades, or the last 2 hours the park is open; not a good use of FastPass+. **Special comment** Must be 35″ tall to ride. **Authors' rating** Great for little ones but not worth the wait for adults; ★★. **Duration of ride** About 53 seconds. **Average wait in line per 100 people ahead of you** 7 minutes. **Loading speed** Slow.

Rough   Scary

Remember that the height requirement for this ride is 35 inches. If you want to see how your child handles riding coasters, The Barnstormer is the perfect testing ground. (Seven Dwarfs Mine Train would be the next to try.)

Liliane

Yours truly screamed big-time from start to end (thankfully it only lasted a minute), and no way would I let the apple of my eye ride alone unless he or she were 6 years or older.

Bob

Liliane is a gentle and sensitive soul. Most kids experience rides wilder than The Barnstormer on their tricycles. When I heard Liliane wailing like a banshee on this dinky coaster, I thought that her appendix must have ruptured.

Casey Jr. Splash 'N' Soak Station ★★★

APPEAL BY AGE PRESCHOOL ★★★★½ GRADE SCHOOL ★★★★½ TEENS ★★★
YOUNG ADULTS ★★½   OVER 30 ★★½   SENIORS ★★★

What it is Opportunity to get wet. **Scope and scale** Diversion. **Fright potential** Not frightening in any respect. **Bottleneck rating** 0. **When to go** When it's hot. **Authors' rating** Great way to cool off; ★★★.

Casey Jr., the circus train from *Dumbo,* hosts an absolutely drenching experience outside the Fantasyland Train Station in the Storybook Circus area. Expect a cadre of captive circus beasts to spray water on you in this elaborate water-play area. It puts all other theme park splash areas to soaking shame and is a marvel to watch. Bring a change of clothes and a big towel.

Wet

Dumbo the Flying Elephant *(FastPass+)* ★★★½

APPEAL BY AGE PRESCHOOL ★★★★½ GRADE SCHOOL ★★★★ TEENS ★★★
YOUNG ADULTS ★★★½   OVER 30 ★★★½   SENIORS ★★★½

What it is Disneyfied midway ride. **Scope and scale** Minor attraction. **Fright potential** Very tame; a favorite of most young children. **Bottleneck rating** 10. **When to go** Before 10:30 a.m. or after 3 p.m.; not a good use of FastPass+. **Authors' rating**

Disney's signature ride for children; ★★★½. **Duration of ride** 1½ minutes. **Average wait in line per 100 people ahead of you** 5 minutes. **Loading speed** Slow.

Making sure your kids get their fill of this tame, happy children's ride is what mother love is all about. The 90-second ride is hardly worth the long lines, unless, of course, you're under 7 years old. As part of the Fantasyland expansion, Dumbo moved to the upper-right corner of the land. The attraction's capacity doubled with the addition of a second ride—a clone of the first. These two changes, along with the addition of the newer Fantasyland attractions, have drastically reduced waits to ride. If you do find yourself with a wait, Dumbo also includes a covered queue featuring interactive elements (read: things your kids can play with to pass the time in line).

If you haven't seen Dumbo *(first released in 1941 and winner of an Academy Award for original music score), you have an elephant-size gap in your Disney education. Watch the movie, fun for all ages, when you get home.*

Enchanted Tales with Belle (FastPass+)   ★★★★

APPEAL BY AGE   PRESCHOOL ★★★½ **GRADE SCHOOL** ★★★★½ **TEENS** ★★★½
YOUNG ADULTS ★★★½   **OVER 30** ★★★★   **SENIORS** ★★★★

What it is Interactive character show. **Scope and scale** Minor attraction. **Fright potential** Not frightening in any respect. **Bottleneck rating** 10. **When to go** As soon as the park opens, during the last 2 hours before closing, or use FastPass+. **Authors' rating** The prettiest meet and greet in the park; ★★★★. **Duration of presentation** About 20 minutes. **Probable waiting time** 25 minutes. **Queue speed** Slow.

A multiscene *Beauty and the Beast* experience that takes guests into Maurice's workshop, through a magic mirror, and into Beast's library, where the audience shares a story with Belle.

You enter the attraction by walking through Maurice's cottage, where you see mementos tracing Belle's childhood, including her favorite books, and lines drawn on one wall showing how fast Belle grew every year.

From there you'll enter Maurice's workshop at the back of the cottage. An assortment of Maurice's odd wood gadgets covers every inch of the floor, walls, and ceiling. Take a moment to peruse the gadgets, and then focus your attention on the mirror on the wall to the left of the entry door.

Soon enough, the room gets dark and the mirror begins to sparkle. With magic and some really good carpentry skills, the mirror turns into a full-size doorway, through which guests enter into a wardrobe room. Once you reach the wardrobe room, the attraction's premise is explained: You're supposed to reenact the story of *Beauty and the Beast* for Belle on her birthday, and guests are chosen to act out key parts in the play.

After the parts are cast, everyone walks into the castle's library and takes a seat. Cast members explain how the play will take place and introduce Belle, who gives a short speech about how thrilled she is for everyone to be there. The play is acted out within a few minutes, and the actors get a photo op with Belle and receive a small bookmark as a memento.

Enchanted Tales with Belle is surely the prettiest and most elaborate meet and greet in Disney World. For the relative few who get to act in the play, it's also a chance to interact with Belle in a way that isn't possible in other character encounters.

It's a Small World *(FastPass+)*   ★★★½

APPEAL BY AGE   PRESCHOOL ★★★★½   GRADE SCHOOL ★★★★   TEENS ★★★
YOUNG ADULTS ★★★½   OVER 30 ★★★½   SENIORS ★★★★

Thumbs Up for the Whole Family

What it is World brotherhood–themed indoor boat ride. **Scope and scale** Major attraction. **Fright potential** Not frightening in any respect. **Bottleneck rating** 7. **When to go** Before 11 a.m., during parades, or after 7 p.m.; FastPass+ is unnecessary. **Authors' rating** Exponentially "cute"; ★★★½. **Duration of ride** About 11 minutes. **Average wait in line per 100 people ahead of you** 3½ minutes; assumes busy conditions with 30 or more boats operating. **Loading speed** Fast.

Small boats carry visitors on a tour around the world, with singing and dancing dolls showcasing the dress and culture of each nation. Of course, there's no escaping the brain-numbing tune. Just when you think you've repressed it, the song will resurface without warning to torture you some more.

> This ride is pretty and full of bright colors. It's so cool to see all the outfits that people in different countries wear. It's perfect for small kids, but big kids like it too.

I'm not into this ride—the music gets stuck in your head for the whole day. My mom loves it, though; probably all moms do.

Isaac

Julia

Mad Tea Party *(FastPass+)*   ★★

APPEAL BY AGE   PRESCHOOL ★★★★½   GRADE SCHOOL ★★★★½ TEENS ★★★★
YOUNG ADULTS ★★★½   OVER 30 ★★★½   SENIORS ★★★½

Queasy

What it is Midway-type spinning ride. **Scope and scale** Minor attraction. **Fright potential** Low, but this type of ride can induce motion sickness in all ages. **Bottleneck rating** 9. **When to go** Before 11 a.m. or after 5 p.m.; not a good choice for FastPass+. **Special comment** You can make the teacups spin faster by turning the wheel in the center of the cup. **Authors' rating** Fun but not worth the wait; ★★. **Duration of ride** 1½ minutes. **Average wait in line per 100 people ahead of you** 7½ minutes. **Loading speed** Slow.

Teenagers love to lure unsuspecting adults into the spinning teacups and then turn the wheel in the middle (making the cup spin faster) until the grown-ups are plastered against the sides and on the verge of throwing up. Unless you aspire to be a living physics experiment, don't even *consider* getting on this one with anybody younger than 21. This ride is notoriously slow-loading. Ride the morning of your second day if your schedule is more relaxed.

Spinning the cups as fast as you can is awesome!

Movie Tip

The Mad Tea Party is inspired by the unusual tea party scene in the 1951 Disney adaptation of Lewis Carroll's Alice in Wonderland. *Did you know that the voice of Alice, British voice actress and schoolteacher Kathryn Beaumont, is also the voice of Wendy in* Peter Pan?

Ethan

The Many Adventures of Winnie the Pooh
(FastPass+)   ★★★½

APPEAL BY AGE   PRESCHOOL ★★★★½   GRADE SCHOOL ★★★★   TEENS ★★★½
YOUNG ADULTS ★★★½   OVER 30 ★★★½   SENIORS ★★★★

What it is Indoor track ride. **Scope and scale** Minor attraction. **Fright potential** Frightens a few preschoolers. **Bottleneck rating** 8. **When to go** Before 10 a.m., the last hour the park is open, or use FastPass+. **Authors' rating** Cute as the Pooh bear himself; ★★★½. **Duration of ride** About 4 minutes. **Average wait in line per 100 people ahead of you** 4 minutes. **Loading speed** Moderate.

Thumbs Up for the Whole Family

This attraction is sunny, upbeat, and charming without being saccharine. You ride a Hunny Pot through the pages of a huge picture book into the Hundred-Acre Wood, where you encounter Pooh, Piglet, Eeyore, Owl, Rabbit, Tigger, Kanga, and Roo as they contend with a blustery day. Pooh is a perfect test to assess how your very young children will react to indoor (dark) rides. It's also a good choice for FastPass+ if you have small children and you're touring over two or more days.

Movie Tip

The ride is based on the 1977 Disney animated feature of the same name. Paul Winchell won a Grammy for his voicing of Tigger. He also voiced a Chinese cat in The Aristocats *and Boomer the woodpecker in* The Fox and the Hound; *plus, he provided the voice of the evil Gargamel in the animated TV series* The Smurfs.

Meet Merida at Fairytale Garden ★★★½

APPEAL BY AGE	PRESCHOOL ★★★★★	GRADE SCHOOL ★★★★½	TEENS ★★★½
YOUNG ADULTS ★★★½	OVER 30 ★★★½		SENIORS ★★★

What it is Storytelling session and character meet and greet. **Scope and scale** Diversion. **Fright potential** Not frightening in any respect. **Bottleneck rating** 7. **When to go** See *Times Guide* for schedule. **Authors' rating** Lovely lass, lovely locale; ★★★½. **Duration of presentation** About 10 minutes. **Probable waiting time** 1 hour or more. **Queue speed** Slow.

Merida, the flame-haired Scottish princess from *Brave,* greets guests in Fairytale Garden, in front of Cinderella Castle on the Tomorrowland side, between the castle and Cosmic Ray's Starlight Cafe. Princess meet and greets tend to be quite popular, especially those involving princesses from recent movies, so expect long lines. If meeting Merida is a must-do for your family, get in line early in the morning.

Mickey's PhilharMagic (FastPass+) ★★★★

APPEAL BY AGE	PRESCHOOL ★★★★	GRADE SCHOOL ★★★★½	TEENS ★★★★
YOUNG ADULTS ★★★★½	OVER 30 ★★★★½		SENIORS ★★★★½

What it is 3-D movie. **Scope and scale** Major attraction. **Fright potential** Scares some preschoolers. **Bottleneck rating** 6. **When to go** Before 11 a.m. or during parades; FastPass+ is unnecessary. **Authors' rating** Not to be missed; a zany masterpiece; ★★★★. **Duration of show** About 12 minutes. **Probable waiting time** 12–25 minutes.

A real stunner, *Mickey's PhilharMagic* combines three fabulous ideas: Mickey and Donald mix and meet with latter-day Disney stars such as Aladdin, Jasmine, Ariel, the Beast's pantry servants (such as Lumiere and Mrs. Potts), and Simba; it employs a form of computer-enhanced 3-D video technology that is truly impressive (it's the first time most of these characters have been digitally animated, which will make them more "flexible," so to speak, in the future); and the whole shebang is projected on a 150-foot-wide, 180-degree screen. *Mickey's PhilharMagic* even employs some of those famous Disney scent effects and turns the old sorcerer's apprentice trick back on Mickey.

Where other Disney 3-D movies are loud, in-your-face affairs, this one is softer and cuddlier. Things pop out of the screen, but they're really not scary. It's the rare child who is frightened—but there are always exceptions, as was the case with the 3-year-old child of this North Carolina mom:

Our family found PhilharMagic *way too violent (what seemed like minutes on end of Donald getting the crap kicked out of him by various musical instruments). I had to haul my screaming child out of the theater and submit to a therapeutic carousel ride afterward.*

Happily, an Oregon mom has an easy way to nip the willies in the bud:

My advice to parents is simply to have their kids not wear the 3-D glasses. We took my daughter's off right away, and then she began giggling and having a good time watching the movie.

Peter Pan's Flight *(FastPass+)* ★★★★

APPEAL BY AGE PRESCHOOL ★★★★½ GRADE SCHOOL ★★★★ TEENS ★★★½
YOUNG ADULTS ★★★★   OVER 30 ★★★★   SENIORS ★★★★

What it is Indoor track ride. **Scope and scale** Minor attraction. **Fright potential** Not frightening in any respect. **Bottleneck rating** 8. **When to go** First or last 30 minutes the park is open, or use FastPass+. **Authors' rating** Happy, mellow, and well done; ★★★★. **Duration of ride** A little more than 3 minutes. **Average wait in line per 100 people ahead of you** 5½ minutes. **Loading speed** Moderate–slow.

Thumbs Up for the Whole Family

Peter Pan's Flight is superbly designed and absolutely delightful, with a happy theme uniting some favorite Disney characters, beautiful effects, and charming music. This dark (indoor) ride takes you on a relaxing trip in a "flying pirate ship" over old London and thence to Never Never Land, where Peter saves Wendy from walking the plank and Captain Hook rehearses for *Dancing with the Stars* on the snout of the ubiquitous crocodile. There's nothing here that will jump out at you or frighten young children. An interactive queuing area alleviates the pain of waiting in line as guests go through the Darlings' house before boarding their ride to Never Land.

Because Peter Pan's Flight is very popular, count on long lines all day. Our touring plan software suggests using FastPass+ for Peter Pan's Flight more than any other Walt Disney World attraction.

Movie Tip

Disney's animated film version of Peter Pan is, of course, the inspiration for this wonderful ride. While the original is easy to find, the sequel, Return to Never Land, *is not. Try to get a copy at a library or find a used one at* **amazon.com** *and reunite with Peter, Wendy, Tinker Bell, Mr. Smee, the Lost Boys, and Captain Hook. But most of all: Never grow up.*

Pete's Silly Sideshow *(FastPass+)* ★★★½

APPEAL BY AGE PRESCHOOL ★★★★½ GRADE SCHOOL ★★★★½ TEENS ★★★★
YOUNG ADULTS ★★★★   OVER 30 ★★★★   SENIORS ★★★★½

What it is Character greeting venue. **Scope and scale** Minor attraction. **Fright potential** Not frightening in any respect. **Bottleneck rating** 8. **When to go** Before 11 a.m. or in the last 2 hours the park is open; rarely a good use of FastPass+.

Authors' rating Well themed, with unique character costumes; ★★★½. **Duration of experience** 7 minutes per character. **Average wait in line per 100 people ahead of you** 25 minutes. **Queue speed** Slow.

Pete's Silly Sideshow is a circus-themed character greeting area in the Storybook Circus part of Fantasyland. The characters' costumes are distinct from the ones normally used around the parks. Characters available include Goofy as The Great Goofini, Donald Duck as The Astounding Donaldo, Daisy Duck as Madame Daisy Fortuna, and Minnie Mouse as Minnie Magnifique. On non–Extra Magic Hour days, Pete's opens 45 minutes later than the rest of the park and usually closes at the same time as the first *Wishes* fireworks show. The queue is indoors and air-conditioned. Note that there is one queue for the male characters (Goofy and Donald) and a second queue for the female characters (Minnie and Daisy). You can meet two characters at once but must line up twice to meet all four.

Prince Charming Regal Carrousel ★★★

APPEAL BY AGE	PRESCHOOL ★★★★½	GRADE SCHOOL ★★★★	TEENS ★★★½
YOUNG ADULTS ★★★½		OVER 30 ★★★½	SENIORS ★★★½

What it is Merry-go-round. **Scope and scale** Minor attraction. **Fright potential** Not frightening in any respect. **Bottleneck rating** 7. **When to go** Anytime. **Special comment** Adults enjoy the beauty and nostalgia of this ride. **Authors' rating** A beautiful children's ride; ★★★. **Duration of ride** About 2 minutes. **Average wait in line per 100 people ahead of you** 5 minutes. **Loading speed** Slow.

You'll have a long wait, but the beauty of the carousel (formerly known as Cinderella's Golden Carrousel) captures everyone. The carousel, built in 1917, was discovered in New Jersey, where it was once part of an amusement park. It is beautifully maintained and especially magical at night when all the lights are on. Check out your children's delighted expressions as the painted ponies go up and down.

A shy and retiring 9-year-old girl from Rockaway, New Jersey, thinks our rating of the carousel for grade-schoolers should be higher:

> *I want to complain. I went on the Prince Charming Regal Carrousel four times and I loved it! Raise those stars right now!*

One horse on the carousel has a gold ribbon on its tail. It's supposed to be Cinderella's favorite (at least that's what the Fairy Godmother told me).

Alex

Princess Fairytale Hall *(FastPass+)* ★★★

APPEAL BY AGE	PRESCHOOL ★★★★★	GRADE SCHOOL ★★★★½	TEENS ★★★★
YOUNG ADULTS ★★★★		OVER 30 ★★★½	SENIORS ★★★½

What it is Character greeting venue. **Scope and scale** Minor attraction. **Fright potential** Not frightening in any respect. **Bottleneck rating** Cinderella, Rapunzel, and Snow White: 9; Anna and Elsa: off the charts. **When to go** Before 10:30 a.m., after 4 p.m., or use FastPass+—if you can get it. **Authors' rating** You want princesses? We got 'em; ★★★. **Duration of experience** 7–10 minutes (estimated). **Average wait in line per 100 people ahead of you** 35 minutes (estimated) for Cinderella and company, exponentially longer for Anna and Elsa. **Queue speed** Slow . . . or, in the case of Anna and Elsa, potentially as glacial as Arendelle.

Princess Fairytale Hall is royalty central in the Magic Kingdom. Inside are two greeting venues, with each holding a small reception area for two royals. Thus, there are four royals meeting and greeting at any time, and you can see two of them at once. Signs outside the entrance tell you which line leads to which royal pair and how long the wait will be. Rapunzel usually leads one side, typically paired with Snow White, Cinderella, or another princess, while Anna and Elsa from *Frozen* reign on the other side.

Around 5–10 guests at a time are admitted to each greeting area, where there's plenty of time for small talk, a photo, and a hug from each princess. Enough time is given to each family, in fact, that we ran out of things to say to Rapunzel and shuffled quietly over to Snow White.

Fairytale Hall first opened with Cinderella headlining one of the attraction's two rooms, but Cindy was drawing roughly half the crowds Rapunzel did. When Anna and Elsa debuted to 5-hour lines at Epcot's Norway Pavilion, Cinderella was demoted to backup and the Scandinavians moved to the Magic Kingdom.

Anna and Elsa are the hottest character greeting ticket in all of Walt Disney World. If your child absolutely must meet them, use FastPass+— good luck with that, by the way—or head to Fairytale Hall first thing in the morning. Understand, though, that even if you're on hand at park opening, waits can easily top 2 hours—and often much, much more than that.

Seven Dwarfs Mine Train *(FastPass+)* ★★★★

APPEAL BY AGE PRESCHOOL ★★★★   GRADE SCHOOL ★★★★½ TEENS ★★★★
YOUNG ADULTS ★★★★   OVER 30 ★★★★   SENIORS ★★★★

Thumbs Up for the Whole Family

What it is A musical roller-coaster journey into the diamond mine of the Seven Dwarfs. **Scope and scale** Super-headliner. **Fright potential** Marginally wild ride, dark scenes, and special effects may frighten children age 7 and younger. **Bottleneck rating** 10. **When to go** As soon as the park opens, or use FastPass+. **Special comments** The swinging effect is more noticeable the farther back you're seated on the train; 38″ minimum height requirement. **Authors' rating** Great family coaster; not to be missed; ★★★★. **Duration of ride** About 4 minutes. **Average wait in line per 100 people ahead of you** 4 minutes. **Loading speed** Fast.

Seven Dwarfs Mine Train is geared to older grade-school kids who've been on amusement park rides before. There are no loops, inversions, or rolls in the track, and no massive hills or steep drops; the Mine Train's trick is that your ride vehicle's seats swing side to side as you go through turns. And— what a coincidence!—Disney has designed a curvy track with steep turns. An elaborate indoor section shows the dwarfs' underground operation. The exterior design includes waterfalls, forests, and landscaping and is meant

DISNEY DISH WITH JIM HILL

MINING INSPIRATION FROM THE PAST In Seven Dwarfs Mine Train's main mine scene, the Imagineers built the animation of the marching Seven Short Dudes using rotoscoped images directly from the "Heigh-Ho" number in the movie.

to join together all of the surrounding Fantasyland's various locations, including France and Germany.

The Mine Train was highly anticipated, but while it's a charming ride in a lovely setting, Liliane wasn't smitten. See her review of this and other New Fantasyland attractions at **tinyurl.com/newfantasylandreview.**

This mom from Utah concurs with Liliane:

Seven Dwarfs Mine Train is the most overrated ride EVER. My kids (ages 6 and 7) were completely bored standing in line and unimpressed with the ride. If you have kids over 40" tall, skip it and save your time and FastPass+ for Space Mountain and Big Thunder Mountain Railroad.

If you have only a day to see the Magic Kingdom, make advance Fast-Pass+ reservations for around 9:30 a.m. at Big Thunder Mountain Railroad and around 3:30 p.m. at Space Mountain. On the day of your visit, ride Seven Dwarfs Mine Train as soon as the park opens, then Splash Mountain. If you have two mornings, do Seven Dwarfs Mine Train, Splash Mountain, and Big Thunder Mountain on one day and Space Mountain the next.

Ricky

Seven Dwarfs Mine Train is a good roller coaster because you don't really feel it sway side to side too much. And if you have to be stuck in a line, at least there are fun things to do in this one.

Under the Sea: Journey of the Little Mermaid
(FastPass+) ★★★½

APPEAL BY AGE	PRESCHOOL ★★★★½		GRADE SCHOOL ★★★★	TEENS ★★★½
YOUNG ADULTS ★★★★		OVER 30 ★★★★		SENIORS ★★★★

What it is Dark ride retelling the film's story. **Scope and scale** Major attraction. **Fright potential** Evil Ursula and dark effects frighten kids under age 7 years. **Bottleneck rating** 8. **When to go** Before 10:30 a.m. or the last 2 hours the park is open; rarely a good choice for FastPass+. **Authors' rating** Cute, but most effects are too simple for an attraction this big; ★★★½. **Duration of ride** About 5½ minutes. **Average wait in line per 100 people ahead of you** 3 minutes. **Loading speed** Fast.

Under The Sea takes riders through almost a dozen scenes retelling the story of *The Little Mermaid* film, with Audio-Animatronics, video effects, and a vibrant 3-D set the size of a small theater. Guests board a clamshell-shaped ride vehicle running along a continuously moving track (similar to The Haunted Mansion's). Once you're on board, the ride descends "under water," past Ariel's grotto and to King Triton's undersea kingdom. The most detailed animatronic is Ursula the octopus, and she's a beauty. Other scenes hit the film's highlights, including Ariel meeting Prince Eric, her deal with Ursula to become human, and, of course, the happy couple at the end.

Try to ride early in the morning or late at night.

Liliane

I was disappointed! The ride feels very much like a clone of The Seas with Nemo & Friends at Epcot. The interactive queuing area is whimsical, but who wants to be stuck in a queuing area?

TOMORROWLAND

AT VARIOUS POINTS IN ITS HISTORY, Tomorrowland's attractions presented life's possibilities in adventures ranging from the modern-day to the distant future. The problem that stymied Disney repeatedly was that the future came faster and looked different than what they'd envisioned.

Today, Tomorrowland's theme makes the least sense of any area in any Disney park. Its current attractions are based on gas-powered race cars, rocket travel (two rides), a look back at 20th-century technology, two rides with aliens, and a comedy show with monsters. It's not so much a vision of the future as it is a collection of attractions that don't fit anywhere else in the park.

Astro Orbiter ★★

APPEAL BY AGE	PRESCHOOL ★★★★	GRADE SCHOOL ★★★★	TEENS ★★★½
YOUNG ADULTS ★★★		OVER 30 ★★★	SENIORS ★★½

What it is Buck Rogers–style rockets revolving around a central axis. **Scope and scale** Minor attraction. **Fright potential** Visually intimidating waiting area for a relatively tame ride. **Bottleneck rating** 10. **When to go** Before 11 a.m. or the last hour the park is open. **Special comment** This attraction is not as innocuous as it appears. **Authors' rating** Not worth the wait; ★★. **Duration of ride** 1½ minutes. **Average wait in line per 100 people ahead of you** 13½ minutes. **Loading speed** Slow.

Parents, beware! If you're prone to motion sickness, this ride a) spins round and round; b) is faster than Dumbo; and c) for added "fun," a joystick lets you raise and lower the rocket throughout your 1½-minute journey. We like to ride the Astro Orbiter at night. The combination of lighting and the view is spectacular.

I just went on this ride for the first time recently. You take an elevator up, and you get to fly your own rocket ship. I like being up so high because you can see pretty much all of Disney World from up there.

Julia

Buzz Lightyear's Space Ranger Spin
(FastPass+) ★★★★

APPEAL BY AGE	PRESCHOOL ★★★★½	GRADE SCHOOL ★★★★½	TEENS ★★★★
YOUNG ADULTS ★★★★		OVER 30 ★★★★	SENIORS ★★★★

What it is Combination space travel–themed indoor ride and shooting gallery. **Scope and scale** Minor attraction. **Fright potential** Dark ride with cartoonlike aliens may frighten some preschoolers. **Bottleneck rating** 8. **When to go** First or last hour the park is open, or use FastPass+. **Authors' rating** A real winner! ★★★★. **Duration of ride** About 4½ minutes. **Average wait in line per 100 people ahead of you** 3 minutes. **Loading speed** Fast.

Once you get the hang of it, you'll come back for more, to infinity and beyond!

This is my favorite ride at the Magic Kingdom. I like how you earn points and how you get to compare your score with your friends and family in the end. It's so cool that the cars spin around while your ride.

Ethan

Toy Story is my favorite Disney movie. It's fun to shoot the targets. It's even better when I can get a higher score than my little brother.

Isaac

The ride is based on the space-commando character Buzz Lightyear from the 1995 Disney-Pixar feature Toy Story. *Did you know that Tom Hanks and Tim Allen are the voices of Woody and Buzz?*

I love this ride. There's a funny part when you get to see yourself shooting the aliens. I always look so serious!

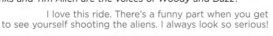
Julia

Monsters, Inc. Laugh Floor (*FastPass+*) ★★★½

APPEAL BY AGE PRESCHOOL ★★★★   **GRADE SCHOOL** ★★★★½ **TEENS** ★★★★
YOUNG ADULTS ★★★★   **OVER 30** ★★★★   **SENIORS** ★★★★½

What it is Interactive animated comedy routines. **Scope and scale** Major attraction. **Fright potential** Not much is frightening, but they are monsters, after all. **Bottleneck rating** 8. **When to go** Before 11 a.m. or after 4 p.m. **Special comment** Audience members may be asked to participate in skits. **Author's rating** Good concept; jokes are hit-and-miss; ★★★½. **Duration of show** About 15 minutes including preshow. **Probable waiting time** 25 minutes.

We learned in Disney-Pixar's *Monsters, Inc.* that children's screams could be converted into electricity, which was used to power a town inhabited by monsters. During the film, the monsters discovered that children's laughter was an even better source of energy. In this attraction, the monsters have set up a comedy club to capture as many laughs as possible. Mike Wazowski, the one-eyed character from the film, emcees the club's three comedy acts. Each consists of an animated monster (most not seen in the film) trying out various bad puns, knock-knock jokes, and Abbott and Costello–like routines. Using the same cutting-edge technology as Epcot's popular *Turtle Talk with Crush,* behind-the-scenes Disney employees voice the characters and often interact with audience members during the skits. As with any comedy set, some performers are funny and some are not, but Disney has shown a willingness to experiment with new routines and jokes. A Sioux Falls, South Dakota, mom is a big fan:

> Laugh Floor *was great. It's amazing how the characters interact with the audience—I got picked on twice without trying. Plus, kids can text jokes to Roz.*

> *Monsters, Inc. Laugh Floor* is a cool attraction, but I don't like things where I could get called on.

Ricky

 The show is based on the 2001 Pixar film Monsters, Inc., *starring Billy Crystal (voice) in the role of Mike Wazowski. It won an Oscar for best song.*

Space Mountain (*FastPass+*) ★★★★

APPEAL BY AGE PRESCHOOL ★★★† **GRADE SCHOOL** ★★★★½ **TEENS** ★★★★★
YOUNG ADULTS ★★★★½   **OVER 30** ★★★★½   **SENIORS** ★★★½

†*Some preschoolers love Space Mountain; others are frightened by it.*

What it is Roller coaster in the dark. **Scope and scale** Super-headliner. **Fright potential** Very intense roller coaster in the dark; the Magic Kingdom's wildest ride and a scary roller coaster by any standard. **Bottleneck rating** 10. **When to go** When the park opens or use FastPass+. **Special comments** Great fun and action; much wilder than Big Thunder Mountain Railroad. Must be 44″ tall to ride; children younger than age 7 must be accompanied by an adult. Switching-off option provided (see page 243). **Authors' rating** An unusual roller coaster with excellent special effects; not to be missed; ★★★★. **Duration of ride** Almost 3 minutes. **Average wait in line per 100 people ahead of you** 3 minutes. **Assumes** Two tracks, one dedicated to FastPass+ riders, dispatching at 21-second intervals. **Loading speed** Moderate–fast.

Dark   Rough   Queasy   Scary

Space Mountain is one of Walt Disney World's zippiest (and darkest) rides, lasting a little less than 3 minutes and including numerous abrupt turns and plummets. However, the top speed is only about 28 mph, a leisurely pace by 21st-century standards.

Space Mountain involves sudden blackouts, as do many thrill rides at Disney World. Those who suffer from claustrophobia (Liliane), who tend to panic in the dark (Liliane), or who have vision problems with extremes of light and darkness (Liliane) should avoid this attraction, as should those with neck or back problems or vertigo. Plunged into darkness and bouncing around like a marble in a spittoon, many warmly recall Space Mountain as the longest 3 minutes of their lives. Your kids will love it.

As a headliner, Space Mountain goes through periodic refurbishments to add effects and maintain ride quality. Past improvements include new lighting and effects, an improved sound system and sound track, and interactive games in the queue to help pass the time in line. It may just be from hearing asteroids whiz past your vehicle, but we think the current ride is slightly faster than it used to be. If you don't catch Space Mountain first in the morning, use FastPass+ or try again during the 30 minutes before closing.

I dream of riding Space Mountain at the pace of Spaceship Earth in Epcot. At last, I would be able to enjoy the twinkling lights.

If you're brave, try to get the front seat for this ride. It's dark, it's fast, and you don't know when the next drop or turn comes.

Liliane

Ethan

Stitch's Great Escape! ★★

APPEAL BY AGE	PRESCHOOL ★★½		GRADE SCHOOL ★★½		TEENS ★★½
YOUNG ADULTS ★★½		OVER 30 ★★		SENIORS ★★½	

What it is Theater-in-the-round sci-fi adventure show. **Scope and scale** Major attraction. **Fright potential** Frightens children of all ages. **Bottleneck rating** 6. **When to go** Before 11 a.m. or after 6 p.m.; try during parades. **Special comments** Must be 40" tall. Switching-off option provided (see page 243). **Authors' rating** It stinks—literally; ★★. **Duration of show** About 12 minutes. **Preshow** About 6 minutes. **Probable waiting time** 5–15 minutes.

Dark
Loud
Scary

Stitch, a prisoner of the galactic authorities, is being transferred to a processing facility en route to his final place of incarceration. He manages to escape by employing an efficient though gross trick that knocks out power to the facility. Enough to scare the pants off many kids age 6 and younger—you're held in your seat by overhead restraints and subjected to something weird clambering around you and whispering to you in a theater darker than a stack of black cats.

I love Stitch myself, but I agree with parents of young children who have complained about how scary the show is—the overhead restraint prevents you from leaving your seat to comfort your child if the need arises.

Liliane

Movie Tip

Skip the show, but don't discount the movie. Lilo & Stitch *(released in 2002) is a great family flick. The Hawaiian concept of* 'ohana, *which in Hawaiian means "extended family" including friends, is the cornerstone philoso phy of this wonderful film. The movie reminds children about the importance of good behavior and points out to adults that there is good inside every child, no matter how rotten he or she may behave at times.*

I found this kind of boring. Surprisingly, there was a long line.

Ethan

Tomorrowland Speedway *(FastPass+)* ★★

APPEAL BY AGE	PRESCHOOL ★★★★½	GRADE SCHOOL ★★★★½	TEENS ★★★½
YOUNG ADULTS ★★★		OVER 30 ★★★	SENIORS ★★★

What it is Drive-'em-yourself miniature cars. **Scope and scale** Major attraction. **Fright potential** The noise of the waiting area frightens some preschoolers; otherwise, not frightening. **Bottleneck rating** 9. **When to go** Before 10 a.m. or in the last 2 hours the park is open. **Special comment** Must be 54" tall to drive unassisted. **Authors' rating** Boring for adults; great for preschoolers; ★★. **Duration of ride** About 4¼ minutes. **Average wait in line per 100 people ahead of you** 4½ minutes; assumes 285-car turnover every 20 minutes. **Loading speed** Slow.

The sleek cars and racetrack noise will get your younger kids hopped up to ride this extremely prosaic attraction. The minimum height requirement of 54 inches means the younger (or shorter) set will have to ride with an adult. We suggest that you work the accelerator and brakes and let your future Danica Patrick steer the car. The loading and unloading speeds are excruciatingly slow, and the attraction offers hardly any protection from the sun.

Tomorrowland Transit Authority PeopleMover ★★★½

APPEAL BY AGE	PRESCHOOL ★★★★	GRADE SCHOOL ★★★★	TEENS ★★★★
YOUNG ADULTS ★★★★		OVER 30 ★★★★	SENIORS ★★★★½

What it is Scenic tour of Tomorrowland. **Scope and scale** Minor attraction. **Fright potential** Not frightening in any respect. **Bottleneck rating** 3. **When to go** During hot, crowded times of day (11:30 a.m.–4:30 p.m.). **Special comments** A good way to check out the lines at Space

Thumbs Up for the Whole Family

Mountain and the Speedway. **Authors' rating** Scenic and relaxing; ★★★½. **Duration of ride** 10 minutes. **Average wait in line per 100 people ahead of you** 1½ minutes; assumes 39 trains operating. **Loading speed** Fast.

There is never a line, and the ride is ideal for taking a break. It's also a great way to see Tomorrowland all aglow at night. The route gives a sneak preview of Buzz Lightyear's Space Ranger Spin, and you can check on those screams emanating from Space Mountain. Most of the time cast members will let you ride several times in a row without having to get off. This last thing, according to many moms, makes the ride a great option for nursing.

Ethan

This is good to ride when your feet hurt.

Walt Disney's Carousel of Progress ★★★

APPEAL BY AGE	PRESCHOOL ★★★	GRADE SCHOOL ★★★	TEENS ★★★½
YOUNG ADULTS ★★★★		OVER 30 ★★★★	SENIORS ★★★★½

What it is Audio-Animatronic theater production. **Scope and scale** Major attraction. **Fright potential** Not frightening in any respect. **Bottleneck rating** 4. **When to go** Anytime. **Authors' rating** Nostalgic, warm, and happy; ★★★. **Duration of show** 21 minutes. **Preshow** Documentary on the attraction's long history. **Probable waiting time** Less than 10 minutes.

Walt Disney's Carousel of Progress offers a nostalgic look at how technology and electricity have changed the lives of an animatronic family over several generations from circa 1900 to 1990. The family is easy to identify with, and a cheerful, sentimental tune bridges the generations. Adults will be amused at the references to laser discs and car phones as examples of modern technology; kids will be confused.

The *Carousel* handles big crowds effectively and is a good choice during busier times of day. Because of its age, this attraction seems to have more minor operational glitches than most attractions, so you may be subjected to the same dialog and songs several times. Look at it as extra air-conditioning.

LIVE ENTERTAINMENT *and* PARADES *in the* MAGIC KINGDOM

IT'S IMPOSSIBLE TO TAKE IN all the many live-entertainment offerings at the Magic Kingdom in a single day. To experience both the attractions and the live entertainment, we recommend that you allocate at least two days to this park. In addition to parades, stage shows, and fireworks, check the daily entertainment schedule (*Times Guide*) or ask a cast member about concerts in Fantasyland, the Flag Retreat at Town Square, and the appearances of the various bands, singers, and street performers that roam the park daily. WDW live-entertainment guru Steve Soares usually posts the Magic Kingdom's performance schedule about a week in advance at **wdwent.com.**

Parades at the Magic Kingdom are full-fledged spectaculars with dozens of Disney characters and amazing special effects. Remember that parades disrupt traffic, making it nearly impossible to move around the park when one is going on. Parades also draw thousands of guests away from the attractions, making parade time the perfect moment to catch your favorite attraction with a shorter line. Finally, be advised that the Walt Disney World Railroad shuts down during parades.

The best place to view a parade is the upper platform of the **Walt Disney Railroad station,** but you'll have to stake out your position 30–45 minutes before the event. Try also, especially on rainy days, the **covered walkway between Liberty Tree Tavern and The Diamond Horseshoe Saloon,** on the border of Liberty Square and Frontierland.

Following is a short list of daily events with special appeal for families with children:

LILIANE The parade is a must-see—great music, outstanding costumes, and more than 100 live performers. The 26-foot-tall Maleficent dragon is awe-inspiring. Disney really went big with this one.

AFTERNOON PARADE Usually staged at 3 p.m., this parade features floats and marching Disney characters. A new production, **Festival of Fantasy** (★★★★), debuted in 2014, with an original score and new floats paying tribute to *The Little Mermaid*, *Brave*, and *Frozen*, among other Disney films. Many of the floats' pieces spin and swing to extremes not normally found in Disney parades: The *Tangled* platform has characters riding swinging wood hammers from one side of the street to the other. The most talked-about float is Maleficent (the villain from *Sleeping Beauty*) in dragon form—she spits actual fire at a couple of points along the route.

BAY LAKE AND SEVEN SEAS LAGOON FLOATING ELECTRICAL PAGEANT ★★★★ Performed at nightfall at about 9 p.m. most of the year on Seven Seas Lagoon and Bay Lake, this pageant is the perfect culmination of a wonderful day. You have to leave the Magic Kingdom to see the show—take the monorail to the Polynesian Village Resort, get the kids a snack and yourself a drink, and walk to the end of the pier to watch. Pure magic, less the crowds. You can also watch the show at the Grand Floridian at 9:15 p.m. and at the Contemporary at 10:05 p.m.

CASTLE FORECOURT STAGE ★★★½ The 20-minute *Dream-Along with Mickey* live show features Mickey, Minnie, Donald, Goofy, and a peck of princesses and other secondary characters, plus human backup dancers, in a show built around the premise that—*quelle horreur!*—Donald doesn't believe in the power of dreams. Crisis is averted through a frenetic whirlwind of song and dance.

CELEBRATE THE MAGIC ★★★★½ In one of the most imaginative shows yet, videos and special effects are set to music and projected nightly on Cinderella Castle. The effects are tremendous: In one vignette, the entire castle becomes a kaleidoscope of brightly colored Mickeys and Donalds; in another, flames appear throughout the castle's windows to emulate a scene from the Pirates of the Caribbean ride. Best of all, Disney regularly

LILIANE If all you want is a serene spot to watch the fireworks or the Bay Lake and Seven Seas Lagoon Floating Electrical Pageant, you don't need to spend big bucks. The gardens of the Grand Floridian are perfect for the fireworks, and the beach of the Polynesian Village Resort does the trick for the pageant.

FAVORITE EATS IN MAGIC KINGDOM

LAND | SERVICE LOCATION | FOOD ITEM

MAIN STREET
- **Main Street Bakery** | Homemade goodies & crisped-rice treats

ADVENTURELAND
- **Tortuga Tavern** *(open seasonally)* | Quesadillas for kids

FANTASYLAND
- **Friar's Nook** | Hot dogs with chips
- **The Pinocchio Village Haus** | Mac and cheese & pizza

FRONTIERLAND
- **Pecos Bill Tall Tale Inn & Cafe** | Burgers & great fixin's station

LIBERTY SQUARE
- **Columbia Harbour House** | Soup & sandwiches • **Sleepy Hollow** | Funnel cake

TOMORROWLAND
- **Cosmic Ray's Starlight Cafe** | Rotisserie chicken, ribs, & kosher choices
- **The Lunching Pad** | Coney Island dogs, pretzels, & frozen soda

updates the show's content to keep it fresh. While the show's sound track is invariably excessively sentimental, the visuals more than make up for it. We rate this as not to be missed.

For the winter holidays, *Celebrate the Magic* gets a *Frozen*-inspired retheming. Titled **A Frozen Holiday Wish,** the castle's projections include Anna, Elsa, Olaf, and other stars from that blockbuster, plus the usual cavalcade of classic Disney characters.

CHARACTER SHOWS AND APPEARANCES A number of characters are usually on hand to greet guests when the park opens. Because they snarl pedestrian traffic and stop most kids dead in their tracks, this is sort of a mixed blessing. Check your daily *Times Guide* for character greeting locations and times, or see our table on pages 246 and 247.

EVENING PARADE Evening parade performances vary by season, happening as often as twice a night during the busy times of year, to two or three times a week during the less busy seasons. We rate the evening parade as not to be missed.

The **Main Street Electrical Parade (MSEP; ★★★★)** is the current nightly cavalcade at the Magic Kingdom. Its sound track—*Baroque Hoedown*—is a bubbly, synthesizer-heavy late-1960s period piece. In our opinion, the Magic Kingdom's nighttime parade is always the best in Walt Disney World, and the Electrical Parade is the standard against which everything else is judged. Disney is known to swap out parades and may do so at any time, so if you're at Disney World while MSEP is running, make a special trip to see it.

BOB FastPass+ is available for premium areas to view the afternoon and evening parades. You still need to show up early for a good spot, though.

FLAG RETREAT At 5 p.m. daily at Town Square (railroad-station end of Main Street). Sometimes performed with great fanfare and college marching bands, sometimes with a smaller Disney band.

MAGIC KINGDOM BANDS Banjo, Dixieland, steel-drum, and marching bands play daily throughout the park.

MOVE IT! SHAKE IT! DANCE AND PLAY IT! STREET PARTY ★★★½ Starting at the railroad end of Main Street, U.S.A., and working toward the Central Plaza, this short walk incorporates about a dozen guests with a handful of floats, Disney characters, and entertainers. An original tune called "Party Up!" serves as the theme song, and there's a good amount of interaction between the entertainers and the crowd.

MICKEY'S HALLOWEEN AND CHRISTMAS PARTIES The Magic Kingdom hosts special after-hours, holiday-themed events in September, October, November, and December, celebrating Halloween and Christmas. These events require separate admission (see pages 47–55 for details) and can sell out. For full details—including photos, the best days to go, touring advice, and more—go to **blog.touringplans.com** and search for "Halloween Party" or "Christmas Party."

TINKER BELL'S FLIGHT This nice special effect in the sky above

Cinderella Castle heralds the beginning of the fireworks show (when the park is open late).

WISHES FIREWORKS SHOW *FASTPASS+/*★★★★★ Memorable vignettes and music from beloved Disney films combine with a stellar fireworks display while Jiminy Cricket narrates a lump-in-your-throat story about making wishes come true.

If you have FastPass+ reservations for the fireworks, your viewing location will be somewhere in the Central Plaza area, between the end of Main Street, U.S.A., and Cinderella Castle. Otherwise, anywhere along Main Street is fine, especially if you plan to leave the park immediately afterward. If we intend to remain in the park, our two favorite spots are in Fantasyland, between Seven Dwarfs Mine Train and *Enchanted Tales with Belle,* or on the bridge between the Central Plaza and Tomorrowland.

A spot we'd previously recommended, in the **Tomorrowland Terrace** area, was apparently so good that Disney decided to start charging for it. To view *Wishes* from this location now costs $49 per adult and $29 per child. The viewing area is available starting 1 hour before the show, and the event includes a dessert buffet and nonalcoholic beverages. Reservations can be made 60 days in advance by calling ☎ 407-WDW-DINE (939-3463). If you make a reservation more than two weeks in advance, you'll be given a default reservation time of 6 p.m. for the dessert party and told to call back within two weeks of your trip for the actual time.

KIERAN If you're like me and you don't care about seeing Tinker Bell fly, then go behind the castle to watch the fireworks. The view is fantastic and the crowds are much smaller. We usually grab a seat at one of the outdoor restaurants and enjoy the show. It's nice to sit down after a long day.

WISHES FIREWORKS CRUISE For a different view, you can watch the fireworks from Seven Seas Lagoon aboard a chartered pontoon boat. The charter costs $293 for up to 8 people and just under $350 for 10 (tax included). Chips, soda, and water are provided; sandwiches and more-substantial food items may be arranged through reservations. Your Disney captain will take you for a little cruise and then position the boat in a perfect place to watch the fireworks. Life jackets are provided, but wearing them is at your discretion. To reserve a charter, call ☎ 407-WDW-PLAY (939-7529) at exactly 7 a.m. Eastern time about 180 days before the day you want to cruise.

EXIT STRATEGIES

ARMIES OF GUESTS leave the Magic Kingdom after evening parades and fireworks. The Disney transportation system gets overwhelmed, causing long waits in boarding areas.

BOB Digital displays at the Magic Kingdom exit show the wait to board the monorails and ferry—take the one with the shorter line.

If you're parked at the Transportation and Ticket Center (TTC) and are intent on beating the crowd, view the early parade from the Town Square end of Main Street, leaving the park as soon as the parade ends and before the fireworks begin. If you're staying at a hotel serviced by the ferry, try to catch the ferry that will be crossing Seven Seas Lagoon while the fireworks are in progress. The best vantage point is on the top deck to the right of the pilothouse as you face the Magic Kingdom. If you don't want to board the boat that's loading, stop at the gate and let people pass you. You'll be the first to board the next boat.

If you don't have a stroller (or are willing to forgo the $1 return refund for rental strollers), catch the Walt Disney World Railroad in Frontierland and ride to the park exit at Main Street. Don't cut it too close—the train stops running during the parade.

If you're on the Tomorrowland side of the park, a new passageway runs from between The Plaza Restaurant and Tomorrowland Terrace, behind the east side of Main Street, to Tony's Town Square Restaurant near the park exit. If you're on the Adventureland side of the park, another new path runs from First Aid to the Main Street Fire Station near the park exit. However, these passageways aren't always open.

If the new path is closed, cut through Tomorrowland Terrace. Before you reach Main Street, bear left into the side door of the corner shop. Main Street shops have interior doors allowing you to pass from one shop to the next without having to get on Main Street. Work your way from shop to shop until you reach Town Square. At Town Square, bear left and move to the train station and the park exit.

This strategy won't work if you're on the Adventureland side of the park because when you pop out of the Emporium at Town Square, you'll be trapped by the parade. As soon as the last float passes, however, you can bolt for the exit.

Strollers, wheelchairs, and ECVs make navigating the crowds even more difficult. If you have one of these, or you're staying at a Disney hotel not served by the monorail and must depend on Disney transportation, watch the early parade and fireworks, and then enjoy the attractions until about 20–25 minutes before the late parade is scheduled to begin. Then leave the park using one of the strategies listed above, and catch the Disney bus or boat back to your hotel.

MAGIC KINGDOM TOURING PLANS

BOB Don't worry that other people will be following the plans and render them useless. Fewer than 2 in every 100 people in the park will have been exposed to this information.

OUR STEP-BY-STEP TOURING PLANS are field-tested, independently verified itineraries that will keep you moving counter to the crowd flow and allow you to see as much as possible in a single day with minimum time wasted in line.

We developed many of these plans when we were preparing to visit the Magic Kingdom with our own children (ages 2–8). Some plans offer a midday break of at least 3 hours back at your hotel. It's debatable whether the kids will need the nap more than you, but you'll thank us later, we promise.

If you have just one day to spend in the Magic Kingdom, our **single-day plans** will allow you to see the best attractions for kids while avoiding crowds and long waits in line. If you're looking for a more relaxed, less structured tour of the park, try the **one-and-a-half, two-day,** or **Sleepyhead plan.** These alternatives have less backtracking. The Sleepyhead plan assumes that you'll get to the park around 11 a.m., so it's great for mornings when you don't feel like getting out of bed early.

LILIANE Switching off allows adults to enjoy the more adventuresome attractions while keeping the group together.

We generally recommend eating lunch outside of the Magic Kingdom, but if you can get an Advance Reservation for **Be Our Guest** restaurant, go for it—it serves the best food in the Magic Kingdom. Our other favorites in the park are the **Columbia Harbour House** in Liberty Square, **Pecos Bill's** in Frontierland, and **Cosmic Ray's** in Tomorrowland.

The different touring plans are described below and on the following page. The descriptions will tell you for whom (for example, tweens, parents with preschoolers, grandparents, and so on) or for what situation (such as sleeping late) the plans are designed. The actual touring plans are located on pages 455–463. Each plan includes a numbered map of the park to help you find your way around.

We've also listed the attractions most likely to need FastPass+ and the approximate return times for which you should try to make reservations. Check **touringplans.com** for the latest information.

MAGIC KINGDOM HAPPY FAMILY ONE-DAY TOURING PLAN This is a one-day touring plan that includes something for everyone in the family: small children, tweens (children ages 8–12), teenagers, parents, and seniors. The plan keeps the entire family together for most of the day, plus lunch and dinner. A midday break is integrated into the day's touring.

The plan includes attractions for the whole family, such as *Enchanted Tales with Belle* and Seven Dwarfs Mine Train in Fantasyland and The Magic Carpets of Aladdin in Adventureland. For older kids and teens, we recommend thrill rides such as Space Mountain and Big Thunder Mountain, with both groups getting back together when each is done.

MAGIC KINGDOM ONE-DAY TOURING PLAN FOR GRANDPARENTS WITH SMALL CHILDREN The attractions in this touring plan are generally those rated at least three stars (out of five) by both seniors and small children, plus a handful of senior-friendly attractions that children just love. Attractions include Seven Dwarfs Mine Train and *Enchanted Tales with Belle* in Fantasyland and Jungle Cruise and Pirates of the Caribbean in Adventureland. We don't try to cover the entire park, either: Most of Tomorrowland is left as an option toward the end if time permits and everyone's feeling up for it.

MAGIC KINGDOM ONE-DAY TOURING PLAN FOR TWEENS AND THEIR PARENTS A one-day plan for parents with children ages 8–12, it includes most attractions rated three stars and higher by this age group and sets aside ample time for lunch and dinner. Includes newer attractions (Seven Dwarfs Mine Train, Under the Sea: Journey of the Little Mermaid, and Pete's Silly Sideshow) along with Magic Kingdom classics (Space Mountain, Splash Mountain, and Big Thunder Mountain).

MAGIC KINGDOM TWO-DAY TOURING PLAN FOR PARENTS WITH SMALL CHILDREN This is a two-day touring plan designed specifically to eliminate extra walking and backtracking. It is a comprehensive touring plan of the Magic Kingdom and includes nearly every child-friendly attraction in the park. The plan features long midday breaks for lunch and naps outside the park.

MAGIC KINGDOM TWO-DAY SLEEPYHEAD TOURING PLAN FOR PARENTS WITH SMALL CHILDREN Another version of the two-day touring plan described above, this plan allows families with young children to sleep in, arrive at the park in the late morning, and still see the very best attractions in the Magic Kingdom over two days. The plan uses FastPass+ to reduce your waits at the most popular attractions, including *Enchanted Tales with Belle,* Peter Pan's Flight, and Seven Dwarfs Mine Train in Fantasyland.

PARENTS' MAGIC KINGDOM TOURING PLAN—ONE AFTERNOON AND ONE FULL DAY This day-and-a-half plan works perfectly if you're arriving in Orlando late in the morning of your first vacation day and can't wait to start touring. It also works great for families who want to sleep in one morning after spending a full day in the Magic Kingdom the day before.

The attractions in these plans are the same as those found in the standard one-day plans for parents with small children, so these day-and-a-half itineraries also work as relaxed versions of those plans. Both plans employ FastPass+ and take advantage of lower evening crowds to visit other popular attractions. The plans should work well during the more crowded times of the year.

PRELIMINARY INSTRUCTIONS FOR ALL MAGIC KINGDOM TOURING PLANS

ON DAYS OF MODERATE-TO-HEAVY ATTENDANCE, follow your chosen touring plan exactly, deviating only:

1. When you aren't interested in an attraction it lists. Simply skip it and proceed to the next step.

2. When you encounter a very long line at an attraction the touring plan calls for. Crowds ebb and flow at the park, and an unusually long line may have gathered at an attraction to which you're directed. For example, you arrive at The Haunted Mansion and find extremely long lines. It's possible that this is a temporary situation caused by several hundred people arriving en masse from a recently concluded performance of *The Hall of Presidents* nearby. If this is the case, skip The Haunted Mansion and go to the next step, returning later to retry.

BEFORE YOU GO

1. Call ☎ 407-824-4321 or check **disneyworld.com** the day before you go to check the official opening time.

2. Purchase admission and make FastPass+ reservations before you arrive.

3. Familiarize yourself with park-opening procedures (described on page 228) and reread the touring plan you've chosen.

MAGIC KINGDOM TRIVIA QUIZ

1. What is the name of the latest role-playing game at the Magic Kingdom?
  a. The Pirates League
  b. Agent P Strikes Back
  c. A Pirate's Adventure
  d. The Many Adventures of Cap'n Jack

2. Where do Anna and Elsa, the heroines from *Frozen,* greet guests?
  a. Storybook Circus
  b. Town Square Theater
  c. Fairytale Garden
  d. Princess Fairytale Hall

3. Whom does Princess Tiana marry in *The Princess and the Frog*?
  a. Prince Eric
  b. Prince Naveen
  c. Prince Charming
  d. Prince Philip

4. What body of water does the *Liberty Belle* Riverboat travel?
  a. The Sassagoula River
  b. Seven Seas Lagoon
  c. The Rivers of America
  d. Echo Lake

5. Which character does *not* meet guests at Pete's Silly Sideshow?
  a. Mickey
  b. Minnie
  c. Donald
  d. Daisy

6. What was the Prince Charming Regal Carrousel formerly called?
  a. Merida's Wild Ride
  c. Cinderella's Golden Carrousel
  b. Ariel's Carrousel Under the Sea
  d. Prince Eric's Royal Carrousel

7. Who plays Madame Leota in the *Haunted Mansion* movie?
  a. Jennifer Tilly
  b. Demi Moore
  c. Raquel Alessi
  d. Eva Mendes

8. What is inside Beast's Castle?
  a. A store
  b. A ride
  c. A restaurant
  d. A show

9. Which attraction is inspired by the movie *Song of the South*?
  a. It's a Small World
  b. Splash Mountain
  c. *Walt Disney's Enchanted Tiki Room*
  d. *Enchanted Tales with Belle*

10. What is the name of the new attraction that opened in 2014 at Fantasyland?
  a. Pete's Silly Sideshow
  b. Ariel's Grotto
  c. Seven Dwarfs Mine Train
  d. Casey Jr. Splash 'N' Soak Station

Answers can be found on page 437.

PART EIGHT

EPCOT

EDUCATION, INSPIRATION, AND CORPORATE IMAGERY are the focus at Epcot, the most adult of the Walt Disney World theme parks. What it gains in taking a futuristic, visionary, and technological look at the world, it loses, just a bit, in warmth, happiness, and charm. Some people find the attempts at education to be superficial; others want more entertainment and less education. Most visitors, however, are in between, finding plenty of amusement *and* information.

Epcot's themed areas are distinctly different. **Future World** combines Disney creativity and the technological resources of major corporations to examine where humankind has come from and where it's going. **World Showcase,** which features landmarks, cuisine, and culture from almost a dozen nations, is meant to be a sort of permanent world's fair.

Epcot is more than twice as large as the Magic Kingdom, so unless one day is all you have, plan on spending two days at Epcot to savor all it has to offer. Unlike the Magic Kingdom, Epcot may not seem to be a natural for kids at face value, but rest assured that families can have as much fun here as at any of the other theme parks.

Now for the practical stuff: Future World always opens first; that's where you start your day. While most of its attractions stay open until the entire park closes, a few close around 7 p.m. most of the year. If you're lodging at a Disney hotel, consider visiting when the park offers morning or evening Extra Magic Hours.

Once you arrive, pick up a park map and the *Times Guide* daily entertainment schedule, which lists all the attractions open during both regular hours and Extra Magic Hours. If you intend to stay for Extra Magic Hours in the evening, each member of your party will need to have his or her MagicBand.

Stroller, wheelchair, and **ECV/ESV rentals** are available inside the main entrance to the left, toward the rear of the Entrance Plaza. For **storage lockers,** turn right at Spaceship Earth. The **Baby Care Center** is on the World Showcase side of the Odyssey Center complex, to the rear of Test Track. At the same location are the **First Aid Center** and **Lost Persons.** For a live-entertainment schedule and dining reservations, stop at **Guest Relations,** to the left of Spaceship Earth. **Lost and Found** is located at the main entrance. **ATMs** are available outside the main entrance, on the Future World Bridge, and in World Showcase at the Germany Pavilion. Across from Disney's Port Orleans Resort, **Best Friends Pet Resort** provides a comfortable home away from home for Fido, Fluffy, and all their pet pals.

FASTPASS+ ATTRACTIONS AT EPCOT

EPCOT OFFERS FASTPASS+ for 11 attractions in two tiers:

TIER A *(Choose one per day)*	TIER B *(Choose two per day)*
• *IllumiNations* (or its replacement)	• *Captain EO*
• Living with the Land	• Epcot Character Spot
• Soarin'	• Journey into Imagination with Figment
• Test Track	• Mission: Space (Green or Orange)
	• Spaceship Earth
	• The Seas with Nemo & Friends
	• *Turtle Talk with Crush*

(*Note:* **Frozen Ever After** and the **Royal Sommerhus Meet and Greet** will most likely be FastPass+ attractions as well, but we won't know the tier until closer to their opening dates in 2016.)

Because the tiers limit the number and combinations of FastPass+ attractions you can experience, much of our Epcot touring strategy is dictated by the popular **Soarin'** and **Test Track** in Tier A—long lines at these two mean that you'll want to get one of them out of the way first thing in the morning. (**Living with the Land,** also in Tier A, is rarely a good use of FastPass+ as it doesn't get the same crowds as the other two.)

Our most frequent FastPass+ recommendation is for **Spaceship Earth** in Future World, usually around lunch. Because wait times can reach 30–40 minutes, it's one of the best choices in Tier B.

On the other hand, we've identified four attractions for which Fast-Pass+ is *never* necessary: *Captain EO,* **Journey into Imagination with Figment,** the nonspinning **Mission: Space (Green),** and **Epcot Character Spot.** In addition to these four, *IllumiNations* (or its successor) is a must-see, and FastPass+ gets you into a special viewing area for the show, but you still have to arrive a good 30–40 minutes in advance to get a good spot. What's more, there are so many other good viewing spots around World Showcase Lagoon that it's difficult to recommend FastPass+ for *IllumiNations.*

Look for Epcot FastPass+ kiosks in the following locations:

- At the Soarin' entrance, downstairs in The Land
- At the MyMagic+ Service Center, between Spaceship Earth and Innoventions East
- At the International Gateway entrance to the park

Continued on page 302

Epcot

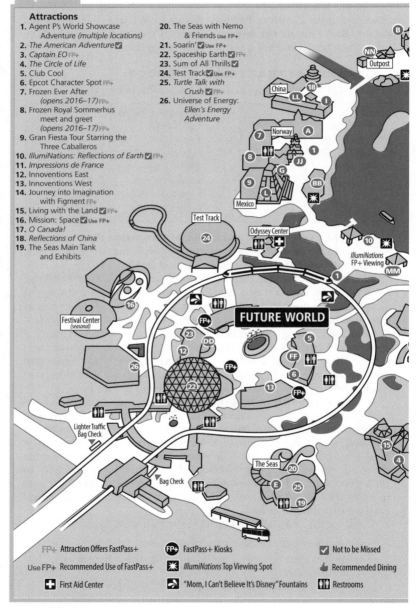

Attractions

1. Agent P's World Showcase Adventure *(multiple locations)*
2. *The American Adventure* ☑
3. *Captain EO* FP+
4. *The Circle of Life*
5. Club Cool
6. Epcot Character Spot FP+
7. Frozen Ever After *(opens 2016–17)* FP+
8. Frozen Royal Sommerhus meet and greet *(opens 2016–17)* FP+
9. Gran Fiesta Tour Starring the Three Caballeros
10. *IllumiNations: Reflections of Earth* ☑ FP+
11. *Impressions de France*
12. Innoventions East
13. Innoventions West
14. Journey into Imagination with Figment FP+
15. Living with the Land ☑ FP+
16. Mission: Space ☑ Use FP+
17. *O Canada!*
18. *Reflections of China*
19. The Seas Main Tank and Exhibits
20. The Seas with Nemo & Friends Use FP+
21. Soarin' ☑ Use FP+
22. Spaceship Earth ☑ FP+
23. Sum of All Thrills ☑
24. Test Track ☑ Use FP+
25. *Turtle Talk with Crush* ☑ FP+
26. Universe of Energy: *Ellen's Energy Adventure*

FP+ Attraction Offers FastPass+

Use FP+ Recommended Use of FastPass+

✚ First Aid Center

FP+ FastPass+ Kiosks

✴ *IllumiNations* Top Viewing Spot

🔁 "Mom, I Can't Believe It's Disney" Fountains

☑ Not to be Missed

👍 Recommended Dining

🚻 Restrooms

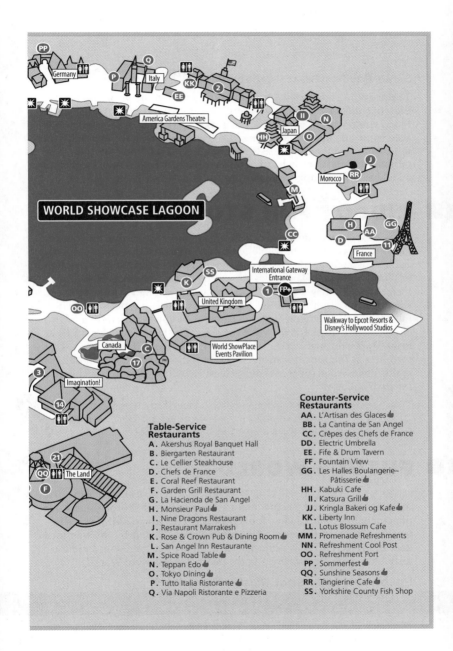

WORLD SHOWCASE LAGOON

Germany

Italy

America Gardens Theatre

Japan

Morocco

Canada

Imagination!

The Land

Canada

Morocco

France

International Gateway Entrance

United Kingdom

World ShowPlace Events Pavilion

Walkway to Epcot Resorts & Disney's Hollywood Studios

Table-Service Restaurants

A. Akershus Royal Banquet Hall
B. Biergarten Restaurant
C. Le Cellier Steakhouse
D. Chefs de France
E. Coral Reef Restaurant
F. Garden Grill Restaurant
G. La Hacienda de San Angel
H. Monsieur Paul 👍
I. Nine Dragons Restaurant
J. Restaurant Marrakesh
K. Rose & Crown Pub & Dining Room 👍
L. San Angel Inn Restaurante
M. Spice Road Table 👍
N. Teppan Edo 👍
O. Tokyo Dining 👍
P. Tutto Italia Ristorante 👍
Q. Via Napoli Ristorante e Pizzeria

Counter-Service Restaurants

AA. L'Artisan des Glaces 👍
BB. La Cantina de San Angel
CC. Crêpes des Chefs de France
DD. Electric Umbrella
EE. Fife & Drum Tavern
FF. Fountain View
GG. Les Halles Boulangerie–
    Pâtisserie 👍
HH. Kabuki Cafe
II. Katsura Grill 👍
JJ. Kringla Bakeri og Kafe 👍
KK. Liberty Inn
LL. Lotus Blossum Cafe
MM. Promenade Refreshments
NN. Refreshment Cool Post
OO. Refreshment Port
PP. Sommerfest
QQ. Sunshine Seasons 👍
RR. Tangierine Cafe 👍
SS. Yorkshire County Fish Shop

Continued from page 299

- In the Future World East walkway, on the way to Mission: Space
- In the Future World West walkway, on the way to The Land

Same-Day FastPass+ Availability

The preceding advice tells you which attractions to focus on when making your *advance* FastPass+ reservations before you get to the park. Once you're in the park, you can make more FastPass+ reservations once your advance reservations have been used or have expired (you must cancel your expired FastPass+ before you can book another). The table at right shows which attractions are likely to have day-of FastPasses available, and the approximate times at which they'll run out.

KIDCOT FUN STOPS

THIS PROGRAM, designed to make Epcot more interesting for younger visitors, is basically a movable feast of simple arts-and-crafts projects. Tables are set up at some locations in Future World and at each pavilion in World Showcase. The tables are staffed by cast members who discuss their native country with the children and engage them in a craft project. Look for the brightly colored Kidcot signs. Participation is free. For a memento and to augment the experience, you can purchase a World Showcase Passport Kit for your children. The kits are sold for $10 at most stores throughout Epcot. As you visit the different lands, cast members at the Kidcot stations will stamp the passport. If your child is really interested in different lands, Guest Relations offers free fact sheets for each country.

Children as young as age 3 will enjoy the Kidcot Fun Stops. If you don't want to spring for the passport, the Disney folks will be happy to stamp an autograph book or just about anything else, including your child's forehead.

Bob

FUTURE WORLD

IMMENSE, GLEAMING FUTURISTIC STRUCTURES define the first themed area beyond Epcot's main entrance. Broad thoroughfares are punctuated with billowing fountains, all reflected in shiny space-age facades. Front and center is **Spaceship Earth,** flanked by **Innoventions East and West.** Pavilions dedicated to mankind's past, present, and future technological achievements ring the perimeter of Future World.

Epcot Character Spot *(FastPass+)* ★★★

APPEAL BY AGE	PRESCHOOL ★★★★½	GRADE SCHOOL ★★★★½	TEENS ★★★★
YOUNG ADULTS ★★★★		OVER 30 ★★★★	SENIORS ★★★

What it is Character greeting venue. **Scope and scale** Diversion. **Fright potential** Not frightening in any respect. **Bottleneck rating** 7. **When to go** Before 11 a.m., or use FastPass+. **Authors' rating** Indoors and air-conditioned; ★★★.

EPCOT
When Same-Day FP+ Runs Out, by Crowd Level

ATTRACTION	LOW CROWDS*	MODERATE CROWDS*	HIGH CROWDS*
Captain EO (if open)	6 p.m.		6–7 p.m.
Epcot Character Spot	4–5 p.m. (all crowd levels)		
IllumiNations (or replacement)	1–2 p.m.	noon–1 p.m.	11 a.m.–noon
Journey into Imagination with Figment	6 p.m.	5–6 p.m.	4–5 p.m.
Living with the Land	6 p.m. (all crowd levels)		
Mission: Space (Orange)	1–3 p.m.	11 a.m.–noon	10 a.m.–noon
The Seas with Nemo and Friends	6–7 p.m.		3–5 p.m.
Soarin'	1–3 p.m.	noon–1 p.m.	11 a.m.
Spaceship Earth	6–7 p.m.	4–5 p.m.	noon–1 p.m.
Test Track	1–3 p.m.	noon–1 p.m.	10 a.m.–noon
Turtle Talk with Crush	6–7 p.m. (all crowd levels)		
* LOW CROWDS (Levels 1–3 on touringplans.com Crowd Calendar)			
* MODERATE CROWDS (Levels 4–7 on touringplans.com Crowd Calendar)			
* HIGH CROWDS (Levels 8–10 on touringplans.com Crowd Calendar)			

Duration of experience 8 minutes. **Probable waiting time** 20–40 minutes. **Queue speed** Slow.

In Future World West, to the right of The Fountain restaurant, Epcot Character Spot offers the chance to meet Disney characters indoors, in air-conditioned comfort. Characters on hand typically include Mickey Mouse, Minnie Mouse, and Pluto. You may also find Chip 'n' Dale outside. Make Epcot Character Spot your first stop of the day at Epcot if you have small kids.

DISNEY DISH WITH JIM HILL

WILL THE FORCE AWAKEN IN INNOVENTIONS WEST? The Imagineers have a temporary solution to the problem of technology progressing faster than Disney can build shows: to turn this part of Future World into an exhibition of props and costumes from the upcoming *Star Wars Episode VII: The Force Awakens.* Why Epcot instead of Hollywood Studios? Because the current plan for 2016 is to start building the new *Star Wars* land at the Studios, making it a major construction zone.

Innovations East and West ★★½

APPEAL BY AGE   PRESCHOOL ★★★½   GRADE SCHOOL ★★★★   TEENS ★★★½   YOUNG ADULTS ★★★   OVER 30 ★★★½   SENIORS ★★★½

What it is Static and hands-on exhibits relating to products and technologies of the near future. **Scope and scale** Minor diversion. **Fright potential** Not frightening in any respect. **Bottleneck rating** 8. **When to go** On your second day at Epcot or after seeing all major attractions. **Special comments** Most exhibits demand time and participation to be rewarding; not much gained here by a quick walk-through. **Authors' rating** We're hoping for a spectacular refurbishment; ★★½.

Note: Currently all of Innovations West and a good chunk of Innovations East are closed for refurbishment, with no reopening date announced.

Innovations—a huge, busy collection of hands-on walk-through exhibits sponsored by corporations—consists of two huge, crescent-shaped, glass-walled structures separated by a central plaza. Electronics and entertainment technology exhibits play a prominent role, as do ecology and "how things work" displays.

However, the future arrives faster and different than expected, so exhibits based on cutting-edge technology have approximately the same shelf life as a sesame bagel. As a result, large chunks of Innovations are either closed or somewhat outdated.

Some exhibits are definitely worth stopping for, however. Our favorite attraction is Raytheon's **Sum of All Thrills** (see below). We also like **Habit Heroes,** which requires you to do calisthenics to save the planet from sloth and gluttony (not kidding).

Spend time at Innovations on your second day at Epcot. If you have only one day, visit late if you have the time and endurance. (The exception is Sum of All Thrills, which you should visit in the morning after Soarin', Test Track, and Mission: Space.) Skip exhibits with waits of more than 10 minutes, or experience them first thing in the morning on your second day, when there are no lines.

Kieran

Don't get confused by the two Innovations—they're not different entrances to Epcot but home to completely different attractions. Make sure you visit both!

CLUB COOL

Attached to the fountain side of Innovations West is a sort of international soda fountain called Club Cool. This Coca-Cola–sponsored exhibit provides free unlimited samples of soft drinks from around the world. Kids will love to fill their own tasting cups and move from one sampling station to the next. In Peru, bubble gum–flavored Inka Kola is in; in Zimbabwe, a raspberry cream soda called Sparberry is popular. Club Cool lives up to its name—it's air-conditioned and it makes a good meeting place.

Kieran

Make sure you stop by Club Cool for unlimited free soda samples. Try them all and give your parents a cup of Beverly whilst trying not to laugh!

SUM OF ALL THRILLS ★★★★

APPEAL BY AGE PRESCHOOL ★★★½ GRADE SCHOOL ★★★★½ TEENS ★★★★½
YOUNG ADULTS ★★★★½ OVER 30 ★★★★½ SENIORS ★★★★

What it is Hands-on exhibit and ride simulator. **Scope and scale** Minor attraction. **Fright potential** Intense simulation of a roller coaster may frighten some kids. **Bottleneck rating** 8. **When to go** Before 10:30 a.m. or after 5 p.m. **Special comments** 48" minimum height requirement, 54" for track designs with inversions. **Authors' rating** Not to be missed; ★★★★. **Duration of attraction** 15 minutes. **Average wait in line per 100 people ahead of you** 40 minutes; assumes all simulators operating. **Loading speed** Slow.

Sum of All Thrills is a design-your-own-roller-coaster simulator in which you use a computer program to specify the drops, curves, and loops of a coaster track before boarding an industrial robotic arm to experience your creation. Three vehicle options are available: bobsled, roller coaster, and jet aircraft. In addition to the vehicle, you select the kinds of turns, loops, and hills in your track design. Choices range from mild, broad curves to extreme multiple-loop inversions. This customization makes it easy to ride Sum of All Thrills many times without experiencing the same track twice. Because of its low capacity, you should ride as early in the morning as possible.

Mission: Space *(FastPass+)*   ★★★★

What it is Space flight simulation ride. **Scope and scale** Super-headliner. **Fright potential** Intense thrill ride may frighten guests of any age. Switching-off option provided (see page 243). **Bottleneck rating 9. When to go** First or last hour the park is open, or use FastPass+. **Special comments** Not recommended for pregnant women or people prone to motion sickness; must be 44" tall to ride; a gentler nonspinning version is also available. **Authors' rating** Impressive; ★★★★. **Duration of ride** About 5 minutes plus preshow. **Average wait in line per 100 people ahead of you** 4 minutes. **Loading speed** Moderate–fast.

Rough   Queasy

In this attraction, you join three other guests in a four-person crew to fly a space mission. Each guest plays a role (commander, pilot, navigator, or engineer) and is required to perform certain functions during the flight. A cleverly conceived, technological marvel, Mission: Space also has a less intense nonspinning version. If you want to experience the spinning version of the ride, join the Orange team, but if you prefer to check it out without those pesky g-forces, join the Green team.

Definitively choose the more intense ride. Nothing beats feeling those g-force winds.
Isaac

Liliane

Follow the Orange brick road; it's much more fun. The ride is too intense for little ones and people prone to motion sickness, but grade-schoolers, teens, and brave moms and dads will love it!

The host during your expedition is Gary Sinise, known for his roles in the space flicks Apollo 13 *and* Mission to Mars.

Movie Tip

THE "MOM, I CAN'T BELIEVE IT'S DISNEY!" FOUNTAINS

On a broiling Florida day, when you think you might suddenly combust, fling yourself into one of these two fountains and dance, skip, sing, jump, splash, stick your toes down the spouts, or catch the water in your mouth! Toddlers and preschoolers, along with hippies, especially love the fountain. Pack a pair of dry shorts and turn the kids loose, but make sure they don't go into the fountain with sneakers—wet shoes are a recipe for blisters.

Spaceship Earth *(FastPass+)*   ★★★★

Thumbs Up for the Whole Family

What it is Educational dark ride through past, present, and future. **Scope and scale** Headliner. **Fright potential** Dark and imposing presentation intimidates a few preschoolers. **Bottleneck rating 7. When to go** Before 10 a.m., after 4 p.m., or use FastPass+. **Special comment**

If lines are long when you arrive, try again after 4 p.m. **Authors' rating** One of Epcot's best; not to be missed; ★★★★. **Duration of ride** About 16 minutes. **Average wait in line per 100 people ahead of you** 3 minutes. **Loading speed** Fast.

This ride spirals through the 18-story interior of Epcot's premier landmark, taking guests through Audio-Animatronic scenes depicting mankind's development in communications, from cave painting to the Internet. It's actually more fun than it sounds and is carried off with a lot of humor. Spaceship Earth draws crowds like a magnet first thing in the morning because it's so close to the park entrance.

> This is a great ride if you need a break. I have to be honest, though—it might remind you of being at school!

> I like this ride because it goes all the way up to the top of the earth ball. It's cool to see how much technology has changed over the years.

Julia

Isaac

Universe of Energy: *Ellen's Energy Adventure* ★★★½

APPEAL BY AGE **PRESCHOOL** ★★★ **GRADE SCHOOL** ★★★½ **TEENS** ★★★
YOUNG ADULTS ★★★½ **OVER 30** ★★★ **SENIORS** ★★★★

What it is Combination dark ride–theater presentation. **Scope and scale** Major attraction. **Fright potential** Dinosaur segment frightens some preschoolers; visually intense, with some intimidating effects. **Bottleneck rating** 7. **When to go** Anytime. **Special comment** Don't be dismayed by long lines; 580 people enter the pavilion each time the theater changes audiences. **Authors' rating** Fun and informative, but showing its age; ★★★½. **Duration of presentation** About 26½ minutes. **Preshow** 8 minutes. **Probable waiting time** 14 minutes.

Scary

Join Ellen DeGeneres and Bill Nye the Science Guy, who star in this 26-minute presentation about energy. Visitors are seated in what appears to be an ordinary theater. After a short film, the theater seats divide into six 97-passenger traveling cars that glide among swamps and through a prehistoric forest full of animatronic dinosaurs. The ride is smooth, though some children are frightened by the dinosaurs. The dialogue between DeGeneres and Nye is humorous and upbeat, but the script was written almost 20 years ago—so don't expect to hear calls to action on climate change or carbon footprints, or much more than a passing reference to alternative energy sources.

> *Ellen DeGeneres lent her voice to the role of Dory, a fish with short-term memory loss, in the animated Disney-Pixar film* Finding Nemo.

TEST TRACK PAVILION

SPONSORED BY CHEVROLET, this pavilion consists of the Test Track attraction and Inside Track, a collection of transportation-themed exhibits and multimedia presentations. The pavilion is the last one on the left before World Showcase. We think Test Track is one of the most creatively conceived attractions in Disney World.

Test Track *(FastPass+)* ★★★★

APPEAL BY AGE **PRESCHOOL** ★★★★ **GRADE SCHOOL** ★★★★★ **TEENS** ★★★★½
YOUNG ADULTS ★★★★½ **OVER 30** ★★★★½ **SENIORS** ★★★★

What it is Automobile test-track simulator ride. **Scope and scale** Super-headliner.
Fright potential Intense thrill ride may frighten guests of any age. Switching-off

option provided (see page 243). **Bottleneck rating** 10. **When to go** First 30 minutes the park is open, just before closing, or use FastPass+. **Special comment** Must be 40" tall to ride. **Authors' rating** Not to be missed; ★★★★. **Duration of ride** About 4 minutes. **Average wait in line per 100 people ahead of you** 4½ minutes. **Loading speed** Moderate–fast.

Rough   Scary

Test Track takes you through the process of designing a new vehicle and then "testing" your car in a high-speed drive through and around the pavilion. After hearing about auto design, you enter the Chevrolet Design Studio to create your own concept car. Using a large touch screen interface (like a giant iPad), groups of up to three guests drag their fingers to design their car's body, engine, wheels, trim, and color. Next, you board a six-seat ride vehicle, attached to a track on the ground, for an actual drive through Chevrolet's test track. The vehicle's tests include braking maneuvers, cornering, and acceleration, culminating in a spin around the outside of the pavilion at speeds of up to 65 miles per hour.

Test Track is a favorite attraction of teens. If nobody in your family wants to join you on the ride and you don't have FastPass+ reservations, join the single-rider line, which moves much faster.

I was very disappointed with this ride. You spend lots of time making a car on a computer screen, and when you finally get to ride, it's just some special effects and speeding around curves.

The ride was really cool because I could design my own car and test it at top speed. It was fun to feel the wind in my hair when racing around the track.

Erin

Ethan

IMAGINATION! PAVILION

THIS MULTIATTRACTION PAVILION is situated on the west side of Innoventions West and down the walk from The Land. Outside are an "upside-down" waterfall and "jumping water," a fountain that hops over the heads of unsuspecting passersby.

Captain EO (FastPass+)   ★★★

| APPEAL BY AGE | PRESCHOOL ★★★ | GRADE SCHOOL ★★★ | TEENS ★★★ |
| YOUNG ADULTS ★★½ | | OVER 30 ★★½ | SENIORS ★★★ |

What it is 3-D film with special effects. **Scope and scale** Headliner. **Fright potential** Intense visual effects and loudness frighten young children. **Bottleneck rating** 5. **When to go** Anytime—FastPass+ is unnecessary. **Special comments** Adults shouldn't be put off by the sci-fi theme or rock music. **Authors' rating** ★★★. **Duration of show** About 17 minutes. **Preshow** 8 minutes. **Probable waiting time** 15 minutes.

DISNEY DISH WITH JIM HILL

EO OUT, INSIDE OUT IN Due to the huge success of Pixar's *Inside Out* (2015), Disney is considering putting Joy, Sadness, Anger, Fear, and Disgust in the 3-D theater that housed *Honey, I Shrunk the Audience* and currently shows *Captain EO*. Pixar is reportedly already hard at work on a brand-new, only-at-the-Disney-parks adventure that would take place at Headquarters (that is, inside Riley's brain).

Dark Loud Scary

In response to Michael Jackson's death in 2009, Disney brought back his 3-D space-themed musical film *Captain EO,* which originally ran 1986–1994, for a "limited" engagement. In early 2015, Disney preempted *EO* to show previews of upcoming theatrical releases. *EO* returned for the summer, but its long-term status is tenuous. It's possible that *EO* could stick around, or the previous film (*Honey, I Shrunk the Audience*) could make a comeback, or something else entirely could appear (see Disney Dish, page 307). Stay tuned.

We think *Captain EO* is still worth seeing if it's playing. Directed by Francis Ford Coppola, it's a 3-D space fantasy with lasers, fiber optics, cannons, and other special effects in the theater, plus some audience participation.

Liliane

Captain EO's loud sound track has a tendency to scare little kids. If they still want to see the show, I recommend letting them watch first without the 3-D glasses and with earplugs.

Journey into Imagination with Figment *(FastPass+)* ★★½

APPEAL BY AGE   PRESCHOOL ★★★★   GRADE SCHOOL ★★★½   TEENS ★★★ YOUNG ADULTS ★★★   OVER 30 ★★★   SENIORS ★★★½

What it is Dark fantasy-adventure ride. **Scope and scale** Major-attraction wannabe. **Fright potential** Frightens a few preschoolers. **Bottleneck rating** 6. **When to go** Anytime—FastPass+ is unnecessary. **Authors' rating** *Meh;* ★★½. **Duration of ride** About 6 minutes. **Average wait in line per 100 people ahead of you** 2 minutes. **Loading speed** Fast.

"One little spark of inspiration is at the heart of all creation," croons the ever-popular Figment, as he takes you on a tour of the Imagination Institute with the help of your five senses. Young children will love the little purple dragon, but grown-ups and teens will be only mildly amused (and probably bored), though Amber, our editor, has fond memories of Figment.

A funny purple dragon and a goofy doctor take you on a ride to help you learn about the five senses and your imagination. The dragon is always getting into trouble. Spoiler alert: Beware of the skunky smell!

Julia

THE LAND PAVILION

THE LAND IS A HUGE PAVILION containing three attractions and two restaurants. When the pavilion was originally built, its emphasis was on farming, but now it focuses on environmental concerns. Dry as that sounds, kids really enjoy The Land's attractions. Note that The Land gets super-crowded during mealtimes.

The Circle of Life   ★★★½

APPEAL BY AGE   PRESCHOOL ★★★½   GRADE SCHOOL ★★★½   TEENS ★★★½ YOUNG ADULTS ★★★½   OVER 30 ★★★   SENIORS ★★★½

What it is Film exploring man's relationship with his environment. **Scope and scale** Minor attraction. **Fright potential** Not frightening in any respect. **Bottleneck rating** 5. **When to go** Anytime. **Authors' rating** Highly interesting and enlightening; ★★★½. **Duration of show** About 20 minutes. **Probable waiting time** 10–15 minutes.

The Swahili saying *hakuna matata* ("no worries") doesn't apply to this movie. On the contrary, Simba, Pumbaa, and Timon from Disney's animated feature *The Lion King* offer a sugarcoated lesson on how to protect and care for the environment.

Did you know that Elton John wrote the music to the song "Hakuna Matata"?

Living with the Land *(FastPass+)* ★★★★

APPEAL BY AGE   PRESCHOOL ★★★½   GRADE SCHOOL ★★★½   TEENS ★★★★   YOUNG ADULTS ★★★★   OVER 30 ★★★★   SENIORS ★★★★½

Thumbs Up for the Whole Family

What it is Indoor boat-ride adventure through the past, present, and future of US farming and agriculture. **Scope and scale** Major attraction. **Fright potential** Not frightening in any respect, but loud. **Bottleneck rating** 9. **When to go** Before 11 a.m., after 1 p.m., or use FastPass+. **Special comments** Go early and save other Land attractions (except for Soarin') for later in the day. The ride is on the pavilion's lower level. **Authors' rating** Informative without being dull; not to be missed; ★★★★. **Duration of ride** About 14 minutes. **Average wait in line per 100 people ahead of you** 3 minutes; assumes 15 boats operating. **Loading speed** Moderate.

This boat ride through four experimental growing areas is inspiring and educational. Kids like seeing the giant fruits and vegetables. Teens will be fascinated by the imaginative ways to grow crops—without soil, hanging in the air, and even on a space station. A lot of the produce grown here is served to guests in the restaurants at Epcot.

> They grow food in unique ways here. Vegetables are grown in sand instead of dirt, and some just seem to float around in the air. I thought the fish tanks were a little weird, though.

Ethan

Soarin' *(FastPass+)* ★★★★½

APPEAL BY AGE   PRESCHOOL ★★★★½   GRADE SCHOOL ★★★★★   TEENS ★★★★½   YOUNG ADULTS ★★★★½   OVER 30 ★★★★½   SENIORS ★★★★★

What it is Flight-simulation ride. **Scope and scale** Super-headliner. **Fright potential** Frightens almost no one who meets the minimum height requirements, except those with a fear of heights. **Bottleneck rating** 10. **When to go** First 30 minutes the park is open or use FastPass+. **Special comments** Entrance on the lower level of The Land Pavilion. May induce motion sickness; must be 40" tall to ride; switching-off option provided (see page 243). **Authors' rating** Exciting and mellow at the same time; not to be missed; ★★★★½. **Duration of ride** 5½ minutes. **Average wait in line per 100 people ahead of you** 4 minutes; assumes 2 concourses operating. **Loading speed** Moderate.

This is the closest you'll come to hang gliding without trying the real thing. Once you're "airborne," IMAX-quality aerial images of California are projected all around you, and the flight simulator moves in sync with the movie. The images are well chosen and drop-dead beautiful. Special effects include wind, sound, and even smell. The ride itself is thrilling but perfectly smooth. Any child (or adult) who meets the 40-inch minimum height requirement will love Soarin'. See it before 9:30 a.m. or book FastPass+ reservations up to 60 days in advance; expect all reservations to be gone by 1 p.m. on days of moderate attendance or as early as 11 a.m. on busier days.

A new ride film should premier at Soarin' in 2016, along with a third ride theater to increase ride capacity by 50%. The new film should incorporate flyover sequences from around the world, possibly with different, random sequences each time you ride.

I felt like I was really flying, but I didn't like the long line.
Riding without FastPass+ is a no-go for me.

Isaac

THE SEAS WITH NEMO & FRIENDS PAVILION

FEATURING CHARACTERS from Disney-Pixar's *Finding Nemo*, this area encompasses one of America's top marine aquariums, a ride that tunnels through the aquarium, an interactive animated film, and a number of first-class educational walk-through exhibits. Altogether it's a stunning package, and not to be missed.

The Seas Main Tank and Exhibits ★★★½

APPEAL BY AGE PRESCHOOL ★★★★½ GRADE SCHOOL ★★★★½ TEENS ★★★★
YOUNG ADULTS ★★★★   OVER 30 ★★★★   SENIORS ★★★★

What it is A huge saltwater aquarium, plus exhibits on oceanography, ocean ecology, and sea life. **Scope and scale** Major attraction. **Fright potential** Not frightening in any respect. **Bottleneck rating** 7. **When to go** Before 11:30 a.m. or after

Thumbs Up for the Whole Family

5 p.m., or especially after 9 p.m. during evening Extra Magic Hours. **Authors' rating** An excellent marine exhibit; ★★★½. **Average wait in line per 100 people ahead of you** 3½ minutes. **Loading speed** Fast.

Take a *Finding Nemo*–themed ride to Sea Base Alpha to start your discovery of The Seas' main tank and exhibits, which feature fish, mammals, and crustaceans in a simulation of an ocean ecosystem. Visitors can observe the activity through windows below the surface (including inside the Coral Reef Restaurant). Children will be enchanted to discover the substantial fish population and the many exhibits offered. With The Seas with Nemo & Friends and *Turtle Talk with Crush*, The Seas is one of Epcot's more popular venues. We recommend experiencing the ride and *Turtle Talk* in the morning before the park gets crowded, saving the exhibits for later.

The Seas with Nemo & Friends *(FastPass+)* ★★★

APPEAL BY AGE PRESCHOOL ★★★★½ GRADE SCHOOL ★★★★ TEENS ★★★½
YOUNG ADULTS ★★★½   OVER 30 ★★★½   SENIORS ★★★★

What it is Ride through a tunnel in The Seas' main tank. **Scope and scale** Major attraction. **Fright potential** Not frightening in any respect. **Bottleneck rating** 7. **When to go** Before 10:30 a.m., after 3 p.m., or use FastPass+. **Authors' rating** Educational *and* fun; ★★★. **Duration of ride** 4 minutes. **Average wait in line per 100 people ahead of you** 3½ minutes. **Loading speed** Fast.

Upon entering The Seas, you proceed to the loading area, where you'll be made comfortable in a "clamobile" for your journey through the aquarium. The technology used makes it seem as if the animated characters are swimming with the live fish. Meet characters from *Finding Nemo*, such as Mr. Ray, and help Dory, Bruce, Marlin, Squirt, and Crush find Nemo. This cool ride attracts lots of the lovable clown fish's fans, so ride early.

Nemo & Friends is scary if you're afraid of the dark or you get scared by fish.
The anglerfish is terrifying!

Ricky

See Finding Nemo *before your visit if you haven't already. You won't soon forget this superb family movie, which won the 2004 Oscar for best animated feature. And stay tuned for* Finding Dory *(2016), a sequel to* Finding Nemo *that brings back Ellen DeGeneres as the voice of the adorably forgetful blue tang.*

Turtle Talk with Crush (FastPass+) ★★★★

**APPEAL BY AGE PRESCHOOL ★★★★½ GRADE SCHOOL ★★★★½ TEENS ★★★★
YOUNG ADULTS ★★★★   OVER 30 ★★★★   SENIORS ★★★★**

What it is An interactive animated film. **Scope and scale** Minor attraction. **Fright potential** Not frightening in any respect. **Bottleneck rating** 9. **When to go** Before 11 a.m., after 3 p.m., or use FastPass+. **Authors' rating** A real spirit-lifter; not to be missed; ★★★★. **Duration of presentation** 17 minutes. **Preshow entertainment** None. **Probable waiting time** 10–20 minutes.

This interactive theater show starring the 150-year-old surfer-dude turtle from *Finding Nemo* starts like a typical theme park movie but quickly turns into an interactive encounter, as Crush begins conversing with guests in the audience. *Awesome!* It's unusual to wait more than one or two shows to get in. If you find long lines in the morning, try back after 3 p.m., when more of the crowd has moved on to World Showcase, or use FastPass+.

WORLD SHOWCASE

EPCOT'S OTHER THEMED AREA, World Showcase is an ongoing world's fair encircling a picturesque 40-acre lagoon. The cuisine, culture, history, and architecture of almost a dozen countries—and one make-believe kingdom—are permanently displayed in individual pavilions spaced along a 1.2-mile promenade. The pavilions replicate familiar landmarks and present representative street scenes from the host countries.

I love World Showcase and enjoy experiencing the different cultures.

Erin

Agent P's World Showcase Adventure ★★★★

**APPEAL BY AGE PRESCHOOL ★★★½ GRADE SCHOOL ★★★★ TEENS ★★★★½
YOUNG ADULTS ★★★½   OVER 30 ★★★½   SENIORS ★★★½**

What it is Interactive scavenger hunt in select World Showcase pavilions. **Scope and scale** Minor attraction. **Fright potential** Not frightening in any respect. **Bottleneck rating** 1. **When to go** Anytime. **Authors' rating** Fun activity, especially for return visitors. It's best experienced if your group has at least two pairs; ★★★★. **Duration of experience** Allow 30 minutes per adventure. **Probable waiting time** None.

Thumbs Up for the Whole Family

In their eponymous Disney Channel show, Phineas and Ferb have a pet platypus named Perry. In the presence of humans, Perry doesn't do a whole lot. When the kids aren't looking, though, Perry takes on the role of Agent P—a fedora-wearing, James Bond–esque secret agent who battles the evil Dr. Doofenshmirtz to prevent world domination.

In Agent P's World Showcase Adventure, you're a secret agent helping Perry, and you receive a cell phone–like device before you're dispatched on a mission to your choice of seven World Showcase pavilions. Once you arrive at the pavilion, the device's video screen and audio provide various clues to help you solve a set of simple puzzles necessary for defeating Doofenshmirtz's plan.

Playing the game is free, but you'll need proof of park admission to sign up before you play. You can choose both the time and location of your adventure; register and pick up your devices at the Italy or Norway Pavilion, the International Gateway (near the UK Pavilion), or the east side of the main walkway from Future World to World Showcase.

> You get to be a secret agent and fight an evil guy. There are lots of special effects and clues to be discovered as you run through seven countries. This is so much fun for the whole family.
>
> Julia

NOW, MOVING CLOCKWISE around the World Showcase promenade, here are the nations represented and their attractions:

MEXICO PAVILION

SPANISH 101	
HELLO: Hola	**Pronunciation:** *Oh-la*
GOODBYE: Adios	**Pronunciation:** *Ah-dee-ohs*
THANK YOU: Gracias	**Pronunciation:** *Grah-see-ahs*
MICKEY MOUSE: El Ratón Miguelito	**Pronunciation:** *El Rah-tone Mee-gell-lee-toe*

A PRE-COLUMBIAN PYRAMID dominates the architecture of this exhibit. Inside you will find authentic and valuable artifacts, a village scene complete with restaurant, and the **Gran Fiesta Tour** boat ride. Don't miss **Mariachi Cobre,** the 12-piece Mexican band that entertains regularly at the Mexico Pavilion. The meet and greet for **Donald Duck** is outside on the right-hand side of the pavilion.

Gran Fiesta Tour Starring the Three Caballeros ★★½

APPEAL BY AGE	PRESCHOOL ★★★★		GRADE SCHOOL ★★★½	TEENS ★★★½
YOUNG ADULTS ★★★		OVER 30 ★★★½		SENIORS ★★★½

Thumbs Up for the Whole Family

What it is Indoor boat ride. **Scope and scale** Minor attraction. **Fright potential** Not frightening in any respect. **Bottleneck rating** 5. **When to go** Before noon or after 5 p.m. **Authors' rating** Light and relaxing; ★★½. **Duration of ride** About 7 minutes (plus 1½-minute wait to disembark). **Average wait in line per 100 people ahead of you** 4½ minutes; assumes 16 boats in operation. **Loading speed** Moderate.

Gran Fiesta Tour's story line features Donald Duck, José Carioca (a parrot), and Panchito (a Mexican charro rooster) from the 1944 Disney film *The Three Caballeros;* the story has our heroes racing to Mexico City for a gala reunion performance. Guests are treated to detailed scenes done in eye-catching colors.

NORWAY PAVILION

SURROUNDING A COURTYARD is an assortment of traditional Scandinavian buildings, including a replica of the 14th-century **Akershus**

NORWEGIAN 101	
HELLO: God dag	**Pronunciation:** *Good dagh*
GOODBYE: Ha det	**Pronunciation:** *Hah deh*
THANK YOU: Takk	**Pronunciation:** *Tahk*
MICKEY MOUSE: Mikke Mus	**Pronunciation:** *Mikeh Moose*

Castle, now home to princess-hosted character meals. The major attraction is the boat ride **Frozen Ever After.**

> It's hard to say no to the mouthwatering pastries at **Kringla Bakeri Og Kafe** in Norway. This is my favorite stop at the end of the day to pick up my next day's breakfast.
>
> Liliane

Frozen Ever After *(opens 2016)* *(FastPass+)*

What it is Indoor boat ride. **Scope and scale** Major attraction. **Fright potential** Dark; previous ride ended with a plunge down a 20-foot flume; at press time, it was unknown if the new boat ride will keep that aspect. **Bottleneck rating** 10. **When to go** Before noon, after 7 p.m., or use FastPass+. **Authors' rating** Not open at press time. **Duration of ride** 4½ minutes. **Average wait in line per 100 people ahead of you** 4 minutes; assumes 12 or 13 boats operating. **Loading speed** Fast.

Dark

Frozen Ever After replaces Maelstrom, Norway's original boat ride. Expect to see all of the major *Frozen* characters, including Marshmallow, Olaf, Sven, and Wandering Oaken. Scenes in the ride will include Troll Valley and, of course, Elsa belting out "Let It Go."

Royal Sommerhus Meet and Greet *(opens 2016)* *(FastPass+)*

What it is Meet and greet with the *Frozen* royalty. **Scope and scale** Minor attraction. **Fright potential** Not frightening in any respect. **Bottleneck rating** 10. **When to go** Before noon, after 7 p.m., or use FastPass+. **Authors' rating** Not open at press time. **Duration of greeting** N/A. **Average wait in line per 100 people ahead of you** N/A.

Scheduled to open in 2016 along with Frozen Ever After, this is a character greeting for Anna and Elsa. While *Frozen* wasn't explicitly set in Norway, Disney says the meet and greet will feature Norwegian architecture and crafts.

CHINA PAVILION

CHINESE (MANDARIN) 101	
HELLO: Ni hao	**Pronunciation:** *Knee how*
GOODBYE: Zai jian	**Pronunciation:** *Zy jehn*
THANK YOU: Xiè xie	**Pronunciation:** *Chi-eh chi-eh*
MICKEY MOUSE: Mi Lao Shu	**Pronunciation:** *Me Lah-oh Su*

THERE IS NO RIDE AT THE CHINA PAVILION, but the majestic half-size replica of the **Temple of Heaven** in Beijing will surely make it into your photo album. See *Reflections of China,* an impressive film about the people and natural beauty of China. Children will enjoy the regularly scheduled performances of **Chinese acrobats;** check your *Times Guide* for showtimes. **Mulan** holds court outside most of the time, or inside the Temple of Heaven during inclement weather.

> In China you can buy a fan and get it personalized for free, with your name written in Chinese on it.

Alex

Reflections of China ★★★½

APPEAL BY AGE PRESCHOOL ★★★ GRADE SCHOOL ★★★½ TEENS ★★★★
YOUNG ADULTS ★★★★ OVER 30 ★★★★ SENIORS ★★★★½

What it is Film about the Chinese people and country. **Scope and scale** Major attraction. **Fright potential** Not frightening in any respect. **Bottleneck rating** 4. **When to go** Anytime. **Special comment** Audience stands throughout performance. **Authors' rating** Beautifully produced film; ★★★½. **Duration of presentation** About 14 minutes. **Probable waiting time** 10 minutes.

Warm and appealing, *Reflections of China* is a brilliant (albeit politically sanitized) introduction to the people and natural beauty of China.

GERMANY PAVILION

GERMAN 101	
HELLO: Hallo	**Pronunciation:** *Hall-o*
GOODBYE: Auf wiedersehen	**Pronunciation:** *Owf veeh-der-zain*
THANK YOU: Danke	**Pronunciation:** *Dan-keh*
MICKEY MOUSE: Micky Maus	**Pronunciation:** *Me-key Mouse*

THE GERMANY PAVILION HAS NO RIDES. The main focus is **Biergarten,** a full-service (reservations suggested) restaurant serving German food and beer. Yodeling, folk dancing, and oompah band music are regularly performed during mealtimes. Be sure to check out the large, elaborate model railroad just beyond the restrooms as you walk from Germany toward Italy. **Snow White** signs autographs at the well just as you reach the Germany Pavilion.

> The Germany Pavilion is the perfect place to introduce your kids to a great snack: *Gummibärchen* (gummy bears), my favorite candy.

Liliane

ITALY PAVILION

ITALIAN 101	
HELLO: Buon giorno	**Pronunciation:** *Bon jor-no*
GOODBYE: Ciao (informal)	**Pronunciation:** *Chow*
THANK YOU: Grazie	**Pronunciation:** *Grah-zee-eh*
MICKEY MOUSE: Topolino	**Pronunciation:** *To-po-lee-no*

THE ENTRANCE TO ITALY is marked by an 83-foot-tall **campanile (bell tower)** intended to mirror the one in St. Mark's Square in Venice. Left of the campanile is a replica of the 14th-century **Doge's Palace.**

Streets and courtyards in the Italy Pavilion are among the most realistic in the World Showcase. You really do feel as if you're in Italy. Because there's no film or ride, you can tour anytime.

Sergio, an Italian mime and juggler, performs daily. New and not to be missed is the energetic flag corps **Sbandieratori Di Sansepolcro.** The group is accompanied by drum and horn players.

Via Napoli serves the best pizza. I go back to England and brag about it to my friends.

Alex

I love the Italian restaurant **Tutto Italia.** After a long day of walking around, I get to sit down in air-conditioning, rest my legs—and eat pasta. YUM!

Julia

UNITED STATES PAVILION

THE UNITED STATES PAVILION is an imposing brick structure reminiscent of Colonial Philadelphia and is home to a very moving and patriotic, albeit sanitized, retrospective of US history.

The American Adventure ★★★★

| APPEAL BY AGE | PRESCHOOL ★★½ | GRADE SCHOOL ★★★½ | TEENS ★★★½ |
| YOUNG ADULTS ★★★★ | OVER 30 ★★★★ | | SENIORS ★★★★½ |

What it is Patriotic mixed-media and Audio-Animatronic theater presentation on US history. **Scope and scale** Headliner. **Fright potential** Not frightening in any respect. **Bottleneck rating** 6. **When to go** Anytime. **Authors' rating** Disney's best historic/patriotic attraction; not to be missed; ★★★★. **Duration of presentation** About 29 minutes. **Preshow** Voices of Liberty chorale singing. **Probable waiting time** 25 minutes.

Thumbs Up for the Whole Family

The 29-minute multimedia show is narrated by animatronic Mark Twain and Ben Franklin. *The American Adventure* reminds you of a contest: Tell us everything you love about America in 30 minutes or less. Only four female figures are among the 12 personified ideals around the theater, one of them representing the rather ambiguous "tomorrow" by virtue of holding a baby. The North American continent seemingly did not exist before the landing of the *Mayflower.*

Don't miss the performances of **Voices of Liberty,** an a cappella choir that performs regularly either in the rotunda of the United States Pavilion or across the plaza in the **America Gardens Theatre,** Epcot's premier venue for concerts and stage shows.

Liliane

JAPAN PAVILION

JAPANESE 101	
HELLO: Konnichiwa	**Pronunciation:** *Ko-nee-chee wah*
GOODBYE: Sayonara	**Pronunciation:** *Sigh-yo-nah-ra*
THANK YOU: Arigato	**Pronunciation:** *Ah-ree-gah-to*
MICKEY MOUSE: Mikki Mausu	**Pronunciation:** *Mikkee Mou-su*

THE FIVE-STORY, BLUE-ROOFED PAGODA, inspired by a 17th-century shrine in Nara, sets this pavilion apart. A hill garden behind it encompasses waterfalls, rocks, flowers, lanterns, paths, and rustic bridges. There are no attractions unless you count the huge Japanese retail venue. Not to be missed, though, are the **Matsuriza Taiko drummers.** The drums can often be heard throughout the World Showcase, but you need to be up close to see the graceful way they're played.

Sadly, Miyuki Sugimori, the only woman (and 1 of only 15 people in the entire world) trained in the 250-year-old art of candy sculpting, is no longer entertaining guests in Japan. There seems to be a hit out on performers at Disney World—the Ziti Sisters in Italy also got the axe in early 2014—and I don't like it one bit.

Liliane

I really enjoy looking around all the stores in each pavilion. My mum treats me to a little Japanese sweet of my choice if I don't moan about walking so much!

Alex

MOROCCO PAVILION

ARABIC 101	
HELLO: Salaam alekoum	**Pronunciation:** *Sah-lahm ah-leh-koom*
GOODBYE: Ma'salama	**Pronunciation:** *Mah sah-lah-mah*
THANK YOU: Shoukran	**Pronunciation:** *Shoe-krah-n*
MICKEY MOUSE: Mujallad Miki	**Pronunciation:** *Muh-jahl-lahd Me-key*

THE BUSTLING MARKET, WINDING STREETS, lofty minarets, and stuccoed archways re-create the romance and intrigue of Marrakesh and Casablanca. Attention to detail makes Morocco one of the most exciting World Showcase pavilions. And while there are no attractions, don't miss **B'net Al Houwariyate,** a music and dance group that takes guests on a journey of Moroccan folk music. Performances take place on select days; check your *Times Guide* for details. The Morocco Pavilion is also home to **Jasmine** and **Aladdin. Spice Road Table** serves up tasty tapas-style Mediterranean dishes and excellent views of *IllumiNations*—along with high prices. At the full-service **Restaurant Marrakesh,** guests can dine while enjoying traditional music and belly dancing.

FRANCE PAVILION

FRENCH 101	
HELLO: Bonjour	**Pronunciation:** *Bon-jure*
GOODBYE: Au revoir	**Pronunciation:** *Oh reh-vwa*
THANK YOU: Merci	**Pronunciation:** *Maer-si*
MICKEY MOUSE: Mickey	**Pronunciation:** *Mee-keh*

WELCOME AND *BIENVENUE* to Paris, the Eiffel Tower, and more. There's not much for kids here, but you won't have any trouble luring them into **Les Halles Boulangerie-Pâtisserie** for scrumptious French pastries or **L'Artisan des Glaces** for yummy ice cream. Kids will also enjoy **Serveur Amusant,** a balancing act of waiters performed on select days in front of Les Chefs de France restaurant. **Givenchy,** the famed

French fashion and beauty house, has a shop at the pavilion and is the only retail location in the United States that offers the full line of Givenchy makeup and skin-care products, as well as a large selection of fragrances. **Belle** and **Aurora** are regularly found here for photo opportunities and autographs. Character appearances are intermittent, so check your *Times Guide.*

> Everyone should try the pastries and the baguettes with cheese and ham on real French bread. They're amazing!
>
> Alex

Impressions de France ★★★½

APPEAL BY AGE	PRESCHOOL ★★★½	GRADE SCHOOL ★★★½	TEENS ★★★½
YOUNG ADULTS ★★★★		OVER 30 ★★★★	SENIORS ★★★★½

What it is Film essay on the French people and country. **Scope and scale** Major attraction. **Fright potential** Not frightening in any respect. **Bottleneck rating** 7. **When to go** Anytime. **Authors' rating** Exceedingly beautiful film; ★★★½. **Duration of presentation** About 18 minutes. **Probable waiting time** 15 minutes.

France, here we come! This truly lovely 18-minute movie will make you want to pack your suitcase. An added bonus is that the showing is *très civilizé,* as you get to sit down and rest your weary feet.

UNITED KINGDOM PAVILION

A BLEND OF ARCHITECTURE ATTEMPTS to capture Britain's city, town, and rural atmospheres. One street alone has a thatched-roof cottage, four-story timber-and-plaster building, a pre-Georgian plaster building, a formal Palladian exterior of dressed stone, and a city square with a Hyde Park bandstand (whew!). There are no attractions, but don't miss **The British Revolution.** The band performs the greatest UK hits from the Beatles to the music of Led Zeppelin and The Who. New to the pavilion is the **Paul McKenna Band,** performing contemporary Scottish folk music on select days in the United Kingdom courtyard. **Alice in Wonderland** and **Mary Poppins** greet their fans outside the little English cottage.

> If your child loves Mary Poppins, your best chance to meet her is here.
>
> Liliane

CANADA PAVILION

CANADA'S CULTURAL, NATURAL, AND architectural diversity are reflected in this large, impressive pavilion. Older kids will be interested in the 30-foot-tall totem poles that embellish a Canadian Indian village.

Canada is also home to the **Canadian Lumberjacks,** a medley of axe throwing, wood chopping, chain sawing, and then some; they perform on the Mill Stage between Canada and the United Kingdom. The lumberjacks replaced the punk–Celtic–country band Off Kilter in October 2014, but in our opinion, the new show neither reflects the beautiful cultural heritage of our neighbor to the north nor furthers the illusion that you're in Canada.

> Of all the new entertainment acts that came to Epcot in 2015, the lumberjacks are the only performers I don't enjoy—honestly, if I were Canadian, I would be insulted. I want my fiddles and bagpipes back!
>
> Liliane

O Canada! ★★★½

What it is Film essay on the Canadian people and their country. **Scope and scale** Major attraction. **Fright potential** Not frightening in any respect. **Bottleneck rating** 5. **When to go** Anytime. **Special comment** Audience stands during performance. **Authors' rating** Makes you want to catch the first plane to Canada! ★★★½. **Duration of presentation** About 15 minutes. **Probable waiting time** 9 minutes.

O Canada! showcases Canada's natural beauty and population diversity and demonstrates the immense pride that Canadians have in their country. A film starring Martin Short features clips of Canada's stunning landscape, all the way from Swift Current to Moose Jaw. (Just kidding, eh. From Prince Edward Island to Vancouver.) Visitors leave the theater through **Victoria Gardens,** which was inspired by the famed Butchart Gardens of British Columbia.

Cast members often run a preshow quiz on Canadian trivia outside the theater before the show. Here are some helpful tips: Canada's capital is Ottawa; its $1 coin is nicknamed the Loonie, after the bird engraved on it; and the $2 coin is the Toonie—not, unfortunately, the Doubloonie.

This large-capacity attraction (guests must stand) gets fairly heavy late-morning attendance, as Canada is the first pavilion encountered as one travels counterclockwise around World Showcase Lagoon.

LIVE ENTERTAINMENT *at* EPCOT

IN FUTURE WORLD

KIDS WILL LOVE THE CREW of drumming janitors (**The JAMMitors**), as well as the **dancing-fountains show** in the plaza between Innoventions East and West.

AROUND WORLD SHOWCASE

STREET PERFORMANCES IN AND AROUND World Showcase are what set live entertainment at Epcot apart from the other Disney theme parks. A mariachi group can be found in Mexico; street actors in France; the **Voices of Liberty** and **American Music Machine** in the United States; traditional drummers in Japan; a Scottish folk music group in the United Kingdom; Moroccan folk music in Morocco; and a lumberjack show in Canada, among other acts. Check your *Times Guide* for performance times. Some restaurants get in on the act too: You can enjoy raucous Oktoberfest entertainment at Germany's **Biergarten** and see belly dancing at Morocco's **Restaurant Marrakesh.**

The street entertainment at Epcot underwent quite a few changes during 2015, and while some of the new acts are great, one major complaint we have is that the frequency of the performances has been reduced substantially.

Liliane

FAVORITE EATS AT EPCOT

PAVILION | SERVICE LOCATION | FOOD ITEM

THE SEAS Coral Reef Restaurant* | Food with a view—fish menu.
The aquarium will keep the kids happy for quite some time.

THE LAND Sunshine Seasons | Healthy choices—our all-time favorite

MEXICO La Cantina de San Angel | Children's plate with empanada, chips, & beverage

NORWAY Kringla Bakeri Og Kafe | Salmon sandwiches & pastries

CHINA Lotus Blossom Café | Beef & chicken rice bowls, vegetable curry, & egg rolls

GERMANY Sommerfest | Bratwurst & frankfurter with kraut & apple strudel

ITALY Tutto Italia* | Good pasta & kids' menu | **Via Napoli** | Best pizza in WDW

UNITED STATES Liberty Inn | If you're craving all-American food

JAPAN Katsura Grill | Beef & chicken teriyaki

MOROCCO Tangierine Cafe | Shawarma, hummus, couscous, & kids' meals;
 outdoor seating

FRANCE Crêpes des Chefs de France | Crêpes & espresso
Les Halles Boulangerie–Pâtisserie | Croissants, chocolate mousse, & yummy
sandwiches on baguettes

UNITED KINGDOM The Tea Caddy | You must have an English Cadbury bar
once in your life.

*Table service only—Advance Reservations highly recommended

WDW live-entertainment guru Steve Soares usually posts the Epcot
performance schedule about a week in advance at **wdwent.com.**

AMERICA GARDENS THEATRE

THIS AMPHITHEATER ON THE LAGOON across from the United
States Pavilion features pop (and oldies pop) musical acts throughout
much of the year, as well as Epcot's popular **Candlelight Processional** for
the Christmas holidays. Showtimes are listed on a board outside the exits
and in the daily *Times Guide*.

IlumiNations: Reflections of Earth (FastPass+) ★★★★½

**APPEAL BY AGE PRESCHOOL ★★★½ GRADE SCHOOL ★★★★½ TEENS ★★★★½
YOUNG ADULTS ★★★★½   OVER 30 ★★★★½   SENIORS ★★★★½**

What it is Nighttime fireworks and laser show at World Showcase Lagoon. **Scope
and scale** Super-headliner. **Fright potential** Not frightening in any respect. **Bottleneck rating** 7 when leaving. **When to go** Stake out a viewing position 60–100
minutes before the show (45–90 minutes during less-busy periods); FastPass+ not
recommended except as noted on the following page. **Special comments** Showtime is listed in the daily entertainment schedule (*Times Guide*); audience stands.
Authors' rating Epcot's most impressive entertainment event; ★★★★½. **Duration of show** About 18 minutes.

Epcot's great outdoor spectacle integrates fireworks, laser lights, neon, and
music in a stirring tribute to the nations of the world. It's the climax of every
Epcot day, and not to be missed.

This enchanting and ambitious show (it tells the history of the universe starting with the big bang) is well worth keeping the kids up late. The best places to view the show are from the lakeside veranda of **La Hacienda de San Angel** at the Mexico Pavilion, **Spice Road Table** in Morocco, or the **Rose & Crown Pub** at the UK Pavilion. Come early and relax with a drink or snack. The drawback is—you guessed it—that you will have to claim this spot at least 90 minutes before *IllumiNations.*

As noted earlier, FastPass+ gets you into a special viewing area for the show—in **Showcase Plaza,** on the south shore of World Showcase Lagoon, directly north of Future World—but you still have to arrive a good half hour or so in advance to get a good spot. What's more, there are so many other good viewing spots around the lagoon that *IllumiNations* really isn't a good use of FastPass+—the consequence is an hour-long wait at either Soarin' or Test Track. The one exception is if you're visiting World Showcase for an evening, as there are no other Tier A attractions here.

For other great viewing spots, check out the map on page 321. Note that the boat dock opposite Germany may be exposed to a lot of smoke from the fireworks because of Epcot's prevailing winds.

IllumiNations is the climax of every day at Epcot, so keep in mind that once the show is over, you'll be leaving the park and so will almost everybody else. For suggested exit strategies, see below.

Word around the lagoon is that a new nighttime extravaganza will replace *IllumiNations* sometime in late 2015 or early 2016. While we don't know the plot, we're reasonably sure it'll contain lasers, fireworks, and music. There are hints that it'll contain some sort of interactive element.

For a really good view of the show, you can charter a pontoon boat for about $350. Captained by a Disney cast member, the boat holds up to 10 guests. Your captain will take you for a little cruise and then position the boat in a perfect place to watch *IllumiNations.* For more information, call ☎ 407-WDW-PLAY.

ILLUMINATIONS EXIT STRATEGIES

MORE GROUPS GET SEPARATED AND MORE CHILDREN lost after *IllumiNations* than at any other time. Make sure that you've pre-selected a meeting point in the Epcot entrance area, such as the fountain just inside the main entrance. Warn your group not to leave through the exit turnstiles until everyone is reunited.

- If you're staying at the Swan, Dolphin, Yacht & Beach Club Resorts, or BoardWalk Inn & Villas, watch *IllumiNations* from somewhere between Italy and the United Kingdom, and exit the park through the International Gateway between France and the United Kingdom. You can walk or take a boat back to your hotel.

- If you have a car in the Epcot lot, find a viewing spot at the Future World end of World Showcase Lagoon (Showcase Plaza) and leave immediately after *IllumiNations* ends. The problem is not the traffic in the parking lot—it actually moves pretty well—it's making your way to, and finding, your car. Make sure that you write down or take a picture of where you're parked—this is not the time to rely on your

Where to View IllumiNations

memory. If you're parked near the entrance, skip the tram and walk. If you walk, watch your children closely and hang on to them for all you're worth. The parking lot is pretty wild at this time of night.

EPCOT TOURING PLANS

OUR STEP-BY-STEP TOURING PLANS are field-tested, independently verified itineraries that will keep you moving counter to the crowd flow and allow you to see as much as possible in a single day with minimum time wasted in line. We present three Epcot one-day touring plans specifically geared toward visiting with children. We also offer, and recommend, a two-day touring plan that is much more relaxing and far less tiring.

Touring Epcot is much more strenuous and demanding than touring the other theme parks. Epcot requires about twice as much walking. And, unlike the Magic Kingdom, Epcot has no effective in-park transportation—wherever you want to go, it's always quicker to walk. Our plans will help you avoid crowds and bottlenecks on days of moderate-to-heavy attendance, but they can't shorten the distance you have to walk. (Wear comfortable shoes.) On days of lighter attendance, when crowd conditions aren't a critical factor, the plans will help you organize your tour.

We love Epcot, and because we spend so much time there, we really wanted our small children to enjoy it too. The challenge was figuring out how to get the kids connected to the theme or presentation at each pavilion, especially in Future World. Let's face it—even with Test Track and Sum of All Thrills, a 7-year-old is only going to take so much talk about hydroponic vegetables, nuclear fission, or communication systems before tuning out. The key for us was to brief our children on what they were likely to see in each attraction and then tie it back to something they could relate to in their everyday lives. During the tour of the greenhouse in Living with the Land, for example, we made a game of finding foods they like. (They have cocoa beans—chocolate—so we think that covers almost everyone.) While riding Test Track, we asked the kids to figure out which parent's driving was most like the ride's. Epcot's Future World attractions can be a lot more palatable to young children if they're engaged and prepared going in. It's all about presentation.

The different touring plans are described on below. The descriptions will tell you for whom or for what situation the plans are designed. The actual touring plans are located on pages 464–468. Each plan includes a numbered map of the park to help you find your way around.

To help with FastPass+, we've listed the approximate return times for which you should attempt to make reservations for specific attractions. (The touring plan should work with anything close to the times shown.) Check **touringplans.com** for the latest developments and information.

EPCOT ONE-DAY TOURING PLAN FOR PARENTS WITH SMALL CHILDREN This plan is designed for parents of children ages 3–8 who wish to see the very best age-appropriate attractions in Epcot. Every attraction has a rating of at least three stars (out of five) from preschool and grade-school children surveyed by *The Unofficial Guide*. Special advice is provided for touring the park with small children. The plan keeps walking and backtracking to a minimum.

EPCOT ONE-DAY SLEEPYHEAD TOURING PLAN FOR PARENTS WITH SMALL CHILDREN A relaxed plan that allows families with small children to sleep late and still see the highlights of Epcot. The plan begins around 11 a.m., sets aside ample time for lunch, and includes the very best child-friendly attractions in the park.

EPCOT ONE-DAY TOURING PLAN FOR TWEENS AND THEIR PARENTS A one-day touring plan for parents with children ages 8–12. It includes attractions rated three stars and higher by this age group, and it sets aside ample time for lunch and dinner.

PARENTS' EPCOT TOURING PLAN—ONE AFTERNOON AND ONE FULL DAY This touring plan is for families who want to tour Epcot comprehensively over two days. Day one uses early-morning touring opportunities. Day two begins in the afternoon and continues until closing.

BEFORE YOU GO

1. Call ☎ 407-824-4321 or check **disneyworld.com** the day before you go to verify official opening time.

2. Make reservations at the Epcot full-service restaurant(s) of your choice 180 days before your visit.

3. Make FastPass+ reservations 60 or 30 days in advance.

EPCOT TRIVIA QUIZ

1. Who is no longer performing at World Showcase?
a. Mariachi Cobre
b. The British Revolution
c. Mo'Rockin
d. Voices of Liberty

2. What is the fastest attraction at Epcot?
a. Soarin'
b. Test Track
c. Mission: Space
d. Spaceship Earth

3. Which Disney princess is *not* found at Epcot?
a. Aurora
b. Mulan
c. Merida
d. Snow White

4. Which character's meet and greet do you encounter at the Mexico Pavilion?
a. Donald Duck
b. Goofy
c. Mickey
d. Pluto

5. Which country do you find between France and Canada?
a. Germany
b. United Kingdom
c. Morocco
d. Japan

6. Where can you find the Frozen Ever After ride?
a. Canada
b. China
c. Norway
d. Italy

7. Which team do you join if you want to experience the spinning version of Mission: Space?
a. The Red team
b. The Green team
c. The Orange team
d. The Blue team

8. Who is the musical superstar featured in *Captain EO*?
a. Steven Tyler
b. Michael Jackson
c. Freddie Mercury
d. Mick Jagger

9. What kind of ride is Living with the Land?
a. A simulation ride
b. A boat ride
c. A water-flume ride
d. A roller coaster

10. What kind of animals do guest meet in *Ellen's Energy Adventure*?
a. Frogs
b. Cats and dogs
c. Dolphins
d. Dinosaurs

Answers can be found on page 437.

PART NINE

DISNEY'S ANIMAL KINGDOM

WITH ITS LUSH FLORA, winding streams, meandering paths, and exotic setting, Disney's Animal Kingdom is a stunningly beautiful theme park. Add a population of more than 1,000 animals, replicas of Africa's and Asia's most intriguing architecture, and a diverse array of attractions, and you have the most distinctive of all Walt Disney World theme parks. The Animal Kingdom's five sections, or "lands," are **The Oasis, Discovery Island, DinoLand U.S.A., Africa,** and **Asia.**

> I thought Animal Kingdom would be just a big zoo, but it wasn't. There were many rides, including my favorite, Expedition Everest.
>
> Erin

On Discovery Island, on your left just before you cross the bridge to Africa, are the **Baby Care Center** and **First Aid. Garden Gate Gifts** at the main entrance and **Mombasa Marketplace** in Africa will save the day if you run out of memory cards or other camera supplies. To your right before the turnstiles, you'll find an **ATM.** As you pass through the turnstiles, **wheelchair** and **stroller rentals** (at Garden Gate Gifts) are to your right. **Guest Relations**—the park headquarters for information, handout park maps, entertainment schedules, missing persons, and lost and found—is to the left. **Lockers** are just inside the main entrance to the left. Across from Disney's Port Orleans Resort, **Best Friends Pet Resort** provides a comfortable home away from home for Fido, Fluffy, and all their pet pals.

If you're staying at a Disney resort, we suggest that you use Disney transportation. The Animal Kingdom parking lot often opens only 15 minutes before the park, causing long lines and frustration for drivers.

The park is arranged somewhat like the Magic Kingdom. The lush, tropical Oasis serves as Main Street, funneling visitors to Discovery Island, the park's retail and dining center. From Discovery Island, guests can access the respective theme areas: Africa, Asia, and DinoLand U.S.A.

Animal Kingdom holds morning Extra Magic Hours on select days; no evening EMHs are currently offered.

For now, **Kilimanjaro Safaris** and the **Pangani Forest Exploration Trail** close around 30–60 minutes before sunset. Thus, as days get shorter with the change of seasons, the attractions close earlier in the day. In the fall, Disney closes all animal exhibits as early as 4:45 p.m.

A major construction project begun in March 2014 will bring the flora and fauna of James Cameron's *Avatar* to Disney's Animal Kingdom sometime in 2017. The area formerly known as Camp Minnie-Mickey has been demolished and its attractions relocated to other areas of the park to make way for the new land, tentatively called **Pandora: The Land of Avatar.**

Finally, Animal Kingdom will, for the first time ever, have a nighttime spectacular. Called *Rivers of Light,* the show will debut in 2016 and will take place on the Discovery River, between Discovery Island and Expedition Everest. It will feature live music, floating lanterns, water screens, and swirling animal imagery as well as amphitheater-style viewing areas facing the Discovery River. (See profile on page 335.)

In addition to *Rivers of Light,* Disney is planning to add live performers and a nighttime version of the Safaris, expected to open in late 2015 or early 2016. The Pangani Trail may also stay open later, though nothing official has been announced. To accommodate the expected increase in park attendance, a new parking lot (**Yeti**) has been built.

FASTPASS+ ATTRACTIONS AT DISNEY'S ANIMAL KINGDOM

FASTPASS+ IS OFFERED at 9 (soon to be 10) attractions:

AFRICA	DINOLAND U.S.A.
• *Festival of the Lion King*	• Dinosaur
• Kilimanjaro Safaris	• *Finding Nemo—The Musical*
ASIA	• Primeval Whirl
• Expedition Everest	**DISCOVERY ISLAND**
• Kali River Rapids	• *It's Tough to Be a Bug!*
• *Rivers of Light* (opens 2016)	• Meet Favorite Disney Pals at Adventurers Outpost

Our touring plans most frequently recommend FastPass+ reservations for **Kali River Rapids** and **Kilimanjaro Safaris.** Using FastPass+ for these allows you to experience other important attractions early in the morning, when lines are short, while still giving you relatively short lines at Kali and Safaris to contend with when you arrive.

Dinosaur and the **Adventurers Outpost** character meet and greet show up on our Animal Kingdom touring plans for parents with small children. Using FastPass+ for these will generally save you more time in line than using it at any other child-friendly attraction in our plans.

Expedition Everest is our least frequently suggested FastPass+ attraction. While posted wait times can average 60–80 minutes during summer and more during holidays, getting to Everest first thing in the morning lets you avoid those lines and save FastPass+ for something else. Plus, it has a single-rider line—a great option if you can't get a FastPass+ reservation and you don't mind splitting up your group to ride.

Continued on page 328

Disney's Animal Kingdom

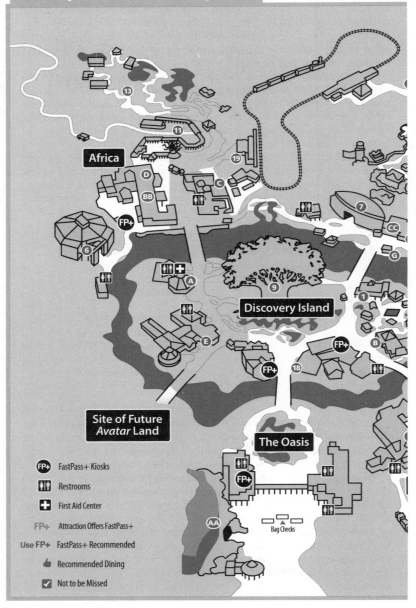

Africa

Discovery Island

Site of Future
Avatar Land

The Oasis

Bag Checks

FP+   FastPass+ Kiosks

Restrooms

First Aid Center

FP+   Attraction Offers FastPass+

Use FP+   FastPass+ Recommended

Recommended Dining

Not to be Missed

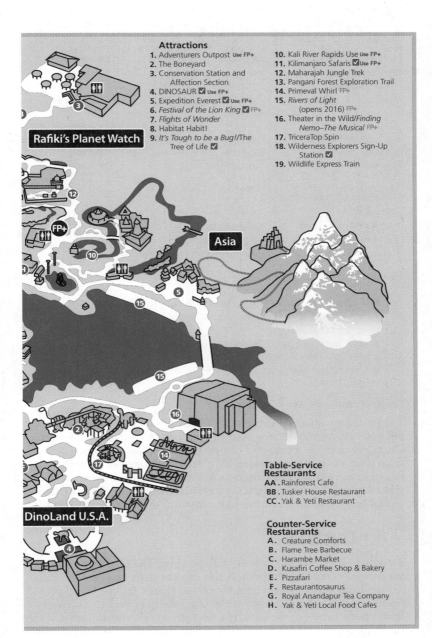

Attractions

1. Adventurers Outpost Use FP+
2. The Boneyard
3. Conservation Station and Affection Section
4. DINOSAUR ☑ Use FP+
5. Expedition Everest ☑ Use FP+
6. *Festival of the Lion King* ☑ FP+
7. *Flights of Wonder*
8. Habitat Habit!
9. *It's Tough to be a Bug!*/The Tree of Life ☑
10. Kali River Rapids Use FP+
11. Kilimanjaro Safaris ☑ Use FP+
12. Maharajah Jungle Trek
13. Pangani Forest Exploration Trail
14. Primeval Whirl FP+
15. *Rivers of Light* (opens 2016) FP+
16. Theater in the Wild/*Finding Nemo–The Musical* FP+
17. TriceraTop Spin
18. Wilderness Explorers Sign-Up Station ☑
19. Wildlife Express Train

Rafiki's Planet Watch

Asia

DinoLand U.S.A.

Table-Service Restaurants

AA . Rainforest Cafe
BB . Tusker House Restaurant
CC . Yak & Yeti Restaurant

Counter-Service Restaurants

A. Creature Comforts
B. Flame Tree Barbecue
C. Harambe Market
D. Kusafiri Coffee Shop & Bakery
E. Pizzafari
F. Restaurantosaurus
G. Royal Anandapur Tea Company
H. Yak & Yeti Local Food Cafes

ANIMAL KINGDOM
WHEN SAME-DAY FP+ RUNS OUT, BY CROWD LEVEL

ATTRACTION	LOW CROWDS*	MODERATE CROWDS*	HIGH CROWDS*
Dinosaur	3–4 p.m.	4 p.m.	11 a.m.–2 p.m.
Expedition Everest	3–4 p.m.	4 p.m.	11 a.m.–2 p.m.
Festival of the Lion King	2–3 p.m.	2–3 p.m.	1–2 p.m. (Levels 8–9), 5 p.m. (Level 10)
Finding Nemo—The Musical	3–4 p.m.	4 p.m.	1–3 p.m.
It's Tough to Be a Bug!	3–4 p.m.	4–5 p.m.	5–6 p.m.
Kali River Rapids	2–3 p.m.	3–4 p.m.	1–4 p.m.
Kilimanjaro Safaris (daytime version)	1–2 p.m.	1–2 p.m.	noon–1 p.m.
Meet Mickey and Minnie at Adventurers Outpost	noon–1 p.m.	noon–3 p.m.	1–2 p.m.
Primeval Whirl	3–4 p.m.	4–5 p.m.	5–6 p.m.

* **LOW CROWDS** (Levels 1–3 on touringplans.com Crowd Calendar)

* **MODERATE CROWDS** (Levels 4–7 on touringplans.com Crowd Calendar)

* **HIGH CROWDS** (Levels 8–10 on touringplans.com Crowd Calendar)

Continued from page 325

FastPass+ kiosk locations in Animal Kingdom are as follows:

- To the left of Expedition Everest's entrance in Asia
- Near Dawa Bar in Asia
- In front of the Disney Outfitters store on Discovery Island and across the walkway near Island Mercantile
- In front of the MyMagic+ Service Center, to the left of the entrance at The Oasis

Same-Day FastPass+ Availability

The preceding advice tells you which attractions to focus on when making your *advance* FastPass+ reservations before you get to the park. Once you're in the park, you can make more FastPass+ reservations once your advance reservations have been used or have expired (you must cancel your expired FastPass+ before you can book another). The table above shows which attractions are likely to have day-of FastPasses available, and the approximate times at which they'll run out.

The OASIS

THOUGH THE FUNCTIONAL PURPOSE of The Oasis is to funnel guests to the center of the park, it also sets the stage and gets you into the right mood to enjoy Animal Kingdom. There's no one broad thoroughfare, but rather multiple paths; each delivers you to Discovery Island at the center of the park, but the path you choose and what you see along the way are up to you. The natural-habitat zoological exhibits are primarily designed for the comfort and well-being of the animals. A sign will identify the animal(s) in each exhibit, but there's no guarantee that the animals will be immediately visible. Because most habitats are large and provide ample terrain for the occupants to hide, you must linger and concentrate, looking for small movements in the vegetation. The Oasis is a place to linger and appreciate—if you're a blitzer in the morning, definitely set aside some time here on your way out of the park. The Oasis usually closes 30–60 minutes after the rest of the park.

When you first walk into Animal Kingdom, all you see are trees, and it feels like you're entering a forest.

Ricky

DISCOVERY ISLAND

DISCOVERY ISLAND IS an island of tropical greenery and whimsical equatorial African architecture. Connected to the other lands by bridges, the island is the hub from which guests can access the park's various themed areas; it's also the park's central shopping, dining, and services headquarters. Here you'll find **First Aid** and the **Baby Care Center,** along with FastPass+ kiosks. For the best selection of Disney merchandise, try **Island Mercantile.** Counter-service food and snacks, but no full-service restaurants, are available. In addition to several wildlife exhibits, Discovery Island's **Tree of Life** hosts the film *It's Tough to Be a Bug!* The indoor **Adventurers Outpost** character meet and greet is just before the bridge to Asia.

Walking trails winding behind The Tree of Life offer several animal-viewing opportunities, from otters and kangaroos to lemurs, storks, and porcupines. Besides the animals, you'll find verdant landscaping, waterfalls, and quiet spots to sit and reflect on your relationship with nature.

Meet Favorite Disney Pals at Adventurers Outpost
(FastPass+) ★★★½

| APPEAL BY AGE | PRESCHOOL ★★★★ | GRADE SCHOOL ★★★★½ | TEENS ★★★★ |
| YOUNG ADULTS ★★★★ | OVER 30 ★★★★ | | SENIORS ★★★★ |

What it is Character-greeting venue. **Scope and scale** Minor attraction. **Fright potential** Not frightening in any respect. **Bottleneck rating** 7. **When to go** First thing in the morning, after 5 p.m., or use FastPass+. **Authors' rating** Nicely themed (and air-conditioned); ★★★½. **Duration of experience** About 2 minutes. **Probable waiting time** About 20 minutes. **Queue speed** Fast.

An indoor, air-conditioned character-greeting location for Mickey and Minnie, Adventurers Outpost is decorated with photos, memorabilia, and souvenirs from the Mouses' world travels. Two air-conditioned greeting rooms house two identical sets of characters, so lines move fairly quickly. Good use of FastPass+ if you have kids too small to ride Expedition Everest or Dinosaur.

The Tree of Life / *It's Tough to Be a Bug!* (FastPass+)
★★★★

| APPEAL BY AGE | PRESCHOOL ★★★½ | GRADE SCHOOL ★★★★ | TEENS ★★★★ |
| YOUNG ADULTS ★★★★ | OVER 30 ★★★★ | | SENIORS ★★★★½ |

What it is 3-D theater show. **Scope and scale** Major attraction. **Fright potential** Very intense and loud, with special effects that startle viewers of all ages and potentially terrify young children. **Bottleneck rating** 9. **When to go** Anytime. **Special comment** The theater is inside the tree. **Authors' rating** Zany and frenetic; ★★★★. **Duration of show** Approximately 8 minutes. **Probable waiting time** 12–20 minutes.

DISNEY DISH WITH JIM HILL

GETTING TO THE ROOT OF THE PROBLEM The Tree of Life got a great new photo op spot in February 2015, when the Imagineers widened the walkway in front of this 14-story-tall structure and built a network of carved "roots" in the shapes of rams, crocodiles, and other animals; look for these along the Discovery Island walkway to Africa, on the front left side of the tree. Disney hopes this new spot will become the perfect framework for family photos.

Before entering the show, take a close look at The Tree of Life, the remarkable home of this 3-D movie. The primary icon and focal point of Animal Kingdom, the tree features a trunk with high-relief carvings depicting 325 animals.

It's Tough to Be a Bug! is cleverly conceived but very intense. For starters, the show is about bugs, and bugs always rank high on the ick-factor scale. That, coupled with some startling special effects and a very loud sound track, make *It's Tough to Be a Bug!* a potential horror show for the age-7-and-under crowd, but you can prepare your kids by watching *A Bug's Life* before you leave home—many of the characters are the same.

The closing lines of the show tipped me off when it was announced that "honorary bugs [read: audience members] remain seated while all the lice, bedbugs, maggots, and cockroaches exit first." In other words, if you don't like bugs crawling on you, even simulated ones, keep your feet off the floor.

Liliane

This one never gets old. Beware, though: Some parts are a tad scary for little kids. You feel like you're inside a real tree. Very cool!

Julia

Wilderness Explorers ★★★★

What it is Park-wide scavenger hunt and puzzle-solving adventure game. **Scope and scale** Diversion. **Fright potential** Not frightening in any respect. **Bottleneck rating** 6. **When to go** Sign up first thing in the morning and complete activities throughout the day. **Special comment** Collecting all 32 badges takes 3–5 hours, which can be done over several days. **Authors' rating** One of the best attractions in any Disney park; not to be missed; ★★★★.

Wilderness Explorers is a scavenger hunt based on Russell's Boy Scout–esque troop from the movie *Up*. Players earn "badges"—stickers given out by cast members—for completing predefined activities throughout the park. For example, to earn the Gorilla Badge, you walk the Pangani Forest Exploration Trail to observe how the primates behave, and then mimic that behavior back to a cast member to show what you've seen. Register for the game near the bridge from The Oasis to Discovery Island. You'll be given an instruction book and a map showing the park location for each badge to be earned. It's tons of fun for kids and adults; we play it every time we're in the park. Activities are spread throughout the park, including areas to which many guests never venture. You have to ride specific attractions to earn certain badges, so using FastPass+ for those will save time.

I love a good scavenger hunt! Collecting the badges and stickers from the Wilderness Explorers is great. You'll learn about animals, and the cast members are very knowledgeable and friendly.

Alex

AFRICA

AFRICA IS THE LARGEST of the Animal Kingdom's lands. Guests enter through **Harambe,** Disney's idealized and immensely sanitized version of a modern rural African town, with shops, a sit-down buffet, limited counter service, and snack stands. Harambe serves as the gateway to the African veldt habitat, Animal Kingdom's largest zoological exhibit. Access to the veldt is via the **Kilimanjaro Safaris** attraction. Harambe is also the departure point for the train to **Rafiki's Planet Watch** and **Conservation Station** (the park's veterinary headquarters), as well as the home of a long-running live theatrical show.

Festival of the Lion King (FastPass+) ★★★★

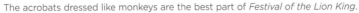

APPEAL BY AGE PRESCHOOL ★★★★½ GRADE SCHOOL ★★★★½ TEENS ★★★★½
YOUNG ADULTS ★★★★½   OVER 30 ★★★★½   SENIORS ★★★★★

What it is Theater-in-the-round stage show. **Scope and scale** Major attraction. **Fright potential** A bit loud but otherwise not frightening. **Bottleneck rating 9. When to go** Before 11 a.m., after 4 p.m., or use FastPass+; check the handout park map or *Times Guide* for showtimes. **Authors' rating** Upbeat and spectacular; not to be missed; ★★★★. **Duration of show** 30 minutes. **Probable waiting time** 20–35 minutes.

Fantastic pageantry, dazzling costumes, a mini–Broadway show, and air-conditioning too. *Festival of the Lion King* at the Animal Kingdom was the precursor of the Broadway production of *The Lion King*. The Festival of the Lion King moved to its new location in Africa in June 2014.

Liliane

Try to score front-row seats. Kids are invited to play musical instruments and join the performance.

Movie Tip

The show is based on the animated feature The Lion King, *a must-see movie. Did you know that James Earl Jones, the voice behind Mufasa (father of Simba), is also the voice behind Darth Vader in* Star Wars?

Ricky

The acrobats dressed like monkeys are the best part of *Festival of the Lion King.*

Kilimanjaro Safaris (FastPass+) ★★★★★

APPEAL BY AGE PRESCHOOL ★★★★½ GRADE SCHOOL ★★★★½ TEENS ★★★★½
YOUNG ADULTS ★★★★½   OVER 30 ★★★★½   SENIORS ★★★★★

What it is Truck ride through an African wildlife reservation. **Scope and scale** Super-headliner. **Fright potential** A "collapsing" bridge and the proximity of real animals make a few young children anxious. **Bottleneck rating 10. When to go** As soon as the park opens, in the 2 hours before closing, or use FastPass+. **Authors' rating** Truly exceptional; ★★★★★.

Thumbs Up for the Whole Family

Duration of ride About 20 minutes. **Average wait in line per 100 people ahead of you** 4 minutes; assumes full-capacity operation with 18-second dispatch interval. **Loading speed** Fast.

Off you go in an open safari vehicle through a simulated African savanna, looking for hippos, zebras, giraffes, lions, and rhinos. Many readers have asked us whether fewer animals are visible from Kilimanjaro Safaris around lunchtime than at park opening, out of concern that the animals might be less active in the midday heat. To help answer that question, we sent a team of researchers to ride continuously during one week in the summer and had them count the number of animals visible at different times of day. We subdivided our counting into large animals (elephants, hippos, and lions, for example), small (deer and other ungulates), and birds. Our results indicate that you'll probably see the same number of animals regardless of when you visit. This finding is almost certainly due to Disney's deliberate placement of water, food, and shade near the safari vehicles. We hear the Safaris will begin offering nighttime tours in late 2015 or early 2016, probably around the time that *Rivers of Light* (see page 335) makes its debut.

The best thing about this ride is that you almost always get to see lions, and it feels like there's no fence to stop the animals from attacking you!

Ricky

Winding through the safari is **Disney's Wild Africa Trek,** a behind-the-scenes walking tour of the Animal Kingdom that takes you into several of Kilimanjaro Safaris' animal enclosures.

Bob

Don't ride just once—you can see different animals at different times of day. Ride the Safaris first thing in the morning and again late in the afternoon.

Pangani Forest Exploration Trail ★★★★

**APPEAL BY AGE PRESCHOOL ★★★★ GRADE SCHOOL ★★★★ TEENS ★★★★
YOUNG ADULTS ★★★★½   OVER 30 ★★★★   SENIORS ★★★★½**

What it is Walk-through zoological exhibit. **Scope and scale** Major attraction. **Fright potential** Not frightening in any respect. **Bottleneck rating** 9. **When to go** Before 11 a.m. or after 2:30 p.m. **Authors' rating ★★★★**. **Duration of tour** About 20–25 minutes.

The Pangani Forest Exploration Trail is lush, beautiful, and jammed to the gills with people much of the time—particularly unpleasant if you have to wiggle your way through with a stroller. Walk the trail before 11 a.m. or after 2:30 p.m., or schedule a FastPass+ reservation for Kilimanjaro Safaris 60–90 minutes after the park opens. That's long enough for an uncrowded, leisurely tour of the trail and a quick snack before you go on safari.

RAFIKI'S PLANET WATCH

THIS AREA ISN'T REALLY a "land" and not really an attraction either. Disney uses the name as an umbrella for Conservation Station, the petting zoo, and the environmental exhibits accessible from Harambe via the Wildlife Express Train. Presumably, Disney hopes that invoking Rafiki (a beloved character from *The Lion King*) stimulates guests to make the effort to check out things in this far-flung outpost of the park. As for your kids seeing Rafiki, don't bet on it. He rarely appears here.

Conservation Station and Affection Section ★★★½

What it is Behind-the-scenes walk-through educational exhibit and petting zoo.
Scope and scale Minor attraction. **Fright potential** Not frightening in any
respect. **Bottleneck rating** 6. **When to go** Anytime. **Special comment** Opens
30 minutes after rest of park. **Authors' rating** ★★★½.

This is the Animal Kingdom's veterinary and conservation headquarters.
Guests can meet wildlife experts, observe some of the ongoing projects,
and learn about the operations of the park. A rehabilitation area for
injured animals, a nursery for recently born (or hatched) critters, and a
petting zoo are included.

What you see will largely depend on what's going on when you arrive.
Some readers think there isn't enough happening to warrant waiting in
line twice (coming and going) for the train, but others have had better
luck, as a university biologist from Springfield, Missouri, attests:

> If you get to Conservation Station between 10 a.m. and noon, you can see the vet
> techs actually doing some routine procedures as they maintain the health of the
> animals. Our aspiring 7-year-old vet LOVED visiting with the technician. She spent
> 20 minutes asking her all kinds of questions.

Conservation Station is interesting, but you have to invest a little effort,
and it helps to be inquisitive. Because it's so removed from the rest of
the park, you'll never bump into Conservation Station unless you take
the train round-trip from Harambe.

This was just OK. Little kids probably like it, but next time I'll skip it.

This is kind of a petting zoo. Not too impressive
unless a goat tries to eat your brother's shorts.

Isaac

Ethan

If you want to see the vets at work, try to get to
Rafiki's Planet Watch before 11 in the morning.
Last summer I saw a tiger having a tooth removed.

Alex

Habitat Habit!

Located on the pedestrian path between the train station and Conservation Station, Habitat Habit! consists of a tiny collection of signs (about
coexistence with wildlife) and a few animals. Park maps call it an attraction, which we find absurd.

Wildlife Express Train ★★

What it is Scenic railroad ride to Rafiki's Planet Watch and Conservation Station.
Scope and scale Minor attraction. **Fright potential** Not frightening in any
respect. **Bottleneck rating** 7. **When to go** Anytime. **Special comment** Opens
30 minutes after the rest of the park. **Authors' rating** Ho hum; ★★. **Duration of ride**
About 5–7 minutes one-way. **Average wait in line per 100 people ahead of
you** 9 minutes. **Loading speed** Moderate.

Take the train only if you have small kids who would really enjoy the Affection Section petting zoo at Rafiki's Planet Watch. If you have a future

veterinarian in your family, it's also worth checking out the behind-the-scenes exhibits at Conservation Station.

ASIA

CROSSING THE BRIDGE FROM DISCOVERY ISLAND, you enter this land through the village of **Anandapur,** a veritable collage of Asian themes inspired by the architecture and ruins of India, Thailand, Indonesia, and Nepal. Anandapur provides access to an animal exhibit and to Asia's two feature attractions, the **Kali River Rapids** whitewater raft ride and **Expedition Everest.** Also in Asia is *Flights of Wonder,* an educational production about birds.

Expedition Everest (FastPass+) ★★★★½

**APPEAL BY AGE PRESCHOOL ★★★½ GRADE SCHOOL ★★★★½ TEENS ★★★★★
YOUNG ADULTS ★★★★★   OVER 30 ★★★★★   SENIORS ★★★★**

What it is High-speed outdoor roller coaster through Nepalese mountain village. **Scope and scale** Super-headliner. **Fright potential** Frightens guests of all ages. **Bottleneck rating 8. When to go** Before 9:30 a.m., after 3 p.m., or use FastPass+. **Special comments** Must be 44" to ride; switching-off option provided (see page 243). **Authors' rating** Not to be missed; ★★★★½. **Duration of ride** 3½ minutes. **Average wait in line per 100 people ahead of you** Just under 4 minutes; assumes 2 tracks operating. **Loading speed** Moderate–fast.

Lose Things

Scary

As you enjoy one of the most spectacular panoramas in Walt Disney World, you wish this expedition would never end. But you get over that in a hurry as the train starts whirring through the guts of Disney's largest man-made mountain. After a high-speed encounter with a large, smelly (and often AWOL) yeti and a dead stop at the top of the mountain, the 50-mph chase continues backward. The ride is very smooth and rich both in visuals and special effects. The backward segment is one of the most creative and exciting 20 seconds in roller coaster annals.

> The best part is when you get to the broken tracks and you start going backward really fast. Be prepared to scream—that adds to it.
>
> Ethan

Flights of Wonder ★★★★

**APPEAL BY AGE PRESCHOOL ★★★★ GRADE SCHOOL ★★★★½ TEENS ★★★★
YOUNG ADULTS ★★★★½   OVER 30 ★★★★½   SENIORS ★★★★½**

What it is Stadium show about birds. **Scope and scale** Major attraction. **Fright potential** Swooping birds startle some younger children. **Bottleneck rating 6. When to go** Anytime. **Special comment** Performance times are listed in the handout park map or *Times Guide*. **Authors' rating** Unique; ★★★★. **Duration of show** 30 minutes. **When to arrive** 20–30 minutes before showtime.

Thumbs Up for the Whole Family

Humorously presented, the show is ideal for kids. Don't expect parrots riding unicycles though: *Flights of Wonder* is about the natural talents and characteristics of various bird species. If your child is comfortable with you sitting a few rows behind, encourage him or her to take a seat in the up front "for kids only" section. When the show is over, stick around and talk to the bird trainers and meet the feathery cast of the show up close and personal. It's a great opportunity to ask questions and take pictures. *Flights of Wonder* plays at the stadium located near the Asia bridge on the walkway between Asia and Africa. Though the stadium is covered, it's not air-conditioned; thus, early-morning and late-afternoon performances are more comfortable.

Kali River Rapids *(FastPass+)*   ★★★½

**APPEAL BY AGE   PRESCHOOL ★★★★   GRADE SCHOOL ★★★★½   TEENS ★★★★
YOUNG ADULTS ★★★★½   OVER 30 ★★★★½   SENIORS ★★★★½**

What it is Whitewater raft ride. **Scope and scale** Headliner. **Fright potential** Potentially frightening and certainly wet for guests of all ages. **Bottleneck rating** 9. **When to go** First or last hour the park is open, or use FastPass+. **Special comments** Must be 38" tall to ride; you're guaranteed to get wet; opens 30 minutes after the rest of the park. Switching-off option provided (see page 243). **Authors' rating** Short but scenic; ★★★½. **Duration of ride** About 5 minutes. **Average wait in line per 100 people ahead of you** 5 minutes. **Loading speed** Moderate.

Wet   Scary

This tame raft ride lets you take in the outstanding scenery as you drift through a dense rain forest, past waterfalls and temple ruins. There are neither big drops nor terrifying rapids; nevertheless, Disney still manages to drench you. Nonriding park guests will take great pleasure squirting water at the rafters from above. The water-squirting elephant stations are a great consolation prize for those who don't meet the 38-inch height requirement.

If you ride early in the morning or on a cool day, use raingear and make sure your shoes stay dry. Touring in wet clothes is no fun, and walking all day in soaked sneakers is a recipe for blisters.

Liliane

You get absolutely soaked. Love it—my mom, not so much.

Isaac

Maharajah Jungle Trek   ★★★★

**APPEAL BY AGE   PRESCHOOL ★★★★   GRADE SCHOOL ★★★★   TEENS ★★★★
YOUNG ADULTS ★★★★½   OVER 30 ★★★★   SENIORS ★★★★½**

What it is Walk-through zoological exhibit. **Scope and scale** Headliner. **Fright potential** Some children may balk at the bat exhibit. **Bottleneck rating** 5. **When to go** Anytime. **Special comment** Opens 30 minutes after the rest of the park. **Authors' rating** A standard-setter for natural habitat design; ★★★★. **Duration of tour** About 20–30 minutes.

The Jungle Trek is less congested than the Pangani Forest Exploration Trail and is a good choice for midday touring. Tigers, gibbons, bats, and birds are waiting to be discovered along a path winding through the fabulous ruins of the maharajah's palace.

Rivers of Light *(opens 2016)*

What it is Nighttime spectacular. **Scope and scale** Major attraction. **When to go** Check your *Times Guide* for showtimes.

Animal Kingdom has never had a nighttime event along the lines of the Magic Kingdom's *Wishes* or Disney's Hollywood Studios' *Fantasmic!* In preparation

---

DISNEY DISH WITH JIM HILL

ROCKIN' OUT THE RHINOS When *Rivers of Light* opens, it will dazzle Animal Kingdom visitors with its mix of music, live performers, and elaborate pageantry. What it *won't* do, or so Disney hopes, is frighten the animals in the park: For months before the show begins, the show's sound track will be played in the backstage barns and corrals where the animals bed down for the night. The idea is to familiarize the animals with the show's sounds, effects, and even audience noise.

---

for the 2017 opening of Pandora: The Land of Avatar, though, Animal Kingdom is adding both the *Rivers of Light* nighttime spectacular and, rumor has it, a nighttime version of Kilimanjaro Safaris in Africa (see page 331).

The show will be staged in the middle of the Discovery River. Disney hasn't released many details about the show's plot, but we do know it will feature sprayed water screens onto which animal- and nature-related films will be projected. Disney also promises "floating lanterns" and live music. We think there will also be dramatic lighting effects, but no fireworks.

Judging from the construction going on around the Discovery River, we expect there to be two seating areas, at least one of them dedicated to FastPass+. One seating area will be in Asia, on the riverfront next to Expedition Everest; the second will be in DinoLand U.S.A.

DINOLAND U.S.A.

THIS MOST TYPICALLY DISNEY of Animal Kingdom's lands is a cross between an anthropological dig and a quirky roadside attraction. Accessible via the bridge from Discovery Island, DinoLand U.S.A. is home to a children's play area, a nature trail, a 1,500-seat amphitheater, and **Dinosaur**, one of Animal Kingdom's three thrill rides. *Finding Nemo—The Musical* is shown at Theater in the Wild.

The Boneyard ★★★

APPEAL BY AGE PRESCHOOL ★★★★½ GRADE SCHOOL ★★★★½ TEENS ★★★★
YOUNG ADULTS ★★★½   OVER 30 ★★★   SENIORS ★★★

What it is Elaborate playground. **Scope and scale** Diversion. **Fright potential** Not frightening in any respect. **Bottleneck rating** 5. **When to go** Anytime. **Special comment** Opens 30 minutes after the rest of the park. **Authors' rating** Stimulating fun for children; ★★★.

> If it's a very hot day, don't go to The Boneyard. It doesn't have a lot of shade—all the slides get red-hot, and you'll burn your bum.
>
> — Alex

Time to play! This elaborate playground for kids age 12 and younger is a great place for them to let off steam and get dirty (or at least sandy). The playground equipment consists of skeletal replicas of *Triceratops, Tyrannosaurus rex, Brachiosaurus,* and the like. In addition, there are climbing mazes, plus sandpits where little ones can scrounge for bones and fossils.

The Boneyard can get very hot in the scorching Florida sun, so make sure your kids are properly hydrated and protected against sunburn. The playground is huge, and parents might lose sight of a small child. Fortunately, however, there's only one entrance and exit. Your little ones are going to love The Boneyard, so resign yourself to staying awhile.

Dinosaur *(FastPass+)* ★★★★

| APPEAL BY AGE | PRESCHOOL ★★★ | GRADE SCHOOL ★★★★ | TEENS ★★★★½ |
| YOUNG ADULTS ★★★★ | | OVER 30 ★★★★ | SENIORS ★★★★ |

What it is Motion-simulator dark ride. **Scope and scale** Super-headliner. **Fright potential** High-tech thrill ride rattles riders of all ages. **Bottleneck rating** 8. **When to go** Before 10:30 a.m., after 4:30 p.m., or use FastPass+. **Special comments** Must be 40″ tall to ride; switching-off option provided (see page 243). **Authors' rating** Not to be missed; ★★★★. **Duration of ride** 3½ minutes. **Average wait in line per 100 people ahead of you** 3 minutes; assumes full-capacity operation with 18-second dispatch interval. **Loading speed** Fast.

Dark   Rough   Scary

Here you board a time capsule to return to the Jurassic age in an effort to bring back a live dinosaur before a meteor hits the Earth and wipes them out. The bad guy in this epic is the little-known *Carnotaurus,* an evil-eyed, long-in-the-tooth, *Tyrannosaurus rex*-type fellow. A combination track ride and motion simulator, Dinosaur is not for the fainthearted—you get tossed and pitched around in the dark, with pesky dinosaurs jumping out at you. Dinosaur has left many an adult weak-kneed. Most kids under age 9 find it terrifying.

Primeval Whirl *(FastPass+)* ★★★

| APPEAL BY AGE | PRESCHOOL ★★★½ | GRADE SCHOOL ★★★★ | TEENS ★★★★ |
| YOUNG ADULTS ★★★½ | | OVER 30 ★★★½ | SENIORS ★★★ |

What it is Small roller coaster. **Scope and scale** Minor attraction. **Fright potential** Scarier than it looks. **Bottleneck rating** 9. **When to go** During the first hour the park is open, in the hour before park closing, or use FastPass+. **Special comments** Must be 48″ tall to ride; switching-off option provided (see page 243). **Authors' rating** Wild Mouse on steroids; ★★★. **Duration of ride** Almost 2½ minutes. **Average wait in line per 100 people ahead of you** 4½ minutes. **Loading speed** Slow.

Scary   Rough   Queasy

This tricky little coaster has short drops, curves, and tight loops—not to mention the coaster cars spin. The problem is that, unlike with those evil teacups, you can't control the spinning. Complete spins are fun, but watch out for the screeching-stop half-spins.

This ride doesn't get much attention because it's far from the main attractions, but my little brother, Max, and I love it and ride it over and over again.

Erin

Theater in the Wild / *Finding Nemo—The Musical* *(FastPass+)* ★★★★

| APPEAL BY AGE | PRESCHOOL ★★★★½ | GRADE SCHOOL ★★★★½ | TEENS ★★★★ |
| YOUNG ADULTS ★★★★½ | | OVER 30 ★★★★½ | SENIORS ★★★★½ |

Thumbs Up for the Whole Family

What it is Open-air venue for live stage shows. **Scope and scale** Major attraction. **Fright potential** Generally not frightening—but see below. **Bottleneck rating** 6. **When to go** Anytime. **Special comment** Performance times are listed in the handout park map or *Times Guide*. **Authors' rating ★★★★**. **Duration of show** 30 minutes. **When to arrive** 30 minutes before showtime.

Based on the Disney-Pixar animated feature, *Finding Nemo—The Musical* is an elaborate stage show headlining puppets, dancers, acrobats, and special effects. It is arguably the most elaborate live show in any Disney World park. A few scenes, such as one in which Nemo's mom is eaten (!), may be too intense for some very small children. Some of the mid-show musical numbers slow the pace, so the main concern for parents is whether the kids can sit still for an entire show. With that in mind, we advise parents to catch an afternoon performance after seeing the rest of Animal Kingdom.

To get a seat, show up 20–25 minutes in advance for morning and late-afternoon shows and 30–35 minutes in advance for shows scheduled noon–4:30 p.m. Access to the theater is via a relatively narrow pedestrian path; if you arrive as the previous show is letting out, you'll feel like a salmon swimming upstream.

When the line is very long, don't assume that you'll get into the next show just by queuing up. Disney cast members monitor the line—ask them whether you're likely to get into the next show.

Liliane

TriceraTop Spin   ★★

APPEAL BY AGE	PRESCHOOL ★★★★½	GRADE SCHOOL ★★★★	TEENS ★★★
YOUNG ADULTS ★★★	OVER 30 ★★★		SENIORS ★★★½

What it is Hub-and-spoke midway ride. **Scope and scale** Minor attraction. **Fright potential** May frighten preschoolers. **Bottleneck rating** 9. **When to go** Before noon or after 3 p.m. **Authors' rating** Dumbo's prehistoric forebear; ★★. **Duration of ride** 1½ minutes. **Average wait in line per 100 people ahead of you** 10 minutes. **Loading speed** Slow.

Instead of Dumbo, you get Dino spinning around a central axis. Fun for little ones, but this slow-loader is infamous for inefficiency and long waits.

LIVE ENTERTAINMENT *at* ANIMAL KINGDOM

WDW LIVE-ENTERTAINMENT GURU Steve Soares usually posts the Animal Kingdom performance schedule about a week in advance at **wdwent.com.**

ANIMAL ENCOUNTERS Throughout the day, Disney staff conduct impromptu short lectures on specific animals at the park. Look for a cast member in safari garb holding a bird, reptile, or small mammal.

Winged Encounters—The Kingdom Takes Flight is sort of like *Flights of Wonder* (see page 334) on a smaller scale. The outdoor show features macaws and their handlers on Discovery Island, across from Flame Tree Barbecue. Guests can to talk to the animals' trainers and see the birds fly around the middle of the park. Check your *Times Guide* for the performance schedule.

GOODWILL AMBASSADORS A number of Asian and African cast members are on hand throughout the park. Gracious and knowledgeable,

DISNEY DISH WITH JIM HILL

ON A WING AND A PRAYER If you want an especially good photo of the *Winged Encounters* birds in action, here's a tip: After the birds take off, turn so that the Tree of Life is to your back, and you're facing the bridge that leads to the exit of Animal Kingdom. You'll be perfectly positioned as this colorful flock of macaws comes swooping back in over the heads of the crowd.

they're delighted to discuss their native countries and the wildlife in them. Look for them in Harambe and along the Pangani Forest Exploration Trail in Africa, and in Anandapur and along the Maharajah Jungle Trek in Asia. They can also be found near the main entrance and at The Oasis.

KIDS' DISCOVERY CLUB Activity stations offer kids ages 4–8 a structured learning experience as they tour Animal Kingdom. Set up along walkways in six themed areas, Discovery Club stations are manned by cast members who supervise a different activity at each station. A souvenir logbook, available free, is stamped at each station when the child completes a craft or exercise. Kids enjoy collecting the stamps and noodling puzzles in the logbook while in attraction lines.

STREET PERFORMERS Far and away the most intriguing is the performer you can't see—at least not at first. A perfect fusion between fantasy and reality, **DiVine** (★★★★) is an artist best described as half vine and half creeping plant. She blends perfectly with the foliage at Animal Kingdom and is noticeable only when she moves—which can be quite startling if you're not aware of her presence. DiVine travels around the park but seems to love the path between Asia and Africa and The Oasis; if you don't encounter her, ask a cast member where she can be found. Video of her is available at **YouTube** (go to **youtube.com** and search for "DiVine Disney's Animal Kingdom").

But DiVine isn't the only performer at Animal Kingdom worth seeing. Make sure you take a moment to enjoy **Viva Gaia Street Band** at

FAVORITE EATS AT ANIMAL KINGDOM

LAND | SERVICE LOCATION | FOOD ITEM

DISCOVERY ISLAND   Flame Tree Barbecue | Ribs & chicken with baked beans
Pizzafari | Pizza & chicken Caesar salad, breadsticks

AFRICA   Tamu Tamu Eats & Refreshments | Dole Whips & sundaes
Tusker House Restaurant | Rotisserie chicken, curried rice, & couscous. Tusker House has a character breakfast, lunch, and dinner featuring Donald, Daisy, Goofy, & Mickey. | *Buffet*

ASIA   Royal Anandapur Tea Company | Teas & specialty coffees
Yak & Yeti Restaurant | *Kalbi* steak & coconut shrimp | *Table service only*

DINOLAND U.S.A.   Restaurantosaurus | Kid's cheeseburger comes with grapes & carrot sticks & choice of 1% milk or bottled water

OUTSIDE ENTRANCE   Rainforest Cafe | Breakfast, lunch, & dinner in a tropical rain forest setting with a huge saltwater aquarium, gorillas going wild once in a while, & simulated thunderstorms. The place to take the kids if you want to sit down! They'll love you for it— cross my heart and hope to die. | *Table service only*

Discovery Island; **Burudika Band** and the **Tam Tam Drummers** in Africa; and Liliane's favorite, **DJ Anaan** in Asia. **Gi-Tar Dan** performs at Rafiki's Planet Watch, and little ones will love the **DinoLand Dance-a-Palooza**.

ANIMAL KINGDOM TOURING PLANS

OUR STEP-BY-STEP TOURING PLANS ARE FIELD-TESTED, independently verified itineraries that will keep you moving counter to the crowd flow. The plans will also allow you to see as much as possible in a single day with minimum time wasted in line. Because Animal Kingdom has fewer attractions than the other parks, you can take them in during a single day, even when traveling with young children.

The different touring plans are described below. The descriptions will tell you for whom (for example, tweens, parents with preschoolers, and so on) or for what situation (such as sleeping late) the plans are designed. The actual touring plans are located on pages 469–472. Each plan includes a numbered map of the park to help you find your way around.

We've also listed the attractions most likely to need FastPass+ and the FastPass+ return times for which you should attempt to make reservations. Check **touringplans.com** for the latest information.

ANIMAL KINGDOM ONE-DAY TOURING PLAN FOR PARENTS WITH SMALL CHILDREN This plan is designed for parents of children ages 3–8 who wish to see the very best age-appropriate attractions in the Animal Kingdom. Every attraction has a rating of at least three stars (out of five) from preschool and grade-school children surveyed by *The Unofficial Guide*. Special advice is provided for touring the park with small children, including restaurant recommendations. The plan keeps walking and backtracking to a minimum, with no crisscrossing of the park.

ANIMAL KINGDOM ONE-DAY SLEEPYHEAD TOURING PLAN FOR PARENTS WITH SMALL CHILDREN A relaxed plan that allows families with small children to sleep late and still see the highlights of the Animal Kingdom. The plan begins around 11 a.m., sets aside ample time for lunch, and includes the very best child-friendly attractions in the park.

ANIMAL KINGDOM ONE-DAY TOURING PLAN FOR TWEENS AND THEIR PARENTS A one-day plan for parents with children ages 8–12. It includes every attraction rated three stars and higher by this age group and sets aside ample time for lunch.

ANIMAL KINGDOM ONE-DAY HAPPY FAMILY TOURING PLAN A plan for families of all ages. Includes time-saving tips for teens and adults visiting the Animal Kingdom's thrill rides, as well as age-appropriate attractions for parents with small children. The entire family stays together as much as possible (including lunch), but this plan allows groups with different interests to explore their favorite attractions without having everyone wait around.

BEFORE YOU GO

1. Call ☎ 407-824-4321 or check **disneyworld.com** for operating hours.
2. Buy your admission and make FastPass+ reservations before you arrive.

DISNEY'S ANIMAL KINGDOM TRIVIA QUIZ

1. Which attraction is inside the iconic Tree of Life?
   a. Pocahontas and Her Forest Friends   **b.** *It's Tough to Be a Bug!*
   c. Wilderness Explorers   **d.** *Flights of Wonder*

2. What parade ran for 14 years at Animal Kingdom?
   a. Festival of Fantasy Parade   **c.** Mickey's Jammin' Jungle Parade
   b. *Festival of the Lion King* Parade   **d.** Mickey's Soundsational Parade

3. In which land do you find Kali River Rapids?
   a. Africa   **c.** Thailand
   b. India   **d.** Asia

4. What show plays at Theater in the Wild?
   a. *Indiana Jones Epic Stunt Spectacular!*
   b. *Voyage of the Little Mermaid*
   c. *Finding Nemo—The Musical*
   d. *Beauty and the Beast—Live on Stage*

5. Which restaurant can be accessed without paying entrance to Animal Kingdom?
   a. Tusker House   **c.** Flame Tree Barbecue
   b. Rainforest Cafe   **d.** Yak & Yeti

6. The new land being added to Animal Kingdom is based on which movie?
   a. *The Jungle Book*   **c.** *Tarzan*
   b. *Avatar*   **d.** *A Bug's Life*

7. Which one of the following attractions can only be experienced in a vehicle?
   a. Pangani Forest Exploration Trail   **c.** Kilimanjaro Safaris
   b. Wilderness Explorers   **d.** Maharajah Jungle Trek

8. What is the closest water park to Animal Kingdom?
   a. Wet 'n Wild   **c.** Blizzard Beach
   b. Typhoon Lagoon   **d.** The Splash Zone

9. What is Animal Kingdom's interactive adventure game?
   a. Yak & Yeti's Adventures   **c.** *Finding Nemo*
   b. Wilderness Explorers   **d.** Expedition Everest

10. What was the first animal to be born in Animal Kingdom?
   a. A black rhino   **c.** A Masai giraffe
   b. A Micronesian kingfisher chick   **d.** A kudu (a large African antelope)

Answers can be found on page 437.

PART TEN

DISNEY'S HOLLYWOOD STUDIOS

ABOUT HALF OF DISNEY'S HOLLYWOOD STUDIOS is set up as a theme park; the other half is off-limits to guests. Though modest in size, the Studios' open-access areas are confusingly arranged (a product of the park's hurried expansion in the early 1990s). As at the Magic Kingdom, you enter the park and pass down a main street, only this time it's the **Hollywood Boulevard** of the 1920s and 1930s. Though the park is largely organized by street names rather than by "lands," the easiest way to navigate it is by landmarks and attractions using the park map.

LILIANE If you're interested in visiting a theme park devoted to TV, movies, and music, **Universal Studios Florida** is a better value than DHS.

After Disney severed its relationship with MGM in 2008, the park formerly known as Disney-MGM Studios was renamed Disney's Hollywood Studios. But the *Studios* in "Disney's Hollywood Studios" is of little significance today: Movie and TV production ceased here long ago, and only a handful of aging attractions remain that offer a peek behind the scenes.

In 2015, the iconic Sorcerer's Hat in front of the Chinese Theatre was removed. The great view upon entering the park has been restored; however, the former icon, the much more appropriate Earffel Tower, is no longer accessible to guests with the closing of the Studio Backlot Tour. Disney CEO Bob Iger also announced that the park—which no longer bears any resemblance to a studio—will be renamed in the near future. The leading candidate for a new moniker is something along the lines of Disney's Hollywood Adventure.

Persistent rumors of a *Star Wars* land coming to the park signal what we hope will be a much-needed makeover for the Studios. When will guests be able to experience this proposed upgrade? The answer seems to be "in a time far, far away."

Guest Relations, on your left as you enter, serves as the park headquarters and information center, similar to City Hall in the Magic Kingdom. Go there for a schedule of live performances, lost persons, package pickup, lost and found (on the right side of the entrance), general information, or in an emergency. If you haven't picked up a

DISNEY DISH WITH JIM HILL

A GALAXY FAR, FAR AWAY GETS A LITTLE CLOSER
It's taken far longer than expected for Disney's board of directors to approve plans for the Studios' new *Star Wars*–themed land, planned for the vicinity of Streets of America and Mickey Avenue. But because Disney is reportedly spending upward of $500 million, it wants enough "wow" to ensure it can compete with The Wizarding World attractions at Universal. Look for construction to get started in 2016.

map of the Studios, get one here. To the right of the entrance are **locker, stroller,** and **wheelchair rentals.**

The **Baby Care Center** is located at Guest Relations, and **Oscar's** sells baby food and other necessities. Camera supplies for those precious moments can be purchased at **The Darkroom,** on the right side of Hollywood Boulevard just past Oscar's. The closest **ATM** is just outside the park, to the right of the turnstiles. Across from Disney's Port Orleans Resort, **Best Friends Pet Resort** provides a comfortable home away from home for Fido, Fluffy, and all their pet pals.

Guests enter the park on **Hollywood Boulevard,** a palm-lined street reminiscent of the famous Hollywood main avenue of the 1930s. The best way to navigate is to decide what you really want to see and go for it! If you want the whole enchilada, you can easily do it all in a day.

Architecture on Hollywood Boulevard is streamlined modern with Art Deco touches. Service facilities are interspersed with eateries and shops. Merchandise includes Disney trademark items and movie-related souvenirs. Hollywood characters and roving performers entertain.

Sunset Boulevard, evoking the 1940s, is a major component of DHS. The first right off Hollywood Boulevard, this area provides another venue for dining, shopping, and street entertainment.

Entering the Studios feels like there's a lot of action going on. I always expect something to happen, like someone jumping off a building.

Ricky

FASTPASS+ ATTRACTIONS AT DHS

THE STUDIOS IMPLEMENTS tiering (see below) to restrict the number of FastPass+ reservations you can have at its headliners:

TIER A (Choose one per day)
- *Beauty and the Beast—Live on Stage*
- *Fantasmic!*
- The Great Movie Ride
- Rock 'n' Roller Coaster
- Toy Story Midway Mania!

TIER B (Choose two per day)
- *Disney Junior—Live on Stage!*
- *For the First Time in Forever—A Frozen Sing-Along Celebration*

- *Indiana Jones Epic Stunt Spectacular!*
- *Jim Henson's Muppet-Vision 3-D*
- *Lights, Motors, Action! Extreme Stunt Show*
- Star Tours—The Adventures Continue
- The Twilight Zone Tower of Terror
- *Voyage of the Little Mermaid*

ENTERTAINMENT & PARADES
- *The Comedy Warehouse Holiday Special* (seasonal)

Continued on page 346

Disney's Hollywood Studios

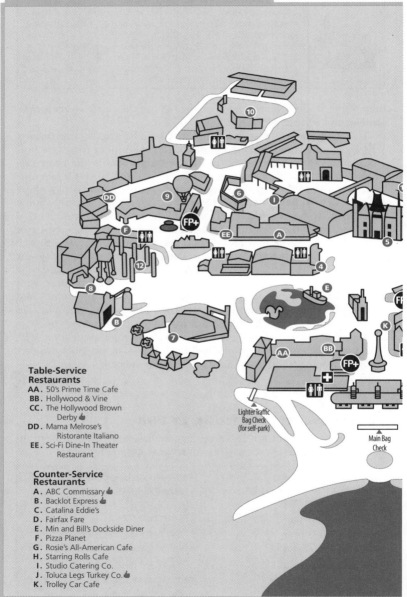

Table-Service Restaurants

AA. 50's Prime Time Cafe
BB. Hollywood & Vine
CC. The Hollywood Brown
    Derby 🍴
DD. Mama Melrose's
    Ristorante Italiano
EE. Sci-Fi Dine-In Theater
    Restaurant

Counter-Service Restaurants

A. ABC Commissary 🍴
B. Backlot Express 🍴
C. Catalina Eddie's
D. Fairfax Fare
E. Min and Bill's Dockside Diner
F. Pizza Planet
G. Rosie's All-American Cafe
H. Starring Rolls Cafe
I. Studio Catering Co.
J. Toluca Legs Turkey Co. 🍴
K. Trolley Car Cafe

Attractions

1. *Beauty and the Beast—Live on Stage/Theater of the Stars* FP+
2. *Disney Junior—Live on Stage!* FP+
3. *Fantasmic!* ☑ Use FP+
4. *For the First Time in Forever: A Frozen Sing-Along Celebration* FP+
5. The Great Movie Ride ☑ Use FP+
6. Honey, I Shrunk the Kids Movie Set Adventure
7. *Indiana Jones Epic Stunt Spectacular!* FP+
8. *Jedi Training Academy*
9. *Jim Henson's Muppet-Vision 3-D* ☑ FP+
10. *Lights, Motors, Action! Extreme Stunt Show* FP+
11. Rock 'n' Roller Coaster ☑ Use FP+
12. Star Tours—The Adventures Continue ☑ Use FP+
13. Toy Story Midway Mania! ☑ Use FP+
14. The Twilight Zone Tower of Terror ☑ Use FP+
15. *Voyage of the Little Mermaid* FP+
16. *Walt Disney: One Man's Dream*

FP+ FastPass+ Kiosks
🚻 Restrooms
✚ First Aid Center
👍 Recommended Dining

FP+ Attraction Offers FastPass+
Use FP+ FastPass+ Recommended
☑ Not to be Missed

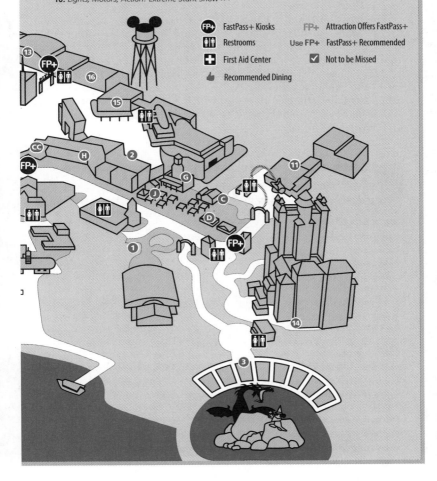

Continued from page 343

FastPass+ is offered at more than a dozen Studios attractions, but there are really only a few you need to worry about most of the year.

Families with children too small to ride Rock 'n' Roller Coaster or Tower of Terror make a beeline to **Toy Story Midway Mania!** first thing in the morning, and lines grow quickly. Waits at Toy Story can reach 90 minutes or more on a busy day—in many of our touring plans, we recommend getting a FastPass+ reservation for 9–10 a.m., even when Toy Story is the first step in the plan. The two benefits to doing this are that (1) you'll shave off at least 10 minutes of waiting, and (2) you don't have to line up as early at park opening to join the mad rush to Toy Story.

For teens and adults especially, the initial morning priorities will be Toy Story, Rock 'n' Roller Coaster, and Tower of Terror, possibly with The Great Movie Ride while they're in the area. This makes **Star Tours** a great choice for a mid- or late-morning FastPass+ reservation.

Many of our touring plans place **The Twilight Zone Tower of Terror** in the evening: generally 7–8 p.m. This allows you to focus on other attractions in the morning, which reduces your waits in line, and it makes for a short walk to *Fantasmic!* after you ride Tower of Terror.

DISNEY'S HOLLYWOOD STUDIOS
When Same-Day FP+ Runs Out, by Crowd Level

ATTRACTION	LOW CROWDS*	MODERATE CROWDS*	HIGH CROWDS*
Beauty and the Beast—Live on Stage	4–5 p.m.	4–5 p.m.	2–3 p.m.
Disney Junior—Live on Stage!	4–5 p.m.	3 p.m.	1–3 p.m.
Fantasmic!	3 p.m.	4–6 p.m.	6–8 p.m.
For the First Time in Forever: A Frozen Sing-Along Celebration	2–4 p.m.	1–3 p.m.	noon
The Great Movie Ride	6–7 p.m.	6–7 p.m.	5–7 p.m.
Indiana Jones Epic Stunt Spectacular!	5 p.m.	5 p.m.	2–4 p.m.
Jim Henson's Muppet-Vision 3-D	6–7 p.m.	7–8 p.m.	8–9 p.m.
Lights, Motors, Action! Extreme Stunt Show	4 p.m.	3–4 p.m.	1–2 p.m.
Rock 'n' Roller Coaster	2–4 p.m.	noon–1 p.m.	10 a.m.–noon
Star Tours—The Adventures Continue	6 p.m.	2–5 p.m.	noon–2 p.m.
Toy Story Midway Mania!	noon–1 p.m.	10 a.m.–noon	No day-of availability
The Twilight Zone Tower of Terror	2–4 p.m.	10 a.m.–noon	noon
Voyage of the Little Mermaid	5–6 p.m.	2–4 p.m.	2–4 p.m.

* **LOW CROWDS** (Levels 1–3 on touringplans.com Crowd Calendar)

* **MODERATE CROWDS** (Levels 4–7 on touringplans.com Crowd Calendar)

* **HIGH CROWDS** (Levels 8–10 on touringplans.com Crowd Calendar)

FastPass+ kiosk locations at the Studios are as follows:

- At the MyMagic+ Service Center, immediately to the left just past the entrance turnstiles
- At the wait-times board on the corner of Hollywood and Sunset Boulevards
- Near Toy Story Midway Mania!, on Pixar Place
- Outside The Twilight Zone Tower of Terror, to the left of the entrance
- Near *Jim Henson's Muppet-Vision 3-D,* just off Streets of America

Same-Day FastPass+ Availability

The preceding advice tells you which attractions to focus on when making your *advance* FastPass+ reservations before you get to the park. Once you're in the park, you can make more FastPass+ reservations once your advance reservations have been used or have expired (you must cancel your expired FastPass+ before you can book another). The table on the previous page shows which attractions are likely to have day-of Fast-Passes available, and the approximate times at which they'll run out.

DISNEY'S HOLLYWOOD STUDIOS ATTRACTIONS

Beauty and the Beast—Live on Stage/ Theater of the Stars ★★★★

APPEAL BY AGE	PRESCHOOL ★★★★½	GRADE SCHOOL ★★★★	TEENS ★★★★
YOUNG ADULTS ★★★★		OVER 30 ★★★★	SENIORS ★★★★½

What it is Live musical, featuring Disney characters; performed in an open-air theater. **Scope and scale** Major attraction. **Fright potential** Not frightening in any respect. **Bottleneck rating** 5. **When to go** Anytime; evenings are cooler. **Special comment** Performances are listed in the daily *Times Guide.* **Authors' rating** Excellent; ★★★★. **Duration of show** 25 minutes. **Preshow** Sometimes. **Probable waiting time** 20–30 minutes.

Join Cogsworth, Lumiere, Chip, and Mrs. Potts as they help Belle to break the spell. This 25-minute musical stage show of Disney's *Beauty and the Beast* will charm everybody. The show is popular, so show up 30 minutes early to get a seat.

The decor, the costumes, the actors, the music: Everything is in perfect harmony. Little girls fond of Belle will want that ball gown, and young boys will be eager to teach that mean Gaston a lesson!

Lillane

Once I was picked to be Belle's special princess—I got to go to the front of the stage, and I received a rose from Belle herself. It was the best day of my life!

Alex

Disney Junior—Live on Stage! ★★★★

APPEAL BY AGE	PRESCHOOL ★★★★★	GRADE SCHOOL ★★★★	TEENS ★★½
YOUNG ADULTS ★★★		OVER 30 ★★★	SENIORS ★★★

What it is Live show for children. **Scope and scale** Minor attraction. **Fright potential** Not frightening in any respect. **Bottleneck rating** 8. **When to go** Per the daily entertainment schedule. **Special comment** Audience sits on the floor. **Authors' rating** A must for families with preschoolers; ★★★★. **Duration of show** 20 minutes. **Probable waiting time** 30 minutes.

The show features characters from the Disney Channel's *Mickey Mouse Clubhouse, Jake and the Never Land Pirates, Doc McStuffins,* and *Sofia the First,* plus other Disney Channel characters. *Disney Junior* uses elaborate puppets instead of live characters on stage. A simple plot serves as the platform for singing, dancing, some great puppetry, and a great deal of audience participation. The characters, who ooze love and goodness, rally throngs of tots and preschoolers to sing and dance along with them. All the jumping, squirming, and high-stepping is facilitated by having the audience sit on the floor so that kids can spontaneously erupt into motion when the mood strikes. Even for adults without children, it's a treat to watch the tykes rev up. For preschoolers, *Disney Junior* will be the highlight of their day, as a Thomasville, North Carolina, mom attests:

> *The show was fantastic! My 3-year-old loved it. The children danced, sang, and had a great time.*

The Florida mother of a 4-year-old agrees:

> *My daughter absolutely LOVED the show! I saw it advertised on the Disney Junior channel and didn't think it looked all that great, but in person it was really fun. If you have preschoolers, this is a MUST!*

Disney Junior is the third iteration of the stage show since 2007. All three versions replaced live characters with puppets, a fact that has left some parents less than thrilled. These comments from a Virginia Beach, Virginia, couple are typical:

> *We were disappointed. The show did not consist of live characters, and I think the kids' level of excitement was lower because of this. The kids enjoyed it, but you would think they would be more excited when the show has some of their favorite characters.*

The show is staged in a huge building to the right of the former Animation tour. Show up at least 25 minutes before showtime. Once inside, pick a spot on the floor and take a breather until the performance begins.

The Great Movie Ride ★★★½

APPEAL BY AGE	PRESCHOOL ★★★	GRADE SCHOOL ★★★½	TEENS ★★★½
YOUNG ADULTS ★★★½		OVER 30 ★★★½	SENIORS ★★★★

What it is Movie-history indoor adventure ride. **Scope and scale** Headliner. **Fright potential** Intense in parts, with very realistic special effects and some visually intimidating sights. **Bottleneck rating** 8. **When to go** Before 11 a.m. or after 8 p.m. **Special comment** Elaborate, with several surprises. **Authors' rating** Unique; ★★★½. **Duration of ride** About 19 minutes. **Average wait in line per 100 people ahead of you** 2 minutes. **Assumes** All trains operating. **Loading speed** Fast.

Inside the re-creation of Hollywood's Grauman's Chinese Theatre awaits a trip down memory lane. From *Casablanca* to *Raiders of the Lost Ark,* classic movies are showcased in this ride through some of the movies' most memorable sets. Young movie buffs might be flipped out along the way (*Alien* is one of the movies represented), but the wonderful Munchkins from *The Wizard of Oz* scene will make up for it—the Wicked Witch of the North notwithstanding.

In early 2015, as part of an agreement with Turner Classic Movies, the Great Movie Ride's preshow film trailer and ride-film finale were updated with commentary from TCM host and film historian Robert Osborne. In addition, the finale was entirely reedited with a mix of classic clips, new scenes from previously featured films, and a handful of more-recent movies. It's not the dramatic overhaul we would have hoped for, but it's certainly a step in the right direction.

For the First Time in Forever: A Frozen Sing-Along Celebration (FastPass+) ★★★★

APPEAL BY AGE   PRESCHOOL ★★★★½   GRADE SCHOOL ★★★★★   TEENS ★★★★½   YOUNG ADULTS ★★★★   OVER 30 ★★★   SENIORS ★★★

What it is Sing-along based on the popular 2013 film *Frozen*. **Scope and scale** Major attraction for *Frozen* fans; minor attraction for everyone else. **Fright potential** Not frightening in any respect. **Bottleneck rating** 8. **When to go** Per the daily entertainment schedule. **Special comment** If you have *Frozen* fans in your family, save your sanity and get FastPass+ for this attraction. **Authors' rating** A must for families with preschoolers and grade-school kids; ★★★★. **Duration of show** 25 minutes. **Probable waiting time** 30 minutes if you don't have FastPass+.

This sing-along show based on the 2013 film *Frozen* started out as a seasonal event in 2014 at the Premiere Theater, near the San Francisco section of Streets of America. As *Frozen* mania took hold, the show moved to a more permanent home at the Hyperion Theater, the former residence of *The American Idol Experience*. Using FastPass+ on this attraction grants you access to a preferred-seating section near the front of the stage, while standby guests are seated in whatever seats are left.

Honey, I Shrunk the Kids Movie Set Adventure ★★½

APPEAL BY AGE   PRESCHOOL ★★★★½   GRADE SCHOOL ★★★★½   TEENS ★★★½   YOUNG ADULTS ★★★   OVER 30 ★★★   SENIORS ★★★

What it is Small but elaborate playground. **Scope and scale** Diversion. **Fright potential** Everything is oversize, but nothing is scary. **Bottleneck rating** 8. **When to go** Before 11 a.m. or after dark. **Special comment** Opens 1 hour later than the rest of the park. **Authors' rating** Great for young children, more of a curiosity for adults; ★★½. **Average wait in line per 100 people ahead of you** 20 minutes.

This elaborate playground appeals particularly to kids age 11 and younger. Tunnels, slides, rope ladders, and oversize props offer lots of fun. However, the place is too small to accommodate all the children who would like to play, and supervision inside the jam-packed and poorly ventilated playground can be trying. Last but not least, kids play as long as parents allow, so be prepared for this stop to take a big chunk of time out of your touring day. If you visit during the warmer months and want your children to experience the playground, get them in and out before 11 a.m. By late morning, this attraction is way too hot and crowded for anyone to enjoy. A mom from Tolland, Connecticut, found the playground exasperating:

We thought Honey, I Shrunk the Kids would be relaxing. NOT! You have three choices: 1) Let your kids go anywhere and hope that if they try to get out without your permission, someone will stop them. 2) Go everywhere with your kids—this takes stamina and some athleticism. If you care about appearances, this could be a problem because you look pretty stupid coming down those slides. 3) Try to visually keep track of your kids. This is impossible, so you will likely be in the middle of an anxiety attack the whole time you're there.

Indiana Jones Epic Stunt Spectacular! ★★★½

APPEAL BY AGE PRESCHOOL ★★★½ **GRADE SCHOOL** ★★★★½ **TEENS** ★★★★
YOUNG ADULTS ★★★★   **OVER 30** ★★★★   **SENIORS** ★★★★

Thumbs Up for the Whole Family

What it is Movie-stunt demonstration and action show. **Scope and scale** Headliner. **Fright potential** An intense show with powerful special effects, including explosions. Presented in an educational context that young children generally handle well. **Bottleneck rating** 8. **When to go** First two shows or last show. **Special comment** Performance times posted on a sign at the entrance to the theater. **Authors' rating** Done on a grand scale; ★★★½. **Duration of show** 30 minutes. **Preshow** Selection of "extras" from audience. **Probable waiting time** None.

Professional stunt men and women demonstrate dangerous stunts with a behind-the-scenes look at how it is done. Most kids handle the show well. The show always needs a few "extras." To be chosen from the audience, arrive early, sit down front, and display unmitigated enthusiasm. Unfortunately "victims" must be 18 years old and up.

An amazing show with fiery explosions and nonstop action. Did you know that the folks at Disney have a vault filled with sound effects ranging from gunshots to magical twinkles? When a show is created, they pick and choose from this treasure chest and upload the sounds into their state-of-the-art computerized mixing table.

Lillane

Huh? What's a magical twinkle sound like? But now that I think about it, I sure remember the noise my innards made after eating about a dozen magical twinkles.

Bob

Those were Twinkies, Mr. Tiki-Birdbrain!

Lillane

Jedi Training Academy ★★★½

APPEAL BY AGE PRESCHOOL ★★★★½ **GRADE SCHOOL** ★★★★★ **TEENS** ★★★★
YOUNG ADULTS ★★★★   **OVER 30** ★★★★½   **SENIORS** ★★★★

What it is Outdoor stage show. **Scope and scale** Minor attraction. **Fright potential** It does involve battle with Darth Vader, but the good guys always win; children typically love it. **Bottleneck rating** 8. **When to go** First two shows of the day. **Special comment** Volunteers from the audience go on stage to fight Darth Vader. **Authors' rating** A treat for young *Star Wars* lovers; ★★★½. **Duration of show** About 20 minutes. **When to arrive** 15 minutes before showtime.

Jedi Training Academy is to the left of the Star Tours building entrance, opposite Backlot Express. Young Skywalkers-in-training are taught the ways of The Force and do battle against Darth Vader. If all this sounds too intense, it's not—Storm Troopers provide comic relief and, just as in the movies, the Jedi always wins. Space is limited, and kids ages 4–12 must register early in the day to make it into the show. To register, see a cast member at the ABC Sound Studio building (near Star Tours) as soon as the park opens, or check for cast members near the entrance just before and after park opening. A Windham, New Hampshire, mother of three describes a common dilemma:

> Many families will have to choose between racing to Toy Story Midway Mania! to ride or racing to sign up for Jedi Training Academy (children MUST be present at sign-up). We hopped on Toy Story, and then crossed the park to sign up for the Academy. By the time we got there, we were pushed to the 2:20 p.m. show, which eliminated the possibility of leaving for a nap after lunch.

Jim Henson's Muppet-Vision 3-D ★★★★

APPEAL BY AGE **PRESCHOOL** ★★★★ **GRADE SCHOOL** ★★★★ **TEENS** ★★★★
YOUNG ADULTS ★★★★ **OVER 30** ★★★★ **SENIORS** ★★★★½

What it is 3-D movie starring the Muppets. **Scope and scale** Major attraction. **Fright potential** Intense and loud but not frightening. **Bottleneck rating** 8. **When to go** Anytime. **Authors' rating** Uproarious; not to be missed; ★★★★. **Duration of show** 17 minutes. **Preshow** Muppets on television. **Probable waiting time** 12 minutes.

Kermit, Miss Piggy, and the rest of the gang will lift your spirits as they unleash their hilarious mayhem. Because adults tend to associate Muppet characters with the children's show *Sesame Street,* many bypass this attraction. Big mistake. *Muppet-Vision 3-D* operates on several planes, and there's as much here for oldsters as for youngsters. The presentation is intense and sometimes loud, but most preschoolers handle it well. If your child is a little scared, encourage him to watch without the 3-D glasses at first. A New Brunswick, Canada, reader thinks the Muppets are heaven-sent:

> Muppet-Vision 3-D *is a godsend: 1) It NEVER has a line (even on our visit on New Year's Day). 2) Everyone ages 1–100 gives the show high marks. 3) Between the preshow and the movie, it's half an hour seated comfortably in an air-conditioned theater. 4) Between the live actors and animatronics, it's so much more than just another silly 3-D movie. 5) IT'S THE MUPPETS! Who doesn't love these hysterical creatures and their 3-D shenanigans?*

Lights, Motors, Action! Extreme Stunt Show ★★★½

APPEAL BY AGE **PRESCHOOL** ★★★★ **GRADE SCHOOL** ★★★★½ **TEENS** ★★★★½
YOUNG ADULTS ★★★★½ **OVER 30** ★★★★ **SENIORS** ★★★★

What it is Auto stunt show. **Scope and scale** Headliner. **Fright potential** Loud with explosions but not scary. **Bottleneck rating** 5. **When to go** Anytime. **Authors' rating** Good stunt work, slow pace; ★★★½. **Duration of show** 33 minutes. **Preshow** Selection of audience "volunteers." **When to arrive** 25–30 minutes before showtime.

This show features cars and motorcycles in a blur of chases, crashes, jumps, and explosions. The secrets behind the special effects are explained after each stunt sequence. The show runs about 30 minutes, and small children may become restless. Teens, however, will be gobsmacked.

Loud

Lillane

The stunts and the special effects are fabulous, but less would be more.

It's cool to see behind-the-scenes and learn how they make the car races and explosions look so realistic.

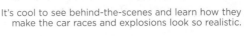
Isaac

Rock 'n' Roller Coaster *(FastPass+)* ★★★★

APPEAL BY AGE PRESCHOOL ★★½ GRADE SCHOOL ★★★★½ TEENS ★★★★★
YOUNG ADULTS ★★★★★   OVER 30 ★★★★½   SENIORS ★★★★

What it is Rock music–themed roller coaster. **Scope and scale** Headliner. **Fright potential** Extremely intense for all ages; the ride is one of Disney's wildest. **Bottleneck rating** 10. **When to go** First 30 minutes the park is open, or use FastPass+. **Special comments** Must be 48" tall to ride; children younger than age 7 must ride with an adult. Switching-off option provided (see page 243). **Authors' rating** Not to be missed; ★★★★. **Duration of ride** Almost 1½ minutes. **Average wait in line per 100 people ahead of you** 2½ minutes; assumes all trains operating. **Loading speed** Moderate–fast.

Dark Lose Things Rough Queasy Scary

Aerosmith once did a tour called Route of All Evil, and this notorious ride at the Studios makes good on their fans' expectations. Loops, corkscrews, and drops that make Space Mountain seem like the Jungle Cruise is what to expect and what is delivered—pronto. You are launched from 0 to 57 miles per hour in less than 3 seconds, and by the time you enter the first loop, you'll be pulling five g's—two more than astronauts experience at liftoff on a space shuttle. If Space Mountain or Big Thunder Mountain Railroad pushes your limits, stay away from Rock 'n' Roller Coaster.

A good strategy for riding Rock 'n' Roller Coaster, Toy Story Midway Mania!, and Tower of Terror with minimum wait is to make a midmorning FastPass+ reservation for Toy Story and an evening FastPass+ reservation for Tower of Terror up to 60 days in advance. Then, when you visit, rush first thing after opening to ride Rock 'n' Roller Coaster. If you can't make FastPass+ reservations before you arrive, ride Rock 'n' Roller Coaster or Toy Story Midway Mania! first, and then find the nearest FastPass+ kiosk to make the other reservations.

Aerosmith describes this ride best in one of their songs: "Living on the Edge."

Lillane

Great ride with awesome tunes that really get you pumped! It ROCKS!

This ride is my favorite ride in the park. It's fun to listen to the music while going superfast through all the loops.

Isaac

Erin

Star Tours—The Adventures Continue *(FastPass+)* ★★★½

APPEAL BY AGE PRESCHOOL ★★★★ GRADE SCHOOL ★★★★½ TEENS ★★★★½
YOUNG ADULTS ★★★★½   OVER 30 ★★★★½   SENIORS ★★★★½

What it is Indoor space flight–simulation ride. **Scope and scale** Headliner. **Fright potential** Extremely intense visually for all ages; too intense for children under age 8. Switching-off option provided (see page 243). **Bottleneck rating** 8. **When to go** Before 10 a.m., after 6 p.m., or use FastPass+. **Special comments** Expectant mothers and anyone prone to motion sickness are advised against riding. Must be 40" tall to ride. **Authors' rating** ★★★½. **Duration of ride** About 7 minutes. **Average wait in line per 100 people ahead of you** 5 minutes. **Assumes** All simulators operating. **Loading speed** Moderate–fast.

Based on the *Star Wars* movie series, the ride, based on the pod racing scene from *Star Wars Episode 1: The Phantom Menace,* uses 3-D special effects and interactive elements. The ride has lots of dips, twists, and climbs as your vehicle goes through an intergalactic version of the chariot race in *Ben-Hur.* Characters from the prequel films released 1999–2005 were included in the 2011 makeover. The ride has more than 50 combinations of scenes!!

Every year (mid-May to mid-June) Walt Disney World hosts four Star Wars weekends. Celebrities from the saga and fans converge at the park in celebration of George Lucas's epic series. Even Mickey turns into a Jedi and joins Ewoks, Jawas, and Wookies for a ride to a galaxy far, far away.

Oh, no! We're caught in a tractor beam!

Star Tours tricks your brain so you really feel like you're flying through space!

Streets of America ★★★

APPEAL BY AGE	PRESCHOOL ★★½	GRADE SCHOOL ★★★½	TEENS ★★★½
YOUNG ADULTS ★★★½		OVER 30 ★★★½	SENIORS ★★★★

What it is Walk-through back lot movie set. **Scope and scale** Diversion. **Fright potential** Not frightening in any respect. **Bottleneck rating** 1. **When to go** Anytime. **Authors' rating** Interesting, with great detail; ★★★. **Probable waiting time** None.

There is never a wait to enjoy the Streets of America; save your visit here until you have seen those attractions that develop long lines. During the holiday season, Streets of America, decorated with millions of Christmas lights, serve as a backdrop for the Osborne Family Spectacle of Lights.

Toy Story Midway Mania! *(FastPass+)* ★★★★½

APPEAL BY AGE	PRESCHOOL ★★★★½	GRADE SCHOOL ★★★★★	TEENS ★★★★½
YOUNG ADULTS ★★★★½		OVER 30 ★★★★½	SENIORS ★★★★½

What it is 3-D ride through indoor shooting gallery. **Scope and scale** Headliner. **Fright potential** Dark ride may frighten some preschoolers. **Bottleneck rating** 10. **When to go** As soon as the park opens, or use FastPass+ (if available). **Authors' rating** ★★★★½. **Duration of ride** About 6½ minutes. **Average wait in line per 100 people ahead of you** 6½ minutes. **Loading Speed** Fast.

This is an interactive shooting gallery much like Buzz Lightyear's Space Ranger Spin, but in Toy Story Midway Mania! your vehicle passes through a totally virtual midway, with booths offering such games as ring toss and ball throw. The pull-string cannon on your ride vehicle takes advantage of computer imaging to toss rings, shoot balls, and even throw eggs and pies. Each game booth is manned by a *Toy Story* character who is right beside you in 3-D glory cheering you on. You also experience vehicle motion, wind, and water spray. The ride begins with a training round to familiarize you with the nature of the games and then continues through a number of games in which you compete against your riding mate for a higher score. The technology has the ability to self-adjust the level of difficulty, and there are plenty of easy targets for small children to reach. *Tip:* Let the pull-string retract all the way back into the cannon before pulling it again.

DISNEY DISH WITH JIM HILL

PUMPING UP PIXAR PLACE Disney wants to turn Hollywood Studios into a full-day theme park. To do that, a number of Pixar-themed rides are now in the works. Some will be simple spinners and flat rides similar to the ones that were recently installed at Hong Kong Disneyland and Walt Disney Studios in Paris. Others will be wildly ambitious, such as an indoor version of Radiator Springs Racers at Disneyland. It's going to take almost five years to complete this Pixar Place expansion, but it should be a real winner once it's running.

Toy Story Midway Mania! is the biggest bottleneck in Disney World, surpassing even Test Track at Epcot. Ride first thing after the park opens, or use FastPass+. In March 2015, Disney announced an expansion of the ride in the form of an extra track, which should increase guest throughput. The expansion is expected to be completed by late 2016.

Erin

> You get to play awesome 3-D games. Definitely worth the wait.
>
> The concept of this ride is cool, but it's not very exciting (my little brother, Max, loved it, though). You absolutely need FastPass+ because the waiting time was 180 minutes. I would *never* wait that long for a ride.

Ethan

The Twilight Zone Tower of Terror *(FastPass+)* ★★★★★

APPEAL BY AGE PRESCHOOL ★★★	**GRADE SCHOOL** ★★★★	**TEENS** ★★★★½
YOUNG ADULTS ★★★★★	**OVER 30** ★★★★½	**SENIORS** ★★★★

What it is Sci-fi–themed indoor thrill ride. **Scope and scale** Super-headliner. **Fright potential** Visually intimidating to young children; contains intense, realistic special effects. The plummeting elevator at the ride's end frightens many adults. Switching-off option provided (see page 243). **Bottleneck rating** 10. **When to go** First or last 30 minutes the park is open, or use FastPass+. **Special comment** Must be 40″ tall to ride. **Authors' rating** Disney World's best attraction; not to be missed; ★★★★★. **Duration of ride** About 4 minutes plus preshow. **Average wait in line per 100 people ahead of you** 4 minutes. **Assumes** All elevators operating. **Loading speed** Moderate.

Dark   Rough   Scary

And suddenly the cable went *snap*. If riding a capricious elevator in a haunted hotel sounds like fun to you, this is your ride. Erratic yet thrilling, the Tower of Terror is an experience to savor. The Tower has great potential for terrifying young children and rattling more mature visitors. Random ride-and-drop sequences keep you guessing about when, how far, and how many times the elevator drops. We suggest using teenagers in your party as experimental probes. If they report back that they really, really liked the Tower of Terror, run quickly in the opposite direction. This is one of the hottest tickets in the park. If you're up to it, experience the ride first thing in the morning or use FastPass+.

Kieran

> I was 4 when I first rode the Tower of Terror. My dad asked me if I liked it and I said no, but when he asked if I wanted to ride it again, I said yes. All I'm saying is that the thought of it is more daunting than the ride itself, which is epic.
>
> This ride is great. It kind of freaks you out every time it stops and drops AGAIN and AGAIN and AGAIN.

Ethan

Erin

So very scary because we didn't know what was going to happen next. Going up and dropping down again was intense.

Voyage of the Little Mermaid ★★★½

| APPEAL BY AGE | PRESCHOOL ★★★★½ | GRADE SCHOOL ★★★★ | TEENS ★★★★ |
| YOUNG ADULTS ★★★½ | | OVER 30 ★★★½ | SENIORS ★★★★ |

Thumbs Up for the Whole Family

What it is Musical stage show featuring characters from the Disney movie *The Little Mermaid*. **Scope and scale** Major attraction. **Fright potential** Ursula the sea witch may frighten preschoolers. **Bottleneck rating** 10. **When to go** Before 9:45 a.m. or just before closing. **Authors' rating** Romantic, lovable, and humorous in the best Disney tradition; ★★★½. **Duration of show** 15 minutes. **Preshow** Taped ramblings about the decor in the preshow holding area. **Probable waiting time** Before 9:30 a.m., 10–30 minutes; after 9:30 a.m., 35–70 minutes.

This most tender and romantic stage show is a winner, appealing to every age. Once inside the theater, the audience is transported into the wonderful underwater world of Ariel and her friends. Very young children might be frightened by Ursula the sea witch, a 12-foot-tall puppet.

Because it's well done and located at a busy pedestrian intersection, *Voyage of the Little Mermaid* plays to capacity crowds all day. When the theater doors open, pick a row of seats, and let 6–10 people enter the row ahead of you. The strategy is twofold: to get a good seat and be near the exit.

Walt Disney: One Man's Dream ★★★

| APPEAL BY AGE | PRESCHOOL ★★½ | GRADE SCHOOL ★★★½ | TEENS ★★★★ |
| YOUNG ADULTS ★★★★ | | OVER 30 ★★★★½ | SENIORS ★★★★½ |

What it is Tribute to Walt Disney. **Scope and scale** Minor attraction. **Fright potential** Not frightening in any respect. **Bottleneck rating** 2. **When to go** Anytime. **Authors' rating** Excellent! ★★★. **Duration of presentation** 25 minutes. **Preshow** Disney memorabilia. **Probable waiting time** For film, 10 minutes.

One Man's Dream is a long-overdue tribute to Walt Disney. The attraction consists of an exhibit area showcasing Disney memorabilia, followed by a film documenting Disney's life. Teens and adults, especially those who are old enough to remember Walt Disney, will enjoy this homage to the man behind the Mouse!

My son, a cinematographer, used to take me to this attraction during every visit, and today, when visiting, he still sees the show in what he calls "paying tribute to the man who started it all." Hands off! Don't even think of packing this gem off!

Liliane

LIVE ENTERTAINMENT
at DISNEY'S
HOLLYWOOD STUDIOS

THE STUDIOS LIVE ENTERTAINMENT, which is generally as good or better than comparable acts found at the other Disney theme parks, includes theater shows; musical acts; street performers; and *Fantasmic!*, a nighttime water, fireworks, and laser show that draws rave reviews. Read on for the details. We'd be remiss if we didn't tell you to catch a show of **Mulch, Sweat, & Shears,** a group of landscaping "brothers" who form a rock-and-roll cover band playing everything from AC/DC to Journey. Guests standing near the front may be invited into the act.

LILIANE Disney's Hollywood Studios is the only Disney World park without an interactive game. I vote for a *Star Wars*-themed game with trading cards and all.

DISNEY CHARACTERS *Toy Story*'s Buzz and Woody are in Pixar Place in front of Toy Story Midway Mania!, while Mike and Sulley from *Monsters, Inc.*, are farther down the same walkway near what used to be the Backlot. Sorcerer Mickey can be found near the Studio Catering Co., and Minnie holds court in front of The Great Movie Ride. Disney Junior stars are next to *Disney Junior—Live on Stage!* Disney Channel's Phineas and Ferb, plus the cast of Pixar's *Cars* franchise, are found along the Streets of America. Check the *Times Guide* for times and locations of character appearances.

FROZEN SUMMER FUN Running from mid-June to at least September 2015, this collection of *Frozen*-themed special events is held from late morning through park closing. **Frozen Royal Welcome** is a 10-minute mini-parade held on Hollywood Boulevard twice a day. Anna and Elsa roll out in a horse-drawn sleigh, accompanied by Kristoff, "skaters" and "skiers," and flag twirlers. **Olaf's Summer Cool Down** features the dorky snowman in his own stage show, which takes place several times a day on the event stage in front of The Great Movie Ride. At 5:30 p.m. each day on a stage in front of the Chinese Theatre, the **Coolest Summer Ever Dance Party** features live music from Mulch, Sweat, & Shears, plus *Frozen* tunes from a DJ. **Frozen Fireworks** is presented nightly, usually around 9:45 p.m. *Frozen* characters join the crowd in watching fireworks set to the movie's sound track.

MULCH, SWEAT, & SHEARS—LIVE IN CONCERT Known as Los Lawn Boys outside of the Studios, this Central Florida rock act (★★★½) puts on a 30-minute show several times during the day, except on Wednesdays, at Streets of America. Check *Times Guide* for performance times.

STREET ENTERTAINMENT ★★★½ The Studios has the best roving street performers in all of Walt Disney World. Appearing primarily on Hollywood and Sunset Boulevards, the cast of characters includes Hollywood stars and wannabes, their agents, film directors, and gossip columnists, as well as police officers and Hollywood public-works crews.

The performers are not shy about asking you to join in their skits, and you may be asked anything from explaining why you came to "Hollywood" all the way to reciting a couple of lines in one of the directors' new films.

Fantasmic! (FastPass+) ★★★★½

APPEAL BY AGE	PRESCHOOL ★★★★	GRADE SCHOOL ★★★★½	TEENS ★★★★½
YOUNG ADULTS ★★★★½		OVER 30 ★★★★½	SENIORS ★★★★½

What it is Mixed-media nighttime spectacular. **Scope and scale** Super-headliner. **Fright potential** Loud and intense with fireworks and some scary villains, but most young children like it. **Bottleneck rating** 9. **When to go** Check *Times Guide* for schedule; if two shows are offered, the second is less crowded. **Special comment** Disney's best nighttime event. **Authors' rating** Not to be missed; ★★★★½. **Duration of show** 25 minutes. **Probable waiting time** 50–90 minutes for a seat; 35–40 minutes for standing room.

Loud   Scary

Fantasmic! is far and away the most dazzling outdoor spectacle ever attempted in any theme park and a must-see for the whole family. Starring Mickey Mouse in his role as the sorcerer's apprentice from *Fantasia,* the production uses lasers, images projected on a shroud of mist, dazzling fireworks, lighting effects, and powerful music. *Fantasmic!* has the potential to frighten young children. Prepare your children for the show, and make sure that they know that, in addition to all the favorite Disney characters, the maleficent dragon and the evil Jafar will make appearances. To give you an idea, picture the evil Jafar turning into a cobra 100 feet long and 16 feet high. Rest assured, however, that during the final parade, your kids will cheer on Cinderella and Prince Charming, Belle, Snow White, Ariel and Prince Eric, Jasmine and Aladdin, Donald Duck, Minnie, and Mickey. You can alleviate the fright factor somewhat by sitting back a bit. Also, if you are seated in the first 12 rows, you will get sprayed with water at times.

The theater is huge, but so is the popularity of the show. If there are two performances, the second show will almost always be less crowded. If you attend the first (or only) scheduled performance, show up at least 1 hour in advance. If you opt for the second show, arrive 50 minutes early. Plan to use that time for a picnic. If you forget to bring munchies, not to worry; there are food concessions in the theater.

Unless you buy a *Fantasmic!* dinner package, you will not have reserved seats, so arrive early for best choice. Try to sit in the middle three or four sections, a bit off-center. Understand that you are out of luck if *Fantasmic!* is canceled due to weather or other circumstances.

Disney offers FastPass+ reservations for *Fantasmic!,* but we don't think it should be one of your first three choices—you still have to arrive 30–60 minutes beforehand to guarantee a good spot. Plus, using FastPass+ for *Fantasmic!* prevents you from using it at Toy Story Midway Mania! and Rock 'n' Roller Coaster. Getting a day-of FastPass (if available) or booking the dining package (see below) makes better sense to us. At press time, Disney had just ended its testing period of assigning seats to FastPass+ holders. If Disney implements assigned seating for *Fantasmic!,* we still recommend getting a day-of FastPass+ instead of making it one of your three reservations.

> By far the best show in any park. There are scary parts,
> so be prepared to cover your eyes at times. The finale is excellent.
> I love it even more each time I see it.
>
> Julia

Fantasmic! Dining Packages

Three restaurants offer a ticket voucher for the members of your dining party to enter *Fantasmic!* via a special entrance and sit in a reserved section of seats. The package consists of a buffet at Hollywood & Vine,

---

FAVORITE EATS AT DISNEY'S HOLLYWOOD STUDIOS

LAND	SERVICE LOCATION	FOOD ITEM

ECHO LAKE   ABC Commissary | Chicken nuggets with fruit or veggies
Backlot Express | Great burgers & fixin's

STREETS OF AMERICA   Pizza Planet | THE place for pizza
Sci-Fi Dine-In Theater | It's not about the food (dismal) but about eating in a vintage convertible car watching old sci-fi movie previews. Teens love it! Great place to cool off.
Table service only

SUNSET BOULEVARD   Studio Catering Co. | Good place for a break while your kids check out Honey, I Shrunk the Kids Movie Set Adventure

---

or a fixed-price dinner at Mama Melrose's Ristorante Italiano or The Hollywood Brown Derby (full-service restaurants). Call ☎ 407-WDW-DINE up to 180 days in advance to request the *Fantasmic!* dinner package. This is a real reservation and must be guaranteed by a credit card at the time of booking. There's a 48-hour cancellation policy.

Included in the package are fixed-price menus for all three restaurants as follows; respective prices are for adults and kids ages 3–9: *Hollywood & Vine:* buffet dinner, $38/$21; *The Hollywood Brown Derby:* lunch and dinner, $61/$18; *Mama Melrose's:* lunch and dinner, $40/$14. Soft drinks and tax are included; park admission and tips are not. Prices fluctuate according to season, so call ☎ 407-WDW-DINE to find out the exact dinner charge for a particular date. If there are two scheduled performances in one night, the lunch package will only grant you reserved seating for the first performance.

Allow at least 2 hours to eat. You will receive the ticket vouchers at the restaurant. After dinner, report to the *Fantasmic!* sign on Hollywood Boulevard next to Oscar's (just inside the front entrance to the park) no later than 35 minutes prior to showtime. A cast member will escort you to the reserved section. If *Fantasmic!* is canceled for any reason, such as weather or technical problems, you will not receive a refund. However, you can go to Guest Relations to receive a voucher for another (next) performance. This only works if you are still in town when *Fantasmic!* is on next and if you are willing to pay another admission to the Studios. If you're still around and you have a Park Hopper, go for it!

If there are two *Fantasmic!* performances during the time of your visit, you really have no reason to spend extra money on the dining package. Just grab some food, enter the theater at least 30 minutes prior to the show, and relax!

EXIT STRATEGIES

EXITING THE STUDIOS at the end of the day following *Fantasmic!* is not nearly as difficult as leaving Epcot after *IllumiNations.* We recommend that you take it easy and make your way out of the park after the first wave of guests has departed. Pick a spot inside the park and give instructions that nobody is to go through the turnstiles before the group is reunited. Most important, latch on to your kids.

DISNEY'S HOLLYWOOD STUDIOS TOURING PLANS

OUR STEP-BY-STEP TOURING PLANS ARE FIELD-TESTED, independently verified itineraries that will keep you moving counter to the crowd flow and allow you to see as much as possible in a single day with a minimum of time wasted in line. You can take in all the attractions at DHS in one day, even when traveling with young children. If you aren't interested in an attraction on the touring plan, simply skip it and proceed to the next step. Likewise, if you encounter a very long line at an attraction, skip it. Use of FastPass+ is factored into the touring plans.

The different touring plans are described below. The descriptions will tell you for whom (for example, tweens, parents with preschoolers, and so on) or for what situation (such as sleeping late) the plans are designed. The actual touring plans are on pages 473–476 and include a numbered map of the park to help you find your way around.

DISNEY'S HOLLYWOOD STUDIOS ONE-DAY TOURING PLAN FOR PARENTS WITH SMALL CHILDREN This plan is for parents of children ages 3–8 who wish to see the very best age-appropriate attractions and shows in Hollywood Studios. Every attraction has a rating of at least three stars (out of five) from preschool and grade-school children surveyed by *The Unofficial Guide*. The plan includes a midday break outside the park so families can rest, relax, and regroup. The plan keeps walking and backtracking to a minimum, with no crisscrossing of the park.

DISNEY'S HOLLYWOOD STUDIOS ONE-DAY SLEEPYHEAD TOURING PLAN FOR PARENTS WITH SMALL CHILDREN A relaxed plan that allows families with small children to sleep late and still see the highlights of DHS. The plan begins around 11 a.m., sets aside ample time for lunch and dinner, and includes the very best child-friendly attractions and shows in the park. Special advice is provided for touring the park with small children. The plan points out where FastPass+ can best be used.

DISNEY'S HOLLYWOOD STUDIOS ONE-DAY TOURING PLAN FOR TWEENS AND THEIR PARENTS A one-day plan for parents with children ages 8–12. It includes every attraction rated three stars and higher by this age group and sets aside ample time for lunch and dinner.

DISNEY'S HOLLYWOOD STUDIOS ONE-DAY HAPPY FAMILY TOURING PLAN A one-day itinerary for multigenerational families, this plan allows teens and older children to experience the Studios' thrill rides while parents and small children visit more age-appropriate attractions. The family stays together most of the day, including lunch and dinner, and each attraction in the plan is rated three stars or higher.

BEFORE YOU GO

1. Call ☎ 407-824-4321 or visit **disneyworld.com** to verify the park's operating hours.

2. Buy your admission and make FastPass+ reservations before you arrive.

3. Make lunch and dinner Advance Reservations or reserve the *Fantasmic!* dinner package (if desired) before you arrive by calling ☎ 407-WDW-DINE.

4. The schedule of live entertainment changes from week to week and even from day to day. Review the daily *Times Guide* handout, available free throughout Disney's Hollywood Studios.

DISNEY'S HOLLYWOOD STUDIOS TRIVIA QUIZ

1. Who is not part of *Disney Junior—Live on Stage*?
a. Baby Einstein
b. Doc McStuffins
c. Princess Sofia
d. Miss Piggy

2. Which famous rock band stars in Rock 'n' Roller Coaster?
a. The Rolling Stones
b. Aerosmith
c. The Who
d. Queen

3. The Twilight Zone Tower of Terror is based on which TV series?
a. *The Tower of Terror*
b. *Hotel California*
c. *The Twilight Hotel*
d. *The Twilight Zone*

4. What is the name of the lake at Disney's Hollywood Studios?
a. Echo Lake
b. Bay Lake
c. Studio Lake
d. Lake Buena Vista

5. What was the original name of Disney's Hollywood Studios?
a. Pixar Studios
b. Paramount Studios
c. Dreamworks
d. Disney-MGM Studios

6. Where does *Beauty and the Beast—Live on Stage* take place?
a. Theater of the Stars
b. American Gardens Theatre
c. Castle Forecourt Stage
d. Hollywood Hills Amphitheater

7. For four weekends Disney's Hollywood Studios hosts a special parade. Which one?
a. Festival of Fantasy Parade
b. Star Wars Parade
c. Mickey's Very Merry Christmas
d. Mickey's Not So Scary Halloween

8. What restaurant is not located in Disney's Hollywood Studios?
a. Hollywood & Vine
b. Cosmic Ray's Starlight Cafe
c. Mama Melrose's Ristorante
d. Starring Rolls Cafe

9. What is the name of the nighttime spectacular held at Disney's Hollywood Studios?
a. *Wishes*
b. *Cinematic Spectacular*
c. *IllumiNations: Reflections of Earth*
d. *Fantasmic!*

10. Which street is not found at Disney's Hollywood Studios?
a. Main Street
b. Hollywood Boulevard
c. Sunset Boulevard
d. Mickey Avenue

Answers can be found on page 437.

PART ELEVEN

UNIVERSAL ORLANDO *and* SEAWORLD

█ UNIVERSAL ORLANDO

UNIVERSAL ORLANDO is a complete destination resort, with two theme parks; four hotels; and a shopping, dining, and entertainment complex. A system of roads and two multistory parking facilities is connected by moving sidewalks to **CityWalk,** a shopping, dining, and nighttime-entertainment complex that also serves as a gateway to **Universal Studios Florida (USF)** and **Universal's Islands of Adventure (IOA)** theme parks.

Universal has developed into a major, world-class, multifaceted resort destination—one we can no longer adequately cover in the several dozen pages allocated here. Therefore, we're excited to announce *The Unofficial Guide to Universal Orlando,* by Seth Kubersky with Bob Sehlinger and Len Testa. This brand-new guide is the most comprehensive on Universal Orlando in print, with almost 400 pages devoted to the subject. Though we'll continue to cover Universal Orlando in this book, we strongly recommend the new guide for all of the tips, insights, elaborations, and attention to detail that we can't accommodate in these pages.

LODGING AT UNIVERSAL ORLANDO

UNIVERSAL HAS FOUR RESORT HOTELS. The 750-room **Portofino Bay Hotel** is a gorgeous property set on an artificial bay and themed like an Italian coastal town. The 650-room **Hard Rock Hotel** is an ultracool "Hotel California" replica, and the 1,000-room, Polynesian-themed **Royal Pacific Resort** is sumptuously decorated and richly appointed. All three resorts are on the pricey side. The retro-style **Cabana Bay Beach Resort,** Universal's largest hotel, has 1,800 moderate- and value-priced rooms, plus amenities (bowling alley, lazy river) not seen at comparable Disney resorts. Universal's newest hotel, **Loews Sapphire Falls Resort,** opens in summer 2016. The

LILIANE If your kids are *Despicable Me* fans, check out the 18 two-room, Minion-themed kids' suites that opened at Portofino Bay in 2014.

Continued on page 364

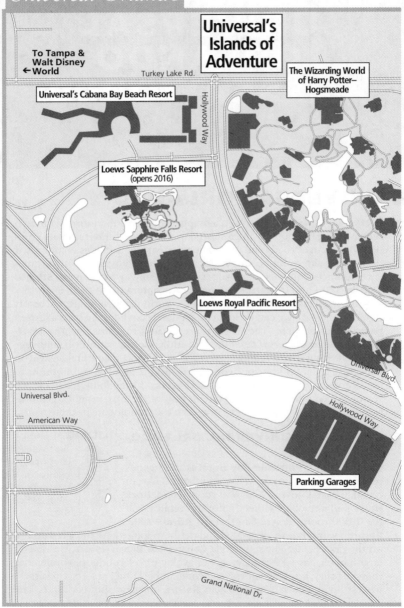

Universal Orlando

Universal's Islands of Adventure

To Tampa &
Walt Disney
← World

Turkey Lake Rd.

Hollywood Way

Universal's Cabana Bay Beach Resort

The Wizarding World
of Harry Potter–
Hogsmeade

Loews Sapphire Falls Resort
(opens 2016)

Loews Royal Pacific Resort

Universal Blvd.

Universal Blvd.

American Way

Hollywood Way

Parking Garages

Grand National Dr.

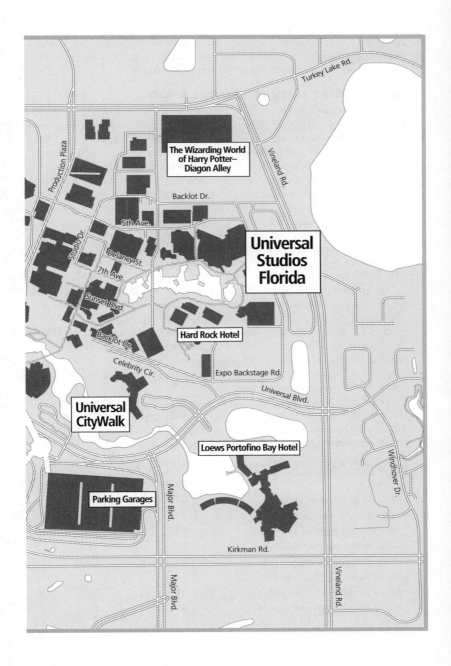

Continued from page 361

resort has a Caribbean theme and is priced between the Royal Pacific and the Cabana Bay Beach Resorts. The hotel will have water taxi service to the parks but no complimentary Universal Express Passes.

ARRIVING AT UNIVERSAL ORLANDO

THE UNIVERSAL ORLANDO COMPLEX can be accessed from eastbound I-4 by taking Exit 75A and turning left at the top of the ramp onto Universal Boulevard. Traveling westbound on I-4, use Exit 74B and then turn right on Hollywood Way. Entrances are also off Kirkman Road to the east, Turkey Lake Road to the north, and Vineland Road to the west. Universal Boulevard connects the International Drive area to Universal via an overpass bridging I-4. Turkey Lake and Vineland Roads are particularly good alternatives when I-4 is gridlocked. Once on-site, you'll be directed to park in one of two multitiered parking garages. Parking runs $17 for cars and $22 for RVs. From the garages, (sometimes) moving sidewalks deliver you to Universal CityWalk; it takes about 8–20 minutes to get from the garages to the parks. From CityWalk, you can access the main entrances of both USF and IOA.

Given that it's hard to find your car among 20,000 other cars, we strongly recommend that you write down or take a picture of the name and number of your section, level, and row. Sections are named for movies such as *Jurassic Park, King Kong,* and so on. The first numeral of the number following the section name tells you what deck level you're on and the remaining numbers specify the row. So if a sign tells you that you're on King Kong 410, you're in the King Kong section on the fourth floor in Row 10.

Universal offers one-day, two-day, three-day, and four-day passes for one park or two parks, as well as annual passes for both parks. Passes can be obtained in advance on the phone at ☎ 800-711-0080 or **universalorlando.com.** Prices below include sales tax.

UNIVERSAL ORLANDO ADMISSIONS (online purchase)		
	ADULTS	**CHILDREN (Ages 3-9)**
1-Day Single-Park Admission	$109	$103
1-Day Park-to-Park Admission	$157	$151
2-Day Single-Park Admission	$160	$149
2-Day Park-to-Park Admission	$208	$197
3-Day Single-Park Admission	$170	$160
3-Day Park-to-Park Admission	$218	$208
4-Day Single-Park Admission	$181	$170
4-Day Park-to-Park Admission	$229	$218

Be sure to check Universal Orlando's website for seasonal deals and specials. You can save as much as $20 by buying your tickets online. A five-park, 14-day pass called the **Orlando Flex Ticket** allows unlimited entry to Universal Studios, Islands of Adventure, SeaWorld, Aquatica, and Wet 'n Wild and costs $335.95 for adults and $315.95 for children ages 3–9, plus tax. For just $20 more, you can add access to Busch Gardens with the **Flex Ticket Plus** (includes free shuttle to Tampa). At **Undercover Tourist,** a reputable whole-saler, you can obtain the Flex Tickets at substantial savings; visit **undercovertourist.com.**

The **Three-Park Unlimited** ticket is good for 14 consecutive days of park-to-park admission at both USF and IOA, plus Wet 'n Wild. Three-Park Unlimited tickets are sold by a number of third-party vendors but not directly by Universal itself at this time. Only a few dollars more than the four-day park-to-park ticket, this ticket is poorly publicized but a great value if you like waterslides and aren't buying an annual pass for your extended stay.

The main Universal Orlando information number is ☎ 407-363-8000. Reach Guest Services at ☎ 407-224-4233, or schedule a character lunch at **universalorlando.com**. The numbers for lost and found are ☎ 407-224-4244 (USF) and 407-224-4245 (IOA).

A WORD ABOUT CROWDS

YOU'VE PROBABLY READ ABOUT the huge crowds that inundate the Wizarding World outposts at both Universal parks. The reports are true, but they present an unbalanced view of the crowds at the Universal parks overall. To get a quantitative grip on crowding, let's look at attendance figures compared with the size of the parks. On a day of average attendance, USF and Disney's Hollywood Studios see about the same number of guests per acre. However, USF has 26 attractions, while DHS has only 17. Therefore, the crowds are distributed among more attractions at USF, making it seem less crowded. Contrasting the Magic Kingdom with IOA, the latter averages 203 guests per day, per acre, while the Magic Kingdom—the attendance leader of all the world's theme parks—registers a whopping 495 guests per day, per acre. Depending on how you define *attractions*, however, the Magic Kingdom has about 42, versus 26 at Islands of Adventure. Even so, there are still one-and-a-half as many guests for each Magic Kingdom attraction as for each IOA attraction.

LILIANE In order, Mondays, Sundays, and Saturdays are the best days to visit Universal Orlando.

UNIVERSAL EXPRESS

SIMILAR TO DISNEY WORLD'S FASTPASS+, Universal Express is a system whereby any guest can "skip the line" and experience an attraction via a special queue with little or no waiting. While Disney's system requires scheduling your ride reservation hours or days ahead of time, Universal Express involves no advance planning; simply visit any eligible operating attraction whenever you choose, no return time windows required. In addition, unlike FastPass+, Universal Express is not free for everyone.

Universal Express is a complimentary perk for guests at all Universal hotels *except* Cabana Bay Beach and Sapphire Falls Resorts; they may use the Express lines all day long simply by flashing the pass they get at check-in. This perk far surpasses any benefit accorded to guests of Disney resorts and is especially valuable during peak season.

Day guests or guests staying at Cabana Bay or Sapphire Falls can purchase Universal Express for an extra $35–$150 (depending on the season), which provides line-jumping privileges at each Universal Express attraction at a given park. (All Universal hotel guests, including those staying at Cabana Bay and Sapphire Falls, may enter both parks' Wizarding World of Harry Potter themed areas 1 hour before they open to the public.)

You can purchase Universal Express for one or both parks and for either single (one ride only on each participating attraction) or unlimited use. The number of Express Passes is limited each day, and they can sell out, so increase your chances of securing passes by buying and printing them at home off Universal's website.

Speaking of participating attractions, more than 90% of rides and shows are covered by Universal Express, a much higher percentage than those covered by FastPass+ at Walt Disney World. The notable exceptions are **Harry Potter and the Forbidden Journey** and **Pteranodon Flyers** at IOA, along with **Harry Potter and the Escape from Gringotts** at USF and the interpark **Hogwarts Express** train.

You can also buy Universal Express at the theme parks' ticket windows, just outside the front gates, but it's faster to do so inside the parks. At Universal Studios Florida, it's available at **Super Silly Stuff;** at Islands of Adventure, you can buy it at **Jurassic Outfitters, Toon Extra,** and the **Marvel Alterniverse Store.** It's also available up to eight months in advance at **universalorlando.com.** You'll need to know when you plan on using it, though, because prices vary depending on the date.

IS UNIVERSAL EXPRESS WORTH IT? The answer depends on the season you visit, hours of park operation, and crowd levels. Attendance has jumped at both parks since the opening of each Harry Potter land, especially at Universal Studios Florida now that Diagon Alley has opened. However, the big-ticket rides in Hogsmeade and Diagon Alley don't participate in Universal Express, so you don't get to cut in line at Universal's most in-demand attractions. Still, if you want to sleep in and arrive at a park after opening, Express is an effective, albeit expensive, way to avoid long lines at the non-Potter headliner attractions, especially during holidays and busy times.

If, however, you arrive 30 minutes before park opening and you use our Universal Orlando touring plans (see pages 477–480), you should experience the lowest possible waits at both USF and IOA. We encourage you to try the touring plans first, but if waits for rides become intolerable, you can always buy Express in the parks.

A father from Snellville, Georgia, discovered that it was cheaper for his family to stay at a Universal resort than to buy Universal Express:

The benefits of staying on-property are worth it, with early entry to The Wizarding World and unlimited Express privileges at both parks. We got a room at the Royal Pacific Resort for $349 on a Saturday *night, which allowed us to use Universal Express Saturday and Sunday. The room cost $43.63 per person per day, while an [à la carte] Express Pass this same weekend would have cost $56 per person per day, and we still would have had to pay for a hotel.*

U-BOT

THIS RIDE-RESERVATION SYSTEM works much like Disney's FastPass+ but incorporates the small U-Bot device. Guests can purchase access to the device at any Express kiosk (buying access online is currently not an option). Once you have your U-Bot, you can use it to reserve ride times for any Universal Express attraction, but note that you can make only one reservation at a time. The U-Bot will vibrate and display a message telling you when it's time to ride. Next, you take your U-Bot to the ride's Express entrance, where the attraction greeter will scan your device and admit you to the Express queue. U-Bot costs considerably less than an Express Pass (usually by about $10–$20).

SINGLES LINES

SEVERAL ATTRACTIONS HAVE THIS SPECIAL LINE for guests riding alone. As Universal employees will tell you, this line is often just as fast as the Express line. We strongly recommend using the singles line whenever possible—it will decrease your overall wait and leave more time for repeat rides or just bumming around the parks. Note, though, that some queues (particularly Forbidden Journey's and Escape from Gringotts') are attractions in themselves and deserve to be experienced during your first ride.

LOCKERS

UNIVERSAL ENFORCES A MANDATORY locker system at its big thrill rides. Lockers outside these attractions are free for an amount of time that depends on the length of the standby line. So if the line is 30 minutes, for example, and the ride itself is 10 minutes, you get 40 minutes plus a small cushion of about 15 minutes. The lockers then cost $3 for each half hour after that, with a $20 maximum.

The locker banks are easy to find; each bank has a small computer in the center. When the sun is bright, the screen is almost impossible to read, so have someone block the sun or use a different computer. After selecting your language, you press your thumb onto the keypad and have your fingerprint scanned. We've seen people walk away cursing at this step, having repeated it over and over with no success. Don't press down too hard—the computer can't read your thumbprint that way. Instead, take a deep breath and lightly place your thumb on the scanner.

After you do your thumb scan, you'll receive a locker number. Write it down! When you return from your ride, go to the same kiosk machine, enter your locker number, and scan your thumb again. Family-size lockers are available for $8–$10 for the entire day, but remember that only the person who used his or her thumb to get the locker can retrieve anything from it.

UNIVERSAL DINING PROGRAMS

CITYWALK MEAL AND MOVIE DEAL This deal includes a ticket to any movie playing at the Universal Cineplex and a meal from a limited menu at participating CityWalk restaurants. The meal includes one entrée and a coffee, tea, or soft drink. This combination costs $21.95 for all ages. Buy your Meal and Movie Deal tickets at the CityWalk Guest Services ticket window or at all Destination Universal locations, or call a CityWalk sales coordinator at ☎ 407-224-2691. Additional charges apply for IMAX, IMAX 3-D, and 3-D movies.

CHARACTER DINING Every Sunday, **Jake's** at the Royal Pacific Resort offers a character breakfast ($29 for adults and $16 for kids). On select evenings, resort theme park characters visit guests during dinner at **Trattoria del Porto** at the Portofino Bay Hotel, **The Kitchen** at Hard Rock Hotel, and the **Islands Dining Room** at the Royal Pacific Resort. For information and reservations, call ☎ 407-503-3463. On Fridays, 4–7 p.m., guests can meet the Minions or SpongeBob SquarePants in the lobby of Cabana Bay Beach Resort. At times, Marilyn Monroe even makes an appearance.

LILIANE Cabana Bay offers wake-up calls from the Blue Man Group, the Cat in the Hat, Transformers, Olive Oyl, Betty Boop, Spider-Man, and the Grinch.

At Universal Studios Florida, try the **Superstar Character Breakfast** at Cafe La Bamba, with characters from Universal's Superstar Parade. Guests can interact with Minions from *Despicable Me* and Sponge-Bob SquarePants, and even get an autograph from Dora and Diego. Later in the day, you get special VIP viewing access to the Superstar Parade; the private viewing area is near the bus stop by Revenge of the Mummy and Finnegan's Bar and Grill. The breakfast costs $27.50 for adults and $14 for kids. After purchasing your dining experience online, you must call ☎ 407-224-3663 up to 24 hours before arriving to confirm your table. Separate theme park admission is required.

ONE-DAY COCA-COLA FREESTYLE SOUVENIR CUP This perk entitles you to one day of unlimited fountain soft drinks at all participating Coca-Cola Freestyle locations at both Universal Studios Florida or Islands of Adventure. Cost is $12 for all ages ($6 if added to a dining plan); add an extra day for $6.

***UNIVERSAL'S CINEMATIC SPECTACULAR* DINING EXPERIENCE** First have dinner at Lombard's Seafood Grille; choose from an array of entrées, including fresh seafood, pasta, sandwiches, and more. Afterward, enjoy a spectacular view of *Universal's Cinematic Spectacular* nighttime show in an exclusive area at the restaurant's waterfront boardwalk. The experience is available for $45 per adult and $13 per child. After reserving and purchasing your dining experience online, you must call ☎ 407-224-7554 up to 24 hours before arriving to confirm your table. Separate theme park admission is required.

UNIVERSAL DINING PLAN This plan is available exclusively to guests who book a hotel package with Universal. The plan includes one counter-service meal (entrée and nonalcoholic beverage), one table-service meal (entrée, dessert, and nonalcoholic beverage), one snack (from a cart or counter-service location), and one additional beverage (from a cart or counter-service location) each day. Select CityWalk locations and most in-park dining locations participate. Gratuity is not included, and no substitutions may be made. Eligible menu items and restaurants are indicated by a Universal Dining Plan logo. Price per day is $52 for adults and $18 for children. To book your vacation package with the Universal Dining Plan, visit **universalorlando.com.**

The **Quick Service Dining Plan** provides one counter-service meal with drink, another soft drink, and one snack. The cost is $20 for adults and $13 for kids age 9 and younger, plus tax. It's valid at most counter-service eateries in both parks (including Three Broomsticks in Hogsmeade, the Leaky Cauldron in Diagon Alley, and Fast Food Boulevard in Springfield U.S.A.) and a smattering at Universal CityWalk, but not at the hotels.

UNIVERSAL, KIDS, AND SCARY STUFF

THOUGH THERE'S PLENTY FOR YOUNGER CHILDREN to enjoy at the Universal parks, most major attractions can potentially make kids under age 8 wig out. At Universal Studios Florida, forget *Disaster!*, Hollywood Rip Ride Rockit, Men in Black Alien Attack, Revenge of the Mummy, The Simpsons Ride, *Terminator 2: 3-D,* Transformers: The Ride 3-D, and *Twister . . . Ride It Out.* The first part of the E.T. Adventure ride is a little intense for a few preschoolers, but the end is all happiness and harmony. There are some scary visual effects on both the Hogwarts Express train that runs between the two parks and Harry Potter and the Escape from Gringotts dark ride–roller coaster, but both are billed as family rides. Interestingly, very few families report problems with *Beetlejuice Graveyard Revue* or *Universal Orlando's Horror Make-Up Show.* Anything we haven't listed is pretty tame.

At Universal's Islands of Adventure, watch out for The Amazing Adventures of Spider-Man, Doctor Doom's Fearfall, Dragon Challenge, Harry Potter and the Forbidden Journey, The Incredible Hulk Coaster, Jurassic Park River Adventure, and *Poseidon's Fury.* Popeye & Bluto's Bilge-Rat Barges is wet and wild, but most younger children handle it well. Dudley Do-Right's Ripsaw Falls is a toss-up, to be considered only if your kids like water-flume rides. *The Eighth Voyage of Sindbad* includes some explosions and startling special effects, but again, kids generally tolerate it well. Nothing else should pose a problem.

CHILD SWAP Switching off at Universal is similar to Disney's version. The entire family goes through the whole line together before being split into riding and nonriding groups near the loading platform. The nonriding parent and child(ren) wait in a designated room, usually with some sort of entertainment (for example, Harry Potter and the Forbidden Journey at IOA shows the first 20 minutes of *Harry Potter and the Sorcerer's Stone* on a loop), a place to sit down, and sometimes restrooms with changing tables. At any theme park, the best tip we can give is to ask the greeter in front of the attraction what you're supposed to do.

BLUE MAN GROUP

UNIVERSAL STUDIOS FLORIDA'S Sharp Aquos Theater, near Universal CityWalk, is home to the Blue Man Group. The theater can be accessed from inside or outside USF; we recommend getting seats at least 15 rows back from the stage.

The three blue men are just that—blue—and bald and mute. Wearing black clothing and skullcaps slathered with bright-blue grease paint, they deliver a fast-paced show that uses music (mostly percussion) and multimedia effects to make light of contemporary art and life in the information age. The 1-hour, 45-minute production was updated and reimagined in 2012 to reflect cultural changes in the use of technology in daily life.

Tickets start at $60 for adults and $30 for children ages 3–9 and can be purchased online or at the Universal box office; tickets purchased at the box office cost $10 more.

UNIVERSAL CITYWALK

AT CITYWALK you will find a number of great restaurants, clubs, shops, outdoor entertainment, a concert hall (Hard Rock Live), and the Universal Cineplex 20 movie theater. CityWalk has a number of combination restaurants and clubs. Open to families with kids until 9 p.m., many of the venues offer live entertainment.

For Mom and Dad's night out, great entertainment is available at **CityWalk's Rising Star,** a karaoke joint where singers are backed by a live band; reggae at **Bob Marley—A Tribute to Freedom;** a **Pat O'Brien's** dueling-pianos club; **Fat Tuesday,** specializing in New Orleans–style daiquiris; a **Hard Rock Cafe** and **Hard Rock Live** concert venue; **Jimmy Buffett's Margaritaville;** the **Red Coconut Club,** a two-story upscale cocktail lounge with live music and dancing; and a dance club called **the groove,** with high-tech lighting and visual effects. If you want to go clubbing, $12 plus tax admits you to all of the clubs. For details, call Universal CityWalk information at ☎ 407-224-2691.

How To Make It Work

CityWalk is open daily, 11 a.m.–2 a.m., and parking is available in the same garages that serve the theme park at the rate of $17 a day for cars and $22 for RVs, trailers, and other large rigs. Regular parking drops to $5 6 p.m.–10 p.m. and is free after 10 p.m. If you stay at one of the Universal resorts, it's a short walk, but water taxi and bus transportation are also available to transport you to CityWalk. For added fun, try one of the pedicabs that will take you from CityWalk to your resort for a modest tip. Call ☎ 407-224-FOOD (3663) for dinner reservations. Visit **universalorlando.com** and select "At CityWalk" under "Events" for special events.

UNIVERSAL'S ISLANDS
of ADVENTURE

WHEN IOA OPENED IN 1999, it provided Universal with enough critical mass to actually compete with Disney. Doubly interesting is that the second Universal park is pretty much just for fun—in other words, a direct competitor to Disney's Magic Kingdom, the most-visited theme park in the world.

And though Universal played second fiddle to Disney for many years, times have changed: Universal's Islands of Adventure is a state-of-the-art park competing with a Disney park that is more than 35 years old and did not add a new super-headliner attraction for many years until the Fantasyland expansion begun in 2010 launched in phases, from 2012 to 2014.

Incidentally, 2010 marked IOA's coming-out party. In one of the greatest seismic shifts in theme park history, Universal secured the rights to build a Harry Potter–themed area within the park. Harry P. is possibly the only fictional character extant capable of trumping Mickey Mouse, and Universal has gone all-out, under J. K. Rowling's watchful and exacting eye, to create a setting and attractions designed to be the envy of the industry.

Disney and Universal officially downplay their fierce competition, pointing out that any new theme park or attraction makes Central Florida a more marketable destination. Behind closed doors, however, the two companies share a Pepsi-versus-Coke rivalry that keeps both working hard to gain a competitive edge. The good news is that all this translates into bigger and better attractions for you to enjoy.

BEWARE OF THE WET AND WILD

LILIANE Consider yourself warned: Several attractions at Islands of Adventure will drench you to the bone.

THOUGH WE HAVE DESCRIBED Universal's Islands of Adventure as a direct competitor to the Magic Kingdom, there is one major qualification you should be aware of: Whereas most Magic Kingdom attractions are designed to be enjoyed by guests of any age, attractions at Islands of Adventure are largely created for an under-40 population. The roller coasters at Universal are serious with a capital S, making Space Mountain and Big Thunder Mountain look about as tough as Dumbo. In fact, seven out of the nine top attractions at Islands are thrill rides, and of these, there are three that not only scare the bejabbers out of you but also drench you with water.

BOB Roller coasters at Islands of Adventure are the real deal—not for the timid or for little ones.

For families, there are three interactive playgrounds as well as six rides that young children will enjoy. Of the thrill rides, only the two

Continued on page 374

Universal's Islands of Adventure

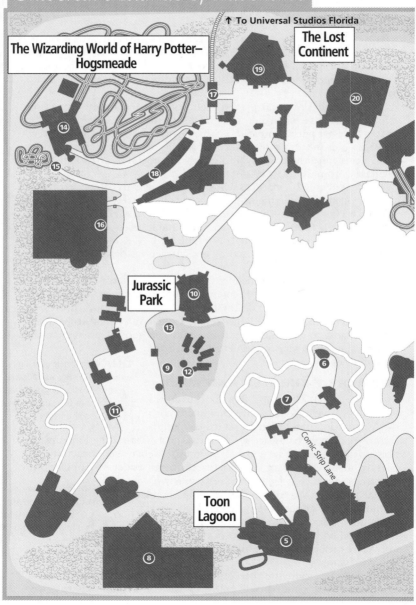

↑ To Universal Studios Florida

The Wizarding World of Harry Potter–Hogsmeade

The Lost Continent

Jurassic Park

Toon Lagoon

Comic Strip Lane

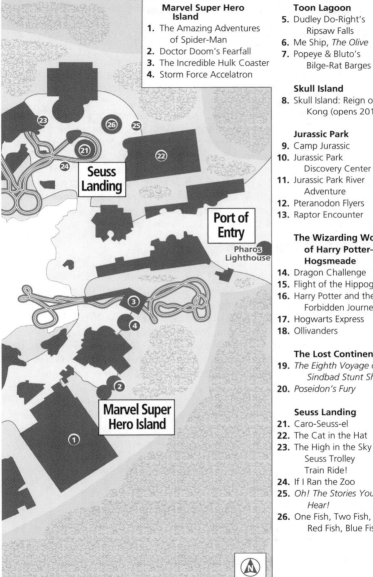

Marvel Super Hero Island
1. The Amazing Adventures of Spider-Man
2. Doctor Doom's Fearfall
3. The Incredible Hulk Coaster
4. Storm Force Accelatron

Toon Lagoon
5. Dudley Do-Right's Ripsaw Falls
6. Me Ship, *The Olive*
7. Popeye & Bluto's Bilge-Rat Barges

Skull Island
8. Skull Island: Reign of Kong (opens 2016)

Jurassic Park
9. Camp Jurassic
10. Jurassic Park Discovery Center
11. Jurassic Park River Adventure
12. Pteranodon Flyers
13. Raptor Encounter

The Wizarding World of Harry Potter– Hogsmeade
14. Dragon Challenge
15. Flight of the Hippogriff
16. Harry Potter and the Forbidden Journey
17. Hogwarts Express
18. Ollivanders

The Lost Continent
19. *The Eighth Voyage of Sindbad Stunt Show*
20. *Poseidon's Fury*

Seuss Landing
21. Caro-Seuss-el
22. The Cat in the Hat
23. The High in the Sky Seuss Trolley Train Ride!
24. If I Ran the Zoo
25. *Oh! The Stories You'll Hear!*
26. One Fish, Two Fish, Red Fish, Blue Fish

Seuss Landing

Port of Entry

Pharos Lighthouse

Marvel Super Hero Island

Continued from page 371

in Toon Lagoon (described later) are marginally appropriate for little kids, and even on these rides your child needs to be fairly hardy.

GETTING ORIENTED AT ISLANDS OF ADVENTURE

BOTH UNIVERSAL THEME PARKS are accessed via the Universal CityWalk entertainment complex. Crossing CityWalk from the parking garages, you can bear right to Universal Studios Florida or left to Universal's Islands of Adventure.

Islands of Adventure is arranged much like Epcot's World Showcase (in a large circle surrounding a lake), but its themed areas are self-contained "lands" reminiscent of the Magic Kingdom. You first encounter the Moroccan-style **Port of Entry,** where you'll find Guest Services, lockers, stroller and wheelchair rentals, ATM banking, lost and found, and shopping. From Port of Entry, moving clockwise around the lagoon, you access **Marvel Super Hero Island, Toon Lagoon, Jurassic Park, The Wizarding World of Harry Potter–Hogsmeade, The Lost Continent,** and **Seuss Landing.**

DECISIONS, DECISIONS

WHEN IT COMES TO TOURING IOA efficiently, you have two basic choices, and as you might expect, there are trade-offs. The Wizarding World of Harry Potter–Hogsmeade sucks up guests like a Hoover. If you're keen to experience **Harry Potter and the Forbidden Journey** first thing, be at the turnstiles waiting to be admitted at least 30 minutes before the park opens. Once you're admitted, move as swiftly as possible to The Wizarding World and then ride Forbidden Journey, followed by Flight of the Hippogriff and Dragon Challenge, in that order. You can get Hogsmeade out of the way in about an hour, and be off to other must-see attractions before the park gets crowded. Then come back to The Wizarding World late in the day to explore Hogsmeade and the shops.

If you can't be at the park when it opens, skip Potterville first thing and enjoy other attractions in IOA, starting at Marvel Super Hero Island. The good news is that The Wizarding World usually clears out in the afternoon even on busy days, so you can ride Forbidden Journey with a minimal wait if you get in the queue shortly before closing time.

ISLANDS *of* ADVENTURE ATTRACTIONS

MARVEL SUPER HERO ISLAND

THIS ISLAND, WITH ITS FUTURISTIC AND RETRO-FUTURE design and comic-book signage, offers shopping and attractions based on Marvel Comics characters.

UNIVERSAL UNDERCOVER WITH JIM HILL

WHERE'S WALDO—UH, STAN? Marvel Comics founder Stan Lee angles for a cameo appearance in any film featuring the characters he helped create, so the Universal creative team decided to get in on the fun by folding him into the recently retooled Spider-Man ride. Lee appears in four scenes in the attraction: as the truck driver who swerves to miss your SCOOP vehicle early in the ride, in the crowd as Spidey and Doc Ock duke it out in New York City's Theater District, in the street after your vehicle falls to the ground, and finally with the cops as the stolen Statue of Liberty is being flown back into place. He also is the voice that bids you farewell before disembarking.

The Amazing Adventures of Spider-Man
(Universal Express) ★★★★★

**APPEAL BY AGE   PRESCHOOL ★   GRADE SCHOOL ★★★★★   TEENS ★★★★★
YOUNG ADULTS ★★★★½   OVER 30 ★★★★½   SENIORS ★★★★**

What it is Indoor adventure simulator ride based on *Spider-Man*. **Scope and scale** Super-headliner. **Fright potential** Intense; kids tall enough to ride usually take it in stride. **Bottleneck rating** 9. **When to go** The first 40 minutes the park is open. **Special comment** Must be 40" tall to ride. **Authors' rating** One of the best attractions anywhere; ★★★★★. **Duration of ride** 4½ minutes. **Average wait in line per 100 people ahead of you** 4 minutes. **Loading speed** Fast.

Dark

Rough

Scary

Soar above buildings without ever leaving the ground! The Amazing Adventures of Spider-Man—covering 1½ acres and combining moving ride vehicles, 3-D film, and live action—was enhanced in 2012 with a complete high-definition digital upgrade. It's frenetic, fluid, and astounding. The visuals are rich, and the ride is wild but not jerky. Though the attractions are not directly comparable, Spider-Man is technologically ahead of The Twilight Zone Tower of Terror at Disney's Hollywood Studios—which is to say that it will leave you in awe. In fact, it's considered by many to be the best theme park attraction on the planet.

The story line is that you're a reporter for the *Daily Bugle* newspaper (where Peter Parker, also known as Spider-Man, works as a mild-mannered photographer), when it's discovered that evildoers have stolen—we promise we're not making this up—the Statue of Liberty. You're drafted on the spot by your cantankerous editor to go get the story. After speeding around and being thrust into a battle between good and evil, you experience a 400-foot "sensory drop" from a skyscraper roof all the way to the pavement. Because the ride is so wild and the action so continuous, it's hard to understand the plot, but you're so thoroughly entertained that you don't really care. Ride several times to take in all the details.

If you were on hand at park opening, ride after experiencing Harry Potter and the Forbidden Journey, Dragon Challenge, and The Incredible Hulk Coaster. If you elect to bypass all the congestion at Forbidden Journey, ride after Dragon Challenge and the Hulk. If you arrived more than 15 minutes after park opening, skip Wizarding World attractions and ride Spider-Man after the Hulk.

As amazing as Spider-Man himself, and the 3-D effects rock!

You feel like you're flying and really climbing up and down buildings, and Spidey even lands on your car. You do get moved around a lot, but it's not scary at all, not even for little kids.

Julia

Doctor Doom's Fearfall (*Universal Express*) ★★★

APPEAL BY AGE	PRESCHOOL ★	GRADE SCHOOL ★★★★½	TEENS ★★★★½
YOUNG ADULTS ★★★★		OVER 30 ★★★½	SENIORS ★★

What it is Vertical ascent and free fall. **Scope and scale** Headliner. **Fright potential** Frightening for all ages. **Bottleneck rating** 10. **When to go** The first 40 minutes the park is open. **Special comment** Must be 52" tall to ride. **Authors' rating** More bark than bite; ★★★. **Duration of ride** 40 seconds. **Average wait in line per 100 people ahead of you** 18 minutes. **Loading speed** Slow.

Lose Things   Scary

Here you are strapped into a seat with your feet dangling, blasted 200 feet up in the air, and then allowed to partially free-fall back down. The scariest part of the ride by far is the apprehension that builds as you sit, strapped in, waiting for the ride to launch; blasting up and falling down are actually pleasant. We've seen glaciers that move faster than the line to Doctor Doom. If you want to ride without investing half a day, be one of the first in the park to ride.

The Incredible Hulk Coaster (*Universal Express*)
★★★★½

APPEAL BY AGE	PRESCHOOL ★	GRADE SCHOOL ★★★★½	TEENS ★★★★★
YOUNG ADULTS ★★★★★		OVER 30 ★★★★½	SENIORS ★★

What it is Roller coaster. **Scope and scale** Super-headliner. **Fright potential** Frightening for all ages. **Bottleneck rating** 10. **When to go** The first 40 minutes the park is open. **Special comment** Must be 54" tall to ride. **Authors' rating** A coaster-lover's coaster; ★★★★½. **Duration of ride** 2¼ minutes. **Average wait in line per 100 people ahead of you** 9 minutes. **Loading speed** Moderate.

Lose Things   Queasy   Scary

The Hulk is a great roller coaster, one of the best in Florida, providing a ride comparable to Montu (Busch Gardens) with the added thrill of an accelerated launch. Hulk's steel track doesn't supply the side-to-side head shaking or uncomfortable jerkiness of Rip Ride Rockit next door. The Hulk gives Dragon Challenge a run as the park's most popular coaster. Arrive before park opening and, when admitted, ride after Harry Potter and the Forbidden Journey and Dragon Challenge.

You-know-who made me ride it, and for the duration of the ride, I lost my very polite Europea

Liliane

Unfortunately, Liliane lost her very polite European ways at about 140 decibels. My ears hurt for days.

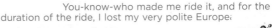

This was the first roller coaster I've ever been on. I love the countdown at the beginning, just before you shoot out like a cannonball.

Ethan

Storm Force Accelatron (*Universal Express*) ★★½

APPEAL BY AGE	PRESCHOOL ★★★★★	GRADE SCHOOL ★★★½	TEENS ★★★
YOUNG ADULTS ★★★½		OVER 30 ★★½	SENIORS —

What it is Spinning ride. **Scope and scale** Minor attraction. **Fright potential** Nauseating but not frightening. **Bottleneck rating** 9. **When to go** The first hour the park is open. **Authors' rating** Teacups in the dark; ★★½. **Duration of ride** 1½ minutes. **Average wait in line per 100 people ahead of you** 21 minutes. **Loading speed** Slow.

Storm Force is a spiffed-up version of Disney's nausea-inducing Mad Tea Party. Ride early or late to avoid long lines. Skip it if you're prone to motion sickness.

TOON LAGOON

THIS LAND TRANSLATES cartoon art into real buildings and settings. Whimsical and gaily colored, with rounded and exaggerated lines, Toon Lagoon is Universal's answer to Storybook Circus in the Magic Kingdom—only you have about a 60% chance of drowning at Universal's version. **Comic Strip Lane** is the main street of Toon Lagoon. Here you can visit the domains of Beetle Bailey, Hagar the Horrible, Krazy Kat, the Family Circus, and Blondie and Dagwood, among others of whom your kids have never heard. Shops and eateries tie in to the cartoon strip theme. This is a great place for photo ops with cartoon characters.

Dudley Do-Right's Ripsaw Falls (*Universal Express*) ★★★½

APPEAL BY AGE	PRESCHOOL ★½	GRADE SCHOOL ★★★★½	TEENS ★★★★
YOUNG ADULTS ★★★★		OVER 30 ★★★★½	SENIORS ★★★★

What it is Flume ride. **Scope and scale** Major attraction. **Fright potential** The big drop frightens guests of all ages. **Bottleneck rating** 8. **When to go** Before 11 a.m. **Special comment** Must be 44" tall to ride. **Authors' rating** A minimalist Splash Mountain; ★★½. **Duration of ride** 5 minutes. **Average wait in line per 100 people ahead of you** 9 minutes. **Loading speed** Moderate.

Inspired by the *Rocky and Bullwinkle* cartoons, this ride features Canadian Mountie Dudley Do-Right as he attempts to save his girlfriend, Nell Fenwick, from the evil Snidely Whiplash. Story line aside, it's a flume ride, with the inevitable big drop at the end. Universal claims that this is the first flume ride to "send riders plummeting 15 feet below the surface of the water." In reality, though, you're just plummeting into a tunnel. The flume is as good as Splash Mountain's at the Magic Kingdom, and the final drop is a whopper, but the theming and the visuals aren't even in the same league.

This ride will get you wet, but on average not as wet as you might expect (it looks worse than it is). If you want to stay dry, however, arrive prepared with a poncho or at least a big garbage bag with holes cut out for your head and arms. While younger children are often intimidated by the big drop, those who ride generally enjoy themselves. Ride first thing in the morning after experiencing the Marvel Super Hero rides.

Small children will be intimidated by the big drop. Try Popeye & Bluto's Bilge-Rat Barges first.

Right, Liliane. Popeye & Bluto's Bilge-Rat Barges is perfect for small children . . . as long as they have wet suits and life jackets.

Me Ship, *The Olive* ★★★

APPEAL BY AGE	PRESCHOOL ★★★★★	GRADE SCHOOL ★★★★½	TEENS ★★
YOUNG ADULTS ★★		OVER 30 ★★½	SENIORS ★★

What it is Interactive playground. **Scope and scale** Minor attraction. **Fright potential** Not frightening in any respect. **Bottleneck rating** 4. **When to go** Anytime. **Authors' rating** Colorful and appealing for kids; ★★★.

The Olive is Popeye's three-story boat come to life as an interactive playground. Younger kids can scramble around in Swee'Pea's Playpen, while older sibs shoot water cannons at riders trying to survive the adjacent Bilge-Rat Barges. If you're into the big rides, save this for later in the day.

Popeye & Bluto's Bilge-Rat Barges
(*Universal Express*) ★★★★

APPEAL BY AGE	PRESCHOOL ★½	GRADE SCHOOL ★★★★★	TEENS ★★★★½
YOUNG ADULTS ★★★★		OVER 30 ★★★★	SENIORS ★★★★

What it is Whitewater-raft ride. **Scope and scale** Major attraction. **Fright potential** Ride is wild and wet but not frightening. **Bottleneck rating** 8. **When to go** Before 10:30 a.m. **Special comment** Must be 42" tall to ride. **Authors' rating** Bring your own soap; ★★★★. **Duration of ride** 4½ minutes. **Average wait in line per 100 people ahead of you** 7 minutes. **Loading speed** Moderate.

This whitewater-raft ride for the whole family is engineered to ensure that everyone gets drenched; the ride even provides water cannons for highly intelligent nonparticipants ashore to fire at those aboard. The rapids are rougher and more interesting, and the ride longer, than Animal Kingdom's Kali River Rapids. If you didn't drown on Dudley Do-Right, here's a second chance.

Rough   Wet

Remember that you *will* get wet. That's OK on a hot summer day, unless it's first thing in the morning. Now is the time to use the raingear or plastic bags to protect yourselves. Most important, keep your footwear dry to avoid blisters later.

Liliane

SKULL ISLAND

SKULL ISLAND: REIGN OF KONG is both an attraction and an entire "island" unto itself, located between Dudley Do-Right's Ripsaw Falls and Thunder Falls Terrace.

Skull Island: Reign of Kong (*opens summer 2016*)

What it is Indoor/outdoor truck safari with 3-D effects. **Fright potential** Extremely intense; if you or your little one has a fear of darkness, insects, or man-eating monsters, you may want to forgo the monkey. **Bottleneck rating** 10. **Scope and scale** Super-headliner. **When to go** Immediately after park opening or just before closing. **Special comment** Must be 34" tall to ride. **Authors' rating** Not yet rated; not to be missed. **Duration of ride** More than 4½ minutes. **Probable waiting time per 100 people ahead of you** N/A. **Loading speed** N/A.

The ride is an original adventure set in the 1930s, which begins as you pass beneath a stone archway, shaped like a massive monkey skull, and start exploring the elaborate,

Dark   Scary

immersive queue. Pathways wind through dense foliage and an ancient temple inhabited by a hostile indigenous tribe before leading you to your transportation: an oversize open-sided "expedition vehicle" that superficially resembles Animal Kingdom's Kilimanjaro Safari trucks. Visit Skull Island first thing in the morning, or immediately following the Hogsmeade attractions if you're using Early Park Admission.

JURASSIC PARK

JURASSIC PARK (for anyone who's been asleep for 20 years) is a Steven Spielberg film franchise about a fictitious theme park with real dinosaurs. Jurassic Park at Universal's Islands of Adventure is a real theme park (or at least a section of one) with fictitious dinosaurs.

Camp Jurassic ★★★½

APPEAL BY AGE	PRESCHOOL ★★★★★	GRADE SCHOOL ★★★★½	TEENS ★
YOUNG ADULTS ★★	OVER 30 ★★★		SENIORS ★★

What it is Interactive play area. **Scope and scale** Minor attraction. **Fright potential** Not frightening in any respect. **Bottleneck rating** 3. **When to go** Anytime. **Authors' rating** Creative playground; confusing layout; ★★★½.

Camp Jurassic is a great place for children to run and explore. Sort of a Jurassic version of Tom Sawyer Island, kids can explore lava pits, caves, mines, and a rain forest.

Jurassic Park Discovery Center ★★½

APPEAL BY AGE	PRESCHOOL ★★★	GRADE SCHOOL ★★★★	TEENS ★★★
YOUNG ADULTS ★★★	OVER 30 ★★★		SENIORS ★★★

What it is Interactive natural-history exhibit. **Scope and scale** Minor attraction. **Fright potential** Not frightening in any respect. **Bottleneck rating** 3. **When to go** Anytime. **Authors' rating** ★★½.

The Discovery Center is an interactive educational exhibit that mixes fiction from the movie *Jurassic Park,* such as using fossil DNA to bring dinosaurs to life, with various skeletal remains and other paleontological displays. Cycle back after experiencing all the rides or on a second day. Most folks can digest this exhibit in 10–15 minutes.

Don't skip the Discovery Center. On a hot summer day, it's a great place to cool off. The best exhibit of all is the one where an animatronic raptor hatches from an egg. Young children will delight in the hatching and are afforded an opportunity to name the baby dino.

Liliane

Jurassic Park River Adventure *(Universal Express)* ★★★★

APPEAL BY AGE	PRESCHOOL ★	GRADE SCHOOL ★★★★	TEENS ★★★★
YOUNG ADULTS ★★★★	OVER 30 ★★★★½		SENIORS ★★★★★

What it is Indoor/outdoor adventure river-raft ride based on the *Jurassic Park* movies. **Scope and scale** Super-headliner. **Fright potential** Visuals and big drop frighten guests of all ages. **Bottleneck rating** 9. **When to go** Before 11 a.m. **Special comment** Must be 42″ tall to ride. **Authors' rating** Better than its Hollywood cousin; ★★★★. **Duration of ride** 6½ minutes. **Average wait in line per 100 people ahead of you** 5 minutes. **Loading speed** Fast.

Wet Scary

Guests board boats for a water tour of Jurassic Park. Everything is tranquil as the tour begins, and then, as word is received that some of the carnivores have escaped their enclosure, the tour boat is accidentally diverted into Jurassic Park's maintenance facilities. Here, the boat and its riders are menaced by an assortment of hungry meat-eaters. At the climactic moment, the boat and its passengers escape by plummeting over an 85-foot drop. Young children must endure a double whammy on this ride: First, they are stalked by giant, salivating (sometimes spitting) reptiles, and then they're sent catapulting over the falls. Unless your children are fairly hardy, wait a year or two before you spring the River Adventure on them.

This ride is relaxing in the beginning, but it sure gets tense when the animals escape. The big drop at the end is a lot of fun.

Ethan

Don't be fooled by the mellow beginning of this ride—the very big drop at the end is scary and fast. I love to see the expression on my face in the picture they snap at the end of the ride; I'm always screaming!

Julia

Pteranodon Flyers ★★

**APPEAL BY AGE PRESCHOOL ★★★½ GRADE SCHOOL ★★★★ TEENS ★★★★
YOUNG ADULTS ★★★½ OVER 30 ★★★ SENIORS ★★★★**

What it is Slow as Christmas. **Scope and scale** Minor attraction. **Fright potential** Not frightening in any respect. **Bottleneck rating** 10. **When to go** When there's no line. **Special comment** Adults and older children must be accompanied by a child 36"–52" tall. **Authors' rating** All sizzle, no steak; ★★. **Duration of ride** 1¼ minutes. **Average wait in line per 100 people ahead of you** 28 minutes. **Loading speed** More sluggish than a hog in quicksand.

This ride swings you along a track that passes over a small part of Jurassic Park. We recommend that you skip this one. Why? Because the next ice age will probably end before you reach the front of the line! And your reward for all that waiting? A 1-minute-and-15-second ride.

This ride is awful.
Sorry, folks—totally boring.

Isaac

Raptor Encounter ★★★½

**APPEAL BY AGE PRESCHOOL ★★ GRADE SCHOOL ★★★★ TEENS ★★★★
YOUNG ADULTS ★★★½ OVER 30 ★★★½ SENIORS ★★★**

What it is Photo op with lifelike dinosaur. **Scope and scale** Minor attraction. **Fright potential** The velociraptor makes loud, growling noises and sudden, snapping movements that startle even some adults. **Bottleneck rating** 8. **When to go** Check park map or attraction for appearance times. **Authors' rating** Sure to scare the spit out of small kids; ★★★½. **Duration of encounter** About a minute. **Probable waiting time per 100 people ahead of you** 30 minutes.

Several times each hour, the blue siren lights around the sunken predator paddock signal the arrival of Lucy or Ethel, the park's new semi-tame velociraptor stars. A game warden briefs one family at a time regarding proper safety procedures (convey calm assurance, move in slowly, and try not to smell like meat) before they step up for a photo. Don't peer too closely over the edge of the raptor enclosure; you'll spot the cleverly camouflaged legs of the puppeteer inside and spoil the illusion. Selfies are encouraged—just don't be surprised if the dino snaps when you say, "Smile!" Don't try to touch the raptor, or you may come home minus a hand—surreptitiously feeding your offspring to the dinosaurs is also discouraged by management.

If appearance times aren't printed on the park map, check with a team member outside the paddock entrance and arrive at least 15 minutes before a scheduled session; 20-minute appearances begin around 11 a.m. and occur about every half hour until 6 p.m.

THE WIZARDING WORLD OF HARRY POTTER–HOGSMEADE

IN WHAT MAY PROVE TO BE THE COMPETITIVE COUP of all time between archrivals Disney and Universal, the latter inked a deal with Warner Brothers Entertainment to create a fully immersive Harry Potter–themed environment based on the best-selling children's books by J. K. Rowling and the companion blockbuster movies from Warner Brothers. The project was blessed by Rowling, who is known for tenaciously protecting the integrity of her work. In the case of the films, she demanded that Warner Brothers be true, almost to an unprecedented degree, to the books on which the films were based.

We don't have room to explain all the Potter allusions and icons incorporated into The Wizarding World. Because they so accurately replicate scenes from the books and films, it helps immeasurably to be well versed in all things Harry. If it's been awhile since you've seen one of the movies or read one of the novels, you can brush up by watching the first four flicks in the series, in particular *Harry Potter and the Goblet of Fire* and *Harry Potter and the Sorcerer's Stone* (*Harry Potter and the Philosopher's Stone* outside India and the United States). For an easy memory jog, check out the films' trailers at **YouTube.** If you know nothing at all about Harry Potter, you'll still have fun, but to truly appreciate the nuance and detail, we suggest you hit the books.

The 20-acre Wizarding World draws its inspiration from all the *Harry Potter* movies and books, creating an amalgamation of landmarks, sights, creatures, and themes that are faithful to the films. The themed area is situated in the northwest corner of the park, between The Lost Continent and Jurassic Park. From the IOA entrance, the most direct route there is through Port of Entry then right, through Seuss Landing (staying to the left of the Green Eggs and Ham Cafe) and The Lost Continent, to the Hogsmeade main gate. The alternative route is to cross the bridge connecting The Lost Continent with Jurassic Park, and then turn right after entering the latter area. (Note that the bridge is closed on slower days.) For the moment, though, let's begin our exploration at The Wizarding World's main entrance, on the Lost Continent side.

BOB The only restrooms in The Wizarding World at IOA, labeled PUBLIC CONVENIENCES, are in the middle of Hogsmeade. Remember where they are—especially if you're planning to ride Forbidden Journey or Dragon Challenge and you're prone to motion sickness.

Passing beneath a stone archway, you enter the village of **Hogsmeade.** Depicted in winter, the village setting is rendered in exquisite detail:

Stone cottages and shops have steeply pitched slate roofs; bowed multipaned windows; gables; and tall, crooked chimneys.

Your first taste—literally—of the Harry Potter universe comes courtesy of **Honeydukes.** Specializing in Potter-themed candy such as Acid Pops (no flashbacks, guaranteed), Tooth Splintering Strong Mints, and Fizzing Whizzbees, the sweet shop offers no shortage of snacks that administer an immediate sugar high. There's also a small bakery inside; while we highly recommend the Cauldron Cakes, the big draw is the elaborately boxed Chocolate Frogs. The chocolate inside isn't anything special, but the packaging looks as if it came straight from a Harry Potter film, complete with lenticular wizard trading card.

Next door to Honeydukes and set back from the main street is **Three Broomsticks,** a rustic tavern serving English staples such as fish-and-chips, shepherd's pie, Cornish pasties, and turkey legs; kids' fare includes mac and cheese and chicken fingers. To the rear of the tavern is the **Hog's Head** pub, which serves a nice selection of beer as well as The Wizarding World's signature nonalcoholic brew, Butterbeer. (Outdoor vendors also sell it, but the wait at the Hog's Head is generally 10 minutes or less, versus half an hour or more in the lines outside. Also, the outdoor vendors charge a few cents more, and don't honor annual pass discounts.) To dine at Three Broomsticks anytime from its opening until roughly 8 p.m., you'll have to wait in a long queue during busier times of year. In summer 2015, waiting times for Three Broomsticks were upwards of 30 minutes much of the day (though additional capacity had been added in 2013 by replacing space-hogging booths with tables).

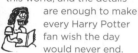

LILIANE Once you enter The Wizarding World of Harry Potter, be ready to get stuck in a time warp. The attractions are out of this world, and the details are enough to make every Harry Potter fan wish the day would never end.

Roughly across the street from the pub, you'll find benches in the shade at the **Owlery,** where animatronic owls (complete with lifelike poop) ruffle and hoot from the rafters. Next to the Owlery is the **Owl Post,** where you can have mail stamped with a Hogsmeade postmark before dropping it off for delivery (an Orlando postmark will also be applied by the real USPS). The Owl Post also sells stationery, toy owls, and the like. Here, once again, a nice selection of owls preens on the timbers overhead. You access the Owl Post in either of two ways: through an interior door following the wand-choosing demonstration at Ollivanders (see below) or through **Dervish and Banges,** a magic-supplies shop that's interconnected with the Owl Post. You can't enter through the Owl Post's front door on busy days, when it serves exclusively as an exit. Because it's so difficult to get into the Owl Post, IOA sometimes stations a team member outside to stamp your postcards with the Wizarding World postmark.

ISAAC Picking out my own wand was great, and I liked the show even though the wand did not pick me.

Next to the Owl Post is the previously mentioned **Ollivanders** (★★★★), a musty little shop stacked to the ceiling with boxes of magic wands. Here, following a script from the Potter books, you can pick out a wand or, in an interactive experience, let it pick you. This is one of the most truly imaginative elements of The Wizarding World: A Wandkeeper sizes you up and presents a wand, inviting you to try it out; your attempted spells produce unintended, unwanted, and highly amusing consequences. Ultimately, a wand chooses you, with all the attendant special effects. It's great fun, but the tiny shop can accommodate only about 24 guests at a time. Usually just one person in each group gets to be chosen by a wand, and then the whole group is dispatched to the Owl Post and Dervish and Banges to make purchases. Wand prices range from $25 for a no-frills model to $45 for an interactive gizmo that triggers special effects hidden inside shop windows throughout Hogsmeade. The wand experience is second in popularity only to Harry Potter and the Forbidden Journey—lines build quickly after opening, and there's little to no shade. If Ollivanders is a priority, go there first thing in the morning or after 7:30 p.m. The average wait time during summer and other busy periods is 45–85 minutes between 9:30 a.m. and 7:30 p.m. If you're just looking to buy a wand without the interactive experience, a cart is usually set up between Filch's Emporium of Confiscated Goods and the Flight of the Hippogriff exit, with little to no wait.

At the far end of the village, the massive **Hogwarts** castle comes into view, set atop a rock face and towering over Hogsmeade and the entire Wizarding World. Follow the path through the castle's massive gates to the entrance of Harry Potter and the Forbidden Journey. Below the castle and to the right, at the base of the cliff, are the **Forbidden Forest, Hagrid's Hut,** and the **Flight of the Hippogriff** children's roller coaster. In the village, near the gate to Hogwarts Castle, is **Filch's Emporium of Confiscated Goods,** which offers all manner of Potter-themed gear, including Quidditch clothing, magical-creature toys, film-inspired chess sets, and, of course, Death Eater masks (breath mints extra).

At the end of the village and to the left is the walkway to **Jurassic Park,** the themed area contiguous to The Wizarding World.

Accessing The Wizarding World

Crowds are certainly larger during summer and holidays, but because of The Wizarding World's overwhelming popularity, you'll encounter lines even at slower times of year. During peak periods, hotel guests may be allowed into IOA 1 hour before the general public, while all guests are usually admitted through the turnstiles into Port of Entry 30 minutes before the official opening time.

Wizarding World crowd management has been a work in progress for Universal. Now, with six years of operation under its belt, Universal has settled on a flexible system predicated on the expected level of attendance for any given day. (Similar procedures are in place at Diagon Alley; see page 407.) No matter the crowd level, if you're staying in one of Universal's on-site hotels and you have early-entry privileges for The Wizarding World, use them, arriving as early during the early-entry period as possible.

On most days of the year, from the slowest off-season through the busiest summer weeks, you can enter and depart The Wizarding World of Harry Potter–Hogsmeade as you please. The waits for the rides will still be more than an hour at times, but gaining entry to the themed area itself is not an issue.

On days when the park is busiest, such as during spring break or between December 25 and January 1, access to Hogsmeade may be limited for part of the day. Barricades are placed at both entrances to The Wizarding World–Hogsmeade once the area reaches maximum occupancy. You can then go to touch screen ticket kiosks outside the Jurassic Park Discovery Center and obtain a free return ticket (not unlike the old paper Fastpasses at Walt Disney World) to come back during your choice of designated time windows. You do not need your admission ticket to receive a timed return ticket, and one person can retrieve a time for your entire party (up to nine people). At the specified time, return to the Lost Continent entrance and present your pass to the barricade crew to gain entry.

BOB If you leave The Wizarding World while the entrance barriers are in place and you wish to return, you'll either have to wait in line to get another pass (provided they haven't all been distributed) or wait until late in the day, when the barricades come down as crowds disperse.

The return time on your pass depends on crowd conditions and how many Universal resort guests are in The Wizarding World–Hogsmeade before the park opens to the general public. Depending on demand, your possible return times may be many hours in the future, and it's possible (though extremely rare) for return tickets to run out entirely. Another factor that will affect your wait is how well Harry Potter and the Forbidden Journey is operating because this is what those in line are waiting for. If the ride comes up on schedule and runs trouble-free, everything runs smoothly. If Forbidden Journey experiences problems, though, especially first thing in the morning, it gums up the works for everyone.

On these peak days, a standby queue may also be erected in the waterfront landing behind the Jurassic Park Discovery Center; because more guests can enter only as others leave, this line can be painfully slow, so a return ticket is strongly suggested. It is common for the entrance barricades to be removed during the last hour or two the park is open, thus presenting the opportunity to come and go as you please.

Once admitted to Hogsmeade, you'll still have to wait for each ride, store, and concession, as well as for the area's one restaurant. Because Hogsmeade has less elbow room than Diagon Alley, it will reach maximum occupancy and require return tickets on days when Diagon does not, and feel more crowded once you finally get inside.

Note that guests arriving on Hogwarts Express disembark outside of Hogsmeade and must still retrieve a ticket before entering. The timed returned tickets are neither needed nor accepted for Hogwarts Express itself.

However complicated, it's all doable, as a multigenerational Grosse Pointe, Michigan, family attests:

> *Convinced of your rectitude, we went without fear to Universal. We made it to Harry Potter by 8:05, were out of the Forbidden Journey and on the Hippogriff by 8:30, and had our Butterbeer by 9.*

WIZARDING WORLD-HOGSMEADE ATTRACTIONS
Dragon Challenge *(Universal Express)* ★★★★

APPEAL BY AGE   PRESCHOOL ★   GRADE SCHOOL ★★★★★   TEENS ★★★★½
YOUNG ADULTS ★★★★★   OVER 30 ★★★★½   SENIORS ★★★

What it is Roller coaster. **Scope and scale** Headliner. **Fright potential** Frightening to guests of all ages. **Bottleneck rating 4. When to go** After Harry Potter and the Forbidden Journey. **Special comment** Must be 54" tall to ride. **Authors' rating** As good as the Hulk coaster; ★★★★. **Duration of ride** 2½ minutes. **Average wait in line per 100 people ahead of you** 9 minutes. **Loading speed** Moderate.

Lose Things   Rough   Queasy

The story line here is that you're preparing to compete in the Triwizard Tournament from *Harry Potter and the Goblet of Fire.* As you wind through the long, long queue, you pass through tournament tents and dark passages that are supposed to be under the stadium. You'll see the Goblet of Fire on display and hear the distant roar of the crowd in the supposed stadium above you.

Riders board one of two coasters—Chinese Fireball or Hungarian Horntail—that are launched moments apart on tracks that are closely intertwined. The tracks are configured so that you get a different experience on each. The trains are dispatched sequentially instead of simultaneously, so it looks as if one train is chasing another.

Because this is an inverted coaster, your view of the action is limited unless you're sitting in the front row. Dragon Challenge is the highest coaster in the park and also claims the longest drop at 115 feet, plus five inversions. It's a smooth ride all the way.

Coaster fans argue about which seat on which train provides the wildest ride. We prefer the front row on either train, but coaster loonies hype the front row of Fireball and the last row of Horntail.

Waits for Dragon Challenge, one of the best coasters in the country, rarely exceed 30 minutes before 11 a.m. Ride after experiencing Harry Potter and the Forbidden Journey. If you don't have time to ride both coasters, the *Unofficial* crew unanimously prefers Chinese Fireball.

By now everybody knows that yours truly hates roller coasters, but the decorations along the queuing line were well worth 60 seconds of near-death experience. Next time I'll grab that Goblet of Fire!

Liliane

Flight of the Hippogriff *(Universal Express)* ★★★

APPEAL BY AGE   PRESCHOOL ★★★½   GRADE SCHOOL ★★★★   TEENS ★★★
YOUNG ADULTS ★★½   OVER 30 ★★★½   SENIORS ★★★

What it is Children's roller coaster. **Scope and scale** Minor attraction. **Fright potential** Frightens a small percentage of preschool riders. **Bottleneck rating** 5. **When to go** First 90 minutes the park is open. **Special comment** Must be 36" tall to ride. **Authors' rating** A good beginner coaster; ★★★. **Duration of ride** 1 minute. **Average wait in line per 100 people ahead of you** 14 minutes. **Loading speed** Slow.

Below and to the right of Hogwarts Castle next to Hagrid's Hut, the Hippogriff is short and sweet but not worth much of a wait. Fortunately, waits usually don't exceed 20 minutes, even in the non-Express line. Have your kids ride soon after the park opens, while older sibs enjoy Dragon Challenge. Even if you don't ride, it's worth a stroll down to see the castle from the cliff bottom and to check out Hagrid's Hut, above the path for the regular line.

I'm sure this ride is great for little kids, but it definitely won't be high on the list for older kids.

Isaac

Harry Potter and the Forbidden Journey ★★★★★

APPEAL BY AGE   PRESCHOOL ★   GRADE SCHOOL ★★★★½   TEENS ★★★★★
YOUNG ADULTS ★★★★★   OVER 30 ★★★★★   SENIORS ★★★★★

What it is Motion simulator dark ride. **Scope and scale** Super-headliner. **Fright potential** Intense special effects and wild ride. **Bottleneck rating** Off the charts. **When to go** Immediately after park opening. **Special comments** Expect *long* waits in line; must be 48" tall to ride. **Authors' rating** Marvelous for Muggles; not to be missed; ★★★★★. **Duration of ride** 4⅓ minutes. **Average wait in line per 100 people ahead of you** 4 minutes. **Loading speed** Fast.

Dark   Rough   Queasy   Scary

This ride provides the only opportunity at Universal Orlando to come in contact with Harry, Ron, Hermione, and Dumbledore as portrayed by the original actors. Half of the attraction is a series of preshows that sets the stage for the main event, a dark ride. To understand the story line and get the most out of the attraction, it's critical to see and hear the entire presentation in each of the queue's preshow rooms. You can get on the ride in only 10–25 minutes using the single-rider line, but everyone should go through the main queue at least once. If you see a complete iteration of each of the preshows in the queue and then experience the 4½-minute ride, you'll invest 25–35 minutes even if you don't have to wait.

From Hogsmeade you reach the attraction through the imposing Winged Boar gates and progress along a winding path. Entering the castle on a lower level, you walk through a sort of dungeon festooned with various icons and prop replicas from the Potter flicks, including the Mirror of Erised from *Harry Potter and the Sorcerer's Stone.* You later emerge back outside and into the Hogwarts greenhouses. Cleverly conceived and executed, with some strategically placed mandrakes to amuse you, the greenhouses compose the larger part of the Forbidden Journey's queuing area. If you're among the first in the park and in the queue, you'll move through this area pretty quickly. Otherwise . . . well, we hope you like plants. The greenhouses are not air-conditioned, but fans move the (hot) air around. Blessedly, there are water fountains but, alas, no restrooms—take care of that before getting in line for the attraction.

Having finally escaped horticulture purgatory, you reenter the castle, moving along its halls and passageways. One chamber you'll probably remember from the films is a multistory gallery of portraits, many of whose subjects come alive when they take a notion. You'll see for the first time the four founders of Hogwarts: Helga Hufflepuff holding her famous cup, Godric Gryffindor and Rowena Ravenclaw nearby, and the tall, moving portrait of Salazar Slytherin straight ahead. The founders argue about Quidditch and Dumbledore's controversial decision to host an open house at Hogwarts for Muggles (garden-variety mortals). Don't rush through the gallery—the effects are very cool, and the conversation is essential to understanding the rest of the attraction.

Next up, after you've navigated some more passages, is Dumbledore's office, where the chief wizard appears on a balcony and welcomes you to Hogwarts. The headmaster's appearance is your introduction to Musion Eyeliner technology—a high-definition video-projection system that produces breathtakingly realistic, three-dimensional, life-size moving holograms. The technology uses a special foil that reflects images from HD projectors, producing holographic images of variable sizes and incredible clarity. After his welcoming remarks, Dumbledore dispatches you to the Defence Against the Dark Arts classroom to hear a presentation on the history of Hogwarts.

As you gather to await the lecture, Harry, Ron, and Hermione pop out from beneath an invisibility cloak. They suggest you ditch the lecture in favor of joining them for a proper tour of Hogwarts, including a Quidditch match. After some repartee among the characters and a couple of special effects surprises, it's off to the Hogwarts Official Attraction Safety Briefing and Boarding Instructions Chamber—OK, we made up the name, but you get the picture. The briefing and instructions are presented by animated portraits, including an etiquette teacher. Later on, even the famed Sorting Hat gets into the act. All this leads to the Room of Requirement, where hundreds of candles float overhead and you board the ride.

After all the high-tech stuff in your queuing odyssey, you'll naturally expect to be wowed by your ride vehicle. Surely it's a Nimbus 3000 turbo-broom, a phoenix, a hippogriff, or at least the Weasleys' flying car. But no, what you'll ride on the most technologically advanced theme park attraction in America is . . . a *bench*? Yep, a bench.

But as benches go, it's a doozy, mounted to a Kuka robotic arm that can be programmed to replicate all the sensations of flying, including broad swoops, steep dives, sharp turns, sudden stops, and fast acceleration. The ride vehicle moves you through a series of alternating sets and domes where scenes are projected all around you. The movement of the Kuka arm is synchronized to create the motion that corresponds to what is happening in the set or film. When everything works correctly, it's mind-blowing: You'll soar over Hogwarts Castle, narrowly evade an attacking dragon, spar with the Whomping Willow, get tossed into a Quidditch match, and fight off Dementors inside the Chamber of Secrets.

Universal has toned down the Kuka programming to help reduce motion sickness, but we nonetheless recommend that you not ride on an empty stomach. If you start getting queasy, fix your gaze on your feet and try to exclude as much from your peripheral vision as possible. If you have a child who doesn't meet the minimum height requirement of 48 inches, a child-swapping option is provided at the loading area.

Liliane

Even if your child meets the height requirement, consider carefully whether Forbidden Journey is an experience he or she can handle. Because the seats on the benches are compartmentalized, kids can't see or touch Mom or Dad if they get scared.

The seats accommodate a wide variety of body shapes and sizes. Each bench has specially modified seats at either end. Though these allow many more people to ride, it's possible that guests of size can't fit in them. The best way to figure out whether you can fit in a regular seat or one of the modified ones is to sit in one of the test seats outside the queue or just inside the castle. After you sit down, pull down on the safety harness as far as you can. One of three safety lights will illuminate: A green light indicates you can fit into any seat, a yellow light means you should ask for one of the modified seats on the outside of the bench, and a red light means the harness can't engage enough for you to ride safely. For you to be cleared to ride, the overhead restraint has to click three times. If you don't pass muster, you'll be escorted to a place where you can wait for the rest of your party.

Upon entering Forbidden Journey's outside queue, you have two choices: left line or right line. They are unmarked, but the left line is for those who have bags or loose items and therefore require a locker (no charge). Our wait-time research has shown that in some cases, not needing a locker can save you as much as 30 minutes of standing in line. If you do need to stow your stuff, be aware that the Forbidden Journey locker area is small, crowded, and confusing. It may make more sense to pay the $3 to stash your things in the lockers beside Dragon Challenge.

The single-rider line is equally unmarked, and relatively few guests use it. Typically, on most attractions, the wait in the single-rider line is one-third the wait of the standby line. At Forbidden Journey it can be as much as one-tenth! Because the ride experience is individual (you can't see the other riders, including members of your party), the single-rider line is a great option. To get there, enter the right (no-bags) line and keep left all the way into the castle. After passing the locker area, take the first left into the unmarked single-rider line. If you use the single-rider line, however, you will miss much of the interior of the castle.

A good way to experience the castle *and* cut your waiting time is to tell the greeter at the castle entrance that you want to take the **castle-only tour.** This self-guided tour allows guests who don't want to experience the ride to view the many features of the castle via an alternative queuing lane. The beauty of the Castle Only Tour is that you can pause as long as you desire in each of the various chambers and take in the preshows at your leisure without being herded along. At the end, if you want to ride, ask to be guided to the single-rider line. Using this strategy you'll maximize your enjoyment of the castle while minimizing your wait for the ride. Note that the castle-only tour is often unavailable on peak attendance days.

This is an awesome ride and the effects are amazing—but hold on to your stuff. My dad lost his sunglasses, and we weren't able to get them back. Dad was NOT happy.

Isaac

Hogwarts Express ★★★★½

What it is Transportation attraction. **Scope and scale** Super-headliner. **Fright potential** Potter villains and spirit creatures menace the train. **Bottleneck rating** 10+. **When to go** Immediately after park opening. **Special comments** Expect lengthy waits in line; Park-to-Park ticket required to enter Universal Studios. **Authors' rating** Not to be missed; ★★★★½. **Duration of ride** 4 minutes. **Probable wait in line per 142 people ahead of you** 10 minutes. **Loading speed** Moderate.

See page 413 for a full description. Because the Hogsmeade Station doesn't include the cool Platform 9¾ effect found at the King's Cross end, expect waits for the one-way trip to be shorter here. If you wish to experience the train going from IOA to USF, make it your first stop of the day, but remember that you must wait in a slow standby line to take a same-day return ride.

Wizarding World Entertainment

Nearly every retail space sports some sort of animatronic or special effects surprise. At **Dervish and Banges,** the fearsome *Monster Book of Monsters* rattles and snarls at you as Nimbus 2001 brooms strain at their tethers overhead. At the Hog's Head pub, the titular porcine part, mounted behind the bar, similarly thrashes and growls. Street entertainment at the Forbidden Journey end of Hogsmeade includes the **Frog Choir** (★★★), composed of four singers, two of whom are holding large amphibian puppets sitting on pillows; and the **Triwizard Spirit Rally** (★★★½), showcasing dancing, martial arts, and acrobatics. Performances run about 15 minutes.

THE LOST CONTINENT

THIS AREA IS AN EXOTIC MIX of Silk Road bazaar and ancient ruins, with Greco-Moroccan accents. (And you thought your decorator was nuts.) This is the land of mythical gods, fabled beasts, and expensive souvenirs.

The Eighth Voyage of Sindbad (Universal Express) ★★

APPEAL BY AGE	PRESCHOOL ★★	GRADE SCHOOL ★★★½	TEENS ★★★
YOUNG ADULTS ★★★		OVER 30 ★★½	SENIORS ★★½

What it is Theater stunt show. **Scope and scale** Major attraction. **Fright potential** Special effects startle preschoolers. **Bottleneck rating** 4. **When to go** Anytime as per the daily entertainment schedule. **Authors' rating** Not inspiring; ★★. **Duration of show** 17 minutes. **Probable waiting time** 15 minutes.

A story about Sindbad the Sailor is the glue that (loosely) binds this stunt show featuring water explosions, 10-foot-tall circles of flame, and various other eruptions and perturbations. Not unlike an action movie that substitutes a mind-numbing succession of explosions, crashes, and special effects for plot and character development, the production is so vacuous and redundant (not to mention silly) that it's hard to get into the action. See *Sindbad* after you've experienced the rides and the better-rated shows.

I place seeing *Sindbad* in the same category as colonoscopies—once every 10 years is enough.

Bob

Not to be missed is the Mystic Fountain at the entrance to the theater. The fountain may not grant you wishes, but it will talk to you. But watch out: It's a fountain with attitude. Keep your umbrella handy.

Liliane

Poseidon's Fury *(Universal Express)*   ★★★½

APPEAL BY AGE	PRESCHOOL ★★	GRADE SCHOOL ★★★½	TEENS ★★½
YOUNG ADULTS ★★★		OVER 30 ★★★	SENIORS ★★★

What it is High-tech theater attraction. **Scope and scale** Headliner. **Fright potential** Intense visuals and special effects frighten some preschoolers. **Bottleneck rating** 7. **When to go** After experiencing all the rides. **Special comment** Audience stands. **Authors' rating** ★★★½. **Duration of show** 17 minutes, including preshow. **Probable waiting time** 25 minutes.

The Greek god Poseidon tussles with an evil wizardish guy using fire, water, lasers, smoke machines, and angry lemurs. (*Note:* Lemurs aren't actually part of the show—just seeing if you're paying attention.) The plot unfolds in installments as you pass from room to room and finally into the main theater. There's some great technology at work here. *Poseidon* is by far and away the best of the Islands of Adventure theater attractions (it only has to compete with *Sindbad*). Frequent explosions and noise may frighten younger children, so exercise caution with preschoolers. We recommend catching *Poseidon* after experiencing your fill of the rides.

SEUSS LANDING

A 10-ACRE THEMED AREA BASED ON Dr. Seuss's famous children's books. As at the old Mickey's Toontown in the Magic Kingdom, all of the buildings and attractions replicate a whimsical, brightly colored cartoon style with exaggerated features and rounded lines. There are four rides at Seuss Landing; an interactive play area, **If I Ran the Zoo,** populated by Seuss creatures; and *Oh, the Stories You'll Hear!,* a live musical show.

If you have only young children in your party, Seuss Landing is the place to spend lots of happy time. A great stop in Seuss Landing is Dr. Seuss's All the Books You Can Read bookstore. Last but not least, if your kids can't get enough of Dr. Seuss, check out **seussville.com**.

Liliane

Caro-Seuss-el *(Universal Express)*   ★★★

APPEAL BY AGE	PRESCHOOL ★★★★★	GRADE SCHOOL ★★★★	TEENS ★★★
YOUNG ADULTS ★★★		OVER 30 ★★★½	SENIORS ★★★★

What it is Merry-go-round. **Scope and scale** Minor attraction. **Fright potential** Not frightening in any respect. **Bottleneck rating** 8. **When to go** Before 11 a.m. **Authors' rating** Wonderfully unique; ★★★. **Duration of ride** 2 minutes. **Average wait in line per 100 people ahead of you** 9 minutes. **Loading speed** Slow.

Totally outrageous, the Caro-Seuss-el is a full-scale, 56-mount merry-go-round made up exclusively of Dr. Seuss characters. If you're touring with young children, try to get them on early in the morning.

The Cat in the Hat *(Universal Express)*   ★★★½

APPEAL BY AGE	PRESCHOOL ★★★★½	GRADE SCHOOL ★★★★	TEENS ★★½
YOUNG ADULTS ★★½		OVER 30 ★★½	SENIORS ★★★

What it is Indoor adventure ride. **Scope and scale** Major attraction. **Fright potential** Not frightening in any respect. **Bottleneck rating** 8. **When to go** Before 11:30 a.m. **Special comment** Must be 36″ to ride. **Authors' rating** Dr. Seuss would be proud; ★★★½. **Duration of ride** 3½ minutes. **Average wait in line per 100 people ahead of you** 5 minutes. **Loading speed** Moderate.

A must for preschoolers, guests ride on "couches" through 18 different sets inhabited by animatronic Seuss characters, including The Cat in the Hat, Thing 1, Thing 2, and the beleaguered goldfish who tries to maintain order in the midst of bedlam. Well done overall, with nothing that should frighten younger children. This is fun for all ages. Try to ride early.

The High in the Sky Seuss Trolley Train Ride!
(Universal Express)   ★★★½

APPEAL BY AGE PRESCHOOL ★★★★★ **GRADE SCHOOL** ★★★½ **TEENS** ★★★ **YOUNG ADULTS** ★★★   **OVER 30** ★★★   **SENIORS** ★★★★

What it is Elevated train. **Scope and scale** Major attraction. **Fright potential** Not frightening in any respect. **Bottleneck rating** 8. **When to go** Before 11:30 a.m. **Authors' rating** ★★★½. **Special comments** Relaxed tour of Seuss Landing; must be 34" tall to ride. **Duration of ride** 3½ minutes. **Average wait in line per 100 people ahead of you** 9 minutes. **Loading speed** Molasses.

Trains putter along elevated tracks, while a voice reads one of four Dr. Seuss stories over the train's speakers. As each train makes its way through Seuss Landing, it passes a series of animatronic characters in scenes that are part of the story being told. Little tunnels and a few mild turns make this a charming ride. The trains are small, fitting about 20 people, and the loading speed is glacial. Save the train ride for the end of the day or ride first thing in the morning.

If I Ran the Zoo (Universal Express) ★★½

APPEAL BY AGE   PRESCHOOL ★★★★ **GRADE SCHOOL** ★★★★   **TEENS** — **YOUNG ADULTS** —   **OVER 30** —   **SENIORS** —

What it is Interactive playground. **Scope and scale** Minor attraction. **Fright potential** Not frightening in any respect. **Bottleneck rating** 2. **When to go** Anytime. **Authors' rating** Whimsical and funny; great for preschoolers; ★★½.

A playground with 19 different interactive elements, this area is great silly-dilly fun for little tykes. How silly? The sign at the entrance of this crazy zoo should give you a clue: "Keep track of adults. They get lost all the time." And yes, you should know by now that there is no way the kids will stay dry.

Oh! The Stories You'll Hear! ★★★

APPEAL BY AGE PRESCHOOL ★★★★½ **GRADE SCHOOL** ★★★ **TEENS** ★★ **YOUNG ADULTS** ★   **OVER 30** ★★★   **SENIORS** ★★½

What it is Character-filled storytelling show. **Scope and scale** Minor attraction. **Fright potential** Not frightening in any respect. **Bottleneck rating** 2. **When to go** Scheduled showtimes. **Special comment** Audience stands. **Authors' rating** Warm and fuzzy; ★★★. **Duration of show** 9 minutes. **Probable waiting time** Negligible.

Featuring many of Dr. Seuss's most beloved characters (including The Lorax, The Grinch, Thing 1 and Thing 2, Sam I Am, and the Cat in the Hat), *Oh! The Stories You'll Hear!* is a fun singing and dancing show staged in an outdoor area between One Fish, Two Fish, Red Fish, Blue Fish and The Cat in the Hat Ride. After each 9-minute show, the characters separate for individual meet and greets and autographs.

FAVORITE EATS AT UNIVERSAL'S ISLANDS OF ADVENTURE		
LAND	SERVICE LOCATION	FOOD ITEM		
PORT OF ENTRY Croissant Moon Bakery	Croissants & panini		
TOON LAGOON Blondie's	Sandwiches		
JURASSIC PARK Pizza Predattoria	Pizza		
THE WIZARDING WORLD OF HARRY POTTER–HOGSMEADE Three Broomsticks	Shepherd's pie & fish-and-chips		
LOST CONTINENT Fire Eater's Grill	Gyro Mythos Restaurant	Risotto & meze platter	*Table service only*		
SEUSS LANDING Circus McGurkus Cafe Stoo-pendous	Fried chicken & mashed potatoes with gravy		
Green Eggs and Ham Cafe *(open seasonally)*	Green eggs & ham sandwich platter (Green herbs, not food coloring, are the reason for the green eggs.)		

Shows run daily, starting usually by 11:30 a.m. and continuing every hour until about 5 p.m. on a schedule published in the park map. During inclement weather, the show takes place within the Circus McGurkus Cafe Stoopendous restaurant nearby. On Sundays, they skip the show but still do the meet and greets on schedule.

One Fish, Two Fish, Red Fish, Blue Fish
(Universal Express) ★★★

APPEAL BY AGE PRESCHOOL ★★★★★ **GRADE SCHOOL** ★★★½ **TEENS** ★★½		
YOUNG ADULTS ★★★½ **OVER 30** ★★★ **SENIORS** ★★★		

What it is Wet version of Dumbo the Flying Elephant. **Scope and scale** Minor attraction. **Fright potential** Not frightening in any respect. **Bottleneck rating** 8. **When to go** Before 10 a.m. **Authors' rating** Who says you can't teach an old ride new tricks? ★★★. **Duration of ride** 2 minutes. **Average wait in line per 100 people ahead of you** 9 minutes. **Loading speed** Slow.

Imagine Dumbo with Seuss-style fish instead of elephants and you've got half the story—the other half involves yet another opportunity to drown. Guests steer their fish up or down 15 feet in the air while traveling in circles. At the same time, they try to avoid streams of water projected from "squirt posts."

I followed Dr. Seuss's advice: If you never did, you should. These things are fun. These things are good. And all wet there I stood! My favorite ride in Seuss Landing!

Liliane

ISLANDS *of* ADVENTURE TOURING PLAN

ISLANDS OF ADVENTURE ONE-DAY TOURING PLAN FOR FAMILIES *(page 477)*

THIS TOURING PLAN is for guests without Park-to-Park tickets and is appropriate for groups of all sizes and ages. It includes thrill rides that may induce motion sickness or get you wet. If the plan calls for you to experience an attraction that doesn't interest you, simply skip it and go to the next step. Be aware that the plan calls for some backtracking.

Because there are so many attractions with the potential to frighten young children, be prepared to skip a few things and to practice switching off (works generally the same way as at Walt Disney World; see page 243). For the most part, attractions designed especially for young children, such as playgrounds, can be enjoyed anytime. Work them into the plan at your convenience.

Be aware that in this park, there are an inordinate number of attractions that will get you wet. If you want to experience them, come armed with ponchos, large plastic garbage bags, or some other protective covering. Failure to follow this prescription will make for a squishy, sodden day.

See page 416 for a description of **The Best of Universal Orlando in One Day** plan.

UNIVERSAL STUDIOS FLORIDA

UNIVERSAL STUDIOS FLORIDA OPENED IN JUNE 1990. At the time, it was almost four times the size of Disney's Hollywood Studios (which today is the larger of the two parks), and much more of the facility was accessible to visitors. USF is spacious, beautifully landscaped, meticulously clean, and delightfully varied in its entertainment. Rides are exciting and innovative and, like many Disney attractions, focus on familiar and/or beloved movie characters or situations.

USF is laid out in a *P*-configuration, with the rounded part of the *P* sticking out disproportionately from the stem. Beyond the main entrance, a wide boulevard stretches past several shows and rides to the park's New York area. Branching off this pedestrian thoroughfare to the right are four streets that access other areas of the park and intersect a promenade circling a large lake. The area of USF open to visitors is a bit smaller than Epcot.

BOB Get to the park with your admission already purchased about 30–45 minutes before official opening time. Arrive 45–60 minutes before official opening time if you need to buy admission. **Be aware that you can't do a comprehensive tour of both Universal parks in a single day.**

The park is divided into seven areas: **Hollywood, New York, Production Central, San Francisco, Woody Woodpecker's KidZone, World Expo,** and **The Wizarding World of Harry Potter–Diagon Alley. Springfield U.S.A.** is considered part of World Expo. Except for Diagon Alley, where one area begins and another ends is blurry, but no matter. Guests orient themselves by the major rides, sets, and landmarks and refer, for instance, to "New York," "the waterfront," "over by E.T.," or "by Mel's Diner."

Continued on page 396

Universal Studios Florida

1. *Animal Actors on Location*
2. *Beetlejuice Graveyard Revue*
3. *The Blues Brothers Show*
4. Curious George Goes to Town
5. *A Day in the Park with Barney*
6. Despicable Me Minion Mayhem
7. *Disaster!*
8. E.T. Adventure
9. *Fear Factor Live*
10. Fievel's Playland
11. Harry Potter and the Escape from Gringotts
12. Hogwarts Express
13. Hollywood Rip Ride Rockit
14. Kang & Kodos' Twirl 'n' Hurl
15. *Lucy—A Tribute*
16. Men in Black Alien Attack
17. Ollivanders
18. Revenge of the Mummy
19. *Shrek 4-D*
20. The Simpsons Ride
21. *Terminator 2: 3-D*
22. Transformers: The Ride 3-D
23. *TWISTER . . . Ride It Out*
24. *Universal's Cinematic Spectacular* (seasonal)
25. *Universal Orlando's Horror Make-Up Show*
26. Woody Woodpecker's Nuthouse Coaster

Parade Route: • • • • • • • • • • •

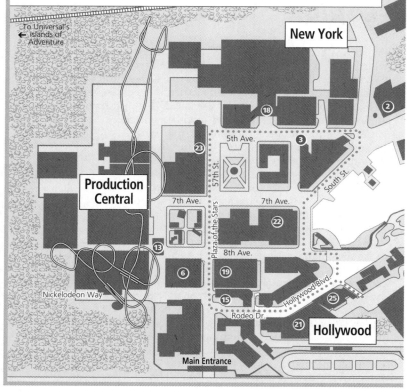

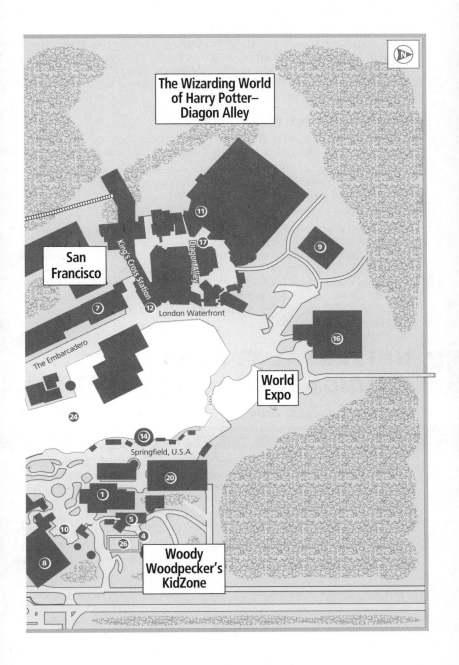

Continued from page 393

The park offers all standard services and amenities, including stroller and wheelchair rental, lockers, diaper-changing and infant-nursing facilities, car assistance, and foreign-language assistance. Most of the park is accessible to disabled guests, and TDDs are available for the hearing-impaired. Almost all services are in the **Front Lot,** just inside the main entrance.

HOW MUCH TIME TO ALLOCATE

TOURING UNIVERSAL STUDIOS FLORIDA, including one meal and a visit to Diagon Alley, takes about 10–12 hours. One reader laments:

> There's a lot of "standing" at USF, and it isn't as organized as DHS. Many of the attractions don't open until 10 a.m. We weren't able to see nearly as many attractions at Universal as we were at DHS during the same amount of time.

As the reader observes, some USF attractions don't open until 10 a.m. or later. Most theater attractions don't schedule performances until 11 a.m. or after. This means that early in the day, all park guests are concentrated among the limited number of attractions in operation.

As a postscript, you won't have to worry about any of this if you use our Universal Studios touring plan. We'll keep you one jump ahead of the crowd and make sure that any given attraction is running by the time you get there.

UNIVERSAL STUDIOS FLORIDA ATTRACTIONS

Animal Actors on Location (Universal Express) ★★★

APPEAL BY AGE	PRESCHOOL ★★★★	GRADE SCHOOL ★★★★	TEENS ★★★
YOUNG ADULTS ★★★		OVER 30 ★★★	SENIORS ★★★★

What it is Animal tricks and comedy show. **Scope and scale** Major attraction. **Fright potential** Not frightening in any respect. **Bottleneck rating** 4. **When to go** After you've experienced all rides. **Authors' rating** Cute li'l critters; ★★★. **Duration of show** 20 minutes. **Probable waiting time** 25 minutes.

Julia

Successful touring of Universal Studios with young children is absolutely possible, and *Animal Actors on Location* is a must-see!

Liliane

If you sit in the front rows, you have a great chance to be part of the show. I was picked as a volunteer, and a huge dog came and sat on my lap and licked my whole face. Everyone was laughing!

This show integrates video segments with live sketches, jokes, and animal tricks performed on stage. Live animals, some of which are veterans of television and movies (and many of which were rescued from shelters), take part, and kids are invited to participate. Where else can you get the chance to hold an 8-foot albino reticulated python in your lap? Check the daily entertainment schedule for showtimes.

Beetlejuice Graveyard Revue
(Universal Express) ★★★

APPEAL BY AGE   PRESCHOOL ★★★★   GRADE SCHOOL ★★★★   TEENS ★★★★
YOUNG ADULTS ★★★½   OVER 30 ★★★½   SENIORS ★★★

What it is Rock-and-roll stage show. **Scope and scale** Almost major attraction.
Fright potential Costumes and loud noises scare the under-7 crowd. **Bottleneck
rating** 2. **When to go** At your convenience. **Authors' rating** Capable of waking
the dead; ★★★. **Duration of show** 18 minutes. **Probable waiting time** None.

Beetlejuice Graveyard Revue features Dracula, the Wolfman, and
Frankenstein and his bride singing pop music from the 1980s,
such as Michael Jackson, Alice Cooper, and Mötley Crüe hits, with
a few recent pop songs thrown in for the kids. Beetlejuice, the
title character from the 1988 film of the same name, serves as the show's
emcee, adding monster jokes, groan-worthy puns, and pop-culture references between songs. In February 2014, the longtime cheerleader characters Hip and Hop were replaced by Cleopatra, a female mummy; Phantasia,
a female Phantom of the Opera; and a quartet of ghoulish backup dancers. In response to concerns from parents, Beetlejuice's formerly risqué
dialogue has been made more family-friendly; still, keep an eye on BJ in
the background for some snarky sight gags.

The show is based on the popular movie Beetlejuice,
which won an Oscar in 1989 for Best Makeup.

The Blues Brothers Show ★★★½

APPEAL BY AGE   PRESCHOOL ★★★   GRADE SCHOOL ★★★½   TEENS ★★★½
YOUNG ADULTS ★★★½   OVER 30 ★★★★   SENIORS ★★★★

What it is Blues concert. **Scope and scale** Diversion. **Fright potential** Not
frightening in any respect. **Bottleneck rating** 1. **When to go** Scheduled showtimes. **Special comment** A party in the street. **Authors' rating** Energetic;
★★★½. **Duration of presentation** 12 minutes.

Held on the corner of the New York area, across from the lagoon, *The
Blues Brothers Show* features Jake and Elwood performing a few of the hit
songs from the classic 1980 movie musical, including "Soul Man" and
"Sweet Home Chicago." The brothers are joined on stage by Jazz the sax-
ophone player and his girlfriend, Mabel the waitress, who belts a cover of
"Respect" to start the show. The concert is a great pick-me-up, and the
short run time keeps the energy high.

A Day in the Park with Barney *(Universal Express)* ★★★

APPEAL BY AGE   PRESCHOOL ★★★★★   GRADE SCHOOL ★★★   TEENS ★★
YOUNG ADULTS ★★★   OVER 30 ★★★   SENIORS ★★★

What it is Live character stage show. **Scope and scale** Major children's attraction.
Fright potential Toddlers may balk at Barney's size. **Bottleneck rating** 4. **When
to go** Anytime. **Authors' rating** Great hit with preschoolers; ★★★. **Duration of
show** 20 minutes, plus 5-minute preshow and character greeting. **Probable waiting time** 15 minutes.

I love you, you love me . . . this show should be
a top priority if you have little ones.

Liliane

Barney, the cuddly purple dinosaur of public-television fame, leads a sing-along with the help of the audience and sidekicks Baby Bop and BJ. A short preshow gets the kids lathered up before they enter Barney's Park (the theater). Interesting theatrical effects include wind, falling leaves, clouds and stars in the simulated sky, and snow. After the show, Barney poses for photos with parents and children in the indoor playground at the theater exit. If your child likes Barney, this show is a must. Unfortunately, we heard rumors at press time that Barney may be calling it quits at USF in the near future.

Despicable Me Minion Mayhem
(Universal Express) ★★★★

APPEAL BY AGE	**PRESCHOOL** ★★★★	**GRADE SCHOOL** ★★★★	**TEENS** ★★★★
YOUNG ADULTS ★★★★		**OVER 30** ★★★★	**SENIORS** ★★★★

What it is Motion simulator 3-D ride. **Scope and scale** Major attraction. **Fright potential** Ride is wild and jerky but not frightening. **Bottleneck rating** 10. **When to go** First hour after park opening or after 5 p.m. **Special comment** Expect long waits in line. **Authors' rating** Great fun; ★★★★. **Duration of ride** 5 minutes. **Average wait in line per 100 people ahead of you** 7 minutes; assumes all simulators in use. **Loading speed** Moderate.

 This motion-simulator system premiered as the Funtastic World of Hanna-Barbera when the park opened in 1990; was used again in Jimmy Neutron's Nicktoon Blast, which replaced the former in 2003; and was retained for the attraction's third incarnation as Despicable Me Minion Mayhem, which opened in summer 2012.

As with the former attractions, Despicable Me Minion Mayhem involves the motion simulators moving and reacting in sync with a cartoon projected on an IMAX-like screen. Though the simulators have been updated, the most significant upgrade is incorporated in the projection system, which employs high-definition 3-D digital technology.

The story combines elements from the animated movie *Despicable Me,* starring Gru, the archvillain, along with his adopted daughters and his diminutive yellow Minions. During the queue and preshow, you visit Gru's house and are then ushered into his lab, where you're turned into a Minion. The ride ends with a 3-minute dance party that you join as you exit.

If you're on hand at park opening and you ride Despicable Me first, you'll have a short wait; however, you'll set yourself up for a long wait at nearby Hollywood Rip Ride Rockit. If the coaster is a priority for you, ride it first and then return to Despicable Me immediately afterward. If by that time the wait is intolerable, try again in the late afternoon. Stationary seating is available for those prone to motion sickness and for children than 40 inches tall.

This 3-D ride really makes you feel like you're a Minion. There's a lot of motion going on. The wait is long but absolutely worth it.

Julia

Disaster! (Universal Express) ★★★½

APPEAL BY AGE	**PRESCHOOL** ★★★	**GRADE SCHOOL** ★★★★	**TEENS** ★★★★
YOUNG ADULTS ★★★★		**OVER 30** ★★★★	**SENIORS** ★★★★

What it is Combination theater presentation and adventure ride. **Scope and scale** Major attraction. **Fright potential** Special effects frighten those age 8 and under. **Bottleneck rating** 7. **When to go** In the morning or late afternoon. **Authors' rating** Shaken, not stirred; ★★★½. **Duration of presentation** 20 minutes. **Probable waiting time** 18 minutes. **Loading speed** Moderate.

Loud   Scary

Guests are recruited for roles in a film called *Mutha Nature,* directed by the conceited Frank Kincaid (Christopher Walken). After the recruiting, the audience enters a soundstage where a number of seemingly random scenes are filmed starring the guests-volunteers. The filming demonstrates various techniques for integrating sets, blue screens, and matte painting with live-action stunts. Next, guests board a faux subway, where they experience a simulated earthquake. For younger children the earthquake is pretty intense; older kids will love it, though. Following the quake, while the subway returns to the station, guests view a finished cut of *Mutha Nature* that incorporates the soundstage shots.

Liliane

Yours truly was recruited for a part in Mutha Nature. I am so happy that the movie is shown only once!

Bob

Yep, I saw that movie. Liliane starred as the earthquake.

Isaac

This is fun, especially when you get picked to be in the show. My mom was chosen, and she had to wear a hard hat and fake her fear as rocks fell on her head. It was hilarious.

E.T. Adventure *(Universal Express)* ★★★½

**APPEAL BY AGE   PRESCHOOL ★★★★   GRADE SCHOOL ★★★★   TEENS ★★★
YOUNG ADULTS ★★★   OVER 30 ★★★★   SENIORS ★★★★**

Thumbs Up for the Whole Family

What it is Indoor adventure ride based on the *E.T.* movie. **Scope and scale** Major attraction. **Fright potential** Too intense for some preschoolers. **Bottleneck rating** 8. **When to go** During the first 90 minutes the park is open. **Special comment** Must be 34″ to ride. **Authors' rating** A happy reunion; ★★★½. **Duration of ride** 4½ minutes. **Average wait in line per 100 people ahead of you** 5 minutes. **Loading speed** Moderate.

Guests aboard a bicycle-like conveyance escape with E.T. from earthly law enforcement officials and then journey to his home planet. The attraction is similar to Peter Pan's Flight at the Magic Kingdom but is longer and has more elaborate special effects. Make sure that you give the attendant your name—we recommend that you just state your name; don't try to spell it—and relish the end of the ride as E.T. will personalize his goodbye message. Lines build quickly after 10 a.m., and waits can be more than 2 hours on busy days. Ride in the morning or late afternoon.

Very cute. Liliane wants to phone home . . .

Movie
Tip

*E.T. Adventure is based on Steven Spielberg's film
E.T.: The Extra-Terrestrial—a great family movie
that won four Oscars in 1982.*

Liliane

Isaac

Definitely not the most exciting ride in the park, but it is kind of cool to see E.T. pop up in your bike basket.

Fear Factor Live *(Universal Express)* ★★½

APPEAL BY AGE	PRESCHOOL ★	GRADE SCHOOL ★★	TEENS ★★★★
YOUNG ADULTS ★★★		OVER 30 ★★★	SENIORS ★★

What it is Live version of the gross-out-stunt TV show. **Scope and scale** Headliner. **Fright potential** The stuff of nightmares. **Bottleneck rating** 6. **When to go** Six to eight shows daily; crowds are smallest at the first and second-to-last shows. **Authors' rating** *Ewwww;* ★★½. **Duration of show** 30 minutes. **Probable waiting time** 25 minutes.

Fear Factor Live is a stage version of the stomach-turning reality show that ran on NBC from 2001 to 2006 and again from 2011 to 2012. Six volunteers compete for one prize (a package that contains Universal goodies ranging from park tickets to T-shirts) by doing dumb and yucky things such as swimming with eels and eating bugs. The show is really payback for adults; adolescents will enjoy watching Mom squirm during the icky parts. For children age 8 and under, *Fear Factor Live* is nightmare material. Whether you participate or simply watch, this show will keep your innards in an uproar.

Fievel's Playland ★★★

APPEAL BY AGE	PRESCHOOL ★★★★	GRADE SCHOOL ★★★★	TEENS —
YOUNG ADULTS —		OVER 30 —	SENIORS —

What it is Children's play area with waterslide. **Scope and scale** Minor attraction. **Fright potential** Not frightening in any respect. **Bottleneck rating** 1. **When to go** Anytime. **Authors' rating** A much-needed attraction for preschoolers; ★★★. **Probable waiting time** 20–30 minutes for the waterslide; otherwise, no waiting. **Loading speed** Slow for the waterslide.

> Fievel's Playland is another must for a successful visit to Universal Studios with small children. The playground is themed after the 1991 Steven Spielberg movie *Fievel Goes West.* Young children will love to identify with the tales of Fievel Mousekewitz.

Liliane

This is a great playground that features ordinary household items reproduced on a giant scale, seen as a mouse would experience them. Preschoolers and grade-schoolers can climb nets, walk through a huge boot, splash in a sardine-can fountain, seesaw on huge spoons, and climb onto a cow skull. Most of the playground is reserved for preschoolers, but a combination waterslide and raft ride is open to all ages. There's almost no waiting in line here, and you can stay as long as you want. Younger children love the oversize items, and there's enough to keep teens and adults busy while little ones cut loose. The waterslide–raft ride is extremely slow-loading and carries only 300 riders per hour. With an average wait of 20–30 minutes, we don't think the 16-second ride is worth the trouble, and, yes, you *will* get soaked.

Hollywood Rip Ride Rockit *(Universal Express)* ★★★★

APPEAL BY AGE	PRESCHOOL —	GRADE SCHOOL ★★★★	TEENS ★★★★½
YOUNG ADULTS ★★★★½		OVER 30 ★★★★½	SENIORS ★★★½

What it is Super-high-tech roller coaster. **Scope and scale** Headliner. **Fright potential** Frightening for all ages. **Bottleneck rating** 9. **When to go** Immediately after park opening. **Special comments** Expect long waits in line; must be 51″ tall to ride. **Authors' rating** Woo-hoo! Not to be missed; ★★★★. **Duration of ride** 2½ minutes. **Average wait in line per 100 people ahead of you** 6–8 minutes. **Loading speed** Moderate.

  Hollywood Rip Ride Rockit has some features that we've never seen before. Let's start with the basics: Rip Ride Rockit is a sit-down X-Car coaster that runs on a 3,800-foot steel track, with a maximum height of 167 feet and a top speed of 65 mph. X-Car vehicles are more maneuverable than most other kinds and use less restrictive restraints, making for an exhilarating ride.

You ascend—vertically—at 11 feet per second to crest the 17-story-tall first hill, the highest point reached by any roller coaster in Orlando, until Mako opens at SeaWorld in 2016. The drop is almost vertical, too, and launches you into Double Take, a loop inversion in which you begin on the inside of the loop, twist to the outside at the top (so you're upright), and then twist back inside the loop for the descent. Double Take stands 136 feet tall, and its loop is 103 feet in diameter at its widest point. You next hurl (not that hurl—it comes later) into a stretch of track shaped like a musical treble clef. As on Double Take, the track configuration on Treble Clef is a first.

The ride starts in the Production Central area; weaves into the New York area near *Twister,* popping out over the heads of guests in the square below; and then storms out and over the lagoon separating Universal Studios from Islands of Adventure. Each row is outfitted with color-changing LEDs and high-end audio and video technology for each seat. Like the Rock 'n' Roller Coaster at Disney's Hollywood Studios, this coaster features a musical sound track. With Rip Ride Rockit, however, you can choose the genre of music you want to hear as you ride: classic rock, country, disco, pop, or rap. After the ride, Universal flogs a digital-video "rip" of your ride, complete with the sound track you chose, that you can upload to YouTube, Facebook, and the like. Your only chance to ride without a long wait is to be one of the first to enter the park when it opens.

 The incentive for me to try out this thingy has not been invented. Therefore, Bob, stop asking me to ride the monster. The answer is NO.

Liliane, I'm still half-deaf from the last roller coaster I rode with you.

Kang & Kodos' Twirl 'n' Hurl ★★★

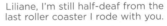

APPEAL BY AGE   PRESCHOOL ★★★★   GRADE SCHOOL ★★★   TEENS ★★★
YOUNG ADULTS ★★★   OVER 30 ★★★   SENIORS ★★

What it is Spinner ride. **Scope and scale** Minor attraction. **Fright potential** Like Dumbo, only louder. **Bottleneck rating** 10. **When to go** After The Simpsons Ride. **Special comment** Rarely has a long wait. **Authors' rating** The world's wittiest spinner; ★★★. **Duration of ride** 1½ minutes. **Average wait in line per 100 people ahead of you** 21 minutes. **Loading speed** Slow.

 The Twirl 'n' Hurl is primarily eye candy for the Springfield U.S.A. section of the park (where the Simpsons live), which was added to create a themed area around The Simpsons Ride. Think of it as Dumbo with Bart's sense of humor: Kang and Kodos are tentacled aliens who hold pictures of Simpson characters for you to blast away at with a ray gun as you ride in a little flying saucer (who thinks this stuff up?). All the while Kang is exhorting you (loudly) to destroy Springfield and making insulting comments about humans. Preschoolers enjoy the ride while older kids crack up over the snarky narration.

Lucy—A Tribute ★★★

APPEAL BY AGE	PRESCHOOL ★	GRADE SCHOOL ★★	TEENS ★★
YOUNG ADULTS ★★	OVER 30 ★★★		SENIORS ★★★

What it is Walk-through tribute to Lucille Ball. **Scope and scale** Diversion. **Fright potential** Not frightening in any respect. **Bottleneck rating** 0. **When to go** Anytime. **Authors' rating** A touching remembrance; ★★★. **Probable waiting time** None.

The life and career of Lucille Ball are spotlighted, with emphasis on her role as Lucy Ricardo in *I Love Lucy.* Well designed and informative, the exhibit succeeds admirably in recalling the talent and temperament of the beloved redhead. See Lucy during the hot, crowded midafternoon or on your way out of the park. By the time you read this, however, the attraction may be shuttered and converted into an interactive Hello Kitty store.

> The well-deserved tribute is not for young children, and most teenagers will lack a frame of reference. As for me? I love Lucy.

Liliane

Men in Black Alien Attack *(Universal Express)* ★★★★½

APPEAL BY AGE	PRESCHOOL ★★	GRADE SCHOOL ★★★★★	TEENS ★★★★★
YOUNG ADULTS ★★★★★	OVER 30 ★★★★★		SENIORS ★★★★

What it is Interactive dark thrill ride. **Scope and scale** Super-headliner. **Fright potential** Dark and intense; frightens many children age 10 and under. **Bottleneck rating** 9. **When to go** In the morning after Revenge of the Mummy. **Special comments** May induce motion sickness; must be 42" tall to ride. Switching-off option provided (see page 243). **Authors' rating** Buzz Lightyear on steroids; not to be missed; ★★★★½. **Duration of ride** 2½ minutes. **Average wait in line per 100 people ahead of you** 5 minutes. **Loading speed** Moderate-fast.

Dark

Scary
Queasy

Based on the movie of the same name, the story line has you volunteering as a Men in Black (MIB) trainee. After an introduction warning that aliens "live among us" and articulating MIB's mission to round them up, Zed expands on the finer points of alien spotting and familiarizes you with your training vehicle and your weapon, an alien "zapper." Following this, you load up and are dispatched on an innocuous training mission that immediately deteriorates into a situation where only you are in a position to prevent aliens from taking over the universe. Now, if you saw the movie, you understand that the aliens are mostly giant exotic bugs and cockroaches and that zapping the aliens involves exploding them into myriad gooey body parts. Thus, the meat of the ride (no pun intended) consists of careening around Manhattan in your MIB vehicle and shooting aliens. Each of the 120 or so alien figures has sensors that activate special effects and respond to your zapper. Aim for the eyes and keep shooting until the aliens' eyes turn red. Avoid a long wait and ride during the first 90 minutes the park is open, or try the single-rider line if you don't mind splitting your group. You can reride by following the signs for the child swap at the top of the exit stairs.

Revenge of the Mummy *(Universal Express)* ★★★★½

What it is Combination dark ride and roller coaster. **Scope and scale** Super-headliner. **Fright potential** Scary for all ages. **Bottleneck rating** 8. **When to go** The first hour the park is open or after 6 p.m. **Special comments** Must be 48" tall to ride; switching-off option provided (see page 243). **Authors' rating** Killer! ★★★★½. **Duration of ride** 4 minutes. **Average wait in line per 100 people ahead of you** 7 minutes. **Loading speed** Moderate.

Revenge of the Mummy is an indoor dark ride based on the *Mummy* flicks, where guests fight off "deadly curses and vengeful creatures" while flying through Egyptian tombs and other spooky places on a high-tech roller coaster. The special effects are cutting-edge, integrating the best technology from such attractions as *Terminator 2: 3-D* and The Amazing Adventures of Spider-Man (the ride). The ride begins slowly, passing through various chambers, including one where flesh-eating scarab beetles descend on you. Suddenly your vehicle stops, then drops backward and rotates. Next thing you know, you're shot at high speed up the first hill of the roller coaster. Though it's a wild ride by anyone's definition, the emphasis remains as much on the visuals, robotics, and special effects as on the ride itself. Note that the queue contains enough scary stuff to frighten small children all on its own. Try to ride during the first hour the park is open. If lines are long, the singles line is often more expedient than Universal Express.

The mummy scared the willies out of me.
This one is definitely not for young children.

Shrek 4-D *(Universal Express)* ★★★½

What it is 3-D movie. **Scope and scale** Headliner. **Fright potential** Loud but not frightening. Preshow area is a little macabre. **Bottleneck rating** 7. **When to go** The first hour the park is open or after 4 p.m. **Authors' rating** Warm, fuzzy mayhem; ★★★½. **Duration of show** 20 minutes. **Probable waiting time** 16 minutes.

The preshow presents the villain from the movie, Lord Farquaad, as he appears on various screens to describe his posthumous plan to reclaim his lost bride, Princess Fiona, who married Shrek. The plan is posthumous since Lord Farquaad ostensibly died in the movie, and it's his ghost making the plans, but never mind. Guests then move into the main theater, don their 3-D glasses, and recline in seats equipped with "tactile transducers" and "pneumatic air propulsion and water spray nodules capable of both vertical and horizontal motion." As the 3-D film plays, guests are also subjected to smells relevant to the on-screen action (oh boy).

Take off the 3-D glasses if it is all too scary, and consider earplugs.
Did you know that *Shrek* in German means "the scare"?
This attraction is a real winner. It's irreverent, frantic, laugh-out-loud funny, and iconoclastic. Concerning the last, the film takes a good poke

at Disney, with Pinocchio, the Three Little Pigs, and Tinker Bell (among others) all sucked into the mayhem. In contrast to Disney's *It's Tough to be a Bug!*, *Shrek 4-D* doesn't generally frighten children under age 7.

The Simpsons Ride *(Universal Express)* ★★★★

APPEAL BY AGE	PRESCHOOL ★★	GRADE SCHOOL ★★★★	TEENS ★★★★
YOUNG ADULTS ★★★★		OVER 30 ★★★★	SENIORS ★★★½

What it is Mega-simulator ride. **Scope and scale** Super-headliner. **Fright potential** Visuals not scary but very wild ride. **Bottleneck rating** 9. **When to go** First thing after park opening. **Special comments** Must be 40" tall to ride; not recommended for pregnant women or people prone to motion sickness. Switching-off option provided (see page 243). **Authors' rating** Despicable Me Minion Mayhem with attitude; ★★★★. **Duration of ride** 4⅓ minutes. **Average wait in line per 100 people ahead of you** 5 minutes. **Loading speed** Moderate.

Rough

Queasy

This attraction is a simulator ride similar to Star Tours at Disney's Hollywood Studios and Despicable Me Minion Mayhem at USF, but with a larger screen more like that of Soarin' at Epcot.

The attraction takes a wild and humorous poke at thrill rides, dark rides, and live shows. Two preshows involve *Simpsons* characters speaking sequentially on different video screens in the queue; their comments help define the characters for guests who are unfamiliar with the TV show. The story line has the conniving Sideshow Bob secretly arriving at Krustyland amusement park and plotting his revenge on Krusty the Clown and Bart, who, in a past *Simpsons* episode, revealed that Sideshow Bob had committed a crime for which he'd framed Krusty. Sideshow Bob gets even by making things go wrong with the attractions that the Simpsons (and you) are riding.

Like the show on which it's based, The Simpsons Ride definitely has an edge—and more than a few wild hairs. Like *Shrek 4-D,* it operates on several levels. There will be jokes and visuals that you'll get but will fly over your children's heads—and most assuredly vice versa. You can expect large crowds all day. Some parents may find the humor a little too coarse for younger children.

> You don't even have to know the TV show to enjoy this ride—that's how funny it is!
>
> Ethan

Street Scenes ★★★★★

APPEAL BY AGE	PRESCHOOL ★★★	GRADE SCHOOL ★★★★★	TEENS ★★★★★
YOUNG ADULTS ★★★★★		OVER 30 ★★★★★	SENIORS ★★★★★

What it is Elaborate outdoor sets for making films. **Scope and scale** Diversion. **Fright potential** Not frightening in any respect. **Bottleneck rating** 0. **When to go** Anytime. **Special comment** You'll see most sets without special effort as you tour the park. **Authors' rating** One of the park's great assets; ★★★★★.

Unlike at Disney's Hollywood Studios, all Universal Studios Florida's back lot sets are accessible for guest inspection. You'll see most as you walk through the park. Enjoy a New York City street, San Francisco's waterfront, Rodeo Drive, and Hollywood Boulevard. The sets make for great photo ops!

Terminator 2: 3-D (Universal Express) ★★★★

APPEAL BY AGE	**PRESCHOOL ★★★**	**GRADE SCHOOL ★★★★**	**TEENS ★★★★**
YOUNG ADULTS ★★★★★		**OVER 30 ★★★★★**	**SENIORS ★★★★**

What it is 3-D thriller mixed-media presentation. **Scope and scale** Super-headliner. **Fright potential** Intense; will frighten children age 7 and under. **Bottleneck rating** 7. **When to go** After 3:30 p.m. **Special comment** The nation's best theme park theater attractions. **Authors' rating** Furiously paced high-tech experience; not to be missed; ★★★★. **Duration of show** 20 minutes, including an 8-minute preshow. **Probable waiting time** 20–40 minutes.

Dark   Loud   Scary

The evil "cop" from *Terminator 2* battles Arnold Schwarzenegger's T-100 cyborg character. In case you missed the *Terminator* flicks, here's a refresher: A bad robot arrives from the future to kill a nice boy. Another bad robot—who has been reprogrammed to be good—pops up to save the boy. The bad robot chases the boy and the good robot, menacing the audience in the process.

The attraction, like the films, is all action, and you really don't need to understand much. What's interesting is that it uses 3-D film and a theater full of sophisticated technology to integrate the real with the imaginary. Images seem to move in and out of the film, not only in the manner of traditional 3-D but also in actuality. Remove your 3-D glasses momentarily and you'll see that the guy on the motorcycle is actually onstage. *Terminator 2: 3-D* has been eclipsed a bit by newer attractions such as Revenge of the Mummy, Hollywood Rip Ride Rockit, and Despicable Me Minion Mayhem. We suggest that you save *Terminator* and other theater presentations until you have experienced all of the rides. Families with young children should know that the violence characteristic of the *Terminator* movies is largely absent from the attraction. There's suspense and action but not much blood and guts.

Transformers: The Ride 3-D ★★★★★

APPEAL BY AGE	**PRESCHOOL ★★★**	**GRADE SCHOOL ★★★★★**	**TEENS ★★★★★**
YOUNG ADULTS ★★★★★		**OVER 30 ★★★★★**	**SENIORS ★★★★**

What it is Multisensory 3-D dark ride. **Scope and scale** Super-headliner. **Fright potential** Loud, intense, and violent; prepare 7-and-unders by previewing a movie trailer before you visit. **Bottleneck rating** 10. **When to go** The first 30 minutes the park is open or after 4 p.m. **Special comments** Must be 40" tall to ride; children 40–48" must be accompanied by a rider 14 years or older. **Authors' rating** ★★★★★. **Duration of ride** 4½ minutes. **Average wait in line per 100 people ahead of you** 4½ minutes. **Loading speed** Moderate–fast.

Dark   Rough   Loud   Scary

Hasbro's Transformers—those toy robots from the 1980s that you turned and twisted into trucks and planes—have been, er, transformed into director Michael Bay's blockbuster movie franchise and then to a theme park attraction befitting their pop-culture idols. Recruits to this cybertronic war enlist by entering the N.E.S.T. Base (headquarters of the heroic Autobots and their human allies). Inside, in the queue, video monitors catch you up on the backstory. Basically, the Decepticon baddies are after the

Allspark, source of cybernetic sentience. Your job is to safeguard the shard. The vastly annoying top villain, Megatron, and his pals Starscream and Devastator threaten the mission, but don't worry—you have Sideswipe and Bumblebee on the bench to back you up.

The plot amounts to little more than a giant game of keep-away, and the uninitiated will likely be unable to tell one meteoric mass of metal from another, but you'll be too dazzled by the debris whizzing by to notice. The ride's mix of detailed set pieces and high-tech video projections brings these colossi to life in one very intense and immersive thrill ride.

This ride draws crowds—your only solace is that The Wizarding World of Harry Potter–Diagon Alley draws even larger throngs. Follow our touring plan to minimize waits. The single-rider line will get you on board faster, but as singles lines go, this is the pokiest we've seen. Finally, it's hard to focus on the fast-moving imagery from the front row; center seats in the second and third rows provide the best perspective.

Transformer characters Optimus Prime, Bumblebee, and Megatron appear regularly on the streets of Universal Studios.

Twister . . . Ride It Out *(Universal Express)*   ★★★½

**APPEAL BY AGE   PRESCHOOL ★★   GRADE SCHOOL ★★★★   TEENS ★★★★
YOUNG ADULTS ★★★★   OVER 30 ★★★★   SENIORS ★★★**

What it is Theater presentation featuring special effects from the movie *Twister*. **Scope and scale** Major attraction. **Fright potential** Will frighten children age 7 and under. **Bottleneck rating** 7. **When to go** Should be your first show after experiencing all rides. **Authors' rating** Gusty; ★★★½. **Duration of show** 15 minutes. **Probable waiting time** 20 minutes.

Loud

Scary

Twister combines an elaborate set and special effects, climaxing with a five-story-tall simulated tornado created by circulating 2 million cubic feet of air per minute. The wind, pounding rain, and freight-train sound of the tornado are deafening, and the entire presentation is exceptionally intense. Schoolchildren are mightily impressed, while younger children are terrified and overwhelmed. Unless you want the kids hopping in your bed whenever they hear thunder, try this attraction yourself before taking your kids.

Universal Orlando's Horror Make-Up Show
(Universal Express)   ★★★★½

**APPEAL BY AGE   PRESCHOOL ★★★   GRADE SCHOOL ★★★★   TEENS ★★★★
YOUNG ADULTS ★★★★★   OVER 30 ★★★★   SENIORS ★★★★**

Thumbs Up for the Whole Family

What it is Theater presentation on the art of makeup. **Scope and scale** Major attraction. **Fright potential** Gory but not frightening; may upset young children. **Bottleneck rating** 6. **When to go** After you have experienced all rides. **Authors' rating** A gory knee-slapper; ★★★★½. **Duration of show** 25 minutes. **Probable waiting time** 20 minutes.

Lively, well-paced look at how makeup artists create film monsters, realistic wounds, severed limbs, and other unmentionables. Exceeding most guests' expectations, the *Horror Make-Up Show* is the sleeper attraction at Universal. Its humor and tongue-in-cheek style transcend the gruesome effects, and most folks (including preschoolers) take the blood and guts in stride. It usually isn't too hard to get into.

Woody Woodpecker's Nuthouse Coaster and Curious George Goes to Town ★★½

APPEAL BY AGE	PRESCHOOL ★★★★	GRADE SCHOOL ★★★½	TEENS —
YOUNG ADULTS —	OVER 30 —		SENIORS —

What it is Interactive playground and kid's roller coaster. **Scope and scale** Minor attraction. **Fright potential** Not frightening in any respect. **Bottleneck rating** 5. **When to go** Anytime. **Special comment** Must be 36″ tall to ride coaster. **Authors' rating** *The* place for rambunctious kids; ★★½. **Average wait in line per 100 people ahead of you** 5 minutes for the coaster. **Loading speed** For the coaster, *slooow.*

The KidZone consists of Woody Woodpecker's Nuthouse Coaster and an interactive playground called Curious George Goes to Town. The child-size roller coaster is small enough for kids, though its moderate speed might unnerve some smaller children. The Curious George playground exemplifies the Universal obsession with wet stuff; in addition to innumerable spigots, pipes, and spray guns, two giant roof-mounted buckets periodically dump *a thousand gallons* of water on unsuspecting visitors below. Kids who want to stay dry can mess around in the foam-ball playground, also equipped with chutes, tubes, and ball blasters. The playground is creatively designed and a great place for kids to cut loose after being in tow all day.

> Have the kids wear a bathing suit under their clothes so they can enjoy the water features. Simpler still, let the 4-and-unders frolic in their underwear (bring an extra pair).

Liliane

THE WIZARDING WORLD OF HARRY POTTER–DIAGON ALLEY

WHEN UNIVERSAL OPENED The Wizarding World of Harry Potter at Islands of Adventure, it created a paradigm shift in the Disney–Universal theme park rivalry. Not only did Universal trot out some groundbreaking ride technology, but it also demonstrated that it could trump Disney's most distinctive competence: the creation of infinitely detailed and totally immersive themed areas. To say that The Wizarding World was a game-changer is an understatement of the first order.

It was immediately obvious that Universal would build on its Potter franchise success—but how and where? Universal's not sitting on 27,000-plus acres like Disney, so real estate was at a premium. If Potterville was going to grow, something else had to go. Conventional wisdom suggested that the Wizarding World expansion would gobble up the Lost Continent section of Islands of Adventure, and that may happen yet. But looking at the ledger, it was clear that the older Universal Studios theme park could use a boost. Concurring, we remember sitting at the foot of the escalators monitoring traffic coming from the parking garages. For every guest who tacked right, toward the Studios, 15 made a beeline for IOA and Harry Potter.

It just so happened that a substantial chunk of turf at the Studios was occupied by the aging Jaws ride and its contiguous Amity themed area. The space would allow for substantial development; plus, its isolated location—in the most remote corner of the park—was conducive to creating a totally self-contained area where Potter themes could be executed absent any distraction from neighboring attractions. In short, it was perfect.

So how would the new Potter area tie in to the original at IOA? And what Harry Potter literary icons could be exploited? It was pretty clear that a new suburb of Hogsmeade wasn't going to cut it. Turns out that the answer was virtually shouting from the pages of the Harry Potter novels, which observe a clear dichotomy of place—plots originate in London and then unfold at distant Hogwarts.

Three London sites figure prominently in the Potter saga: the house where Harry once lived with his adoptive family; Diagon Alley, a secret part of London that is a sort of sorcerers' shopping mall; and the King's Cross railroad station, where wizarding students embark for the train trip to Hogwarts. There wasn't much to milk from Harry's house, but Diagon Alley and the train station brimmed with possibilities.

Following much deliberation and consultation with Warner Bros. and author J. K. Rowling, the final design called for a London-waterfront street scene flanking Universal Studios Lagoon. The detailed facades, anchored by the **King's Cross** railroad station on the left and including **Grimmauld Place** and **Wyndham's Theatre,** recall West London scenes from the books and movies. **Diagon Alley,** secreted behind the London street scene, is accessed through a secluded entrance in the middle of the facade. Like Hogsmeade at IOA, Diagon Alley features shops and restaurants in addition to three attractions and live entertainment.

Diagon Alley covers 20 acres—about the same area as the Hogsmeade original—but offers about two-and-a-half times the pedestrian space, since it doesn't have space- (and people-) eating outdoor roller coasters. With only one high-capacity ride (**Harry Potter and the Escape from Gringotts**), along with an enlarged version of the **Ollivanders** wandshop experience in Hogsmeade and the **Hogwarts Express** train connecting the two Wizarding Worlds, the new area's increased elbow room is somewhat offset by a relatively reduced hourly attraction capacity, making Diagon Alley's maximum capacity approximately 8,000, about double Hogsmeade's occupancy limit.

In the attraction department, Universal once again came out swinging for the fences. As before with Harry Potter and the Forbidden Journey, the headliner attraction for the expansion is high-tech and cutting-edge—and once again a dark ride, but this time of the roller coaster genre. The labyrinthine passages and caverns of Gringotts Wizarding Bank, the financial institution of choice for the wizarding set, are the setting of this plot-driven 3-D dark ride–coaster.

Though the Gringotts attraction is Diagon Alley's headliner, the most creative element in the two-park Potter domain is the Hogwarts Express, which re-creates the train trip from London to Hogwarts and vice versa. Serving as both an attraction and transportation between USF and IOA, the Express unifies the two disparately located Wizarding Worlds into a continuous whole.

Diagon Alley in Detail

Diagon Alley and its London Waterfront are sandwiched between the San Francisco and World Expo areas of the park, about as far from Universal Studios Florida's main entrance as you can get. From the park entrance, turn right on Rodeo Drive to Mel's Diner; from here, circumnavigate the lagoon counterclockwise, keeping the body of water to your left until you reach the entrance to the London Waterfront, where wrought iron fencing surrounds a parklike promenade. You can also access the London Waterfront from the San Francisco area by walking clockwise around the lagoon and then taking a shoreline bypass along the embankment to the World Expo side of the Potter themed area. Here you can access London through the gateway closest to the *Fear Factor Live* stadium. A third option is to take the Hogwarts Express from Islands of Adventure—exit the London Waterfront–Diagon Alley area into San Francisco.

Having arrived at the London area, take a moment to spot Kreacher (the house elf regularly peers from a second-story window above 12 Grimmauld Place) and chat with the Knight Bus conductor and his Caribbean-accented shrunken head. Also notable are snack and souvenir stands and a towering statue-topped fountain.

Now enter Diagon Alley next to the Leicester Square marquee in the approximate center of the building facades. As in the books and films, the unmarked portal is concealed within a magical brick wall that is ordinarily reserved for wizards and the like. (Unfortunately, the wall doesn't actually move, due to safety concerns.) The endless queue of Muggles (plain old humans) in shorts and flip-flops will leave little doubt where that entryway is.

Once admitted, look down the alley to the rounded facade of **Gringotts Wizarding Bank,** where a 40-foot fire-breathing Ukrainian Ironbelly dragon (as seen in *Harry Potter and the Deathly Hallows: Part 2*) perches atop the dome. To your left is the **Leaky Cauldron,** the area's flagship restaurant, serving authentically hearty British pub fare such as bangers and mash, cottage pie, and Guinness stew. You order and get your drinks at a counter; then you're seated with a candle that helps servers deliver food direct to your table. You can top off your meal with potted chocolate and sticky toffee pudding for dessert, or step around the corner to **Florean Fortescue's Ice-Cream Parlour** for Butterbeer soft-serve or unusual hard-pack flavors like clotted cream, Earl Grey and lavender, and chocolate chili. If all that eating makes you thirsty, a variety of alcoholic and virgin novelty drinks are poured at **The Hopping Pot** and **Fountain of Fair Fortune.** Try the Wizard's Brew (a heavy porter) or Dragon Scale (a hoppy amber), or the Fishy Green Ale (mint boba tea with balls of blueberry juice) or Gillywater, which can be spiked with four different flavored elixirs. Of course, you can also get your Butterbeer or Pumpkin Juice fix.

LILIANE I want to sneak into the Wizarding World through the Leaky Cauldron pub. OK, I'll take the Hogwarts Express.

Shopping is a major component of Diagon Alley in Potter lore; while Hogsmeade visitors went wild for the few wizardy shops there, Diagon Alley is the planet's wackiest mall, with a vastly expanded array of enchanted tchotchkes to declare bankruptcy over. Shops include **Weasleys' Wizard Wheezes,** a joke shop with many of the toys previously found in Hogsmeade's Zonko's, plus new gags like Skiving Snackboxes and Decoy Detonators. Look up through the three-story store's glass ceiling for fireworks. **Wiseacre's Wizarding Equipment,** at the exit of Escape from Gringotts, sells crystal balls, compasses, and hourglasses. **Madam Malkin's Robes for All Occasions** stocks school uniforms, Scottish wool sweaters, and dress robes for wizards and witches. Adopt a plush cat, rat, owl, or hippogriff from the **Magical Menagerie. Shutterbutton's** will film your family in front of a green screen and insert you into a DVD of Potter scenes (about $70); **Quality Quidditch Supplies** sells golden snitches and jerseys for your favorite teams; and **Scribbulus** carries quills, notebooks, and similar school supplies. You can pay for all this loot in Gringotts bank notes, which you can purchase inside a money exchange overseen by an imperious interactive animatronic goblin, and then spend it anywhere within Universal Orlando (think Disney Dollars). In general, Diagon Alley's stores are larger and more plentiful than the tiny shops over in Hogsmeade, with carefully planned external and internal queues to corral waiting customers.

To the right of Escape from Gringotts is **Carkitt Market,** a canopy-covered plaza where short live shows are staged every half hour or so. *Celestina Warbeck and the Banshees* (★★★★) showcases the singing sorceress swinging to jazzy tunes titled and inspired by J. K. Rowling herself, and *Tales of Beedle the Bard* (★★★½) recounts the Three Brothers fable from *Deathly Hallows* with puppets crafted by Michael Curry (*Festival of the Lion King, Finding Nemo—The Musical*).

Intersecting Diagon Alley near the Leaky Cauldron is **Knockturn Alley,** a labyrinth of twisting passageways where the Harry Potter bad guys hang out. A covered walk-through area with a projected sky creating perpetual night, it features spooky special effects in the faux shop windows (don't miss the creeping tattoos and crawling spiders) and **Borgin and Burkes,** which sells objects from the dark side of magic (watch out for the mummified hand!).

Touring Strategy

The Wizarding World of Harry Potter–Diagon Alley is the queen of the hop in the theme park world. Because of the crowds, experiencing Diagon Alley without interminable waits is a challenge—if you visited The Wizarding World of Harry Potter–Hogsmeade during its first three years at IOA, you know of what we speak. Hogsmeade opened with three rides and Ollivanders; now it has four rides plus the wand shop. As discussed earlier, Diagon Alley has another Ollivanders and only two rides, one of which, Hogwarts Express, it shares with Hogsmeade in IOA. Because only half of each day's total train passengers can board at the USF station, Diagon Alley in essence has only one-and-a-half rides, plus Ollivanders and the various shops, to entertain the expected masses. In other words, it's crazy, folks.

If you're a Universal hotel guest, use your early-entry privileges. Arrive at the turnstiles at least 65 minutes *before the beginning* of the early-entry hour. You'll be admitted to the park after about a half hour and held in place until early entry begins. At that time, the crowd will essentially be walked to Diagon Alley. Do and see everything in Diagon Alley before you leave. If you want back in, try back about 4 p.m.

As at IOA, Universal has multiple operational options for allowing guests into USF's Wizarding World. On low-attendance days, you may be able to stroll in and out of Diagon Alley without restriction. On busy days, barricades may limit access to the London Waterfront in the morning (usually to be removed by lunchtime). If this happens, timed-entry return tickets specifying when you can visit may be distributed from touch screen kiosks located between Men in Black and *Fear Factor Live*. Guests are given a selection of 1-hour return windows, assuming any are still available. Once your time comes, report to the gates at the end of London near *Fear Factor Live*. On the busiest days, standby queues may snake from *Fear Factor Live* behind Men in Black toward The Simpsons, but waiting in these is strongly discouraged; by late afternoon you should almost always be able to waltz right into Diagon Alley without a wait. (Gringotts is, of course, another story.)

Circling the lagoon clockwise to the waterfront is the shortest route to the Hogwarts Express, but it's also the route that about 70% of guests take. Hustling to the waterfront counterclockwise through the Simpsons area is the most direct path to the ticket kiosks.

On the upside, the rush to Diagon Alley diminishes crowds and waits at other attractions. The downside to that upside: Those who can't enter Diagon Alley right away spread to nearby attractions, particularly *Disaster!*, Men in Black Alien Attack, and to a lesser extent The Simpsons Ride and Revenge of the Mummy. Diagon Alley spillover affects wait times at these attractions all day, so experience them as early as possible.

Heading first to The Wizarding World–Hogsmeade at IOA and lining up for Hogwarts Express may be the best way to experience both the train plus Gringotts in the least amount of time. Hogsmeade won't be hit with a morning inundation comparable to that of USF, and the queue there isn't slowed by a Platform 9¾ effect, so waits for the train from there should be less onerous. You'll want to grab a Diagon Alley return ticket from the opposite end of the area immediately upon arrival. If you're among the first on the train in the morning, you shouldn't be too far behind the first wave of guests who entered USF directly.

WIZARDING WORLD-DIAGON ALLEY ATTRACTIONS

Harry Potter and the Escape from Gringotts ★★★★★

APPEAL BY AGE	PRESCHOOL ★★	GRADE SCHOOL ★★★★	TEENS ★★★★★
YOUNG ADULTS ★★★★★		OVER 30 ★★★★★	SENIORS ★★★★

What it is Super-high-tech 3-D dark ride with roller coaster elements. **Scope and scale** Super-headliner. **Fright potential** All scary elements are heaped on this one, though the ride itself is less intense than Forbidden Journey at IOA. **Bottleneck rating** 10+. **When to go** Immediately after park opening or just before closing. **Special comments** Expect *looong* waits in line; must be 42″ to ride. **Authors' rating** Not to be missed; ★★★★★. **Duration of ride** 4½ minutes. **Probable waiting time per 100 people ahead of you** 4 minutes. **Loading speed** Moderate–fast.

Owned and operated by goblins, Gringotts is the Federal Reserve of the wizarding economy, as well as the scene of memorable sequences from the first and final Potter installments. It's known for its toppling column facade, chandelier-adorned lobby, and bottomless caverns, as well as the heart-stopping rail carts running through them. The theme park adaptation is the centerpiece of Diagon Alley.

Like Forbidden Journey at IOA, Harry Potter and the Escape from Gringotts incorporates a substantial part of the overall experience into its elaborate queue, which (like Hogwarts Castle) even nonriders should experience. You enter through the bank's lobby, where you're critically appraised by glowering animatronic goblins. Your path takes you to a "security checkpoint" where your photo will be taken (to be purchased afterward as an identity lanyard in the gift shop, natch) and past animated newspapers and office windows where the scenario is set up.

Unlike Forbidden Journey, Gringotts doesn't rush you through its queue, but rather allows you to experience two full preshows before approaching the ride vehicles. In the first, goblin banker Blordak and Bill Weasley (Ron's curse-breaking big brother) prepare you for an introductory tour of the underground vaults. Then you're off for a convincing simulated 9-mile plunge into the earth aboard an "elevator" with a bouncing floor and ceiling projections. All this is before you pick up your 3-D glasses (identical to those at Transformers: The Ride 3-D) and ascend a spiral staircase into the stalactite-festooned boarding cave where your vault cart awaits.

Visitors enter the bank at the exact moment that Harry, Ron, Hermione, and Griphook have arrived to liberate the Hufflepuff Cup Horcrux from Bellatrix Lestrange's vault. Only in this retelling of *Deathly Hallows: Part 2*'s iconic action scene, you (as Muggles opening new bank accounts) are ingeniously integrated into the action. Familiar film moments featuring the vaults' guardian dragon play out in the ride's background as Bellatrix and Voldemort appear to menace you with snakes and sinister spells, whereupon the heroic trio pauses its quest to save your hapless posteriors.

Gringotts's ornately industrial ride vehicles consist of two-car trains, each holding 24 people in rows of four. The ride merges Revenge of the Mummy's indoor-coaster aspects with The Amazing Adventures of Spider-Man's seamless integration of high-resolution 3-D film and massive sculptural sets, while adding a few new tricks such as independently rotating cars and motion-simulator bases built into the track.

As far as physical thrills go, Gringotts falls somewhere between Seven Dwarfs Mine Train and Space Mountain, with only one short (albeit unique) drop and no upside-down flips. It was designed to be less intense (read: less nauseating) than Forbidden Journey and therefore more appealing to families, with fewer height, weight, and size restrictions. The restraints are similar to the Mummy's, with bars across your lap and shins, but slightly more restrictive. Use the test seat to the left of the front entrance if you're unsure, and request the third or sixth row for additional legroom.

The ride feels noticeably different depending on where you're seated. The front row is closest to the action and has the scariest view of the drop; 3-D effects look better farther back. The sixth row gets the most coaster action, but the screens are slightly distorted. Row three may be the sweet spot.

Gringotts is the pot of gold at the end of Universal's rainbow that a kazillion crazed guests are racing toward. Though the interior line is gorgeous and air-conditioned, the mostly unshaded outdoor extended queue holds 4,000 guests—you don't want to be at the end of it. If you're a Universal resort guest and you qualify for early entry, use it. Otherwise, try the attraction in the late afternoon; wait times usually peak after opening but become reasonable later in the day. Just beware that the queue may close to new arrivals 2–3 hours before the park closes, or even earlier if the ride breaks down.

Hogwarts Express   ★★★★½

What it is Transportation attraction. **Scope and scale** Super-headliner. **Fright potential** Potter villains and spirit creatures menace the train. **Bottleneck rating** 10+. **When to go** Immediately after park opening. **Special comments** Expect lengthy waits in line; Park-to-Park ticket required to enter Islands of Adventure. **Authors' rating** Not to be missed; ★★★★½. **Duration of ride** 4 minutes. **Probable wait in line per 142 people ahead of you** 10 minutes. **Loading speed** Moderate.

Part of the genius of creating Diagon Alley at USF is that it's connected to Hogsmeade at Islands of Adventure by the Hogwarts Express, just as in the novels and films. The counterpart to Hogsmeade Station in IOA is Universal Studios's King's Cross station, a landmark London train depot that has been re-created a few doors down from Diagon Alley's hidden entrance. (It's important to note that King's Cross has a separate entrance and exit from Diagon Alley: You can't go directly between them without crossing through the London Waterfront.)

The passage to Platform 9¾, from which Hogwarts students depart on their way to school, is concealed from Muggles by a seemingly solid brick wall, which you'll witness guests ahead of you dematerializing through. (Spoiler: The Pepper's Ghost effect creates a clever but congestion-prone photo op, but you experience only a dark corridor with whooshing sound effects when crossing over yourself.)

Once on the platform, you'll pass a pile of luggage before being assigned to one of the three train cars' seven compartments. The train itself looks exactingly authentic to the nth degree, from the billowing steam to the brass fixtures and upholstery in your eight-passenger private cabin. Along your one-way Hogwarts Express journey, you'll see moving images projected beyond the windows of the car rather than the park's backstage areas, with the streets of London and the Scottish countryside rolling past outside your window. You experience a different presentation coming and going, and in addition to pastoral scenery there are surprise appearances by secondary characters (Fred and George Weasley, Hagrid) and threats en route (bone-chilling Dementors, licorice spiders), augmented by sound effects in the cars.

One-way passengers will need a valid two-park ticket. Disembarking passengers must enter the second park and, if desired, queue again for their return trip. You'll be allowed (nay, encouraged) to upgrade your 1-Park Base Ticket at the station entrance. Universal Express is, ironically, unavailable for Hogwarts Express, at least for the time being.

In addition, if the line becomes too long, Universal may limit you to only one one-way ride per day.

Park-to-park ticket-purchasing Potterphiles should make the train their second stop of the day after Escape from Gringotts if going from Diagon Alley to Hogsmeade. Or, if Diagon Alley is your top priority of the day, enter Islands of Adventure as early as possible and line up at the Hogsmeade Station for the train to London King's Cross. If the wait is less than 30 minutes, it is typically quicker to take the train than it is to walk to the other Wizarding World.

Ollivanders ★★★★

APPEAL BY AGE   PRESCHOOL ★★★★   GRADE SCHOOL ★★★★★   TEENS ★★★★
YOUNG ADULTS ★★★★   OVER 30 ★★★½   SENIORS ★★★½

What it is Combination wizarding demonstration and shopping op. **Scope and scale** Major attraction. **Fright potential** Special effects may startle 6-and-unders. **Bottleneck rating** 10. **When to go** After riding Harry Potter and the Escape from Gringotts. **Special comment** Audience stands. **Authors' rating** Enchanting; ★★★★. **Duration of presentation** 6 minutes. **Average waiting time in line per 100 people ahead of you** 7 minutes.

Ollivanders, located in Diagon Alley in the books and films, somehow sprouted a branch location in Hogsmeade at IOA (see page 382). Potter scholars pointed out this misplacement, but the wand shop stayed and became one of the most popular features of The Wizarding World. It also became a horrendous bottleneck, with long lines where guests roasted in an unshaded queue. In The Wizarding World–Diagon Alley, Ollivanders assumes its rightful place, with much larger digs. At IOA, only 24 guests at a time can experience the little drama where wands choose a wizard (rather than the other way around). At the Studios, the shop has three separate choosing chambers, turning it from a popular curiosity into an actual attraction. As for the IOA location, it continues to operate.

If your young 'un is selected to test-drive a wand, be forewarned that you'll have to buy it if you want to take it home.

LIVE ENTERTAINMENT *at* UNIVERSAL STUDIOS

IN ADDITION TO THE SHOWS profiled earlier, Universal offers a wide range of street entertainment. Costumed comic-book and cartoon characters (Shrek, Donkey, SpongeBob SquarePants, and Woody Woodpecker) roam the park for photo ops, along with movie star look-alikes, plus the Frankenstein monster, who can be said to be neither. The handout park map has a section called "Character Zones" that provides times and places for character appearances and shows. Musical acts include Blues Brothers impersonators dancing and singing in the New York section of the park.

The Disney-like **Universal's Superstar Parade** (★★★½) features dancers and performers, four large and elaborate floats inspired by cartoons, and a very mixed bag of street-prowling Universal characters. The parade stops twice for a highly choreographed ensemble number. Though impressive in its scope and coordination, the performance is well-nigh impossible to take in from any given viewing spot. The same floats are trotted out individually at various times of day for mini-shows and character meet and greets.

The parade begins at the gate between Louie's Pizza, in the New York area of the park, and *Beetlejuice Graveyard Revue*, in San Francisco. From there it proceeds along 5th Avenue, past Revenge of the Mummy. At the end of 5th Avenue, the parade takes a left onto Plaza of the Stars and heads toward the front of the park, where it makes another left onto Hollywood Boulevard, from whence it disappears backstage across from Mel's Diner. The best viewing spots are along 5th Avenue, on the front steps of faux buildings in New York.

If you miss part of the parade in the New York area, you can scoot along the waterfront to Mel's Diner and catch it as it comes down Hollywood Boulevard. If after watching the parade on the New York streets you plan to leave the park, you can use the same route to access Hollywood Boulevard and the park exit before the parade arrives.

Universal's Cinematic Spectacular: 100 Years of Movie Memories ★★★½ *(seasonal when park is open late)*

| APPEAL BY AGE | PRESCHOOL ★★★ | GRADE SCHOOL ★★★★ | TEENS ★★★½ |
| YOUNG ADULTS ★★★★ | | OVER 30 ★★★★ | SENIORS ★★★★ |

What it is Fireworks, dancing fountains, and movies. **Scope and scale** Major attraction. **Fright potential** Loud and intense with fireworks and some scary villains, but most young children like it. **Bottleneck rating** 9. **When to go** 1 show a day, usually at park closing. **Authors' rating** Good effort; ★★★½. **Special comment** Movie trailers galore. **Duration of presentation** 15–20 minutes. **Probable waiting time** None.

This is USF's big nighttime event, designed to cap your day at the park. Shown on the lagoon in the middle of the Studios, the presentation runs through clips and music from the first 100 years of Universal's biggest movies. The scenes are projected onto three enormous "screens" made by spraying water from the lagoon into the air (similar to *Fantasmic!* at Disney's Hollywood Studios). Fireworks and colored lights are also used to good effect throughout the presentation, which is narrated by Morgan Freeman. It's an enjoyable way to end your day.

The best spot is directly across the lagoon from Richter's Burger Co., where the sidewalk makes a small protrusion overlooking the water.

Because acquiring a spot here can be very difficult, we recommend arriving at least 45 minutes ahead of time.

Before the show begins, realize that not all of the movie clips may be suitable for young viewers. The horror montage, for example, mixes excerpts from hoary black-and-white monster movies with potentially fright-inducing clips from films such as *The Birds, Halloween, Psycho, The Silence of the Lambs,* and *Tales from the Crypt.*

UNIVERSAL STUDIOS FLORIDA TOURING PLANS

UNIVERSAL STUDIOS FLORIDA ONE-DAY TOURING PLAN (page 478)

THIS PLAN IS FOR GUESTS without Park-to-Park tickets and includes every recommended attraction at USF. If a ride or show is listed that you don't want to experience, skip that step and proceed to the next. Move quickly from attraction to attraction, and if possible, hold off on lunch until after experiencing at least six rides.

THE BEST OF UNIVERSAL ORLANDO IN ONE DAY (pages 479–480)

THIS TOURING PLAN is for guests with one-day Park-to-Park tickets who wish to see the highlights of Universal Studios Florida and Islands of Adventure in a single day. The plan uses Hogwarts Express to get from one park to the other and then back again; you can walk back to the first park for the return leg if the line is too long. The plan includes a table-service lunch at Mythos (make reservations online a few days before your visit) and dinner at the Leaky Cauldron; during holiday periods, you may need to substitute a quick-service snack for one or both meals to fit in all of the plan's attractions.

FAVORITE EATS AT UNIVERSAL STUDIOS		
LAND	**SERVICE LOCATION**	**FOOD ITEM**
PRODUCTION CENTRAL	Classic Monsters Cafe	Chicken, salads, & hot dogs
NEW YORK Finnegan's Bar and Grill	Irish pub with fish-and-chips, frequently features live music	*Table service only* **Louie's Italian Restaurant**	Pasta	
SAN FRANCISCO Richter's Burger Co.	Burgers	
THE WIZARDING WORLD OF HARRY POTTER–DIAGON ALLEY Leaky Cauldron	Bangers & mash, fish-and-chips, & cottage pie		
WORLD EXPO Fast Food Boulevard	Several eateries with food inspired by *The Simpsons* TV series. We love the tacos at **Bumblebee Man's Taco Truck.**	
WOODY WOODPECKER'S KIDZONE KidZone Pizza Company	Pizza	
HOLLYWOOD Mel's Drive-In	Old-fashioned root beer float	

SEAWORLD

MANY DOZENS OF READERS have written to extol the virtues of SeaWorld. The following are representative. An English family writes:

BOB Discount coupons for SeaWorld admission are available in the free visitor magazines found in most (but not Disney) hotel lobbies.

> *The best-organized park is SeaWorld. The park map we got on arrival included the show schedule and told us which areas were temporarily closed due to construction. Best of all, there was almost no queuing. Overall, we rated this day so highly that it is the park we would most like to visit again.*

A woman in Alberta, Canada, gives her opinion:

> *We chose SeaWorld as our fifth day at the "World." What a pleasant surprise! It was every bit as good (and in some ways better) than WDW itself. Well worth the admission, an excellent entertainment value, educational, well run, and better value for the dollar in food services. Perhaps expand your coverage to give them their due!*

OK, here's what you need to know (for additional information, call ☎ 407-351-3600 or 888-800-5447, or visit **seaworld.com/orlando**). SeaWorld is a world-class marine-life theme park near the intersection of I-4 and the Beachline Expressway. It's about 10 miles east of Walt Disney World. Opening daily at 9 a.m. and closing between 5:30 and 10 p.m., depending on the season, SeaWorld charges about $97 for adults and $92 for children ages 3–9 at the gate (prices include tax). If you purchase online at the website above, the same tickets will cost you about $20 less. Several multipark tickets are available as well, including the five-park **Orlando Flex Ticket,** which includes admission to SeaWorld, Aquatica, Universal Studios, Islands of Adventure, and Wet 'n Wild. **Fun Card** offers by far the best deal. This annual pass for Florida residents costs $240 for access to SeaWorld, Aquatica, and Busch Gardens. There are no blackout dates, and parking fees are waived. Check SeaWorld's website for all ticket options. Parking is $17 per car, $22 per RV or camper.

BOB If you don't purchase your admission in advance, take advantage of the automatic admission machines located to the right of the main entrance. The machines are a pain in the rear, asking for your name, age, home zip code, and billing zip code, but if you have a credit card, the machines are a lot faster than standing in line at the ticket windows.

Figure 8–9 hours or more to see everything, 6 or so if you stick to the big deals. **Discovery Cove** (see page 418) is directly across the Central Florida Parkway from SeaWorld. Parking at Discovery Cove is free.

SeaWorld is about the size of the Magic Kingdom and requires about the same amount of walking. In terms of size, quality, and creativity, it's unequivocally on par with Disney's major theme parks. Unlike Walt Disney World, SeaWorld primarily features stadium shows or walk-through exhibits. This means that you will spend about 80% less time waiting in

BOB Be forewarned that you can't take food or drinks into SeaWorld or its swimming park, Aquatica.

FAVORITE EATS AT SEAWORLD		
LAND	SERVICE LOCATION	FOOD ITEM
KEY WEST AT SEAWORLD Captain Pete's Island Eats	Hot dogs & fresh funnel cakes		
THE WATERFRONT Voyager's Smokehouse	Barbecue ribs & chicken		
SHARK ENCOUNTER Sharks Underwater Grill	Fish, pasta, & coconut chicken tenders; floor-to-ceiling glass allows guests to observe some 50 sharks and fish.	*Table service only*		
WILD ARCTIC Mango Joe's	Turkey, ham, or chicken salad sandwich; fruit salad		
FRONT GATE PLAZA Sweet Sailin' Candy Shop	Candies & hand-dipped chocolate turtles		

line during 8 hours at SeaWorld than you would for the same-length visit at a Disney park.

But you'll notice immediately as you check the performance times that the shows are scheduled so that it's almost impossible to see them back-to-back. A Cherry Hill, New Jersey, visitor confirms this rather major problem, complaining:

> *The shows were timed so we could not catch all the major ones in a 7-hour visit.*

Much of the year, you can get a seat for the stadium shows by showing up 10 or so minutes in advance. When the park is crowded, however, you need to be at the stadiums at least 20 minutes in advance (30 minutes in advance for a good seat). All of the stadiums have splash zones, specified areas where you're likely to be drenched with ice-cold salt water by whales, dolphins, and sea lions. Finally, SeaWorld has three of the best coasters—**Journey to Atlantis, Manta,** and **Kraken**—in Florida. If you're a coaster lover, be on hand before park opening and ride all three rides as soon as the park opens. **Mako** will be the tallest, longest, and fastest roller coaster in Orlando when it opens in 2016.

DISCOVERY COVE

ALSO OWNED BY SEAWORLD, this intimate park is a welcome departure from the hustle and bustle of other Orlando parks. Its slower pace could be the overstimulated family's ticket back to mental health.

The main draw at Discovery Cove is the chance to swim with an **Atlantic bottlenose dolphin** from among the 45 here. The 50-minute experience (30 minutes in the water) is open to visitors age 6 and up who are comfortable in the water. The experience begins with an orientation led by trainers and an opportunity for participants to ask questions. Next, small groups wade into shallow water to get an introduction to the dolphin in its habitat. The experience culminates with guests swimming into deeper water for closer interaction with the dolphin before being towed back to shore by the dolphin.

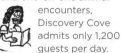 **LILIANE** With a focus on personal guest service and one-on-one animal encounters, Discovery Cove admits only 1,200 guests per day.

STAR RATINGS FOR SEAWORLD ATTRACTIONS

★★★★★	Manta (roller coaster)
★★★★½	Antarctica: Empire of the Penguin
★★★★½	*One Ocean* (high-tech Shamu and killer whale show)
★★★★½	*Shamu's Celebration: Light Up the Night* (seasonal killer whale show at night)
★★★★	Dolphin Cove (2-acre outdoor dolphin habitat)
★★★★	Kraken (roller coaster)
★★★½	*Clyde and Seamore Sea Lion High* (sea lion, walrus, and otter show)
★★★½	Manta Aquarium (more than 3,000 marine animals; the pop-up aquarium lets kids feel like they're in the aquarium)
★★★½	Shamu's Happy Harbor (children's play area with two teacup-style rides, a children's roller coaster, a carousel, a net climb, a gently rocking boat, and a mild 20-foot drop tower)
★★★½	Shark Encounter
★★★½	Wild Arctic (simulation ride and Arctic-wildlife viewing)
★★★	*Blue Horizons* (dolphin and bird show)
★★★	Pacific Point Preserve (sea lions and seals)
★★★	*Pets Ahoy!* (show with performing birds, cats, dogs, and a pig)
★★★	Shamu Underwater Viewing (whale viewing area)
★★★	TurtleTrek (3-D film about sea turtles; animal habitats)
★★½	*Journey to Atlantis* (combination roller coaster–flume ride)
★★½	Stingray Lagoon
★★	Dolphin Nursery (outdoor pool for expectant dolphins or mothers and calves)
★★	Pelican Preserve
★★	Sky Tower (400-foot tower with a bird's-eye view of Orlando)
N/A	Mako (tallest, longest, fastest coaster in Orlando; opens 2016)

Other exhibits at Discovery Cove include the **Grand Reef,** the **Freshwater Oasis,** and the **Explorer's Aviary.** Snorkel or swim in the Grand Reef, which houses thousands of exotic fish as well as an underwater shipwreck and hidden grottoes. The Freshwater Oasis is a swimming and wading experience where you can get up close and personal with otters and marmosets. In the Explorer's Aviary, you can touch and feed gorgeous tropical birds. The park is threaded by the **Wind-Away River,** in which you can float or swim, and dotted with beaches that serve as pathways to the attractions.

All guests are required to wear flotation vests when swimming, and lifeguards are omnipresent. You'll need your swimsuit, pool shoes, and a cover-up. On rare days when it's too cold to swim in Orlando, guests are provided with free wet suits. Discovery Cove also provides fish-friendly sunscreen samples; guests may not use their own sunscreen.

LILIANE The price is high, but the prize is right. Swimming with a dolphin across the bay was one of the most amazing things I have ever done in my life.

Discovery Cove is open 8 a.m.–5:30 p.m. daily; check-in begins at 7:15 a.m. Admission is limited, so purchase tickets well in advance; call ☎ 877-557-7404 or visit **discoverycove .com.** Prices vary seasonally from $276 per person to $361, including tax (no children's discount). Prices for Florida residents start at $219. Admission includes the dolphin swim; self-parking; Continental breakfast; a substantial lunch; snacks and drinks; use of beach umbrellas, lounge chairs, towels, lockers, and swim and snorkel gear; and unlimited admission to SeaWorld and Aquatica water park (see page 427) for 14 days surrounding your visit to Discovery Cove.

If you're not interested in the dolphin swim, you can visit Discovery Cove for the day for $180–$212 per person, including tax, depending on the season. For only $25 more you can add unlimited admission to Busch Gardens in Tampa Bay for 14 consecutive days. The passes are valid before or after your Discovery Cove visit.

For an additional $59 per person, you can experience **SeaVenture,** a 25-minute underwater stroll on the bottom of the Grand Reef aquarium. Participants wear diving helmets (large enough to accommodate eyeglasses), and no experience or scuba certification is necessary. Minimum age is 10 years.

PART TWELVE

THE BEST
of the REST

The WATER THEME PARKS

WALT DISNEY WORLD has two swimming theme parks. **Typhoon Lagoon** is the most diverse Disney splash pad, while **Blizzard Beach** takes the prize for the most slides and most bizarre theme (a ski resort in meltdown). Blizzard Beach has the best slides, but Typhoon Lagoon has a surf pool where you can bodysurf. Both parks have excellent and elaborate themed areas for toddlers and preschoolers.

BOB During summer and holiday periods, Typhoon Lagoon and Blizzard Beach fill to capacity on weekdays and close their gates before 11 a.m.

Admission costs for each park, including tax, are $62 per day for adults and $54 per day for children (ages 3–9). Seasonal tickets are $5 cheaper and available year-round, except May 23–August 30. Florida residents may purchase a no-blackout-date Annual Pass granting them daily access to both water parks from 2 p.m. until closing; prices are $70 for adults and $64 for kids, tax included.

Disney water parks allow one cooler per family or group, but no glass and no alcoholic beverages. Both parks charge the following rental prices: towels are $2; lockers are $8 small, $10 large (plus $5 refundable deposit); life jackets are available at no cost. Strollers are welcome but unavailable for rent.

The best way to avoid standing in lines is to visit the water parks when they're not very crowded. We recommend going on a weekend, when most visitors are traveling, or on a Monday. While Disney once offered morning and evening Extra Magic Hours at its water parks, it's been a couple of years since we last saw them on the operating schedule. It's Disney's prerogative to change its mind, however, especially during summer, so check the schedules online a couple of days before you plan to go.

BOB If you have a car, drive instead of taking a Disney bus.

Just as at the theme parks, the key to a successful visit to the Disney water parks is to get up early, have breakfast, and arrive at the park

BLIZZARD BEACH

ATTRACTION | HEIGHT REQUIREMENT | WHAT TO EXPECT

CHAIR LIFT UP MT. GUSHMORE | 32 inches | Great ride even if you go up only for the view. When the park is packed, use the single-rider line.

CROSS COUNTRY CREEK | None | Lazy river circling the park; grab a tube.

DOWNHILL DOUBLE DIPPER | 48 inches | Side-by-side tube-racing slides. At 25 mph, the tube races through water curtains and free falls. It's a lot of fun but rough.

MELT-AWAY BAY | None | Wave pool with gentle, bobbing waves. The pool is great for younger swimmers.

RUNOFF RAPIDS | None | Three corkscrew tube slides to choose from. The center slide is for solo raft rides; the other two slides offer one-, two-, or three-person tubes. The dark, enclosed tube makes the ride feel as if you've been flushed down a toilet.

SKI PATROL TRAINING CAMP | 60 inches for T-Bar | A place for preteens to train for the big rides.

SLUSH GUSHER | 48 inches | A 90-foot double-humped slide. Ladies, cling to those tops—all others hang on to live.

SNOW STORMERS | None | Three mat-slide flumes; down you go on your belly.

SUMMIT PLUMMET | 48 inches | A 120-foot free fall at 60 mph. This ride is very intense. Make sure that your child knows what to expect. Being over 48 inches tall does not guarantee an enjoyable experience. If you think you'd enjoy washing out of a 12th-floor window during a heavy rain, then this slide is for you.

TEAMBOAT SPRINGS | None | 1,200-foot whitewater group raft flume. Wonderful ride for the whole family.

TIKE'S PEAK | 48 inches and under only | Kid-size version of Blizzard Beach. This is the place for little ones.

TOBOGGAN RACERS | None | Eight-lane race course. You go down the flume on a mat. The ride is less intense than Snow Stormers.

30 minutes before opening. Wear your bathing suit under shorts and a T-shirt so you don't have to bother with lockers or dressing rooms. Wear shoes—paths are relatively easy on bare feet, but there's a lot of ground to cover. If you or your children have tender feet, wear protective footwear that can be worn in and out of the water as you move around the park. Shops in the parks sell sandals and waterproof shoes.

Obviously, you'll need a towel, sunblock, and money. Carry enough money for the day and your Disney resort ID (if you have one), or use your MagicBand to pay for stuff. Though no location is completely safe, we've felt comfortable hiding our money in our cooler—nobody disturbed our stuff, and our cash was easy to reach. If, however, you're carrying a wad or you're simply a worrywart when it comes to money, rent a locker. Another great device is a water-resistant case with a lanyard to hold park tickets, a credit card, some cash, and your hotel key/card. You can buy these cases at the water parks for about $10; more-sophisticated versions are available at any good outdoors or sporting-goods shop.

LILIANE Wallets and purses get in the way, so lock them in your car's trunk or leave them at your hotel.

Personal swim gear (fins, masks, rafts, and so on) is not allowed—everything you need is either provided free or available to rent. If you forget your towel, you can rent one (cheap!). If you forgot your swimsuit or lotion, you can buy it on-site; disposable waterproof cameras

TYPHOON LAGOON

ATTRACTION | HEIGHT REQUIREMENT | WHAT TO EXPECT

BAY SLIDES | 60 inches and under | A miniature, two-slide version of Storm Slides, specifically designed for small children. Kids splash down into a far corner of the surf pool.

CASTAWAY CREEK | None | Half-mile lazy river in a tropical setting. Wonderful!

CRUSH 'N' GUSHER | 48 inches | Water roller coaster where you can choose from among three slides: Banana Blaster, Coconut Crusher, and Pineapple Plunger, ranging 410–420 feet long. This thriller leaves you wondering what exactly happened—if you make it down in one piece, that is. It's not for the faint of heart. If your kids are new to water-park rides, this is not the place to break them in, even if they're tall enough to ride.

GANG PLANK FALLS | None | Whitewater raft flume in a multiperson tube.

HUMUNGA KOWABUNGA | 48 inches | Speed slides that hit 30 mph. A five-story drop in the dark rattles the most courageous rider. Ladies should ride this in a one-piece swimsuit.

KEELHAUL FALLS | None | Fast whitewater ride in a single-person tube.

KETCHAKIDDEE CREEK | 48 inches and under only | Toddlers and preschoolers love this area reserved only for them. Say "splish splash" and have lots of fun.

MAYDAY FALLS | None | The name says it all. Wild single-person tube ride. Hang on!

SHARK REEF | None; kids under age 10 must be accompanied by an adult | After you're equipped with fins, a mask, a snorkel, and a life vest, you get a brief lesson in snorkeling. Then off you go to the other side of the saltwater pool, where you swim with small colorful fish, rays, and very small leopard and hammerhead sharks. If you don't want to swim with the fish, visit the underwater viewing chamber. Surface Air Snorkeling—a SCUBA-like pursuit involving a "pony" tank, a small regulator, and a buoyancy vest—is also offered. Participants must be at least 5 years old. To sign up and get more information, visit the kiosk near the entrance to Shark Reef.

STORM SLIDES | None | Three body-slides down and thru Mount Mayday.

SURF POOL | None; minimum age is 8; adult supervision required | World's largest inland surf facility with waves up to 6 feet high. Monday–Friday, in the early morning before the park opens, or evenings after the park has closed (hours vary), surfing lessons are offered (surfboard provided). Cost is $150 for 2½ hours; class size is 12. Call ☎ 407-wdw-surf (939-7873). The price does not include park admission.

are available for sale as well, though you can find them cheaper at area drugstores.

Establish your base for the day. Beautiful sunning and lounging spots are plentiful throughout both swimming parks; arrive early so you can have your pick. The breeze is best along the beaches of the lagoon at Blizzard Beach and the surf pool at Typhoon Lagoon. At Typhoon Lagoon, if children younger than age 6 are in your party, choose an area to the left of Mount Mayday near the children's swimming area.

Though Typhoon Lagoon and Blizzard Beach are huge parks with many slides, armies of guests overwhelm them almost daily. If your main reason for going is the slides and you hate long lines, try to be among the first guests to enter the park. Go directly to the slides and ride as many times as you can before the park fills. When lines for the slides become intolerable, head for the surf or wave pool or the tube-floating streams. The lazy rivers at both parks are perfect for

LILIANE While I don't feel any better on a water roller coaster than I do on the dry thing, I love the water parks. My all-time favorite water ride is Teamboat Springs, the 1,200-foot white-water raft flume at Blizzard Beach.

FAVORITE EATS AT THE WATER PARKS

LAND | SERVICE LOCATION | FOOD ITEM

BLIZZARD BEACH • **Avalunch** | Hot dogs & cheesecake • **Cooling Hut** | Popcorn, nachos, & Itzakadoozie • **Lottawatta Lodge** | Pizza, burgers, salads, & kids' meals • **Warming Hut** | Hot dogs & chicken wraps

TYPHOON LAGOON • **Happy Landings** | Ice cream, cookies, & waffle cones. *Garbage Pail:* Ice cream, fudge, nuts, & sprinkles in a pail with shovel. • **Leaning Palms** | Pizza & kids' meals in a sand pail with shovel • **Lowtide Lou's** (*seasonal*) | Chicken wraps & tuna sandwiches • **Typhoon Tilly's** | Fish, barbecue pork, & kids' meals in a sand pail with shovel. Great beer selection for the grown-ups.

Refillable mugs: If you or the kids enjoy soda, your best bet is to get a refillable mug, available at both water parks. For the price of the mug ($10), you are entitled to free refills throughout the day (only on the day of purchase). Select locations.

relaxation. Float through caves, beneath waterfalls, past gardens, and under bridges. Did you know that in the winter months Disney actually heats all the water-park pools?

Both water parks are large and require almost as much walking as the theme parks. Add to this wave surfing, swimming, and climbing to reach the slides, and you'll definitely be pooped by day's end. Consider a low-key activity for the evening. A Waterloo, Ontario, mom found Typhoon Lagoon to be more strenuous than she anticipated:

LILIANE Lost-children stations at the water parks are so out of the way that neither you nor your child will find them without help from a Disney cast member. Explain to your children how to recognize cast members (by their distinctive name tags) and how to ask for help.

I wish I had been prepared for the fact that we'd have to haul the tubes up the stairs of the Crush 'n' Gusher slides. My daughter was not strong enough to carry hers, so I had to lug the tubes up by myself. I was EXHAUSTED by the end of the day, and my arms ached for a couple of days afterward.

It's as easy to lose a child or become separated from your party at one of the water parks as it is at a major theme park. On arrival, pick a very specific place to meet in the event you are separated. If you split up on purpose, establish times for checking in.

KIERAN Every day, one kid is selected to be the Ski Captain at Blizzard Beach. I was picked once and got to enter the park first and open it officially for everyone. You have to arrive very early, though—50-60 minutes before the park opens—so be patient and look cute

Children under age 14 must be accompanied by an adult. The water parks are great fun for the whole family, but if you have very young children or if you are not a thrill-seeking water puppy, the pool of your hotel might serve just as well. The water parks, however, were made to order for teens. Note that during the winter months, Disney closes Blizzard Beach and Typhoon Lagoon for refurbishing, alternating maintenance in such a way that one water park will be open at all times. If it is very wintry, Disney will close both parks.

Blizzard Beach and Typhoon Lagoon offer premium spaces for rental that can accommodate up to six people and cost

$345 including tax for the full day. There are four premium spaces in each water park, and they include the personalized services of an attendant, private lockers, all-day drink mugs, cooler with bottled water, lounge furniture, tables, and rental towels. You can also rent a premium beach chair space at both parks. The deal includes two lounge chairs, umbrella, cocktail table, and two towels. Limit is up to four people; if you have more than four people in your party, a second reservation is needed. These rentals are also available on a same-day basis if any locations are left (check at Shade Shack for Blizzard Beach and at High and Dry Rentals for Typhoon Lagoon). Cost is $58 including tax and must be paid at time of reservation. Reserve the premium or beach chair spaces in advance by calling ☎ 407-WDW-PLAY (939-7529). Cancellations must be made no later than 9 a.m. the day prior to the reservation to avoid a penalty.

ALEX The Garbage Pail ice cream bucket is delicious and great for families. There's enough ice cream for everybody, plus you get to keep the bucket!

Alex

BEFORE YOU GO

1. Call ☎ 407-939-6244 before you go to get the official park opening time.
2. Purchase admission tickets online before you arrive.
3. Decide if you want to picnic or not, and then plan or pack accordingly. Pets are not allowed at the water parks.

A WORD FROM THE WEATHERMAN

THUNDERSTORMS ARE COMMON in Florida. On summer afternoons, such storms often occur daily, forcing the water parks to close temporarily while the threatening weather passes. If the storm is severe and prolonged, it can cause a great deal of inconvenience. The park may actually close for the day, launching a legion through the turnstiles to compete for space on the Disney resort buses. If you depend on Disney buses, leave the park earlier, rather than later, when you see a storm moving in. Most important, though, instruct your children to immediately return to home base at the sight of lightning or when they hear the first rumble of thunder.

We recommend that you monitor the local weather forecast the day before you go, checking again in the morning before leaving for the water park. Scattered thunderstorms are to be expected and usually cause no more than a temporary inconvenience, but moving storm fronts are to be avoided.

We get a lot of questions about the water parks during cold-weather months. Orlando area temperatures can vary from the high 30s to the low 80s during December, January, and February. When it's warm, though, these months can serve up a dandy water-park experience, as this Batavia, Ohio, woman recounts:

Going to Blizzard Beach in December was the best decision ever! They told us that if the park didn't reach 100 people by noon, they would be closing. . . . There was no wait for anything all day! In June we waited

WET 'N WILD

ATTRACTION | HEIGHT REQUIREMENT | WHAT TO EXPECT

AQUA DRAG RACER | 42 inches | At six stories tall, it propels guests through four lanes of head-to-head competition at the speed of 15 feet per second.

THE BLACK HOLE | 48 inches if riding alone; 36 inches if riding with an adult | Two-person tube; 1,000 gallons of water per minute; all this in the dark. Do we need to say more? While not the wildest ride in town, it sure is dark in there.

THE BLAST | 48 inches if riding alone; 36 inches if riding with an adult | Two-person tube ride inside a waterworks where all the pipes are broken. You cannot get any wetter.

THE BOMB BAY | 48 inches | You stand on a pair of doors that open, dropping you down a 76-foot slide. You're gonna need a lot of nerve to stand on those doors and wait for the drop.

BRAIN WASH | 48 inches | Extreme six-story tube ride with a 53-foot vertical drop into a 65-foot funnel; tube holds two or four riders.

DER STUKA | 48 inches | Speed flume descending from a six-story tower.

DISCO H2O | 48 inches if riding alone; 36 inches if riding with an adult | Four persons in a raft are ushered down a tube into a 1970s-era nightclub complete with lights, music, and a disco ball.

THE FLYER | 48 inches if riding alone; 36 inches if riding with an adult | A calmer toboggan-style ride more suitable for families with smaller children.

MACH 5 | 48 inches | Mat slide. For a really fast ride, grab a newer mat.

THE STORM | 48 inches | Half slide, half toilet bowl. This ride is exhilarating and disorienting; when the lifeguard begins hollering, just stumble toward his voice and give him a thumbs-up.

THE SURGE | 48 inches if riding alone; 36 inches if riding with an adult | Four-person raft ride sends you flying down 600 feet of banked turns. Wild!

in line for an hour for Summit Plummet. In December it took us only the amount of time to walk up the stairs. We had the enormous wave pool to ourselves. We did everything in the entire park and had lunch in less than 3 hours. The weather was slightly chilly at 71° and overcast with very light rain, but the water is heated, so we were fine.

SAFETY FIRST

TOO MUCH FUN IN THE SUN isn't a good thing if you get sunburned or become dehydrated. Drink lots of fluids, use sunscreen, and bring a T-shirt and a hat for extra protection. Lifeguards are on duty throughout the parks. At Typhoon Lagoon, a first-aid station is located behind Leaning Palms. The Blizzard Beach first-aid station is between Lottawatta Lodge and Beach Haus.

WET 'N WILD

WET 'N WILD (ON INTERNATIONAL DRIVE IN ORLANDO, one block east of I-4 at Exit 75A; ☎ 800-992-WILD (9453) or 407-351-9453; **wetnwildorlando.com**) is a non-Disney water-park option. If you're looking for a colorful atmosphere, Wet 'n Wild doesn't deliver, but it's packed with incredible slides, flumes, and activities for all ages.

Note: Wet 'n Wild, a Universal property, will close December 31, 2016, to make way for Universal's new water park, **Volcano Bay,** scheduled to open in 2017.

Tickets at the main gate cost $61 for adults and $56 for kids ages 3–9, including tax; call or check online for special deals and discounts (especially for AAA members, Florida residents, and members of the military). An annual pass for Florida residents costs $97, including tax and free parking, if you buy it online. Parking fees are $13 for cars and vans and $17 for RVs. Lockers can be rented for $6–$11 plus tax depending on size, and towel rental is $4; both require a refundable deposit of $3. Life vests are provided for free. Pets aren't allowed inside the park.

Mears Transportation operates a shuttle to Wet 'n Wild that stops three times a day at Disney hotels. Cost is $20 for guests age 3 and older. If you're staying on International Drive, you can take the International Drive trolley (visit **iridetrolley.com** for schedules and fees).

As with all thrill slides, lines can become unbearably long, so arrive early. Also keep in mind that most slides are geared more toward older children. Check the height requirements in the table on the previous page.

LILIANE What I like best about Wet 'n Wild is that the park is open 9:30 a.m.–9 p.m. daily throughout the summer. This is a huge advantage over the Disney water parks, which generally close 6–7 p.m.

Wet 'n Wild attractions include **Blastaway Beach,** which offers a kid-size version of the adult menu, and the 17,000-square-foot wave pool at **Surf Lagoon,** perfect for body bobbing. If you prefer to ride the waves with tubes, you can rent those at the main rental stand. Another great way to relax is the **Lazy River.**

When you get hungry, the main food pavilions are the centrally located **Bubba's Fried Chicken and Ribs, Manny's Pizza,** and **Surf Grill,** together offering such staples as burgers, pizza, and barbecue-pork sandwiches, as well as more-nutritious (and nontraditional) items such as veggie burgers and tabbouleh.

You can take in all the attractions at Wet 'n Wild in a single day, especially in the summer when the park is open until 9 p.m.

BEFORE YOU GO

1. Call ☎ 800-992-WILD (9453) or 407-351-9453, or visit **wetnwildorlando .com,** the day before you go to find out the official park opening time.

2. Purchase admission tickets online before you arrive.

3. Visit the website to determine what attractions are appropriate for the kids in your party.

AQUATICA *by* SEAWORLD

AQUATICA IS LOCATED across International Drive from the back side of SeaWorld. From Kissimmee, Walt Disney World, and Lake Buena Vista, take I-4 East, exit onto the Central Florida Parkway, and then

AQUATICA BY SEAWORLD

ATTRACTION | HEIGHT REQUIREMENT* | WHAT TO EXPECT

CUTBACK COVE AND BIG SURF SHORES | None | One cove serves up bodysurfing waves, while the other puts out gently bobbing floating waves. A spacious beach arrayed around the coves is the park's primary sunning venue. Shady spots, courtesy of beach umbrellas, ring the perimeter of the area for sun-sensitive guests.

DOLPHIN PLUNGE | 48 inches; must be able to maintain proper riding position unassisted | Corkscrewing romp through a totally arced tube until you blast through the clear tube at the end. The viewing of the dolphins is nearly impossible because you're flushed through the clear tube so fast and with so much water splashing in your face, the ride is over before you've seen anything.

HOOROO RUN | 42 inches | A six-story open-air run down a steep, straight, undulating slide.

IHU'S BREAKAWAY FALL | 48 inches | Opened in May 2014, the ride is Orlando's tallest and steepest multidrop tower slide. This is not a mild journey. Brace yourself, and make sure your swimsuit is securely fastened to your body!

KATA'S KOOKABURRA COVE | 48 inches and under only | Wading pool and slides for the preschool crowd.

LOGGERHEAD LANE | must be in a single or double tube | Take a tube and enjoy this lazy river, which at one point passes through the Fish Grotto, a tank populated by hundreds of exotic tropical fish.

OMAKA ROCKA | 48 inches | A wide diameter, enclosed, one-person tube ride. The name is derived from the wave action inside the tube, which washes you alternately up one side of the tube and then the other.

ROA'S RAPIDS | 51 inches and under required to wear a life vest | Floating stream with a very swift current but without any rapids. There is only one place to get in and out.

TASSIE'S TWISTERS | must be able to maintain proper riding position while holding on to both handles unassisted | An enclosed slide tube spits you into an open bowl, where you careen around the edge much in the manner of the ball in a roulette wheel.

TAUMATA RACER | 42 inches; must be able to maintain proper riding position unassisted | A high-speed mat ride down a steep hill.

WALHALLA WAVE | 42 inches; must be able to maintain proper riding position unassisted | Circular raft that can accommodate up to four people and splashes down a six-story enclosed twisting tube.

WALKABOUT WATERS | 36–42 inches for slides into main pool and over 42 inches tall for larger slides | 15,000-square-foot children's adventure area. If your children are under the age of 10, this alone may be worth the admission price. It's impossible not to get wet and impossible not to have fun!

WHANAU WAY | must be able to maintain the proper riding position while holding on to both handles unassisted | Tubes carry one or two passengers down one of four slides with a few twists and one corkscrew.

*Guests under 48 inches are required to wear a life vest.

bear left on International Drive. From Universal Studios, take I-4 West to FL 528 and from there exit onto International Drive.

Admission prices at the gate are $61 for adults and $56 for kids, tax included. Tickets purchased online are $20 cheaper, and off-season specials online can reduce admission to as little as $17. Standard parking is $13 ($17 for RVs or preferred parking). If you don't want to wait in line to buy tickets, buy them in advance at **aquatica**

byseaworld.com, or use the ticket machines to the left of Aquatica's main entrance. An Aquatica/SeaWorld/Busch Gardens combo ticket starts at $119 online.

Aquatica is comparable in size to other water theme parks in the area. Attractively landscaped with palms, ferns, and tropical flowers, it's far less themed than Disney's Typhoon Lagoon and Blizzard Beach. You can take in all the attractions in one day, but as with all water parks, remember that an entire day of action in the Florida sun will wear out the most active kids and most grown-ups too.

As at other water parks, there are lockers, towels, wheelchairs, and strollers to rent; gift shops to browse; and places to eat. The three restaurants at Aquatica are **WaterStone Grill,** offering specialty sandwiches, fried fish, wraps, and salads; **Banana Beach Restaurant,** an all-you-can-eat venue dishing up burgers, hot dogs, and chicken; and **Mango Market,** a diminutive eatery serving pizza and chicken tenders. WaterStone Grill and Mango Market serve beer. If you're looking for the best dining value during your stay, consider Banana Beach. Unlimited visits to the all-you-can-eat buffet cost $16 for adults and $11 for kids.

BEFORE YOU GO

1. Call ☎ 888-800-5447 or 407-351-3600, or visit **aquaticabyseaworld .com,** the day before you go to find out the official park opening time.

2. Purchase admission tickets online before you arrive.

3. Visit the website to determine which attractions are appropriate for the kids in your party.

▮▮ DISNEY SPRINGS

THIS SPRAWLING DINING, SHOPPING, and entertainment complex is strung along the banks of Village Lake, on the east side of Walt Disney World. It consists of the **Marketplace, The Landing,** the **West Side,** and, coming in 2016, **Town Center.** You can roam, shop, and eat without paying any sort of entrance fee.

If you have a car, use it. There is bus transportation from all the Disney resorts to Disney Springs, and some resorts offer boat transportation. The problem is that buses make stops at a number of locations at Disney Springs, so you might sit on the bus for 20 minutes or more before you finally disembark for your destination. The boats are better than the buses but take about four times as long as driving your car. The boat route, however, is very pretty and a good choice if you're not in a hurry. Shops open as early as 9:30 a.m.

There are five ATMs at Disney Springs. All major credit cards are accepted, and if you're a Disney resort guest, you can have your shopping purchases delivered to your hotel (this only works if you are not checking out the next day). Pickup is usually at the primary gift shop

Continued on page 432

Disney Springs

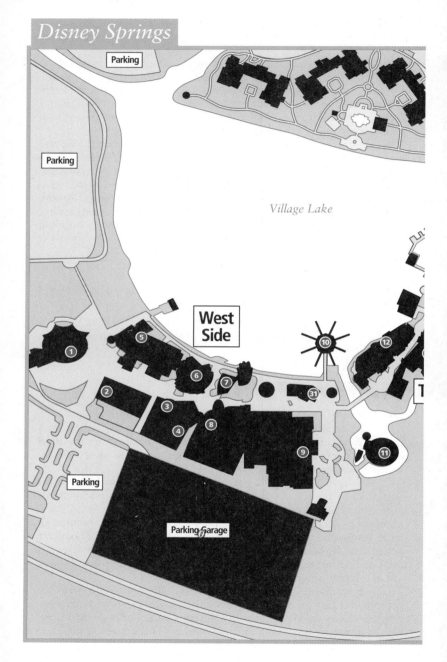

Parking

Parking

Village Lake

West Side

Parking

Parking Garage

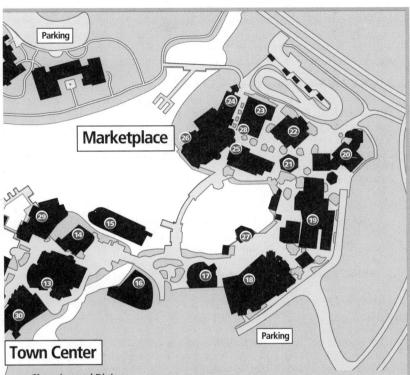

Parking

Marketplace

Parking

Town Center

Shopping and Dining
1. Cirque du Soleil *La Nouba*
2. DisneyQuest *(closes 2016)*
3. Curl by Sammy Duvall/Fit2Run
4. Splitsville
5. House of Blues
6. Wolfgang Puck Grand Cafe
7. Bongos Cuban Cafe
8. AMC Downtown Disney 24 Theatres
9. *Specialty shopping:*
   Disney's Candy Cauldron
   D-Street
   Orlando Harley-Davidson
   Pop Gallery
   Something Silver
   Sosa Family Cigars
   Sunglass Icon
   Super Hero Headquarters
10. Characters in Flight
11. Planet Hollywood
12. Paradiso 37
13. Raglan Road/Cookes of Dublin

14. Portobello
15. Fulton's Crab House
16. T-REX
17. LEGO Imagination Center
18. World of Disney/ Bibbidi Bobbidi Boutique
19. *Specialty shopping:*
    Arribas Brothers
    Basin
    Ghirardelli Soda Fountain & Chocolate Shop
    Marketplace Co-op
    Tren-D
20. Once Upon a Toy
21. Disney's Pin Traders
22. Earl of Sandwich/Mickey's Pantry/The Spice & Tea Exchange
23. Wolfgang Puck Express Cafe
24. *Specialty shopping:*
    The Art of Disney
    Disney Design-a-Tee

24. *Specialty shopping (continued):*
    Disney's Wonderful World of Memories
25. *Specialty shopping:*
    Goofy's Candy Co.
    littlemissmatched
    Marketplace Fun Finds
26. Rainforest Cafe
27. Waterside Stage
28. Disney's Days of Christmas
29. The Boathouse
30. *Specialty shopping:*
    Art of Shaving
    Apex by Sunglass Hut
    Chapel Hats
    Havaianas
    Erin McKenna's Bakery NYC
    Sanuk
    Sound Lion
    Vivoli Gelateria
31. Starbucks

Continued from page 429

of your resort (no room delivery), but even so, it beats the heck out of lugging stuff around. Pets are not allowed at Disney Springs.

Most of the construction in Disney Springs should be finished in 2016. A number of major projects, including parking garages to address the notoriously bad traffic, have already been completed.

DISNEY SPRINGS MARKETPLACE

THOUGH THE MARKETPLACE offers interactive fountains, a couple of playgrounds, a lakeside amphitheater, and watercraft rentals, it's primarily a shopping and dining venue. The centerpiece of shopping is the 50,000-square-foot **World of Disney,** the largest store in the world selling Disney-trademarked merchandise. Kids will particularly enjoy the **LEGO Imagination Center.** You'll know you're there when you see Brickley, the 30-foot sea serpent made out of more than a million LEGO blocks that lives in the lake right in front of the store. Outside the store is a play area filled with LEGO blocks for children to enjoy.

Once Upon a Toy is a joy. The biggest draws at this 16,000-square-foot store are classic toys with a Disney twist. Here you can find Mr. Potato Head with Mickey Ears or a sorcerer's hat and the classic game Clue set in The Haunted Mansion.

Bibbidi Bobbidi Boutique transforms your little girl into a princess, albeit for a price. A Fairy Godmother–in–training (the shop manager) and her helpers offer salon services for princesses age 3 and up. Hair-style and makeup cost $55, adding a manicure will cost you $60, and the royal makeover (including your choice of a princess costume with accessories and a photo shoot with imaging package) starts at $190. Hairstyling for your young Prince Charming is also available.

LILIANE Save money by getting just the hairstyle and makeup at Bibbidi Bobbidi and taking your own pictures.

DISNEY SPRINGS WEST SIDE

THE BEST THING at Disney Springs—and probably in all of Walt Disney World—is **Cirque du Soleil's** *La Nouba. Mesmerizing, thrilling, superb,* and *beautiful* hardly do the show justice, but it's all of those and more. Tickets range $67–$160 for adults and $55–$133 for kids ages 3–9 (tax included). Florida residents are eligible for a 20% discount. Book online at **cirquedusoleil.com/lanouba** or call ☎ 407-939-7600.

Splitsville, an upscale bowling, billiards, and dining venue, covers 45,000 square feet on two levels. Or try **Characters in Flight,** where you ascend 400 feet over Disney Springs in a tethered balloon (the characters are painted on the balloon—don't expect to float around up there with Br'er Fox). The weather-dependent ride is 8–10 minutes and runs $18 for adults (age 10 and up) and $12 for children (ages 3–9). Operating 8:30 a.m.–midnight, the balloon ride is wheelchair accessible.

RICKY Splitsville is the best place on Earth! You can bowl, and they bring you food, and you can mix your own soda flavors.

Ricky

Harley Davidson offers motorcycle apparel, including leather vests. **Fit2Run** sells running gear, and **Sunglass Icon** stocks designer shades.

Catch the latest box-office hits at the state-of-the-art **AMC Downtown Disney 24 with Dine-In Theatres Orlando,** showing flicks and serving food in an Art Deco setting. For showtimes and ticket sales, go to **amctheatres.com,** click "Find a Theatre," and select "AMC Downtown Disney 24 w/ Dine-In Theatres Orlando" from the "Orlando/Daytona Beach" list.

Restaurants include **House of Blues,** which serves Cajun specialties, and **The Smokehouse,** a quick-service barbecue joint operated by HOB; **Planet Hollywood,** offering basic American fare amid movie memorabilia; **Bongos Cuban Cafe,** serving Cuban favorites; a **Starbucks;** and **Wolfgang Puck Grand Cafe,** featuring California cuisine.

The West Side's **Exposition Park** food trucks include **Namaste Café,** serving Indian-inspired cuisine; **Superstar Catering,** offering meatballs in a variety of sandwiches; **Fantasy Fare,** selling ham-and-cheese sandwiches, corn dogs, and noodle salads; and **World Showcase of Flavors,** with beef sliders, a lobster roll, and pierogies. (Food-truck offerings and schedules vary daily.)

DISNEYQUEST (CLOSES 2016) This so-called virtual theme park is contained in a modest five-story building. It's more of a quaint game museum than anything high-tech, though: Your smartphone probably has better graphics and more computing power than most of the games, and nostalgia is more common than cutting-edge technology.

BOB Weekday mornings are least crowded at DisneyQuest.

Visitors to DisneyQuest arrive at the **VenturePort,** the third floor of the building, by elevator. They can then take either stairs or another elevator to the other floors, or zones. We like the attractions that are truly interactive. **CyberSpace Mountain** (second floor, **Create Zone**) lets you design and ride your own virtual roller coaster, and while it isn't as advanced as the similar Sum of All Thrills in Epcot, it's still pretty fun. Despite graphics that are rather primitive by today's standards, **Virtual Jungle Cruise** and **Pirates of the Caribbean—Battle for Buccaneer Gold,** both on the first floor's **Explore Zone,** score points with us for active—and sometimes exhausting—physical interaction. Kids will enjoy **Mighty Ducks Pinball Spin,** and **Buzz Lightyear's AstroBlasters** is a fun take on bumper cars, with the added bonus of shooting basketballs at your opponents' cars (protected by a cage).

Anyone who remembers changing dollar bills for quarters at the mall will enjoy the classic video games and air hockey in the **Replay Zone** (floors five and three; all games are set for free play). We've even played games we've never seen before, such as the head-to-head versions of **Pac-Man** and **Tetris,** with up to four players on a large screen. Hidden among the classics is a one-of-a-kind, real-life **Fix-It Felix Jr.,** from the Disney animated movie *Wreck-It Ralph.*

We don't recommend any of the virtual-reality games that require you to wear VR goggles, such as **Aladdin's Magic Carpet Ride.** The graphics, rudimentary at best, have a strong likelihood of inducing motion sickness in even the strongest of stomachs.

While nearly every game at DisneyQuest is free to play with your admission, there are some exceptions. Like all things Disney, admission to DisneyQuest is not cheap. A one-day admission is $48 for adults and $42 for kids ages 3–9 (prices include tax). Children under age 10 must be accompanied by a responsible person 16 years or older. Kids under the age of 3 are admitted free of charge, but strollers are not permitted inside DisneyQuest (you can leave them at the coat check on the first floor).

Four attractions have height restrictions: Buzz Lightyear's Astro-Blasters, 51 inches; CyberSpace Mountain, 51 inches; Mighty Ducks Pinball Slam, 48 inches; and Pirates of the Caribbean—Battle for Buccaneer Gold, 35 inches.

No need to leave DisneyQuest when hunger strikes. **Wonderland Cafe** and **FoodQuest** serve the usual fare, and once you are ready to leave, the exit is through the obligatory gift shop.

DisneyQuest will close in 2016 to make way for **The NBA Experience,** featuring a National Basketball Association–themed restaurant, shop, and exhibits. Interactive activities, designed for guests of most ages, will focus on basketball skills as well as test agility, reflexes, and mobility.

THE LANDING AND TOWN CENTER

FEATURING WATERFRONT WALKWAYS and merchandise kiosks, **The Landing** has seen the most reimagining, with new shopping and dining areas. What was once a bottleneck for guests (and their strollers) trying to go from the West Side to the Marketplace is now a much more open area, with multiple pathways to alleviate pedestrian traffic, plus sweeping views of the water and Saratoga Springs Resort.

Still under construction is **Town Center,** a brand-new area situated between The Landing and the parking garage. Anchoring this area is the **Planet Hollywood** restaurant (still open during construction).

Family-friendly shops and restaurants include **Raglan Road,** an Irish pub and restaurant featuring live Celtic music; **Curl by Sammy Duvall,** a surf shop; and several outdoor food-and-beverage locations. **Paradiso 37** features the cuisines of the Americas (that would be North, Central, and South) served both indoors and out.

The newest kid on the block is **The Boathouse,** which offers upscale waterfront dining. The restaurant is also the launching pad for the **Venezia,** a 40-foot wooden Italian water taxi. Kids will enjoy the guided **Amphicar** rides, which take guests on a 20-minute tour of the landmarks of Disney Springs, albeit at an exorbitant price.

Art of Shaving offers high-end grooming essentials for the modern dad, **Sanuk** sells creatively inspired footwear, and **Sound Lion** comes in handy should you need new headphones or earbuds. The latest sports sunglasses can be found at **Apex by Sunglass Hut,** and **Havaianas** is your

FAVORITE EATS AT DISNEY SPRINGS

LAND | SERVICE LOCATION | FOOD ITEM

MARKETPLACE
- **Earl of Sandwich** | Sandwich paradise
- **Ghirardelli Soda Fountain & Chocolate Shop** | Ice cream & chocolate treats
- **T-REX** | Burgers, ribs, pasta, & kids' menu in Jurassic setting with animatronic dinosaurs | *Table service only*
- **Wolfgang Puck Express Cafe** | Soups, salads, & pizza

WEST SIDE
- **House of Blues** | Cajun food & kids' menu. For shows in the music hall next door, check out **hob.com.** | *Table service only*
- **Planet Hollywood** | Burgers. Great for teens who will love checking out the Hollywood memorabilia. | *Table service only*
- **Starbucks** | Bistro boxes, coffee & tea, croissants, pastries, & salads
- **Wetzel's Pretzels** | Pretzels with a twist

THE LANDING
- **Raglan Road** | Irish food & live music | *Table service only*

place to go for cool flip-flops plus options to design your own. **Vivoli Gelateria** serves panini and gelato made with fresh, seasonal ingredients.

Liliane's two favorite new additions are **Chapel Hats** ("I really had to control myself to keep from buying a fascinator for the next Kentucky Derby") and **Erin McKenna's Bakery NYC,** the world's premier vegan and gluten-free bakery.

In fall 2015, **Morimoto Asia** will serve pan-Asian food. Guests can take in the view with waterside seating, or enjoy the show from the exhibition kitchens. In 2016 **The Edison** will amaze kids with its 1920s-era power plant setting. The restaurant will serve American food and feature live entertainment, including DJs, cabaret dancers, palm readers, and more.

OUTDOOR RECREATION

WALT DISNEY WORLD OFFERS a wealth of fun stuff for families besides theme parks, water parks, eating, and shopping. You can fish, canoe, hike, bike, boat, play tennis and golf, ride horses, work out, take cooking lessons, and even watch the Atlanta Braves' spring training.

Your kids will go nuts for the **Wilderness Lodge Resort,** and so will you. While you're there, have a family-style meal at the kid-friendly **Whispering Canyon Cafe** and rent bikes for a ride on the paved paths of adjacent **Fort Wilderness Resort & Campground.** The outing will be a great change of pace. The only downside is that your kids might not want to go back to their own hotel.

Find more fun at **ESPN Wide World of Sports Complex,** a 220-acre competition and training center. During late winter and early spring, the venue is the spring-training home of the Atlanta Braves. It's also home to Orlando's Major League Soccer team, the Orlando City Soccer

Club. Orlando City's schedule usually runs February–mid-September. Disney guests are welcome at the sports complex as paying spectators, but none of the facilities are available for guests to use. Prices vary; to book tickets and to learn what events (including Major League Baseball exhibition games) are scheduled during your visit, call ☎ 407-939-GAME (4267) or visit **espnwwos.com.**

Located 40–60 minutes south of Walt Disney World is the **Disney Wilderness Preserve,** a wetlands-restoration area with hiking trails and an interpretive center, operated by The Nature Conservancy in partnership with Disney. The preserve is open Monday–Friday, 9 a.m.–5 p.m.; closed on most holidays. Admission is free, though donations are appreciated. If you're interested, call the preserve directly at ☎ 407-935-0002 or visit **tinyurl.com /disneywildernesspreserve.**

GOLF

IF GOLF IS YOUR THING, call ☎ 407-938-GOLF (4653) or visit **golfwdw.com** for information, tee times, and greens fees at **Palm Golf Course** (★★★★), **Magnolia Golf Course** (★★★½), **Lake Buena Vista Golf Course** (★★★), or **Oak Trail Golf Course** (★★½).

There is, of course, golf beyond Mickey's Kingdom. The greater Orlando area has enough high-quality courses to rival better-known golfing meccas, such as Scottsdale and Palm Springs. But unlike these destinations with their endless private country clubs, Orlando is unique because almost all its courses are open for some sort of public play. We compiled a list of off-Disney golf courses for Dad's or Mom's special day off (see the table below).

GOLF BEYOND WALT DISNEY WORLD

- **ARNOLD PALMER'S BAY HILL CLUB & LODGE** ★★★★ ☎ 407-876-2429, **bayhill.com**

- **CHAMPIONSGATE INTERNATIONAL COURSE** ★★★★ ☎ 407-787-4653, **championsgategolf.com**

- **CHAMPIONSGATE NATIONAL COURSE** ★★★½ ☎ 407-787-4653, **championsgategolf.com**

- **CROOKED CAT** ★★★★ ☎ 407-656-2626, **ocngolf.com**

- **FALCON'S FIRE GOLF CLUB** ★★★★ ☎ 407-239-5445, **falconsfire.com**

- **GRAND CYPRESS GOLF CLUB** ★★★★½ ☎ 407-239-4700, **grandcypress.com**

- **PANTHER LAKE GOLF COURSE** ★★★★½ ☎ 407-656-2626, **ocngolf.com**

- **REUNION RESORT: NICKLAUS, PALMER, AND WATSON COURSES** ★★★★ ☎ 407-396-3199, **reunionresort.com/golf/courses**

- **TRANQUILO GOLF CLUB AT FOUR SEASONS RESORT ORLANDO** (Too new to rate) ☎ 800-267-3046, **tinyurl.com/tranquilogolfclub**

MINIATURE GOLF

FUN FOR THE WHOLE FAMILY ABOUNDS at **Fantasia Gardens Miniature Golf,** across the street from the Walt Disney World Swan, and **Winter Summerland,** right next to Blizzard Beach. Fantasia Gardens is a beautifully landscaped course with fountains, animated statues, topiaries, and flower beds. Winter Summerland offers two 18-hole courses—one has a "blizzard in Florida" theme, while the other sports a tropical-holiday theme, with Christmas ornaments hanging from palm trees.

Fantasia Gardens is quite demanding and not nearly as whimsical as Winter Summerland. Adults and older teens will enjoy the challenge of Fantasia Gardens, but if your group includes children younger than 12, head to Winter Summerland. Another Winter Summerland plus is that it can be reached easily via Disney transportation. To access Fantasia Gardens you must take a bus to the Swan and walk to the course from there. Admission to both courses is $14 for adults and $12 for children ages 3–9, tax included. Opening hours are 10 a.m.–11 p.m. For more information call ☎ 407-WDW-PLAY (939-7529).

Our favorite minigolf in Orlando is **Hollywood Drive-In Golf,** in Universal CityWalk (☎ 407-802-4848; **hollywooddriveingolf.com**). One hole has the Creature from the Black Lagoon spitting water over the walkway you need to pass through; another hole has a huge alien ship that you need to walk through and for which you need to press a button so that a door opens, *Star Trek*–style, to let you out. It's a nonstop barrage of clever in-jokes, insanely well-designed holes, and unique lighting elements. There's also an iPhone app for keeping score and misting fans for keeping cool. Open daily, 9 a.m.–2 a.m.; cost (including tax) is $16 for adults, $14 for children ages 3–9.

THEME PARK TRIVIA QUIZ ANSWERS

MAGIC KINGDOM

1. (C) **2.** (D) **3.** (B) **4.** (C) **5.** (A) **6.** (C) **7.** (A) **8.** (C) **9.** (B) **10.** (C)

EPCOT

1. (D) **2.** (B) **3.** (C) **4.** (A) **5.** (B) **6.** (C) **7.** (C) **8.** (B) **9.** (B) **10.** (D)

DISNEY'S ANIMAL KINGDOM

1. (B) **2.** (C) **3.** (D) **4.** (C) **5.** (B) **6.** (A) **7.** (C) **8.** (C) **9.** (B) **10.** (D)

DISNEY'S HOLLYWOOD STUDIOS

1. (D) **2.** (B) **3.** (D) **4.** (A) **5.** (D) **6.** (A) **7.** (B) **8.** (C) **9.** (D) **10.** (A)

INDEX

Aashirwad Indian Cuisine, 137
ABC Commissary, 155, 165, 344–45, 358
accommodations, 78–133
  Animal Kingdom, 13, 100–101
  babysitting in, 91
  Bonnet Creek, 98–100, 104–5
  child-care options, 91
  childproofing, 133
  commuting time to/from, 81–84
  condominiums, 130–32
  convenience of, 83–84
  costs, 79–81, 129–30
  dining in, 84
  discounts/good deals, 105–7
  Disney Springs, 98–100, 104–5
  ease of access, 86
  Epcot, 12, 96–98
  Extra Magic Hours with. *See* Extra Magic Hours
  good deals, 106, 129–30
  Good Neighbor hotels, 113
  group size and, 84–85
  guaranteed admission with, 91
  holiday decorations in, 54
  information chart, 108–10
  International Drive, 113–14, 116–21
  internet sites, 129–30
  Lake Buena Vista and I-4 corridor, 114–15, 121–27
  locations, 79–81
  Magical Express service, 89–90
  Magic Kingdom, 12, 92–96
  parking with, 91
  reservations for, 129–30
  selection, 79–86
  swimming areas, 89
  themes, 87–89
  transportation options, 79–81
  travel agent help with, 110–11
  travel packages, 111–12
  Universal Orlando, 114, 361
  US 192 (Irlo Bronson Memorial Hwy.), 115, 127–29
  vacation homes, 130–32
  in Walt Disney World, 87–112
  outside Walt Disney World, 81–84, 113–32
Ace Plus Chinese Buffet, 135
acting out, 34–35
admission, 59–71
  Aquatica by SeaWorld, 427
  discounts for, 37
  Discovery Cove, 418–19
  DisneyQuest, 434
  Disney's Hollywood Studios, 365
  guaranteed, 91
  SeaWorld, 417
  Universal Orlando, 365
  water parks, 421
  Wet 'n Wild, 426
Advance Reservations, for dining, 141–44, 254–55
Adventureland (Magic Kingdom)
  attractions, 264–65, 270–72
    Enchanted Tiki Room, 264–65, 272
    Jungle Cruise, 264–65, 270
    Magic Carpets of Aladdin, 270–71
    Pirates of the Caribbean, 271–72

    Swiss Family Treehouse, 264–65, 272
  dining, 291
  FastPass+, 266–67
Adventurers Outpost (Animal Kingdom), 325
Affection Station (Animal Kingdom), 190, 326–27, 333
Africa (Animal Kingdom), 190, 326–29, 331–34
age considerations, 21–24
  4–6, 24
  ideal age, 24
  infants, 21–24, 133, 214
  teenagers, 24–26
  toddlers, 21–24, 133, 214
Agent P's World Showcase Adventure (Epcot), 300–301, 311–12
agriculture exhibit (Epcot), 300–301, 308–10
airports, transportation to/from, 89–90
Akershus Royal Banquet Hall, 142, 170, 252, 255, 300–301
Aladdin, Magic Carpets of (Magic Kingdom), 270–71
All About Kids, 72
All Star Vacation Homes, 131–32
allears.net, 41
All-Star Resorts, 80–81, 85, 88, 90, 101–2, 108
Aloha Isle, 157, 264–65
Amazing Adventures of Spider-Man, The (IOA), 372–73, 375–76
AMC Downtown Disney movie theater, 14, 433
America Adventure Rotunda, 53
America Gardens Theatre (Epcot), 52, 315
American Adventure, The (Epcot), 300–301, 315
American Gymkhana (restaurant), 136
American Music Machine, 318
Amura (restaurant), 136
Andiamo (restaurant), 124
animal(s). *See also* Animal Kingdom
  Animal Actors on Location (USF), 394–97
  SeaWorld, 417–20
Animal Kingdom, 324–41
  accommodations, 13, 100–101
  attractions, 326–38
    Affection Section, 190, 326–27, 333
    Boneyard, The, 326–27, 336–37
    Conservation Station, 190, 326–27, 333
    Dinosaur, 190, 325–28, 337
    Discovery Island, 190, 326–27, 329–31, 339
    Expedition Everest, 190, 325–28, 334
    Festival of the Lion King, 190, 326–28, 331
    Finding Nemo: The Musical, 326–28, 337–38
    Flights of Wonder, 190, 326–28, 334–35
    fright potential, 190
    Habitat Habit!, 333
    Harambe Village, 331
    height requirements, 242
    It's Tough to Be a Bug!, 190, 326–30
    Kali River Rapids, 190, 326–28, 335
    Kilimanjaro Safaris, 190, 326–28, 331–32
    Maharajah Jungle Trek, 190, 326–28, 335
    Pandora: The Land of Avatar, 325
    Pangani Forest Exploration Trail, 326–28, 332
    Primeval Whirl, 190, 326–28, 337
    Rafiki's Planet Watch, 332
    Theater in the Wild, 326–28, 337–38
    Tree of Life, The, 190, 326–30
    TriceraTop Spin, 190, 326–28, 338
    Wilderness Explorers, 326–27
    Wildlife Express Train, 190, 326–28, 333–34

Winged Encounters—The Kingdom Takes Flight, 338
Christmas celebration, 54
dining, 155, 164–65, 168, 252, 326–27, 339
FastPass+, 325, 328
first aid, 324, 329
Island Mercantile, 329
live entertainment, 338–40
lost persons, 258–60
map, 326–27
opening procedures and operating hours, 222, 228
overview, 13, 324–25
parades, 54
touring plans, 340–41
tours of, 76
Animal Kingdom Lodge and Villas, 54, 72, 73, 79–81, 85, 88, 90–91, 100–101, 109
Animation Courtyard (DHS), 191
Anna, Princess. *See Frozen* characters and events
Annual Passes, 63–64, 364
Anthony's Coal-Fired Pizza, 136
apps, 41
aquariums, The Seas with Nemo and Friends Pavilion (Epcot), 300–301, 310–11
Aquatica by SeaWorld, 427–29
archery experience, 75
Ariel's Grotto (Magic Kingdom), 264–65, 277–78
L'Artisan des Glaces (restaurant), 160, 300–301, 316
Artist Point (restaurant), 51, 144, 170
Artist's Palette (restaurant), 170
Art of Animation Resort, 80–81, 85, 88–90, 102–3, 108
Asia (Animal Kingdom), 190, 326–27, 334–36, 339
Astro Orbiter (Magic Kingdom), 264–65, 286
Atlanta Braves, 48
ATMs. *See* banking services
attractions. *See also specific locations*
dark, 194
Fastpass for. *See* FastPass+
height requirements, 241–42
intensity, 194
last-minute cold feet, 245
loud, 195
protection from water, 213
switching off, 243, 245, 369, 370
tactile, 195
types, 222–23
visual impact, 194
autographs, 227
Avatar land (Animal Kingdom), 13, 325
aviary (Discovery Cove), 419

B Resort, 81, 104–5, 121–22
Baby Care Centers, 23
Animal Kingdom, 324
Disney's Hollywood Studios, 343
Epcot, 298
Magic Kingdom, 262
supplies at, 214
Universal Studios Florida, 396
babysitting, 16, 71–73, 91
Backlot Express (restaurant), 155, 165–66, 344–45, 358
Bahama Breeze, 125
Ball, Lucille, tribute to (USF), 394–95, 402
banking services
Animal Kingdom, 324

Disney Springs, 429
Epcot, 299
Islands of Adventure, 374
Magic Kingdom, 262
Barney show (USF), 394–95, 397–98
Barnstormer (Magic Kingdom), 264–65, 278
base tickets, 60–64
baseball team, 48
Bay Lake Tower, 79, 85, 90, 92, 108, 291
Be Our Guest Restaurant, 141–44, 152–53, 157, 168, 264–65
Beach Club Resort and Villas, 54, 71–72, 79, 80–81, 85, 88, 97–98
Beaches & Cream (restaurant), 154
bears, *Country Bear Jamboree* (Magic Kingdom), 264–65, 273
Beauty and the Beast—Live on Stage (DHS), 344–47
Beetlejuice Graveyard Revue (USF), 394–95, 397
behavior, 30–35
Behind the Seeds Tour, 73
Belle, Enchanted Tales with (Magic Kingdom), 264–65, 279
Benihana (restaurant), 124
beourguestpodcast.blogspot.com, 42
Best Friends Pet Resort, 262, 299
Best Western LBV Resort, 104–5
Bibbidi Bobbidi Boutique (Disney Springs), 77, 432
Bice Orlando Ristorante, 136
Biergarten, 153, 167–68, 300–301, 318
Big Thunder Mountain Railroad (Magic Kingdom), 265–67, 273
Bio Brazil Churrascaria, 137
birds
Explorer's Aviary (Discovery Cove), 419
Flights of Wonder (Animal Kingdom), 190, 326–28, 334–35
Walt Disney's Enchanted Tiki Room (Magic Kingdom), 264–65, 272
Winged Encounters—The Kingdom Takes Flight (Animal Kingdom), 338
birthdays, 76–77
blisters, 198–200
Blizzard Beach, 13, 61–63, 242, 421–26
Blondie's (restaurant), 392
Blue Man Group (USF), 370
Blues Brothers, The (USF), 394–95, 397
bluezoo (restaurant), 145
B'net al Houwariyate, 316
Boardwalk, Disney's, 14
BoardWalk Inn and Villas, 79–81, 85, 88, 90, 96, 109
boat rides
Gran Fiesta Tour Starring the Three Caballeros (Epcot), 190, 300–301, 312
IllumiNations (Epcot), 53, 190, 299–301, 319–21
It's a Small World (Magic Kingdom), 264–65, 280
Jungle Cruise (Magic Kingdom), 264–65, 270
Jurassic Park River Adventure (IOA), 372–73, 379–80
Kali River Rapids (Animal Kingdom), 190, 326–28, 335
Liberty Belle Riverboat (Magic Kingdom), 264–65, 276
Living with the Land (Epcot), 299, 300–301, 309
Pirates of the Caribbean (Magic Kingdom), 264–65, 271–72

Popeye & Bluto's Bilge-Rat Barges (IOA), 372–73, 378

Splash Mountain (Magic Kingdom), 264–65, 274

to Tom Sawyer Island (Magic Kingdom), 264–65, 274–75

Boathouse, The (restaurant), 169

Boma (restaurant), 76

Bonefish Grill (restaurant), 137

Boneyard, The (Animal Kingdom), 326–27, 336–37

Bongos Cuban Cafe, 14, 169, 433

Bonnet Creek, accommodations, 98–100, 104–5

Boo to You Parade, 50

Boston Lobster Feast, 138

bottlenecks, avoiding, 222–23

breakfast, 138–39, 149–52, 250–54

breast-feeding, 23–24, 215–16

British Revolution Band, The (Epcot), 317

Bubbalou's Bodacious Bar-B-Que, 136

Buena Vista Palace Hotel & Spa, 81, 104–5, 122

buffets, 135, 137–39, 146

Bull & Bear (restaurant), 137

Bumblebees Man's Taco Truck, 416

Burudika Band, 340

Butterbeer, 382, 409

Buzz Lightyear's Space Ranger Spin (Magic Kingdom), 264–65, 286

Cabana Bay Beach Resort, 120–21, 361, 366

Cafe La Bamba, 368

Café Mineiro, 137

California Grill, 144, 169, 170

Camp Jurassic (IOA), 372–73, 379

campfire, Fort Wilderness Resort, 255

camping, 92–93

Canada Pavilion (Epcot), 190, 300–301, 317–18

Canadian LumberJacks, 317

Candlelight Processional (Epcot), 52–53, 319

La Cantina de San Angel, 160, 169, 300–301, 319

Capa (restaurant), 123

Cape May Cafe, 253

caps, as sun protection, 208

Captain EO (Epcot), 300–301, 307–8

Captain Jack Sparrow's Pirate Tutorial (Magic Kingdom), 264–65, 270

Captain Pete's Island Eats, 418

Caribbean Beach Resort, 74, 80–81, 85, 88, 90, 96–97, 108

Carkitt Market (USF), 410

Caro-Seuss-el (IOA), 372–73, 390

carousel(s)

Caro-Seuss-el (IOA), 372–73, 390

Prince Charming's Regal Carrousel (Magic Kingdom), 264–65, 283

Carousel of Progress (Magic Kingdom), 264–65, 289–90

cars

Test Track (Epcot), 189, 299–301, 305

Tomorrowland Speedway (Magic Kingdom), 245, 264–65, 289

Casey Jr. Splash N Soak (Magic Kingdom), 264–65, 278

Casey's Corner (restaurant), 158, 264–65

Castaway Cay, 15, 17

castles

Akershus, 312–13

Beast's, 279

Cinderella, 264–66, 291

Hogwarts, 383

Cat in the Hat, The (IOA), 372–73, 390–91

Catalina Eddie's (restaurant), 166, 344–45

Celebrate the Magic (Magic Kingdom), 291–92

Celebration Toon Tavern, 137

Celestina Warbel and the Banshees, 410

Le Cellier Steakhouse, 142, 169, 300–301

cell phones, charging stations for, 212

Centra Care, 43

Central Plaza (Magic Kingdom), 264–65

Character Spot (Epcot), 300–303

characters

Disney. *See* Disney characters

Universal Orlando, 368

Characters in Flight (Disney Springs), 432

charging stations, for electronic equipment, 212

Chef Mickey's, 252

Les Chefs de France, 167, 169–70, 300–301

Chevy's Fresh Mex, 136

child-care centers, 71–73, 91

childproofing rooms, 133

China Pavilion, 53, 190, 300–301, 313–14

Chinese buffets, 135

Chinese Fireball (IOA), 372–73, 385

Chinese New Year, 48

Christmas celebration, 51–55, 76, 292

Churrascarias, 137–38

Cinderella Castle, 141–44, 264–66, 291

Cinderella's Royal Table, 141–44, 152–53, 168, 252, 254–55, 264–65

Cinematic Spectacular—100 Years of Memories (USF), 368, 394–95, 415–16

Circle of Life, The (Epcot), 300–301, 308–9

Circus McGurkus Cafe Stoo-pendous, 392

Cirque du Soleil (Disney Springs), 14, 55, 432

Citricos, 51, 144

City Hall (Magic Kingdom), 264–65

CityWalk (Universal Orlando), 361–64, 370, 392

Christmas celebration, 55

Halloween events at, 51

Clarion Suites Maingate, 127

Classic Monsters Cafe, 416

clothing, 144–45, 203, 206

Club Cool (Epcot), 300–301, 304

Coca Cola freestyle souvenir cup, 368

CoCo Key Hotel and Water Resort—Orlando, 116

Columbia (restaurant), 136

Columbia Harbour House, 153, 158, 264–65, 291

comedy, *Monsters, Inc. Laugh Floor* (Magic Kingdom), 264–65, 287

Comic Strip Lane, 372–73, 390–91

communication, devices for, 210, 212–13

condominiums, 130–32

Conservation Station (Animal Kingdom), 190, 326–27, 333

Contemporary Resort, 80, 85, 88–90, 92, 108

convention schedule, 47

coolers, 209–10

Coolest Summer Dance Party (DHS), 356

Le Coq au Vin (restaurant), 136

Coral Reef (Discovery Cove), 419

Coral Reef Restaurant, 153, 167–68, 300–301, 319

Coronado Springs Resort, 80–81, 85, 88, 90, 103, 108

Cosmic Ray's Starlight Cafe, 158, 264–65, 291

costs
    accommodations, 79–81, 129–30
    admission, 59–71
    Aquatica by SeaWorld, 428
    condominiums, 130–32
    dining, 139–41
        character meals, 254
        counter-service, 150–51
        by cuisine, 178–83
        discounts in, 134–35, 151–152
    Discovery Cove, 418–19
    DisneyQuest, 433
    Disney's Hollywood Studios, 364
    price increases, 65
    typical day at WDW, 67–68
    Universal Studios Florida, 364, 365
    vacation home rental, 130–32
    water parks, 421
counter service, 157–67
    author's favorite, 152–53, 155
Country Bear Jamboree (Magic Kingdom), 264–65,
    273
coupons, for meal discounts, 139
Covington Mills Restaurant, 124
Creature Comforts (restaurant), 164, 326–27
credit cards, 106
Crêpes des Chefs de France, 168, 300–301, 319
Croissant Moon Bakery, 392
crowds
    avoiding, 222–23
    Crowd Calendar, 36
    day of week, 55
    Extra Magic Hours. See Extra Magic Hours
    holiday, 47–55
    lost children in, 260
    seasonal, 44–47
    Universal Orlando vs. Walt Disney World, 365
    water parks, 421
    Wizarding World of Harry Potter, 383–84
cruise line, 14–18, 38
Crystal Palace, The, 152–53, 168, 252, 264–65
Curious George Goes To Town (USF), 394–95, 407

daily itinerary, planning, 224, 226
Darkroom, The (DHS), 343
David's Disney Vacation Club Points, 107, 110
Day in the Park with Barney, A (USF), 394–95, 397–98
day of week, for visit, 55
day packs, 208
DDRA (Downtown Disney Resort Area), 79, 98–100,
    104–5
dehydration, 209
Dervish and Banges (IOA), 382
Despicable Me Minion Mayhem (USF), 394–95, 398
DHS. See Disney's Hollywood Studios
diapers, 214
dining, 134–83
    in accommodations, 84
    advance reservations for, 141–44, 254–55
    with an animal specialist, 73
    Animal Kingdom, 155, 164–65, 168, 326–27, 339
    Blizzard Beach, 424
    breakfast, 138–39, 149–52, 250–54
    buffets, 135, 137–39, 146
    choices, 148
    costs, 134–35, 139–41, 150–52, 178–83

counter service, 146, 157–67
cruise ships, 15–16
by cuisine, 178–83
Diagon Alley, 382
dinner shows, 176–78
discounts for, 134–35, 139
with Disney characters, 148, 176, 249–55
Disney Springs, 168–69, 433, 434
Disney's Hollywood Studios, 155, 165–66, 368
dress recommendations, 144–45
Epcot, 153, 160–64, 167–70
ethnic foods, 137–40, 178–83
family-style, 146
fast casual, 146
fast food, 148–52
food allergies, 145
food courts, 146
full-service restaurants, 146, 167–71
healthful, 149
Islands of Adventure, 392
Magic Kingdom, 147, 152–53, 157–60, 168, 291
Magic Your Way plan, 171–76
money-saving, 139, 151–52, 210
quality, 140, 156
ratings and rankings, 178–83
readers' comments, 156–57
reservations, 40–41
restaurant categories in, 145–47
romantic, 195–96
SeaWorld, 418
smoking in, 145
snacks, 150–52, 154
special diets, 145
Thanksgiving, 51
time saving in, 149–50
touring plans and, 148
Typhoon Lagoon, 424
Universal Studios Florida, 368, 416
vendor food, 147
outside Walt Disney World, 135–40
water parks, 424
Wizarding World of Harry Potter, 409–10
dinner shows, 143, 176–78
DinoLand Dance-a-Palooza, 340
DinoLand U.S.A. (Animal Kingdom), 190, 326–27,
    336–38
Dinosaur (Animal Kingdom), 190, 326–27, 337
disabled visitors
    guidebook for, 38
    Universal Studios Florida, 393
Disaster! (USF), 394–95, 398–99
discipline, 30–35
discounts
    accommodations, 105–7
    for admission, 37
    dining, 134–35, 139
    on websites, 41
Discovery Center, Jurassic Park (IOA), 372–73, 379
Discovery Cove (SeaWorld), 418–19
Discovery Island (Animal Kingdom), 190, 326–27,
    329–31, 339
discussion boards, 42
Disney Character Warehouse, 69
Disney characters, 245–55
    autographs, 227
    costumes, 196–97

dining with, 148, 176, 249–55
Disney's Hollywood Studios, 356
face, 196
friends of, 254
greeting, 265, *See also* meet and greets; *individual characters by name*
headpiece, 196–97
lost children and, 249, 260
meeting, 196–97
Princess Fairytale Hall, 263–65, 283–84
types, 196–97
watching, 245–58
Disney Cruise Line, 14–18
Disney Junior—Live on Stage! (DHS), 191, 344–45, 347–48
Disney Marketplace, 430–32
Disney Parks Christmas Day Parade, 51
Disney Perfectly Princess Party, 75
Disney Rewards Visa Cards, 106
Disney Signature restaurants, 172
Disney Springs, 13–14, 429–35
accommodations, 98–100, 104–5
Christmas celebration, 54–55
dining, 168–69
holiday decorations, 55
Disney Vacation Club Points, 107, 110
Disney, Walt, tribute to, *One Man's Dream* (DHS), 191, 344–45, 355
Disney Wilderness Preserve, 434, 436
DisneyQuest, 14, 242, 433–34
Disney's Boardwalk, 14
Disney's Holiday D-Lights, 76
Disney's Hollywood Studios, 342–60
attractions, 344–55
Animation Courtyard, 191
Beauty and the Beast—Live on Stage, 344–47
Disney Junior—Live on Stage!, 191, 344–45, 347–48
Fantasmic!, 143–44, 191, 344–45, 356–58
For the First Time in Forever: A Frozen Sing-Along Celebration, 344–45, 349
fright potential, 191
Great Movie Ride, The, 191, 344–45, 348–49
height requirements, 242
Honey, I Shrunk the Kids Movie Set Adventure, 344–45, 349–50
Indiana Jones Epic Stunt Spectacular, 191, 344–45, 350
Jedi Training Academy, 344–45, 350–51
Jim Henson's Muppet-Vision 3-D, 191, 344–45, 351
Lights! Motors! Action! Extreme Stunt Show, 191, 344–45, 351
One Man's Dream, 191, 344–45, 355
Rock 'n' Roller Coaster, 191, 344–45, 352
Star Tours: The Adventure Continues, 191, 344–45, 352–53
Streets of America, 353
touring plans, 359–60
Toy Story Midway Mania!, 191, 344–46, 353–54
Twilight Zone Tower of Terror, The, 191, 344–46, 354–55
Voyage of the Little Mermaid, 191, 344–45, 355
Christmas celebration, 53–54
dining, 147, 155, 165–66, 253, 358
Disney characters in, 356

exit strategies, 358
Extra Magic Hours, 231–32
FastPass+, 343, 346–47
Halloween parade, 50
live entertainment, 355–58
lost persons, 258–60
map, 344–45
opening procedures and operating hours, 222, 228
overview, 13, 342–43
services, 342–43
touring plans, 359–60
vs. Universal Studios Florida, 393, 396
Disney's West Side, 430–34
Disney's Yuletide Fantasy tour, 76
Disney speak, 18
DisneyWorld.com, 39–40, 106
diversions, 223
DiVine (Animal Kingdom), 339
DJ Anaan, 340
Doge's Palace, 314
Dole Whip, 154, 339
dolphin(s)
Aquatica by SeaWorld, 427–29
SeaWorld, 418–19
Dolphin Resort, 71–72, 80–81, 85, 88–90, 97, 109
DoubleTree by Hilton Orlando at SeaWorld, 116–17
DoubleTree Guest Suites, 81, 104–5
Downtown Disney. *See* Disney Springs
Dragon Challenge (IOA), 372–73, 385
Dragon Court Chinese Buffet & Sushi Bar, 135
Dr. Doom's Fearfall (IOA), 372–73, 376–77
Dream Along with Mickey (Magic Kingdom), 291
Dream Girls, Disney's, 43
dress recommendations, 144–45, 203, 206
drugs, 209
Dudley Do-Right's Ripsaw Falls (IOA), 372–73, 377
Dumbo the Flying Elephant (Magic Kingdom), 264–65, 278–79
D-Zone, 212

Earl of Sandwich, 435
Easter Parade, 48–49
eating. *See* dining
Echo Lake (DHS), 191
ECV/ESV rental
Animal Kingdom, 324
Epcot, 298
Magic Kingdom, 262
educational programs, 73–77
Eighth Voyage of Sindbad, The (IOA), 372–73, 389
El Patron (restaurant), 136
electric conveyance or standing vehicle rental. *See* ECV/ESV rental
Electric Umbrella Restaurant, 160–61, 300–301
electronic devices, 210, 212–13
elephant ride, 264–65, 278–79
elephants, Dumbo the Flying Elephant (Magic Kingdom), 266–67
Ellen's Energy Adventure (Epcot), 189, 300–301, 306
Elsa, Queen. *See* Frozen characters and events
Empress Package (Magic Kingdom), 74
Enchanted Tales with Belle (Magic Kingdom), 264–65, 274
Enchanted Tiki Room (Magic Kingdom), 264–65, 272
energy presentation, Epcot, 189, 300–301, 306

Epcot, 298–323. *See also* Future World; World Showcase
- accommodations, 12, 96–98
- attractions
  - fright potential, 189–90
  - Future World, 300–311
  - height requirements, 241–42
  - World Showcase, 171–76, 300–301, 311–21
- Christmas celebration, 52–53
- dining, 147, 153, 160–64, 167–70, 255
- ECV/ESV rental, 298
- exit strategies, 320–21
- Extra Magic Hours, 231–32
- FastPass+, 298, 302
- first aid, 298
- Guest Relations, 300
- Kidcot Fun Stops, 302
- live entertainment, 318–20
- lost persons, 258–60
- Main Entrance, 300
- map, 300–301
- Monorail Station, 300
- New Year's celebration, 55
- opening procedures and operating hours, 222, 228, 300
- overview, 12, 298–99
- rentals, 298–99
- services, 298–99
- Showcase Plaza, 321
- touring plans, 321–22
- World Showcase attractions, 311–18, 311–21

Epcot International Flower & Garden Festival, 48
Epcot International Food & Wine Festival, 49–50
Escape to Walt's Wilderness, 76
ESPN Wide World of Sports Complex, 14, 435–36
E.T. Adventure (USF), 394–95, 399
ethnic foods, 137–40, 178–83
evening parade (Magic Kingdom), 292
expectant mothers, tips for, 214–15
expedia.com, 106
Expedition Everest (Animal Kingdom), 190, 326–28, 334
Exposition Park (food trucks), 433
expresswayauthority.com, 42
Extra Magic Hours (EMHs), 56–59, 87
- Epcot, 298
- opening hours and, 222
- touring plans with, 231–32
- water parks, 421

Fairfax Fare, 166, 344–45
Fairy Godmothers, 72
Fairytale Hall (Magic Kingdom), 283–84
Fairy Tale Weddings, Disney's, 17
family magic tour, 73
Fantasia Gardens Miniature Golf, 436
Fantasmic! (DHS), 143–44, 191, 344–45, 356–58
Fantasy Fare, 433
Fantasyland (Magic Kingdom)
- attractions, 277–85
  - Ariel's Grotto, 264–65, 277–78
  - Barnstormer, 264–65, 278
  - Beast's Castle, 279
  - Casey Jr. Splash N Soak, 264–65, 278
  - Dumbo the Flying Elephant, 264–65, 278–79
  - *Enchanted Tales with Belle*, 264–65, 279
  - It's a Small World, 264–65, 280
  - Mad Tea Party, 264–65, 280
  - Many Adventures of Winnie the Pooh, The, 264–65, 280–82
  - Meet Merida at Fairytale Garden, 264–65, 281
  - *Mickey's PhilharMagic*, 264–65, 281–82
  - Peter Pan's Flight, 264–65, 282
  - Pete's Silly Sideshow, 264–65, 282–83
  - Prince Charming's Regal Carrousel, 264–65, 283
  - Princess Fairytale Hall, 263–65, 283–84
  - Seven Dwarfs Mine Train, 263, 264–65, 284–85
  - Under the Sea: Journey of the Little Mermaid, 264–65, 285
- dining, 291
- FastPass+, 266–67

fast food, 148–52
Fast Food Boulevard (USF), 416
FastPass+, 39–40, 232–41
- Animal Kingdom, 325, 328
- Disney's Hollywood Studios, 343, 346–47
- Epcot, 298, 302
- guidelines, 233–36
- information, 37
- limits, 237
- Magic Kingdom, 266–67
- obtaining, 234–36
- reservations in advance, 233–36
- reservations on arrival, 236–37
- returning to ride, 236–37
- rules, 237–38
- switching off with, 243, 245
- tiers, 235–38
- touring plans and, 238–40
- vs. Universal Express, 365–67
- waiting time with, 238
- World Showcase, 299, 302

Fear Factor Live (USF), 394–95, 400
ferry dock, 264–65
Festival of Fantasy (Magic Kingdom), 290
Festival of the Lion King (Animal Kingdom), 190, 326–28, 331
Fievel's Playland (USF), 394–95, 400
Fife & Drum Corps, Spirit of America (Epcot), 315
Fife & Drum Tavern, 161, 300–301
50's Prime Time Cafe, 51, 155, 168, 344–45
Figment, Journey into Imagination with (Epcot), 300–301, 308
Filch's Emporium of Confiscated Goods (IOA), 383
films
- at AMC Downtown Disney movie theater, 14, 433
- *Captain EO* (Epcot), 300–301, 307–8
- *Cinematic Spectacular—100 Years of Memories*, 368, 394–95, 415–16
- *Circle of Life, The* (Epcot), 300–301, 308–9
- *Impressions de France* (Epcot), 190, 300–301, 316–17
- *It's Tough to Be a Bug!* (Animal Kingdom), 190, 326–30
- *Jim Henson's Muppet-Vision 3-D* (DHS), 191, 344–45, 351
- *Mickey's PhilharMagic* (Magic Kingdom), 264–65, 281–82
- *O Canada* (Epcot), 190, 300–301, 317–18
- *One Man's Dream* (DHS), 191, 344–45, 355
- *Reflections of China* (Epcot), 190, 300–301, 313–14
- *Shrek 4-D* (USF), 394–95, 403–4

Terminator 2: 3-D (USF), 394–95, 405
Turtle Talk with Crush (Epcot), 189, 300–301, 311
Finding Nemo: The Musical (Animal Kingdom), 326–28, 337–38
Finnegan's Bar and Grill, 368
Fire Eater's Grill, 392
fireworks
    Christmas celebration, 55
    Cinematic Spectacular—100 Years of Memories (USF), 368, 394–95, 415–16
    Fantasmic! (DHS), 143–44, 191, 344–45, 356–58
    Frozen, 356
    IllumiNations (Epcot), 53, 190, 299–301, 319–21
    Magic Kingdom, 293
    New Year's celebration, 55
    Wishes fireworks show and cruise (Magic Kingdom), 293
first aid, Epcot, 298–99
First Mate Package, 74
flag retreat, 292
Flame Tree Barbecue, 155, 164, 326–27, 339
Flamingo Crossings, 115–16
Flex Ticket Plus (Universal Orlando), 365
Flight of the Hippogriff (IOA), 372–73, 385–86
flight simulation rides
    Mission: SPACE (Epcot), 300–301, 305
    Soarin' (Epcot), 189, 299–301, 309–10
    Star Tours: The Adventure Continues (DHS), 191, 344–45, 352–53
Flights of Wonder (Animal Kingdom), 190, 326–28, 334–35
Florean Fortescue's Ice-Cream Parlour, 409
Florida Guide, 38, 129
Florida-resident passes, 64
Flower & Garden Festival (Epcot), 48
flume rides
    Dudley Do-Right's Ripsaw Falls (IOA), 372–73, 377
    Jurassic Park River Adventure (IOA), 372–73, 379–80
    Splash Mountain (Magic Kingdom), 264–65, 274
Flying Fish Cafe, 144, 170
Fogo de Chão (restaurant), 138
foot care and footwear, 198–200
Forbidden Journey, Harry Potter and the (IOA), 372–73, 379–80, 386–88
Forest Exploration Trail, Pangani (Animal Kingdom), 326–27, 332
Fort Langhorn (Magic Kingdom), 264–65, 274–75
Fort Wilderness Resort & Campground, 50–51, 75–76, 79, 80, 85, 90, 92–93, 109, 177, 255, 435
fountain(s), Epcot, 305
Fountain View (restaurant), 161, 300–301
4 Rivers Smokehouse, 136
Four Seasons Resort Orlando at Walt Disney World Resort, 122–23
Fourth of July celebration, 49
France Pavilion (Epcot), 53, 190, 300–301, 316–17
French Quarter, Port Orleans Resort, 99, 109
Freshwater Oasis (SeaWorld), 419
Friar's Nook (restaurant), 158, 264–65, 291
friends, inviting, 26–27
Frog Choir, 389
Frontierland (Magic Kingdom)
    attractions, 264–65, 272–75
    Big Thunder Mountain Railroad, 263–67, 273
    Country Bear Jamboree, 264–65, 273

    Frontierland Shootin' Arcade, 264–65, 274
    Splash Mountain, 264–65, 274
    Tom Sawyer Island, 264–65, 274–75
    dining, 291
    FastPass+, 266–67
Frontierland Shootin' Arcade (Magic Kingdom), 264–65, 274
Frozen characters and events, 300–301
    Coolest Summer Dance Party, 356
    For the First Time in Forever: A Frozen Sing-Along Celebration, 344–45, 349
    Frozen Ever After, 312–13
    Frozen Fireworks, 356
    A Frozen Holiday Wish, 292
    Frozen Royal Welcome, 356
    Frozen Summer of Fun (DHS), 356
    Olaf's Summer Cool Down, 356
    at Princess Fairytale Hall, 283–84
    Royal Sommerhus Meet and Greet, 313
full-service restaurants, 167–71
Future World
    attractions, 300–311
        Captain EO, 300–301, 307–8
        Circle of Life, The, 300–301, 308–9
        Club Cool, 300–301, 304
        FastPass+, 299, 302
        fright potential, 189
        Imagination Pavilion, 300–301, 307–8
        Innoventions, 300–301, 303–4, 318
        Journey into Imagination with Figment, 300–301, 308
        Living with the Land, 299, 300–301, 309
        Mission: SPACE, 300–301, 305
        "Mom, I Can't Believe It's Disney" Fountain, 305
        Odyssey Center, 300
        Seas with Nemo and Friends Pavilion, The, 300–301, 310–11, 319, 321
        Soarin', 189, 299–301, 309–10
        Spaceship Earth, 189, 300–301, 305–6
        Sum of All Thrills, 300–301, 304–5
        Test Track, 189, 299–301, 305
        Turtle Talk with Crush, 189, 311
        Universe of Energy: *Ellen's Energy Adventure,* 189, 300–301, 306
    dining, 153
    Epcot Character Spot, 300–303
    live entertainment, 318
    overview of, 12

games
    Agent P's World Showcase Adventure (Epcot), 300–301, 311–12
    DisneyQuest, 433–34
    A Pirate's Adventure: Treasures of the Seven Seas (Magic Kingdom), 264–65, 271
    Sorcerers of the Magic Kingdom, 264–65, 268–69
garden festival, 48
Garden Grill Restaurant, The, 252, 300–301
Garden Grove Cafe, 253
Gaston's Tavern, 158–59, 264–65
Gaylord Palms Hotel & Convention Center, 127–28
gays and lesbians, Gay Days, 49
Germany Pavilion (Epcot), 53, 190, 300–301, 314, 319, 321
Ghirardelli Soda Fountain and Chocolate Shop, 154, 435

Gi-Tar Dan, 340
Givenchy, 316
Golden Corral, 125, 138-39
Golden Oak Outpost (restaurant), 159, 264-65
golf, 436
goodwill ambassadors, 338-39
Gran Fiesta Tour Starring the Three Caballeros (Epcot), 190, 300-301, 312
Grand Floridian Resort & Spa/Grand Floridian Villas, 54, 74-75, 79, 80, 85, 88, 90, 93-94, 109
Grand Reef (SeaWorld), 419
grandparents, 28-29
Great Movie Ride, The (DHS), 191, 344-45, 348-49
Green Eggs and Ham Cafe, 392
greeting venues. See meet and greets; *individual characters by name*
Gringotts, Harry Potter and the Escape from (USF), 394-95, 409, 411-13
grocery stores, 152
Guest Relations/Services
    Animal Kingdom, 324
    Disney's Hollywood Studios, 342
    Epcot, 302
    Islands of Adventure, 374
    Magic Kingdom, 262
    Universal Studios Florida, 396
Guidebook for Guests with Disabilities, 38

Habitat Habit! (Animal Kingdom), 326-27, 333
La Hacienda de San Angel (restaurant), 153, 300-301, 320
Les Halles Boulangerie-Patisserie, 153-54, 161, 300-301, 316
Hall of Presidents, The (Magic Kingdom), 264-65, 275
Halloween Horror Nights (Universal Orlando), 51
Halloween Party, 50-51, 292
Hanukkah celebration, 53
Harambe Market, 164, 326-27
Harambe Village (Animal Kingdom), 331
Harambe Wildlife Reserve, 76
Hard Rock Café, 117
Hard Rock Hotel Orlando, 117, 361
Harmony Barber Shop, 77
Harry Potter and the Escape from Gringotts (USF), 394-95, 411-13
Harry Potter and the Forbidden Journey (IOA), 372-73, 386-88
hats, 208
Haunted Mansion, The (Magic Kingdom), 50, 264-65, 266, 276
headliners, 223
height requirements, 241-42
High in the Sky Seuss Trolley Train Ride, The (IOA), 372-73, 391
Hilton in the Walt Disney World Resort, 105
Hilton Orlando Lake Buena Vista, 81, 124
hip packs, 207
Hippogriff ride (IOA), 372-73, 386-87
Hog's Head pub (IOA), 382
Hogsmeade (IOA), 381-89
Hogwarts Castle (IOA), 383
Hogwarts Express (IOA), 372-73, 388-89, 408
Holiday D-Lights, Disney's, 76
Holiday Inn in the WDW Resort, 81
Holiday Inn Resort Lake Buena Vista, 124
Holiday Inn Walt Disney World Resort, 104-5

holidays from around the world, 53
Hollywood (USF), 394-95, 416
Hollywood & Vine, 155, 168, 253, 344-45, 358
Hollywood Boulevard (DHS), 191, 343
Hollywood Brown Derby, 155, 344-45, 358
Hollywood Drive-In Golf, 437
Hollywood Rip Ride Rockit (USF), 394-95, 400-401
Honeydukes (IOA), 382
Honey, I Shrunk the Kids Movie Set Adventure (DHS), 344-45, 349-50
Hoop-Dee-Doo Musical Review, 143, 177
Hopping Pot, The, 409
horror, make-up for, 394-95, 406-7
hotelcoupons.com, 38, 129
hotels. *See* accommodations
House of Blues, 14, 169, 433, 435
Hungarian Horntail (IOA), 372-73, 385
Hyatt Regency Grand Cypress, 124-25

I-4 corridor, accommodations, 121-27
If I Ran the Zoo (IOA), 372-73, 391
IllumiNations (Epcot), 53, 190, 299-301, 319-21
Il Mulino New York Trattoria, 145
Imagination Pavilion (Epcot), 300-301, 307-8
Impressions de France (Epcot), 190, 300-301, 316-17
Incredible Hulk Coaster, The (IOA), 372-73, 376
Independence Day, 49
Indian buffets, 137
Indiana Jones Epic Stunt Spectacular (DHS), 191, 344-45, 350
infants, 21-24. *See also* Baby Care Centers
    childproofing rooms for, 133
    strollers for. *See* strollers
    supplies for, 214
Information, 36-44
    accommodations, 129-30
    Animal Kingdom, 324
    Aquatica by SeaWorld, 428
    Disney's Hollywood Studios, 343
    Epcot, 299
    Magic Kingdom, 262
    planning DVDs and videos, 195
    podcasts, 42-43
    publications, 38
    SeaWorld, 417
    Universal Orlando, 365
    websites, 36-44
Innoventions (Epcot), 300-304, 319, 321
insider websites, 42
International Drive, accommodations, 113-14, 116-21
Irlo Bronson Memorial Hwy., accommodations, 115, 127-29
Island Mercantile (Animal Kingdom), 329
Islands Dining Room, 368
Islands of Adventure, 371-93
    admission, 364-65
    arrival, 364-65
    attractions, 372-73
        Amazing Adventures of Spider-Man, The, 372-73, 375-76
        Camp Jurassic, 372-73, 379
        Caro-Seuss-el, 372-73, 390
        Cat in the Hat, The, 372-73, 390-91
        Dragon Challenge, 372-73, 385
        Dr. Doom's Fearfall, 372-73, 376-77
        Dudley Do-Right's Ripsaw Falls, 372-73, 377

Eighth Voyage of Sindbad, The, 372–73, 389
Flight of the Hippogriff, 372–73, 385–86
Harry Potter and the Forbidden Journey, 372–73, 386–88
High in the Sky Seuss Trolley Train Ride, The, 372–73, 391
If I Ran the Zoo, 372–73, 391
Incredible Hulk Coaster, The, 372–73, 376
Jurassic Park Discovery Center, 372–73, 379
Jurassic Park River Adventure, 372–73, 379–80
Lost Continent, The, 372–73, 389–90
Marvel Super Hero Island, 372–77
Me Ship, *The Olive,* 372–73, 378, 390
Oh! The Stories You'll Hear!, 391–92
One Fish, Two Fish, Red Fish, Blue Fish, 372–73, 392
Popeye & Bluto's Bilge-Rat Barges, 372–73, 378
Poseidon's Fury, 372–73, 390–92
Pteranodon Flyers, 372–73, 380
Seuss Landing, 372–73, 390
Skull Island: Reign of Kong, 378–79
Storm Force Accelatron, 372–73, 376–77
Toon Lagoon, 372–73, 377–78
dining, 392
maps, 372–73, 394–95
overview, 374
services, 374
touring plans, 392–93
Italy Pavilion (Epcot), 53, 190, 300–301, 314–15, 319, 321
It's a Small World (Magic Kingdom), 264–65, 280
It's Tough to Be a Bug! (Animal Kingdom), 190, 326–30

Jake and the Never Land Pirates Package (Magic Kingdom), 74
Jake's (restaurant), 368
Jambo House, Animal Kingdom, 100–101
JAMMitors, The, 318
Japan Pavilion (Epcot), 53, 190, 300–301, 315–16, 319, 321
Jedi Training Academy (DHS), 344–45, 350–51
Jiko—The Cooking Place, 144, 170
Jim Henson's Muppet-Vision 3-D (DHS), 191, 344–45, 351
jimhillmedia.com, 42
Johnnie's Hideaway, 136
Journey into Imagination with Figment (Epcot), 308
Journey of the Little Mermaid (Magic Kingdom), 264–65, 285
Jungle Cruise, 270
Jurassic Park (IOA), 372–73, 379–81, 392
Jurassic Park River Adventure (IOA), 372–73, 379–81

Kabuki Cafe, 161, 300–301
Kali River Rapids (Animal Kingdom), 190, 325–28, 335
Kang & Kodos' Twirl 'n' Hurl (USF), 394–95, 401–2
Katsura Grill, 153, 161, 300–301, 319
kayak.com, 130
Key to the World (KTTW) card, 65–66
Kidani Village, Animal Kingdom, 100–101
Kidcot Fun Stops, 302
Kid's Discovery Club (Animal Kingdom), 339
Kids Eat Free Card, 134
Kid's Night Out, 72
KidZone Pizza Company, 416

Kilimanjaro Safaris (Animal Kingdom), 190, 325–28, 331–32
Kimonos (restaurant), 169
Kissimmee Guest Services, 66
Kissimmee Visitor's Guide, 38
Kitchen, The, 117, 368
Knife, The (restaurant), 137
Kringla Bakeri og Kafe, 153, 162, 300–301, 319
Kusafiri Coffee Shop, 164, 326–27
Kwanzaa celebration, 53

labels, for clothing, 206
La Cantina de San Angel, 160, 169, 300–301, 319
La Hacienda de San Angel, 153, 300–301, 320
Lake Buena Vista, accommodations, 114–15, 121–27
Land Pavilion, The (Epcot), 300–301, 308–10, 319, 321
Landing, The, Disney Springs, 14, 434–35
La Nouba (Disney Springs), 14, 52,432
L'Artisan des Glaces, 160, 300–301, 316
laser shows
  Cinematic Spectacular—100 Years of Memories, 368, 394–95, 415–16
  IllumiNations (Epcot), 53, 190, 299–301, 319–21
Last Minute Villas, 132
Leaky Cauldron, 409, 416
Le Cellier Steakhouse, 142, 169, 300–301
Le Coq au Vin (restaurant), 136
LEGO Imagination Center (Disney Springs), 432
Les Chefs de France, 167, 169–70, 300–301
Les Halles Boulangerie-Patisserie, 153–54, 161, 300–301, 316
Liberty Belle Riverboat (Magic Kingdom), 264–65, 276
Liberty Inn (restaurant), 162, 300–301, 319
Liberty Square (Magic Kingdom), 275–76
  attractions, 264–65, 275–76
    Hall of Presidents, The, 264–65, 275
    Haunted Mansion, The, 50, 264–66, 276
    Liberty Belle Riverboat, 264–65, 276
  dining, 291
Liberty Tree Tavern, 51, 152–53, 168, 264–65
Lights! Motors! Action! Extreme Stunt Show (DHS), 191, 344–45, 351–52
Lilo's Playhouse, 71–72
Lines (app), 37, 228
Lion King, Festival of the (Animal Kingdom), 190, 326–28, 331
Little Mermaid, Journey of the (Magic Kingdom), 264–65, 285
live entertainment. *See also* music
  Animal Kingdom, 338–40
  Disney's Hollywood Studios, 355–58
  Epcot, 318–20
  on holidays, 47–55
  Magic Kingdom, 290–94
  SeaWorld, 417–20
  Universal Studios, 414–16
Living with the Land (Epcot), 299–301, 309
lobster buffets, 138
lockers
  Animal Kingdom, 324
  Disney's Hollywood Studios, 343
  Epcot, 298
  Islands of Adventure, 374
  Magic Kingdom, 262
  Universal Orlando, 367–68
  water parks, 422

lodging. *See* accommodations
Loews Portofino Bay Hotel, 117–18, 361
Loews Royal Pacific Resort, 118–19, 361
Loews Sapphire Falls Resort, 119–20, 361, 366
Lombard's Seafood Grille, 368
lost and found
    Animal Kingdom, 324
    Disney's Hollywood Studios, 343
    Epcot, 299
    Islands of Adventure, 374
    Magic Kingdom, 262
    phone numbers, 43
    Universal Studios Florida, 396
Lost Continent, The (IOA), 372–73, 389–90, 392
lost persons, 258–61
    Animal Kingdom, 258–60, 324
    Disney character meeting and, 249
    Disney's Hollywood Studios, 258–60, 343
    Epcot, 258–60, 299
    Magic Kingdom, 258–60
    water parks, 424
Lotus Blossom Cafe, 162, 300–301, 319
Louie's Italian Restaurant, 416
Lucy—A Tribute (USF), 394–95, 402
Lunching Pad, The, 159, 264–65, 291

Mad Tea Party (Magic Kingdom), 264–65, 280
Magical Express service, 89–90
MagicBands, 39, 65–66, 69–71
Magic Behind Our Steam Trains, The, Disney's, 73–74
Magic Carpets of Aladdin (Magic Kingdom), 264–65, 270–71
Magic Kingdom, 262–97
    accommodations, 12, 92–96
    attendance, 46
    attractions
        Adventureland, 270–72
        Fantasyland, 277–85
        Frontierland, 264–65, 272–75
        height requirements, 242
        Liberty Square, 264–65, 275–76
        Main Street, U.S.A., 266–69
        Tomorrowland, 264–65, 285–90
    Christmas celebration, 52
    City Hall, 266–67
    dining, 147, 152–53, 157–60, 168, 252, 291
    ECV/ESV rental, 262
    evening parade, 292
    exit strategies, 293–94
    Extra Magic Hours, 231–32
    family magic tour, 73
    FastPass+, 263, 266–67
    first aid, 262
    handout park map, 262
    live entertainment, 290–94
    lost children, 258–60
    map, 264–65
    Monorail Station, 264–65
    opening procedures and operating hours, 222, 228
    overview, 12, 262–63
    parades, 290–91
    rentals, 262
    services, 262
    Times Guide, 262
    touring plans, 294–97
    transportation to/from, 83–84

Magic Your Way Deluxe Dining, 173
Magic Your Way package, 62–64, 111–12, 171–76
    dining plans, 171–76
    maximizing, 64
    purchasing options, 66–67
Magic Your Way Platinum Package, 173
Magic Your Way Premium Package, 173
Maharajah Jungle Trek (Animal Kingdom), 190, 326–28, 335
Main Street Bakery, 158, 291
Main Street Electrical Parade (Magic Kingdom), 292
Main Street, U.S.A. (Magic Kingdom), 12, 266–69, 291
    attractions, 266–69
    FastPass+, 266–67
    parade, 292
major attractions, 223
make-up show, *Universal Orlando's Horror Make-Up Show* (USF), 394–95, 406–7
Mama Melrose's Ristorante Italiano, 155, 168, 344–45, 358
Mandolin's (restaurant), 129
Mango Joe's, 418
Many Adventures of Winnie the Pooh, The (Magic Kingdom), 264–65, 280–81
Maple Leaf Tickets, 66–67
maps. *See specific locations*
marathons, 48
Mardi Gras, 48
Mariachi Cobre (Epcot), 312
marine animals, SeaWorld, 417–20
Marketplace, Disney Springs, 13, 432
Marriott Village at Lake Buena Vista, 125
Marvel Super Hero Island (IOA), 372–77
Matsuriza Taiko drummers (Epcot), 316
Me Ship, *The Olive* (IOA), 372–73, 378, 390
medication, 209
Meet Merida at Fairytale Garden (Magic Kingdom), 264–65, 281
meet and greets
    Animal Kingdom, 329
    Ariel's Grotto, 264–65, 277–78
    Discovery Island, 324
    Epcot, 300–303, 312–13, 315–16
    Magic Kingdom, 292
    Pete's Silly Sideshow, 264–65, 282–83
    Princess Fairytale Hall, 283–84
    Town Square Theater, 264–65, 269
    venues for, 246–47
Mel's Drive-in, 416
memories, 217–18
Memories of India, 136
Memory Maker Service, 70
Men in Black Alien Attack (USF), 394–95, 402
Merida, meeting, 264–65, 281
Mermaid, Little, Journey of the (Magic Kingdom), 264–65, 285
Mermaid, Little, Voyage of the (DHS), 191, 344–45, 355
Mermaid Package (Magic Kingdom), 74
merry-go-rounds
    Caro-Seuss-el (IOA), 372–73, 390
    Prince Charming's Regal Carrousel (Magic Kingdom), 264–65, 283
Mexico Pavilion (Epcot), 53, 190, 300–301, 312, 319, 321
Mickey Avenue (DHS), 191
Mickey's Backyard BBQ, 143, 177–78

Mickey's Not-So-Scary Halloween Party, 50
Mickey's Once upon a Chrismastime Parade, 52
Mickey's PhilarMagic (Magic Kingdom), 264–65, 281–82
Mickey's Very Merry Christmas Party, 52
Mighty St. Patrick's Day Festival, 48
Min and Bill's Dockside Diner, 155, 166, 344–45
Ming Court, 136
miniature golf, 437
mini-fridges, 209
minor attractions, 223
Mission: Space (Epcot), 300–301, 305
mobissimo.com, 130
"Mom, I Can't Believe It's Disney" Fountain (Epcot), 305
Mom's Panel, 41
Monorail Station
    Epcot, 300
    Magic Kingdom, 264–65
Monsieur Paul, 144, 153, 169, 170, 300–301
Monsters, Inc. Laugh Floor (Magic Kingdom), 264–65, 287
Morocco Pavilion (Epcot), 53, 190, 300–301, 316
mousesavers.com, 42, 66, 106
Mouseworld Radio, 42
Move It! Shake It! Dance and Play it! Street Party (Magic Kingdom), 292
movies. *See* films
Mulch, Sweat, & Shears—Live in Concert (DHS), 356
Muppet-Vision 3-D (DHS), 191, 344–45, 351
music, 292
    America Gardens Theatre (Epcot), 315, 319–20
    British Revolution band, The (Epcot), 317
    Epcot, 306–20
    Matsuriza Taiko drummers (Epcot), 316
    Sounds Like Summer Concert Series, 49
    United States Pavilion, 315–16
My Disney Experience, 39–41, 233–34
My Disney Girl's Perfectly Princess Tea Party (Magic Kingdom), 75
MyMagic +, 39
Mythos Restaurant, 392

Nagoya Sushi, 136
Namaste Café, 433
naps, 224
Narcoossee's (restaurant), 144
natural history exhibit, Discovery Center (IOA), 372–73, 379
nature reserves, 436
NBA Experience, 434
Nemo and Friends, The Seas with (Epcot), 300–301, 310–11, 319, 321
New Year's celebration, 54–55
New York (USF), 394–95, 416
Nickelodeon Suites Resort, 120
Nicktoons Cafe, 120
Night of Joy music festival, 49
Nine Dragons Restaurant, 170, 300–301
1900 Park Fare, 252, 255
Norway Pavilion (Epcot), 53, 190, 252, 300–301, 312–13, 319, 321
#1 Dream Homes, 132

O Canada (Epcot), 190, 300–301
Oasis, The, 190, 326–29

Odyssey Center (Epcot), 300–301
Official Ticket Center, 66
Official Visitor Center, Orlando, 139
'Ohana, 51, 253
Olaf's Summer Cool Down (DHS), 356
Old Key West Resort, 79, 80–81, 85, 88, 90, 98, 108
Olive, The (IOA), 372–73, 378, 390
Ollivanders (IOA), 382–83, 408
Ollivanders (USF), 414
Once Upon a Toy (Disney Springs), 432
One Fish, Two Fish, Red Fish, Blue Fish (IOA), 372–73, 392
One Man's Dream (DHS), 191
One Travel website, 106
opening procedures, 222, 228
operating hours
    Animal Kingdom, 222
    Disney's Hollywood Studios, 222
    Epcot, 222, 298
    Magic Kingdom, 222
    with small crowds, 46
Orange Lake Resort, 128
Orlando Magicard, 38, 129
Orlando, map, 8–9
Orlando's Finest Vacation Homes, 132
Orlando Stroller Rentals, 256–57
Osborne Family Spectacle of Dancing Lights, 53–54
Oscar's (DHS), 343
Osceola County Welcome Center and History Museum, 139
Outback Steakhouse, 127
Owlery and Owl Post (IOA), 382

Palm Restaurant, 117
Pandora: The Land of Avatar (Animal Kingdom), 325
Pangani Forest Exploration Trail (Animal Kingdom), 190, 326–27, 332
parades
    Halloween, 50
    lost children at, 260
    Magic Kingdom, 51–52, 290–91
    Universal Orlando, 415
parents
    activities for, 195–96
    children sharing room with, 91
    single, 27–28
park hopping, 61–63
Park Ticket Calculator, 60
parking
    at accommodations, 91
    Universal Orlando, 364
passports, World Showcase, 302
Paul McKenna Band, 317
Pecos Bill's Tall Tale Inn & Cafe, 159, 264–65, 291
Peter Pan's Flight (Magic Kingdom), 264–65, 282
Pete's Silly Sideshow (Magic Kingdom), Fantasyland, 264–65, 282–83
petting zoos
    Affection Section (Animal Kingdom), 190, 326–27, 333
    Rafiki's Planet Watch (Animal Kingdom), 332
Phineas and Ferb scavenger hunt (Epcot), 311–12
phone numbers, Walt Disney World, 45–46
PhotoPass, 70
photos, 217–18
Pinocchio Village Haus, The, 159, 264–65, 291

pirate activities
    adventures, 74
    Captain Jack Sparrow's Pirate Tutorial (Magic
        Kingdom), 264–65, 270
    Pirate's Adventure: Treasures of the Seven Seas,
        A, (Magic Kingdom), 264–65, 271
    Pirate's League, The, 74
Pirates of the Caribbean (Magic Kingdom), 264–65,
    271–72
Pixar Place (DHS), 191
Pizzafari, 164–65, 326–27, 339
Pizza Hut, 125, 129
Pizza Planet, 166, 344–45, 358
Pizza Predattoria, 392
pizza scams, 140
Planet Hollywood (restaurant), 169, 433, 435
Planet Watch (Animal Kingdom), 332
planning, 36–77
    accessories, 206–14
    admission options, 59–71
    for attractions, 222–24
    babysitting, 71–73
    birthdays, 76–77
    clothing, 203, 206
    daily itinerary, 224, 226
    day of week, 55
    Disney character meeting, 196–97
    Extra Magic Hours. *See* Extra Magic Hours
    holidays, 47–55
    importance, 184
    information for, 36–44
    logistic preparation, 203–16
    master plan, 201–3
    memory recording, 217–18
    for parents' enjoyment, 195–96
    physical preparation, 197–201
    for rest, 200–201
    seasons to visit, 44–47
    special events, 47
    special programs, 73–77
    telephone numbers, 45–46
    time allocation, 44–59
    trial run, 219–20
playgrounds
    Boneyard, The (Animal Kingdom), 326–27, 336–37
    Camp Jurassic (IOA), 372–73, 379
    Curious George Goes To Town (USF), 394–95, 407
    Fievel's Playland (USF), 394–95, 400
    If I Ran the Zoo (IOA), 372–73, 391
    Me Ship, *The Olive* (IOA), 372–73, 378, 390
    for relaxation, 224
    Tom Sawyer Island (Magic Kingdom), 264–65,
        274–75
    Woody Woodpecker's KidZone (USF), 394–95,
        407
Plaza Restaurant, The, 152–53, 264–65
podcasts, 42–43
Polynesian Village Resort, Villas, & Bungalows, 71–72,
    79, 80, 82, 85, 88, 90–91, 94, 108, 178
ponchos, 208–9
Ponderosa (restaurant), 138
Pop Century Resort, 80–81, 85, 88, 90, 103–4, 109
Popeye & Bluto's Bilge-Rat Barges (IOA), 372–73, 378
Port of Entry (IOA), 374, 392
Port Orleans Resort, 54, 74, 85, 88, 90, 99, 109–11
Portofino Bay Hotel, 117–18, 361

Poseidon's Fury (IOA), 372–73, 390–92
post office, Wizarding World of Harry Potter, 382
Potter, Harry, The Wizarding World of (IOA), 381–89
    at Islands of Adventure. *See* Wizarding World of
        Harry Potter, The—Hogsmeade (IOA)
    at Universal Studios Florida. *See* Wizarding
        World of Harry Potter, The—Diagon Alley
        (USF)
pregnant visitors, tips for, 214–15
Premium Annual Pass, 60, 63–64
Presidents, The Hall of (Magic Kingdom), 264–65, 275
Presidents' Day, 48
preview sites, for WDW, 41
price increases, 65
priceline.com, 106
Primeval Whirl (Animal Kingdom), 190, 326–27, 337
Prince Charming's Regal Carrousel (Magic Kingdom),
    264–65, 283
Princess Fairytale Hall (Magic Kingdom), 263–65,
    283–84
Princess Half-Marathon, 48
Production Central (USF), 394–95, 416
Promenade Refreshments, 162, 300–301
Pteranodon Flyers (IOA), 372–73, 380
Publix Market, 152
Punjab Indian Restaurant, 137, 138

Quick Service dining plan, 173–75, 369
Quidditch match (IOA), 387

radio-frequency identification, 65–66, 69–71
radio stations, 42
Radisson Resort Orlando-Celebration, 128–29
Rafiki's Planet Watch (Animal Kingdom), 332
Raglan Road, 434–35
railroads
    Big Thunder Mountain Railroad (Magic King-
        dom), 263–67, 273
    High in the Sky Seuss Trolley Train Ride, The
        (IOA), 372–73, 391
    Seven Dwarfs Mine Train (Magic Kingdom), 189,
        263–65, 284–85
    Tomorrowland Transit Authority PeopleMover
        (Magic Kingdom), 189, 264–65, 289
    Walt Disney World Railroad (Magic Kingdom),
        73–74, 264–65, 269–70, 272
    Wildlife Express Train (Animal Kingdom), 190,
        326–28, 333–34
Rainforest Cafe, 14, 155, 168–70, 326–27, 339
raingear, 208–9
Ravenous Pig, The, 136
Red Lobster, 127
Reflections of China (Epcot), 190, 300–301, 313–14
Refreshment Cool Post, 162, 300–301
Refreshment Port, The, 162–63, 300–301
Reign of Kong (IOA), 378–79
rentals
    Animal Kingdom, 324
    ECV/ESV, 262, 298, 324
    Epcot, 298–99
    lockers, 262, 324
    Magic Kingdom, 262
    strollers. *See* strollers
    wheelchairs. *See* wheelchairs
reservations
    for accommodations, 129–30

for dining, 40–41, 141–44, 254–55
U-Bot device, 367
rest, 200–201, 224
restrooms
diaper changing facilities in, 22
lost children at, 259
Restaurant Marrakesh, 153, 300–301, 316, 318
Restaurantosaurus, 165, 326–27, 339
restaurants. *See* dining
Revenge of the Mummy (USF), 394–95, 403
Richter's Burger Co., 416
rides. *See* attractions
River Adventure, Jurassic Park (IOA), 372–73, 379–80
Riverside, Port Orleans Resort, 99, 109–11
Rivers of Light (Animal Kingdom), 325–26, 335–36
Rock 'n' Roller Coaster (DHS), 190, 344–45, 352
roller coasters
Barnstormer (Magic Kingdom), 264–65, 278
Big Thunder Mountain Railroad (Magic Kingdom), 263–67, 273
Dragon Challenge (IOA), 372–73, 385
Expedition Everest (Animal Kingdom), 190, 326–28, 334
Hollywood Rip Ride Rockit (USF), 394–95, 400–401
Incredible Hulk Coaster, The (IOA), 372–73, 376
Primeval Whirl (Animal Kingdom), 190, 326–28, 337
Revenge of the Mummy (USF), 394–95, 403
Rock 'n' Roller Coaster (DHS), 190, 344–45, 352
SeaWorld, 418
Space Mountain (Magic Kingdom), 189, 264–65, 287–88
Universal Orlando, 371
Woody Woodpecker's Nuthouse Coaster (USF), 394–95, 407
romantic activities, 195–96
Rose & Crown Pub, 153, 163, 300–301, 320
Rosie's All-American Cafe, 166, 344–45
routines, in vacation schedule, 201–3
Rowling, J. K., 381, 408
Royal Anandapur Tea Company, 165, 326–27, 339
Royal Pacific Resort, 361
Royal Sommerhus Meet and Greet (DHS), 313

safety
childproofing rooms for, 133
information, 42
for teenagers, 25–26
water parks, 426
website for (safetytat.com), 206, 261
St. Patrick's Day Festival, 48
salad buffets, 138
San Angel Inn (restaurant), 167–68, 170, 300–301
San Francisco (USF), 394–95, 416
Sanaa (restaurant), 73, 170
Sapphire Falls Resort, 119–20, 361, 366
Saratoga Springs Resort & Spa, 79, 80–81, 85, 88, 90, 99–100, 110
Sbandieratori Di Sanspolcro, 315
scavenger hunts
Agent P's World Showcase Adventure (Epcot), 300–301, 311–12
Animal Kingdom, 326–27, 331
school calendar, attendance and, 45–46

Sci-Fi Dine-In Restaurant, 155, 168, 344–45, 358
scooter rental, 262, 298, 324
seafood buffets, 138
Seas with Nemo and Friends Pavilion, The (Epcot), 189, 300–301, 310–11, 319, 321
seasons
opening procedures and, 228
to visit, 44–47, 223
SeaWorld, 417–20
Aquatica by, 427–29
SeaVenture (Discovery Cove), 420
Segway-type vehicle rental, 262, 298, 324
senior citizens, 28–29
Serveur Amusant, 316
services
Animal Kingdom, 324
Disney's Hollywood Studios, 342–43
Epcot, 298–99
Islands of Adventure, 374
Magic Kingdom, 262
Universal Studios Florida, 396
Seuss Landing (IOA), 372–73, 390–92
Seven Dwarfs Mine Train (Magic Kingdom), 189, 263–65, 284–85
Seven Seas Lagoon Floating Electrical Pageant (Magic Kingdom), 291
Shades of Green, 80, 90, 95, 111
Sharks Underwater Grill, 418
Sharp Aquos Theater (USF), 370
Sheraton Lake Buena Vista Resort, 125
Sheraton Vistana Resort Villas, 126
shoes, 198–200
Shoney's, 139
Shootin' Arcade (Magic Kingdom), 264–65, 274
shooting galleries, Toy Story Midway Mania! (DHS), 191, 344–46, 353–54
shopping
Diagon Alley (USF), 382–83
Disney Springs, 429–35
Hogsmeade (IOA), 382
Islands of Adventure, 374
Wizarding World of Harry Potter, 382–83, 410
Showcase Plaza (Epcot), 320
shows
American Adventure, The (Epcot), 190, 300–301, 315
Animal Actors on Location (USF), 395–97
Aquos Theater (USF), 370
Beauty and the Beast—Live on Stage (DHS), 344–47
Beetlejuice Graveyard Revue (USF), 394–95, 397
Blue Man Group (USF), 370
Blues Brothers, The (USF), 394–95, 397
Celebrate the Magic (Magic Kingdom), 291
Cinematic Spectacular—100 Years of Memories (USF), 368, 394–95, 415–16
Cirque du Soleil (Disney Springs), 432
Country Bear Jamboree (Magic Kingdom), 264–65, 274
Day in the Park with Barney, A (USF), 394–95, 397–98
dinner, 176–78
Disaster! (USF), 394–95, 398–99
Disney Junior—Live on Stage! (DHS), 191, 344–45, 347–48
Dream Along with Mickey (Magic Kingdom), 291

Eighth Voyage of Sindbad, The (IOA), 372–73, 389

Enchanted Tales with Belle (Magic Kingdom), 264–65, 279

Enchanted Tiki Room (Magic Kingdom), 264–65, 272

Fantasmic! (DHS), 143–44, 191, 344–45, 356–58

Fear Factor Live (USF), 394–95, 400

Festival of the Lion King (Animal Kingdom), 190, 326–28, 331

Finding Nemo—The Musical (Animal Kingdom), 326–28, 337–38

Flights of Wonder (Animal Kingdom), 190, 326–28, 334–35

Hall of Presidents, The (Magic Kingdom), 264–65, 275

Indiana Jones Epic Stunt Spectacular (DHS), 191, 344–45, 350

Jedi Training Academy (DHS), 344–45, 350–51

Little Mermaid, Voyage of the (DHS), 191, 344–45, 355

lost children, 259

Poseidon's Fury (IOA), 372–73, 390–92

Rivers of Light (Animal Kingdom), 335

SeaWorld, 417–20

Stitch's Great Escape (Magic Kingdom), 189, 264–65, 288

Theater in the Wild (Animal Kingdom), 326–28, 337–38

Tree of Life, The (Animal Kingdom), 326–28

Twister (USF), 394–95, 406

Universal Orlando's Horror Make-Up Show (USF), 394–95, 406–7

Voyage of the Little Mermaid (DHS), 191, 344–45, 355

Walt Disney's Carousel of Progress (Magic Kingdom), 189, 264–65, 289–90

Winged Encounters—The Kingdom Takes Flight (Animal Kingdom), 338

Shrek 4-D (USF), 394–95, 403–4

Shula's Steakhouse, 145, 169

shuttle services, to/from accommodations, 79–81, 83

Simpsons Ride, The (USF), 394–95, 404

simulator rides

Despicable Me Minion Mayhem (USF), 394–95, 398

Harry Potter and the Forbidden Journey (IOA), 372–73, 386–88

Sindbad, The Eighth Voyage of (IOA), 372–73, 389

sing-alongs, *For the First Time in Forever: A Frozen Sing-Along Celebration,* 344–45, 349

single parents, 27–28

singles lines (Universal Orlando), 367

Sizzler (restaurant), 138

Skipper's Cantina, 168

Skull Island: Reign of Kong (IOA), 378–79

sleep, 200–201

"sleigh" rides, 54

Small World, It's A (Magic Kingdom), 189, 264–65, 280

Smokehouse, The, 433

smoking, in restaurants, 145

snacks, 150–52, 154, 210

Soarin' (Epcot), 189, 299–301, 309–10

social media, 42

soda fountains, Epcot, 300–301, 304

Sommerfest restaurant, 153, 163, 300–301, 319

Sonny's Real Pit Bar-B-Q, 139

Sorcerers of the Magic Kingdom, 264–65, 268–69

Sounds Like Summer Concert Series, 49

Sounds of Disney, 43

South American buffets, 137–38

Space Mountain (Magic Kingdom), 189, 264–65, 287–88

Spaceship Earth (Epcot), 189, 300–301, 305–6

Sparrow, Jack, pirate tutorial (Magic Kingdom), 264–65, 270

special children's programs, 73–77

special events, 47–55

Spice Road Table (Epcot), 168, 300–301, 316, 320

Spider-Man, The Amazing Adventures of (IOA), 372–73, 375–76

Spirit of Aloha dinner show, 143, 178

Splash Mountain (Magic Kingdom), 264–65, 274

Splitsville, 14, 432

Sports, Wide World of Sports, 14, 435–36

SpringHill Suites, 116

Star Tours: The Adventure Continues (DHS), 191, 344–45, 352–53

Star Wars weekends, 49

Starbucks, 433, 435

Starring Rolls Cafe, 166, 344–45

Stitch's Great Escape (Magic Kingdom), 189, 264–65, 288

Storm Force Accelatron (IOA), 372–73, 376–77

Street Scenes (USF), 394–95, 404–5

Streets of America (DHS), 191, 344–45, 353

strollers, 23, 200, 255–58

Animal Kingdom, 324

Disney's Hollywood Studios, 343

Epcot, 298

Islands of Adventure, 374

Magic Kingdom, 262

sunburn in, 209

Universal Studios Florida, 396

Studio Catering Co., 146, 167, 344–45, 358

stunt shows

Eighth Voyage of Sindbad, The (IOA), 372–73, 389

Indiana Jones Epic Stunt Spectacular (DHS), 191, 344–45, 350

Lights! Motors! Action! Extreme Stunt Show (DHS), 191, 344–45, 351–52

Subway, 127

Sum of All Thrills (Epcot), 300–301, 304–5

sunglasses, 207

sunscreen, 211

Sunset Boulevard (DHS), 191, 343

Sunshine Seasons (Epcot), 146, 163, 170, 300–301, 319

super-headliners, 223

Superstar Catering Co., 433

Superstar Character Breakfast, 368

Super Target store, 152

Swan Resort, 71–72, 80–81, 85, 88, 90, 97, 110

Sweet Sailin' Candy Shop, 418

Sweet Tomatoes (restaurant), 138

swimming, 89. *See also* water parks

Swiss Family Treehouse (Magic Kingdom), 264–65, 272

switching off, at attractions, 243, 245, 369–70

T. G. I. Friday's, 127

Tales of Beedle the Bard (USF), 410

Tam Tam Drummers, 340

Tamu Tamu Eats and Refreshments, 339

Tangierine Cafe, 153, 163, 300–301, 319
tantrums, 34–35
Taquitos Jalisco (restaurant), 137
tattoos, temporary, 206, 261
Tchoup Chop (restaurant), 119
Tea Caddy, The (Epcot), 319
tea cup ride, Magic Kingdom, 188, 264–65, 280
tea party, 75
teenagers, 16, 24–26
telephone numbers, Walt Disney World, 45–46
temperature, 46
Temple of Heaven, China Pavilion (Epcot), 313–14
temporary tattoos, 206, 261
Teppan Edo, 170, 300–301
Terminator 2: 3-D (USF), 394–95, 405
Test Track (Epcot), 189, 299–301, 305
Texas de Brazil, 137–38
Thai Silk, 137
Thai Thani, 137
Thanksgiving celebration, 50
Theater in the Wild (Animal Kingdom), 326–27, 337–38
Theater of the Stars (DHS), 191
Three Broomsticks (IOA), 382, 392
Three Caballeros, Gran Fiesta Tour Starring (Epcot), 190, 300–301, 312
Three-Park Unlimited ticket, 365
tickets. *See* admission
Tinker Bell's flight, 292–93
Tinker Bell, Town Square Theater, 264–65, 269
Todd English 's bluezoo, 145
toddlers, 21–24. *See also* Baby Care Centers
    childproofing rooms for, 133
    strollers for. *See* strollers
    supplies for, 214
Tokyo Dining, 300–301
Toluca Legs Turkey Company, 167, 344–45
Tomorrowland (Magic Kingdom)
    attractions, 264–65, 285–90
        Astro Orbiter, 189, 264–65, 286
        Buzz Lightyear's Space Ranger Spin, 189, 264–65, 286
        Carousel of Progress, 189, 264–65, 289–90
        fright potential, 189
        Monsters, Inc. Laugh Floor, 189, 264–65, 287
        Space Mountain, 189, 264–65, 287–88
        Stitch's Great Escape, 189, 264–65, 288
        Tomorrowland Speedway, 189, 245, 264–65, 289
        Tomorrowland Transit Authority PeopleMover, 189, 264–65, 289
    dining, 291
    FastPass+, 266–67
Tomorrowland Speedway (Magic Kingdom), 189, 245, 264–65, 289
Tomorrowland Terrace Restaurant, 264–65
Tomorrowland Transit Authority PeopleMover (Magic Kingdom), 189, 264–65, 289
Tom Sawyer Island (Magic Kingdom), 264–65, 274–75
Tony's Town Square Restaurant, 264–65
Toon Lagoon (IOA), 372–73, 377–78, 392
Tortuga Tavern, 160, 264–65, 291
tour(s)
    Behind the Seeds, 73
    Escape to Walt's Wilderness, 76
    magic, 73–74
    steam trains, 73–74

Ultimate Day for Young Families or Day of Thrills—VIP Tour Experience, 75
touring plans
    Animal Kingdom, 340–41
    bouncing around with, 229–30
    computer-optimized, 36
    Disney's Hollywood Studios, 359–60
    Epcot, 321–22
    expectations for, 227
    with Extra Magic Hours, 231–32
    FastPass+ and, 238–40
    for high-attendance days, 228–29
    interruption, 228
    Islands of Adventure, 392–93
    for low-attendance days, 231
    Magic Kingdom, 294–97
    for obsessive-compulsive readers, 230
    opening procedures and, 228
    rejection, 229–31
    revision, 229
    selection, 229–32
    Universal Studios, 410–11
    variables affecting, 227–28
touringplans.com, 36–38
Tower of Terror (DHS), 191, 344–46, 354–55
Town Center, 14, 430–31, 434–35
TownePlace Suites, 116
Town Square Theater (Magic Kingdom), 264–65, 269
Toy Story Midway Mania! (DHS), 191, 344–46, 353–54
traffic, 42
trains
    Big Thunder Mountain Railroad (Magic Kingdom), 263–67, 273
    High in the Sky Seuss Trolley Train Ride, The (IOA), 372–73, 391
    Hogwarts Express (IOA), 388–89, 408
    Seven Dwarfs Mine Train (Magic Kingdom), 189, 263–65, 284–85
    Tomorrowland Transit Authority PeopleMover (Magic Kingdom), 189, 264–65, 289
    Universal Studios, 388–89
    Walt Disney World Railroad (Magic Kingdom), 73–74, 264–65, 269–70, 272
    Wildlife Express Train (Animal Kingdom), 190, 326–28, 333–34
Transformers: The Ride 3-D (USF), 394–95, 405–6
transportation
    to/from accommodations, 79–81
    for teenagers, 25–26
Transportation and Ticket Center, 82
Trattoria del Porto (restaurant), 368
travel agents, 111–12
travel packages, 111–12
travelocity.com, 106
Treasures of the Seven Seas (Magic Kingdom), 271
Tree of Life, The (Animal Kingdom), 190, 326–30
Treehouse, Swiss Family (Magic Kingdom), 264–65, 272
Treehouse Villas at Disney's Saratoga Springs Resort & Spa, 80, 85, 88
tree-lighting ceremony, 52
T-REX restaurant, 169–70, 435
TriceraTop Spin (Animal Kingdom), 190, 326–27, 338
Trivia quiz
    Animal Kingdom, 341
    Disney's Hollywood Studios, 360

Epcot, 323
Magic Kingdom, 297
Triwizard Spirit Rally (IOA), 389
Trolley Car Cafe, 167, 344–45
truck rides
Kilimanjaro Safaris (Animal Kingdom), 190, 326–28, 331–32
Skull Island, 378–79
Turf Club Bar & Grill, 171
Turtle Talk with Crush (Epcot), 189, 300–301, 311
Tusker House Restaurant, 155, 168, 252, 326–27, 339
Tutto Italia (restaurant) (Epcot), 300–301, 315, 319
Twilight Zone Tower of Terror, The (DHS), 191, 344–46, 354–55
Twister (USF), 394–95, 406
Typhoon Lagoon, 13, 61–63, 242, 421–26

U-Bot device, 367
Ultimate Day for Young Families or Day of Thrills—VIP Tour Experience, 75
Undercover Tourist, 66, 365
Under the Sea: Journey of the Little Mermaid (Magic Kingdom), 189, 264–65, 285
United Kingdom Pavilion (Epcot), 53, 190, 300–301, 317, 319, 321
United States Pavilion (Epcot), 53, 190, 300–301, 315, 319, 321
Universal CityWalk. *See* CityWalk (Universal Orlando)
Universal Express, vs. FastPass+, 365–67
Universal Orlando. *See also* Islands of Adventure; Universal Studios Florida
accommodations near, 115, 361
admission, 364–65
arrival, 364–65
dining, 368
map, 394–95
overview, 364–65
parking, 364
time allocation for, 396
Universal Orlando's Horror Make-Up Show (USF), · 394–95, 406–7
Universal Studios Florida, 393–414
accommodations, 361
admission, 364–65
arrival, 364–65
attractions, 394–414
Animal Actors on Location, 395–97
Beetlejuice Graveyard Revue, 394–95, 397
Blues Brothers, 394–95, 397
Cinematic Spectacular—100 Years of Memories, 394–95, 415–16
Day in the Park with Barney, A, 394–95, 397–98
Despicable Me Minion Mayhem, 394–95, 398
Disaster!, 394–95, 398–99
vs. Disney's Hollywood Studios, 393, 396
E.T. Adventure, 394–95, 399
Fear Factor Live, 394–95, 400
Fievel's Playland, 394–95, 400
Hollywood Rip Ride Rockit, 394–95, 400–401
Kang & Kodos' Twirl 'n' Hurl, 394–95, 401–2
Lucy—A Tribute, 394–95, 402
Men in Black Alien Attack, 394–95, 402
Revenge of the Mummy, 394–95, 403
Shrek 4-D, 394–95, 403–4
Simpsons Ride, The, 394–95, 404
Street Scenes, 394–95, 404–5

Terminator 2: 3-D, 394–95, 405
Transformers: The Ride 3-D, 394–95, 405–6
Twister, 394–95, 406
Universal Orlando's Horror Make-Up Show, 394–95, 406–7
Woody Woodpecker's KidZone, 394–95, 407
costs, 364
dining, 416
vs. Disney's Hollywood Studios, 393, 396
live entertainment, 414–16
maps, 394–95
overview, 393, 396
services, 396
touring plans, 410–11
Universal Express, 365–67
Universal's Cabana Bay Beach Resort, 120–21, 361, 366
Universe of Energy: *Ellen's Energy Adventure (Epcot),* 189, 300–301, 306
US 192 (Irlo Bronson Memorial Hwy.), accommodations, 115, 127–29

vacation home rental, 130–32
Vacation Rentals 411, 132
vendor food, 148
Very Merry Christmas Parade, 52
Via Napoli, 153, 169, 300–301, 315
Victoria & Albert's, 144–45, 170
Victoria Gardens, 318
video cameras, 217–18
Village Coffee House, 125
Village Grill, 125
Villains' Mix and Mingle, 50
VIP experiences, 77
virtual games, DisneyQuest, 433–34
Visa Card, Disney Rewards, 106
Visit Orlando Official Visitor Center, 139
Vito's Chop House, 137
Viva Gala Street Bank, 339–40
Voices of Liberty choral ensemble (Epcot), 315, 318
Voyage of the Little Mermaid (DHS), 191, 344–45, 355
Voyager's Smokehouse, 168

waiting-line strategies, 241–45
Waldorf Astoria Orlando, 126
walking, foot care for, 198–200
wallets, 207
Walt Disney Theater, 16
Walt Disney Travel Company Florida Vacations Brochure and DVD, 38
Walt Disney World, map, 10–11
Walt Disney World Marathon, 48
Walt Disney World Railroad (Magic Kingdom), 73–74, 264–65
Walt Disney's Carousel of Progress (Magic Kingdom), 189, 264–65, 289–90
Walt Disney's Enchanted Tiki Room (Magic Kingdom), 264–65, 272
wand store (IOA), 382–83
water bottles, 209
Water Park Fun and More (WPFAM), 61–64
water parks, 421–29
admission, 61–63
Aquatica by SeaWorld, 427–29
Blizzard Beach, 61–63, 242, 421–26
costs, 421
eating in, 424

height requirements, 242
overview, 13
safety in, 426
Typhoon Lagoon, 61-63, 242, 421-26
weather and, 425-26
Wet 'n Wild, 426-27
water play areas
Casey Jr. Splash N Soak (Magic Kingdom), 264-65, 278
"Mom, I Can't Believe It's Disney" Fountain (Epcot), 305
wdwtoday.com, 42
weather
cool, 206
raingear, 208-9
seasonal, 44-47
for water park use, 425-26
websites, 36-44
West Side (Disney Springs), 13-14, 432-34
Wet 'n Wild water park, 426-27
Wetzel's Pretzels, 435
whales, SeaWorld, 417-18
wheelchairs
Animal Kingdom, 324
Disney's Hollywood Studios, 343
Epcot, 298
Islands of Adventure, 374
Magic Kingdom, 262
Universal Studios Florida, 396
Whispering Canyon Cafe, 435
whitewater raft rides
Kali River Rapids (Animal Kingdom), 190, 325-28, 335
Popeye & Bluto's Bilge-Rat Barges (IOA), 372-73, 378
Wide World of Sports Complex, 14, 435-36
Wild Africa Trek, 76
Wilderness Explorers (Animal Kingdom), 326-27, 330-31
Wilderness Lodge and Villas, 54, 71-72, 79, 80, 85, 87-88, 90, 95-96, 110, 435
Wilderness Preserve, Disney's, 436
Wildlife Express Train (Animal Kingdom), 190, 326-27, 333-34
Wind-Away River (SeaWorld), 419
Wine and Dine Half-Marathon, 51
wine festivals, 49-50
Winged Encounters—The Kingdom Takes Flight (Animal Kingdom), 338
Winn-Dixie Marketplace, 127, 152
Winnie the Pooh, The Many Adventures of (Magic Kingdom), 189, 264-65, 280-81
Winter Summerland miniature golf, 437
Wishes fireworks show and cruise (Magic Kingdom), 293
Wizarding World of Harry Potter, The—Diagon Alley (USF), 407-14
attractions, 411-14
dining, 409-10
map, 362-63
overview of, 407-8
shopping, 382-83, 410
touring strategy, 410-11
Wizarding World of Harry Potter, The—Hogsmeade (IOA), 381-89

attractions, 372-73, 385-89
Diagon Alley, 394-95
dining, 392
map, 362-63
shopping in, 382-83
Wolfgang Puck Express Cafe, 435
Wolfgang Puck Grand Cafe, 14, 169, 433
Wonderland Cafe, 434
Wonderland Tea Party (Magic Kingdom), 74-75
Woody Woodpecker's KidZone (USF), 394-95, 407
Woody Woodpecker's Nuthouse Coaster (USF), 394-95, 407
World Expo (USF), 394-95
World Showcase
attractions, 300-301, 311-18
Agent P's World Showcase Adventure, 300-301, 311-12
American Adventure, The, 190, 300-301, 315
China Pavilion, 53, 190, 300-301, 313-14, 319, 321
France Pavilion, 53, 190, 300-301, 316-17
fright potential, 190
Germany Pavilion, 53, 190, 300-301, 314, 319, 321
Gran Fiesta Tour Starring the Three Caballeros, 190, 312
Impressions de France, 190, 300-301, 316-17
Italy Pavilion, 53, 190, 300-301, 314-15, 319, 321
Japan Pavilion, 53, 190, 300-301, 315-16, 319, 321
Mexico Pavilion, 53, 190, 300-301, 312, 319, 321
Morocco Pavilion, 53, 190, 300-301, 316
Norway Pavilion, 190, 252, 300-301, 312-13, 319, 321
O Canada, 190, 300-301, 318-20
Outpost, 300
Reflections of China, 190, 300-301, 313-14
United Kingdom Pavilion, 53, 190, 300-301, 319, 321
United States Pavilion, 53, 190, 300-301, 315, 319, 321
dining, 153
FastPass+, 299, 302
International Gateway Entrance, 300-301
live entertainment, 318-20
overview of, 12
World Showcase Lagoon (Epcot), 300-301
World Showcase of Flavors, 433
wristbands, 39, 65-66, 69-71
Wyndham Bonnet Creek Resort, 127
Wyndham Lake Buena Vista Resort, 81, 104-105

Yacht Club Resort and Villas, 54, 71-72, 74, 80, 85, 88, 90, 97-98, 110
Yachtsman Steakhouse, 144
Yak & Yeti Local Food Cafes, 155, 165, 326-27
Yak & Yeti Restaurant, 155, 168, 326-27, 339
Yorkshire County Fish Shop, 163-64, 300-301
YouTube, 41
Yuletide Fantasy tour, Disney's, 76

zoologic exhibits, Maharajah Jungle Trek (Animal Kingdom), 190, 326-28, 335

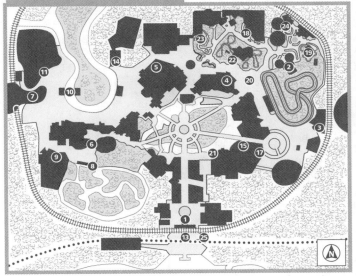

The Magic Kingdom

MAGIC KINGDOM HAPPY FAMILY ONE-DAY TOURING PLAN

1. If you're a Disney resort guest, arrive 30 minutes before opening. Otherwise, arrive 50 minutes before opening. Obtain park maps and the *Times Guide*. Stroller rentals are under the train station on Main Street.

2. PARENTS: Ride Dumbo the Flying Elephant in Fantasyland.

3. TEENS: Ride Space Mountain in Tomorrowland.

4. FAMILY: Ride The Many Adventures of Winnie the Pooh in Fantasyland.

5. FAMILY: Ride Peter Pan's Flight using your FastPass+ reservation.

6. PARENTS: Experience The Magic Carpets of Aladdin in Adventureland.

7. TEENS: Ride Splash Mountain using your FastPass+ reservation.

8. FAMILY: Take the Jungle Cruise.

9. FAMILY: Ride Pirates of the Caribbean.

10. PARENTS: Take the raft to Tom Sawyer Island. Allow at least 30–45 minutes to run around the island.

11. TEENS: Ride Big Thunder Mountain Railroad and then meet the rest of the family on Tom Sawyer Island.

12. FAMILY: Eat lunch. Good nearby choices are Pecos Bill Tall Tale Inn and Columbia Harbour House.

13. PARENTS: Take a midday break of 3–4 hours back at your hotel.

14. TEENS: See The Haunted Mansion in Liberty Square. Explore the rest of the park for the next few hours.

15. FAMILY: See *Monsters, Inc. Laugh Floor* in Tomorrowland.

16. FAMILY: Eat dinner. Good choices nearby are Cosmic Ray's Starlight Cafe and The Plaza Restaurant.

17. FAMILY: Ride Buzz Lightyear's Space Ranger Spin.

18. FAMILY: Ride Under the Sea: Journey of the Little Mermaid in Fantasyland.

19. PARENTS: Ride The Barnstormer.

20. FAMILY (OR JUST KIDS): Take a spin on Mad Tea Party.

21. FAMILY: See the evening parade and fireworks from Main Street. A good viewing spot is between The Plaza Restaurant and Tomorrowland Terrace.

22. FAMILY: Ride Seven Dwarfs Mine Train in Fantasyland.

23. FAMILY: See *Enchanted Tales with Belle* using your FastPass+ reservation.

24. FAMILY: Meet Goofy and Donald at Pete's Silly Sideshow.

25. Depart the Magic Kingdom.

Suggested start times for FastPass+ reservations: Peter Pan's Flight: 10:15 a.m.; *Enchanted Tales with Belle:* 7 p.m. Teens might use their third FastPass+ on Splash Mountain around 11:30 a.m., while parents might consider using theirs to meet characters. Also check for *Wishes* FastPass+ reservations after you've used your first three FastPasses or after 4 p.m. (whichever is later).

The Magic Kingdom

MAGIC KINGDOM ONE-DAY TOURING PLAN FOR GRANDPARENTS WITH SMALL CHILDREN

1. If you're a Disney resort guest, arrive 30 minutes before opening. Otherwise, arrive 50 minutes before opening. Obtain park maps and the *Times Guide* when you pass through the turnstiles. Stroller rentals are under the train station on Main Street.

2. Ride The Many Adventures of Winnie the Pooh in Fantasyland.

3. See *Enchanted Tales with Belle*.

4. Ride Seven Dwarfs Mine Train using your FastPass+ reservation.

5. Ride Mad Tea Party.

6. See *Mickey's PhilharMagic*.

7. Ride It's a Small World.

8. Ride Peter Pan's Flight using your FastPass+ reservation.

9. See *Country Bear Jamboree* in Frontierland.

10. Take a spin on The Magic Carpets of Aladdin in Adventureland.

11. Ride Pirates of the Caribbean using your FastPass+ reservation.

12. Eat lunch outside the park and return to your hotel for a midday break.

13. Return to the park and explore the Swiss Family Treehouse in Adventureland.

14. Take the Jungle Cruise.

15. Take the raft to Tom Sawyer Island. Allow 30–45 minutes to explore.

16. Take the railroad from Frontierland to Fantasyland.

17. Eat dinner.

18. Ride Dumbo the Flying Elephant in Fantasyland.

19. Ride Under the Sea: Journey of the Little Mermaid.

20. Ride Buzz Lightyear's Space Ranger Spin in Tomorrowland.

21. Ride the Tomorrowland Transit Authority PeopleMover.

22. Ride the Tomorrowland Speedway.

23. See *Monsters, Inc. Laugh Floor*.

24. See the evening parade and fireworks from Main Street. A good viewing spot is between The Plaza Restaurant and Tomorrowland Terrace.

25. Depart the Magic Kingdom.

You can customize this touring plan and get real-time updates while you're in the park! See **touringplans.com** for details. Suggested start times for FastPass+ reservations: Seven Dwarfs Mine Train: 9 a.m.; Peter Pan's Flight: 10 a.m.; Pirates of the Caribbean: 11 a.m. After you've used your first three FastPass+ reservations, see if reservations are available for Jungle Cruise (suggested start time: 3:30 p.m.) and *Wishes*.

The Magic Kingdom

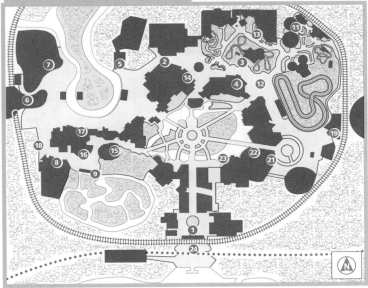

MAGIC KINGDOM ONE–DAY TOURING PLAN FOR TWEENS AND THEIR PARENTS

1. If you're a Disney resort guest, arrive 30 minutes before opening. Otherwise, arrive 50 minutes before opening. Obtain park maps and the *Times Guide* when you pass through the turnstiles. Stroller rentals are under the train station on Main Street.

2. Ride Peter Pan's Flight in Fantasyland.

3. Ride Seven Dwarfs Mine Train using your FastPass+ reservation.

4. Try The Many Adventures of Winnie the Pooh.

5. See The Haunted Mansion in Liberty Square.

6. Ride Splash Mountain in Frontierland.

7. Ride Big Thunder Mountain Railroad using your FastPass+ reservation.

8. Experience Pirates of the Caribbean in Adventureland.

9. Take the Jungle Cruise using your FastPass+ reservation.

10. Eat lunch.

11. Meet Goofy and Donald at Pete's Silly Sideshow in Fantasyland.

12. Take a spin on the Mad Tea Party.

13. Ride Under the Sea: Journey of the Little Mermaid.

14. See *Mickey's PhilharMagic.*

15. Explore the Swiss Family Treehouse in Adventureland.

16. See *Walt Disney's Enchanted Tiki Room.*

17. See *Country Bear Jamboree.*

18. If time permits, play a round of A Pirate's Adventure in Adventureland. Sign up along the walkway between Pirates of the Caribbean and Splash Mountain.

19. Ride Space Mountain in Tomorrowland.

20. Eat dinner. Good choices nearby are Cosmic Ray's Starlight Cafe and The Plaza Restaurant.

21. Ride Buzz Lightyear's Space Ranger Spin.

22. See *Monsters, Inc. Laugh Floor.*

23. See the evening parade and fireworks from Main Street. A good viewing spot is between The Plaza Restaurant and Tomorrowland Terrace.

24. Depart the Magic Kingdom.

You can customize this touring plan and get real-time updates while you're in the park! See **touringplans.com** for details. Suggested start times for FastPass+ reservations: Seven Dwarfs Mine Train: 9 a.m.; Big Thunder Mountain Railroad: 10 a.m.; Jungle Cruise: 11 a.m. After you've used your first three FastPass+ reservations, see if reservations are available for Space Mountain (suggested start time: 4 p.m.) and *Wishes.*

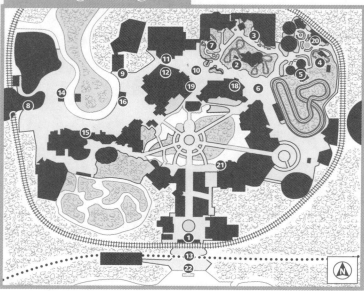

The Magic Kingdom

MAGIC KINGDOM TWO-DAY TOURING PLAN FOR
PARENTS WITH SMALL CHILDREN: DAY ONE

1. If you're a Disney resort guest, arrive 30 minutes before opening. Otherwise, arrive 50 minutes before opening. Obtain park maps and the *Times Guide* when you pass through the turnstiles. Stroller rentals are under the train station on Main Street.

2. Ride Seven Dwarfs Mine Train in Fantasyland using your FastPass+ reservation.

3. Ride Under the Sea: Journey of the Little Mermaid.

4. Try The Barnstormer.

5. Ride Dumbo the Flying Elephant.

6. Take a spin on the Mad Tea Party.

7. See *Enchanted Tales with Belle* using your FastPass+ reservation.

8. Ride Splash Mountain in Frontierland.

9. See The Haunted Mansion in Liberty Square.

10. Take a spin on the Prince Charming Regal Carrousel in Fantasyland.

11. Ride It's a Small World.

12. Ride Peter Pan's Flight using your FastPass+ reservation.

13. Eat lunch and return to your hotel for a midday break of 3–4 hours.

14. Return to the park and take the raft to Tom Sawyer Island in Frontierland. Allow 30–45 minutes to explore the island. Try the barrel bridges and tour Fort Langhorn.

15. See *Country Bear Jamboree.*

16. Experience the *Liberty Belle* Riverboat.

17. Eat dinner.

18. Ride The Many Adventures of Winnie the Pooh in Fantasyland.

19. See *Mickey's PhilharMagic.*

20. Take the Walt Disney World Railroad from Fantasyland to Main Street.

21. See the evening parade and fireworks. A good viewing spot is between the Plaza and Tomorrowland Terrace restaurants.

22. Depart the Magic Kingdom.

You can customize this touring plan and get real-time updates while you're in the park! See **touringplans.com** for details. Suggested start times for FastPass+ reservations: Seven Dwarfs Mine Train: 9 a.m.; *Enchanted Tales with Belle:* 10 a.m.; Peter Pan's Flight: 11 a.m. After you've used your first three FastPass+ reservations, see if reservations are available for Splash Mountain (suggested start time: 5 p.m.) and *Wishes.*

The Magic Kingdom

MAGIC KINGDOM TWO-DAY TOURING PLAN FOR
PARENTS WITH SMALL CHILDREN: DAY TWO

1. If you're a Disney resort guest, arrive 30 minutes before opening. Otherwise, arrive 50 minutes before opening. Obtain park maps and the *Times Guide* when you pass through the turnstiles. Stroller rentals are under the train station on Main Street.

2. In Tomorrowland, ride Buzz Lightyear's Space Ranger Spin.

3. Ride the Astro Orbiter.

4. Ride the Tomorrowland Speedway.

5. Ride the Magic Carpets of Aladdin in Adventureland.

6. Ride Pirates of the Caribbean.

7. If time permits, play a round of A Pirate's Adventure in Adventureland. Sign up along the walkway between Pirates of the Caribbean and Splash Mountain.

8. Take the Jungle Cruise.

9. Explore the Swiss Family Treehouse.

10. See *Walt Disney's Enchanted Tiki Room*.

11. Eat lunch, and return to your hotel for a midday break.

12. Take a round-trip on Walt Disney World Railroad from Main Street.

13. See *Monsters, Inc. Laugh Floor* in Tomorrowland.

14. Ride the Tomorrowland Transit Authority PeopleMover.

15. Eat dinner.

16. See the evening parade and fireworks if you haven't already done so. A good viewing spot is between the Plaza and Tomorrowland Terrace restaurants.

17. Depart the Magic Kingdom.

You can customize this touring plan and get real-time updates while you're in the park! See **touringplans.com** for details. Note that Day Two does not require FastPass+. This means that all of your waits should be less than 10 minutes, and you can use in-park FastPass+ (if reservations are available) to revisit favorite attractions.

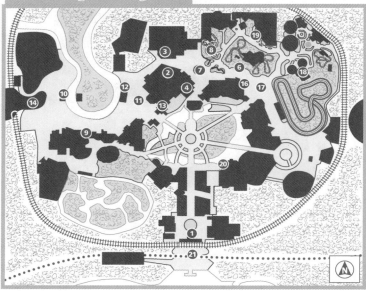

The Magic Kingdom

MAGIC KINGDOM TWO-DAY SLEEPYHEAD TOURING PLAN
FOR PARENTS WITH SMALL CHILDREN: DAY ONE

1. Arrive around 11 a.m. Obtain park maps and the *Times Guide* when you pass through the turnstiles. Stroller rentals are under the train station on Main Street.
2. Ride Peter Pan's Flight in Fantasyland using your FastPass+ reservation.
3. Ride It's a Small World.
4. See *Mickey's PhilharMagic*.
5. Eat a quick lunch.
6. Ride Seven Dwarfs Mine Train using your FastPass+ reservation.
7. Experience the Prince Charming Regal Carrousel.
8. See *Enchanted Tales with Belle* using your FastPass+ reservation.
9. See *Country Bear Jamboree* in Frontierland.
10. Take the raft to Tom Sawyer Island. Allow 30–45 minutes to explore the island.
11. See the afternoon parade from Liberty Square.
12. Experience the *Liberty Belle* Riverboat.
13. See *The Hall of Presidents*.
14. Ride Splash Mountain in Frontierland.
15. Eat dinner.
16. Ride The Many Adventures of Winnie the Pooh in Fantasyland.
17. Take a spin on the Mad Tea Party.
18. Ride Dumbo the Flying Elephant.
19. Ride Under the Sea: Journey of the Little Mermaid.
20. See the evening parade and fireworks. A good viewing location for the fireworks is between The Plaza Restaurant and Tomorrowland Terrace.
21. Depart the Magic Kingdom.

You can customize this touring plan and get real-time updates while you're in the park! See **touringplans.com** for details. Suggested start times for FastPass+ reservations: Peter Pan's Flight: 11 a.m.; Seven Dwarfs Mine Train: 12:15 p.m.; *Enchanted Tales with Belle:* 1:15 p.m. After you've used your first three FastPass+ reservations, see if reservations are available for Splash Mountain (suggested start time: 4:30 p.m.), The Many Adventures of Winnie the Pooh (suggested start time: 6:15 p.m.), and *Wishes*.

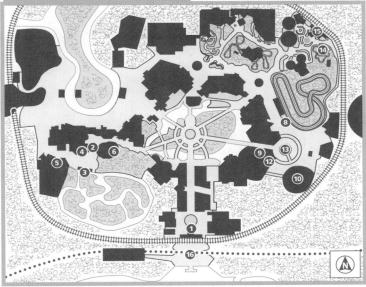

MAGIC KINGDOM TWO-DAY SLEEPYHEAD TOURING PLAN
FOR PARENTS WITH SMALL CHILDREN: DAY TWO

1. Arrive around 11 a.m. Obtain park maps and the *Times Guide* when you pass through the turnstiles. Stroller rentals are under the train station on Main Street.

2. Ride The Magic Carpets of Aladdin in Adventureland.

3. Take the Jungle Cruise using your FastPass+ reservation.

4. See *Walt Disney's Enchanted Tiki Room*.

5. Ride Pirates of the Caribbean using your FastPass+ reservation.

6. Explore the Swiss Family Treehouse.

7. Eat a quick, late lunch.

8. Ride the Tomorrowland Speedway using your FastPass+ reservation.

9. See *Monsters, Inc. Laugh Floor*.

10. Ride the Tomorrowland Transit Authority PeopleMover.

11. Eat dinner.

12. Ride Buzz Lightyear's Space Ranger Spin.

13. Take a spin on the Astro Orbiter.

14. Ride The Barnstormer in Fantasyland.

15. Take the Walt Disney World Railroad from Fantasyland to Main Street, U.S.A.

16. Depart the Magic Kingdom.

You can customize this touring plan and get real-time updates while you're in the park! See **touringplans.com** for details. Suggested start times for FastPass+ reservations: Jungle Cruise: 11 a.m.; Pirates of the Caribbean: noon; Tomorrowland Speedway: 1:30 p.m. After you've used your first three FastPass+ reservations, see if reservations are available for Buzz Lightyear's Space Ranger Spin (suggested start time: 6:30 p.m.).

The Magic Kingdom

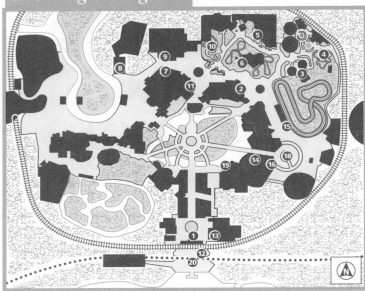

PARENTS' MAGIC KINGDOM PLAN: ONE AFTERNOON AND ONE FULL DAY (FULL DAY)

1. If you're a Disney resort guest, arrive 30 minutes before opening. Otherwise, arrive 50 minutes before opening. Obtain park maps and the *Times Guide* when you pass through the turnstiles. Stroller rentals are under the train station on Main Street.

2. Ride The Many Adventures of Winnie the Pooh in Fantasyland.

3. Ride Dumbo the Flying Elephant.

4. Ride The Barnstormer.

5. Ride Under the Sea: Journey of the Little Mermaid.

6. Ride Seven Dwarfs Mine Train using your FastPass+ reservation.

7. Ride Peter Pan's Flight using your FastPass+ reservation.

8. See The Haunted Mansion in Liberty Square.

9. Ride It's a Small World.

10. See *Enchanted Tales with Belle* using your FastPass+ reservation.

11. See *Mickey's PhilharMagic.*

12. Leave the park for lunch and a midday break.

13. Return to the park and see Mickey Mouse at Town Square Theater.

14. See *Monsters, Inc. Laugh Floor* in Tomorrowland.

15. Ride the Tomorrowland Speedway.

16. Ride Buzz Lightyear's Space Ranger Spin.

17. Eat dinner.

18. Take a spin on the Astro Orbiter.

19. See the evening parade and fireworks. A good viewing spot is between The Plaza Restaurant and Tomorrowland Terrace.

20. Depart the Magic Kingdom.

You can customize this touring plan and get real-time updates while you're in the park! See **touringplans.com** for details. Suggested start times for FastPass+ reservations: Seven Dwarfs Mine Train: 9 a.m.; Peter Pan's Flight: 10 a.m.; *Enchanted Tales with Belle:* 11 a.m. After you've used your first three FastPass+ reservations, see if reservations are available for Buzz Lightyear's Space Ranger Spin (suggested start time: 4:30 p.m.) and *Wishes*.

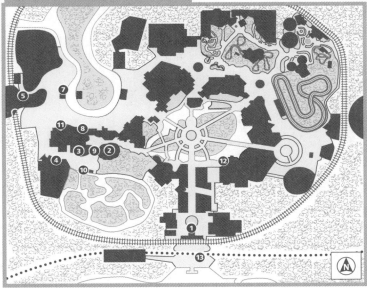

PARENTS' MAGIC KINGDOM PLAN: ONE AFTERNOON AND ONE FULL DAY (AFTERNOON)

1. Arrive at the Magic Kingdom entrance around 4 p.m. Obtain park maps and the *Times Guide* when you pass through the turnstiles. Stroller rentals are under the train station on Main Street.

2. Climb the Swiss Family Treehouse.

3. See *The Enchanted Tiki Room*.

4. Ride Pirates of the Caribbean in Adventureland using your FastPass+ reservation.

5. Ride Splash Mountain in Frontierland using your FastPass+ reservation.

6. Eat dinner.

7. Take the raft to Tom Sawyer Island. Allow 30–45 minutes to run around the island. Be sure to try the barrel bridges and tour Fort Langhorn.

8. See *Country Bear Jamboree*.

9. Ride The Magic Carpets of Aladdin.

10. Take the Jungle Cruise using your FastPass+ reservation.

11. See the evening parade from Frontierland if you haven't already. A good viewing spot is in front of the doors to the Frontierland candy shop.

12. See the evening fireworks from Main Street if you haven't already. A good viewing location for the fireworks is between the Plaza and Tomorrowland Terrace restaurants.

13. Depart the Magic Kingdom.

You can customize this touring plan and get real-time updates while you're in the park! See **touringplans.com** for details. Suggested start times for FastPass+ reservations: Pirates of the Caribbean: 4 p.m.; Splash Mountain: 5 p.m.; Jungle Cruise: 6:30 p.m. After you've used your first three FastPass+ reservations, see if reservations are available for *Wishes*.

Epcot

EPCOT ONE-DAY TOURING PLAN FOR PARENTS WITH SMALL CHILDREN

1. Arrive 40 minutes before opening. Rent strollers if needed. Get guide maps and the *Times Guide*.

2. As soon as the park opens, head to the Epcot Character Spot in Innovations West.

3. Ride Soarin' in The Land using your FastPass+ reservation.

4. See *The Circle of Life*.

5. In the Imagination! Pavilion, experience Journey into Imagination with Figment.

6. Ride Spaceship Earth using your FastPass+ reservation.

7. Eat lunch and take a midday break back at your hotel.

8. Experience Universe of Energy: *Ellen's Energy Adventure*.

9. See The Seas with Nemo & Friends and *Turtle Talk with Crush*.

10. Ride Living with the Land.

11. Tour Mexico and ride the Gran Fiesta Tour.

12. In Norway, try the new Frozen Ever After boat ride (if open) using your FastPass+ reservation, and visit the stave church.

13. Play a game of Agent P's World Showcase Adventure. Sign up between the Mexico and Norway Pavilions.

14. Eat dinner.

15. See *The American Adventure*.

16. Tour Canada and see *O Canada!*

17. See *IllumiNations*: Prime viewing spots are along the lagoon between Canada and France. You could also try for a lagoon-side table at La Cantina de San Angel or La Hacienda de San Angel in Mexico (Advance Reservations needed at the latter), or Spice Road Table in Morocco.

18. Depart Epcot.

You can customize this touring plan and get real-time updates while you're in the park! See **touringplans.com** for details. Suggested start times for FastPass+ reservations: Soarin': 9 a.m.; Spaceship Earth: 11 a.m.; Frozen Ever After (if open): after 6 p.m. Check for FastPass+ reservations for *IllumiNations* after you've used your first three FastPasses or after 6 p.m. (whichever is later).

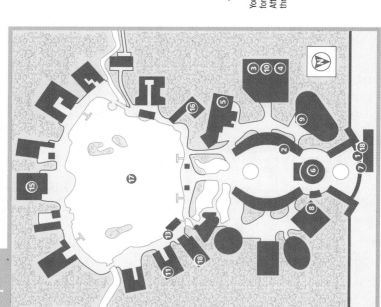

EPCOT ONE-DAY SLEEPYHEAD TOURING PLAN FOR PARENTS WITH SMALL CHILDREN

1. Arrive at the entrance around 11 a.m. Pick up a park map and daily entertainment schedule when entering the park. Stroller rentals are just inside the main entrance and to the left.

2. Ride Journey Into Imagination with Figment at the Imagination! Pavilion.

3. Ride Soarin' in the Land Pavilion using your FastPass+ reservation.

4. See The Seas with Nemo and Friends.

5. Experience *Turtle Talk with Crush* using your FastPass+ reservation.

6. Eat lunch. The Land's Sunshine Seasons food court is the best counter-service option in Future World.

7. Take the Gran Fiesta Tour Starring the Three Caballeros in Mexico.

8. Sign up for Agent P's World Showcase Adventure between Mexico and Norway.

9. In Norway, try the new Frozen Ever After boat ride (if open) using your FastPass+ reservation, and visit the stave church.

10. Play a round of Agent P's World Showcase Adventure in Mexico, Norway, China, or Germany.

11. See *The American Adventure*.

12. See *Captain EO* at the Imagination! Pavilion.

13. See *The Circle of Life* in The Land.

14. Take the Living with the Land boat ride.

15. Ride Spaceship Earth using your FastPass+ reservation.

16. Eat dinner.

17. Get character autographs at the Epcot Character Spot in Future World Plaza.

18. See the *O Canada!* film in Canada. Don't forget to stop at the Kidcot Fun Stops throughout World Showcase.

19. See *IllumiNations*. Excellent viewing locations can be found along the walkway around World Showcase Lagoon.

20. Depart Epcot.

You can customize this touring plan and get real-time updates while you're in the park! See **touringplans .com** for details. Suggested start times for FastPass+ reservations: Soarin': 10:50 a.m. (not a typo—see **touringplans.com** for a detailed explanation); *Turtle Talk with Crush*: 11:30 a.m.; Frozen Ever After (if open): 1:30 p.m. After you've used your first three FastPass+ reservations, see if reservations are available for the Epcot Character Spot meet and greet (suggested start time: 5 p.m.) and *IllumiNations*.

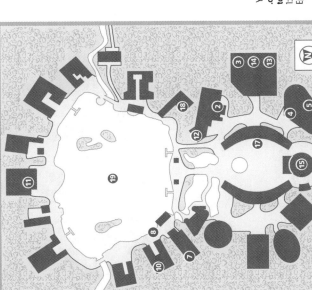

Epcot

EPCOT ONE-DAY TOURING PLAN
FOR TWEENS AND THEIR PARENTS

1. Arrive at the entrance to Epcot 30 minutes prior to opening. Pick up a park map and daily entertainment schedule when entering the park. Stroller rentals are just inside the main entrance and to the left.

2. Ride Test Track in Future World East.

3. Ride Mission: Space (Orange).

4. Ride Sum of All Thrills in Innoventions East.

5. Ride Soarin' in the Land Pavilion using your FastPass+ reservation.

6. Ride Spaceship Earth near the park entrance using your FastPass+ reservation.

7. See *Captain EO* at the Imagination! Pavilion.

8. Eat lunch.

9. Take the Living with the Land boat ride.

10. Experience The Seas with Nemo and Friends.

11. Begin a clockwise tour of World Showcase at the Mexico Pavilion.

12. Take the Gran Fiesta Tour boat ride.

13. At Norway, sign up for Agent P's World Showcase Adventure and tour the pavilion.

14. Ride Frozen Ever After (if open) in Norway using your FastPass+ reservation.

15. Play a round of Agent P's World Showcase Adventure in Mexico, Norway, China, Germany, Japan, France, or the United Kingdom.

16. Tour the China Pavilion.

17. See the *Reflections of China* film.

18. Tour the Italy Pavilion.

19. See *The American Adventure*.

20. Tour the Japan Pavilion.

21. Eat dinner.

22. Visit the Morocco Pavilion.

23. Explore the France Pavilion.

24. See the film *Impressions de France*.

25. Tour the Canada Pavilion and see the *O Canada!* film if time permits.

26. See *IllumiNations*. Excellent viewing locations can be found along the walkway near Canada and the United Kingdom.

27. Depart Epcot.

You can customize this touring plan and get real-time updates while you're in the park! See **touringplans.com** for details. Suggested start times for FastPass+ reservations: Soarin': 10 a.m.; Spaceship Earth: 11 a.m.; Frozen Ever After (if open): 2 p.m. Check for FastPass+ reservations for *IllumiNations* after you've used your first three FastPasses or after 1 p.m. (whichever is later).

Epcot

Epcot

PARENTS' EPCOT TOURING PLAN: ONE AFTERNOON AND ONE FULL DAY (FULL DAY)

1. Arrive at the entrance to Epcot 30 minutes prior to opening. Pick up a park map and daily entertainment schedule when entering the park.

2. In Future World East, ride Test Track.

3. In Innoventions East, ride Sum of All Thrills.

4. Ride Mission: Space (Orange) using your FastPass+ reservation.

5. In Future World Plaza, get character autographs at the Epcot Character Spot.

6. Ride Soarin' using your FastPass+ reservation.

7. Eat lunch. Sunshine Seasons has the best food in Future World. The Coral Reef in the Seas Pavilion is the closest sit-down restaurant. Or try the counter-service restaurant at Mexico in World Showcase.

8. Ride Living with the Land.

9. Ride Journey into Imagination with Figment at the Imagination! Pavilion.

10. See *Captain EO* at the Imagination! Pavilion.

11. Sign up for Agent P's World Showcase Adventure between Norway and Mexico. There's enough time in this plan to play several games around World Showcase.

12. Experience the Gran Fiesta Tour boat ride at Mexico. This begins a clockwise tour of World Showcase.

13. Ride Frozen Ever After (if open) in Norway using your FastPass+ reservation.

14. See *Reflections of China*.

15. Tour Germany.

16. Visit Italy.

17. See *The American Adventure*.

18. Eat dinner.

19. Explore Japan.

20. Visit the Morocco Pavilion.

21. Depart Epcot.

You can customize this touring plan and get real-time updates while you're in the park! See **touringplans.com** for details. Suggested start times for FastPass+ reservations: Mission: Space (Orange): 9:45 a.m.; Soarin': 11:15 a.m.; Frozen Ever After (if open): 2:30 p.m.

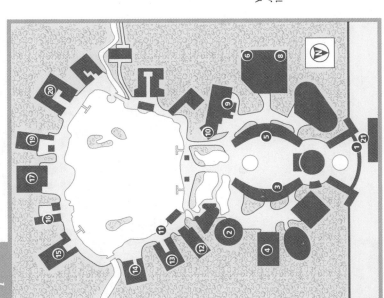

Epcot

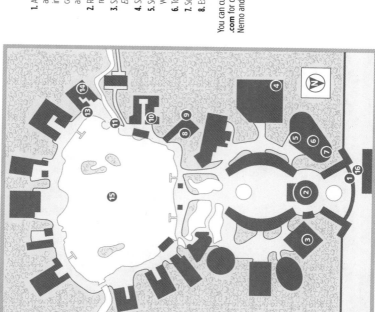

PARENTS' EPCOT TOURING PLAN: ONE AFTERNOON AND ONE FULL DAY (AFTERNOON)

1. Arrive at Epcot at 1 p.m. Pick up a park map and daily entertainment schedule when entering the park. Make dining reservations by calling ☎ 407-WDW-DINE if you have not already done so.

2. Ride Spaceship Earth using your FastPass+ reservation.

3. See the Universe of Energy: *Ellen's Energy Adventure*.

4. See *The Circle of Life* at the Land Pavilion.

5. See The Seas with Nemo and Friends using your FastPass+ reservation.

6. Tour The Seas Main Tank and Exhibits.

7. See *Turtle Talk with Crush*.

8. Explore the Canada Pavilion.

9. See *O Canada!*

10. Visit the United Kingdom Pavilion.

11. If you have not already done so, sign up for Agent P's World Showcase Adventure between the United Kingdom and France Pavilions.

12. Eat dinner. Good nearby restaurants include Le Cellier at Canada, Restaurant Marrakesh at Morocco, and Teppan Edo at Japan. Reservations are recommended.

13. Visit the France Pavilion.

14. In France, see *Impressions de France*.

15. See *IllumiNations* using your FastPass+ reservation. Good viewing spots can be found along the waterway between France and Canada.

16. Depart Epcot.

You can customize this touring plan and get real-time updates while you're in the park! See **touringplans .com** for details. Suggested start times for FastPass+ reservations: Spaceship Earth: 1 p.m.; The Seas with Nemo and Friends: 2 p.m.; *IllumiNations*: 8:45 p.m.

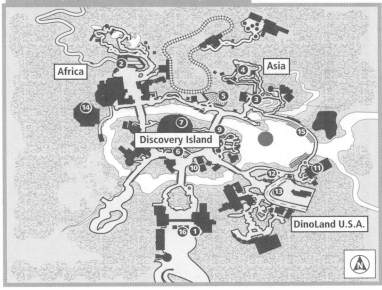

ANIMAL KINGDOM ONE-DAY TOURING PLAN
FOR PARENTS WITH SMALL CHILDREN

1. Arrive 25 minutes prior to opening (40 minutes mid-June–mid-August and during holidays). Pick up a park map and entertainment schedule. Stroller rentals are just past the entrance, to the right.

2. As soon as the park opens, experience the Kilimanjaro Safaris in Africa.

3. Ride Kali River Rapids in Asia using your FastPass+ reservation. You *will* get wet, so use ponchos or plastic bags to keep dry.

4. Walk the Maharajah Jungle Trek.

5. See *Flights of Wonder.* Check the daily entertainment schedule for showtimes.

6. See *It's Tough To Be a Bug!* on Discovery Island.

7. See the exhibits at the Tree of Life and walk the Discovery Island trails.

8. Eat lunch. Good nearby locations include Flame Tree Barbecue and Pizzafari. Tusker House has an all-you-can-eat buffet.

9. Get character autographs at Adventurers Outpost, across from Flame Tree Barbecue, using your FastPass+ reservation.

10. Earn a few badges at Wilderness Explorers.

11. Check the next performance time of *Finding Nemo—The Musical* in DinoLand U.S.A.

12. Let the kids play at The Boneyard.

13. Try TriceraTop Spin.

14. See *Festival of the Lion King* in Africa.

15. See *Rivers of Light* in Asia using your FastPass+ reservation.

16. Depart Animal Kingdom.

You can customize this touring plan and get real-time updates while you're in the park! See **touringplans.com** for details. Suggested start times for FastPass+ reservations: Kali River Rapids: 9:15 a.m.; Adventurers Outpost meet and greet: 12:30 p.m.; *Rivers of Light:* Check *Times Guide* for performance schedule.

Disney's Animal Kingdom

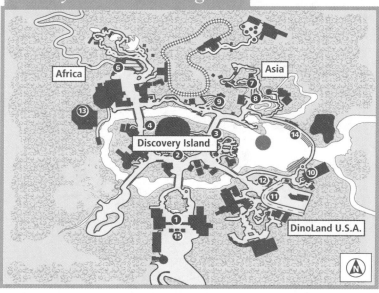

ANIMAL KINGDOM ONE-DAY SLEEPYHEAD TOURING PLAN
FOR PARENTS WITH SMALL CHILDREN

1. Arrive around 11 a.m. Pick up a park map and entertainment schedule. Stroller rentals are just past the entrance, to the right.

2. See *It's Tough to Be a Bug!* on Discovery Island.

3. Get character autographs at Adventurers Outpost, across from Flame Tree Barbecue, using your FastPass+ reservation.

4. See the exhibits at the Tree of Life and walk the Discovery Island trails.

5. Eat lunch. A good nearby location is Flame Tree Barbecue on Discovery Island.

6. Experience Kilimanjaro Safaris in Africa using your FastPass+ reservation.

7. Walk the Maharajah Jungle Trek in Asia.

8. Ride Kali River Rapids using your FastPass+ reservation. You *will* get wet, so use ponchos or plastic bags to keep dry.

9. See the next showing of *Flights of Wonder*.

10. See *Finding Nemo—The Musical* in DinoLand U.S.A.

11. Ride TriceraTop Spin.

12. Visit The Boneyard playground.

13. See *Festival of the Lion King* in Africa.

14. See *Rivers of Light* in Asia.

15. Depart Animal Kingdom.

You can customize this touring plan and get real-time updates while you're in the park! See **touringplans.com** for details. Suggested start time for FastPass+ reservations: Adventurers Outpost meet and greet, 11 a.m.; Kilimanjaro Safaris: noon; Kali River Rapids: 1 p.m. After you've used your first three FastPass+ reservations, see if reservations are available for *Rivers of Light* (check *Times Guide* for performance schedule).

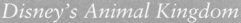

Disney's Animal Kingdom

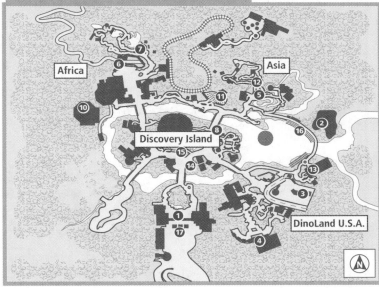

ANIMAL KINGDOM ONE–DAY TOURING PLAN
FOR TWEENS AND THEIR PARENTS

1. Arrive 25 minutes prior to opening (40 minutes mid-June–mid-August and during holidays). Pick up a park map and entertainment schedule. Stroller rentals are just past the entrance, to the right.

2. As soon as the park opens, ride Expedition Everest in Asia using your FastPass+ reservation.

3. Ride Primeval Whirl in DinoLand U.S.A.

4. Ride Dinosaur.

5. Take a ride on Kali River Rapids in Asia. You *will* get wet, so use ponchos or plastic bags to keep dry.

6. Ride Kilimanjaro Safaris in Africa using your FastPass+ reservation.

7. Walk the Pangani Forest Exploration Trail.

8. Get character autographs at Adventurers Outpost, across from Flame Tree Barbecue, using your FastPass+ reservation.

9. Eat lunch.

10. See *Festival of the Lion King* in Africa.

11. See the *Flights of Wonder* show in Asia.

12. Take the Maharajah Jungle Trek.

13. See *Finding Nemo—The Musical* in DinoLand U.S.A.

14. Earn a few badges by playing Wilderness Explorers.

15. See *It's Tough to Be a Bug!* on Discovery Island.

16. See *Rivers of Light* in Asia.

17. Depart Animal Kingdom.

You can customize this touring plan and get real-time updates while you're in the park! See **touringplans.com** for details. Suggested start times for FastPass+ reservations: Expedition Everest: 9 a.m.; Kilimanjaro Safaris: 10 a.m.; Adventurers Outpost meet and greet: 11 a.m. After you've used your first three FastPass+ reservations, see if reservations are available for *Rivers of Light* (check *Times Guide* for performance schedule).

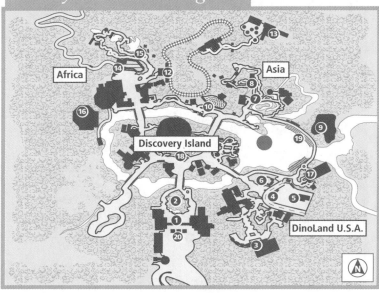

Disney's Animal Kingdom

Africa

Asia

Discovery Island

DinoLand U.S.A.

ANIMAL KINGDOM ONE-DAY
HAPPY FAMILY TOURING PLAN

1. Arrive 25 minutes prior to opening (40 minutes mid-June–mid-August and during holidays). Pick up a park map and entertainment schedule. Stroller rentals are just past the entrance, to the right.

2. PARENTS: Don't feel the need to rush to an attraction. Explore The Oasis on Discovery Island, pointing out any unusual animals. Hungry? Find the Royal Anandapur Tea Company between Kali River Rapids and Expedition Everest in Asia.

3. TEENS: Ride Dinosaur in DinoLand U.S.A.

4. PARENTS: Ride TriceraTop Spin.

5. TEENS: Ride Primeval Whirl.

6. PARENTS: Check out The Boneyard playground.

7. FAMILY: Take a ride on Kali River Rapids in Asia. You *will* get wet, so use ponchos or plastic bags to keep dry.

8. FAMILY: Take the Maharajah Jungle Trek.

9. TEENS: Ride Expedition Everest using your FastPass+ reservation.

10. FAMILY: See the *Flights of Wonder* show.

11. FAMILY: Eat lunch.

12. FAMILY: Take the Wildlife Express train to Rafiki's Planet Watch and Conservation Station.

13. FAMILY: Tour Conservation Station. Note the writing on the bathroom walls. Take the train back to Africa when you're done.

14. FAMILY: Ride Kilimanjaro Safaris in Africa using your FastPass+ reservation.

15. FAMILY: Walk the Pangani Forest Exploration Trail.

16. PARENTS: See *Festival of the Lion King*.
TEENS: Free time. Revisit favorite attractions or explore the rest of the park.

17. FAMILY: See *Finding Nemo—The Musical* in DinoLand U.S.A.

18. FAMILY: See *It's Tough to Be a Bug!* on Discovery Island.

19. FAMILY: See *Rivers of Light* in Asia using your FastPass+ reservation.

20. Depart Animal Kingdom.

You can customize this touring plan and get real-time updates while you're in the park! See **touringplans.com** for details. Suggested start times for FastPass+ reservations: Expedition Everest (teens): 11 a.m.; Kilimanjaro Safaris (family): 1:30 p.m.; *Rivers of Light* (family): Check *Times Guide* for performance schedule.

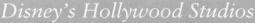

Disney's Hollywood Studios

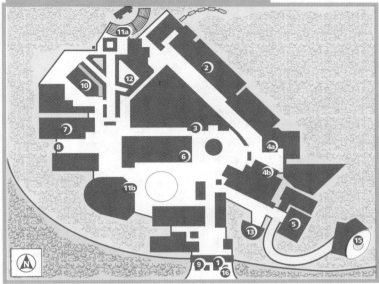

DISNEY'S HOLLYWOOD STUDIOS ONE-DAY TOURING PLAN
FOR PARENTS WITH SMALL CHILDREN

1. Arrive 30 minutes prior to opening (40 minutes during summer, holidays, and special events). Grab a park map and daily entertainment schedule when you enter the park. Rent strollers as needed at the gas station on the right side of the park entrance, just past the turnstiles.

2. Ride Toy Story Midway Mania! using your FastPass+ reservation.

3. Take The Great Movie Ride.

4. Catch a performance of a) *Voyage of the Little Mermaid* or b) *Disney Junior—Live on Stage!* Check the daily entertainment schedule for showtimes.

5. If your kids are tall enough and willing, ride The Twilight Zone Tower of Terror using your FastPass+ reservation.

6. See *For the First Time in Forever: A Frozen Sing-Along Celebration.*

7. Ride Star Tours—The Adventures Continue.

8. See *Jedi Training Academy.* Check the daily entertainment schedule for showtimes.

9. Eat lunch and return to your hotel for a midday break of 3–4 hours.

10. Return to the Studios and see *Muppet-Vision 3-D.*

11. See a) the *Lights, Motors, Action! Extreme Stunt Show* or b) the *Indiana Jones Epic Stunt Spectacular!* Check the daily entertainment schedule for showtimes.

12. Let the kids play on the Honey, I Shrunk the Kids Movie Set Adventure.

13. See *Beauty and the Beast—Live on Stage.* Check the daily entertainment schedule for showtimes.

14. Eat dinner.

15. See *Fantasmic!* Plan on arriving 60 minutes early to get good seats, or 30 minutes early for standing room only.

16. Depart the Studios.

You can customize this touring plan and get real-time updates while you're in the park! See **touringplans.com** for details. Suggested start times for FastPass+ reservations: Toy Story Midway Mania!: 9 a.m.; The Twilight Zone Tower of Terror: 10 a.m.; *For the First Time in Forever: A Frozen Sing-Along Celebration:* 11 a.m. After you've used your first three FastPass+ reservations, see if reservations are available for *Fantasmic!* (check *Times Guide* for performance schedule).

Disney's Hollywood Studios

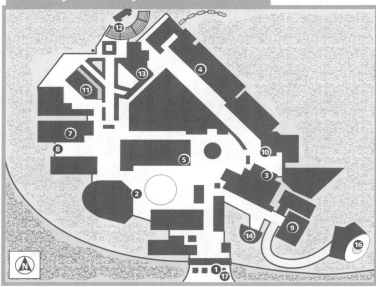

DISNEY'S HOLLYWOOD STUDIOS ONE-DAY SLEEPYHEAD TOURING PLAN FOR PARENTS WITH SMALL CHILDREN

1. Arrive at the entrance to Disney's Hollywood Studios around 11 a.m. Grab a park map and daily entertainment schedule when you enter the park. Rent strollers as needed at the gas station on the right side of the park entrance, just past the turnstiles.

2. See the *Indiana Jones Epic Stunt Spectacular!* Check the daily entertainment schedule for showtimes.

3. See *Disney Junior—Live on Stage!* Check the daily entertainment schedule for showtimes.

4. Ride Toy Story Midway Mania! at Pixar Place using your FastPass+ reservation.

5. See *For the First Time in Forever: A Frozen Sing-Along Celebration.*

6. Eat lunch.

7. If your children meet the height requirement (40"), ride Star Tours—The Adventures Continue using your FastPass+ reservation.

8. See *Jedi Training Academy.* Check the daily entertainment schedule for showtimes.

9. Ride The Twilight Zone Tower of Terror using your FastPass+ reservation.

10. See *Voyage of the Little Mermaid.*

11. See *Muppet-Vision 3-D.*

12. See the *Lights, Motors, Action! Extreme Stunt Show.* Check the daily entertainment schedule for showtimes.

13. Let the kids play on the Honey, I Shrunk the Kids Movie Set Adventure.

14. See *Beauty and the Beast—Live on Stage.* Check the daily entertainment schedule for showtimes.

15. Eat dinner.

16. See *Fantasmic!* Plan on arriving 60 minutes early to get good seats, or 30 minutes early for standing room only.

17. Depart the Studios.

You can customize this touring plan and get real-time updates while you're in the park! See **touringplans.com** for details. Suggested start times for FastPass+ reservations: Toy Story Midway Mania!: 12:15 p.m.; Star Tours—The Adventures Continue: 1:30 p.m.; The Twilight Zone Tower of Terror: 2:30 p.m. After you've used your first three FastPass+ reservations, see if reservations are available for *Fantasmic!* (check *Times Guide* for performance schedule).

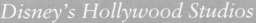

Disney's Hollywood Studios

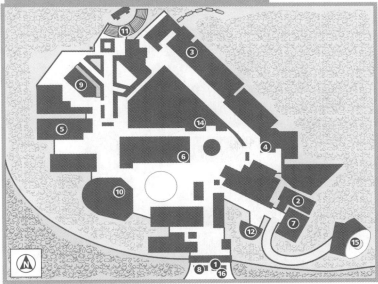

DISNEY'S HOLLYWOOD STUDIOS ONE-DAY TOURING PLAN
FOR TWEENS AND THEIR PARENTS

1. Arrive at the entrance to Disney's Hollywood Studios 30 minutes prior to opening (40 minutes during summer, holidays, and special events). Grab a park map and daily entertainment schedule when you enter the park. Rent strollers as needed at the gas station on the right side of the park entrance, just past the turnstiles.

2. Ride the Rock 'n' Roller Coaster.

3. Ride Toy Story Midway Mania! using your FastPass+ reservation.

4. See *Voyage of the Little Mermaid.*

5. Ride Star Tours—The Adventures Continue using your FastPass+ reservation.

6. See *For the First Time in Forever: A Frozen Sing-Along Celebration.*

7. Ride The Twilight Zone Tower of Terror using your FastPass+ reservation.

8. Eat lunch and return to your hotel for a midday break of 3–4 hours.

9. See *Muppet-Vision 3-D.*

10. See the *Indiana Jones Epic Stunt Spectacular!* Check the daily entertainment schedule for showtimes.

11. See the *Lights, Motors, Action! Extreme Stunt Show.* Check the daily entertainment schedule for showtimes.

12. See *Beauty and the Beast—Live on Stage.* Check the daily entertainment schedule for showtimes.

13. Eat dinner. Tweens will enjoy Pizza Planet.

14. Take The Great Movie Ride.

15. See *Fantasmic!* Plan on arriving 60 minutes early to get good seats, or 30 minutes early for standing room only.

16. Depart the Studios.

You can customize this touring plan and get real-time updates while you're in the park! See **touringplans.com** for details. Suggested start times for FastPass+ reservations: Toy Story Midway Mania!: 9 a.m.; Star Tours—The Adventures Continue: 10 a.m.; The Twilight Zone Tower of Terror: 11 a.m. After you've used your first three FastPass+ reservations, see if reservations are available for *Fantasmic!* (check *Times Guide* for performance schedule).

Disney's Hollywood Studios

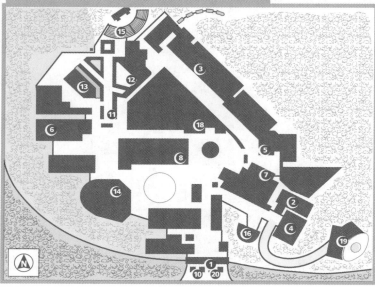

DISNEY'S HOLLYWOOD STUDIOS ONE-DAY
HAPPY FAMILY TOURING PLAN

1. Arrive at the entrance to Disney's Hollywood Studios 30 minutes prior to opening (40 minutes during summer, holidays, and special events). Grab a park map and daily entertainment schedule when you enter the park. Rent strollers as needed at the gas station on the right side of the park entrance, just past the turnstiles.

2. **TEENS:** Ride Rock 'n' Roller Coaster. Consider using the single-rider line if the wait exceeds 25 minutes.

3. **FAMILY:** Ride Toy Story Midway Mania! at Pixar Place using your FastPass+ reservation.

4. **TEENS:** Ride The Twilight Zone Tower of Terror.

5. **PARENTS:** See *Voyage of the Little Mermaid.*

6. **TEENS:** Ride Star Tours—The Adventures Continue using your FastPass+ reservation.

7. **PARENTS:** See *Disney Junior—Live on Stage!* Check the daily entertainment schedule for showtimes.

8. **FAMILY:** See *For the First Time in Forever: A Frozen Sing-Along Celebration* using your FastPass+ reservation.

9. **FAMILY:** Eat lunch.

10. **PARENTS:** Go back to the hotel for a midday break. Come back around 4 p.m. **TEENS:** Explore the rest of the park, or revisit favorite attractions.

11. **FAMILY:** Explore the Streets of America.

12. **PARENTS:** Explore the Honey, I Shrunk the Kids Movie Set Adventure.

13. **FAMILY:** See *Muppet-Vision 3-D.*

14. **FAMILY:** See *Indiana Jones Epic Stunt Spectacular!* Check the daily entertainment schedule for showtimes.

15. **TEENS:** See the *Lights, Motors, Action! Extreme Stunt Show.* Check the daily entertainment schedule for showtimes.

16. **FAMILY:** See *Beauty and the Beast.* Check the daily entertainment schedule for showtimes.

17. **FAMILY:** Eat dinner. Good sit-down choices include Mama Melrose's Ristorante Italiano and The Hollywood Brown Derby.

18. **FAMILY:** Ride The Great Movie Ride.

19. **FAMILY:** See *Fantasmic!* Plan on arriving 60 minutes early to get good seats, or 30 minutes early for standing room only.

20. Depart the Studios.

You can customize this touring plan and get real-time updates while you're in the park! See **touringplans.com** for details. Suggested start times for FastPass+ reservations: Toy Story Midway Mania!: 9:30 a.m.; Star Tours—The Adventures Continue: 10:30 a.m.; *For the First Time in Forever: A Frozen Sing-Along Celebration:* 11:30 a.m. After you've used your first three FastPass+ reservations, see if reservations are available for *Fantasmic!* (check *Times Guide* for performance schedule).

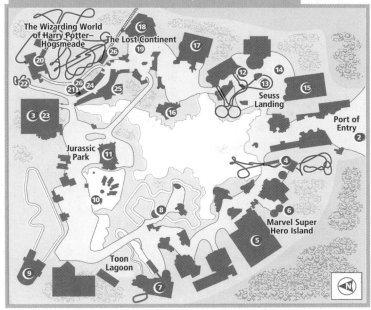

UNIVERSAL'S ISLANDS OF ADVENTURE
ONE-DAY TOURING PLAN

1. Buy your admission in advance and call ☎ 407-363-8000 the day before your visit for the official opening time.

2. Arrive at IOA 75–90 minutes before official opening time if Early Park Admission is offered and you're eligible, or 30–45 minutes before opening for day guests. Get a park map as soon as you enter.

3. Early-entry guests should ride Harry Potter and the Forbidden Journey. Ride Flight of the Hippogriff and Dragon Challenge as well if you have time.

4. Exit Hogsmeade before early entry ends, and head to Marvel Super Hero Island to ride The Incredible Hulk Coaster. Guests without early entry should start at this step.

5. Ride The Amazing Adventures of Spider-Man.

6. Backtrack to ride Doctor Doom's Fearfall.

7. Continue clockwise and ride Dudley Do-Right's Ripsaw Falls in Toon Lagoon.

8. Ride Popeye & Bluto's Bilge-Rat Barges.

9. Take the Jurassic Park River Adventure.

10. Explore Camp Jurassic.

11. Check out the exhibits in the Jurassic Park Discovery Center.

12. Cross the bridge bypassing Hogsmeade to Lost Continent, and ride the High in the Sky Seuss Trolley Train Ride! in Seuss Landing.

13. Ride the Caro-Seuss-el.

14. Ride One Fish, Two Fish, Red Fish, Blue Fish.

15. Ride The Cat in the Hat.

16. Return to Lost Continent and eat lunch at Mythos.

17. Experience *Poseidon's Fury.*

18. See the next scheduled performance of *The Eighth Voyage of Sindbad Stunt Show.*

19. Chat with the Mystic Fountain before or after the *Sindbad* show.

20. Enter Hogsmeade and ride Dragon Challenge, or walk through the queue to see the Triwizard Tournament artifacts.

21. See the *Frog Choir* or *Triwizard Spirit Rally* perform on the small stage outside Hogwarts.

22. Ride Flight of the Hippogriff.

23. Ride Harry Potter and the Forbidden Journey. If the wait is more than 30 minutes, request a castle tour to experience the queue, and then use the single-rider line.

24. See the wand ceremony at Ollivanders.

25. Have dinner at Three Broomsticks.

26. See the stage show you didn't see earlier. Pose for a picture with the Hogwarts Express conductor, and explore the shops and interactive windows around Hogsmeade. Sample (or at least smell) some sweets at Honeydukes.

27. Revisit any favorite attractions, or remain in Hogsmeade until closing, enjoying the atmosphere.

Universal Studios Florida

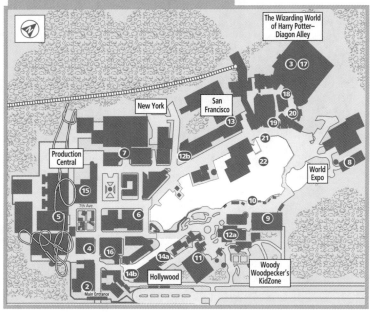

UNIVERSAL STUDIOS FLORIDA ONE-DAY TOURING PLAN
(Assumes: Day guest without Universal Express; 1-Day Base Ticket)

1. Buy your admission in advance and call ☎ 407-363-8000 the day before your visit for the official opening time.

2. Arrive at USF 90–120 minutes before official opening if Early Park Admission is offered and you're eligible, or 30–45 minutes before opening for day guests. Get a park map as soon as you enter.

3. Early-entry guests should ride Harry Potter and the Escape from Gringotts if it's operating. If it's not, enjoy the rest of Diagon Alley but don't get in line.

4. Before early entry ends, hotel guests should exit Diagon Alley and ride Despicable Me Minion Mayhem. Day guests should wait in the front lot until permitted to ride Despicable Me.

5. Ride Hollywood Rip Ride Rockit.

6. Experience Transformers: The Ride 3-D.

7. Ride Revenge of the Mummy in New York.

8. Ride Men in Black Alien Attack in World Expo.

9. Ride The Simpsons Ride.

10. Ride Kang & Kodos' Twirl 'n' Hurl if 50 or fewer people are in line.

11. Ride E.T. Adventure.

12. Work in *Animal Actors on Location* **(12a)** and *Beetlejuice Graveyard Revue* **(12b)** around lunch (we recommend Fast Food Boulevard), according to the daily entertainment schedule.

13. Experience *Disaster!* in San Francisco.

14. See *Universal Orlando's Horror Make-Up Show* **(14a)** and *Terminator 2: 3-D* **(14b)** according to the daily entertainment schedule.

15. See *Twister . . . Ride It Out* in New York.

16. See *Shrek 4-D* in Production Central.

17. Re-enter Diagon Alley and ride Harry Potter and the Escape from Gringotts. If this is your first ride, take the standby queue. For re-rides, use the single-rider line. The queue may close before the rest of the park if the posted wait time exceeds remaining operating hours by more than an hour.

18. See the wand ceremony at Ollivanders.

19. Tour Diagon Alley. Browse the shops, explore the dark recesses of Knockturn Alley, and discover the interactive effects. If you're hungry, try the Leaky Cauldron or Florean Fortescue's Ice Cream Parlour.

20. See the *Celestina Warbeck* and *Tales of Beedle the Bard* shows.

21. Chat with the Knight Bus conductor and his shrunken head. Also look for Kreacher in the window of 12 Grimmauld Place, and listen to the receiver in the red phone booth.

22. If scheduled, see *Universal's Cinematic Spectacular* from Central Park (directly across the lagoon from Richter's), Duff Brewery, or the embankment in front of London.

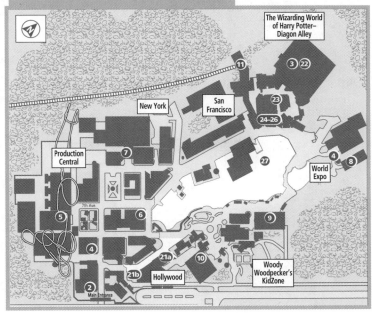

Universal Studios Florida

The Wizarding World of Harry Potter–Diagon Alley

New York

San Francisco

Production Central

World Expo

Hollywood

Woody Woodpecker's KidZone

7th Ave.

Main Entrance

THE BEST OF UNIVERSAL ORLANDO IN A DAY
(Assumes: 1-Day Park-to-Park Ticket)

1. Buy your admission in advance; call ☎ 407-363-8000 the day before your visit for the official opening time.

2. Arrive at USF 90–120 minutes before the official opening time if Early Park Admission is offered and you're eligible, or 30–45 minutes before opening for day guests. Line up at the shortest open turnstile, and get a park map as soon as you enter.
Alternative: If only IOA is open for Early Park Admission and you're eligible, arrive at IOA's turnstiles 75–90 minutes before the official opening time. Ride Harry Potter and the Forbidden Journey. Ride Flight of the Hippogriff and Dragon Challenge as well if you have time. Take the Hogwarts Express to King's Cross Station before USF officially opens for the day, and continue at the next step.

3. Early-entry guests should ride Harry Potter and the Escape from Gringotts if it is operating. If Gringotts is not operating, enjoy the rest of Diagon Alley but don't get in line.

4. Before early entry ends, hotel guests should exit Diagon Alley and ride Despicable Me Minion Mayhem. Day guests should wait in the front lot until permitted to ride Despicable Me.

5. Ride Hollywood Rip Ride Rockit.

6. Experience Transformers: The Ride 3-D in Production Central.

7. Ride Revenge of the Mummy in New York.

8. Ride Men in Black Alien Attack in World Expo.

9. Ride The Simpsons Ride.

10. Ride E.T. Adventure in Woody Woodpecker's KidZone.

11. Ride Hogwarts Express from King's Cross Station to IOA. Have your Park-to-Park ticket ready.

(Continued on next page)

Universal's Islands of Adventure

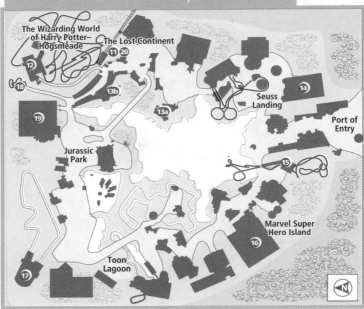

The Wizarding World of Harry Potter–Hogsmeade

The Lost Continent

Seuss Landing

Port of Entry

Jurassic Park

Marvel Super Hero Island

Toon Lagoon

THE BEST OF UNIVERSAL ORLANDO IN A DAY
(continued)

12. Ride Dragon Challenge in The Wizarding World of Harry Potter–Hogsmeade.

13. Eat lunch at Mythos in Lost Continent (**13a**) or Three Broomsticks in Hogsmeade (**13b**).

14. Ride The Cat in the Hat in Seuss Landing.

15. Ride The Incredible Hulk Coaster on Marvel Super Hero Island.

16. Ride The Amazing Adventures of Spider-Man.

17. Continue clockwise through Toon Lagoon, and take the Jurassic Park River Adventure.

18. Enter Hogsmeade, and ride Flight of the Hippogriff if the wait isn't too long.

19. Ride Harry Potter and the Forbidden Journey. If the wait is more than 30 minutes, request a castle tour to experience the queue, and then use the single-rider line.

20. Return to Universal Studios Florida using the Hogwarts Express from Hogsmeade Station, or walk back to the other park if the posted wait exceeds 20 minutes.

See map on previous page for the following steps.

21. See the next showing of *Universal Orlando's Horror Make-Up Show* (**21a**) upon returning to USF. If the remaining *Horror Make-Up* showtimes

aren't convenient, substitute with *Terminator 2: 3-D* (**21b**).

22. By this time, you should be able to enter Diagon Alley without waiting, even on busy days. Ride Harry Potter and the Escape from Gringotts. If this is your first ride, take the standby queue. For re-rides, use the single-rider line. The Gringotts queue may close before the rest of the park if the posted wait time exceeds remaining operating hours by more than 60 minutes.

23. See the wand ceremony at Ollivanders.

24. Tour Diagon Alley. Browse the shops, explore the dark recesses of Knockturn Alley, and discover the interactive effects. If you're hungry, try the Leaky Cauldron or Florean Fortescue's Ice Cream Parlour.

25. See the *Celestina Warbeck* and *Tales of Beedle the Bard* shows.

26. Chat with the Knight Bus conductor and his shrunken head. Also look for Kreacher in the window of 12 Grimmauld Place, and listen to the receiver in the red phone booth.

27. If scheduled, watch *Universal's Cinematic Spectacular* from Central Park (directly across the lagoon from Richter's), Duff Brewery, or the embankment in front of London.